Keywords for Gender and Sexuality Studies

Keywords

Collaborative in design and execution, the books in the Keywords series bring together scholars across a wide range of disciplines in the humanities and social sciences, with each essay on a single term to help trace the contours and debates of a particular field. Keywords are the nodal points in many of today's most dynamic and vexed discussions of political and social life, both inside and outside of the academy. Providing accessible A-to-Z surveys of prevailing scholarly concepts, the books serve as flexible tools for carving out new areas of inquiry.

For more information, visit http://keywords.nyupress.org.

Titles in the series include the following:

Keywords for American Cultural Studies
Edited by Bruce Burgett and Glenn Hendler

Keywords for Children's Literature
Edited by Phillip Nel and Lissa Paul

Keywords for Asian American Studies
Edited by Cathy J. Schlund-Vials, Linda Trinh Võ, and K. Scott Wong

Keywords for Disability Studies
Edited by Rachel Adams, Benjamin Reiss, and David Serlin

Keywords for Environmental Studies
Edited by Joni Adamson, William A. Gleason, and David N. Pelow

Keywords for Media Studies
Edited by Laurie Oulette and Jonathan Gray

Keywords for Latina/o Studies
Edited by Deborah R. Vargas, Nancy Raquel Mirabal, and Lawrence La Fountain-Stokes

Keywords for African American Studies
Edited by Erica R. Edwards, Roderick A. Ferguson, and Jeffrey O. G. Ogbar

Keywords for Comics Studies
Edited by Ramzi Fawaz, Shelley Streeby, and Deborah Elizabeth Whaley

Keywords for Gender and Sexuality Studies
Edited by the Keywords Feminist Editorial Collective

For a complete list of books in the series, see www.nyupress.org.

Keywords for Gender and Sexuality Studies

Edited by

the Keywords Feminist Editorial Collective

Kyla Wazana Tompkins (managing editor), Aren Z. Aizura, Aimee Bahng, Karma R. Chávez, Mishuana Goeman, and Amber Jamilla Musser

NEW YORK UNIVERSITY PRESS New York

NEW YORK UNIVERSITY PRESS
New York
www.nyupress.org

References to internet websites (URLs) were accurate at the time
of writing. Neither the author nor New York University Press is
responsible for URLs that may have expired or changed since the
manuscript was prepared.

Library of Congress Cataloging-in-Publication Data

Title: Keywords for gender and sexuality studies / edited by
The Keywords Feminist Editorial Collective.
Description: New York: New York University Press, [2021] |
Series: Keywords | Includes bibliographical references.
Identifiers: LCCN 2021014000 | ISBN 9781479808137 (hardback) |
ISBN 9781479808151 (paperback) | ISBN 9781479808120 (ebook) | ·
ISBN 9781479808168 (ebook other)
Subjects: LCSH: Women's studies. | Sex role—Terminology. |
Women—Terminology. | Feminism.
Classification: LCC HQ1180 .K49 2021 | DDC 305.42—dc23
LC record available at https://lccn.loc.gov/2021014000

Hardback 9781479808137
Paperback 9781479808151
Consumer Ebook 9781479808120
Library Ebook 9781479808168

New York University Press books are printed on acid-free paper, and
their binding materials are chosen for strength and durability. We
strive to use environmentally responsible suppliers and materials to
the greatest extent possible in publishing our books.

Manufactured in the United States of America

10 9 8 7 6 5 4 3 2 1

Also available as an ebook

Contents

Introduction

Keywords Feminist Editorial Collective

We write this introduction from our isolated homes across the United States in the fall of 2020 while many of us are homeschooling our kids, teaching classes from our kitchen tables, and worrying about the health and economic stability of our families, friends, and communities. We write as the world is witnessing a great upheaval in neoliberal patriarchal white supremacist business as usual. From the start, our collective wanted to address these structures head-on. We had planned to write this introduction together during an editorial retreat over a long weekend away in late March 2020; writing collectively while sharing food, drinks, and camaraderie was central to how we imagined the praxis of creating this volume. Losing the possibility for that type of embodied, collective feminist world making is, in the end, a tiny loss within the unspeakably enormous losses created by the COVID-19 pandemic and the traumatic events of state violence. Yet the many losses and structural inequities that the pandemic exposes and the rising collective voices opposing them are now, and always will be, the context from which we, along with our contributors, produced this volume. Remembering context and history, building and fostering relationships of mutual care, and collectively generating knowledge are central to the feminist approach that we hope *Keywords for Gender and Sexuality Studies* reflects.

While some volumes might begin with an account of what the book is, we intentionally begin this introduction with an account of how it came together. The work of creating this Keywords volume began as a scholarly endeavor that was also a commitment to collectivity, both as politics and as practice. Before the coronavirus shut down our ability to see each other and write in person, we were able to gather together three times to write, plan, and lay out the process for editing the keywords. It was important to us to think about, commemorate, and work in honor of the collective practices that gave birth to some of the most important feminist publishers and texts of our time: Kitchen Table Press, Sister Vision Press, and Third Woman Press and works such as *This Bridge Called My Back*; *All the Women Are White, All the Blacks Are Men, but Some of Us Are Brave*; *Nice Jewish Girls*; "The Combahee River Collective Statement"; *Women of All Red Nations*; and *Indigenous Women and Feminism*. Pushing through the crises that arose during the COVID pandemic, even at the scale of daily life, led many of us to reflect even further on the centrality of care to the labor of editing and writing. We told our contributors and each other that while we were going to continue to push through, we would do so while keeping each other's well-being in mind.

These acts of intellectual, feminist caring ensured that this amazing array of feminist scholars could manifest this book. We arranged writing dates, phone calls, and consults with each other and contributors. We wrote together in pomodoro sessions, brainstormed entries, or sometimes just let deadlines slide until people could manage. When someone stumbled under the weight of family duties, illness, or other burdens, we took up the load for each other.

For many of us, these practices are based in the activist, queer, disabled, immigrant, Indigenous, anarchist, and feminist communities we grew up in, as well as those we have learned from. We are all grateful to have been able to lean on each other and to have created an editorial process that felt smooth, democratic, trusting, and centered on the well-being of its workers.

This melding of theory and practice is a theme of this Keywords volume, as well as, indeed, a theme of the genealogy of feminist studies itself. Gender and sexuality studies has found institutional purchase in universities and colleges throughout North America for almost five decades. Initially organized under the rubric of women's studies, the feminist and queer political struggles that found a home in the university emerged from multiple civil rights and anticolonial efforts ranging from women's and gay liberation, movements against racial oppression and for Indigenous sovereignty, and global struggles against apartheid, colonialism, capitalism, and enslavement. As a reflection of these multiple origins, the field that we are calling "gender and sexuality studies" in this volume continues to be multiple, contested, and fluid. The overlapping investments of queer studies with feminist and gender studies and the emergent field of trans studies also shape the present contours of gender and sexuality studies.

Gender and sexuality studies is a vast set of methods, questions, and concerns that each refract across multiple fields, from the humanities to the social sciences to the sciences, and refuse to be contained by any one discipline. The editors of this volume similarly come from a variety of disciplinary backgrounds and institutional locations. We designed this volume to be geared toward introductory gender/feminist/sexuality/women's studies courses at the undergraduate and graduate levels that serve as gateways into the field. Including our fierce colleague Shona N. Jackson, who later needed to withdraw from the project, and our brilliant research assistant Anisha Ahuja, together the eight of us brainstormed a working list of keywords, cowrote the book proposal, and came up with a list of tentative contributors. We also coconceived and planned out an editorial process that would ensure that each of us carried an equal editorial load and that each keyword would be handled by two editors at all times.

As many of us have taught such introductory courses ourselves, our aspiration for *Keywords for Gender and Sexuality Studies* is that it provides readers, including but not limited to teachers and students, with a set of terms that will aid them in understanding the central methodological and political stakes currently energizing queer and feminist studies in gender and sexuality. Our vision is oriented toward showing the different ways that gender and sexuality must be conceptualized through the prisms of racialization, coloniality, nation, and class. As a result, we worked hard to approach the vastness of this field by centering intersectional feminist knowledge as it is located in relation to anticolonial and civil rights struggles that foreground how gender and sexuality get configured through these other vectors. The ethics of naming origins and practicing correct and thorough citation are central to this project. For instance, we do not use the term *intersectionality* lightly. Rather, we take up intersectionality as "part of a cohort of terms that black feminists created in order to analyze the interconnectedness of structures of domination" (Nash 2019a, 6).

We have fundamentally operated from the knowledge that the term *feminism* has often been appropriated by a white liberal vision of women's empowerment or equality without acknowledging how race, colonialism, political economy, gender, and other structural inequalities differentiate women's experiences. The corollary to that insight is that feminist political concerns have often emerged in political and intellectual spaces not explicitly named or framed as feminist because they did not always foreground "woman" as a primary subject. Gender and sexuality studies in our framework does not regard "woman" as its primary object of study or understand identity and representation as the field's central concerns—in part because we understand that gender binarisms, such as the one that upholds biological womanhood as an essential category, are themselves in league with the project of white supremacy, which reserves normative gender identity for white subjects.

We also take the "wave" model of feminist history—in which feminism can be categorized chronologically as "first wave," "second wave," or "third wave"—as insufficient because the significant events on that time line refer overwhelmingly to white and middle-class feminist history. Instead, in this volume, we are eager to highlight the richness of work that complicates single-axis or linear time line analyses of gender and sexuality. The essays gathered in this volume trace various intellectual strands, sometimes interwoven at key historical moments and sometimes running parallel across disparate contexts. Many essays think with queer of color critique, trans studies, and/or disability studies in their overlapping challenges to normativity; others focalize structural contestations to a range of institutions, from the state and securitization to biomedical health industries and extractive capitalism.

Drawing from Indigenous feminisms, critiques of settler colonialism, and queer engagements with matter and ecology, many keywords call attention to the fundamental assumptions of humanism's political and intellectual debates—from the racialized contours of property and ownership to eugenicist discourses of improvement and development. Across the volume, we see feminisms explicitly working with the cleavages that Blackness produces in concepts of gender and sexuality; transnational critiques that are oriented around subjugated knowledges and decolonial thought; queer studies that prioritize diffuse understandings of relationality, intimacies, and sexualities; and movements for abolition imbricated with analyses of both care and carcerality. Reflecting the disciplinary breadth of the field, the essays in this collection weave together methodologies from science and technology studies, affect theory, and queer historiography. As a whole, these essays move alongside the distinct histories and myriad solidarities of gender and sexuality studies.

In conceptualizing the volume this way, we considered some of the rhetorical dead ends and theoretical cul-de-sacs we often find ourselves in as teachers in gender and sexuality studies classrooms. Some of these dead ends, we thought, consisted in the terms that seem to define the conditions within which we speak to, and labor alongside, each other: oppositions, for instance, between theory and praxis, the university or college and the "real" world, academic and nonacademic communities, speculation and fact. Students and professors alike often use these binaries to challenge the value of the knowledge we produce, leaving us caught in a drama that pits seemingly different kinds of feminist actors against each other: the scholar and the activist, the teacher and the worker, the professor as producer of knowledge and the student as recipient of that knowledge.

What do these inherited conflicts have to do with feminism, queer theory, or gender and sexuality studies today? Often the birth of women's studies is narrated as the institutionalization of what used to be a movement. The story goes like this: Once upon a time, by which we mean the 1960s, there was a political grassroots movement called feminism, or women's liberation, and in the 1970s and 1980s, some in the movement agitated to get their knowledge included in academia, even at the expense of others. Soon those ideas became professionalized as women's studies. At that point, the story tells us, feminism began to lose its political edge. The serious activists and workers stayed in the "real" world, while only the select few joined the privileged ranks of the ivory tower. Academic knowledge regularly superseded that produced from elsewhere. Only certain thinkers became "experts."

Without a doubt, the institutionalization of women's studies produced and continues to produce very real and unequal distributions of institutional access, power, money, social and cultural capital, and precarity between and among feminists. We do not intend to minimize those disparities. But we do wish to ask, What do we lose when we refuse to accept the distance between these terms and the disparities between these feminist actors as simply natural and given, and what might we gain when we become attentive to how they are related? What other histories of activism and theory—past, present, and future—can we see when we refuse these distinctions and this single narrow history?

It is here we might recall the rich tradition of working people's organizing, of feminist consciousness-raising groups, of woman of color caucuses, of community and neighborhood and union study groups, that came together in different historical periods to read what we now think of as critical theory, whether Marxist, socialist, anarchist, gay and lesbian or queer; from the radical Black tradition; or from Black, Chicana/Latina, Asian diasporic, Indigenous, Muslim, or Jewish feminisms as well as other political traditions. For these groups, discussing and exchanging political theory of many sorts were simply ways to think about the project of making

worlds otherwise to the deeply flawed one in which we live. If a text was challenging, the work of unfolding its challenges was part of the raising of a collective understanding, together. Here, again, we can bear witness to historic expressions of collectivity as praxis and as pedagogy. Perhaps it is time to return to these histories of collaborative praxis to rethink what learning can be.

Thus we want to use the occasion of this book to throw out some of the tired old narratives about intellectual and activist labor that continue to haunt us. The university is a workplace, implicated and intertwined with the workings of a state that is also in the world. While professors teach students, students are teaching professors at every step along the way. Many scholars engage in activism even as we teach or become other kinds of workers. Sometimes our workplace is the site of our activism. But writing, too, is valuable labor, not some luxury meant to be pitted against other kinds of work, to the detriment of its social and political value. More than that, feminist and queer theory, particularly as it emerges from woman of color and transnational feminism, is and has always been a knowledge that travels, confusing the professional and disciplinary lines that are meant to unevenly distribute theory's critical value, lines that try to elevate theory into some mythical realm where its trenchant relation to the world as it is, and as it could be, is somehow erased. Feminist knowledge has always traveled from the shelter to the state and back again, from the psychoanalytic couch to the artist's body and back again, from the front lines of racial protest to the poet's notebook and back again, from the reservation to the courtroom and back again, from the kitchen table to the union boardroom and back again, from the dance floor to the text and back again, from the text to the bedroom. And back again.

Theory is praxis and praxis is theory. And nowhere has this ever been so true than in the genealogies of literature, writing, activism, art, and institutional life that have come to constellate the worlds we now call gender and sexuality studies. As the reader will see, then, we frame gender and sexuality studies as an opportunity to deepen analyses of the relationships among race, gender, sexuality, nation, ability, and political economy as foregrounded in the rich history of justice-oriented intersectional movements. This volume centers scholarship enacting these analyses: Black, Indigenous, and woman of color feminisms; transnational feminisms; queer of color critique; trans, disability, and fat studies; feminist science studies; and critiques of the state, law, detention centers, and prisons that emerge from within queer and woman of color justice movements.

We define a keyword as a genealogical inquiry that reflects upon the field in terms of its elaboration across diverse disciplines, geographies, and communities. In *Keywords: A Vocabulary of Culture and Society*, Raymond Williams writes that he aims to examine each of his keywords as "a field of meanings" or "the vocabulary of a crucial area of social and cultural discussion, which has been inherited within precise historical and social conditions and which has to be made at once conscious and critical—subject to change as well as to continuity . . . a shaping and reshaping, in real circumstances and from profoundly different and important points of view" ([1976] 2014, xxxv). A keywords project, Williams argues, is something different from a dictionary project, and although his volume follows the conceit of alphabetical organization, he makes the argument that such a project cannot be, nor should aim to be, encyclopedic.

We agree that keywords projects are partial and perspectival, more generative than definitive; we see that as a strength of the genre. Following the approach laid out by Williams, our goal is that each of the keywords in this volume is a site of explication and critique that generates new political formations and engagements on many possible levels. Some contributors frame their keyword entries to address central debates animating the field. Some contextualize their keywords vis-à-vis related concepts or terms. Others produce critical genealogies of a given term and show how these genealogies have shaped its emergence or critical reception. Many authors speak from their own activist work. For all contributors, though, the main task has been to connect the work each keyword does in its constitutive fields to what it animates in the field of gender and sexuality studies.

Even as this keywords project addresses the need for a discrete volume emphasizing gender and sexuality, we seek to establish a dialogic relationship with other Keywords volumes. This relationship emerges from the multi-institutional and multifield positionality of the editorial team, within whose work gender and sexuality constitute a "gaze from below" reorientation of knowledge production in both disciplinary and interdisciplinary fields. Collectively, the keywords in this volume underscore the integral nature of gender and sex-based distinction as the a priori genre of the human and, as such, central to all aspects of the human experience and thought. While, for example, colonialism, imperialism, and settler colonialism are central to the field of African American studies—as shown in the recently published *Keywords for African American Studies*—locating these keywords in gender and sexuality studies critically reorients our lens to centralize how processes of racialization and colonial and imperial exploitation are deeply gendered and sexualized. Several keywords in this collection overlap with those in *Keywords for Disability Studies*, *Keywords for Environmental Studies*, and *Keywords for Children's Literature*, including *citizenship*, *education*, *gender*, *queer*, *girl*, *race*, *ecology*, *sexuality*, and *space*. Many of our contributors' intersectional orientation to these fields and others, including Asian American studies and Latinx studies, means this volume offers a sustained and far-reaching engagement with the previous volumes. These crossovers are crucially important, as they signal the interrelated development of these fields of study and the necessity of their being in conversation in order to produce a deep and meaningful intersectional understanding of shared core concepts.

Although we have included a robust list of keywords, this would not be a feminist project if we did not pay attention to what was inevitably left out. Throughout this collective editorial process, we have described our approach to the question of what to exclude as one of "tops and bottoms." This playful description obviously signals queer sexual practice. But concretely, it means that we have imagined "tops" to be the dominant terms listed in the table of contents; "bottoms" refers to terms that were subordinate but nonetheless powerful within each essay. For example, *femme* became the keyword under which *butch* is accounted for, in a reversal of the prevailing conception of femme as an adjunct to butch; girl is included but not boy; education but not pedagogy.

Simultaneously, our choice of keywords indexes conceptual frameworks or intellectual traditions rather than specific practices or identity categories; these choices reflect the fact that while popular terms change, the logics governing how knowledges, practices, and identity categories come to circulate have a longer historical reach. Thus we include identity but not specific identity categories; heteronormativity but not marriage; biology but not medicalization, pathologization, or technology; justice but not equality or equity. We include gender, trans, and cis as intellectual and conceptual frameworks rather than identity terms (and not nonbinary, genderqueer, and multiple other terms indexing gender nonconforming practices that are nonetheless referred to in these essays). Relatedly, we have not included any entries that trace the historical genealogies of any particular form of feminism: Black feminism, Indigenous feminism, Latinx or Asian American feminism, or even Liberal feminism. This is because we are committed to an open and changing idea of what those traditions might mean rather than defining their perspectives and limitations and because we did not want to endorse multiculturalist pedagogies that give each of these genealogies a module of their own, ultimately forfeiting their complexities and interweavings. Instead, we simply asked Black, Indigenous, Latinx, Asian American, Arab, Muslim, and other writers to take up the central terms that we thought every queer feminist scholar needed to know.

There were some cases in which important keywords fell beyond the structure of the volume because they seemed too large to cover adequately in a keyword essay, or any essay for that matter. For example, the table of contents does not include some of the biggest terms in the field, such as *feminism*, *violence*, *relationality*, *activism*, *assimilation*, or *resistance*. However, each of these arises over and over again across the volume. One of our more experimental attempts at navigating the tricky terrain of inclusion was an imagined entry titled "LGBTQIAA2S+," indexing the emergence and limitations of acronyms across the recent history of queer and trans politics. Although these particular entries never ended up getting spoken for, we leave the door open for a future edition to take up the project of identifying the ever-expanding umbrella of terms without foreclosing other possibilities we cannot even imagine at this moment.

We also felt that input from those outside the collective was critical to our project, particularly from those who might teach the book. To that end, we reached out to fellow teachers, activists, and thinkers at the 2019 National Women's Studies Association conference in

San Francisco, in part to test our intuitions about what to include and how. We presented our provisional keywords list to our peers at a keywords panel and asked them to tell us what they thought was missing. From that meeting, we gained six more terms—*intersex, lesbian, agency, identity, sports,* and *religion*—that we had either not thought of or eliminated from the earlier list; to the attendees of that panel who so generously and brilliantly helped us resee our own table of contents, we extend our sincerest thanks. While no single volume could successfully encompass the complexity of the frames, investments, and methodologies of these fields or the global complexities that shape them, we believe that this volume ultimately does offer a snapshot of the intellectual depth of the field in its current and emerging forms. Our hope, again, is that this volume will see enough use that in a next edition, we can even further expand what we were not able to accomplish here.

One last word did not end up in our table of contents: *collectivity*. We began the project in deep historical sympathy with and gratitude for our foremothers and our lesbian and queer and trans ancestors who wrote, edited, published, and organized in collective and cooperative formations. And as the state and our social and political worlds broke down around us across 2019 and 2020, the importance of collective action as well as the resurrection of mutual aid, cooperative, and care pod formations in the pandemic and its historic uprisings against state and police violence resounded even more profoundly for each of us in our various locations, as we participated in and witnessed organizing to support Black Lives Matter and abolition movements within the everyday struggle of trying to survive a pandemic.

It is collectivity that has led to what restructuring and redistributions we have had and collectivity that will lead to a just future. Instead of writing that entry, however, we had to step up to write the entry on *race*,

for which we had a great deal of difficulty finding an author—no surprise given the traumas of the last few years. In lieu of a formal entry on collectivity, we offer up this process, this introduction, and our collectively written "race" keyword entry as evidence of the importance of collectivity to feminist praxis. These intersectional, collective engagements are now more than ever important in a world struggling to deal with the violent entanglements of white supremacy.

While we recognize the promise of collectivity, we also do not want to romanticize the term or oversimplify the sometimes contradictory dynamics it implies. These very dynamics call us to confront and grapple with dissensus and even sometimes incommensurability. It is through this powerful, if imperfect, promise of collectivity that we recognize we cannot afford to move forward without supporting each other and imagining new worlds that take into account all of us and the "we"s that might emerge through our collective efforts.

In the classrooms, kitchens, cafés, parks, bookstores, bedrooms, and meeting rooms in which we hope that this volume will have a life, we hope that the reader will take a moment or two to step away from the text to imagine for themselves different, less individualistic, more collectivized ways of being, creating, organizing, living, and thriving. And we hope that this practice and all these words will travel further—back to the kitchen tables and working people's circles, reading groups, unions, and book clubs that foment change and then perhaps back into classrooms again. And then perhaps even further toward a better, more just world.

1

#

micha cárdenas

What does it mean to become a hashtag? When Black and trans people say they do not want to become a hashtag, the statement is, in part, shorthand for saying that they do not want to die. I imagine they do not want to become like #SandraBland or #TrayvonMartin, people who were murdered by police and vigilantes and became hashtags that spurred massive mobilizations for justice by the #BlackLivesMatter movement (cárdenas 2017). Many trans people of color do not even have the privilege of becoming a hashtag because their deaths often do not become causes for such mobilizations. Yet to become a hashtag is to become multiple, to become a massive flow of information and energy that far exceeds the racialized, gendered confines of a single body.

Hashtags as they are popularly known today are corporate commodifications of the means of daily communication and community formation (Jackson, Bailey, and Welles 2020). The # symbol is used by social media platforms such as Twitter to allow a quick search of their database of recent posts that contain particular markers, signified to the algorithms of the platform by the # followed by a series of letters and numbers. This is not new in that it was commonly used as a way to create rooms in older platforms for online conversations like Internet Relay Chat (Losh 2019).

In considering hashtags, scholars of intersectional feminism and trans feminism can consider not just categorization and labels but operators that enable action.

Following Deleuze and Guattari, we can ask not only what a hashtag is but what it does. One thing a hashtag does is allow scholars to study a massive conversation, a huge amount of data being created in real time, through an ongoing process of communication, exchange, databasing, and algorithmic data transfer (cárdenas 2017).

VJ Um Amel, an Egyptian American remix artist, creates artworks that allow viewers to see and hear hashtags. In her article "A Virtual Body Politic on #Gaza: The Mobilization of Information Patterns," she presents an image she created that visualizes over a million tweets about the Egyptian uprising in 2011, all grouped under the hashtag #Egypt (Sakr 2015). Organized with different languages as colors, the image is reminiscent of a ball of cotton candy, or a head of hair, or a sea creature with an uncountable number of strands, with many protrusions curving out, possible threads of conversation, areas of interest, flows of energy devoted to a thread.

In another piece, "#Gaza Audio-Visual Narrative by a Cyborg," Amel (2014) presents a different method of visualizing an impossible amount of data. Instead of an unstructured ball, the artist re-creates a photograph by using the massive number of images referenced by a hashtag, shrinking them down and arranging the images as pixels in the photograph. The image she chooses to represent hashtags including #Gaza and #PalestineResists is deeply haunting, a blurry surveillance camera image of three young Palestinian boys running across a beach before being murdered by the Israeli Defense Forces (IDF). Amel uses the power of a hashtag to visualize the massive scale of violence, assembling thousands of horrific images of murdered Palestinian children alongside images of protest mobilizations, comics commenting on the violence, and Zionist propaganda images arguing the valor of the IDF. In this artwork, she shows the power of a hashtag, the immensity that overwhelms understanding, much like the immensity of violence that the settler colonial project of the state of Israel enacts on Palestinian people.

Amel's artwork visualizing social media posts makes the categorization process perceptible by which settler colonialism utterly devalues the individual lives of these three boys and turns them into multiplicities, into imagined categories of violent racialized others. In her writing about the artwork, Amel wonders if this is what the end of the world looks like, but I would respond with claims from Donna Haraway (2016), building on the work of Black scholars such as Cedric Robinson (1983), that reject apocalyptic thinking and understand the present moment of violence as a plantationocene, or capitalocene: an epoch of time in which the earth is shaped by racial capitalism. The group California Scholars for Academic Freedom (2020) points to the thousands of Palestinians that have been unjustly murdered in the Great March of Return, #GreatReturnMarch, which has been going on since 2018. The huge number of images of Palestinian children murdered by the IDF does not indicate a soon-to-be end to this violence but visualizes a process that has continued since the 1948 attack on Palestine by Israel and continues an even longer trajectory of the murder of millions of Native people in settler colonial projects in places such as the United States.

The use of hashtags such as those in "#Gaza Audio-Visual Narrative by a Cyborg" allow one to see the online community's reaction to three young Palestinian boys joyfully playing soccer on a beach who, due to the racism of the IDF, have their bodies destroyed seconds later by weapons likely supplied by the United States. These boys expand into a process beyond their individual social categories. Hashtags facilitate mediated processes that make perceptible these boys becoming many bodies, many voices, and many, many deaths. The boys' individual hopes, desires, and losses have been obliterated, spread out into billions of lines of data; they have become a hashtag. By considering hashtags, scholars of gender and sexuality studies can consider operations rather than categories, processes rather than reified entities. Hashtags are algorithmic operators used by people on social media to tag content, to enter into a conversation, to add data to a flow. In the hands of artists such as VJ Um Amel, hashtags allow scholars to think gender and sexuality far beyond the bounds of a single body or identity, seeing in a single visual how hashtags create processes where gender, sexuality, race, and nationality interact, spread, and dance across millions of points.

2

Abjection

Leticia Alvarado

There is a widely held understanding of what political art from minoritarian communities looks like: accessible, uplifting, humanizing, unifying. What do scholars and students of gender and sexuality make, then, of politically inclined queer and of color artists who use strategies that seem counterintuitive—that embrace and often embody abstraction, illegibility, and dejection? A useful rubric to help us understand the work of their aesthetic strategies is that of abjection. In everyday use, the word *abjection* signals debasement and extreme societal rejection. Abjection's scholarly genealogy reveals a complex dynamic that might help us understand the ways we are constituted as individuals in relation, imbricated in rubrics of power.

Abjection is commonly understood as the process of social or psychological casting out of undesirables in order to consolidate a norm or ideal but also the condition of being undesirable. Two significant theorists whose writings bring psychoanalysis, aesthetics, and social and political thought together in conversations are Julia Kristeva and Georges Bataille. Kristeva's *Powers of Horror: An Essay on Abjection* and Bataille's writings on abjection and his essay "L'Informe" have had a profound influence on gender and sexuality studies, particularly in those corners of the field that engage theories of political aesthetics, such as cultural studies, performance studies, art history, literary theory, and the production of art itself. Bataille situates abjection within a social matrix, structured in and through biopolitical governmentality. Which is to say, abjection is a process linked to the treatment of bodies in hierarchical cultures that produce "waste societies" structured by class (Tyler 2013, 20; Hennefeld and Sammond 2020, 3). Because, according to Bataille (1999), social abjection is a consequence of proximity to abject things (filth, snot, vermin), this concept is closely linked to his concept of *l'informe*, or "formlessness," which he describes as an active concept that "bring[s] things down in the world . . . squashed like a spider or an earthworm" (1985, 31). For Bataille, what is abject also resists social homogeneity and assimilation into capitalist circulation (Georgelou 2014, 29). Kyla Wazana Tompkins (2017, 266) makes Bataille's emphasis on classlessness and the crude as clear proximal affects to abjection. Bataille's theory of formlessness has been famously taken up, as Tompkins writes, in elaboration of an "anti-modernist art practice" (265) but also in the formulation of an aesthetic, a way of organizing the senses, that counters hierarchical artistic operations with a focus on form and content and prioritizes thinking with concepts of performativity and affect (H. Foster 1998; Bois and Krauss 1997).

Kristeva's Lacanian and psychoanalytic approach in *Powers of Horror* most directly engages abjection as a negative process of subject formation—the ways by which the self comes to be formed in opposition to other entities. Distinguished as something other than "subject" or "object," the abject, for Kristeva, is an "in-between," "ambiguous," and "composite" intermediary entity that helps the subject cohere through its exclusion (Kristeva 1982, 4). The way Kristeva describes it, this process is propelled by the infant's differentiation to the maternal figure as much as by the repulsion to and differentiation from bodily secretions and the wasting body. Once formed, the Kristevan subject is nonetheless invested in the negative process that resulted in its becoming: what is rejected as abject/other becomes foundational to becoming a self. An entity that "disturbs identity, system, order [and] does not respect borders, positions, rules," the abject is then locked in a relationship of simultaneous "attraction and repulsion" with the subject-in-becoming (Kristeva 1982, 4).

While Kristeva's French feminism is engaged with theories of gender formation, particularly in relation to the psychic rejection of the mother's body, and Bataille was thinking in relation to the material world as organized by class, in some ways, both theorized abjection as resolutely ahistorical. Neither theorist overtly engaged the sociopolitical categories of race, colonization, and empire or their imbrication in longer histories of gender formation in the ways that we have come to recognize as part of the work of woman of color feminists, queer of color critique, and gender studies.

However, abjection has proven to be an especially useful rubric for scholars of queer, queer of color, feminist, and critical race theory who explore the historically specific debasement of socially undesirable communities (J. Butler 1993a; Halperin 2007; Ibarra, n.d.; J. Rodríguez 2014; Sandoval-Sánchez 2005; D. Scott 2010; Shimakawa 2002; Vargas 2014). These scholars argue that the formation of normative identities (including, for instance, national identities) coheres through the symbolic and material rejection and degradation of certain kinds of bodies and communities—those Black, brown, queer, disabled, DACAmented, undocumented, and poor—that deviate from a societal ideal, or in Foucault's words, the "norm" (Foucault [1978] 1990). For instance, in her theorization of subject formation through the work of "performativity," the feminist and queer theorist Judith Butler describes "a domain of abject beings" living in "uninhabitable zones" that are variously and "densely" populated by minoritized communities. These zones of abjection help us understand the "exclusionary matrix by which subjects are formed" (J. Butler 1993a, 3).

Centered on the denizens of abjection's uninhabitable zones, scholars of queer, queer of color, feminist, and critical race theory and those writing on queer migration have provided a model to think about abjection as "reclamation": a resistant engagement with identity politics writ large in what has historically been a counterintuitive site from which to imagine collectivity, queer sociality, and power via negative affect (Sandoval-Sánchez 2005; Halperin 2007; Shimakawa 2002; D. Scott 2010; J. Rodríguez 2014; Vargas 2014). For example, in his brief meditation on the politicized possibilities of abjection for queer Latinx men living with AIDS, Alberto Sandoval-Sánchez narrates their abjected bodies as "bodies in revolt that corporalize difference and heterogeneity with the potential to never cease 'challeng[ing their] master' with a boundary crisis, the instability of meaning, and the disruption of order." These queer Latinx men's embrace of abjection, he tells us, "[undoes], in some part, racism, shame, homophobia, and the fear of death, allowing for a source of self-empowerment and a liberating counterhegemonic force" (2005, 549).

Similarly writing about recovering pleasure from shameful desire, Juana María Rodríguez urges us to "consider the possibility of seizing our sexual imaginations to activate abjection as a resource for a reclamation of erotic-self-determination and world-making" (2014, 21). Queer Chicana artist Xandra Ibarra works precisely to "explore abjection and joy and the borders between proper and improper racial, gender, and queer subjects" (A. Patel, n.d.). Often embodying and bringing together demeaned social positions—by combining, for example, the cockroach and the sex worker into one character in performance—Ibarra embraces an aesthetic strategy that helps the spectator see how abjection not only forms the national imaginary but also shapes who gets left out of minoritarian political projects that elevate "respectability," or normative, productive belonging to the state, as the key to accessing more political power (Higginbotham 1993).

In fact, in some ways, we might consider "respectability" to be abjection's Other. *Respectability politics*, a term referencing histories of assimilation and desire for incorporation, ask us to clean up, to make nice, to shed any characteristics dominant culture might find distasteful. Thinking with abjection might instead offer us ways to not imagine communities insistent on normative belonging to an exclusionary order but instead explore modes of being that resist performing cohesion and knowability at the expense of those living, in Butler's terms, in the "zones of exclusion" (J. Butler 1993a, 3). Such a model might encourage us to dwell in the houses of difference famously proposed by Audre Lorde ([1984] 2007b), to do the difficult work of being with one another in and across difference.

3

Affect

Joshua Javier Guzmán

"Can the subaltern feel?" asks José Esteban Muñoz (2006, 677) in response to Gayatri Spivak's well-known dictum "Can the subaltern speak?" According to Spivak (1988), the subaltern, a postcolonial variation of the Gramscian figure of the economically dispossessed, cannot speak, let alone know herself under the neocolonial structures of discourse she seeks to disrupt. But does this also preclude the subaltern from feeling? Muñoz's provocative retort gets to the epistemological problem at the center of affect studies: Can knowing be felt, and is feeling a way of knowing?

The Spivak-Muñoz relay unearths what Judith Butler (1986) names the "Cartesian ghost" haunting western epistemology. In feminist theory, the Cartesian ghost represents the residual though consequential split between mind (i.e., thought, philosophy, consciousness, activity) and body, whereby the former is revered, valued, endowed, and proudly managerial over the latter, which, since antiquity, has been coded as feminine (i.e., the passions, the passive, the body, the corporal, the flesh). Therefore, what affect circumscribes for feminist theorization is how masculine gender norms of western colonial thought emerge as the very "embodiment of denial" of the body (J. Butler 1986, 44). This will have a profound impact on the gender binary system (masculine/feminine), where the body and its potential to feel and be affected are made to succumb to the will of masculine denial sanctified as reason and rationality. Affect's history is a history of the irrational limit of reason, where what one can know is suspended and *how* we come to be—remembering Simone de Beauvoir's watershed claim "One is not born, but rather *becomes*, woman" ([1949] 1989, 267; my emphasis)—takes flight. In other words, the processual is one of affect's earliest articulations in feminist theory.

Yet one cannot forget that Jean-Paul Sartre (1948), de Beauvoir's partner and interlocutor, famously hated emotions, arguing for their irrelevance due to their obstructionist nature to thwart the real world, since in his paradigm, the "magical realm of emotions is something we regress into when under duress," as Muñoz (2020, 71) has put it. Sartre's suspicion of emotions mirrors a similar assessment by Sigmund Freud that emotions are merely spectacular symptoms of something deeper. In fact, the hysteric, the feminine Gothic figure who demonstrates Truth through what Sedgwick (1980, 102) called "the hieroglyphics of the body," "acts out" feelings of betrayal, jealousy, and anxiety but has no language for them, *since these feelings are not hers*. They are projected onto her by her counterpart, the paranoid-schizoid: the masculine, cool, objective investigator/scientist/analysts/philosopher. (Think here of Regan's terrible monstrosity [played by Linda Blair] in the 1973 film *The Exorcist*.)

Perhaps this is what leads Chicana feminist Gloria Anzaldúa to proclaim that she "knew things before Freud" at the moment when she and fellow Chicana theorist Cherríe Moraga were advocating in the 1980s for "a theory in the flesh," "where the physical realities of our lives—our skin color, the land or concrete we grew up on, our sexual longings—all fuse to create a politic born out of necessity. . . . We are the colored in a White feminist movement" (Moraga and Anzaldúa 1981, 21). To be colored here means to be the object of another's projection, imbued with feelings of being indifferent and in contradiction with the norm. Meanwhile, Kyla Schuller (2018) shows how projection was understood

as "impressionability" in nineteenth-century scientific and early psychoanalytic discourses marking the susceptibility of the feminized. Thus, between hysteria and "theories in the flesh," it becomes clear that feelings can be projected; the boundary between interiority/exteriority blurs. Indeed, the processual is transitive in its ability to provisionally hold multiple objects in relation, even if said relations are "partial and ephemeral, subject to change, and altered by changing conditions," as C. Riley Snorton (2017, 7) writes of his sensual archive in *Black on Both Sides: A Racial History of Trans Identity*. And if the processual remains transitive, it can also be transferable.

In the *Transmission of Affect*, Teresa Brennan (2004) reveals how the mood (what Heidegger called Stimmung) or atmosphere of a room registers on the body and thus can be altered by some body through transmission. To ignore or pathologize the way affect *moves* between individuals is to obscure a physical and social environment's conditioning experience. These "public feelings" are apt grounds for social critique, since they question the way the nation-state, for example, mobilizes feelings as modes of control while also providing an opportunity to rethink forms of collectivity in the face of such oppressive regimes.

"Capitalism has made and continues to make money out of cooking, smiling, fucking," says the Italian Marxist feminist Silvia Federici. "They say it is love. We say it is unwaged work" (1975, 1). What is called "affective labor" often looks like care work. Evelyn Nakano Glenn (2010) has forcefully documented this type of work from unpaid family caregivers to home health care workers in *Forced to Care*. Thus, care and love are fraught public feelings, since they entail a further mystification of labor at the expense of women, the poor, immigrants, and the precarious working class. Even online feelings in the form of likes,

AFFECT   JOSHUA JAVIER GUZMÁN

(dis)likes, laughs, and hearts contribute to how capital may insidiously profit from what Jodi Dean (2009) names "communicative labor," a contemporary variation of such affective work. The transmission of affect actively politicizes emotions by making politics emotional (and personal) and in turn illuminates the social structures conditioning certain lives as livable and others as not by rendering certain genres of life as "likable" and others as not. To quote Ann Cvetkovich, "Depressed? It might be political" (2012, 2).

"Ugly feelings" like depression, melancholia, and "shame and its sisters" have been central to anticolonial, anticapitalist, queer, and feminist approaches to affect (S. Ngai 2005; Sedgwick and Frank 1995). Depathologizing negative emotions such as those can be instrumental to political organizing rather than inhibitive to it and have been paramount to queer and feminist work. Cvetkovich's (2003) *An Archive of Feelings* served as a response to the more canonical "trauma studies" by cataloging the ways affects come to be sexualized and thus queer in not only moments of great social strife (the radical feminist movement, the anti-war movement, or AIDS activism) but also everyday life. If affects are transmittable, malleable, and relational, then they can also be mundane, minor, and ordinary.

Sianne Ngai (2005) has demonstrated how "ugly feelings" such as envy and irritation, characteristic of modern life, are engendered as feminine and operate as noncathartic expressions of discontent. These "ordinary affects," to borrow Kathleen Stewart's (2010, 339) description, provide "worlding refrains" by which "forms, rhythms, and refrains" are disclosed through interrelated phenomena and between human and nonhuman actors, by the stuff outside of intentionality. However, Ranjana Khanna (2003) problematizes "worlding" by meeting it at its Heideggerian roots to exhibit how worlding's disclosing characteristic requires a process of violently inscribing the colony into the modern postcolonial world. For Khanna, uncovering what was previously covered, obscured, opaque, dark, and inscrutable into the "world" throws the parochial into the universal, leaving in its trace colonial melancholia as a potentially refashioned ethics of transnational feminism. After all, as Jonathan Flatley (2008) has argued, melancholy is a sign of modernization itself.

Some minoritarian and intersectional analyses foreground this particular affect to interrogate how a politics of loss more often than not shapes the way gender and sexuality studies approach their objects of investigation. In Anne Cheng's (2000) *The Melancholy of Race*, the feeling of melancholia permeates literature on/from marginalized life in the United States. David Eng and Shinhee Han (2018) tag a particular manifestation of loss also as racial melancholia and dissociation in Asian American psychic life. Antonio Viego (2007) reminds us of the political purchase of centering loss in queer Latinx studies, while Maria Josefina Saldaña-Portillo (2016) melancholizes the figure of the *indio barbaro* for machista Chicanos, and Black feminists such as Saidiya Hartman (2008a) have attuned to such loss as the material remains of historical subjugation.

When attenuating to archives, literature, art, and aesthetic practices *about* the emotional lives of those unpermitted to mourn their own "expulsion" from language, history, and thought, "feeling backward" toward a magnetizing lost object can parochialize attachments and thus proliferate them (Love 2009). Lauren Berlant (2011) has long studied how "the public" is affectively constituted through processes of attachments and detachments—"cruel optimism" being the most stubborn form of attachment to that which prevents one's flourishing; Jennifer Doyle (2013) locates this dynamic in the art world as well, underscoring the coextensive work between affect and "relational aesthetics," art work aimed at "moving" or "touching" the spectator and thus implicating her. However, if the capitalist patriarchy racializes the other through "economies of abandonment," then by extension, capitalist patriarchy *proliferates* attachments, relations, and transmissions (Povinelli 2011a). Minoritarian and intersectional scholarship has, for some time now, sought to identify embodied knowledges that identify with such economies in hopes for collectivity and pleasure.

For Juana María Rodríguez, processes of racialization provoke sexual longings, not entirely divorced from racial melancholia though in line with "the ephemera of affect that leaves no trace" (2014, 4). Chasing the ghostly traces of sexual desire opens up ways of knowing through touching and feeling. As Native scholar Dian Million argues in "Felt Theory," "Feelings are theory, important propositions about what is happening in our lives" (2009, 61). Viewed in this light, frustration as a form of inadequate anger indexes how the world, through systems and structures, makes one's life impossible to live. Keep in mind, ugly feelings do not always guarantee political refusal, as Ngai (2005) elaborates after Paul Virilio. Negative emotions can always potentially be deployed and transmitted toward oppressive logics.

In *The Cultural Politics of Emotion*, Sara Ahmed (2004) contends that emotions are sticky, provoking orientations toward or away, under or beyond ideas, bodies, and things. In *Queer Phenomenology* (2006), she develops these arguments to demonstrate how the way one is oriented in space and time (the world) *affects* what objects are within and out of reach. Ahmed's (2017) larger feminist project is one of reorienting academic discourse to alternative worldviews that enable someone like "the feminist killjoy" to refuse the orgiastic "promise of happiness" dangled in front of her and to instead feel her way through movements for social change.

I like to think about Ahmed and other feminist theorists grappling with the affective life of surviving alongside Lizzie Borden's 1983 feminist fiction film *Born in Flames*. The film tells the story of two feminist pirate radio stations broadcasting to the public in a socialist alternative United States. After an international feminist activist mysteriously dies in police custody, the community spurs into action guided by the two stations broadcasting feminist consciousness-raising messages. Shot documentary-style, *Born in Flames* intimately captures the everyday life of sexism and direct action. After both radio stations are mysteriously burned to the ground, they combine forces and broadcast together out of a stolen van, where they interrupt the US president's address to proclaim on air that women should be paid for their housework. The film ends with a shot of the antenna at the top of one of the Twin Towers exploding. *Born in Flames* can be said to be a film about the wielding of public feelings to combat racism, sexism, homophobia, and exploitation. The lo-fi quality of the film mirrors bootleg culture and the undercommons of sensibility crucial to feminist knowledge sharing. With the phallic destruction of mainstream broadcasting closing the film, *Born in Flames* takes seriously the textured ways we come to know about each other's suffering—the *sensing* of commonality—while transmitting a willful desire to feel the world differently.

Feminist approaches to affect studies become more visible when we heed Roderick A. Ferguson's (2004, 134) description of the Combahee River Collective's articulation of the "simultaneity of oppressions" (a phrase he borrows from Barbara Smith) through group *ties*—or affects. For Audre Lorde ([1984] 2007e), "love between women" predicated her thinking of the erotic, that affective force capable of breaking through the enslaver's broadcast like the explosion of an antenna. What Lorde called the "erotic" is not unlike what Chicana feminist

Chela Sandoval has called a "hermeneutics of love" (2000). These ties, or affects, demonstrate how "theory in the flesh" can link pleasure, desire, feeling, and sense at the disjuncture between knowing (differently) and being (different).

4

Agency
Hershini Bhana Young

An enslaved woman brought to the Cape of Good Hope by Dutch slavers, Tryntjie of Madagascar (b. 1688) only appears in the archival records as a result of her criminal conviction. Sentenced to death for several charges—including the attempted poisoning of her enslaver, Elizabeth Lingelbach, and adultery with her enslaver's husband, Willem Menssink—she was publicly executed, her body left hanging from a forked post. The question of who Tryntjie was, her desires, her motivations, and her fears, marks a seething absence in the archive. Reading her archival remains, scholars and students are left only with an impression of her criminalized agency, a distorted fragment that casts a long shadow into the present.

Tryntjie's long-term "adultery" with Menssink—or, more likely, the slave owner's sexual enjoyment of his property—poses a crisis to current vocabularies of agency. Traditional notions of volition, choice, free will, and independent agential actors collapse when confronted by such systems of subjugation. How can scholars who struggle to account for different frames of historical interpretation explain Tryntjie's years of sexual liaisons with Menssink? Was she a victim of the enslaver's sexual predatory acts? An agent negotiating her relationship with him to her benefit? Was Menssink her rapist or her lover? Or both? In order to understand Tryntjie as something more than a rape victim (with no agency) or a lover (with full agency), we need to interrogate our understandings of agency itself.

When opening the Pandora's box of agency, out jumps a virulent host of attendant foundational concepts such as liberal humanism, discrete normal embodiment, and autonomous subjects. Notions of "free will" have their roots in Christian theology, where theologians stressed the moral agency of humans. This notion of free will was later secularized by John Locke (1689), whose emphasis on the individual as the bearer of free will and on society as a social contract between free individuals gave rise to notions of agency, progress, and humanity that dominate popular understandings of agency today.

Agency, understood as an individual's capacity for calculative acts, is embedded in the liberal conceptualization of the subject as one who is able to volitionally enter into social contracts. If the free subject is human and able to make choices, those supposedly incapable of choice were therefore not quite human and necessarily unfree. Children, women, Natives, savages, the insane, and the disabled all become the limit cases of humanity and agency. As Walter Johnson (1999, 15) writes, the enslavers' "phantasms of [their own] independent agency" were based on the enslaved status of Black men and women deemed incapable of choice. Saidiya Hartman and Frank Wilderson (2003) also note the nonrelationality of Blackness to so-called universal forms of subjectivity. The enslaved's difficulty with crafting a story that stages her will, as Tendayi Sithole elaborates, lies in her status as existing "outside the grammar of being human and its ontological constitution" (2020, 26). Thus the impossibility of telling Tryntjie's story lies in her very exclusion from the category of the agential human and her political relegation to being not quite human and unfree.

Social historians have engaged the concept of agency in order to assert the humanity of enslaved people, the disabled, and other groups. Works such as John Blassingame's (1979) *The Slave Community* and Deborah Gray White's (1999) *Ar'n't I a Woman?* insist that it is only by giving them back their agency that we can recover and retrieve the enslaved person's humanity from what Johnson calls "the historical condition of civil objectification and choicelessness" (2003, 115). There are several challenges with this approach. First, agency is usually reinscribed as "grand"—which is to say, white and masculinist gestures of defiance. Conversely, the agency of people of color, and particularly women, becomes reduced to what Stephanie Li calls "an explicit oppositional stance, embodied through certain types of [individual] actions" (2011, 19). The leader of an armed slave rebellion, typically a man, is seen as more free than the Black woman who submits to rape in order to save her life. The enslaved woman's actions have often been interpreted as conformity or as a form of accommodation (Genovese 2011, 598). Second, attempting to prove the enslaved or the disabled person's humanity by recovering their agency ignores the historical grounding of human agency in racial, gender, and ableist hierarchies. Third, we should not assume that agency is legible in the archive. The archive only recognizes the agency of the enslaved and other subjugated people when their will is criminalized or regarded as deviant.

We can never approach the motives for Tryntjie of Madagascar's actions without the development of different modes of research. Rather than the romance of retrieval, I argue that confronting the seething silences around Black will is "not about uncovering what really happened as we don't have access to this, but about uncovering the places where the will can surface through repeated performances of violence and survival" (H. Young 2017, 23). Similarly, Hartman (2008b, 11) calls for a process of "critical fabulation," in which the scholar allows absences in the archive to generate fictional narrations. These sorts of critical approaches move away from the notion of "agency" as volitional acts chosen by capable individual bodies and, instead, toward a genealogy of performance where individual and collective acts operate on a continuum. Such a reconceptualization of agency as a series of embodied performances locates agency as emerging between differentially embodied and not always autonomous bodies. Rather than agency being the provenance of a single rational, thinking man, it can be understood as a sensuous embodiment that connects nonnormative bodies to each other while recognizing how bodies inhabit "variable and changing orientations within the flow of time" (Emirbayer and Mische 1998, 964). Thus Tryntjie's actions can only be understood in relation to the enslaved people who traveled with her in the ship's hold, the diverse community of indentured and enslaved peoples alongside whom she worked, and even her child whom she poisoned. We can only gesture toward the possibility of her agency as she struggled against her violent relegation to the categories of not quite human, unfree, and worthy only of death.

5

Anal
Dredge Byung'ch

Everyone has an anu
hole," does not recei
refers to anything re
its proximate area. As
anal provides an alter............ .... theory
that decenters the phallus and reproduction as well as the normality these impose and imply. By centering the anus rather than the penis, the term becomes a critique of patriarchal values and social hierarchies (Hocquenghem [1972] 1993). The focus of analysis shifts from traditional masculinity to gender ambiguity, from obligatory labor to pleasurable experience, from the chaste to the erotic, from pride to shame. Anality as an orientation, an approach, and a practice seeks to evade heterosexist life-course models.

The back hole is a site of intense anxiety, signifying heteromasculine penetration, power relations, and deviance. Scholars point to Freud's anal stage of psychosexual development in children as the origin of anal thinking (Freud 1905). As the anus produces excrement, that part of the body and associated practices are regarded as dirty (Douglas 1966). Anal sex is aligned with homosexuality and improper heterosexuality, heavily regulated in many cultures at various times. While homosexual penetrative and receptive sex acts are different from gay identity (Halperin 1989), being the male receiving partner in anal sex is considered feminizing in many cultures (Murray 2002). During the early AIDS crisis, anal sex became associated with disease, death, and self-destruction (Bersani 1987).

Subsequently, anal the
and white, provided a r
sociality: an altern?
rejecting or sur
spectabilit
receptiv
cap'

ry, predominantly cis gay adical critique of phallocentric tive political framework based on ndering mastery. Anality, against re-olitics, embraces abject representations of anal sex as aberrant, disease causing, and anti-ist (Bersani 1987). Anal masculinity embraces risk, nger, and disease. Barebacking (sex without condoms) is proof of a "fuck-you" to social, sexual, and medical norms (T. Dean 2009). "Passive" anal intercourse, such as being a "power bottom," could express control and authority that destabilize hierarchies of active/passive: top/bottom (J. Mercer 2012). Perhaps most vexing to heterochrononormativity, the reproductive failure of anal sex denies the possibility of children and thus a future (L. Edelman 2004). This "antisocial" centering of anal queerness destroys both the self and the possible continuation of humanity (Caserio et al. 2006). Anality is revolutionary, reveling in vilification.

This formulation of anal receptive male sex as radical alterity, however, does not account for gender and race. Queer negativity associated with the white cis-gay anus disregards the positioned relationships that allow for the disavowal of white cis-male privilege and the need to align with multiple, often contradictory communities. Modleski (1991) criticizes Bersani (1987) for ignoring the different stakes of passive anal eroticism for men and for women; for the latter, it is not radical to claim passivity as masochism. Critiquing Bersani's celebration of gay male anal sex as a willful surrender of power, Modleski says, "Masochism in the *guise* of powerlessness is . . . frequently the luxury of empowered beings. . . . It is clear that powerlessness *and* masochism have different ideological valences for women than for gay men" (1991, 148–49). Merck (2000) observes that Bersani is describing two different femininities, saying, "His rendition of rectal sex reveals a heroic rhetoric of 'demolition,'

'danger,' and 'sacrifice' . . . that is nowhere attributed to vaginal penetration. Might it be Bersani's view that male 'femininity' is more butch than its female equivalent, precisely because the subject's masculinity is at stake?" (157). Similarly, Fraiman (2003, 136) critiques Lee Edelman's celebration of anal resistance that reinforces the binary logic of "front/female versus back/male," disavowing women's own erotic deployment of anuses and the painful imperatives of heterosexuality. In sum, the openness accorded to men's anuses assumes a privilege that is given up to others courageously, a practice that remains out of women's reach. "Masochism" thus challenges conventional notions of agency, not as abdicating control, but rather as a site linking power relations between bodies and society through race, gender, and other aspects of difference (Musser 2014).

The refusal of power associated with the phallus in favor of the anus is also contingent for those racially deemed to lack a penis. Fung (1991, 153) notes that "Asian and anus are conflated." Fung emphasizes that there is nothing wrong with being a bottom per se; however, Asian men are always consigned to this position in gay porn videos. Eng (2001) argues that this "racial castration" signals the white male subject's refusal to see the penis on the body of an Asian male, which underscores how the psychic traumas of sexual and racial differences powerfully constitute each other. Yet in rejecting the power of the penis, Joon Oluchi Lee (2005) mines the "castrated boy" by denying the very impulse of aggressive self-preservation that has traditionally marked masculinity. Lee says, "Embracing racial castration can be a potentially libratory willingness to embrace femininity as a race and, vice versa, race as femininity" (44). Hence, the value and eroticization of the racialized *Asian* anus as already feminized represents a threat to white cis-patriarchal social order (Nguyen 2014).

ANAL   DREDGE BYUNG'CHU KANG AND NGUYEN TAN HOANG

Anality symbolically references both low social status and debasement that adheres to bodies of color marked as detritus: posterior and already spoiled. However, this positioning can also be used agentively. The "productive perversity" in identifying with "bad" images or creating alternative narratives broadens racial agendas beyond normalcy and standardization (Shimizu 2007). The shame associated with being on the bottom, Black, and queer can be a valuable while painful form of sociality (Stockton 2006). Black debasement is not redemptive but offers new ways of knowing, fosters attractions, and produces aesthetic delight. Connecting the hierarchical and sexual meanings of "bottom," Darieck Scott (2010) redeploys pain and abjection as potential sources of Black pleasure and power. In this vein, Rodríguez (2014) asserts that what is "queer" is a female-bodied femme of color actively asserting herself as a sexual servant, playing a role assumed for her. Thus the rejection of phallocentric investment in mastery is reduced not to the glorification of the anus but to specific anuses, roles, and performances that take on the nuances of gender, race, class, nation, ability, and other forms of subjectification.

Anal theory enables and constrains degraded bottom positioning, be it aesthetic, affective, political, sexual, or social. In recentering race and gender in anal analytics, Nguyen (2014) formulates "bottomhood" as an ethical position that recodes risk, vulnerability, and submission as racialized-gendered pleasure/power. Bottomhood mobilizes expansive coalitional, minoritarian, political projects. The "anal" in gender and sexuality studies is not just a bodily site symbolic of dirty sex but more broadly about the second, the back, the behind, the debased, the under, the shameful. That is, anal disparagement is a metaphor for social marginalization (contra the phallus) that can be deployed as always also agentive, creative, productive: a well of abjection from which gendered and racialized subjects can remake themselves.

6

Bathroom

Perry Zurn

Colloquially and perhaps paradoxically, the term *bathroom* does not primarily refer to a space of bathing. In fact, one typically looks for a bathroom less to get clean than to deposit the stuff from which one must be cleansed. The bathroom is a waste space, a place where excretion is hidden away but also deeply governed. For millennia, innumerable spoken and unspoken rules have constrained who and when and how one can use the bathroom. But those rules have also been contested. As such, bathrooms are spaces of refuse *and* refusal. They are political spaces and spaces of possibility.

As a mix of social practices and material structures, the bathroom has long been a subject of study in history and architecture, law and philosophy, cultural studies and gender and sexuality studies. As a result, bathroom literature is as rich in content as it is in methodology. Here, I take just one path through that landscape. I pair critical phenomenology (Guenther 2019), which attends to how our experiences are informed by our social practices and institutions, with critical genealogy (Koopman 2012), which tracks a term's history in order not only to illuminate our present but also to reimagine our futures.

When one walks into the social institution called "the bathroom," one walks into a world of feeling and of history. With its pristine white, beige, or silver fixtures, the string of open or closed cubicles, and the fluorescent lights, the modern bathroom provides an education in affect, or cultural emotion. People are trained every day to experience a certain disgust at the product of their own flesh and the subsequent pleasure (and relief) of good hygiene (Cavanagh 2010). Dispatching with their animal selves in a private room, they reemerge into public spaces fully human. The story of the modern bathroom, then, is inseparable from the western conceit of the modern individual (Penner 2013). But what exactly makes this place clean? Hygienic and safety regimes are always interwoven in social orders, especially of gender, race, class, and ability. Understanding those social orders allows us not only to appreciate how the bathroom developed but also to ask how it might develop differently.

In the West, the public bathroom—from pail closet to flush toilet—has long been reserved for the full citizen, engaged in public affairs. Just as women, people of color, people with disabilities, and transgender people have had to fight for inclusion in public life, they have also had to fight for bathroom access. (White) women's restrooms, and thus gender-segregated restrooms, arose in the late 1800s as women joined the industrial workforce (Kogan 2007). Gendered restrooms were then used in colonial contexts to impose colonial gender expectations (Moore 2009). Racially segregated restrooms similarly have a long and wide history, stretching from US settler colonies to apartheid South Africa. After the emancipation of enslaved peoples in the United States, restrooms became a standard reminder of second-class status, even if they did replace the common demand for African Americans to simply relieve themselves in a nearby field (Abel 2009). And while accessible restrooms, as legislated by the Americans with Disabilities Act of 1990 (Kafer 2013), and gender-inclusive restrooms for transgender people (L. Crawford 2015; Nirta 2014; Cannon 2019) are becoming more common, both accessible restrooms and gender-inclusive restrooms are quite often spatially set apart from the pack. Winning rights to the public restroom has, in each case, signified a claim—if still an unequal claim—to public life.

But why has the bathroom been a battleground for social equality? Or conversely, why have social hierarchies used the bathroom as one of their primary forces of control? And what can bathrooms, therefore, help us see about western society? Bathrooms institute "civilized" order in a space of bodily disorder, they police purity in a space of fleshly impurity, and they subject our most private moments to keen surveillance (Douglas 1966; Kristeva 1982; Lugones 2003). That order, purity, and privacy, however, are always deeply informed by racialized, ableist, and cis-centric logics (Zurn 2019). The marginalized "Other" is consistently cast as a force of disorder, making a mess of whiteness, the gender binary, and other norms of embodiment. Bathroom exclusions are therefore common, and inclusions are typically piecemeal.

No social order is ever total, however. There is always a remnant that escapes, a liberatory possibility latent in the fabric of everyday life. The bathroom is no exception. Indeed, it is precisely in those moments when bathrooms and their users defy reigning hygienic and safety regimes that visions of a different, even decarceral future appear. Historically, for instance, "colored" restrooms were often multigendered. Today, accessible restrooms are often ungendered and family friendly. While these facts signify a theoretical degendering of people of color and people with disabilities, they can also inspire new acts of radical imagination and coalition. What would it mean for our multiplicitous selves and our intersectional communities to find equal home in the bathroom (Chess et al. 2004; Gershenson 2010; Pryor 2017; I. West 2010)? What would it look like for our intimacies and our interdependencies to take root in this space? Ultimately, how might bathroom culture reflect a larger culture of care?

While critically tracking the term *bathroom* helps us not only understand human social order but also reimagine it, it also generally obscures the necessity of a more-than-human politics. The modern bathroom trains us to forget where our waste goes. In a culture where waste only ever disappears, whether into our pipes, our landfills, or our rivers, intimacies between the human and the nonhuman are systematically erased (J. Bennett 2010). What would it look like were we to refuse to let our refuse out of sight? What kind of accountability might we practice if we honored the intimate ecologies that really constitute us and connect us to the earth (M. Chen 2012)?

There is no denying that the bathroom is a political space. But that is what makes it a space of possibility. As a social-material fixture we use every day, the bathroom has the potential to illuminate, and ultimately to challenge, some of our deepest values and deepest needs. Appreciating the weave of experiences and institutions that have, across time, made the modern bathroom what it is opens up important questions about what it might be. Leaning into the legacy of refusal, we can demand a radical break with logics that have so long masked insidious social hierarchies with calls to order and purity.

7

BDSM
Jennifer DeClue

Imagine heavy steel double doors opening onto a dimly lit, cavernous warehouse space. The concrete walls are painted black and adorned with leather paddles and crops. Bodies writhe, some wrestle, others are bound to iron rings bolted to the walls. At one such station, taut straps lead down to the crossed wrists of a fat woman wearing a leather bodice and strap-on dildo. Her topless, chaps-clad partner whispers in her ear; she nods her head. The partner slowly rolls a spiked wheel across her chest, over her belly, and down the inside of her thigh. This is a play party where couples and small groups role-play and enact fantasies that channel discipline and restraint, pain and release.

BDSM refers to bondage, discipline and/or domination, submission and/or sadism, and masochism. Exploring BDSM and finding supportive kink communities can be liberatory endeavors for feminist, queer, trans, and nonbinary people of color (Musser 2014). *Kink* can be thought of as sexual desires that defy norms and sexual practices that dive headlong into issues of power and pleasure with intention, consent, and purpose. In their embrace of what may be read as abject sexual appetites, kink communities make space to explore desire without shame. Historic and personal trauma will inevitably rise to the surface, and rather than shy away, BDSM communities work to establish trust and consent, find the language to address safety and risk, and contend with nuances of sexuality and harm that lurk in the shadows of bedrooms and in the corners of psyches.

The place of BDSM within feminist circles has been highly contested over the years. A flash point for this contestation erupted through the issue of pornography during the feminist sex wars of the 1970s and 1980s. Antipornography feminists, like Catharine MacKinnon and Andrea Dworkin, argued that pornography is inherently patriarchal and violent. This camp sought redress from the judicial system and advocated for the censorship of pornography. Propornography feminists found liberation through sex positivity, insisted that redress from the state would only hurt minoritarian subjects, and believed that the censorship of pornography suppressed free speech. Those who supported sex radicalism moved beyond the propornography/antipornography debate by exploring their interests in the messiness of sex play as well as the paradoxes embedded in divining pleasure through BDSM (Nash 2014). In particular, a lesbian feminist S/M (sadism/masochism) group, Samois, which openly and defiantly embraced BDSM, emerged during these feminist sex wars; they published two anthologies, *Coming to Power* (Samois 1981) and *The Second Coming: A Leatherdyke Reader* (Califa and Sweeney 1996), that chronicled the experiences of lesbian feminist BDSM practitioners.

The intricacies of BDSM are tangled up with histories of racial violence; pain and pleasure through dominance and submission have complex resonances for Black people in the kink community. Whether it is the long history of enslavement or the everyday threat of violence, murder, and incarceration that peeks through, the afterlife of slavery is an inescapable factor in an arena where BDSM scenes unfold. Instead of ignoring the hum of historic and contemporary racialized and gendered violence, BDSM can be a pathway to explore the quotidian horrors that shape experiences of being Black in the United States.

One exquisitely satisfying scene that illustrates this particular knot is happening with a dominatrix and the enslaved. She is tall and flawless, has dark brown skin and long thick braids, dons thigh-high stiletto boots and a black leather bustier. On her leash is a middle-aged white man wearing a studded collar and a black leather jockstrap. He licks her boot if she puts one before him. She pets him when she is pleased and stings him with her riding crop when she is not. Something recuperative is happening in this scene of a Black woman dominating a white man in open space. The afterlife of slavery is at work here too. The field of play for Black kinky exploration could mean embracing submission and giving up control, on one's own terms, or trying on domination for size and driving the action for someone else. Pleasure and release could work through holding the position as a top, who is in control of the action, or as a bottom, who is relinquishing control, or as a switch, who partakes in both of these positions. The hierarchy of positions is not absolute, and kinky sex provides a way to enter the sexual field to disrupt dominant power, rewrite outmoded tropes, and dissolve concretized roles that limit sexual exploration. Controlling from the bottom is definitely a thing (DeClue 2016).

As BDSM offers a pathway to contend with racial trauma in the realm of the sexual, so too it provides a way to contend with sexual violence and trauma through touch, control, and role-play. Sexual fantasy creates the space to recognize and make explicit the implicit negotiations embedded in sex (J. Rodríguez 2011). BDSM and kinky play launch excursions through a sexual terrain that is rife with fault lines, craters, and steep drop-offs. Rather than occlude this sexual landscape, BDSM moves toward it and through it with awareness. BDSM sets the stage, offers language, and locates the parameters for the kinds of intrepid sexual encounters that can activate grief, trigger trauma, recall violations, and plunge participants into the past. Having sex is bound to bring up difficult feelings simply by having it, but BDSM navigates this complex ground with intention; kinky sex can wrest control and comfort out of that precarious territory.

Importantly, BDSM does not need a redeeming quality to be valuable; kink can exist for the sake of kink. BDSM and other kinky pleasures are tied to the rebuff of sexual convention and the embrace of acts that have been historically pathologized and criminalized. If we travel back to the play party that introduced this keyword, we can hear pops to already tender cheeks, titillated gasps, and hisses of delight. The erotic power of resistance and defiance in the name of shared pleasure and naughty connection is a current that courses through BDSM communities and binds them together.

8

Biology
Banu Subramaniam and Angie Willey

Feminist engagements with biology vary widely in methodological approaches, critical interventions, and knowledge-making projects. Biology can refer to (at least) two different things: the scientific *study* of living organisms or the workings of organisms *themselves* in all their complexity. With respect to the former, biology emerged as a single coherent scientific field, or as the "biological sciences," only in the nineteenth century, but traditions of natural history and medicine date back to ancient times and include multiple traditions and genealogies across the globe. The biological sciences as we know them today were consolidated through histories of colonialism, and the history of biology subsequently coalesced into a larger history of "western science." The idea of a cohesive and universal science emerged through the appropriation of some nonwestern knowledge as science and the relegation of other knowledge to the status of nonscientific beliefs or cosmologies. Indigenous and local sciences were also marginalized as alternate knowledges, away from the mantle of "Science." In fact, the boundaries among these various knowledge-making practices are highly porous, and the success of the "biological sciences" should be understood as a selective project deeply steeped in the history and afterlives of colonization.

The second meaning of biology—the workings of organisms themselves—is also multiple. First, it is a shorthand for "how things work" at multiple scales: the biology of an amoeba or the biology of development, the biology of muscles or the biology of cells. However, the biological too often gets deployed in opposition to the social or aligned and conflated with the "natural." For example, many talk about biological development in contrast to social development. As a result, people put this use of biology (as "the stuff") into common parlance to signal something foundational, innate, and often immutable. Despite considerable experimental and empirical work in genetics that repeatedly indicates that organisms develop as an unfolding of complex interactions between genes and environment, the binaries of biological/social continue to shape how the term *biology* often gets put into play.

A critical feminist science and technology studies lens calls attention to this slippage between the study of biological phenomena and the biological workings themselves and the trouble this slippage creates. The study of an object is *not* the object itself. Data about bodies are not bodies themselves. The study of any object and the knowledge produced by researchers of it are always representations mediated by the positionality of researchers, modes and apparatuses of measurement, and conceptual and narrative resources available. In other words, biology (the study) always necessarily reflects the cultural, historical, economic, and political contexts out of which it emerges. And the stuff of biology (organisms themselves) might be approached and represented in ways that exceed the bounds of what has historically counted as biology (the study). When the field of biology and its objects of study are conflated, worlds of possibility for knowing biologies (the stuff) are rendered unimaginable. Here we offer an overview of feminist engagements with both the study and the stuff of biology and some thoughts on connections between those projects.

Feminists have been engaged with these multiple definitions for many decades. The stakes of knowledge about human bodies and their more-than-human kin are high. For so long, "nature" has been either a devalued counterpoint to a seemingly separate "culture" or a romanticized proxy for the pure, untouched, good, moral, and healthy. To say that the study of biology is political seems an epic understatement! Feminist scholarship has thoroughly disabused us of any notion that science or scientists can ever remove themselves from the context of scientific production—that is, science can never be value neutral or unbiased but rather is always situated (Haraway 1988). Science, instead, can be understood as a mode of telling stories about the world. Storytelling about the natural enables and delimits visions of what is possible for human and more-than-human life. Indeed, the power and authority ceded to the sciences have rendered scientific stories as "Truth" and objective knowledge about the natural. The naturalization of the status quo makes what *is* seem like all that might yet be. Whether people characterize biology (the stuff) as competitive or cooperative, for instance, matters tremendously because that characterization then consistently shapes political, economic, and social understandings of what is possible. For example, what do we make of the fact that elite scientists such as Nobel laureates are consistently white, male, and European? If this is the result of the elite superiority of those groups and sexual and racial minorities are not good at mathematics and the sciences, any social programs for girls and students of color are futile. However, if the status quo is the result of histories of exclusion and discrimination, then such social correctives are critically important. Debates about nature versus nurture continue to haunt biology, in all its complex manifestations. The stories we tell about nature—both dominant stories and counternarratives—are vital to feminist thinking about biology.

One of the key insights of feminist work in the sciences is that even though "nature" is consistently gendered feminine, western science has persistently shaped the workings of nature in its own image—into competitive, male-dominated, cis-heteropatriarchal, European, white, elite norms. The early feminist critiques of science started a long tradition of reading and unpacking scientific studies—from claims of brain size and capacity to stories about social organization of birds, insects, and animals. These studies show consistently that biological storytelling is deeply implicated in the differential valuation of lives. Biological determinism—claims that whole groups of individuals share in common more or less desirable traits that explain the status quo—fuels rationales that support European colonialism (to civilize the savages), keeping various groups away from sites of power such as access to higher education and high-paying jobs, and eugenic programs that rationalize the sterilization and indeed extermination of some groups. This long history of work that has rationalized cis-heterosexism, racism, colonialism, and ableism *as* biology provides the context for a rich and robust history of feminist scholarship seeking to illuminate and redress biology's production of difference and its meanings. Indeed, the social categories of sex, gender, race, sexuality, class, ability, and nation are deeply grounded in the histories of the biological sciences and their embeddedness in colonialism.

If the biological sciences and our stories of biology are so thoroughly grounded in these oppressive histories, how might we reimagine a renewed feminist project of world knowing and world making? Feminists have reimagined the meaning, significance, and practice of biology, thoroughly remaking both the study of biology—that is, institutional locations of study or the biological sciences—and the "stuff" of biology by challenging the silos of disciplinary knowledge and knowledge-making practices. Feminist scholarship has worked to imagine itself not only as a site of critique but as a site of reimagining knowledge making, of retelling old stories and writing new stories about the world.

Fundamental to this reimagining is blurring the boundaries of nature and culture. Rather than vivisecting the world into the natural (that natural scientists study) and the cultural (that the social sciences and humanities study), feminists have instead reimagined the world as one not artificially apportioned to disciplinary silos but whole as *naturecultures* (Haraway 2003). The framework of naturecultures allows us to understand the dense imbrications of how bodies and biologies come to be. For example, we see the long histories of racialization when we track how the field of biology understands the category of race. Despite the deep entanglements of race with histories of slavery and indentured servitude and their continuing legacies in the racial and class politics of many nations, "race" reemerges as a neutral biological category repeatedly in the history of science. Indeed, we are witnessing the reemergence and reinvigoration of old racial categories in population genetics; for example, the first "ethnic" drug, BiDil, a race-based pharmaceutical, was approved by the FDA in 2007 for a single racial-ethnic group, African Americans, in the treatment of congestive heart failure. We have seen an explosion of studies since that attempt to geneticize race in studies of various diseases, including hypertension, diabetes, and coronary heart disease. Feminists and critical race scholars poignantly remind us that race and racism are deeply intertwined, making complex racialized naturecultures (D. Roberts 2011; R. Benjamin 2013; Reardon 2002). The biological body is not some prediscursive blank slate on which culture then writes. Rather, naturecultural biologies are complex unfoldings of histories of oppression and the politics of the present. Indeed, what the historical record shows us is a history of power and privilege. Biological categories of gender, race, sexuality, and nation emerge not as unique and unconnected but through a complex matrix of histories. For this reason, the history and biology of Black women differ from that of Asian women or white women. Feminist science and technology studies has made a compelling case for the critical need for dense and close accounts of how bodies as we know them materialize. For complex naturecultural accounts of biology, we need complex interdisciplinary formations. Contemporary academe and its disciplinary silos will not do.

In critical theory, "materialism" has been mobilized as a capacious way to name approaches to and engagements with the stuff of biologies. Critical feminist materialist scholarship—including and exceeding the bounds of science and technology studies—has developed a variety of conceptual and methodological innovations for naturecultural research. Karen Barad's (2007) theorization of onto-epistemological entanglement famously articulated the naturecultural insight that the stakes of knowledge politics are more than representational. That is to say, how we know shapes the materialization of our worlds, so researchers are responsible not only for describing but for bringing into being. This ethical burden has led to a proliferation of scholarship on the nature and particularity of these entanglements in relation to plants (Subramaniam 2014; L. Foster 2018), nonhuman animals (Woelfle-Erskine 2015; Schrader et al. 2017; H. Weaver 2020), ecosystems (J. Bennett 2010; Alaimo 2016; Bahng 2018), human health (D. Roy 2018; Bailey and Peoples 2017; E. Wilson 2015; Murphy 2012; M. Chen 2012; D. Roberts 1997), and relationality (Pitts-Taylor 2016; Willey 2016; Herzig 2015). Attentiveness to processes of becoming—to the inseparability of history, storytelling, and the physicality of bodies and the worlds within and in relation to which they evolve and become intelligible—might be understood as a constitutive feature of an emerging interdisciplinary

biology in the academy. Indeed, interdisciplinary feminist biologies that understand the redistribution of epistemic authority as central to the redistribution of material benefits of knowledge (Harding 2008) and replace the pretense of neutrality with a commitment to knowledge making in service to more just futures are being imagined and produced in labs and classrooms, in volumes of poetry and fiction, and in activist movements. As we remake biology (both the study and the stuff), we would do well to consider the vast and diverse archives of knowledge from which we might draw inspiration and insight.

9

Biopower

Kyla Wazana Tompkins

Biopower is a theory that describes how political power works by investing itself in the biological life of individuals and populations. First developed by the French philosopher Michel Foucault in his 1978 book *The History of Sexuality*, *biopower* has become a term of critical importance to scholars of gender, sexuality, race, colonialism, and imperialism (Foucault [1978] 1990). The concept of biopower gives us the tools to connect the body, long a site of feminist interest, to the disciplining power of scientific, medical, legal, anthropological, statistical, and aesthetic knowledges while also building a critique of the internal bureaucratic functioning of the liberal state.

The theory of biopower is also a specific elaboration of the relationship that Foucault calls *power-knowledge*, a term that describes how power is made and circulated through accepted forms of knowledge and method, including scientific understanding and forms of empirical "truth." The theory of biopower allows scholars to analyze how power is diffused and connected across multiple scales, from the penetrations of power into our most intimate selves (for instance, at the level of the relationship between our desires and our identities, also known as "sexuality") all the way up to state and nonstate projects, like medicine, psychiatry, and law—institutions that organize how the state distributes unequal chances to life, death, and community flourishing.

Foucault's general theory of biopower encapsulates two central propositions. First, he argues that the nature of political power fundamentally changed during the historical shift from European monarchies to the European liberal nation-state. He argues that political power was first exemplified in the king's right to mete out death as a negative force: you might think of the command "Off with her head!" Across the Enlightenment, however, political power shifted from the monarch to a more diffuse network of penal, medical, and educational institutions (for instance) that exerted power "positively" by seeking to either maximize or rehabilitate life: think here of the educational, parental, state, or medical injunction "It's for your own good." In Foucault's narrative, this diffuse network changed the nature of power from a negative force to a positive one by working *productively* to create ideal and nonideal subjectivity as disciplinary norms. Here you might think of how particular gender formations and identities are rewarded with more social status—heterosexuality over bisexuality or cisgender people over trans and nonbinary genders—than others. This exercise of power at the level of the individual is what Foucault refers to as anatomopolitics. The second part of biopower is called "biopolitics," or what he describes as the penetration and elaboration (or increasing complexity) of these productive forms of power into the nooks and crannies of the biological life of the population. Often, this latter term has come to stand in for the whole of biopower.

It's useful to pause here over the phrase "penetration of power." These words were not chosen casually. Foucault was very interested in how power is also an erotic force, arguing that within the organization of biopower, "pleasure and power function as mechanisms with a double impetus." Famously, he wrote, "The pleasure that comes of exercising a power that questions, monitors, watches, spies, searches out, palpates, brings to light; and on the other hand, the pleasure that kindles at having to evade this power, flee from it, fool it, or travesty it. . . . These attractions, these evasions, these circular incitements have traced around bodies and sexes, not boundaries not to be crossed, but perpetual spirals of power and pleasure" (Foucault [1978] 1990, 120). Biopower, then, is a form of power that is sexual in and of itself because it is highly surveillant in nature: it peeps and seeks out. At the level of the individual, biopower is invested in watching, categorizing, and thus producing typologies of sex and sexuality and then chasing them as erotic objects of interest, often through criminalization; psychiatric, pedagogical, and police harassment; and other forms of sanctioned state violence. Central to these "perpetual spirals of power and pleasure" are "the secret" and "the confession," narrative genres borrowed from religious discourse and ostensibly made secular by psychiatry and other knowledge-power formations.

Foucault argues that within biopower, sexual identity came to signify a personal self-truth whose truth-value was magnified and eroticized by its need to be chased and pursued. This pursuit in turn gives sexual expression its arousing, naughty energy as well as its affiliation with personal freedom. And yet a freedom that must be invoked by a repressive, finger-shaking authority—student affairs, the church, the synagogue, your parents, and so on—is also dependent on that repression to give it titillating value and vice versa.

At a larger scale, biopolitics is a structure of power affiliated with the rise of liberal industrial capitalism. In this relationship, biopower works *through* sexuality as "a dense transfer point of power" with a clear eye to maximizing the population as a labor and energy resource for the capitalist nation-state (Foucault [1978] 1990, 103). Biopower works through surveillance and checkpoint management, as the state and its allies permit themselves to rule over, analyze, study, statistically survey, and regulate the structures that unequally distribute access to well-being. Here one might think of the long-held injunction by the American Medical Association that no birth control could be distributed to women without sexual wellness checks first, including Pap smears and STI checks.

In the fact that the state might have a right to put people with vaginas into stirrups to painfully scrape their cervixes before giving them power over their own reproduction, Foucault's idea of penetrative and surveillant state power becomes literal. As Foucault argues in a discussion of the eighteenth and nineteenth centuries in Europe in the final chapter of *History of Sexuality*, volume 1, the moment of this shift in the nature of power from the "Right of Death [to] Power over Life" was accompanied by the proliferation of medical, statistical, state, psychiatric, educational, and carceral institutions. Foucault argues that each of these was tasked with examining and directing how sexuality was expressed within the borders of the state, with a particular mind to directing the energies of the population toward "norms" of proper and reproductive sexual citizenship. This interest in turn was entirely coordinated with the growth of liberal economics and capitalism, which had a vested interest in having access to broad swaths of workers and consumers in order to keep its labor supply available and profit flowing.

One of Foucault's central proposals was the then radical idea that sexuality can even be understood to *have* a history. In this, Foucault countered psychoanalytic theories of sexuality, derived largely from Sigmund Freud but later expanded by sexologists such as Havelock Ellis and others, that posited the existence of innate and biological human drives and desires. Foucault's theory of productive power posited that the homosexual, for instance, was an invention of the nineteenth-century biopolitical investment in chasing down, taxonomizing, and diagnosing sexual types, in particular in obsessively charting an entire species map of normal and deviant sexualities. Thus, prior to the rise of biopolitical forms of power, an individual might commit illegal acts of indecency—say, sodomy, or masturbation, or cross-dressing. These were considered to be solitary sins that were to be punished, acts to be redeemed with penance. With the emergence of "sexuality" as an object of interest on the part of medicine, psychiatry, an increasingly carceral state, theories of child development and education, and other disciplinary knowledge-power projects, the deviant came to be an identity. In this shift, sometimes referred to as the acts-to-identities shift, the truth of one's desires was characterized as a secret that nestled at the core of one's own self, and sexuality came to characterize the most interior truth of the self. One became a type, studied and categorized by a discipline.

Over the last few decades, Foucault's work has been subjected to a variety of critiques, and as a result, the idea of biopower has expanded in its analytic possibilities. One early response to Foucault, particularly from feminists, is that his theories were not attentive to issues of gender. In *History of Sexuality*, Foucault does point to the psychiatric sexual typologies that impact women, such as the hysterical woman, but after that, he appears uninterested in examining how the workings of biopower differentially impact male and female gender formations, never mind genders outside the binary. He also overlooked most sexual orientations beyond gay cis men.

The most productive critiques of biopower register how Foucault's time line for the historical emergence of biopower tracks with the high period of European colonialism, settler colonialism, empire, and enslavement. Postcolonial theorists and historians of enslavement and settler colonialism have clearly demonstrated that the social formations of metropolitan colonial centers such as Paris, London, Rome, and Amsterdam were not exported to their colonies, like cookie cutters pressing on unformed matter. In actuality, close attention to the historical archive shows that ideas about sexuality, heteronormativity, and forms of gender deviance emerged in direct relation to colonial regimes of race, enslavement, settler colonialism, and empire. This emergence took place through explicit forms of psychic, genocidal, and physical violence in those colonial and imperial spaces.

Scholars of science in the colonial Americas have pointed out that in the early study of the flora, fauna, and even people of the so-called New World, the invention of sexuality and even of gender difference itself can be seen as a side effect of the invention of race, which took place through aggressive taxonomic charting of nonhuman species (LaFleur 2018). This contention has been supported by recent scholarship that examines archives of sexology, obstetrics, natural history, and evolutionary science in the nineteenth and twentieth centuries (Snorton 2017; Schuller 2018). This recent work shows how sexual and gender deviance was always already embedded in notions of racial inferiority, while the gender binary itself, in its purest forms, was constructed to the ends of upholding whiteness. In this sense, the history of sexuality has *always* been the history of race.

Either as colonial comparison or as scientific knowledge that made its way into social policy, those racial and thus sexual formulations found their way back to the metropolitan centers of Europe as racialized, gendered, and classed hierarchies of normativity. As Ann Laura Stoler demonstrates in her work on colonial Indonesia, imperial and colonial outposts were spaces where working-class whites and Indigenous populations often mixed when European white working classes were dispatched to the colonies to serve as low-level administrators or soldiers. When white colonials intermarried or reproduced with Indigenous and local communities, white administrators became anxious about métissage and racial mixing and instituted preventative policy and regulations (Stoler 2010). Thus what would become the class and race hierarchies of the colonial metropoles were worked out in colonial policy, returning to Europe. Such regulations appeared at first as discourses about how and where reproduction could be put to the nationalist purpose of maintaining the population's blood purity. In this formulation, biopower as a fundamentally racialized and racist discourse emerged through colonialism and empire.

Thus, we cannot theorize biopower without rethinking Foucault's theorizations of race as a primary locus of biopolitical intervention. As Stoler shows, Foucault was mainly preoccupied with theorizing race through a concept of state racism. For Foucault, the emergence of state racism in Nazism exemplified the final expression of a biopolitics invested in the metaphorics of blood, or what he called "sanguinary biopolitics." In this, Foucault's theories align with later European theorists such as Giorgio Agamben, who sees the stark and harsh death machineries of the concentration camp as exemplifying biopower as the ultimate expression of how states are constituted by and through the invention of expendable others. But scholars have intervened in this argument with different historical genealogies, making the point that prior to the Third Reich, racial capitalism was a main locus of the regulation of sexuality and violently imposed gender normativity through the enslavement of African populations into plantation labor in the Americas and elsewhere and the displacement of Indigenous and First Nations cultures of gender expression, matrilineage, and kinship.

Turning from the optimization of European life that Foucault saw as central to the project of European state biopolitics, queer, trans, and critical race theorists have turned to a consideration of the centrality of death (the unequal distribution of chances to thrive and live) as similarly central to the biopolitical project. Sharon Holland's germinal work on the centrality of death to queer and Black life, particularly in the age of AIDS, first discussed what came to be named, in the work of African theorist Achille Mbembe, *necropolitics* (Holland 2000; Mbembe 2019). Mbembe's argument with Foucault and Agamben was that we might need to look beyond the concentration camp to the plantation and to other sites of colonial violence to really understand how the murderous impulses of colonial, metropolitan, and imperial biopolitics were actually entirely dependent on meting out death as liberally as they claimed to maximize life. Here it is helpful to consider the construction of Indigenous reservations, which Nazis studied in creating their final solution, as similar death-dealing or necropolitical projects.

This shift from thinking about biopower as a power invested in life to necropolitics as an all-out genocidal project that ranges across modernity has wide-ranging implications for queer, trans, disabled, queer of color, Native, and Black studies. For instance, both Scott Morgensen and Mohawk scholar Audra Simpson have shown how the genocide of Indigenous and First Nations people—especially those who might now be considered or self-identify as Two Spirit, queer, trans, or nonbinary people—was at the heart of how normative biopolitical power was and still is shaped and practiced by settler colonial nations. Morgensen writes, "Colonists interpreted diverse practices of gender and sexuality as signs of a general primitivity among Native peoples. Over time, they produced a colonial necropolitics that framed Native peoples as queer populations marked for death" (2010, 106). For Morgensen, as well as scholars Mark Rifkin (2011) and Kim TallBear (n.d.), both heteronormativity and monogamy are tools of settler colonialism.

Simpson's research, which examines the relationship between settler colonialism and Indigenous women's life and death chances, makes the argument that

> Canada requires the death and so called "disappearance" of Indigenous women in order to secure its sovereignty. . . . Canada is quite simply, a settler society whose multicultural, liberal and democratic structure and performance of governance seeks an ongoing "settling" of this land. . . . This settling thus is not innocent—it is dispossession, the taking of Indigenous lands and it is not over, it is ongoing. It is killing Native women in order to do so and has historically done this to do so. It is this killing that allows me to also qualify the governance project as gendered and murderous. (A. Simpson 2016)

In this formulation, the necropolitics of settler colonialism is understood as "gendered and murderous." Read alongside Mbembe, these critiques and elaborations show that the king's negative power to mete out death never disappeared but rather transferred to the settler colonial state, itself imbricated in the rise of racial capitalism. In this light, Foucault's historical account seems rather optimistic.

Disability activists and scholars have also taken up the relationship between biopolitics and necropolitics by troubling the line between the two: what some have described as bionecropolitics. In Mel Chen's new materialist formulation, disability and racialization are constituted along ideological lines that parallel what they call, borrowing from linguistics, "animacy hierarchies" (M. Chen 2012, 24). Those who might be said to be living or "lively" and those who are variously immobilized or less mobile, impassive, inscrutable, or seemingly affectively flat come to be seen more as objects and less as humans, or as active and agential subjects. The animacy hierarchy, in Chen's analysis, contributes to the social ranking of humans along the scale of desirably human and less than human and includes the social ordering and racialization of affective expression along the scale of ability, with rational agentive action being deemed more human than other forms of living emotionally and psychologically.

Still other critics have pointed to how biopolitics, with its intense affiliation with liberal capitalism, in fact depends on the production of disability—or, in Jasbir Puar's terms, *debility*—to create profit (Puar 2017). Puar's articulation of debility, picking up on Lauren Berlant's theorization of slow death and Anna Jain's idea of prognosis time, argues that "debility"—injury and its resultant exclusions—disability, and capacity together constitute an assemblage that states use to control populations (Berlant 2011; Jain 2007). In Puar's theory, debility and disability are state produced as various populations are differently designated by the state's right—in particular, the police and military's right—to not only kill but maim.

Thinking from the point of view of an intersectional, queer of color, disability perspective also points to where the line between the human and the animal and thus even matter itself gets confused. For instance, in Chen's work, they think about their own chronically ill queer and Asian body as one that has been rendered toxic by mercury poison but then in turn is intoxicated by the cognitive disruptions resulting from mercury poison (M. Chen 2012). This turn to the molecular—to the chemical and biological scales at which biopower works and then in turn to the intersection between those fields and affect and consciousness itself—further dislodges the human subject from the center of biopolitical analysis and opens up new questions. Is the toxically intoxicated body a living body, or has it become an object like the substance that poisons it? And from a cognitively intoxicated perspective—from within a disability epistemology that upends rationality as a normative and therefore disciplinary genre of being—how might we explore other ways of being or knowing that unsettle, ungender, queer, or upend the animacy hierarchies that depend on hierarchical subject/object, animal/human, white/not-white, and living/not-living binarisms?

10

Capital
Grace Kyungwon Hong

In elucidating the concept of *capital* as a keyword of gender, I contend that modern conceptions of gender developed historically out of the emergence of capitalism as a settler colonial, colonial, and racializing regime. Such a regime not only underwrites the modes of accumulation and extraction upon which capitalism depends, but its epistemes also situate racialized and colonized peoples and cultures as the limit or the outside to the modern definition of the human in order to legitimate and naturalize the conditions for accumulation and extraction. Current normative understandings of gender, which structure roles, embodiments, and institutions, are based on this definition of the human, figured as the individuated subject of property for which the corresponding organization of social space is separate and differently gendered public and private spheres. The propertied subject, or "possessive individual," and separate-spheres institutions, while mystified within western liberal capitalist ideologies as natural, universal, and ahistorical, are in fact historically specific, socially constructed, and unevenly available. Thus, understanding the emergence and development of capital requires a *structural* understanding of how political, economic, and cultural institutions normalize certain ways of knowing, being, and relating to others while making others deviant, criminal, or incomprehensible. Yet this process is never complete or totalizing, meaning that racialized, colonial, queer, sexualized, and gender nonnormative formations are constantly enacting alternative modes of relationality.

I begin this entry with a review of Karl Marx's ([1867] 1992) definitions of capitalism as predicated on the accumulation of wealth based on the circulation of value stolen from labor, a process that is dependent on private property relations. I then present a range of feminist and queer imaginaries of social relation and in so doing highlight the limits of Marx's critique of property. That is, while he critiques private property, he reproduces the private/public divide and invests in the rational, secular subject, both of which are foundational to property relations. Each account of capital's foundations offers concomitantly differing visions of where and how resistance to exploitation, extraction, and accumulation occurs and who the agents of that resistance are.

In the most general sense, *capital* means any assets that can be invested to produce more wealth. Rendered more precisely, Marx ([1867] 1992, 247–53 passim) writes that the building block of capital is the process by which the capitalist takes a certain amount of money, invests it, and creates more money. The circulation of value to create more value is what Marx calls capital, and a capitalist economy is one in which this process exists for itself rather than as a means to satisfy the needs and wants of the people in that society. While classical and contemporary liberal and neoliberal economists presume that this production of wealth is of universal benefit to society, radical political economists such as Marx contend that capitalism is predicated on relations of inequality reinforced through violence. Marx argues that all value is produced from labor; however, in a capitalist economy, this value is alienated from laborers, who do not benefit from the wealth that their labor produces. This can only happen, for Marx, in a system predicated on the private ownership of property. Capitalists, owning the means of production, are able to extract surplus value from laborers, who own nothing of worth to the market but their own labor.

This leads Marx to ask, How did this unequal condition, in which some own the conditions of production and others own only their own labor, come about? How did property become private in the first place? Marx scoffs at liberal economists who legitimate inequality through a morality tale in which "long, long ago, there were two sorts of people; one the diligent, intelligent, and above all frugal élite; the other, lazy rascals, spending their substance, and more, in riotous living. . . . Thus it came to pass that the former sort accumulated wealth, and the latter sort finally had nothing to sell except their own skins" ([1867] 1992, 873). Marx argues that "in actual history, it is a notorious fact that conquest, enslavement, robbery, murder, in short, force, play the greatest part" (873–74). Marx narrates the process by which capitalists first accumulated wealth, at "the dawn of the era of capitalist production"—a process he calls "primitive accumulation," by which he means "original"—using historical England as his example (915). From the fourteenth century onward, the monarchy, the church, and the aristocracy pushed agricultural serfs from lands allotted to them for subsistence cultivation, as well as any lands held and used in common, in a process called enclosure. By the nineteenth century, serfs were driven from their lands and became wage laborers, and their lands were claimed by individual property owners who filled the ranks of the capitalists. While this process was a bloody and violent one, for Marx and his co-author, Engels, it was a necessary evil insofar as it led to the creation of an urban proletariat who is the revolutionary subject. This urban proletariat will "[sweep] away by force the old conditions of production," and "in place of the old bourgeois society, with its classes and class antagonisms, we shall have an association, in which the free development of each is the condition for the free development of all" (Marx and Engels [1848] 1998, 62).

Marx's focus on the European urban proletariat predictably means that he is unable to theorize race, colonialism, and gender as central to capitalism. While Marx and Engels reference "the East-Indian and Chinese markets, the colonisation of America, trade with the colonies" in *The Communist Manifesto*, these processes only have significance in that they contributed "to the revolutionary element in the tottering feudal society" ([1848] 1998, 32) that hastened the advent of capitalism and the development of the urban proletariat as the revolutionary class. Marx and Engels also decry the "bourgeois family" that exists only because of "capital, private gain" (53) and assert that communism will "do away with the status of women as mere instruments of production" (54). Yet there is no suggestion that these colonized peoples or the women thus freed by the dissolution of class society might themselves be the agents of revolution.

With the advent of twentieth-century movements for decolonization and liberation, the world could no longer ignore colonized peoples as agents of revolution. In the wake of these movements, scholars theorized the racialized basis of capital as a way to account for racialized and colonized peoples as revolutionary subjects. For instance, Cedric Robinson's (1983) landmark account of racial capitalism *Black Marxism* identifies race as central to western civilization. Robinson departs from Marxist theorizations of capitalism as a *break* from feudal modes of organization, arguing that race organized both feudal and capitalist systems, and traces the emergence of an autonomous Black radical tradition of anticapitalist critique separate from Marxism. Thus, while Marx provides an important initial critique of liberal epistemologies that naturalize capitalist relations of exploitation and advances a different model of social organization, we must turn to subsequent thinkers for alternative possibilities for social relations that do not naturalize the public/private divide or the rational, secular subject, both of which are foundational to the property system.

Indigenous feminists have shown that the very notion of private property has been developed and honed through the processes of colonization and settlement, based on displacing Indigenous understandings of land as *mutual* relation. That is, as Leanne Betasamosake Simpson writes, "our knowledge system, the education system, the economic system, the political system of the Michi Saagiig Nishnaabeg were designed to promote more life . . . not just human life but the life of all living things. . . . It was an emergent system reflective of the relationality of the local landscape" (2017, 3). This relational system, Simpson writes, is antithetical to private property, which allows only ownership as the structure of relation between the self and others. Likewise, she observes the limits of Marx's notions of liberation, writing, "We didn't just control our means of production, we lived embedded in a network of humans and nonhumans that were made up of only producers" (80). In so doing, she critiques both Marx's investment in the (rational and secular) human as the only agential subject and his assumption that "production" happens only in certain (public) settings. While settler states have attempted to impose property relations, Audra Simpson argues that settler colonialism has so far failed. She writes that "colonialism survives in a settler form. In this form, it fails at what it is supposed to do: eliminate Indigenous people; take all their land; absorb them into a white, property-owning body politic" (2014, 7–8). Settler colonial states have had to continually work to suppress Indigenous modes of life and have done so by attempting to implement many cycles of extraction and dispossession stretching to the present day. Indigenous feminist studies scholarship thus undermines Marx's notion of so-called primitive or original accumulation of capital as the precondition of capitalism, instead asserting that it is an ongoing process inherent to capitalism's central functions. In turn, Indigenous sovereignty movements based on alternative modes of relationality offer vibrant and powerful challenges to capitalist extraction and accumulation.

Marxist feminists likewise take issue with Marx's narrative of primitive accumulation but by identifying the domestication and containment of women within Europe as foundational to the development and maintenance of capitalism. They do so by challenging Marx's investment in the public/private split through the naturalization of reproductive labor. Instead, they posit reproductive labor as a central contradiction of capitalism and frame women as best situated to challenge capitalist structures. Marx acknowledges that productive labor requires its own reproduction but characterizes it as a question of the value required to reproduce the laborer: "The value of labour-power is the value of the means of subsistence necessary for the maintenance of its owner" ([1867] 1992, 274). In addition to this daily maintenance, Marx observes that because of human mortality, the reproduction of the laborer evidences that the means of maintenance also has to include "the worker's replacements, i.e., his children" (275). While Marx understands the necessity of reproduction, in both the daily and the generational senses, he tends not to characterize it as a form of labor.

A signal contribution of early Marxist feminism was exactly the labeling of reproductive labor as labor. Mariarosa Dalla Costa's and Selma James's influential 1972 book *The Power of Women and the Subversion of the Community* introduces an account of the shift from feudal agricultural and artisanal modes of production centered on the home and the family to industrial capitalism organized around the factory and wage work. In this shift, only productive labor was compensated through wages, while reproductive labor ensured that "women,

children and the aged lost the relative power that derived from the family's dependence on their labor, *which was seen to be social and necessary*" ([1972] 1975, 24). The same year that the book was published, Dalla Costa and James cofounded the International Wages for Housework Campaign, a global feminist crusade calling for compensation for reproductive labor, among other demands.

Building on the work of Dalla Costa and James, Silvia Federici offers a more developed account of the centrality of gender relations to the emergence of capitalism. In *Caliban and the Witch*, Federici (2004) rewrites Marx's narrative of enclosure as primitive accumulation, arguing that the development of private property through enclosure ensured the separation of public and private and the development of modern gender norms. She observes that simply dispossessing the peasantry from their lands and turning them into wage labor was not enough to create a permanent condition of proletarianization necessary for capitalism to take root. Rather, as European peasant men and women moved to urban areas, production and reproduction were separated into public and private and gender divisions correspondingly hardened. The emergence of capitalism was thus predicated on the constitution of public and private as separate and separately gendered spheres, the relegation of the activities of reproduction to the private, and the disavowal of reproduction as labor requiring compensation. This context of industrialization and urbanization was the foundation for the emergence of Anglo-American gay and lesbian identities in the late nineteenth and early twentieth centuries, which, as John D'Emilio claims, required individual (rather than familial) access to waged labor, which allowed for homosexual desire to coalesce into homosexual identity—that is, "an identity based on the ability to remain outside of the heterosexual family and to construct a personal life based on attraction to one's own sex" ([1983] 1993, 470). Yet as postcolonial feminists have observed, bourgeois domesticity required imperialist arrangements in order to exist, and the work of maintaining a bourgeois domestic home has from the beginning been transferred to working-class, enslaved, racialized, and colonized women workers (George 1998). Those workers who were enslaved were not paid at all for this labor, while others were—albeit poorly—in an unregulated and exploitative industry performing domestic labor in the homes of wealthier families, all the while doing uncompensated reproductive labor at home (Nakano Glenn 1992; Nakano Glenn 1985). If, as early Marxist feminist scholars argue, those who perform the reproductive labor secretly at the foundations of capitalism have the most potential to be agents of revolutionary change, they would necessarily be racialized and colonized workers.

Thus, while Federici writes that "it is the condition of the enslaved woman that most explicitly reveals the truth and the logic of capitalist accumulation" (2004, 89–90), we must turn to Angela Davis's landmark 1971 essay "Reflections on the Black Woman's Role in the Community of Slaves" to understand exactly how. Written and published while Davis was being held in the Marin County jail on charges of murder, kidnapping, and conspiracy, of which she was later acquitted, this essay provides an early theorization of reproductive labor as the site for the creation of new forms of relationality based on care. Here, the context is not urbanization; *industrialization* means "industrial agriculture" rather than "industrial production," and capital accumulates not through the exploitation of waged productive labor (and the concomitant removal of reproductive labor from the market) but through the turning of people into property.

Davis builds on Marx's classical formulation of private property as the foundation of capital but in a way that centers racialization and gendering as central to both the existence of capitalism and its downfall. She reads Marx's differentiation of waged and enslaved labor as a *problem of knowledge* by observing that western epistemologies cast enslaved labor, and by extension enslaved people, not as exploitable people but as "inorganic conditions of production" (A. Y. Davis 1971, 5), much like land or animals, and thus render them a part of nature that is humankind's right to use. In this context, productive and reproductive labor are not differentiated because one is public and waged and the other private and unwaged. Instead, the difference between production and reproduction is in their relationship to alienation and dehumanization. In the realm of production, enslaved people were thoroughly alienated from the products and process of their labor, rendering that site one of utter dehumanization. Yet Davis argues that enslaved Africans refused a definition of themselves as a dehumanized part of nature, as evidenced by the many accounts of insurrections and rebellions. From where would this refusal of dehumanization and desire for freedom come? As Davis writes, "A human being thoroughly dehumanized has no desire to be free" (6).

In sharp distinction to Marx's claim of production as where class consciousness develops, Davis argues that the desire to resist "had to be directly nurtured by the social organization which the slaves themselves improvised" in the areas of their lives most removed from domination—that is, "the living quarters, where the basic needs of physical life were met" (1971, 6). She observes that Black women were tasked with doing the reproductive labor—what she calls "the infinite anguish of ministering to the men and children around her" (7)—that was as necessary to the foundations of a capitalist economy as the productive labor they did in the fields. Through this labor of care, Black women enabled enslaved people to resist dehumanization and imagine themselves as worthy of freedom. Davis thus argues that Black women were the most likely to have created the conditions to enable enslaved people to resist the dehumanization inherent to slavery and to envision a way to freedom. The Black woman, in Davis's words, was "the custodian of a house of resistance" (8). Black women's care work is framed not only as enabling the material reproduction of workers but as creating and sustaining the desire for freedom itself.

An implication of Davis's theorization of Black women's care work is that capitalist exploitation and the violence of property are epistemological, ideological, and ontological processes. The "Black women's role in the community of slaves," then, was to evade what Kara Keeling (2007, 6) would call "currently available common sense" as a regime of affect and being. In so doing, we can think of Black women's care work as Davis describes as somehow bringing into being that which the material world makes impossible but that "can still be felt—like an intuition or a premonition" (1971, 6) of freedom.

The exclusion of racialized, enslaved, and colonized people from normative modes of gendering implied by bourgeois domesticity, private property relations, and the public/private split has thus been a fruitful avenue of analysis for Black, Indigenous, and woman of color feminisms. Building on these insights, Roderick A. Ferguson (2004) has theorized queer of color critique as a means of illuminating how capital requires the differentiation of its workforce by gender, age, and race in order to more efficiently exploit, which is then reinforced by rendering deviant and "queer" those who, by dint of this differentiation, are in excess of the supposedly universal norms of bourgeois heteropatriarchy. These nonnormative formations, however, out of both necessity and invention, conjure other ways to be.

The wide array of investments and positions, then, that we can identify in feminist, antiracist, and queer theorizations of capital provide startlingly heterogeneous and often incommensurable imaginaries of what emerges despite, against, and in excess of extraction, accumulation, and exploitation.

11

Carcerality

Beth E. Richie

Few concepts animate more discussion by interdisciplinary, activist-oriented feminist scholars than the concept of carcerality. The broad context for these discussions is the emerging scholarship exploring the profound impact that mass criminalization has had on the fabric of our society, the shifts in public awareness and opinion about questions of crime and justice, policy reforms at the institutional level, high-profile campaigns on behalf of those wrongfully accused, a surge in on-the-ground activism around questions of systemic violence, excessive punishment, and how state power is implicated in the buildup of a prison nation within the borders of the United States (Chettiar and Raghavan 2019; Gould and Leo 2010; Sered 2019). At the level of the university, these discussions are multidisciplinary: philosophers ask questions about the meaning of justice; scholars of race look at profound disproportionate confinement; historians make conceptual links between chattel slavery, Jim Crow segregation, and current punishment regimes; sociologists look at how crime is socially constructed; critical legal scholars explore the rhetoric and microlevel processes in the criminal legal system; and critical criminologists explore how the national preoccupation with punishment has fundamentally shifted the social order in this country in the last twenty-five years (Hernández, Muhammad, and Thompson 2015; Lerman and Weaver 2014; M. Nagel 2018; Schenwar and Law 2020). Importantly, feminist scholars in these disciplines frame intellectual questions around gender,

sexuality, and heteropatriarchy, interrogating how carcerality is theoretically bound up with issues of power, exploitation, and domination (Carrington 2015; Gruber 2020).

Each of these disciplinary trends has been influenced by (feminist) activism around the political problematics of carcerality. For instance, community activists mobilize campaigns to close jails, coalitions of immigrant rights groups protest mass deportations, transformative justice organizations experiment with radical alternatives to the criminal legal system in cases when harm has been caused, and individuals caught in the tight grip of the perilous punishment industry fight daily for their dignity and survival. Like the scholarship, much of this activism takes an antiracist, anticapitalist posture, linking the specific manifestations of carcerality to larger patterns of social control, forced isolation, degradation, and even annihilation of marginalized people (Western and Pettit 2010). Activists insist that an anticarcerality analysis and praxis must be deeply rooted in an understanding of systematic oppression. As in the case of scholarship, feminist activists have provided leadership in these movements to bring questions of sexuality and class and an analysis of hegemonic gender power to the work (Ball 2016; Cacho 2012; Vitale 2018). Informed by queer politics, disability justice, and international solidarity movements, the feminist work to confront carcerality insists on a focus on abolition, not only on the reform of existing institutions and strategies to be "less or more gently carceral" (Ben-Moshe 2020; Stanley and Smith [2011] 2015).

This accounting of how the concept of carcerality travels across scholarly disciplines and activist spaces serves as the introduction to what the term means. Following a brief definition of carcerality, I provide examples of where it appears in public, professional, academic, and activist spheres. I then identify some of the adjunct terms and issues that circulate around the term *carcerality*. This essay concludes with an unapologetic plea for abolition feminism instead of reforming carcerality.

At the most basic level, the term *carcerality* refers to all things punishment. The "things" encompassed in this definition are those institutions, policies, and ideological positions that are involved or invoked in response to situations when "laws" have been broken, "crimes" have been committed, or norms have been violated. Technically, carcerality is an abstraction of the word *carceral* and refers to the ways that "things" take features of the criminal legal system, extending the reach beyond the system into other aspects of society. By using the terminology "all things" when I am defining carcerality, I am intentionally signaling that there is a connection between the formal institutions, agencies, policies, and legal processes that provide the scaffolding of punishment and the less formal apparatus that dispense sanctions. In this way, carcerality can be understood to be a condition or set of social arrangements that advances a reliance on punishment or incapacitation. It includes the ideological, political instincts, and public investment in deploying the state's punishment apparatus to control nonnormative behaviors from aggressive physical harm to minor nuances that inconvenience people in power.

From the perspective of feminist scholarship and activism, *carcerality* is not merely a descriptive or neutral term. Rather, it renders the presence of prisons and policing problematic, challenging the state's normalized role in judging and controlling the behaviors deemed "bad" as well as the "bad" people who engage in them. Carcerality thus refers to how laws and law enforcement become tools of those with power to legitimately exercise domination of people who have less power by creating rules (laws) that target and sometimes permanently relegate certain groups to criminalized and/or noncitizenship status. In this way, carcerality allows the state to categorize people as dispensable or nonhuman.

A critical dimension of carcerality that renders it problematic is how it promotes de facto law enforcement as the singular answer to problems of threat. This belief plays into an ideological position that sees safety and protection to be the purview of the state's punitive authority and justifies allocating resources to uphold that belief, in contrast to providing resources for community development or healing. Carcerality also explains how these material investments in punishment flow as logical policies, ignoring any rational measure of the effectiveness of these policies to enact positive change. This way of thinking is related to the concept of carceral logic, where a punishment mindset creeps into routine social institutions as if it were "natural."

Carceral logic is but one of several concepts that have emerged from the notion of carcerality, all of which are important for feminist scholars and activists to consider in our work. It helps explain how carcerality swells to influence society beyond confinement in institutions to include drug treatment programs, mental health clinics, facilities for people with disabilities, social services, schools, and other institutions that are allegedly organized to provide assistance but instead replace aid with punishment (A. B. Cox 2017; Hernández, Muhammad, and Thompson 2015; Peterson et al. 2019). Schools, welfare offices, and food stamp eligibility become opportunities to criminalize, and particular issues get targeted like gender-based violence (P. Edelman 2019; Goodwin 2020; Hinton 2016). This change in the character of social institutions and the expansion of carcerality become *logical* to the extent that administrative and legal policies legitimize punishment and authorize punitive state intervention. Such legitimation and authorization become part of bureaucratic routines as institutions reinforce this logic among themselves, resulting in a seemingly coordinated set of institutional policies. Scholar Kayla Martensen has called this coordination the "Web of Detention" (Martensen 2020). The expansion of carcerality beyond actual sites of confinement is important to note.

Carceral creep is a term coined by Mimi Kim, a feminist scholar-activist whose work focuses on using transformative justice approaches to end gender-based violence (Kim 2020). She built this concept to portray how insidious the move toward carcerality is in programs that respond to sexual and intimate partner violence. Even feminist programs are shaped by carcerality, wherein they tend to advance approaches to change by engaging with the punitive state. This move has been called carceral feminism and is widely critiqued by feminists who understand that state intervention that relies exclusively on arrest, prosecution, longer prison sentences, and other strategies associated with retributive justice can actually make violence worse (Russo 2018; Thuma 2019). Black and other woman of color feminists have been in leadership positions articulating this analysis as an extension of work on anti-Black racism in the criminal legal system (Haley 2016; H. Potter 2015; Richie 2012). By erasing the experiences of women of color and other groups who are harmed by carcerality, mainstream programs feed the carceral state. Clarion calls to "dial 911," demanding mandatory arrests of people who use violence, celebrating long sentence terms for people who have abused their domestic partners or children, or permanently disenfranchising people who have committed a sexual assault *even when* there is good evidence that this does not meet the goals of bringing resolution to those who have been harmed, not to mention safety or justice, is evidence of the inextricable power of carcerality in the face of a more rational approach.

It bears repeating that carcerality is an ideological belief that punishment-oriented responses are natural, appropriate, and effective ways to manage a society when harm is understood to be inevitable (M. Cooper 2017). Conservatively, it can be read as the most rational and justifiable strategic approach to creating safety. When the application of the ideology of carcerality is considered in relationship to feminist concerns about gender justice, a very different understanding of its meaning emerges. From here, carcerality implicates the state's role in perpetuating the presumption that because of their behavior, certain groups of people are best responded to with punishment and other sanctions. Carceral humanism is a concept related to this aspect of carcerality (Hirschberg 2015; Nagel 2018).

Feminist activists and scholars whose work is geared toward resisting the trends that carcerality brings—mass criminalization, disproportionate confinement, targeting of Black and other people of color for punishment, and justifying state violence in response to interpersonal harm—are adopting new strategies informed by the politics of abolition feminism. Understood to be an aspirational approach to both dismantling prisons, policing, and other sites where carcerality prevails and building up of communities and their capacity to deal with harm, abolition feminism is a theory of change that refutes "all things punishment" as codified through neoliberalism and depends on an understanding of racial capitalism to inform organizing and resistance movements (Berger, Kaba, and Stein 2017; M. Cooper 2017; Gilmore 2021; C. Robinson [1983] 2019; J. Wang 2018). It advances an agenda that puts people who have been harmed in positions of authority to lead efforts to create safe spaces. Abolition feminism relies on queer theory and embraces the goals of disability justice in the creation of nonhierarchal organizational structures. Transformative justice strategies are used to ensure community safety, and there is an understanding that people can change if they are given the opportunity and material support to do so (Kushner 2019; Kaba and Hassan 2019; Haga 2020; Norris 2020). The carceral state or other institutions that are infused with carceral logics are not required; indeed, they are rendered obsolete. Processes of community accountability, feminist principles of engagement, and coalition building are used to reestablish the health and well-being of communities that are moved into positions to make decisions about their futures (Gilliard 2018). Resources would flow away from carceral institutions into local social change organizations. Abolition feminist is a direct response to carcerality and an exciting approach to liberation, which is why it holds such strong appeal to feminist scholars and activists. Even as an aspirational and experimental approach, it offers a much more solid path to justice in the future than does carcerality.

12

Care
Sandy Grande

On March 11, 2020, the World Health Organization declared the coronavirus outbreak a global pandemic. As of the writing of this entry, there are 85.1 million confirmed cases and just over 1.8 million deaths worldwide, with the United States leading in both categories. The economic implications have been equally catastrophic. The US unemployment numbers hover around 12.6 million, with a disproportionate number of women and Black, Indigenous, and other people of color (BIPOC) workers shouldering the downturn. The budget deficit is at an all-time high, and the disruptions to the global supply chain have exacted irreparable damage to small businesses. These nearly unprecedented conditions have exacerbated the already intolerable gross inequities in housing, health care, education, and welfare suffered disproportionately by the Black, Indigenous, Latinx, queer, and disabled communities. The pandemic has laid bare how the valences of care—its allocation, apportionment, and distribution—have always been imbricated with systems of governance and power.

In one of his first pandemic press conferences, Donald Trump framed COVID-19 as a "foreign virus" spread by international travelers who "seeded" viral clusters in "America" while also vowing to close borders and complete "the wall" (B. Bennett 2020). The racist and xenophobic notion that Americans must be protected (cared for) against foreign contagions is endemic to its founding, whereby the valorization of freedom for white settlers was conditioned upon the dispossession of Black and Indigenous land and labor. Genocide and slavery set the conditions for who was perceived and constructed as a legitimate subject of care and who was conscripted into providing the labor of care (Stoler 2004; Nakano Glenn 2010; Stevenson 2014; Sharpe 2016; Raghuram 2019; Segrest 2020). In an effort to decenter this history from the discussion of care, I focus on those theories and practices that situate care as a means of anticolonial and antiracist struggle—which is to say, on the work of Indigenous, Black, disabled, and queer of color and transnational feminists. In so doing, I draw inspiration from Saidiya Hartman's claim that "care is the antidote to violence" (Maclear 2018, 603).

This compendium of work emerged in tension with notions of care theorized by white liberal feminists who critiqued the sexist and masculinist notions of autonomy and independence prevalent in theories of justice but failed to problematize the racial and heteronormative assumptions of the white female subject (e.g., Gilligan 1982; Noddings 1984). In addition to its conceptual aporias, the lack of intersectional analysis erased the historic role of Black, Indigenous, and migrant women's care labor in the service of white women's children and households and how such dynamics of power continue to condition access to and quality of care (Nakano Glenn 1992, 2010). Materialist feminists and political scientists Joan Tronto and Bernice Fischer troubled the assumptions of liberal feminism, defining care more capaciously as "a species of activity that includes everything we do to maintain, contain, and repair our 'world' so that we can live in it as well as possible" (Fisher and Tronto 1990, 126–36). While at times taken to task for being overly broad, Tronto and Fischer's work is generally upheld for not only calling into question the white middle-class woman as the subject of care and the conflation of feminine, feminist, and mother within heteronormative theorizations of "woman" but also

its materialist analyses of care work as a form of social reproduction.

Black feminists discuss how the feminist analytic of social reproduction is necessary but also grossly insufficient for mapping the intricacies of power, patriarchy, and personhood. More specifically, they developed cogent analyses of how their (care) labors were erased not only within white feminism but also by the male-dominated discourses of Marxist theorists (including the Black radical tradition). Hartman, for example, discusses how the category of labor itself "insufficiently accounts for slavery" and how the (presumed male) figure of the "black worker" fails to recognize the "value produced by and extracted from enslaved women"—and how both constructs erase Black women's bodies as "the definitional sites of racial slavery" (2016, 168–69). On this point, she is worth quoting at length: "The captive female body . . . could be converted into cash, speculated and traded as a commodity, worked to death, taken, tortured, seeded, and propagated like any other crop, or murdered. The value produced by and extracted from enslaved women included productive labor—their labors as farm workers, cotton pickers, tobacco hands, and rice cultivators—and their reproductive capacities created 'future increase' for farms and plantations and human commodities for markets, yoking the prospect of racial slavery to their bodies. Even the unborn figured into the reproductive calculus of the institution" (169). Hartman's analysis reveals how the structure of slavery and forced servitude not only confound the categories of social reproduction and domestic labor but also compound Black women's oppression. She argues that the "afterlife of slavery" persists in multiple forms, including in the extractive and dispossessive relations of domestic labor that relegate Black women to the margins. Transnational feminist and geographer Parvati Raghuram similarly accounts for how care labor continues to be shaped by "racialized encounters" (2019, 618): (1) the ongoing racialization of care workers, (2) the mobility of care workers (i.e., migrants who move as domestic workers), (3) the extraction of care from racialized majority populations by elites, and (4) the globalization of the care industry all evidence the different valuations of care labor based on the racialization of care workers.

The work of social reproduction and/or feminists of color helped move analyses of care as an ethic, value, disposition, or virtue toward understandings of care as a labor practice and political theory. They extend analyses of state care systems that refract dominant arrangements of power and governance and thereby limit access to social benefits (e.g., welfare, Medicare, Medicaid) while continuing to extract the (care) labor of oppressed peoples. Scholars such as Eileen Boris, Jennifer Klein, and Keeanga-Yamahtta Taylor, for example, detail how the exclusions of major social programs such as the New Deal, the National Labor Relations Act, the Social Security Act, and the Fair Housing Act disproportionately impact poor and working-class women of color, denying not only the protections of state care but also the ability to care for their own. Disability justice advocates (e.g., Patty Berne, Leah Lakshmi Piepzna-Samarasinha, and Mia Mingus) experience similar exclusions, working across communities to create spaces of care through the development of intricate care webs and systems of mutual aid.

In sum, the work of QTBIPOC and/or disabled theorists (e.g., Hazel Carby, Grace Chang, Saidiya Hartman, Evelyn Nakano Glenn, Grace Lee Boggs, Audre Lorde, Chandra Mohanty, Premilla Nadasen, Hortense Spillers) critiques notions of care that (1) presume the white middle-class woman as subject; (2) deny the historic and ongoing labors of service and servitude provided by Black, Indigenous, and migrant women in white women's homes; (3) fail to address the heteronormative constructions of "women" and "home"; and (4) theorize the domestic sphere as discrete from the public domain. By contrast, these scholars engage care as a practice and politics aimed at resisting the gendered, biopolitical regimes of settler colonialism and racial capitalism in ways that are often deemed as threatening. Alexis Pauline Gumbs, for example, blurs the lines between care as a practice, as a queer embodiment, and as a politics of writing: "She who refuses to reproduce *property* reveals a dangerous desire for something different. She who refuses to reproduce *properly* bears the mark of the alternative, the mark of the criminal, the mark of the terrorist. She who refuses to reproduce property must be busy teaching us something new. She who refuses to reproduce the status quo threatens to produce a radically different world" (2010, 13–14). Indigenous feminists (e.g., Joanne Barker, Jodi Byrd, Jennifer Denetdale, Mishuana Goeman, Rebecca Jane Hall, Audra Simpson, and Melanie Yazzie) further complicate analyses of care through an anticolonial politics of gender and sexuality grounded in Indigenous relations to land, sovereignty, and self-determination. While they also leverage critiques of social reproduction (an analytic limited to the dialectics of capitalist production and reproduction), they do so through the erasures of noncapitalist or subsistence modes of being that are fundamental to Indigenous lifeways.

In particular, since the dispossession of Indigenous peoples was/is predicated on the theft of land as relation, *not as property* (an understanding that is often missed in analyses of social reproduction, even antiracist ones), Indigenous feminists call attention to how the event of land theft is tied to a broader settler logic and structure that thieves relationality as a mode of kinship and care. The Indigenous political project is, therefore, about registering the import of women's labor not to capitalist (re)production but rather to nurture and sustain lifeways that refuse productivist logics altogether, particularly as the ongoing violences of capitalist accumulation are continually made manifest on the bodies of Indigenous women.

Mohawk feminist Audra Simpson, for instance, details how Indigenous dispossession is enfleshed, fundamentally "born by the living, the dead, and the disappeared corporealities of Native women" (2016, 16). She shows that this is because Indigenous women have been historically "rendered less valuable" because they represent "land, reproduction, Indigenous kinship and governance" (16) and seen as inherently dangerous because their very existence threatens the heteropatriarchal norms of property, personhood, and the heteronormative family. Thus, in ways that are related to but different from the subjugation of Black women, Indigenous women represent the gendered afterlife of settler invasion, whereby their ongoing care for land and communities is structured as threatening.

Today, one in three Indigenous women is a victim of rape, and the lands, waters, and other-than-human relations of Indigenous peoples are incessantly violated. These violences are coconstitutive; the same settler logic perceives Indigenous women and land as nothing more than "matter to be extracted from, used, sullied, taken from, over and over again . . . in a great march to accumulate surplus" (A. Simpson 2016, 15). Thus, the nineteenth-century imperative to "kill the Indian and save *the man*"—set in motion by General Richard H. Pratt, first superintendent of the Carlisle Indian School (Pratt 1973, 260)—manifested in ways that explicitly targeted Indigenous women as well as the expansive relations of making kin: child abduction, religious conversion, dissolution of land into property, imposed citizenship, enforced attendance at boarding and residential schools, forbidding the use of Indigenous languages, issuing of individual land titles, and coercion into heteronormative marriage and monogamy. In other words, "saving the man" was not simply sexist but a deeply misogynist project. Nevertheless, white women played a critical role in this campaign, serving as missionaries, boarding school teachers, domestic overseers, and child abductors, acting as the saviors and caretakers of the settler state (see M. Jacobs 1999, 2009).

As the global pandemic continues to unfold, questions of care—who is "worthy" of care, who can access care, and whose labor will be conscripted and extracted to care for others—reveal the ongoing salience of the foundational exclusions. Given this history, contemporary antiracist, anticolonial, Black, Indigenous, and other feminist and queer scholars continue to organize around the revaluing of care as a *politics of refusal*, one that rejects the exploitative relations of racial capitalism and settler colonialism and asserts, instead, care as a praxis of relationality and kinship critical to the development of just and liberatory futures (e.g., Vora quoted in Boris and Parreñas 2010; Yazzie 2018).

The assertion of care as a praxis extends beyond theorizing about violence and exploitation and engages the purposeful building of coalitions and networks of human and other-than-human kinship. Whether through the "care webs" articulated by queer disability justice activists or the kinship networks of Indigenous water protectors, care remains a central organizing node across social movements. The operating assumption is that modes of care that sustain and reproduce constellations of solidarity and connection fundamentally threaten racial capitalist, settler colonial logics of violence and disconnection.

13

Cis
Finn Enke

The prefix *cis-* derives from the Latin term meaning "on this side of" or "on the same side as." Linguistically, it has long derived its meaning in relation to *trans-*, meaning "across," "through," "on the other side of," or "beyond." Within white, European, and American contexts, people began attaching *cis-* to the words *gender* and *sex* in the late twentieth century to name people who are not transgender. Specifically, cis has functioned as a way to describe the condition in which one's gender identity and sense of self are congruent with the sex/gender assigned to one at birth. By implication, people use cis to mean someone whose gender identity is also congruent with dominant norms and expectations associated with one's anatomically defined sex/gender. The term *cisgender* made its way into print on both sides of the Atlantic by the 1990s, rapidly gained popularity by 2010 with the increasing publication of transgender perspectives and scholarship, and the term ultimately reached near-mainstream status with its incorporation into the *Oxford English Dictionary* in 2016 and *Merriam-Webster* in 2017. Vernacularly, "cis" is used as shorthand for people who are assumed by others to be cisgender or who self-identify as such; "cis" usually carries with it proximity to the privileges of normativity.

Particularly since the early twenty-first century, the mainstreaming of the prefix *cis-* attached to *gender* has encouraged the productive amplification of decolonial, queer of color, Indigenous, transfeminist, and nonbinary critiques of normativizing discourses but has also bolstered binary logics. Both the increased medicalization of transgender and the elaboration of nonbinary articulations owe much to the establishment of cisgender as a concept, label, and ontological status applied to persons. Because gender is an organizing principle that shapes everyone's lives and because all persons (not just trans people) are constituted within the hierarchies, violences, and pleasures of the requirement to "have" and "be" a gender, some scholars have found it useful to name those who are not transgender. One purpose of the term *cisgender* is to make visible and denaturalize what otherwise goes unnamed as the *natural* gender and make clear that being cisgender requires labor, construct, coercion, and reward. Many have argued that cisgender is useful for naming the privileges associated with being perceived to be aligned with the sex/gender one was assigned at birth and performing a normative-enough gender legibility and stability (Koyama 2002; Serano 2014; M. Roberts 2009). Naming the "unmarked" was a radical practice in sync with denaturalizing and queering heterosexuality, illuminating the supremacist logics of whiteness, and uprooting the settledness of ongoing settler colonial violences.

However, while "cisgender" aimed to depathologize "transgender," critiques of its limitations abound. Foremost, when it gets opposed to trans, cis circulates within compulsory binary logics and thus perpetuates systemic binary violences that trans communities sought to counter with the adoption of the term *transgender* in the late 1980s (Bey 2017). Scholarly critiques have had little impact on common parlance, in which *cis* draws on habituated beliefs about individuals presumed not to be trans and the unearned privileges that accrue to them because they are presumably not trans. To wit, a trans person might ask, "Why are all these cisgender people using the only single-occupancy bathroom in this whole building when they could be using the men's or women's room?" By separating the world into cis and trans, binary logics and habits of perception erase the complex embodiments, disabilities, and gender identities of vast numbers of people, including but not limited to trans and other queerly gendered people.

Cisgender privilege is understood to arise when anyone is passed as cisgender, regardless of their past, present, or future identification and embodiment (Enke 2012; Henningsen 2019). It is an established fact that most trans and nonbinary people face innumerable barriers and violences within most social institutions. And yet a minority, rather than a majority, of people are passed so seamlessly that they carry less trauma from their own risk or experience of being colonized, enslaved, objectified, harassed, assaulted, incarcerated, experimented on, misidentified, denied access, or murdered. The gender norms that enable such violence are inseparable from white supremacist and ableist social institutions. Thus, although many people enjoy literally countless passing privileges, trans, nonbinary, intersex, crip, decolonial, and antiracist critiques require bringing a great deal more nuance to assertions that (1) everyone is cisgender and (2) people who appear to be nontransgender have access to the privileges of normativity (Feinberg 2013; Snorton 2017; Bey 2019; R. Ferguson 2004; Clare 2017; Schalk 2018; Samuels 2014; McRuer 2006; Enke 2012; D. Rubin 2017).

This line of critique invites us to see that "cisgender" in practice may have paradoxically little to do with gender. Read intersectionally, it is unlikely that cisgender on its own can serve as a nonviolent *heuristic* with the potential to open critical analysis of the mechanisms through which communities and nation-states establish the boundaries and legitimating violences associated with gender normativity without actually reestablishing those same violences. At stake is no less than our ability to comprehend the full range of queer pasts, presents, and futures. By imposing sharp divisions

between queers who identify as trans and queers who don't and by aligning nontrans people with gender normativity, the uncritical deployment of the concept cisgender contributes to the elision of elaborate vocabularies and communities predicated on the instabilities of gender and sexual identity and expression. To be sure, queer communities themselves—including trans communities—have often fragmented around gender expression and identity. In most eras up to the present, some queer and trans people have worked to garner the privileges of white, able-bodied, and middle-class gender normativity or, alternatively, to distance themselves from those normativities. Notions such as "straight-acting" distance one kind of queerness from another; efforts to curtail "flamboyance" or attempting to exclude from pride parades people who do "drag" outside the confines of drag shows and people who are openly transsexual have served to establish a relative (homo) normativity within queerness predicated on gendered, racialized, ableist, and classist desires to separate queer sexual desire from queer gender expression (Feinberg 2013; Bailey 2013; Bey 2017; Valentine 2007; Mumford 2019; R. Ferguson 2019; Fisher 2016, 2019; Tinsley 2018). Put another way, efforts to secure and reject cisnormativity have fractured and shaped every moment of queer, trans, and nonbinary history, a history in which systemic white supremacy, with its gendered and ableist logics, puts BIPOC, disabled, and queer people (trans and not trans) in precarious and antagonistic relation to each other and any privileges within reach.

Cis/trans binaries also sediment around the insistence that gender and sexuality are two separate things, a distinction marshaled by trans and GLBA people alike often in an effort to distance themselves from and/or educate others about damaging stereotypes and stigmas. But the notion that sexual desire and gender identity and expression are discernably separate must also be contextualized not as a truth but as a rubric developed in relatively recent imperialist, white supremacist, and settler colonial histories (Miranda 2010, 2013; Swarr 2012; Najmabadi 2014; Aizura et al. 2014; Gill-Peterson 2018; Driskill 2016; L. Simpson 2017; Kauanui 2018; Tallie 2019).

In the late twentieth century, the term *transgender* emerged in resistance to the erasures, normativizing and institutionalizing practices that constituted the category "transsexual." Now in the twenty-first century, the increasingly bold line of distinction wrought by the cis-trans binary has encouraged new language that again seeks to reject binaristic thinking. The use of "nonbinary" in non-Indigenous communities and elaborations of Two Spirit in many Indigenous communities express widespread recognition of the failures of the cis/trans and homo/hetero binaries to represent and support the vast field of possibilities through which people experience and express gender, sex, sexuality, embodiment, and community (Driskill 2016; Driskill, Heath Justice, et al. 2011; L. Simpson 2017; Anguksuar Anguksuar / Richard LaFortune 1997). Simply, humans exceed binary definition.

14

Citizenship
Julie Avril Minich

Understood as the status of permanent belonging in a nation-state, *citizenship* is the legal mechanism through which people claim rights in a territory and define their relationship to its government. In liberal states like the United States, citizenship is often said to function independently of race, ability, gender, or sexuality. Schoolchildren in the United States are generally told that all are equal before the law, even as their teachers may tacitly acknowledge that laws have changed with regard to reproductive rights, property ownership, inheritance, and other entitlements of citizenship. US students learn early on that citizenship was initially restricted to white men but that changing attitudes and new legal protections made it available to everyone. By contrast, scholars in fields like ethnic, gender, LGBTQ, disability, and migration studies have shown that access to US citizenship and its benefits continue to be distributed unequally in ways that mirror ongoing patterns of discrimination (Berlant 1997; Carey 2009; Day 2016; Minich 2014; Molina 2014; M. Ngai 2004). Additionally, scholars of Native studies have shown that state citizenship for Indigenous peoples has been experienced as what Kevin Bruyneel calls "a direct colonial imposition, worthy of resistance and refusal" (2007, xxiii). The institution of citizenship is, therefore, a double-edged sword: on one hand, it is the mechanism through which a state confers rights and privileges upon the people residing within its boundaries; on another hand, the means by which people are deemed (in)eligible for (or forced into) citizenship are inherently violent.

By examining citizenship from the perspective of those denied its benefits, we see that simply including the previously marginalized is not as simple a matter as we hear in grade school. Rather, the very value of citizenship depends on the existence of people excluded from its fold. Historically, those excluded were identified by race, gender, and national origin. Examples include the US Naturalization Act of 1790, the first statute defining US citizenship, which declared only nonenslaved white people eligible. While women married to citizens were technically citizens, they lacked many of the rights associated with citizenship (including reproductive and sexual autonomy as well as the rights to vote and to own or manage property). Later laws modified the 1790 law: after the Civil War, formerly enslaved people became citizens, Native Americans living on reservations were forcibly incorporated into the US citizenry in 1924 (Bruyneel 2007; Tuck and Yang 2012), and changing state laws gradually conferred more rights to white women and then to Black and Latinx women. Yet efforts to racially manage the nation's citizenry continued, particularly through immigration laws like the Chinese Exclusion Act of 1882 and the Johnson-Reed Act of 1924, which established national origin quotas favoring immigrants from western Europe. Similarly, immigration law has functioned as an instrument of gender and sexual control throughout much of US history; lesbians and gay men were formally barred from immigrating to the United States until 1990, and LGBTQ migrants (particularly those who are gender nonconforming) continue to face exacerbated violence throughout the migration process, including steep obstacles even to filing asylum claims (Luibhéid and Cantú 2005; Luibhéid and Chávez 2020). While these examples are sometimes explained as aberrations in an otherwise egalitarian history, the practice of restricting eligibility for citizenship continues, although today those deemed ineligible are described not by race or national origin but with words like *criminal*, *undocumented*, or *terrorist* (Michelle Alexander 2012; Cacho 2012; Lowe 2015; Paik 2016; Puar 2007). As of this writing, for instance, approximately eleven million people who live in the United States have no path to becoming citizens: forced to migrate without authorization, upon arrival, they have no means of becoming naturalized citizens or even of resolving their status before US law.

The fact that there are people living in the United States without access to citizenship is a concern because it means that not every resident is promised the same legal rights. But it is also a concern that not all citizens enjoy the rights they are promised. For instance, throughout the early twentieth century, US citizens of Mexican descent were subjected to lynchings, land theft, and deportation (Muñoz Martínez 2018; Balderrama and Rodríguez 1995), while US citizens of Japanese descent were interned in prison camps (M. Ngai 2004; Paik 2016). Such events lead the historian Mae M. Ngai to describe US citizens of Asian and Latin American descent as *alien citizens*: those "who are citizens by virtue of their birth but who are presumed to be foreign" (2004, 2). Meanwhile, although the Fourteenth Amendment granted citizenship to formerly enslaved people in 1868, African Americans were not offered the full rights of citizenship until the 1960s, when the Civil Rights Act of 1964 and the Voting Rights Act of 1965 were passed. Furthermore, many scholars argue that the effects of mass incarceration and ongoing voter suppression efforts mean that many citizens of color, particularly African Americans, are still denied the benefits of citizenship (Michelle Alexander 2012; Combs 2016). Framing the use of the word *citizen* in relation to these facts means understanding that the idea of citizenship as a state of legal documentation is subtended by ideological concepts of who is a desirable citizen worthy of full benefits, privileges, and access to thriving.

Restrictions on eligibility for citizenship and the denial of rights to citizens are often mutually reinforcing processes. In June 2018, US attorney general Jeff Sessions issued a policy on behalf of President Donald Trump's administration that survivors of domestic violence were no longer eligible to apply for political asylum. Although the policy was quickly blocked by a judge and its fate is not settled as of this writing, it offers a particularly potent example of how gender, race, and national origin intersect in the regulation of citizenship. Because the rule was issued at the same time that increased numbers of Central American families—many of whom were requesting asylum—were arriving at the US-Mexico border, it was widely understood as designed to curtail migration specifically from Central America. In other words, a ruling ostensibly focused on gender violence functioned as a racialized restriction, rendering members of particular national origin groups from becoming eligible for citizenship. The rule also has implications for the rights of women and gender minorities more generally. In his decision, Sessions characterized domestic violence as "private behavior" (US Department of Justice 2018, 316), not political persecution. As feminist legal scholars note, such language minimizes gender-based violence as a problem that merits state intervention and public concern (Masulo 2015). In this way, Sessions also sought to create a precedent through which women and other gender minorities vulnerable to domestic abuse can be deprived of the right to a life free of violence.

The Sessions policy thus further illuminates how restrictions on citizenship, while most explicitly linked to racial ideologies, frequently operate through gender-based oppression. The most notorious example of this would be the eugenic sterilizations that were performed without consent on people of color and people with disabilities throughout the twentieth century (Gutiérrez 2008; Ross and Solinger 2017; Stern [2005] 2016). In 2020, news came to light of migrant women subjected to involuntary hysterectomies while detained by Immigration and Customs Enforcement, revealing how eugenic ideologies continue to inform immigration policy. The legacy of eugenics also lives on in less sensational but still devastating attacks on the parental legitimacy of poor people, people of color, and people with disabilities: family cap laws that deny benefits to people who become pregnant while receiving welfare, efforts to end birthright citizenship due to stereotypes about the fertility of immigrant women (particularly Latinas), and the systemic removal of Native American children from their birth families, a practice that was formalized with the establishment of Indian Residential Schools in the mid-nineteenth century and continues through court challenges to the Indian Child Welfare Act (Briggs 2017). These efforts are not all as blunt as forced sterilizations, but like both immigration restrictions and reproductive control, they rely on ideologies about who is fit to birth and raise (and thus to reproduce) citizens.

The above discussion might seem to offer a very dark view of the institution of citizenship, and indeed, many scholars are justifiably wary of its value. As media scholar Hector Amaya puts it, "There is something intrinsically poisonous in citizenship . . . an excess that feeds the power hungry and that convinces otherwise good people that oppression is just" (2013, 4). The "intrinsic poison" of citizenship might lead one to ask, Does the concept have any use at all? Why not abolish it altogether and appeal instead to a higher concept like human rights that is not tied to the laws of a particular nation-state? The problem is that *human rights*—which supposedly supersede the rights conferred by individual states—are themselves exercised through citizenship. Without a state to guarantee them, do rights become meaningless?

Recognizing this conundrum, other scholars have sought to illuminate how people assert their entitlement to the rights and benefits of citizenship even when they lack a legal claim to them. For instance, the field of Latinx studies has not only examined how Latinx peoples are denied the benefits of citizenship; it has also yielded a rich body of work demonstrating how people without legal standing take on the obligations of citizenship through civic participation and in doing so actively lay claim to its rights. This work focuses on what its scholars call *cultural citizenship* (Flores and Benmayor 1997; Oboler 2006; Rosaldo 1997). In theories of cultural citizenship, the citizen and the noncitizen are not so diametrically opposed, and room arises to think about redefining citizenship in ways that go beyond just conferring it on more people. Cultural citizenship, in other words, isn't just about making legal citizenship available to more people but about radically rethinking what citizenship could mean and how it might be enacted. The scholarship on cultural citizenship, therefore, enables us to ask whether the state is the most appropriate entity to function as guarantor of rights and whether there is a way to define citizenship so that its value doesn't depend on exclusion.

What critics of citizenship and advocates of cultural citizenship share is a commitment to dismantling citizenship as an engine of what the cultural critics A. Naomi Paik and Lisa Marie Cacho have separately theorized as *rightlessness*, a state ascribed to both noncitizens and devalued citizens. Paik argues that "there are variegations of rights and gradations of rightlessness" such that "the relatively rightful" and "the rightless" overlap and that "the stories that the rightless tell summon us to see their predicament as our own" (2016, 9). In a similar vein, Cacho suggests that taking seriously the position of those rendered rightless "enables us to privilege the populations who are most frequently and most easily disavowed, those who are regularly regarded with contempt, those whose interests are bracketed at best because to address their needs in meaningful ways requires taking a step beyond what is palatable, practical, and possible" (2012, 31–32). In examining the state of rightlessness, Paik and Cacho offer a framework for thinking about citizenship as well. Although public discourse often seems to present a stark distinction between citizens and noncitizens, the lines are more blurry than they might appear. Not all citizens have access to the same rights, and citizenship itself is more precarious and easily rescinded than many wish to believe. For this reason, the dilemma of the noncitizen is a matter that implicates citizens and must be an ethical concern to all.

15

Colonialism

Geeta Patel

The *Oxford English Dictionary* (*OED*) defines the word *colonialism* as a practice, as a manner of doing things (*OED Online*, "colonialism," n.d.). The word as such emerged in the mid to late nineteenth century in England. However, foreshortened versions such as *colony* and *colonial* have been extant and in use for far longer. "Colony" ostensibly comes from the Latin *colōnia, transported* into Old English in the fourteenth century via the French *colonie*, or "tiller," "farmer," "cultivator," "planter," "settler in a new place." But it has resonances in other European languages such as Spanish, Portuguese, Danish, and Dutch, each constituency shipping in its own, sometimes mottled, history of colonialism. Etymologies often trace the spoor of ideologies. So also with these connotations. They conveyed what was implicated by colonialism, their seeming innocuousness papering over the routes through which settler colonialism found its technologies of occupation, as we will go on to see.

Colonial, as the newer English word, has a shorter history, coming supposedly into common use in 1776 in the *Parliamentary Register* in the United Kingdom, the exact moment of the formation of the United States. However, it is perhaps no accident, as scholars are at pains to submit, that Rome was the birthplace of this keyword. Rome was notorious for its settlements that sought to refashion and assimilate local peoples. It was Roman-Christian religious legislative decrees that bolstered the early modern European push to conquest in the Americas and still hold sway in their seemingly

secular manifestations (Deloria and Treat 1999; R. A. Williams 1990). Roman law was refurbished during different periods of European neoclassical revival. In the late eighteenth century, for instance, it found its secular footing through William Blackstone's *Commentaries on the Laws of England*, which themselves provided the underpinnings for the East India Company's legal directives in India and Africa and in so doing ordained the flow of property through heteromasculinist lineages.

Given these various origin stories, what, then, constitutes the matrices that fall under the rubric of "colonialism"? Scholars who study histories of colonialism speak about it both variously and comparatively. Those who begin with a longer historical trajectory gather under its fold territorial or even nonterritorially sanctioned imperia—ranging from ancient Egypt and Assyria to Byzantium and the Ottoman caliphates of the early sixteenth century. Colonialisms have been as various as their architects. Whether Dutch, Spanish/Portuguese, Danish, French, Italian, or British, they were trafficked as pirates, missionaries, merchants, sailors, soldiers, voyagers, scientists, bankers, prisoners, magistrates, doctors, tax collectors, farmers, pensioners, middlemen, hunters, royal servitors, or corporation-backed colluders. At their collated reach, these varied colonialisms spanned over 80 percent of the planet in some form by the 1930s (Loomba [1995] 2015).

However, what most scholars refer to when they refer to "colonialism" are the various modalities of post-fifteenth-century European expansionism convened under the imprimatur of trade (Cooper and Burbank 2011). Unearthing routes and launching outposts to source and manipulate trade in gold, silver, chocolate, coffee, spices and medicinal plants, cotton, sugar, wood, coir, animal products, slave labor, and later on, opium, tea, and texts: all these furnished the guise under which European powers, nations, and companies justified settler colonialism, runaway territorial possession, and lethal domination. Included under the purview of this latter understanding of colonialism are the conveyances under which they assumed shape—for instance, through conquest, mining, and plantation slavery and finally through the aggressive take-over of land through settler colonialism and Indigenous displacement and planned genocide. Following the work of postcolonial, Black, and Indigenous feminist scholars, we might also understand colonialism as a historical project that serves capital through racialized gender and sexualized racism.

What might this entail? What are its ramifications? Colonial ventures, whether they were orchestrated through procedures associated with what might be called a state or through more indirect itineraries, reconfigured and institutionalized gendered, sexualized, and racialized habits and forms, according value to a select few. Simply stated, colonial economies were nourished and emboldened by regimes of social and biological reproduction. Whether in the context of the Americas or in the practice of British colonial rule in Africa and South and Southwest Asia, Indigenous and African kinship, family, and community formations were attacked and violently displaced, and the property and capitalist value that flowed through them in the literal sense as land, labor, political authorization, cash, credit, and goods were seized in the service of European domination and profit. Colonialisms' fingers (Tadiar 2004) reached deep into the guts of Indigenous and African ontologies and epistemologies and attempted to violently reconstitute them through their own notions of appropriate gender and sexuality. Contrived charges of ineptitude as well as degeneration that relied on arguments of sexual perversity and gendered capriciousness (which focused on queer and trans communities) provided the fodder for "proving" that what

constituencies knew, thought, and imagined were inadequate, primitive, and morally suspect. The effects were virulent and pernicious—damning communities' own sense of what mattered, who belonged in the worlds in which they lived, how they could compose, what genres were significant, how knowledge itself took shape, where and how knowing was to be found, and what was deemed meaningful.

Very abbreviated samplings of the aggressive displacements that also ensued include the diminution of flows of decision-making through clan mothers such as those of the Haudenosaunee in North America, the abbreviation and reforming of Nair matrilineal lineages in Kerala in South India, the deauthorization of Punjabi women in village communities, the refusal to accept women as heads of households in Bengal and Manipur, and the rights to the market transferred from women to men in many parts of Africa (Hill 2017; Mann 2006; S. Wagner 2001; Goeman 2013; Anzaldúa 1987; J. Nair 1996; A. Simpson 2014; Oldenburg 2002). Families were most often officially recognized by the colonial state through monogamous nuclear marriage and blood and racially based units, bolstered by paper certification; adoption, when permitted, was allocated only along caste or racial lines; and property passed via primogeniture that consolidated transformed notions of what many feminists have termed *patriarchy*, or the enforcement of inheritance of property passed down through what has been termed *heterosexuality*.

The racialized grammar of legislative sanctions under "civil" statutes adjudicated financial inheritance and the right to work and converted land from use into property handed over and through men and their direct offspring, while criminal statutes such as antisodomy laws, even when they were hard to enforce legally but sanctioned socially and politically, rendered sexual practices of trans and queer folks illegitimate. Aesthetic devices such as storytelling, dream walking, and the meta-phorics of love were curbed, and lock hospitals for sexually transmitted diseases were established to patrol the sexuality of genders that were not reckoned salutary or curtail entire constituencies by deeming them criminal.

More to the point, as so many scholars and activists, especially those from Indigenous constituencies, point out, the practices and projects that fall under colonialisms' terms are ongoing. The sharpest and most rigorous and nuanced readings of colonialisms are scripted by feminist scholars of colonialism—in particular, settler colonialisms and decolonization, race, Indigeneity, and transnationality—who attend to gender and sexuality in the context of what colonialisms constitute, abridge, and abrade. This expanding cohort of scholars refuses racialized gender/sexuality as a sideline, or as an addendum to political critique. Rather, for them, colonialisms' constitutions of value are routed through and as racialized gender and sexuality (M. J. Alexander 2005; Arondekar 2009; Arondekar and Patel 2016; Barker 2017; I. Chatterjee 2004; Cooper and Stoler 1997; Fiereck, Hoad, and Mupotsa 2020; J. Goldberg 2010; Goeman 2013; Grewal 1997; Hartman 1997; Higginbotham 2001; Kauanui 2008; Levine 2003; Loomba [1995] 2015; L. Mani 1998; Mohanty 2003; Molloy and Irwin 1998; Moraga 2011; J. Nair 1996; G. Patel 2017; Povinelli 2002; Rege 2003; Rifkin 2011; Sarkar 2002; Sangari and Vaid 1990; A. Simpson 2014; Sinha 1995; Spivak 1999; Stoler 2010; Tadiar 2004; Weston 1993).

16

Consent

Emily Owens

When I give public talks about the history of sexual violence, audience members usually ask me about the #MeToo movement and whether things are changing. When I walk into my campus bookstore, I notice glossy book covers that offer scholars' takes on their encounters with Title IX (Education Amendments of 1972, 20 U.S.C. § 1681 (1976)). I also see my students sitting about the bookstore café and recall their generalized discontent with Title IX processes on our own campus. When I walk a bit farther down the street to the beleaguered indie bookstore that serves my small city, I am faced with parenting books that promise lessons on how to raise "our boys" to be "better men." As a feminist parent with disposable income, I might grab one of those parenting books, alongside an illustrated one that will speak directly to my toddler about respect and/or bodies and/or being "a boy who dares to be different." On my drive home, I catch a news story about how teenagers watch a ton of porn. When I settle in for the night, various streaming services pitch shows that fictionalize the very real sexual predation of media men, doctors, coaches, and frat boys. I opt out, going straight to bed. I consider reading my new parenting book, but I'm exhausted, so instead, I pick up a novel; I'm disappointed when I stumble into a scene in which a middle-aged white cis-het guy finds himself naked in a hot tub with a teenager and wonders if it's appropriate. At this moment in the United States, I can't go anywhere without encountering consent.

The current ubiquity of "consent" functions at once as a shorthand for the problems of our sexual culture and for their imagined solution. When scholars, teachers, and activists use consent to think about sex, they extend an intellectual tradition that argues that more choice means more freedom to suggest that more choice and more freedom will also mean better sex.

Consent—traditionally understood as the expression of free will, or choice, of an autonomous subject—emerged in western political thought in Enlightenment-era experiments with democracy (Haag 1999; A. D. Davis 1999; Brewer 2005; Painter 2009) and with the coemergence of capitalism's slavery and wage labor (also called "free labor"; Dru Stanley 1998; Beckert and Rockman 2018). During this period, European intellectuals shifted their focus from theology to the human as the site of knowledge production. That shift was predicated on the belief that humans—a category that was itself developed through imperial encounters in the Atlantic world (J. Morgan 2004)—were "reasonable" subjects who had the capacity to discern the world around them, produce knowledge about it, and make decisions accordingly. In this political-intellectual tradition, reasonable subjects needn't rely on God or his deputies (monarchs) but instead could rule themselves. In this new era, government would draw its legitimacy from its *chosenness*, or as John Locke (2014) famously wrote, from the consent of the governed. Consent, then, was the cornerstone of the liberal political project because the expression of one's will at once confirmed and inaugurated his belonging within the citizenry of reasonable humans.

Consent also gave shape to the boundary between public and private life in the early American republic, for if public men entered public contracts through the utterance "I will," then women's lives were circumscribed by their relationship to the parallel phrase "I do"
(Cott 2003; Freedman 2013). White women, generally deemed unreasonable subjects unfit for full citizenship, nonetheless experienced temporary legal sovereignty over their bodies in their consent to a marriage contract. When they said "I do," their legal person became absorbed in—or "covered" by—the legal person of their husband, thus cementing the property relation of marriage through the doctrine of coverture (L. Edwards 2009; Light 2017). The process through which white women consented to marriage mirrored white men's process of consenting to be governed: the expression of self-sovereignty gave way to someone else's rule, and in the case of white women, this process made their submission to the will of their husband the defining quality of their freedom.

If white men and white women secured their statuses as public and private individuals in the early republic through separate expressions of consent, these new Americans' obsession with the ability to assert individual freedom was bound entirely to the context of the displacement and enslavement of Africans and African Americans and the dispossession and genocide of Indigenous peoples, none of whom were imagined as part of the polity of consenting individuals. New Americans wrote Black and Indigenous inhabitants *out* of the polity by claiming that they did not possess the capacity to reason and thus could not consent to be governed; instead, their unreasonable nature secured them as the abject Other whose very exclusion from the polity gave shape and meaning to ideas about freedom (S. Brooks 2010; Pinto 2020; C. Owens 2020). The free claimed to be masters and in turn endowed themselves with power over those they understood as unfree (McCurry 1995).

The notion that nonwhite inhabitants of the early republic *could* consent was only applied against them. For example, Andrew Jackson legalized his occupation of Creek, Choctaw, and Cherokee ancestral territories through treaties: he covered over the extent to which he had threatened them with annihilation by holding up a series of treaties that, he claimed, gave him legitimate control of their land because they had consented to give it to him (W. Johnson 2013, 2020; Grandin 2019). Slaveholding lawmakers assured themselves of enslaved people's incapacity to reason and inability to consent (to make contracts, to sit on juries, to file lawsuits) but made an exception for criminality, at which level they understood enslaved people as thinking beings who needed to be held responsible for their actions (Hartman 1997). Slaveholders routinely explained their sexual relationships with enslaved women through the fantasy of a fair agreement, in which the woman gave of herself sexually—that is, *freely* consented—in exchange for his withholding of his legal capacity to maim her, kill her, or separate her from her children (E. Owens 2015). Thus even as consent secured the freedom of the few Americans counted within the polity, it also functioned as a tool to justify and maintain the unfreedom of everyone else.

In the middle of the twentieth century, the campaigns of second-wave feminists revived and revised the long-standing Black feminist tradition of critiquing racialized sexual violence and the encroachment of the state on women's bodies (A. Y. Davis 1971; Hunter 1997, 2017; Feimster 2009; Rosen 2009). The pillars of second-wave feminism rested on consent as a negative right when they argued that women had the right to refuse sex—recall the familiar adage "No means no!"—and that the state must remove itself from a woman's right to make choices about her reproductive life (D. Roberts 1997; Schoen 2005; Self 2012; Mathiesen 2016). From the 1980s onward, feminist campaigns continued to imagine "choice" as a foundational tool for protecting people oppressed at the level of their sexuality. Feminists fought to broaden the legal definition of rape to include rape in marriage, raised the age of consent and thus expanded the spectrum of sex acts that would be considered predatory or violent, and defined the contours of sexual harassment law around unwanted—that is, un*chosen*—sexual behavior (MacKinnon and Siegel 2008; Fischel 2016; Wiegman 2019).

In the early 2000s, a surge of undergraduate activists publicized their outrage about the consistently high rates of sexual violence on college campuses. This movement reanimated the existing legal framework of Title IX, catalyzing what Janet Halley has critiqued as "the move to affirmative consent" and, later, the "#MeToo Movement," which extended far beyond campus life (Halley 2016; Know Your IX, n.d.; US Department of Education 2011). If organizers on and off campuses have emphasized that consent is a positive good (Kimmel and Steinem 2014) that invites fundamental changes to our historically broken sexual culture, feminist and queer theorists have raised questions: Is consent pedagogy really an answer to the climate of violence (Nash 2019b; Fischel 2019)? Which processes and approaches might interrupt institutional as well as interpersonal violences (C. Potter 2014)? Do movements that emphasize consent and Title IX encourage cultures of compliance rather than justice (Marine and Nicolazzo 2020)? Do those movements obscure other sites of on-campus violence and the violence of the university itself (Doyle 2015)? Does an emphasis on consent embrace transaction as the heart of sexual contact (E. Owens 2019)? Does an embrace of consent also signal an embrace of state power in intimate life (Essig 2014; Fischel 2019)?

If feminist and queer theorists and activists have troubled the notion that consent can save us, its racial and imperial histories present a more fundamental set of problems. The history of liberal humanism reveals that consent was the rubric of domination, not its opposite. Freedom is consent's conceit, and yet that freedom was indexed at its inception by white imperial and slave-holding will—that is, the ability to dominate as the evidence of freedom. The question of consent, then, is not whether we have gotten it right but rather whether it can be gotten right at all. Can we do consent (can we do freedom) without recuperating the violence in which its original expressions were embedded and upon which its invention was predicated (C. Reddy 2011)?

To situate consent within its historical context, in which the logic of consent authorized violence as often as it prevented it, is to interrupt the fantasy that freedom is best understood in the person of an autonomous subject. If those are freedom's terms, have they ever been achieved by anyone who is not white, wealthy, and male? A choice that pretends to be unperturbed by the pressures of interconnectedness amounts to an embrace of isolationist self-preservation, which is also to say, an embrace of the logic of domination. Consent's historic failures invite a new question: What would it mean to make interconnectedness and the accountability it requires fundamental aspects of political life?

17

Decolonization

Hōkūlani K. Aikau

Since the auspicious moment of European "discovery" five hundred years ago, Native women and Two Spirit / queer (2SQ) folks have resisted the gendered logics and practices of imperialism, colonialism, and settler colonialism. According to Leanne Simpson (2017, 41), "Indigenous bodies, particularly the bodies of 2SQ people, children, and women, represented the lived alternative to heteronormative constructions of gender, political systems, and rules of descent" and thus were treated as political orders needing to be controlled, co-opted, and eliminated. Many Native feminists have argued that imperialism, colonialism, and settler colonialism are not historical processes or events that only took place in the past; rather, they fundamentally constitute the sexual and gender-based violence that targets Indigenous women, children, and 2SQ people today. Furthermore, gender and sexual binaries (re)enforce patriarchy and heteronormativity through legislation, policies, laws, land rights, and treaties. Indigenous peoples continue to adapt their tactics and strategies to respond to the way heteropatriarchy shape-shifts to maintain (white) supremacy.

While decolonial struggle should be traced back to the dawn of European imperialism and account for the myriad ways imperialists and colonialists were tactically and strategically resisted, given the ongoingness of colonization, we must also recognize that gender and sexuality continue to be key to the maintenance of those projects today. According to Walter Mignolo, decolonization as an explicit political project "emerged in contemporary intellectual debates from the critical foundation established in Latin America, by José Carlos Martiátegui in Perú (in the 1920s). . . . And in the 70s it spread all over Latin America" (2007, 163). Decolonization includes but is not limited to resistance, refusal, and dismembering the legal, political, economic, social, and spiritual structures constructed by colonizers. When we approach decolonization as a set of practices intended to make material the liberation of Indigenous land and lives, then we can better see how decolonization cannot and should not be reduced to a metaphor, nor should it stand in for something else (Tuck and Yang 2012).

The grammar of *decolonization*, as a word, also suggests processes that must be engaged with on a continuous basis; decolonization is not a one-off event or act. The prefix *de-* derives from the Latin *dē* (prep), meaning "away from," "out of," "reversal," and "removal," and can be used intensively and pejoratively. *De-* also signifies separation, cessation, or contraction. There is a slight variation in the meaning of *de-* between American English and British English. In the American context, the prefix *de-* seems more instrumental: "away from, off; down; wholly, entirely, reverse the action of; undo." In British English, the prefix forms with verbs to suggest "removal of or from something specified; reversal of something; departure from," thus offering a more nuanced understanding of the conjoined term (*Collins Dictionary*, n.d.). For Mignolo, decolonization/decoloniality conjoins with delinking as it stresses the need to unveil, undo, or uncouple epistemologically from the logics of coloniality. Delinking is necessary for achieving political liberation and independence (decolonization) and epistemic liberation at the level of knowledge and ways of knowing (decoloniality). Decolonization and decoloniality cannot be achieved without delinking from the logics of coloniality.

To be sure, decolonization has a political and material history that includes but should not be reduced to a set of political procedures such as the process of federal acknowledgment in the United States and decolonization via the United Nations. The 1960s marked the formal beginning of global anticolonial movements, with the United Nations establishing procedures whereby colonies—non-self-governing territories—could petition the United Nations and work with administrative powers toward a process of self-governance. Whereas formal procedures for decolonization as set forth by the United Nations focus on the governmental aspects of colonization, they do not, on their own, address the ongoing psychological, social, and cultural realities of colonization, or what Mignolo calls coloniality. Nor do they, on their own, redress the way imperialism and colonialism are gendered, targeting Indigenous women, children, and 2SQ people to transform Indigenous gender and sexual systems.

Native activists, scholars, artists, and politicians have repeatedly noted that even with formal decolonization, the people living under newly independent states are often not free because far too often, the oppressive structures and institutions established under the colonial regime continue under "independence." In other cases, in order to meet the criteria for recognition or independence, Native Nations are required to create social, political, and economic institutions according to colonial models and standards. In both instances, neocolonial infrastructures continue to be based on heteronormativity, heteropatriarchy, capitalist democracy, and white supremacy. And for those Indigenous Nations that are no longer (or never were) listed as non-self-governing territories, such as Native and First Nations in the United States and Canada, respectively, they have yet to experience decolonization in any form. Indeed, more than twenty years ago, Marie Anna Jaimes Guerrero argued that in order to understand the status and struggles of Native women in the United States, "we must also understand the US as an advanced colonial state, because territorial colonization remains integral to the relationship between the state and native peoples" (1997, 101). Joanne Barker asserts that the process of federal recognition in the United States to which Native Nations must succumb is intended not to merely place them under the power and authority of the Congress but to coerce Native people to "*recognize themselves* to be under federal power within federal terms" (2011, 22). The racialization and gendering of membership criteria, as determined by the US federal acknowledgement or recognition terms and conditions, produce what Barker calls "a politics of relationship (un)making, as Native people negotiate the terms of their legal status and rights in relationship to one another as 'Indian members'" (22). For Native Nations in the United States, decolonization is *not* about inclusion as a minority group or recognition as quasi-sovereign nations beholden to the plenary power of the US Congress. Rather, Indigenous Nations want self-determination of their lands, lives, and futures on their own terms, not inclusion in the white supremacist heteropatriarchal settler state.

Native feminists continue to contend that decolonization as a set of political procedures is not up to the task of addressing the capaciousness of colonialism and coloniality, and it certainly does not have as its goal the restoration of Indigenous nationhood and Indigenous freedom (see L. Simpson 2017 for a discussion of Indigenous freedom). What this means in practice is that a field of gender and sexuality studies that does not acknowledge settler colonial states (such as the United States, Canada, Australia, and Aotearoa / New Zealand) as *settler colonial* as well as heteropatriarchal *and then* work to address issues of Indigenous land rights and sovereignty will fail to meet the needs of Native women,

their lands, and their kin and will wittingly or unwittingly prepare for settler futures without Natives (Tuck and Gaztambide-Fernández 2013).

Decolonization and decoloniality require all this and more because in order to bring about Indigenous freedom, we must decolonize *and* recover Indigenous stories, languages, ontologies, and epistemologies. To consider what decolonization wants is to stress that there was a time in the not-so-distant past when many Indigenous peoples "were born into and lived in a universe which was entirely of our making" (L. Smith 1999, 24). In part, returning to a vision of a future where Indigenous peoples are sovereign and self-determined is a commitment to understanding the process by which colonization and occupation occurred. It is not enough to critically analyze the process of colonization, occupation, and imperialism; we must also engage in the how of deconstructing and delinking from those systems. And while our instinct may be to use a sledgehammer to bring down these systems and structures, we may find that we must use a scalpel and a high level of skill, precision, and dexterity to delink from the ideas and practices that have been naturalized and normalized but are colonial imposition.

As scholars, we are trained to use our analytical skills to deconstruct, dissect, and destroy arguments and, far too often, peers and colleagues. What we are not trained to but must do is consider what will come after we have deconstructed, dissected, and destroyed. We should be considering the afterlife of analysis. Once we have delinked from the logics of coloniality, then what? The members of the architecture collective Decolonizing Architecture Art Residency (DAAR) share a similar sentiment when they contend that decolonization "is an ongoing practice of deactivation and reorientation understood both in its presence and its endlessness" (Petti, Hilal, and Weizman 2014, 18). They, too, are concerned about the impact of focusing on the *de-* of decolonization. Rather, they strive for more than demolishing or reusing existing structures and institutions. The members assert, "Decolonization, in our understanding, seeks to unleash a process of open-ended transformation toward visions of equality and justice" (18). For DAAR, subversion offers a third way that is open ended and transformative. From their standpoint as architects attentive to the materiality of decolonization, they recognize the impulse of destruction, the turning back of time, or a reversal upon which new beginnings can take root. However, "destruction generates desolation and environmental damage that may last for decades" (20). They go on to explain that this impulse to destroy all that the colonizers built can result in "a million and a half tons of toxic rubble that poisoned the ground and the water" (20). And while it is tempting to reuse the "existing structures in the very same ways they were used under colonial regimes," they caution against such impulses because these structures reflect a specific political ideology that will be reproduced if inhabited in the same way for the same purposes. Merely swapping out one set of occupants for another does not change the form, function, or ideologies built into that structure or institution. For DAAR, subversion takes existing structures and repurposes them for other ends. As architects, the members of DAAR approach their work by considering and addressing the physicality of the colonial present "and the trash it leaves behind" (31). And if we are going to attend to the materiality of decolonization, we must dwell in the materiality of colonization in all its forms. As DAAR members say of their project, they seek to create neither "an architectural utopia nor . . . a political instrument for 'denouncing' or 'mobilizing public opinion'" (26). Rather, the lesson for gender and sexuality studies is that they have "sought to establish a different balance between withdrawal and engagement,

action in the world and research, fiction and proposal" (26).

Many of us continue to live on stolen Indigenous lands that are still under the jurisdiction of settler colonizers. Decolonization is a commitment to the return of Indigenous lands and waters to Indigenous peoples. Decoloniality also requires delinking from the kinds of institutions and corporations that occupy and abuse Indigenous homelands and people, targeting women, children, and 2SQ people. Decolonizing gender and sexuality studies requires that scholars, students, artists, activists, and allies have the courage and imagination to envision life beyond the logics of coloniality and settler colonial logics of elimination in order to move toward Indigenous resurgence and freedom. Indigenous peoples and their allies engage in decolonial processes and practices day after day, generation after generation, for survival in order to get out in front of the colonizing machines that continue to wreak havoc on Indigenous lands, lives, and futures.

18

Development

Dina M. Siddiqi

The idea that international development is ideologically innocent and essentially a matter of overcoming technical or cultural deficits persists in popular imagination as well as development thought and policy, despite trenchant critiques over the years (A. Escobar 1995; J. Ferguson 1990; Gupta 1998; Rodney 1972). Especially in relation to gender and sexuality, development thought tends to be premised on colonial logics of cultural and economic backwardness (Mohanty 1988; Wynter 1996). In this short entry, I trace the making of hegemonic development narratives and examine the ideological labor performed by specific figurations of "Third World Women and Girls" in a transnational context. Such figurations are central to securing the story of capitalist progress development institutions and national governments like to tell.

Development discourse came into its own during decolonization, as the world order shifted from empires to ostensibly sovereign and equal nation-states. Deeply inflected by Cold War politics, between the 1950s and 1970s, ideological debates over redistribution, growth, and inequality raged across the (post)colonial world. The United States and its allies prevailed: by the 1980s, development came to be synonymous with faith in the ability of a "free" market to deliver national prosperity and individual freedoms (Rist 2008). In this sense, dominant development discourses blunted the radical edge of decolonization. Development was also a profoundly cultural project, steeped in the teleology of capitalist modernity and its many progress narratives all rooted

in heteropatriarchy (Cornwall, Harrison, and Whitehead 2007; Ong 2006). Cast as a moral and economic endeavor, development continues to possess enormous colonizing power (Spivak 1999).

The framework of development provides a way to understand a putatively decolonized world in which fundamental power relations remain unaltered. The conceptual division between a "developed" First World and an "underdeveloped" Third World maps neatly onto long-standing colonial dichotomies in which Europe remains the site of civilizational and moral order. Thus dominant development narratives reprise colonial uplift and rescue projects and reproduce colonial/orientalist hierarchies of race, gender, class, and sexuality (Abu-Lughod 2009; Bacchetta, Maira, and Winant 2019; Haritaworn, Kuntsman, and Posocco 2013). Development conceptualized as a lag (being behind and needing to catch up with the developed world) and a lack (the absence of cultural and other resources) also allows "women's status" to be framed as an outcome of the absence of modernity (which is always assumed to be the property of the Euro-American world and the values with which it is associated). In the temporal order built around the binary of development, underdevelopment involves a historical imagination in which the past and the present are not related (Loftsdottir 2016). This assumption of disconnection works to obscure or erase colonial and imperial histories; once the "debris" of empire is rendered ahistorical (Stoler in Loftsdottir 2016), poverty can be cast as a natural "Third World" condition, from which women and girls must be rescued through First World technical expertise and feminist enlightenment. This binary also works to hide similarities across presumed North-South differences.

In short, development discourse conjures up particular geographies to which certain kinds of gendered and sexualized bodies—unfree, passive, culturally/religiously/sexually oppressed—are relegated. The discursive construction of development as outside politics and culture or tradition as an obstacle to individual women's and national economic prosperity justifies the attention lavished by development institutions, NGOs, and governments on eliminating "backward" kinship norms and "barbaric" cultural practices, in isolation from larger social or political structures (Abu-Lughod 2013; Hammami 2019; Grewal 2013). This emphasis also takes attention away from the overwhelmingly extractive nature of the globalized, neoliberal developmental state and donor-imposed policies of structural adjustment, trade liberalization, and privatization (Bergeron 2003; M. J. Alexander 2005; Sen and Grown 1987).

Further, stripping away history and politics enables a variety of interventions in the name of improving women's lives. The so-called war on terror revived earlier models of imperial salvation to devastating effect, "ethicizing imperialism," producing new subjects of development—oppressed Muslim women and dangerous Muslim men poised to deprive the former of human rights and nations of economic prosperity (Abu-Lughod 2013; Murphy 2017; Razack 2008; Toor 2012).

Postcolonial and transnational feminist scholars pay close attention to the ways gendered histories of the present are embedded in imperial inheritances and constituted through highly uneven global relations of power and inequality (Alexander and Mohanty 1997; Grewal and Kaplan 1994). They note that treating the developmental state as a discrete, self-contained unit not only brackets out histories of conquest, slavery, and setter colonialism but also obscures the contemporary effects of the circulation of capital. This ensures that difficult or awkward questions, such as the role of transnational corporations in creating and perpetuating poverty, are never asked (Appel 2017; T. Li 2017). Rescuing or reforming the conditions of individual women from, for instance, "sweatshops" or sex work rather than attacking root causes becomes key to popular mobilization and development policy (Siddiqi 2009).

Under conditions of neoliberal capitalism, Third World women have gone from being constructed as victims and objects of welfare to figures of efficiency, entrepreneurship, and responsibility. In this version of development discourse, the bodies of girls and women are understood to be sites of financial investment and future value (Murphy 2017, 115). At the same time, neoliberal narratives of female empowerment reproduce the logic of Euro-American modernity, implicitly equating "progress" with culturally specific notions of bodily freedom and entry into the public sphere of wage work. Such assumptions allow once radical feminist discourses of empowerment to be sutured to that of profit maximization, most noticeably in the popularity of microfinance programs (Kabeer 1994; Karim 2011; Moeller 2018; Sharma 2008).

Global microfinance produced early on conditions for more "intimate transactions" between feminist consumer-citizens in the North and poor Third World Women and Girls. No longer at a distance, the latter becomes a visible and accessible figure whose life can be changed meaningfully through consumption or donations (A. Roy 2010). Thus, the figure of the girl child who is assisted in escaping marriage or the microcredit recipient whose future is transformed through loans "anchors a global conscience and transforms the distance of gender and race into a liberal intimacy with the world's poor" (A. Roy 2010).

Late twentieth-century corporatization of development has produced girls as the new flexible and self-enterprising citizens whose bodies are sites of investment for future returns, as potentially productive capital (Moeller 2018). It is now a development axiom that girls' education is the key to individual empowerment *and* global poverty reduction. Represented as a universalized victim in need of saving, the Third World Girl is simultaneously cast as the solution to problems of national development (Khoja-Moolji 2018).

Through their power to circulate globally, these development imaginaries produce shared understandings of progress and empowerment. Such representations are actively marketed through popular campaigns to promote empowerment "elsewhere" through consumption practices. The presumed link between "enlightened" consumption practices of the global citizen and human rights deficiencies "elsewhere" actively elides Euro-American complicity in the production of sustained global inequalities. It also hides the often coercive and violent encounters in the name of development.

Development cannot be reduced to a global project of engineering the world and reshaping subjectivities, however. Alternative imaginations of the good life and experiments with how to achieve it have always existed (A. Escobar 2018; Kothari et al. 2019). For most people in the Global South, an alternative vision of "development" stands in for the aspiration to a better life—if not for themselves, then for their children.

19

Deviance
Kemi Adeyemi

In the United States, some of our favorite deviants have been homosexuals, women, prostitutes, people who have kinky sex, people who are poor, people who are disabled, and people with mental illnesses—especially when these people are nonwhite, don't conform to expected gender roles, have "bad" manners, live in the "wrong" neighborhoods, and so on. Fields like sociology, anthropology, psychology, criminology, and legal and religious institutions played a central role in how these populations were pathologized as deviant. These disciplines' beliefs that deviance and biology were fundamentally linked often extended the scientific racism of the eighteenth and nineteenth centuries (which made false claims about the inherent and inescapable inferiority of nonwhites, nonmales, and non-Europeans) and shaped public opinion and policy to usually devastatingly violent effects. In the last half of the twentieth century, deviance became a more complex frame of analysis as scholars argued it is of course *not* biological and that our ideas of who and what is deviant are socially constructed, are historically situated, and change over time (Goffman 1963; Gagnon and Simon 1967, [1973] 2017; Goode [1978] 2016; Schur 1984; G. Rubin 2002; Worthen 2016; Love 2015; Dennis 2018). Scholars—especially feminists, queer theorists, and critical race theorists—reframed "deviance" not as an aberrance to a stable and unchanging norm but as evidence of how racism, misogyny, ableism, classism, xenophobia, and homophobia shape definitions and everyday understandings of norms and deviance alike

(G. Rubin [1984] 2011; J. Butler [1990] 1999; R. Ferguson 2004; Prohaska and Jones 2017; Puar 2007).

People within and beyond the academy were, moreover, taking deviance up as a powerful position to be reclaimed and rallied around in order to specifically *resist* norms (de Lauretis 1991; Jagose 1996; Warner 1993; L. Edelman 1994; Berlant and Warner 1998; Muñoz 1999; Cohen 2004). Organizations across the demographic spectrum from Lavender Menace (lesbian feminist deviants from the women's movement's focus on heterosexuality) to Gay Shame (antiestablishment deviants within homonormative configurations of US capitalist imperialism) to (re)invigorations of Yellow Peril Supports Black Power (Asian and Asian American deviants within US racial formations) to dyke marches (gender deviants within corporate homonormative nationalism) staked claims to deviance as a platform and strategy for radical political action (R. Brown 1995; Taniwaki 2000; Sycamore 2004; Watkins 2012; Currans 2017). The work of these activists has been reflected in scholarship by and about Black women, femmes, and trans and gender nonconforming people that is especially pointed in illuminating how the label of deviance has been used to violently regulate ways of thinking, feeling, being, and moving. This scholarship showcases Black women, femmes, and trans and gender nonconforming people as skilled outlaws (Evans 1993) and saboteurs (Haley 2016) whose deviant practices press against normative conventions of racialized gender performance and desire, often while interrupting the smooth flow of capitalist extraction that depends on their bodies yet disavows their subjecthood: work slowdowns, redirecting conversation, stealing themselves away from plantations, cross-dressing, forming queer and lesbian bonds with one another, having sex (and filming it), causing disturbances on the chain gang, refusing to speak, and more (Hurston 1935; A. Y. Davis 1971; Hartman 1997; Miller-Young 2014; Cruz 2016; Snorton 2017; E. Johnson 2018).

These studies of deviance also enact a *politics* of deviance by centering the everyday practices of people who are among the most surveilled and disciplined, and they do this by assuming that people's so-called deviance can tell us much about how they interact with and live otherwise to systems of power and control. In her landmark essay "Deviance as Resistance," Cathy Cohen describes a politics of deviance grounded in Black people like unmarried mothers; LGBTQ youth; those who have been incarcerated, are on welfare, and/or have risky sex; people "whose everyday decisions challenge, or at least counter, the basic normative assumptions of a society intent on protecting structural and social inequalities under the guise of some normal and natural order to life" (2004, 32–33). Cohen is careful, however, to argue that deviant practices are valuable sites of radical possibility but that the links between deviance and resistance are not inherent or given; deviance does not always equal resistance. She explains, "Most acts labeled deviant or even defiant of power are not attempts to sway fundamentally the distribution of power in the country or even permanently change the allocation of power among individuals involved in an altercation" (40). Indeed, some forms of gender and sexual deviance are absorbed into normative popular culture, as happened with drag, a historically deviant practice by "deviant" Black and brown people that has been built into a lucrative global industry increasingly important to the mainstreaming of certain expressions of gay male identity and politics. The political neutering of deviance has also been staged in the academy as modes of inquiry (e.g., queer theory) that were once radically deviant from and antagonistic to academic disciplines have become de rigueur within them (J. Butler 1994; Jakobsen 1998).

It is tempting to ascribe political power to a person, gender expression, cultural practice, desire, race or ethnicity, academic discipline, belief, object, theory, or action because they deviate from a norm. But we cannot simply note that a deviant act has transpired or assume that people's deviant acts are intentional, self-aware interrogations of systems of power. What we perceive as deviance is just as often the simple, though endlessly difficult, task of using our limited embodied, emotional, and material resources to make the best out of hard lives (Cohen 2004). Moreover, when we flatten the power and potential of deviance as a political strategy and critical analytic into tidy examples of resistance par excellence, we risk oversimplifying how the norms are themselves constructed and maintained (Wiegman and Wilson 2015; Amin 2017): complex descriptions of deviant acts must go hand in hand with complex descriptions of systemic power that frame and shape their possibilities. Blanket idealizations of deviance can, further, belie our unconscious beliefs in or attachments to the "fundamental" nonnormativity of racial, sexual, and gender minorities, especially women of color, people in the Global South, and queer people (E. Edwards 2015, 146–47). Not every body, life, or act can or should be recuperated into a heroic narrative of deviance; scholars of populations and subjects rendered pathological, different, or abnormal must interrogate whether the impulse to dramatize deviance as resistance is rooted in the materiality of the actions in question or rooted in deep-seated assumptions about the bodies, cultures, and locations of the populations and subjects in question.

An effective politics of deviance is not consumed with the novelty of deviance, or what Lila Abu-Lughod (1990) calls the "romance of resistance." It shifts perspective to ask "not about the status of resistance itself but about what the forms of resistance indicate about the forms of power that they are up against" (47). Studying deviance thus requires a rigorous materialist analysis that tracks how norms transform over time *and* documents how people make conscious and intentional choices to engage and dismantle them. It is particularly urgent to understand how people sense and negotiate the dynamic forms of subjection that are fomented as political actors collude with corporations and militarized police forces to unevenly assert control over and extract resources from people and territories. Thinking more closely with people who self-consciously embody and theorize their own politics of deviance in these times can tell us much about how we commit to and move against diverse regimes of governance as they shape our sensoria and networks of connecting while also imagining new ways of being in the process.

20

Diaspora

Gayatri Gopinath

As a descriptive category, "diaspora" refers to the dispersal and movement of a population (defined by race, religion, ethnicity, nationality, or another coalescing identity) from one national or geographic location to other disparate sites. The word derives from Greek, a combination of *dia* (across or through) and *sperein* (to sow or to scatter). The fraught nature of the term for gender and sexuality studies scholars is reflected in its etymological roots, which are shared with the word *sperm*: "The original meaning of diaspora summons the image of scattered seeds, and . . . thus refers us to a system of kinship reckoned through men and suggests the questions of legitimacy in paternity that patriarchy generates" (Helmreich 1992, 245). Indeed, this traditional articulation of diaspora is apparent in myriad contemporary cultural formations, where all too often diasporas are narrated through relational bonds between men and specifically through an oedipal relation between fathers and sons (Gopinath 2005). Feminist and queer scholars have had to grapple with the patriarchal, patrilineal, and heteronormative underpinnings of the term in order to retool it for their own purposes.

The critical genealogy of "diaspora" that many gender and sexuality studies scholars draw on, negotiate, and rework emerges from Black British cultural studies in the 1980s and 1990s—particularly the foundational work of Stuart Hall and Paul Gilroy—and its articulation of diaspora in relation to questions of culture, identity, race, and nation. Gilroy (1993) theorizes "the

Black Atlantic" as a diasporic formation precipitated by the transatlantic slave trade and the forced migration of African peoples to Europe, the Americas, and the Caribbean. "Diaspora" here is a conceptual category that names the dialectic of commonality and difference that binds African-descended populations to each other across disparate terrains and that is characterized by "a conception of 'identity' which lives in and through, not despite, difference; by hybridity" (S. Hall 1990, 235). By theorizing the Black diaspora as a "changing same," where "routes" mediate and complicate an adherence to "roots" (Gilroy 1993), these scholars were deeply invested in moving "diaspora" away from its conventional association with nostalgic evocations of lost homelands and the desire to preserve and retain an "authentic" culture or tradition. Working against an essentialist notion of identity as static and unchanging rather than as shifting and unstable, they embraced diaspora as a concept for its potential to foreground notions of impurity, hybridity, and heterogeneity that reject the ethnic/racial/religious absolutism at the heart of nationalist projects. Thus the promise of "diaspora" is that it serves as a critique of and alternative to both cultural and state nationalisms and their constitutive investment in the fixity of metaphorical and material borders of identity, culture, and community. As feminist scholar Avtar Brah notes, "Diaspora offers a critique of discourses of fixed origins while taking account of a homing desire, as distinct from a desire for a homeland" (1996, 16). A desire for home and belonging, in other words, is central to diasporic consciousness, even as there is a concomitant recognition of the impossibility of return to an "original" homeland.

It is significant that Brah took as her starting point in theorizing diaspora in the mid-1990s the experience of South Asian women in Britain—first- and second-generation migrants from South Asia and Africa who were often multiply displaced—so that "home" and "homeland" were also multiply constituted. South Asian feminist scholarship on diaspora, such as this, makes clear how contemporary gendered nationalist discourses of tradition, culture, and purity—which trace their genealogy to British colonial ideologies that frame South Asian women as passive, oppressed, and in need of saving—are replicated in the diaspora. Thus there is a double-faced nature to the concept of diaspora: one iteration of diaspora embraces precisely the generative notion of identity not as essence but as "positioning" (S. Hall 1990, 230), while another conservative iteration of diaspora understands questions of identity, culture, community, and tradition as indeed fixed and static. This latter version of diaspora is violently consolidated on the bodies of women, who are meant to serve as symbols of cultural authenticity and communal identity (Grewal 2005; Maira 2002; B. Mani 2012; Niranjana 2006; V. Reddy 2016). Thus feminist theorists of diaspora have been finely attuned to how nationalist and diasporic discourses are not, in fact, always in opposition but rather coconstitutive when it comes to questions of gender. These intersectional framings of diaspora—which locate diasporic formations at the nexus of discourses of masculinity, femininity, nation, race, migration, class, and religion and in the context of colonial histories—make clear the necessity of a gender analysis in theorizing both diaspora and nation.

Drawing on postcolonial and woman of color feminist theorizing of diaspora, queer studies scholars in the late 1990s and 2000s coined the term *queer diaspora* to reference the ways that the meanings and manifestations of sexual desire, subjectivity, and practices shift and transform in the context of diasporic movement, migration, and dwelling (Gopinath 2005; Eng 2010; La Fountain-Stokes 2009; Manalansan 2003; Manalansan and Cruz-Malave 2002; Patton and Sánchez-Eppler

2000; Quiroga 2000). This scholarship illuminates how the communal boundaries of both diaspora and nation are formed not just through discourses of gender but crucially through discourses of sexuality as well. More specifically, these boundaries are consolidated through the institutionalization of heteronormativity and the subsequent abjection and effacement of particular subjects (deemed sexually and morally "perverse" or abnormal and/or simply outside the boundaries of intelligibility) and the reification of others (the category of "woman," for instance; M. J. Alexander 2005). Suturing "queer" to "diaspora," then, allows these scholars to wrest "diaspora" away from its more conservative iterations and to instead recuperate the antiessentialist framings of identity and culture that some articulations of diaspora enable. The concept of queer diaspora provides "new methods of contesting traditional family and kinship structures—of reorganizing national and transnational communities based not on origin, filiation, and genetics, but on destination, affiliation, and the presumption of a common set of social practices or political commitments" (Eng 2003, 4). Queer diasporic expressive culture and everyday forms of queer diasporic world making articulate radically expansive visions of "home" and belonging, kinship and community, that are not beholden to heteronormative and patrilineal logics (Bailey 2013; Diaz, Largo, and Pino 2017; Eng 2010; Gopinath 2005, 2018; Kapadia 2019; Muñoz 1999; J. Rodríguez 2003; R. Rodríguez 2009; Quiroga 2000).

The concept of "queer diaspora" not only productively disorganizes the heteronormative and patrilineal terms of conventional articulations of diaspora; it also disorganizes conventional framings of queerness and its attendant tropes and signifiers, such as the closet, "coming out," and a politics of visibility. Suturing "diaspora" to "queer" pushes queerness outside of a Euro-American frame and instead demands a theorization of queerness in relation to histories of colonialism, migration, and globalization. Queer diaspora studies illuminates how the desires, embodiments, and socialities of racialized diasporic populations are governed by sexual and gender logics that may be unintelligible within standard Euro-American identity formations of "LGBTQ." Queer diaspora scholarship makes apparent how dominant Euro-American formulations of sexual identity adhere to a civilizational discourse that frames sexual subjects that do not cohere within its terms of legibility as premodern, backward, and underdeveloped (Manalansan 2003; Massad 2008). This framing extends to noncosmopolitan sexual subjects in the Global South as well as migrant and racialized populations in the Global North. Instead, queer diaspora studies provides a critical interpretive frame through which to read and register as strategic and oppositional those cultural practices (such as silence, invisibility, or the hyperbolic performance of gender) that would otherwise be dismissed as insufficiently political (Decena 2011; Manalansan 2003; Quiroga 2000).

Scholars working at the intersection of Black diaspora studies and queer studies have powerfully reworked the concept of diaspora inherited from Paul Gilroy and other key figures in the field of Black diaspora studies to foreground the queerness of the Black Atlantic itself (M. J. Alexander 2005; J. Allen 2011; Tinsley 2008; Walcott 2016). In pointing to the same-sex intimacies forged in the hold of the slave ship and that manifest in contemporary formations of same-sex desire, support, and sustenance throughout the Black Atlantic (Wekker 2006), Omise'eke Natasha Tinsley argues that the Black Atlantic has always been the queer Atlantic. These intimacies are "'queer' not in the sense of a 'gay' or same-sex loving identity waiting to be excavated from the ocean floor but as a praxis of resistance" (Tinsley 2008, 199). These Black queer reframings of diaspora reveal how queerness is central to its formation, even as they make the afterlife of transatlantic slavery and the insurgent knowledges and oppositional practices to which it gave rise central to any understanding of queerness.

Given that "diaspora is a fundamentally spatial relation" (Hawthorne 2019, 5), gender and sexuality studies scholars have turned to other spatial scales and frames that address the various limits of diaspora as a conceptual tool. Scholarship on "queer regions," for instance, focuses on the region in both its subnational and supranational senses as a corrective to the diaspora-nation dyad (Gopinath 2018; Herring 2010; Manalansan 2014; Tongson 2011). This work attends to intraregional and transregional resonances between gender and sexual formations within the Global South and between the Global South and the Global North so as to foreground south-south and region-to-region mappings of gender and sexuality that provincialize the Global North (Chiang and Wong 2016; Fajardo 2011; A. Wilson 2006).

Diaspora studies has also drawn criticism for not being sufficiently attentive to the workings of settler colonialism in mapping the ground upon which diasporic communities take root. Indigenous studies scholars have pointed out that the powerful critique of the nation form that diaspora studies offers presumes a settler nation and erases Indigenous understandings of nationhood and sovereignty. In recent years, feminist and queer scholars have been at the forefront of grappling with the relation between diaspora and Indigeneity, given that settler colonial histories have been subsumed or effaced in many theories of diaspora (Byrd 2011; DeLoughrey 2010; Lawrence and Dua 2005; A. Smith 2010). Definitionally, the categories of "diaspora" and "Indigeneity" seem oppositional, with diaspora connoting dispersal and rootlessness and Indigeneity connoting place and rootedness. However, a rich body of gender and sexuality studies scholarship tracks the shared terrain between diaspora and Indigeneity as well as how diasporic populations participate in the project of settler colonialism (Day 2016; S. Jackson 2012; T. King 2019; McKittrick 2006; Miles and Holland 2006).

Diaspora studies' overemphasis on mobility over emplacement has been critiqued by generations of feminist and queer scholars who have importantly moved definitions of diaspora away from a singular focus on displacement and leave-taking and toward an understanding of the geography of diaspora as encompassing itineraries of "staying put" and dwelling as much as of departure (Brah 1996; J. Brown 2005). These scholars have embraced other spatial metaphors that are at once materially grounded and that work alongside diaspora in order to trouble the dwelling/departure dichotomy. Vanessa Agard-Jones, for instance, turns to the materiality and metaphoricity of sand, "this object that exists at the point of nature's hesitation between land and sea," to illuminate "how people with access to only limited forms of mobility, like those of the shifting sands, live their genders and sexualities within the region" (2012, 326–27). Queer diaspora scholarship has also made clear how movement and mobility are often enforced and enjoined upon racialized migrant populations, who are not given the luxury of dwelling. Nayan Shah's (2012) research on early twentieth-century South Asian male migrants in western North America, for instance, excavates the "stranger intimacies" they created in the wake of forced transience. Such work reveals how the gender and sexual logics of diasporic formations are inescapably refracted through histories of racialized labor migrations, and vice versa. In short, gender and sexuality studies scholarship on diaspora has revealed how processes of both diasporic dwelling and leaving are subject to various interlocking systems of juridical, material, and epistemic violence. But this scholarship has also made abundantly clear how those who are subject to these forms of violence nevertheless create vibrant and endlessly imaginative modes of feminist and queer diasporic livability (McKittrick 2006).

21

Difference

Lisa Kahaleole Hall

In the United States, the most complex and grounded analyses of difference have directly arisen from the political and intellectual labor of those who identify themselves as part of woman of color feminism and/or Black feminist traditions. Poet Audre Lorde has been the key architect of theorizing difference as a permanent and endemic dynamic that is commonly ignored or suppressed but that holds the possibility of creative inspiration and growth through friction. The central theme of Lorde's lifework was to examine the creative power of difference in relation to the absolute necessity of examining the specific conditions of our lives in the service of growth and change. In her essay "Age, Race, Class and Sex," first given as a speech at Amherst College in 1980 (and later published in her collection *Sister Outsider*), she insists that "advocating the mere tolerance of difference between women is the grossest reformism. It is a total denial of the creative function of difference in our lives. Difference must be not merely tolerated, but seen as a fund of necessary polarities between which our creativity can spark like a dialectic. Only then does the necessity for interdependency become unthreatening" ([1984] 2007a, 99). In 1981, the anthology published through grassroots feminist presses, *This Bridge Called My Back: Writings by Radical Women of Color*, powerfully named the multiple contradictions that those who are erased from binary narratives of political struggle are forced to constantly reckon with. The anthology formed a creation story of the category "women of color" with its construction of community through shared and unshared difference, solidarity, and contradiction. Contrary to the assumption of a naturalized identity, the category asserted as a political choice to link with other Others. The work that co-editors Cherríe Moraga and Gloria Anzaldúa brought together articulated new understandings of pervasive forms of multiple marginalization as well as expressions of spiritual, creative, and intellectual resistance to those violences.

Moraga describes this epistemological and political process as creating "theory in the flesh":

A theory in the flesh means one where the physical realities of our lives—our skin color, the land or concrete we grew up on, our sexual longings—all fuse to create a politic born out of necessity.

> Here, we attempt to bridge the contradictions in our experience.
> We are the colored in a white feminist movement.
> We are the feminists among the people of our culture.
> We are often the lesbians among the straight.
> We do this bridging by naming our selves and by telling our stories in our own words. (Moraga and Anzaldúa 1981, 21)

These theories in the flesh refused the commonplace conceptual erasures embodied in binary phrases like "women and minorities" and "everyone—Black or white" in order to illuminate the complexity of relationships of solidarity and inequality, complicity and coalition.

During the late 1980s and early 1990s, there were still robust community-based feminist institutions in the United States—most notably around health care and reproductive rights and cultural production through bookstores, bars, and performance spaces. *This Bridge* had just been published and was causing waves of change in the feminist classroom. The "evidence of difference" was everywhere. The title of the first Black women's studies anthology, *All the Women Are White, All the Blacks Are Men, but Some of Us Are Brave* (Hull, Bell Scott, and Smith [1982] 2015), and poet Gwendolyn Brooks's wry observation—"The juice of the tomato is never just called *juice*. It's always called *tomato* juice" (cited in Spelman 1988, 186)—highlighted the whiteness and maleness of unmarked categories of race and gender. Relations of difference productively animated an explosion of work from feminist small presses, such as bell hooks's (1989) *Talking Back: Thinking Feminist, Thinking Black*, Chrystos's (1988) *Not Vanishing*, and Anzaldúa's (1987) *Borderlands / La Frontera*.

These writers were making an epistemological critique about the *theoretical* as well as the political inadequacy of a unitary, unmarked construction of female identity, publicly questioning racist constructions and histories of "womanhood." Norma Alarcón's "The Theoretical Subject(s) of *This Bridge Called My Back* and Anglo-American Feminism" was first published in Anzaldúa's (1990) path-making anthology *Making Face, Making Soul: Haciendo Caras; Creative and Critical Perspectives by Feminists of Color*. In it, Alarcón noted that *This Bridge* revealed that the formation of the female subject could take place in relations of difference and inequality from *other women* and not just from men, and she did so in full command of the theoretical apparatus employed by those she was critiquing. The anthology's section on "'Doing' Theory in Other Modes of Consciousness" put the voices of Alarcón, Barbara Christian, María Lugones, and Trinh T. Minh-ha in collective conversation about difference's modes and meanings (Anzaldúa 1990).

But the tumultuous discussions sparked by US women's analyses of multiply diverse experiences of racialized gender were short-circuited when many academic feminists turned their analytical attention to the valorization of a school of thought that came to be called "French feminism." While some white feminist scholars did combine the concerns of race and gender in this work, for the most part, the question of racialized difference(s) was dropped in the service of linguistic and psychoanalytic *difference*, ultimately deflecting robust discussions of the theoretical critiques being mounted by US women of color. In the 1980s turn toward "theory" in the US academy, France was not conceptualized as a nation-state with its own particular histories of colonialism, settler colonialism, gendered and racialized immigration, and nationalist exclusion. Absent being understood as rooted in a particular context, this version of "French feminist" theory implicitly declared its ideas universal. In the US classroom, this universalizing move enabled those who wished to connect theory to specific contexts and purposes to be dismissed as antitheoretical or "essentialist" or condescendingly portrayed as the intellectually inferior side of a hierarchical "theory" / applied theory divide.

An emblematic example of the refusal to acknowledge US women of color's analyses as theoretical interventions can be seen in the lack of engagement with the arguments Caribbean American feminist literary critic Barbara Christian (1987) made in her much-circulated and oft distorted essay "The Race for Theory," in which she argues that theories and theorizing take many forms and have many histories. Surreally, her plea for recognition of theoretical *multiplicity* is persistently framed as being *anti*theoretical.

Trinh T. Minh-ha's (1986) brilliant meditation in "Difference: 'A Special Third World Women Issue'" is a poignant reminder of both the necessity for the theoretical analysis of difference and what is at stake in the struggle. She understands the historical and epistemological violences directed toward women of color attempting to articulate their experiences within frameworks that contain no conceptual space for them, "the humiliation of having to falsify your own reality, your voice—you know" (Trinh 1986, 6). With regard to the kinds of distorted reception meted out to those outside a hegemonic norm, she observes, "Difference is not difference to some ears, but awkwardness or incompleteness" (6). Trinh presciently notes the ongoing necessity of pushing back against conceptual erasure where crucial differences disappear: "You try and keep on trying to unsay it, for if you don't, they will not fail to fill in the blanks on your behalf and you will be said" (6).

Difference is a keyword that allows for the analysis of relations that depend not on identical subjects but on interrelations. It is the ground of possibility for bringing complexity and nuance to forms of both identity and solidarity. A focus on the political and analytical implications of difference sparked a body of work by US woman of color feminists that has been vastly underrated as a theoretical archive, if not outright ignored. The genealogies of women of color and/or Black feminism contain a rich archive of grappling with what Lorde described as the creative spark of difference as well as sometimes daunting retreats to univocal and one-dimensional constructs of identity and relation. Woman of color feminism continues saying and unsaying how and why difference matters.

22

Disability
Sami Schalk

The term *disability* refers to a wide range of bodymind differences that have accrued a variety of social meanings over time, often with negative associations. I use the term *bodymind* here after Margaret Price, who defines it as a materialist feminist disability studies concept referring to "the imbrication (not just the combination) of the entities usually called 'body' and 'mind'" (2015, 270). The term *bodymind* highlights how "mental and physical processes not only affect each other but also give rise to each other" (269), collectively impacting our experiences of ourselves and the world. Discussions of disability include conditions that are physical (like paralysis or amputation), sensory (like blindness or deafness), psychiatric (like depression or schizophrenia), cognitive/intellectual (like Down's syndrome or autism), and chronic (illnesses and diseases like fibromyalgia or diabetes). Since the early 1990s, however, scholars in disability studies have researched disability as a socially constructed category that cannot be wholly understood through moral or medical models that frame it as a problem to be solved. While disability conceptually overlaps with studies of medicine and health, disability is not the same as health. In disability studies, *disability* is a social and political category describing bodyminds that depart from the bodily, mental, and/or behavioral norms of a society. Scholars in the field are invested in discovering the history and culture of disabled people as well as how the category of disability has developed and changed over time. Discrimination based on disability is referred to as ableism, while benefits within the (dis)ability system are referred to as ability privilege or able-body/able-mind privilege. Some scholars use terms like *(dis)ability*, *ability/disability*, and *dis/ability* to additionally refer to the overarching social system that determines how bodymind differences are valued or devalued to distinguish this concept from the word *disability* alone; *(dis)ability*, *ability/disability*, and *dis/ability*, therefore, operate similarly to concepts like *gender*, *race*, or *sexuality*, which also refer to larger systems of privilege and marginalization (Schalk 2018; Garland-Thomson 2002; Goodley 2014). This entry will use *(dis)ability* to describe the larger social system and *disability* and *ability* to describe, respectively, the marginalized and privileged positions within the (dis)ability system.

Disability studies as a field was largely inspired by work in women's studies, ethnic studies, and LBGTQ studies in much the same way that the disability rights movement took inspiration from the feminist, civil rights, and gay rights movements. It makes sense, therefore, that the field remains in close contact and conversation with gender and sexuality studies today. When scholars combine theories and methods from these two fields, the work is typically referred to as *feminist disability studies*, a term coined by Rosemarie Garland-Thomson, and/or *crip theory*, a term coined by Robert McRuer (Garland-Thomson 2005; McRuer 2006; see also Wendell 1996; Smith and Hutchinson 2004; K. Hall 2011; Kafer 2013). Feminist disability studies generally explores the relationship between gender and disability, particularly through lived experiences and cultural representation, as well as how feminist movements and scholarship have either perpetuated or resisted ableism within their work. Crip theory, on the other hand, takes its inspiration from queer theory and moves away from disability identity politics (as queer theory moves from gay and lesbian identity politics) to critique and understand the creation of the stigmatized category itself. Crip theory, therefore, pushes the edges of disability studies to include more engagement with chronic illnesses and diseases, including psychiatric ones, which were often marginalized or ignored in early disability studies that focused more on physical and sensory disabilities (Kafer 2013, 36, 18).

First and foremost, feminist disability studies and crip theory teach us that (dis)ability matters to the field of gender and sexuality studies because it is a social system that intersects with gender and sexuality. Any intersectional approach to research in gender and sexuality studies, therefore, ought to consider how disability impacts and shapes experiences of gender and sexuality. For instance, while women, especially women of color, have frequently combatted hypersexualization, disabled women are more likely to be desexualized, infantilized, and denied sexual autonomy. Any discussion of the hypersexualization of women, therefore, would benefit from an exploration of how disability impacts that experience for individual women or for women characters in media. To take another example, queer people have historically found community and sexual partners in public spaces like bars, bathhouses, and parks, but when such public spaces are inaccessible for people with disabilities due to stairs, lack of seating, or dim lighting, how do disabled queer people find community and sexual partners? Considering how disability impacts our experiences of gender and sexuality, such as how some marginalized community spaces remain inaccessible to disabled people in that community, is a direct, important way that disability can be incorporated into scholarship in the field.

Researching disability, however, is not exclusively about studying disabled people—though this is still central and important to disability studies. In an essay on the field, Julie Avril Minich writes that "the methodology of disability studies . . . involves scrutinizing not bodily or mental impairments but the social norms that define particular attributes as impairments, as well as the social conditions that concentrate stigmatized attributes in particular populations" (2016, para. 6). In other words, in addition to research on the lives, art, and media representations of disabled people, disability studies also explores how the concept of disability comes to exist and have meaning in a particular time period and culture as well as the material effects of the system on people's lived experiences.

Feminist disability studies and crip theory, along with critical race disability studies and feminist of color disability studies, understand (dis)ability as mutually constitutive with gender, sexuality, race, and class; that is, each of these social systems depends on (dis)ability to function and define its own categories. This concept is reflected in Talila A. Lewis's (2018) working definition of ableism: "A system that places value on people's bodies and minds based on societally constructed notions of normalcy, intelligence and excellence. These societally constructed notions of normalcy, intelligence and excellence are deeply rooted in eugenics, anti-Blackness and capitalism." Lewis's definition is based in the work of the contemporary disability justice movement and draws attention to the relationship between ableism and other oppressions—a key aspect for any work on disability in gender and sexuality studies.

There are numerous examples of the mutual constitution of these concepts historically. For instance, from Aristotle's belief that female bodyminds are simply mutilated versions of males' to Freud's concept of penis envy, women have frequently been understood in western theorizing as abnormal, lesser versions of men who are supposedly limited by biological processes like pregnancy and menstruation (Schalk 2017). Such notions of gender difference as bodymind inferiority are based in the (dis)ability system because they rely on the ableist belief that bodymind differences ought to be valued, ranked, and if possible, fixed or eliminated. To take another example, homosexuality was once labeled a psychiatric disability to be treated with electroshock and other therapies because same-sex desire was considered so far outside of the norms of sexuality that to express such desire meant one was not psychiatrically well and in need of treatment. In terms of race, claims of lesser intellectual abilities were once used to justify the enslavement and segregation of Black people. Across each of these examples, we can see how norms of gender, sexuality, and race depend on ableist rhetoric about inferiority and brokenness to further marginalize and oppress women, queer people, and Black people. As a result of this mutual constitution, historically marginalized groups have attempted to distance themselves from association with disability by claiming able-bodiedness and able-mindedness in their fights for justice; however, doing so has often left unchallenged the notion that disability is inherently negative and that disabled people do not deserve the very rights and liberties being fought for by these groups (Baynton 2001). Further, such distancing from disability among marginalized groups also leads to the further marginalization and erasure of those who occupy multiple oppressed identities such as disabled women, disabled queer people, disabled Black people, and so on.

It is important when discussing disability in gender and sexuality studies, however, not to collapse lived experiences with disability and impairment with the rhetorical or discursive uses of disability to further sexism, racism, homophobia, and transphobia. These are related and overlapping but not the same. For example, discussing how transgender identities have been categorized as psychiatric disabilities in the *Diagnostic and Statistical Manual* under different labels and whether trans identity should be categorized in this way is different from discussing the experiences of disabled trans people, like the work of Eli Clare, and different still from people who understand the experience of transitioning as disabling (Clare 2009; Baril 2015). Each of these issues is about gender and disability specific to trans people but in very different ways. Feminist disability studies and crip theory consider the role of gender and sexuality in conjunction with (dis)ability within lived experiences, representation, and larger theoretical and political questions.

Ultimately, disability studies ought to be understood as a lens for exploring the (dis)ability system as it shapes our material and social worlds, from medicine and psychiatry to the environment and technology, from educational systems and the prison industrial complex to mainstream media and architecture. Disability studies asks, Whose bodyminds are valued, and why? Whose bodyminds are more subject to violence and harm and thus more likely to become sick, ill, or disabled? Who has better access to medicine, care, and support for their bodymind needs? Here again the relationship between (dis)ability and other systems of oppression becomes further apparent: when one is marginalized by one system, including ableism, they are more likely to also be subjected to violence and harm, which can be further disabling to their bodyminds. Jasbir Puar (2017) refers to this slow disabling violence toward poor and racialized people as debility, a state of impairment that isn't fully recognized by the government as disability warranting accommodation and support, a state actually necessary to define the limits of legally, governmentally supported disability status. Debility is a particularly useful concept for thinking about disability transnationally in relation to war and global politics that shape who has access to certain kinds of medical and life-sustaining products and who is most subjected to violence and neglect around the world.

As these broad questions suggest, students and scholars of gender and sexuality ought to attend to and understand the (dis)ability system because it shapes and is shaped by systems of gender, sexuality, race, class, and nation. We cannot understand how gender and sexuality operate, let alone how to dismantle systemic sexism, homophobia, and transphobia, without understanding the rhetorical and material role of (dis)ability as a mutually constitutive system of oppression. The terms *disability* and *(dis)ability* intersect not only with other social categories like gender, sexuality, race, and class but also with other critical terms in the field of gender and sexuality studies such as *biopolitics*, *care*, *institutionalization*, *incarceration*, *colonialism*, *deviance*, *health*, *education*, *fat*, *reproduction*, and *violence*.

For example, scholars in disability studies explore the relationship between institutions such as asylums, psychiatric wards, and hospitals and institutions like jails and prisons to understand the relationship between these spaces as methods of forcible containment of marginalized populations via the removal of rights and freedoms (Ben-Moshe and Carey 2014). To take another example, fatness and disability, similar to the discussion of trans identity and disability above, contain multiple resonances conceptually; however, some are hesitant to talk about fatness as disability. Nonetheless, the connections are plentiful, and several scholars bring together fat studies and disability studies to understand how fat stigma and ableism overlap and intersect as well as how fat liberation and disability justice can and must work together (Schalk 2013; Mollow 2015, 2017). In both of these examples, we can see again how (dis)ability as a social system operates in ways that help us understand how multiple structural oppressions operate—by relying on subtle ableism.

Disability can and should operate as a critical lens for all work in gender and sexuality studies, as the gender and sexuality systems cannot be understood historically or contemporarily apart from the (dis)ability system and ableism. By better understanding the relationship of these terms through further critical analysis and scholarship, we move toward models of justice and social understanding that refuse to leave anyone behind, ones attentive to the realities of our bodyminds living under multiple systems of oppression.

23

Ecology

Kyle Powys Whyte

Conceptualizing ecology is contested terrain. Ecology may generically denote "the study of ecosystems," with etymological roots in terms for home and economy. Most broadly, an ecosystem could refer to any conception of how various beings, entities, elements, and flows relate to one another as members of a network that constitutes a shared environment. In practice, though, there are cases where some people mobilize definitions of ecology in ways that directly or indirectly wield power over others. And how someone understands ecology relates to their perspectives on the concepts of land, property, resilience, and sustainability. Such concepts intersect with gender, sexuality, and power in multiple ways, including but not limited to gendered inheritance laws, racial logics of ownership, and heteronormative assumptions about the natural world. Furthermore, climate change's impacts on how, when, and under what conditions people can work, reproduce, move, and migrate exposes the differential risks borne by women, trans, and gender nonconforming people.

What it means to "define ecosystems" and "study them" depends on where we are coming from based on our histories, embodiments, and life pathways. Reflecting on ecology in relation to my work as a Potawatomi scholar-organizer working for environmental justice, I seek to share about merely one journey tied to my own perspective. Indigenous and numerous other societies have had to develop adaptive approaches to being organized and responsive to constant changes in their lived environments for the sake of their well-being. They had to prepare for annual weather patterns, unexpected extreme weather events, and long-term climatic trends (Trosper 2002; Cochran and Geller 2002; Benton-Banai 2008; J. Armstrong 2007). One of the approaches in the North American context was to develop philosophies of how diverse beings, entities, elements, and flows are dependent on one another for their well-being (J. Armstrong 1998; Shilling and Nelson 2018; Grignon and Kimmerer 2017). Since they are interdependent, these diverse members of ecosystems were understood to have responsibilities to one another.

So the "study" of ecosystems involved learning about mutual responsibility for the sake of societal well-being, wherein "society" need not privilege particular conceptions of membership, such as humanity or personhood. The nature of responsibilities varies across cultures and languages and differs across the diversity of modes of expression belonging to plants, mountains, insects, humans, lakes, animals, forests, and fishes, among others. Some of the oldest articulations of ecosystems maintain that interdependence requires humility and attentive listening, a motivation to exercise caretaking, and a commitment to keeping track of constantly changing environmental conditions (Kawagley 2006; Trosper 1995; Lickers 1997).

The diverse traditions of ecosystems describe various ways to understand the commitments and the responsibilities that members have. In some traditions, different animals are considered to tell their own stories, have bodies of knowledge unto themselves, and make critical choices about how to best behave for the sake of their well-being in relation to others (Arquette 2000; LaPier 2017; Kimmerer 2013). Sometimes different agents are considered to have overlapping commitments and responsibilities. An example is certain Anishinaabe clan systems where human and animal communities are interwoven with one another toward joint action as caretakers of shared lands and waters (Stark 2012; Bohaker 2006).

A number of Indigenous traditions of ecosystems do not convey the separation or distinction of "human" or "person" in some of the ways familiar to users of various dominant English-language conventions. They instead have more open and inclusive concepts of differences across members (Atleo 2002; L. Simpson 2011). In some traditions, hierarchical forms of gendered leadership, such as patriarchy, are widely understood to generate violence that erodes interdependence and mutual responsibility. They instead have gender systems that are open, fluid, and respectful of responsibilities as they are freely taken up by people across diverse genders (Child 2012; Buffalohead 1983; Sinclair 2016; Barker 2017; Morgensen 2011; Sy 2018). Indigenous peoples have sought to recover historic traditions of ecology where gender and sexuality were not organized or interpreted patriarchally. Indigenous environmentalism but also diverse fields like ecofeminism have drawn on recovery work as part of how they ground and frame the possibilities for just and inclusive aspirations toward ecological sustainability and environmental stewardship. For example, in the early 1800s, Ozawwendib was a gender nonconforming Two Spirit person who was an Anishinaabe leader known for their ecological knowledge and environmental stewardship (Sinclair 2016).

Colonialism, capitalism, patriarchy, ableism, and industrialization work to undermine Indigenous responsibilities within shared environments (Rifkin 2011; Maracle 2015; Battiste 2000; Moreton-Robinson 2015). Indigenous peoples currently are engaged in liberatory projects that emphasize many of the aforementioned aspects of ecology tied to responsibility, whether they invoke the term *ecology* or use adjacent terms (Carroll 2014; McGregor 2005; Goeman 2009; Driskill et al. 2011;

Bang et al. 2014). Some scholars are invoking the concept of kinship as a way of describing a relationality with responsibility-based features such as mutual care, reciprocity, and trust (TallBear 2019; Innes 2013; Todd 2017).

As I understand ecology as the study of responsibility across networks of members in shared environments, coalitional dialogue across many communities and people is critical, especially when diverse groups draw from their own perspectives, histories, and traditions. Queer, Two Spirit, and feminist organizing efforts have created generative spaces for the intersections of liberatory gender norms, political action, health care, and environmental protection (Driskill et al. 2011; Gaard 1997). Some diasporic peoples such as African Americans are creating land-based practices that reflect their historic and more recent histories of working toward self-determination in the face of anti-Black racism. Black traditions of agrarianism, environmental ethics, and recreation are seeking to establish sustainable food sovereignty; equal access to clean, safe, and healthy environments; and enjoyment of responsible connections to nonhumans (White 2011; Finney 2014; Bullard 1990). Scholars have invoked Black intellectual traditions, including queer and feminist philosophy, and artistic and literary production to challenge white supremacist conceptions of "the human" (Agard-Jones 2012; Z. Jackson 2020; Wynter 2003).

For me, the field most commonly known as "ecology" today is markedly different from the longer aforementioned traditions. It was generated in the nineteenth and twentieth centuries in imperialistic, settler colonial, patriarchal, and anti-Black contexts and often in association with military actions (especially bombing) and other high-impact industrial activities of the United States and other nations. Certainly, some forms of ecology in the early twentieth century were concerned with environmental protection and human impacts on the environment even when associated with the military. Yet subsequent iterations of ecology, as they became institutionalized, tended to exclude Indigenous, Black, and other people of color from the study of ecological harm and impact (Bocking 1997; DeLoughrey 2013; Kwa 1989). While societies such as the Ecological Society of America have attempted to repair the exclusion of diverse peoples—through regular meetings of a subgroup on traditional ecological knowledge (Ford and Martinez 2000)—certain forms of ecological restoration continue to displace Indigenous peoples and people of color as residents and exclude them as re-creators (Igoe 2004; Finney 2014). So there is still much more work that must happen for generative and global coalitions to be fostered on ecology.

24

Education

Savannah Shange

How did you learn to be careful with fire? Who taught you the best way to console a friend after a breakup or how to manage an encounter with the police? How do you know which pronouns to use for another person or for yourself? Your answers to these questions give a clue to the scale of the educational process, which begins at birth and continues throughout the life course. Learning happens every time you experiment with different smoothie ingredients or get into a debate over gender-reveal parties on Twitter. From the consciousness-raising circles of the 1970s women's liberation movement to online communities to street gangs, teaching and learning are circular social processes that shape how we see the world and ourselves. "Education," in this sense, is the cumulative total of these processes as they unfold in real time. Schooling, conversely, is the formalization of these processes in a physically and logistically separate sphere for teaching and learning. Compulsory schooling is a relatively new phenomenon worldwide and is inextricably tied to both old colonial power structures and newer neoliberal debt paradigms. For instance, across the Global South, structural adjustment programs administered by international financial institutions like the World Bank and International Monetary Fund weaken the state and threaten universal access to primary schooling. At the same time, feminist NGOs have been mobilizing transnationally for girls' education as part of an expansive vision of social transformation that exceeds the narrow measures of gender parity codified during the UN Decade for Women (1975–85). The relationship between schooling, sexuality, and gender is deeply embedded in particular national contexts, and the rest of this entry will focus on K-12 public schools in the United States as but one site of these dynamics. The contours of contemporary US schools, like so much of US social life, emerge from chattel slavery.

Prior to emancipation, it was a crime in most states to teach enslaved Black people how to read, and those who pursued literacy risked their life to do so. During Reconstruction, freedmen's schools served both men and women and provided the foundation for universal public education, marking a massive expansion of access to literacy and social advancement (Du Bois 1935). Despite these lofty origins as tools of social mobility, schools also serve to reproduce and reinforce existing hierarchies of race, gender, and class. Carter G. Woodson (1933) indicted the schools that served Black students for offering only a "miseducation" through a shallow Eurocentric curriculum that taught pupils to be deferent and obedient in the face of systemic racism. While Indigenous and later Latinx students were historically barred from enrolling in most schools serving white children, even after legal integration, the education provided to brown communities was "subtractive schooling" (Valenzuela 1999) that sought to disconnect them from their rich linguistic, cultural, and political heritages. Damien Sojoyner (2016) has dubbed the collusion between state policy, public schooling, and carceral logics an "educational enclosure" that perpetuates hierarchies of race, class, and gender.

As an "educational enclosure," schools are largely a state project that leverages public resources to serve the needs of capital. By displacing the gendered reproductive care labor of child-rearing that had previously belonged in the private sphere, compulsory schooling ensures that all parents and caregivers are available to the market as wage laborers. However, access to the "private sphere" is a privilege that was rarely available to Black and brown women who were employed for generations as domestic workers in the homes of white middle- and upper-class families, leaving the rearing of their own children to the second shift. Once enrolled, schools train the next generation of workers by transferring concrete skills and by acculturating them to the pace, shape, and discourse of capitalist institutions. Finally, schools are workplaces that are central to understanding the relationship between gender, labor, and the state.

Teaching was historically one of the few professions available to women with formal education, and in particular, elementary school teaching was viewed as "women's work." The proportion of women teaching public school increased steadily in recent decades, with 77 percent of public school teachers identifying as women in 2016 (de Brey 2017). Alongside nursing, teaching is a stronghold of unionization among women, and generations of working-class women and women of color have used jobs in K-12 education as footholds into the middle class. Neoliberalism has started to erode the stability of the public sector, siphoning off funding and community control through charter schools, state take-overs, and privatization. While these shifts have a disproportionate impact on women workers in schools, neoliberalization has also created the conditions for a social justice activism rooted in schools and led by the students and teachers that make them work. From 2018's historic nine-day wildcat strike by public school teachers in West Virginia that won a 5 percent pay increase for all the state's public employees to the fifteen-day teachers' strike in Chicago that sought rent control and affordable housing for city residents as part of contract negotiations, the beginning of the twenty-first century witnessed a reclamation of schools as sites of political struggle. Students have organized mass walk-outs and protests against budget cuts, the climate crisis, police violence, and gun violence at the hands of both the cops and their peers.

Rather than an exceptional event that can be summed up on a protest sign or remediated by a policy change, violence is the structural condition of American life. "America" is itself capacitated by ongoing settler colonialism in the wake of chattel slavery. School settings reflect the larger patterns of violence in the United States, from spectacular events like mass shootings to the mundane everyday collusion between school officials and the police departments and immigration agents that seek to cage children. Research on the "school to prison pipeline" reveals the deeply racialized and gendered nature of punishment in schools, where Black and Latinx boys are far more likely to be arrested at school and to be incarcerated as youths (Rios 2011). Black girls, on the other hand, are specifically subject to "adultification" that leads to harsh censure for "disrespect" or "defiance," even though those are developmentally appropriate behaviors for adolescents (M. Morris 2019). Further, while LGBTQ people of all races receive harsher disciplinary sanctions than their cis-het peers, gender nonconforming Black girls are the hardest hit, receiving triple the harsh disciplinary measures of their peers (Mitchum and Moodie-Mills 2014). The structural vulnerabilities of masculine-presenting Black girls (who might be recognized in communities as "studs" or "butches") flummoxes recent efforts to mobilize *femme* as an umbrella term for those targeted by gender violence.

Within many schools, bureaucratic and disciplinary policies target girls and transgender and gender-defiant youth with surveillance, control, and punishment. Dress codes for students reinforce patriarchal, conservative gender norms and prohibit spaghetti straps, crop tops, short skirts, and other "revealing" clothing as either inappropriate or distracting for male students (in the framework of these rules, young women exist primarily as vehicles for male desire and are not perceptible as agents of queer desire). Some schools, particularly parochial and independent institutions, mandate that girl students wear skirts and boys wear pants regardless of their gender expression. Further, Black girls and fat girls are often targeted for violations of dress code because their bodies are viewed as excessive compared to their thinner, paler peers (M. Morris 2019). Beyond constricting self-expression in general, school dress codes serve two purposes: upholding one narrow version of modest, bourgeois femininity and enforcing a polarized gender binary by targeting students assigned male at birth for wearing any clothing associated with femininity simply because of the body they are in. The fatal politics of school dress codes are on display in the response to the murder of Latisha King, a gender-defiant student of color. Latisha wore high heels and lipstick to school, and the principal of her high school defended her right to wear anything she chose within the school dress code. Latisha was shot in the back of the head by a classmate, and at trial, he blamed the school for not enforcing a binary dress code and thus creating the conditions that led to Latisha's death. Rather than transform the culture of patriarchal respectability that constrains all of us, responses like this literally weaponize gender norms against young people who dare to defy them.

Similarly, transantagonistic policies that directly target gender nonconforming students also focus on surveilling and punishing individual young people rather than on changing institutional cultures to engender safety and affirmation for all students. Bathroom and locker-room policies have been some of the most contested institutional norms and generally are justified by a false narrative that trans and gender nonconforming students pose a risk to cisgender students and in particular that trans girls' presence in a sex-segregated space amounts to a social violation that will traumatize cis girls. Locker-room policies create contradictory restrictions on participation in intramural sports, which offer crucial opportunities for social, personal, and physical development in addition to coveted access to scholarships for higher education. Trans students are alternately forced with a choice of playing on teams with their assigned gender or opting out of sports entirely. When provided the opportunity to play on sex-segregated teams, gender nonconforming student athletes are critiqued for having an unfair advantage due to assumed differences in size, strength, and physiognomy. For trans and gender-defiant students at all levels of schooling, the right to be addressed by the correct name and pronouns is imperiled by hostile instructors and peers as well as inflexible bureaucratic systems that hamper even allies who seek to use the correct terms for students. The lived experience of trans and gender nonconforming students is ignored by this suite of policies that seek to legislate them out of existence one rule at a time.

While the discriminatory policies outlined above warrant community outcry and mobilization, it is crucial to recognize that they are often created in response to communities mobilizing for justice and safety. For instance, North Carolina was thrown into the national spotlight as the first state to prohibit trans students from using gender-appropriate bathrooms during the course of the school day. HB2, or the "bathroom bill," was proposed only after the city of Charlotte passed its own citywide antidiscrimination laws protecting the rights of trans and queer city residents. Across the US South, which is stereotyped as more homophobic and conservative than coastal urban areas, there is also a queer and trans activist legacy that produced material wins from accessible bathrooms to the dozens of queer, trans, and gender-defiant prom and homecoming royalty who have been chosen by their peers, including Charlotte's own Blake Brockington, the first openly trans homecoming king in North Carolina.

Brockington was a musician and activist as a teen, raising money to help build schools in Sudan and protesting police killings of unarmed Black people. He went to a high school that was relatively supportive of his transition and even starred in a short film about his election as homecoming royalty. Brockington was a poster child for the recognition sought by decades of mainstream LGBT politics, but visibility didn't protect Blake Brockington from the epidemic of trans self-harm—he took his own life at the age of eighteen. Brockington's death by suicide points to the conflation of visibility and vulnerability for gender-transgressive young people and the ways that Black trans youth in particular live without the protections associated with childhood or even humanity. As C. Riley Snorton reminds us, a narrow "focus on transgender people's abilities to use the bathroom of their choice obscures a more urgent conversation about what modes of dispossession are possible under the ruse of state inclusion" (2017, ix). Audre Lorde is ritually cited by feminist and queer activists for her revelation that "your silence will not protect you" ([1984] 2007d, 41). In the early twenty-first century, it's clear that neither will our visibility.

Policy is an opening for struggle, not an end to it. Gender abolition, or the desire to eliminate gender as a salient social category, produces at times intense tension with community-based traditions and structures of gendered protection, thrival, and cultural development. By engaging schools as battlegrounds in the long fight against miseducation, we can better understand the broad range of political responses that have been used to fight gender inequity, transantagonism, and heterosexism.

25

The Erotic

Sharon Patricia Holland

In a brief moment during my unattached life, I found myself journeying with a small group of lesbians in the Triangle (a region in North Carolina) who gathered to do "lesbian" things together and then, after, share a meal. On that particular prespring day, we found ourselves in Chapel Hill's Internationalist Bookstore—the convergence point for all things radical. The reading that day was billed as a showcase of personal stories and performance pieces from LGBTQ community members focusing on the scope and range of the erotic in their lives. I think that people in my group thought it was going to be sexy. I don't think they paid much attention to the moniker "S/M" that was also in the publicity for the reading. For the next hour and a half, I watched the absolutely stunned faces of the women in my group of lesbians—not the kind of dykes (what we called ourselves when we were reclaiming that language) I knew in my community of lesbians in Ann Arbor, Michigan, really—as the readers talked about their girlhoods, their sexual fantasies, and yes, their sexual proclivities, including being hit in the face and/or bitten while having sex with a partner. Obviously, none of these women had ever spent any time with erotica author Susie Bright and/or traveled much to the Bay Area, where communities embracing such consensual sexual practices are common.

This experience in the bookstore conjures a host of understandings and misunderstandings about what the erotic entails, how people experience "it," and most importantly, what a central place it has in queer life. After all, when gender and sexuality studies scholars think of sexuality, we often go to "queer." What do I mean by this? Think of the important *Lawrence v. Texas* (539 U.S. 558 (2003)) US Supreme Court decision that struck down antisodomy statutes across the country; while some queers do engage in anal sex, I would venture that the number of "homosexuals" who do so probably compares with the number of "heterosexuals" who do so as well, yet solving the problem of sodomy was laid squarely at queer feet as a practice almost exclusive to a certain kind of coupling. Enough said.

In tune with the strain of gender and sexuality studies that encourages queer misreadings and in fact honors the sense that we got here because we didn't get all the cues right (like how to become a heterosexual and really mean it), I want to follow the trajectory of the erotic in the early queer lexicon. Doing so charts how sexuality matters in queer discourse and how what sexuality is in feminist studies in particular can be traced through the rough terrain of opinion it has traveled through.

Much of what we know, say, and do in queer studies—at least when it comes to the "erotic"—stems from Audre Lorde's groundbreaking paper "Uses of the Erotic: The Erotic as Power," delivered at the Fourth Berkshire Conference on the History of Women at Mount Holyoke College on August 25, 1978. The essay was later included in the collection of essays *Sister Outsider* (Lorde [1984] 2007e). Lorde's chief preoccupation in the paper was to secure our understanding of the power of the erotic and to unshackle male-identified (yep, that too!) understandings of women's power to self-determine their own sexual lives. Lorde was also in the crosshairs of a debate about pornography within feminism. When she set the erotic against the pornographic in that work, and in later interviews, she came fully in touch with the growing radical sexual revolution in feminist and

what would become queer studies. This movement cut in so many directions: it produced friction (no pun intended) between male-identified allies in the gay community who thought of sex as merely recreational and autonomous and their sometimes separatist lesbian counterparts. It brought forth the insidious work of "respectability politics" in our sexual cultures, and in feminism, it generated some very strange bedfellows, including the likes of twentieth-century robber baron Charles Keaton and feminists like Andrea Dworkin and Catharine MacKinnon. In short, the erotic in the late 1970s and very early 1980s was a hot mess.

By 1982, feminists had had enough of all the infighting and the drama around who we fucked and how. What came out of that debate is the field of sexuality (and later queer) studies during another important conference at Barnard College in 1982 that produced the volume *Pleasure and Danger: Exploring Female Sexuality*, edited by Carole S. Vance (1984), who was then an anthropologist and epidemiologist at Columbia University and codirector of the Institute for the Study of Sex and History in New York. The names of its contributors serve as a who's who of radical feminist thought on sexuality: Dorothy Allison, Alice Echols, Amber Hollibaugh, Cherríe Moraga, Joan Nestle, Esther Newton, Gayle Rubin, Kaja Silverman, and Hortense J. Spillers, just to name a few.

Through the work of this stunning array of scholars committed to feminist inquiry, the erotic found its home in a diversity of opinion—as it should be in queer feminist scholarship. With the publication of *Pleasure and Danger*, scholar/activists were encouraged to look at the historical predicaments of the erotic—to consider the sequestering of marginalized groups based on their erotic choices (Rubin). They were challenged to think about the difference that region makes when considering its pleasures (Allison). Some were encouraged to think about their erotic selves as women who could "no longer live outside power in sex" (Hollibaugh 1984, 411). Even more were interested in materialist feminist analyses of the sexual lives of others (Newton and Nestle). And still, some began to chronicle the extent to which theories of our racial selves and national imaginaries subtended our erotic lives altogether.

New work in the field by Lyndon Gill (2018) *Erotic Islands: Art and Activism in the Queer Caribbean* or Jafari Allen (2012) *Black Queer Diaspora* ought to remind us that the terrain of the erotic is under constant revision and reimagining. This work pulls us away from the pleasure/pain binary into experiences that encompass embodiments that are not "human"—I am thinking about Mel Chen's (2012) work in *Animacies* in particular. In short, how the erotic embraces us is just as important as a *practice* as is our critique of its power.

26

Experience
Mimi Thi Nguyen

The feminist movement maxim "The personal is political" underscores the connections between personal experiences and larger sociopolitical structures, but what this means in terms of not just what but *how* we know what we know is less clear. The formula has been understood to mean that our experiences are the wellspring of our most authentic politics, our most authentic truths, but what exactly mediates the movement between personal and structural?

One of the tasks of feminist theories has been to challenge conventional epistemologies—ways of knowing, accumulating, and institutionalizing knowledge—in order to make more obvious that these are not the *only* ways of knowing and that these are often ideological in themselves. Or as Catherine Belsey asks, "To what extent is it possible to perceive the world independently of the conventional ways in which it is represented? To what extent is experience contained by language, society, history?" (1980, 13). The idea that experience comes from authentic knowledge is distilled from multiple liberal humanist traditions that assume a rational actor who can evaluate his interests in relation to others and then arrive at proper and proportionate action. But as many observers note, the problems with this set of premises are multiple. Liberal humanism recognizes some forms of reason and not others (for instance, that reason is the province of certain populations, of which others are insensible or incapable), it assumes that knowledge is a clear expression of an unmediated inner truth, and it assumes that the conditions for acting upon what "counts" as reason are always available to all persons.

Nonetheless, the language of experience, of seeing (or sensing) as believing, undergirds much western thought. Experience is not a straight path to an ethical or political sensibility, however; thus social movements posit a process through which experience leads to the articulation of a *shared social consciousness*. This understanding is sometimes referred to as *standpoint epistemology*: the notion that a particular social location can yield a unique set of experiences and thus knowledges, related to the earlier Marxist notion that the oppressed classes themselves hold their own comprehensive truths about the world. Standpoint epistemologies held that an externally imposed obstacle—whether understood in liberal humanism as superstition, in Marxist humanism as the alienation of the proletariat from his own labor, or in the feminist theories of Simone de Beauvoir and Nancy Hartsock as a "slave mentality" or the imposition of a "perverse" masculine order—must be overcome to achieve full or true consciousness (Beauvoir [1949] 1989; Hartsock [1983] 2004). Standpoint epistemologies have thus constituted a central ideological formation for modern political and social theory, including those with radical or revolutionary commitments; standpoint insists that we already know what we need to know. However, the woman of color feminisms of the 1970s, 1980s, and 1990s in particular challenged standpoint epistemologies and their limits for how we understand both political education and affiliation. These theorists pointed out that many revolutionary theories and practices still assumed a self-sufficient, self-knowing individual, replicating the subject of western Enlightenment philosophies. Furthermore, they observed that no standpoint can withstand its contradictions; standpoint theories generally flatten out the complicated ways we become *kinds* of people, *kinds* of

subjects. For instance, putting the category of "woman" in the center of feminist theory negated the work of Black, Indigenous, and non-Black women of color in other liberation movements. As Norma Alarcón writes, "The inclusion of other analytic categories [in a feminist theory based solely on gender] such as race and class becomes impossible for a subject whose consciousness refuses to acknowledge that 'one becomes a woman' in ways that are much more complex than in a simple opposition to men. In cultures in which 'asymmetric race and class relations are a central organizing principle of society,' *one may also 'become a woman' in opposition to other women*" (1994, 360; my emphasis).

One of woman of color feminisms' key insights, then, is that violence may come from men, but it also comes from other women. Some of these violences include regarding race and class as secondary features in social organization or philosophical ontologies and treating the labor of women of color to interpret their experiences as *things* without theorizing their conditions or acknowledging other forms of language—such as Audre Lorde's poems—as theory too (Lorde [1984] 2007c). Woman of color feminisms have repeatedly observed this conundrum. As early as the 1980s, bell hooks describes the racialized division of labor in women's studies classrooms between women of color as objects of knowledge—as persons to learn *about*—against white women as agents of knowledge, as persons to learn *from*. In this division, women of color are confined to experience, while white women make theory.

Another strain of feminist theories challenging the nature of experience follows from semiotics and poststructuralism. Thus Joan Scott observes, "The evidence of experience then becomes evidence for the fact of difference, rather than a way of exploring how difference is established, how it operates, how and in what ways it constitutes subjects who see and act in the world" (1992,

EXPERIENCE MIMI THI NGUYEN

25). Scott argues that to invoke experience as evidence masks the "necessarily discursive nature of these experiences" (31). She does not reject experience, however, but asks us to radically *historicize* it. Subjects do not simply acquire experiences that as *possessions* can sediment a subjectivity, an interiority, that gives rise to already-known modes of critique or politics; experience is not a *thing* to be observed that carries inherent value. It is instead a narration that secures the grounds for meaning making.

The point here is to take note of the *effects* of the claim to experience, to be attentive to the *effects* of our own assent to its transparency. Experience as *evidence* can bring some together, but experience as *truth* can exclude others. Where the ontological "truth" of experience rests on assumptions about how categories of being (such as "woman") should function and therefore generates conjectures (and sometimes condemnations) about how deviations from "true" being are produced, it cannot or will not account for the ways that such measures are made in the first place—and it needs to do so. Observe the trans exclusionary argument that the experience of having certain genitalia binds together a collectivity as "women," presuming that a specific social consciousness follows from that experience, though that experience is not the same even for all persons with those parts. Or consider that the experience of assault does not guarantee a politics to follow: one survivor might support the expansion of policing, while another calls for its abolition. The epistemological certainty of experience thus presents a bind. Recourse to the experience of everyday harm or extraordinary violation has fueled some of the most dynamic social movements of the last century. But experience can also be limiting where there is an uncritical dimension to its recourse. ("Lived experience" continues to hold sway as a conversation killer, invoked to bring an end to a debate.) Making experience "visible" might preclude an analysis of the way ideologies actually work to organize categories and produce differences and elide the premises of what these categories and differences mean, how they operate, and even how we feel about them.

What does it mean to say that experience is a product of interpretation, mediated by language and ideology? It means that we have to consider that our politics come into being not through something we *have*—lived experiences as resolute properties of the self—but through something we *do* or come to *want*, through those contacts, attachments, and investments that take form in encounters with power and knowledge. It means putting less faith in experience as a transcendental placeholder for the production of truth or politics and exerting more pressure on the conditions that produce its significance. Does this make the evidence of experience any less valid or powerful as a source for theorizing and for making change? Not at all. When we witness our own experiences, we are not drawing on some core, intrinsic sense of self, but we are speaking to and about ideology, history, reciprocity, and power. Because we cannot assume a common experience will yield a shared politics, Bernice Johnson Reagon (1983) argues that feminism is not a respite from the world but "a coalition," with all the risk this entails. Similarly, Cathy Cohen calls for a process of movement building "rooted not in our shared history or identity, but in our shared marginal relationship to dominant power that normalizes, legitimizes, and privileges" (1997, 458). Experience is not a fixed point from which one interacts in the world, then, but an ongoing relation with which we might destabilize all our epistemological certainties and through which another world is possible.

27

Fat

Virgie Tovar

Fat is largely understood and used in the United States as a slur. It's usually used to hurt or judge someone or to speak badly or pityingly of them. Few people use the word with love, affection, or respect. People go to extraordinary lengths to stay as far away from this word as possible: fasting, refusing to eat delicious things like ice cream or maple donuts filled with espresso Bavarian cream, living with body shame and hatred, or pushing their bodies to exercise past the point of enjoyment. In fact, it's estimated that in the United States, forty-five million people go on a diet every year. That's a little more than one out of every ten people. Many—maybe even most—people who diet do so primarily because they are afraid of being considered fat.

Just as there are people who put a lot of time, resources, and energy into attempting to avoid being associated with this word, there are people who embrace it. They may identify as fat activists or be described as fat positive. They may not label themselves at all, but their use of the word disrupts a strong cultural taboo against the word *fat*.

It is important to contextualize the fear of fat as something that is not universal. In the West, we have been taught to fear the word *fat*. We were not born associating negative thoughts or feelings with this word. These negative thoughts and feelings lead to the formation of an ideology of bigotry known as fatphobia. Bigotry leads to discrimination. Fat people face hiring discrimination as well as romantic and medical discrimination. For instance, fat people earn less than their thin counterparts, and it is legal to fire or refuse to hire someone because of their body size in every state except Michigan and Washington.

Fatphobia has racial origins in anti-Blackness (Strings 2019). It intersects with other forms of oppression—for instance, sexism due to the disproportionate ways that it negatively impacts the body image of women and feminine people and ableism due to the ways that structures were not built to accommodate fat bodies, that fatness is sometimes associated with physical disability, and that it was classified as a disease by the American Medical Association in 2013. Fatphobia is also inherent in the colonial origins of white supremacy due to the fact that beauty ideals and health standards are based on the white body and that thinness is interpreted as evidence of a relationship to food that is governed by restraint, a value that emerged as part of the colonialist rationalization of violence against racialized people who were seen as incapable of restraint. Different cultures have different attitudes toward the word *fat* and toward fat people. For instance, there are cultures in the world where fat is desirable. In parts of Mauritania and Niger, for example, fat women are considered the most marriageable (Haworth 2016; Meneley and Kulick 2005). In those cultures, fat bodies are considered beautiful and pleasing. Further, scholars have noted that even within the United States, there are different feelings about fat, especially among communities of color where beauty standards may entirely diverge from or hybridize with the prevailing white (and thin) standard. And yet even within those potential subsets, there are a variety of ways that attitudes can still vary and cluster, with some folks seeing fat as a sign of higher class status and others a sign of equal status, for instance.

The word *fat* has a political history. Many fat studies scholars and fat activists situate the beginning of fat activism as the year 1969, the year the National

Association to Advance Fat Acceptance (NAAFA) was founded. A year later, a chapter of NAAFA felt dissatisfied with the organization's focus on acceptance and went rogue, ultimately becoming a group called the Fat Underground (FU). FU was interested in talking about fat discrimination at the doctor, at work, and in their communities as well as understanding fat within a framework that included gender, trauma, desire, and sexuality. This immediately took fat from a single-issue politic to an intersectional politic and facilitated a significant change in approach and ideology. Borrowing from Black feminism, the women's liberation movement, and other liberatory movement ideologies, FU is where the discussion around fat moved from one about acceptance or assimilation (seeking rights and privileges within an established system that had historically marginalized fat people and other minority groups) to one about liberation or anti-assimilation (seeking radical change that fundamentally troubles the system that had historically marginalized fat people and other minority groups).

The conversation that emerged within and around FU was also connected to both the movement for mainstream feminism that emerged in the 1960s and the cultural expressions of radical and lesbian feminism that emerged in the 1970s. Though we don't know how many fat activists at that time identified as queer/gay/lesbian, much of the literature that attempted to reenvision the word and representation around fat (like *Fat Girl: A Zine for Fat Dykes and the Women Who Want Them*) was published by and for lesbians.

The countercultural deployment of the word *fat* thus emerged within one of the most radical sectors of distinct feminisms that were being practiced from the 1970s through the early 2000s. This is important because prevailing conversations happening within white liberal feminism did not trouble or seriously question issues like bigotry against fat women or homophobia. Further, the conversations that lesbian fat activists were having happened without the looming specter of straight cis men, who were (and remain) some of the greatest beneficiaries of misogyny and heteronormativity and who were (and remain) the husbands and partners of many of the leaders and constituents of mainstream feminism. Unencumbered (or, at least, less encumbered) by a commitment to heteronormativity, lesbian fat activists had more latitude than their straight counterparts to imagine possibilities for connection, strategize for justice, break (more) social rules, and center pleasure and intimacy. This version of fat activism is the closest antecedent to the body positivity movement, a growing online movement that "promotes self-love and acceptance of bodies of any shape, size, or appearance" (Cwynar-Horta 2016). Though fat activism has been eclipsed by body positivity, the conversation around the word *fat* is still tied to the queer politics that emerged following the height of lesbian feminism.

For people interested in dismantling fatphobia, using the word *fat* is a strategy that serves multiple purposes for fat people. First, it normalizes and decharges the word from its negative associations, which repositions it as something that can become part of a healing process. Second, it turns the word *fat* into a term of endearment used for in-group conversations (even today, it's not uncommon to hear fat activists refer to each other as "fatties" or "fat babes" or just "fats"). Third, it is an act of reclamation with roots in the Black Power movement and the queer movement through AIDS activism / Queer Nation. For example, "Black is beautiful" emerged in the 1960s against the backdrop of racist assertions that only white people could be considered beautiful. "We're here, we're queer and we'd like to say hello" emerged in the 1990s against the backdrop of homophobia and violence against queer people.

Reclaiming a word that is meant to injure marginalized people can be part of a strategy known as resignification (see J. Butler [1990] 1999), when someone exerts power over a situation. In this case, a fat person flips the script by using the word *fat*, and this immediately creates a change in what's expected, which means the fat person has taken the advantage rather than ceding it.

In this cultural moment in the West, a fat person is considered a failed thin person. In actuality, however, fat is its own autonomous, legitimate, and stand-alone identity. When we use the word *fat*, it's important to contextualize it as a word that has the meaning it does because of where we come from, who we are, and whether we subscribe to the bigoted and discriminatory meanings it holds in the United States now or we seek to lovingly disrupt and creatively reimagine what this word can become.

28

Femme

Ashley Coleman Taylor

Femme (alternatively spelled "fem") is a queer resistive embodied identity liberated from the limits of normative gender (Story 2016). Femme approaches femininity, encompasses it, and then pushes against its boundaries—especially those informed by Eurocentric ideals of "woman." Femme demands repositioning gender as a fluid and creative process of being. When language seeks to confine or define our sexualities and genders, femme marks itself as an ineffable performative gender. In what follows, I trace the historical usage of the term *femme* in US LGBT culture, centering a femme framework that is "bent, unfixed, unhinged, and finally unhyphenated" (Rose 2002, 12). I explore femme across three movements in an effort to describe its "unruliness that struts across time and place" (S. Lewis 2012, 106): the homophile movement of the 1940s to the 1950s, the gay liberation movement of the 1960s to the 1970s, and queer organizing of the 1980s and 1990s. I ask the reader to understand not only the shifting uses of a gendered term but also how reading the past through the language of the present can provide a deep understanding of human experience across time (Snorton 2017; Stryker 2008). Alternatively, the term *movement* asks us to consider the ways that gender is embodied—its rhythms appear in gesture, form, aesthetic, and lived experience. Taken together, femme is movement work characterized by possibility.

Contemporary use of the term *femme* emerged in queer subcultures through midcentury lesbian working-class communities. In the pre-Stonewall era of the homophile movement, "femme" described a feminine lesbian with a sexual and romantic proclivity for butches. The butch/femme dyad marked the core of midcentury lesbian "community, culture, and consciousness" (Kennedy and Davis 2014), offering an outward representation of "homosexual" life and sexual desire at a time when many lived in secrecy to evade abuse, attacks, and ridicule (Nestle 1997). According to Audre Lorde (2011), in the dyke-chic scene fashion of the fifties, clothing choices were unspoken symbols of sexual desire, romantic attraction, and self-stylized gender. This is not to simplify the butch/femme dyad as role-playing, however. As Black femme elder and author Jewelle Gomez explains, femme is "not a role but an identity, as in something embedded inside that manifests externally in many different ways" pointing to a nuanced, internally recognized ontology (quoted in Pulley 2013).

A decade later, trans women Marsha P. Johnson and Sylvia Rivera (who would later form the Street Transvestite Action Revolutionaries) challenged gay and lesbian homophile politics of respectability and ignited the Stonewall rebellion. Although they may not have used the term at the time to describe themselves, the movement work of these femmes sparked what we now know as the antecessor of the contemporary fight for LGBT rights—the gay liberation movement. However, the post-Stonewall lesbian feminism of the seventies critiqued the femme/butch dyad as an antiquated attempt to mirror heterosexual relationships and championed "freedom from cosmetics and high heels" (Gomez 1998, 105). Even as the more masculine-leaning "androgyny" became a norm of cultural feminism, writers like Gomez and Joan Nestle celebrated the femme aesthetic of the era as a form of self-expression and erotic independence (Gomez 1998; Nestle 1992). Paradoxically, by narrowly defining "woman" by anatomy, the lesbian feminism movement reified the very essentialized gender system it critiqued (Smyth and Roof 1998).

After Crystal LaBeija founded the House of LaBeija in the late 1970s, the explosion of the ballroom scene among Black and brown queer and trans subcultures expanded the use of the term *femme* beyond its exclusively lesbian history. Uncoupled from the cis-centered origins, femme-as-performance in the 1980s and 1990s shaped the imaginings and artistry of ballroom culture with categories like "femme queen" represented by trans women. As gendered work, the ritualized planning, design, and implementation of balls by femme "house mothers" also fostered kinship, support networks, and safe spaces for queer and trans "children" otherwise outcasted and ostracized in larger social spheres (Tinsley 2018).

The rise of queer politics and radical leftist resistance of normative gender and sexuality demanded more nuanced discussions of race, class, ethnicity, and other categories of being. Poststructuralist shifts in academic queer theory during this era, largely informed by queer movement work in the shadows of the HIV/AIDS crisis by organizations like ACT UP and Queer Nation, demanded rethinking the essentializing binaries of "man" and "woman," "gay," and "lesbian" (Jagose 1996). Although deconstructing these binaries was not a new practice, critical engagement with gender and sexuality inside and outside the academy required interrogation of the "collapsed and naturalized coupling of femme-ness and femaleness" (Snorton 2017, 174).

Today, femme continues to be further separated from "woman," and gender identities beyond an existence rooted in biologized essentialist discourse keep expanding. *Femme* is not synonymous with *woman*, and *woman* is not synonymous with *femme*. All femmes are not women, and all women are not femmes. These terms must not be conflated. Although patriarchy and embedded power often undervalue femme existence, not all femme lived experiences are parallel, nor do they have the same access to safety. Femme aversion can inform desire in gay men's circles where the term *fem* is used pejoratively to insult feminine men, and femme cis women often experience invisibility in lesbian circles. Trans women and trans femmes of color specifically often end up murdered, missing, or subject to other forms of violence as a result of their gender identities.

Grounding our conversation in femme embodiment can lead us to explore the possibilities of gender expansion. First, femme demands dissolution of gender binaries by conceptualizing a femme whose existence is not dependent on the butch. Femme exists in completion with no opposites and requires no counterpart: iterations of enby femme, gender-fluid femme, femme boi, and trans femme identities emerge to disrupt and deconstruct the normative, narrow concepts of gender.

Second, femme provides a counternarrative for "femininity," rejecting cis-heteronormative beauty and body ideals with roots in Eurocentricity. Femmes of color, in particular, challenge racist, dominant narratives of form and experience and ask questions of the future where the past and present fail us. Centering femmes, whose embodiment troubles the norms of respectability, provides opportunities for freedom from the confines of static gender and "proper" bodies. As Leah Lakshmi Piepzna-Samarasinha (2017) asks in "Femme Futures," "Is there a free future in this femme of color disabled body?"

Third, femme embodiment is informed by erotic subjectivity. This framing centers the body and requires that we "consider how erotic meaning is produced and made pleasurable through acts and articulations, gestures and utterances" (J. Rodríguez 2014, 22). Here, the femme body is the vehicle for the erotic processes of transformation and the politicization of femme materiality. We see this in Fatima Jamal's documentary-in-process *No Fats No Femmes*, which explores the politics of desirability on dating apps. A femme erotic self-articulates notions of pleasure and power within the experiences of subjectivity, using them as fuel to demand a different world (Lorde [1984] 2007c).

Femme disrupts, mocks, and simultaneously rejects cis-heteropatriarchy, demanding that we trouble gender. The untranslatability of *femme* demonstrates that although the term entered our lexicon in the mid-1950s, it has long existed ontologically and phenomenologically in subaltern and fugitive form (Keeling 2007). Femme is theory (Hoskin 2019). Femme is expansive, performative, performed, and deeply felt (Shange 2019). It "makes room for the spectrum of gray-area" (Shelton 2018, 33). It is praxis, becoming and emerging (Ellison 2019). It disrupts the standards to which we have societally clung, propelling us into a future orientation of gender identity beyond the confines of normativity. Femme is movement work.

29

Flesh

Tiffany Lethabo King

My flesh, your flesh, our desire to be flesh-to-flesh, the word became flesh, "I don't eat flesh": invocations of the flesh abound. *Flesh* is a widely circulating term that has purchase for a number of contexts. From the biblical, to the political, and to the phenomenological, many differently situated people have used the term *flesh*. Flesh has indexed various social and ontological positions (states of being and their rank in the hierarchy) that attempt to mark the boundaries of self and other or ideal states of existence. For millennia, sacred texts like the Torah (Hebrew Bible) and the Christian Bible have referred to the flesh as both sacred (transcendent, holy) and profane (immanent, sinful). At times, social actors and scholars have talked about flesh as a stand-in for the body, and in other moments, flesh has been talked about as distinct from the body. The keyword *flesh* is difficult to track and even more difficult to fix to one stable meaning within the field of gender and sexuality studies. One of the reasons for this is that the field draws from and is shaped by various theoretical "turns" or traditions ranging from poststructuralism, phenomenology, Black studies, Indigenous studies, woman of color scholarship, queer of color critique, transgender studies, and new materialisms. All these intellectual and theoretical projects have their own unique concerns, political projects, and points of emphasis. *Flesh* means something different depending on who you are talking to and what conversation they are having at the moment.

During the formative years of the field of women's studies, European and US-based white women scholars at times deployed flesh to grapple with the materiality of the sexed body—specifically the female body—and its circulation within a masculinist symbolic universe. The center of gravity within a field marked by white cis womanhood (hetero and lesbian) often consisted of feminist philosophical explanations of patriarchy understood as the invention of women, sex, and gender through a masculine symbolic system that either subjugated women or erased their very existence. While drawing on masculinist philosophical traditions, poststructuralist French feminists like Luce Irigaray attempted to reappropriate and manipulate masculinist discourse toward feminist goals. For example, in *The Sex Which Is Not One*, Irigaray ([1977] 1985) sought to create a ground for taking seriously the embodied experience of women excised from men's linguistic and symbol universe. One of the ways that Irigaray achieved this was through repurposing Maurice Merleau-Ponty's 1968 text *The Visible and the Invisible*, which theorizes the flesh as a field of relation and "entanglement/intertwining" that overcomes Cartesian subject-object division. For poststructuralists, this is an important intervention that creates the ground for a discussion of subjectivity beyond the space of the normative self-possessed subject. The flesh offers a space of becoming that does not become static or fixed at the site of the overdetermined body. In Irigaray's ([1977] 1985, 1993) *The Sex Which Is Not One* and *An Ethics of Sexual Difference*, she touches upon the flesh as a transgressive space of relationality and ideal ground for her to introduce the feminine as a radical disruption of universality. The flesh—and in this case, the female "labia," or "two lips" that always touch (and are touched)— becomes a privileged site of relationality that stands in for an alternative symbolic universe of a yet-to-be-imagined or yet-to-be-languaged feminine relationality (Irigaray [1977] 1985).

As contemporaries of white feminist scholars, in the early years of the field of women's studies development in the United States, woman of color feminism critiqued both the whiteness and the biological determinism of the field's assumptions (Christian 1987). Black, Indigenous, Latina, Asian, and mixed-race women who identified politically as women of color developed their own modes of "theorizing the flesh." The flesh assumes a prominent role in the 1981 anthology *This Bridge Called My Back* (Moraga and Anzaldúa 1981). The collection assembles the work of woman of color writers whose elaborations upon the notion of flesh span a number of genres and styles, including poems, essays, letters, testimonials, journal entries, conversations, and interviews.

In her preface, Cherríe Moraga explains the materialist claims of the book, asserting that "the materialism in this book lives in the flesh of these women's lives: 'exhaustion,' 'fire in the heart,' 'knife in the back,' 'nausea,' 'hunger,' and 'fear'" (1981, xxix). The anthology defines a theory in the flesh to be "one where the physical realities of our lives—our skin color, the land or concrete we grew up on, our sexual longings—all fuse to create a politic born out of necessity" (Moraga and Anzaldúa 1981, 21). The writers' materialism animated by the flesh includes race, land, and sexuality. Informed by Indigenous and Chicana writers, the invocation of land as flesh disrupts the violent settler binary that separates humans and nonhumans/land. The authors elaborate further that through the flesh, they attempt to "bridge the contradictions of our experiences" (21). As woman of color, often lesbian, and working-class scholars and artists, their politics of the flesh worked as an analytic of interlocking forms of oppression that disrupted spaces of domination. Often responding to their objectification by white feminists and the heteronormative violence within their monoracial communities, in the words of contributor Norma Alarcón (1981, 202), they

had to put "flesh back on the object." For example, Jo Carrillo (1981, 66) speaks back to white feminists and demands that they recognize their "flesh and blood" humanity or risk becoming unsettled by their uncomfortable political demands "in the flesh." The woman of color contributors to *This Bridge Called My Back* understood the political and affective force of the flesh and often chose poetry to convey the flesh's urgency and transformative power. The use of poetics powerfully evinces the limitations of abstract theory that seeks to flatten and capture experience. Theories in the flesh continue to leave their epistemic and methodological imprints on the work of woman and queer of color humanists and social scientists who came after them (Muñoz 1999; E. Johnson 2001; Hurtado 2003).

Included within yet demanding a distinction from woman of color theories of flesh, Black feminist creative writers and scholars have developed their own fleshly poetics and theories. Ranging from Toni Morrison's ([1987] 1988) character Baby Suggs Holy, who delivers the sermon in the clearing on loving your flesh in *Beloved*, to Hortense Spillers's invocation of flesh as distinct from the body in her 1987 essay "Mama's Baby, Papa's Maybe: An American Grammar Book," flesh has proliferated within Black thought. Frustrated with how white academics used Black people's history as "raw material" for inspiration but never as anything that implicated them or that could be used "to explain something in theoretical terms," Spillers attempted to turn poststructuralist language back on itself (Spillers et al. 2007, 300). By giving her own account of the semiotic economy of slavery and its role in constituting language and proper subjecthood through the present, Spillers creates a foundational theory of Black (female) flesh that accounts for both the violent ways that the enslaved are stripped of proper gendered humanity and bodies and the ways that the remaining "ungendered" female flesh paradoxically offers a flip side (Spillers [1987] 2003), or in Harriet Jacobs's terms, a "loophole of retreat" (H. Jacobs [1861] 2009, 146). Reading an expansive archive of slavery from the fifteenth century through its afterlife in the twentieth century (Moynihan Report), Spillers theorizes how captive flesh, like Jacobs's, becomes a space for violent white patriarchal gendered self-making. The stolen African body becomes a captive body that can more appropriately be described as flesh or a state of "seared, divided, ripped-apartness" through its transformation in the hold of the ship (Spillers [1987] 2003, 206). As captive male and female bodies become a "territory of cultural and political maneuver not at all gender related," their flesh bears the marks of "cultural texts whose inside[s] have been turned outside" (206). While emerging from the violent context of the Middle Passage and slavery as a rearranged and disordered cultural text, Black flesh contains a surplus, or a remainder. Flesh offers a different kind of "cultural text" that if acknowledged can reconfigure certain "representational potentialities" for Black life—or more specifically, free it from the constraints of a liberal humanist body wed to patriarchal gender norms like manhood and womanhood (228). Scholars in Black studies have traveled with Spillers's notion of flesh to make important interventions in Black feminisms (Spillers et al. 2007), affect/sensation studies (Musser 2014), transgender studies (Snorton 2017), and new materialisms (Z. Jackson 2020) and as an avenue to developing new Black theoretical traditions like Afropessimism (Wilderson 2010, 2020).

Similarly, Native / First Nations and Indigenous studies scholars in the Americas, particularly Indigenous feminists, have theorized the flesh as double sided or multiple, containing lively capacity and also emerging from the terror of genocide and settler colonialism. Indigenous poetic and world-making traditions often invoke flesh as a space where humans and more

than humans meet. In 1981, invoking flesh, or "skin," Mvskoke Creek poet Joy Harjo penned "Remember": "Remember the earth whose skin you are: / red earth, black earth, yellow earth, white earth, brown earth, we are earth" (1983, 40). In 2016, Mohawk scholar Audra Simpson grounded her article "The State Is a Man" in a theory of flesh. Simpson focuses on Attawapiskat chief Theresa Spence's use of her flesh during a "hunger strike" to demand that Prime Minister Stephen Harper address the state's violence against First Nations peoples (A. Simpson 2016). While marked for genocide by the Canadian nation-state, Spence endures on a fish broth diet during her fast, and white settlers read her flesh as excessive because of its resistance to the telos of Indigenous death. In conversation with Spillers's ([1987] 2003) flesh, María Lugones's (2007) colonial gender system, and transgender studies' critiques, Cherokee scholar Brooklyn Leo theorizes the colonial violence that produced abject Indigenous Two Spirit, trans, and trans of color flesh as the condition of possibility for cis people of color's darkened and degraded colonial binary gender (Leo 2020).

In the context of Native/Indigenous and Black relational theories of flesh that account for the racial violence of slavery and colonialism, theories of (white) flesh like the ones that Merleau-Ponty and Irigaray posit or the dehumanized flesh that cis people of color theorize can be transformed into coherent and legible bodies when thinking relationally. Flesh takes shape and unfurls in ever-shifting and unpredictable ways. As the field of gender and sexuality studies introduces newer feminist and queer materialisms that reconfigure the flesh at the scale of the stem cell (Dixon 2014) or the organs affected by toxins (M. Chen 2012) in ways that move the flesh further away from corporeality and the body as a referent (Dixon 2014), scholars must continue to read these fleshy moves in relation to their temporally and spatially bound fields of power and the multiple forms of flesh the contexts produce. What the aforementioned invocations and theorizations of the flesh reveal is that flesh only gains meaning relationally and contextually.

30

Gender

Jules Gill-Peterson

How often do introductory courses in gender and sexuality studies begin by rehearsing a variation of the following model: "Sex ≠ Gender ≠ Sexuality"? And how pervasive has this relation of embodiment, identity, and desire become given the global export of Anglophone, US epistemologies and taxonomies of gender and sexuality? Part of what is at stake in confrontations over gender is the desire for a proper model, an accurate definition, and the right politics. How many genders are there? Is the twenty-first century defined by the most accurate and inclusive categories of gender to date? Or has the openness of gender "gone too far" in some way, diluting its meaning or undermining social order? What does the success and diffusion of gender mean for non-Anglophone, nonsecular, and nonwestern ways of being and knowing? And where did this very terminology and its distinctions that now anchor academic study come from? Was it not feminists who first introduced the concept and brought it into the mainstream? If what gender *is* and how it can be defined and distinguished from sex and sexuality are never-ending points of debate and discussion, then gender and sexuality studies might ask instead, Where did the contemporary concept of gender actually come from?

The answer may prove surprising. Most accounts of *gender* define it as a social or cultural matter, distinct from the biological domain of sex. Yet gender, as the word is used today, as well as its distinction from sex, was the invention not of feminism but rather of US behavioral psychology and medicine. Gender is thus an incredibly recent invention, dating from the mid-twentieth century. Prior to that era, the category "sex" encompassed a wide variety of phenomena at once somatic, psychic, and social. Phrases like *sex difference, the sexes,* or *sexual differentiation* carried much more than biological significance. What's more, today's concept of a gender *binary* has a much weaker predecessor. For the first several decades of the twentieth century, the western life sciences understood sex to be normally what they termed *bisexual,* which meant that every individual was naturally a mix of male and female. More precisely, these sciences contended that all human life started out in utero with the biological potential to become any sex and that the course of human development led to one sex becoming predominant, though humans never lost the potential to change sex.

A series of medical and psychological experiments on intersex infants, children, and young adults in the United States formed the data set out of which gender was invented, overturning this bisexual paradigm. By 1950, clinicians in urology and endocrinology at the Johns Hopkins Hospital in Baltimore, Maryland, had become somewhat able to coercively alter intersex children's development with new synthetic hormones as well as painful and nontherapeutic plastic surgeries. At the time, doctors routinely made surgical decisions on sex assignment without consulting children or their families, often deciding on their "true sex" based on what kind of plastic surgery was easier to perform. In developing a protocol for assigning a binary sex to these children, clinicians also created the base procedures for the new field of transsexual medicine, which was also emerging at this time in response to transgender people's demands for medical transition. John Money, a psychologist, was hired at Hopkins in the early 1950s to take over the clinic that saw intersex children. His clinical research team published several articles in 1955 in

which they outlined the new concept of "gender role." The first of these, published in the *Bulletin of the Johns Hopkins Hospital,* constitutes the inaugural appearance of the word *gender* in English: "The term gender role is used to signify all those things that a person says or does to disclose himself or herself as having the status of boy or man, girl or woman, respectively. It includes, but is not restricted to sexuality in the sense of eroticism" (Money, Hampson, and Hampson 1955b, 254). For Money and the Hampsons, gender delimited the social and psychological components of what used to all be called "sex."

The introduction of this new term *gender* also allowed for the introduction of a much stricter binary, though not for reasons of biological determinism. Money suppressed the concept of intersex people as a "mix" of two sexes. Still, *gender* referred to a psychosocial dimension *of* sex rather than a separate entity. Gender role was introduced as one of many components of sex that Money and his team (Money, Hampson, and Hampson 1955a) suggested clinicians could look to in intersex children to determine sex assignment. Money was very careful to insist that there was no way to know what caused the formation of gender roles. Rather, for a general theory, he analogized gender to a first language: once acquired, it became nearly impossible to lose, and any languages learned after childhood would never reach the same level of natural fluency. This theory reinforced the binary as a matter of social input, not biology. The concern was not whether human sex was naturally binary or whether any individual patient was truly male or female but rather how "normal" patients felt, which actually meant how well they adapted to the normative expectations of others. With that twist, a gender identity that did not conform to a binary-looking body could be identified as pathological because it might lead to distress from not being perceived as normal. This use of the language of "feeling normal" also narrowed the gender binary's parameters, doubling down on man and woman as rigid social roles. Medicine's new self-appointed task became to normalize the development of people whose gender identities did not "match" their bodies so that they would grow up to be *either* a woman or a man. Armed with the new concept of gender, the reach of medicine and psychiatry into the lives of intersex, trans, and gender nonconforming queer people greatly expanded in the second half of the twentieth century.

For Money, the distinction between sex and gender was a matter of descriptive convenience rather than an ontological claim. However, it was of central interest to the psychiatrist Robert Stoller ([1968] 1994), whose research with queer and especially trans patients in the 1960s popularized the difference between the two. It was this original *sexological* distinction between sex and gender that US feminists borrowed in the 1970s. As Jennifer Germon (2009, 86) and Jemima Repo (2015, 2) point out, this distinction has often been misattributed to 1970s feminists or even to earlier feminist texts like Simone de Beauvoir's declaration in *The Second Sex* that "one is not born, but rather becomes a woman" ([1949] 1989, 267). In reality, 1970s feminism was one of many places that Money's and Stoller's work popularized the distinction. Still, the adaptation from sexology did not occur without alteration. In her now classic article "Gender: A Useful Category of Historical Analysis," the historian Joan Scott (1986, 1054) observes that "in its most recent usage, 'gender' seems to have first appeared among American feminists who wanted to insist on the fundamentally social quality of distinctions based on sex." That is, gender introduced a cultural concept to critique sex stereotypes, sexed hierarchies, and power imbalances between women and men. Kate Millett's (1970) *Sexual Politics*, which concerns the political domination

of women by men, was one of the first books to contend on this basis that sex hierarchies had to be socialized under patriarchy rather than being based in anatomical or biological difference. As Repo explains in a history of the term *gender*, Millett explicitly cited both Money and Stoller to make this point, writing that "sex is biological, gender psychological, *and therefore cultural*" (2015, 80). This early adoption was joined by so many other landmark 1970s Anglophone feminist texts—including those by Germaine Greer, Ann Oakley, and Nancy Chodorow—that subsequently, the reference to Money and Stoller was dropped as the sex/gender distinction became the consensus point of view (27).

For white 1970s feminists, gender had done relatively little to disturb the category "women." (Black feminists, on the other hand, drew on a long lineage critical of exclusions built into "women.") However, the publication of anthropologist Gayle Rubin's ([1975] 1997) essay "The Traffic in Women," which critically analyzed what Rubin called "the sex/gender system," began to adapt gender for new ends that radically questioned the coherence of "women" as a reference point. Rubin's ([1984] 2011) later essay "Thinking Sex," along with Donna Haraway's ([1985] 1991) "A Cyborg Manifesto," served as a bridge to thinking about gender beyond the study of women. Gender became increasingly important because it was distinct from not just sex but *sexuality*, a concern central to the new field of queer theory. Eve Kosofsky Sedgwick's *Epistemology of the Closet* explored this shift by declaring as axiomatic that "*the study of sexuality is not coextensive with the study of gender. . . . But we can't know in advance how they will be different*" (1990, 27). Of course, Judith Butler's ([1990] 1999) *Gender Trouble* has most often been read as the signature text of this queer shift. Butler's theory of gender's performativity was widely interpreted as indexing a shift from "women" as the subject of feminism to a queer analysis of how gender is produced, is regulated, and might be subverted. The original feminist borrowing of the sex/gender distinction from sexology does not appear in *Gender Trouble*. Butler's account of their relation (16–25) comes instead in an argument that "sex" is actually a conceptual back-formation *of* gender, produced retrospectively to lend the appearance of physical substance.

Butler's theories of performativity and the demotion of sex to a discursive aftereffect of gender were both widely read—and hotly debated. Some feminist critics charged, in particular, that the performative theory of gender relegated the material body—its actual flesh and blood—to an unthinkable place, rendering the matter gender is made of more opaque. Feminist materialist theories like Elizabeth Grosz's (1994) *Volatile Bodies* argued on this basis for a feminist theory of sexual difference over a theory of gender. Butler (1993a) published *Bodies That Matter* in part as a clarification of her thinking on the sex/gender relation. However, the critique of that book's reading of race and especially Blackness as the "limit" of gender's performativity is perhaps more instructive in taking stock of this moment in the history of gender. Butler (1990) was critiqued, in particular from the growing field of transgender studies, for her overly allegorical reading of the death of Venus Xtravaganza in the film *Paris Is Burning*. As trans studies scholar Jay Prosser (1998) put it in *Second Skins*, Butler's interpretation of Xtravaganza's transsexuality and desire for the security and safety of a "white picket fence" version of the good life was a self-fulfilling prophecy: Butler read Xtravaganza's gender as unstable while fixing the Black and transsexual body as tragic failures to subvert norms. This debate over sex, gender, and the materiality of the body points to one important way that "gender" as a singular concept obscures its racialization.

Along with Prosser, other trans theories of gender critiqued the queer theory of performativity. Sandy Stone's (1992) foundational essay "The *Empire* Strikes Back: A Posttranssexual Manifesto" treated the trans body as a potentially subversive and semiotic text with the potential to disrupt not just the medical models that force trans people to feign adherence to gender norms but the very stability of gender that rests upon a legibly sexed body. Leslie Feinberg's pamphlet *Transgender Liberation: A Movement Whose Time Has Come* likewise begins by asserting that "all our lives we've been [incorrectly] taught that sex and gender are synonyms" (2013, 5). Feinberg defines gender, instead, as "self-expression, not anatomy" (5). The nascent field of transgender studies also levied an important critique of queer theory's fixation on trans people as mere figures for theorizing the instability and subversion of the gender binary rather than paying attention to the material oppression faced by trans people or their own experiences and theories of gender (Prosser 1998; Namaste 2000; Stryker 2004). As trans of color theory (J. Chen 2019) and decolonial theories of gender (Lugones 2010) further specified, the binary sex and gender system was substantially built through colonialism and racialized bodies of knowledge about cultures deemed nonnormative by white Euro-American structures of political domination.

As gender traveled from sexology to Anglophone feminists and on to women's and gender studies, as well as queer studies and trans studies, it also became integral to theories of intersectionality. Kimberlé Crenshaw's (1989, 1991) initial two essays outlining the concept specifically referred to sex and racial discrimination under US law but also broadly conceived of gender as one of multiple axes (or lanes of traffic in an intersection, per one of its central metaphors) through which Black women experienced oppression. Still, as Jennifer Nash (2019a) observes, a great deal of skepticism could be turned on this entire periodization. Black feminists have articulated complex models for thinking about oppression involving sex and gender since at least the 1970s, when the Combahee River Collective released "A Black Feminist Statement" (Moraga and Anzaldúa 1981, 210–18). Landmark woman of color feminist writing in the 1980s, such as the collection *This Bridge Called My Back* (Moraga and Anzaldúa 1981), also significantly challenged the whiteness and coloniality of Anglophone feminism's singular interest in gender. As Gloria Anzaldúa puts it evocatively in *Borderlands / La Frontera*, "I know things . . . older than gender" (1987, 26).

Theories of gender that center race and colonialism, it should be emphasized, most consistently have *not* borrowed the sex/gender distinction from sexology. Indeed, they often recontextualize sexology as integral to racist projects that make use of gender. C. Riley Snorton's (2017) investigation of how the malleability of gender relies on the concept of pliable and exchangeable Black flesh under transatlantic slavery, for instance, offers an entirely different frame for thinking about gender's emergence in the twentieth century. Likewise, Qwo-Li Driskill's (2016) investigation of the violent imposition of binary sex and gender roles on the Cherokee Nation over nearly five centuries recontextualizes the invention of gender in 1950s as but a small chapter in a still-unfolding Indigenous temporality of survival. Scholarship in Indigenous studies (P. Allen 1986; Deer 2009; L. Simpson 2017), decolonial studies, and Black studies not only breaks from the unacknowledged reiteration of the sexological model of sex/gender by predominately white Anglophone scholars but further recontextualizes gender within a racial and colonial system of violence and governance established over centuries in the Americas (Spillers [1987] 2003; Lugones 2007). One important narrative to disrupt is that this kind of thinking about race, anti-Blackness, and colonialism as central to sex and gender did not come "after" the Anglophone feminist adoption of gender. A global critique of gender, however, might move in a different direction, pointing out that the category is ultimately a narrow western one and cannot be presumed to exist, or have existed, elsewhere in the world, except as an outcome of colonial and neocolonial processes.

If today's category of gender is borne of a racial, colonial, and sexological forge, what does this mean for its ostensibly progressive contemporary shifts that continue to privilege western, Anglophone, academic, and white forms of subjectivity? The emergence and popularity of "gender spectrum" models in recent years could be read, for instance, as a capitulation to sexology: a belief that the value of gender lies in producing taxonomies, expecting everyone to name and express a "true" identity, and strengthening forms of state surveillance (Beauchamp 2019) and everyday violence premised on gendered visibility (Tourmaline, Stanley, and Burton 2017). The rapid emergence and diffusion of the category "cis" may serve to both reinforce the normality of the normative category of gender and minimize its oppressive impacts by converting it into a self-identification (Enke 2012). The misattribution of cisness to nontrans people who do not enjoy the privileges of gender normativity, like Black or Indigenous women, is one of the risks of the unmarked whiteness of the term. Likewise, while *nonbinary* introduces conceptual trouble into the gender binary, its potential to reify hierarchies within trans communities (a new binary, dizzyingly, between nonbinary and binary) and the whiteness and masculine-of-center androgyny with which it is predominately associated have served as points of concern and critique (Rajunov and Duane 2019).

Still, the critique of gender's invention and uptake is not the only story to be told. If gender is, among other things, a system for classifying and governing human beings (Spade 2011)—one employed by the law and the state as well as violent institutions of captivity like schools, prisons, and medicine to restrict individual and collective self-determination (Stanley and Smith [2011] 2015)—should it be abolished? Is the abolition of gender even feasible, or would it produce harm for marginal populations that have struggled to affirm their genders? These are major questions gender and sexuality studies can engage. Still, they are not the only way to approach gender. Those who have been subject to similar patterns of oppression through normative regimes of race, sex, gender, and sexuality (J. Chen 2019), like Black women, Indigenous people, and trans, nonbinary, and intersex people, may have their own competing claims to gender that could push the category in different directions—not just in the future but through past and present ways of being and knowing that have been suppressed. For instance, late in her life, Virginia Prince, a self-identified transvestite woman who had built relationships since the 1960s with many of the clinicians who popularized gender and founded US trans medicine, claimed that Robert Stoller had in fact borrowed the sex/gender distinction *from her*. However true Prince's claim may be, it holds open the door to a different way of understanding gender: from the perspective of those who, having been forced to pay some of the highest prices for the category, might know more about it than any of the usual experts, including scholars.

31

Girl
Karishma Desai

These days, we see images of girls everywhere. Certain celebrity girl-activists like Malala Yousafzai and Greta Thunberg circulate across social media. As empowered girls, they draw attention and compel. It is easy to become stuck to the futures their images promise. The ways girls are configured and subsequently the kinds of futures attached to them certainly range. International development campaigns such as Nike Foundation's Girl Effect mark the adolescent girl in particular as the single best human capital investment for economic growth, community development, and racial uplift in the Global South. And the girl is also figured spearheading social movements across the world. The ubiquitous celebration of girls and their potential demands analytic attention. Girls have long been contested sites of intervention as they have been deployed in colonial humanitarian reasoning and anticolonial nationalist projects. Yet present decades mark an intensified focus on the girl. As she has emerged more prominently in the popular imagination within the past few decades as a subject of concern and object of investment, scholarly and popular writing about the girl continues to amass.

As scholarly inquiry around the girl accrued, girl studies coalesced as a field in the 1990s, and a journal dedicated to the study of girlhood was established in 2008. The white liberal feminist scholars who founded the field and journal maintained that the study of girlhood remained on the margins of both youth studies and women and gender studies. Youth studies was preoccupied with age and generation, and academic analysis focused on young white men as the normative category used to define stages of psychological development and the norm against which young women should be measured despite feminist critiques (McRobbie and Garber 1976). While questions about the girl have always been entangled with the category of woman, space for girlhood within women's studies remained prohibitive as adult-centered logics structured earlier liberal feminist movements and women's studies scholarship (Kearney 2009). Some argue that the assertion of the term *woman* was shaped by the long-standing affronts attached to the term *girl*. "Girl" was used to infantilize economically subservient women, such as domestic servants. And well into the Jim Crow era, the term was used to mark racial hierarchies and attach nonadult status to Black women (Weinbaum et al. 2008). While girlhood studies established itself in the 1990s, until very recently, the field has been preoccupied with white middle-class girlhoods in the United States, Europe, and Australia. Feminist scholars of color have critiqued this preoccupation and the field's failure to attend to how coloniality, race, and global capitalism have structured the category and young women's lives.

Who is a girl, and what defines stages of girlhood? When and how did the girl emerge as a social fact? How have colonial impositions and imperial regimes shaped the category and its circulation? How does age and status define this shifting category? As with other terms, the category of girl is unstable and contested. The term's meaning and its boundaries have varied historically and geographically. This essay is not concerned with the girl as a container that holds empirical onto-epistemic truth. Rather, it considers institutions, public discourses, affects, and rationalities that formulated girl as a category in currently commonplace generational and gendered terms.

Girlhood studies scholars point to British journalist Eliza Lynn Linton's 1868 diatribe titled *The Girl of the Period*, which reflected emerging public anxiety around the "modern girl" in the western industrialized world, as a moment that marks a point of visibility. In contrast to the Victorian feminine ideal of purity and innocence, the modern girl "dies her hair and paints her face, and is only concerned with a life of fun" (Linton 1868, 339). In her essay, Linton laments the loss of purity, dignity, and innocence attached to "the fair young English girl" and argues for her recuperation. The mid to late nineteenth-century figure of the innocent girl was lodged in dominant ideals of Victorian domesticity that centered on family, motherhood, respectability, and managing the life of the home (Driscoll 2002). The girl as future mother within this period of the British Empire needed to be saved from the perils of modernization, as her proper cultivation was required to maintain racial purity, national stability, and imperial expansion. Victorian domesticity traveled through colonial educational interventions based on the racialized biopolitical logic that educating girls in home life would catalyze civilizational progress (Lomawaima 1994; M. Jacobs 2009).

Policies that fixed boundaries between girl and woman, such as the landmark age of consent legislation, were exported to the colonies (Driscoll 2002; Tambe 2019). Several decades later, the category of adolescence as a separate and specific developmental stage between childhood and adulthood was forcefully articulated by US psychologist G. Stanley Hall, who translated evolutionary biology in psychological terms. Racial science undergirded the production and circulation of the adolescent. Hall analogized the maturation of people and national societal progress, arguing that adolescence was the apex of human development and that adolescence was a point at which an individual (or society) jumped from savage to a western superior selfhood or remained unable to mature toward civilization (Lesko 2012). The significance of this stage of adolescence grew in prominence among European and American psychologists in the 1920s and 1930s, traveled to the Global South through western social scientific "expertise" and international development apparatus, and became central to contemporary girl-centered interventions.

Whether Hall's analysis was gendered is contested among historians of girlhood (Simmons 2015). Psychologists later attached gendered specificities to female subjects, and the category of "adolescent girl" was further crystallized. The crisis of confidence and self-esteem connected to the period of female adolescence was established as a social fact through an influential text written in the 1990s by American clinical psychologist Mary Pipher titled *Reviving Ophelia: Saving the Adolescent Girl*. Pipher describes the period of adolescence for young women as a time of chaos where their behaviors and emotions are incomprehensible and a time where they lose touch with their authentic selves (Gonick 2006). This anxiety around young women was paired with promise of recuperation, articulating the desired cultivation of a specific type of girlhood.

As white middle-class girls in the western world became increasingly visible in social and cultural spaces, they were configured as subjects worthy of investment. Liberalization led to global economic restructuring, which relied on the labor of young women, and the advancements of liberal feminism increased opportunities for middle-class women. Moreover, neoliberal notions of responsibility, choice, and innovation converged with white liberal feminist ideals of women's individual freedom and opportunity. Such discourses of liberal feminism converged with discourses and conditions of neoliberalism to craft a specific articulation of empowered girlhood as the ideal subject for investment in the western world. Young women were represented as educationally and economically successful, responsible and self-inventing, delaying motherhood and living glamorous lives of enterprise and consumption (A. Harris 2004). The girl has been imagined, deployed, and captured as a crucial entry point to the discipline of conspicuous consumption by infrastructures of capital such as marketing firms via teen fashion and lifestyle magazines, makeup and hair-care advertisements, and so on.

However, empowered girls have been configured in relation to their at-risk Others. In particular, the bodies of Black, Latinx, and Indigenous working-class girls marked by hypersexuality, teen pregnancy, disordered consumption, and delinquency are perceived as at risk. The overly sexualized girl figures as a monster (Bettie 2014, xxvi) and is deemed to delay national progress. While racial capitalist structures shape the lives of young women of color, their conditions are calculated as cultural deficits and failures of individual subjectivity such as lack of ambition, poor choices, and sexual deviance. In contrast, white middle-class girls who take on neoliberal dispositions are configured as exceptional subjects, most adept to serve nation building in the era of late modernity. Whiteness is erased as race and becomes a universalized form marked as requisite for civilizational progress.

Transnational feminist scholars have pointed to the troubling ways in which this form of normative girlhood proliferates through international development campaigns, policies, and interventions focused on "saving" girls in the Global South (Switzer 2010; Khoja-Moolji 2018). If empowered girls illustrate the potential to bring forth national progress, corporate development paired with neoliberal feminist activism, transnational policy actors, and biopolitical interventions target adolescent girls in the Global South as the ultimate investment for activating Third World potential (Moeller

2018; Desai 2020). Investment in the potential of adolescent girls promises to unleash a cascade of social effects that will alleviate poverty, prevent terrorism, and curb gender-based violence. The assumptions undergirding the global convergence around girls hinge upon the juxtaposition of the postfeminist subject from the Global North with the girl in/from the Global South who is either hypersexualized or veiled but always oppressed by "backward" culture. Postcolonial feminist Chandra Mohanty's analytic of the Third World woman and Lila Abu-Lughod's (2002) critique of the white liberal feminist logic that undergirds the urge to save Muslim women have been important intellectual resources for transnational feminist scholars studying the contemporary preoccupation with saving Third World Girls.

The imperial reasoning undergirding humanitarian interventions is further unsettled by scholars who illustrate the capitalist frenzy to invest in the human capital potential of girls. It is an instantiation of the economization of life (Murphy 2017), a hierarchical value regime that recapitulates colonial racial hierarchies linked to practices that value and govern life in terms of its ability to foster the macroeconomy of the nation-state. Colonial investments in domesticity through education extend through racial logics of measurement in contemporary development regimes. While transnational feminists examining contemporary development have attended to how imperial racial logics and global capitalism shape investment in neoliberal forms of empowered girlhoods, others have examined earlier forms of gendered modernity and globalization. Tracking the modern girl across multiple contexts during the interwar period of the 1920s and 1930s, the Modern Girl around the World research group illustrates the contested and multiple meanings attached to this figure. Scholars in this collective also pay heed to how young women defined themselves in excesses of conventional female roles and as transgressive of national, imperial, and racial boundaries (Weinbaum et al. 2008).

Black and queer feminist scholars, among others, have worked to recuperate wayward, willful girlhoods. These critical interventions illuminate how the "becoming" attached to the category "girl" generates possibilities for thinking otherwise, for bringing forth potential futures outside of and beyond liberal humanism. Saidiya Hartman centers the intimate lives of young Black women in the twentieth century, suggesting that in their experiments and meditations on what a free life might be, they proposed and took up radical visions of Black futures. She calls her account the "fugitive text of the wayward" (2019, xiv), maintaining that young Black women were "radical thinkers who tirelessly imagined ways of living that contested normative boundaries of respectability, and never failed to consider how the world might be otherwise" (xv). Queering the history of the will, Sara Ahmed (2014) opens her text with a vignette of a young girl whose will persists despite being willfully suppressed. She unearths this willful girl within an old Brothers Grimm's tale and in doing so urges attention to willful subjects, strays, or wanderers who refuse to subject their wills and refuse to become willing subjects. Like Hartman, Ahmed brings to light willful girls within textual archives and collects feminist killjoy scenes. Girlhood is queered in this account as willful girlhood entails being without normative heterosexual demands and limits. This orientation, she writes, is necessary for survival, noting that "some have ways of lives because others have lives, some have to be assertive because others have been given self-assertion" (S. Ahmed 2014, x). Willfulness, the refusal of one's will to be governed, is necessary for existence to be possible; this willfulness invites other possible worlds. Attending to how the ordinary, everyday lives of young women hold revolutionary seeds of otherwise that Hartman, Ahmed, and others (see, e.g., Lomawaima 1994; A. M. Cox 2015) illuminate in their archival and ethnographic work affords new directions in understanding the productive potential of the category of the girl.

32

Health

Jenna M. Loyd

Health is a decidedly double-edged keyword. Etymologically, *health* derives from the Old English *hælþ* as related to "being whole, sound or well," and thus the verb *heal* means "to make whole" or "to make robust." Its figurative usage as a biologized descriptor for well-being—of the economy, communities, the environment—is so widespread as to be taken for granted. Much as Raymond Williams suggested about *community*, health, too, "can be the warmly persuasive word" that "seems never to be used unfavorably" ([1976] 2014, 76).

The double-edgedness of *health* hinges on the rhetorical sway of leveraging wholeness, wellness, or the implied opposite of disease to naturalize what are profoundly political projects. As I write in the midst of the COVID-19 pandemic, the director of the Centers for Disease Control (CDC) has invoked his office's public health policing powers to halt requests for asylum made in the US-Mexico borderlands. Meanwhile, Free Them All for Public Health has mobilized health toward abolitionist ends by calling for the release of people held in jails, prisons, and detention centers.

These tensions, if not deep conflicts, over human health in its many facets (public, mental, physical, sexual, spiritual), forms (state, nonprofit, for-profit, mutual aid), and modalities (traditional, holistic, western) are perhaps best understood through gender and sexuality studies. Feminist and queer movements and organizations, particularly those led by BIPOC, have conceptualized health as *entangled with*, not in opposition to, violences that result in health inequities, including premature death (Galtung 1969 and Gilmore 2007 center *premature death* in their influential definitions of structural violence and racism, respectively). In the face of violences that shape bodily vulnerability to environmental, economic, and interpersonal harms, these movements have claimed well-being and healing as visceral cores of radical politics.

The importance of their intersectional understandings of health cannot be overstated, as they clarify how systems of oppression (the -isms) work through health and how these systems often coalesce where the health sector meets the carceral state and/or where it meets militarism (A. Y. Davis 1989, 35–65). As healing justice movement organizers and practitioners Anjali Taneja, Cara Page, and Susan Raffo (2019) explain, the "medical industrial complex emerged as an extension of policing and state violence to control the biology and healing practices and to define the line between 'normal' and not." For example, the power of the state and organized medicine is often mobilized to defend "the body politic" or "the public health" (it is always a "the") through invoking health's (often feminized) opposites: disease, disability, insanity, brokenness, fragility, and so on. The threat that these ubiquitous conditions ostensibly pose betrays the categorical lines of human value that actually are being drawn. Critical disability studies scholars and disability justice and healing justice movements have challenged such epistemic violence by demonstrating how race and disability, race and sanism, are mutually constitutive and inseparable (Erevelles 2014; Samuels 2014; Clare 2017; Ben-Moshe 2020; Breedlove 2020).

I focus this entry on the United States, where health care has become an increasingly important part of the capitalist economy since the end of World War II. As an economic sector, health care has ballooned from 5 percent of US GDP to 17.9 percent of GDP. It currently accounts for 11 percent of the US workforce, 24 percent of government spending, and the largest portion of nonwage compensation for workers (Mikulic 2019; Nunn, Parsons, and Shambaugh 2020). Yet even before the COVID-19 pandemic, some thirty million people did not have health insurance, half of whom were people of color. Black and Native mothers experience childbirth-related death at two to three times the rate of white mothers (Peterson et al. 2019). Approximately one-third of transgender folks report negative treatment by health workers, with higher rates among racialized groups (National Center for Transgender Equality 2016, 97). I invoke these data as evidence of health inequities (defined as systematic, avoidable, and unfair), yet far too often, health officials and politicians use such evidence to blame individuals and rationalize away structural determinants of health and realities of medical abuse and discrimination (see Farrow 2016).

Within a capitalist (health) system, one way in which health is commodified is through medicalization wherein medicine claims as its domain "particular social problems deemed morally problematic and often affecting the body" (Clarke et al. 2003, 164). Healthism can be understood as a highly profitable form of medicalization emerging since the 1970s wherein health becomes an ongoing project accompanied by "mandates for self-regulation" (172) that confer individual worth (R. Crawford 1980). The hegemony of healthism as a capitalist ideology premises our healthiness on our (class-based) capacity to consume and make time for new healthy products, diets, lifestyles, and beauty and wellness regimes. Our (inevitable) failure to be perfectly self-disciplined becomes occasion for body and attitude shaming (Piepzna-Samarasinha 2018; Ehlers and Krupar 2019). As new technoscientific fields and practices—including so-called race-based medicine, genomics, and personal data trackers—expand the terrain of health, our data bodies and practices of self-governance simultaneously become sources of surveillance and wealth extraction for the health care, insurance, and data sectors (Berlant 2011; D. Roberts 2011; Ehlers and Hinkson 2017; Ehlers and Krupar 2019).

The flow of capital through these forms of health also reproduces social and economic hierarchies. Failure to follow a prescribed drug or diet regimen is often called "noncompliance" even though people may not have the money or time to follow health advice. Patterns of disinvestment accumulate health harms along racial, gender, and sexuality lines. In turn, groups that have been abandoned are subject to coercive and degrading treatment, further undermining their well-being. Nirmala Erevelles observes that treating people with disabilities as "unworthy" of receiving health care so they can live an active economic and social life "consigns them to institutional care or active neglect" (2006, 30; also see Wong 2020).

And yet.

Health is not only about normalization. The second utterly fierce and invaluable insight gained from a focus on health from feminist, queer, and trans movements and lenses is their adamant refusal of ableist terms of health and logics of disposability that undergird the medical-industrial complex and broader racial capitalist circuits of value and deservingness. Since the 1960s, the civil rights, women's, disability rights, and LGBT movements have profoundly challenged the authority and paternalism of medicine to define healthy and bodily knowledge, control care, and define cure (J. Nelson 2003; A. Nelson 2011; Loyd 2014; Sharman 2016). Dignity, personal autonomy, and care-fullness of health services are what make a right to health care meaningful.

While "choice" became the dominant framework of reproductive health, contests over that single-issue frame, at the time and in the present, reveal competing registers of the meaning of health. "Choice" can be understood as an iteration of healthism, an individualizing mechanism that differentiates those who "are disciplined for pregnancies or for exercising reproductive autonomy, while others are honored for the very same thing" (Ross and Solinger 2017, 139). The largely white campaign for abortion rights accepted the neo-Malthusian premise that abortions might remedy poverty. "As if," Angela Y. Davis wryly notes, "having fewer children could create more jobs, higher wages, better schools, etc., etc." (1981, 205).

Black and Indigenous women and women of color, meanwhile, steadily created organizations to forcefully challenge the limits of "choice" and uplift the "reproductive dignity and safety of women of color" (Ross and Solinger 2017, 55). Coalitions they formed grew in the 1990s into the reproductive justice movement, an intersectional framework that powerfully links environmental racism, poverty, anti-immigrant policy, criminalization, and incarceration (Silliman and Bhattacharjee 2002; Ross and Solinger 2017; Firmat 2018). Such a perspective is rooted in recognizing that "a combination of pronatalist and antinatalist strategies" has been deployed throughout US history (Ross and Solinger 2017, 18). As part of efforts to usurp Native lands and expand slavery, settlers changed English common law so that the legal status of children would follow mothers; enslavers would thereby appropriate the children of enslaved women (A. Y. Davis 1981; Hartman 2016). In the 1970s, Native activists and antiracist feminists challenged forced sterilization as genocidal. Andrea Smith (2005) built upon this legacy when she named gender and sexual violence against Native women as tools of genocide and ongoing social control. Pro- and antinatalist strategies can also be recognized in federal blood quantum logics, which Kim TallBear observes render Native peoples as perpetually diminishing through intermarriage with white people while simultaneously treating Black-white sexual relations as threatening to whiteness (Tuck 2016).

Natalist politics also informed increasingly restrictive and eugenic migration policies. Legislation enacted between the 1870s and 1920s welded together race, gender, sexuality, poverty, and disability as interrelated bases of undesirability and thereby exclusion. The 1875 Page Law targeted Chinese women, whom white elites viewed as prostitutes who posed health and moral threats to white families (Luibhéid 2002). The category "likely to become a public charge" became law in 1882 to "exclude women who were pregnant outside of marriage" (5). This patriarchal form of racial-class discretion was accompanied by bans on certain classes of criminals and those considered to be "feeble-minded," "imbeciles," or disabled. Eugenicists also implemented state and local policies that encouraged or required sterilization in their efforts to "improve" humanity. Contemporary racist discourses targeting Asian and Latina women as hyperfertile build on these histories (M. Escobar 2016; S. Wang 2017). For Krysta Williams of the Native Youth Sexual Health Network, "Border imperialism perpetuates and upholds violence against Indigenous bodies by the historical and present-day violent reinforcement of the doctrine of discovery and assertion of colonial ownership of Indigenous land and territories" (in Ross and Solinger 2017, 255).

Scholars working on gender, sexuality, and (mental) health have repeatedly shown that medicalization does not neatly cleave control of an issue away from other powerful institutions, such as the church or legal system. Antinatalist strategies have relied on criminalization. "Pregnancy policing" refers to how the war on drugs and antifeticide laws create fear among pregnant people using drugs "about seeking necessary and vital medical attention, even though drug users require health care and support to get clean" (Ross and Solinger 2017, 219; also see Sered and Norton-Hawk 2014). Dorothy Roberts (1997, 157) traces contemporary criminalization of Black women's fertility to histories of gender-racial control that have been mobilized through interlinked controlling figures of the matriarch, welfare queen, and crack mother. Child protective services agencies, as a result, act as intrusive, surveillant agencies that remove far more Black and Native children from their families than white children from white families (A. Smith 2005; D. Roberts 2006).

The oppressive alignment between medicine and the carceral state also can be observed in the medicalization of violence. In the 1970s, activists in California challenged government-funded biomedical research into violence, which "represented not merely an effort to biologize (and medicalize) violence but to do so through resources dedicated to expanding the carceral state" (A. Nelson 2011, 160). Activists in Massachusetts opposed the opening of a "secure" psychiatric facility, arguing that it "would be used discretionarily against imprisoned women who protested their conditions of confinement, and that women of color and lesbian women would be especially vulnerable" (Thuma 2019, 55).

The cooptation of feminist antiviolence work would be realized through deepened connections between medicine and the carceral state (see Law 2014). Procedures of forensic care for rape survivors can become another form of violence because they prioritize the collection of medicolegal evidence over the emotional and physical care and wishes of survivors (Mulla 2014). Further, mandatory reporting obligations for health care providers mean that a survivor's "stop at the hospital . . . potentially enlists processes of incarceration, detention and deportation" (Durazo 2006, 181).

My contention that gender, sexuality, and health articulate with institutions of violence is clear once more with HIV/AIDS. In the 1980s, the federal (non) response to HIV was shaped by existing inequalities in access to health care and racialized, classed, heterogendered perceptions of health and "riskiness" (Cohen 1999). Likewise, Cindy Patton observes that public health researchers did not take much interest in socalled junky pneumonia "because it was not considered remarkable that injecting drug users should get sick and die" (in Cohen 1999, 134–35). Simultaneously, racist conceptions of disease led the CDC to designate Haitians as a nationality a "risk group," resulting in the "carceral quarantine" of HIV+ asylum seekers on the US Navy base at Guantanamo (Paik 2016). Politicians also mobilized antigay and racist panic to propose referenda and pass legislation to mandate HIV testing, require quarantine, and criminalize the transmission of HIV (Center for HIV Law and Policy 2020). Enforcement of these laws transpires in a racialized carceral landscape that heightens vulnerabilities to imprisonment for Black queer, gender nonconforming, and trans people (McTighe 2012; Gossett 2012).

Collective care and direct action responses to AIDS in the 1980s grew from feminist health, gay, and left organizing (Patton 1990; Schulman 2013), demonstrating the many ways of "doing queer love" (Diedrich 2016, 22). Emily Hobson recalls that the first act of civil disobedience to confront AIDS was organized in 1984 by members of Enola Gay, a group of white radical gay men who organized against US militarism, when they poured fake blood on the entrance to a nuclear weapons laboratory. Antimilitarist analyses could be seen on protest signs reading "Money for AIDS, not war" and "Fund condoms, not contras" (Hobson 2016, 164). Nishant

Shahani (2016) notes that such internationalism also informed Bay Area–based ACT UP organizers' opposition to deportation and HIV migration restrictions. For activist Jorge Cortiñas, the federal migration ban "does more than insult and seek to humiliate us. This law perpetuates the epidemic. This law kills queers" (in Shahani 2016, 21).

Lisa Diedrich argues that "co-optation . . . is *the* double-bind of health activism" (2016, 13; my emphasis). We can see this with women's health and antiviolence movements of the 1970s and with HIV/AIDS activism. Feminists who focused on self-help viewed collectivizing reproductive health knowledge as a necessary part of freeing themselves from paternalistic control by medicine and the law, but broader racial-class struggles for rights to health care, childcare, and welfare remain unrealized (Loyd 2014). Likewise, race and class threaded through ideological conflicts within the HIV/AIDS movement between the "treatment" ("drugs into bodies") and "social action" agendas, the latter focusing on how interlocking structural forces "affected both the spread of the virus and access to and efficacy of medical care" (Hobson 2016, 159). The partial absorption of feminist self-help and the treatment agendas into medical practice is an arguably positive development, but it also can diminish the powerful insights and momentum from each of the movement's broader agendas.

Lessons that gender and sexuality studies can draw from these movements suggest that a radical health politics is necessarily intersectional and coalitional. The queer (health) politics Cathy Cohen advanced are coalitional, wherein people with different identities came "together to challenge dominant constructions of who should be allowed and who deserved care" (1997, 460). For example, activists involved in ACT UP's prison project in New York City contended "that the government which denied even wealthy gay men access to drugs to combat this disease must be regarded as the same source of power that denied incarcerated men and women access to basic health care" (460). A more recent example comes from Women with a Vision (WWAV), a Black feminist reproductive justice organization in New Orleans, which successfully challenged Louisiana's Crime Against Nature by Solicitation (CANS) law. Following Hurricane Katrina, many of the Black cis and trans women sex workers with whom WWAV organized were convicted under the CANS law, which had initially been passed to criminalize sex between men. Dismantling the power of this law to determine who could live in New Orleans freely simultaneously was a way "for advancing Black women's health and wellbeing" (McTighe and Haywood 2017, 273). A final example of the necessity of coalitional politics comes from the tragic death of Victoria Arellano, a trans woman and Mexican immigrant who was HIV+, in migration detention after being denied treatment. Queer activists argued that new political coalitions would need to challenge the "good immigrant," heteronormative, and homonormative frames of mainstream immigrant rights LGBT organizations in order to challenge border imperialism, HIV, and heteropatriarchy (Y. Nair 2015; Contreras 2012). Finally, these examples all illustrate the vital importance for sexuality and gender studies to challenge health as a disciplinary modality operationalized through respectability politics (Cohen 1999).

Health and health care are such thickets because health in itself is not progressive, care-full, or rights based. It only is made so through struggles against healthism, ableism, and sanism as three primary elements of health (care) within racial capitalism. This means that health must be unmoored from its roots in wholeness and cure. For Eli Clare, cure operates as an ideology that is tethered to a normalizing narrative of damage wherein "what existed before is superior to what exists currently" (2017, 15). Yet recognizing that relief from illness and pain is desirable, Clare is left "holding it all—sickness and human vulnerability, health and disability, the need for and rejection of cure" (62). Healing justice as a movement was started by BIPOC in the South and established nationally through the 2006 Southeast Social Forum and 2010 US Social Forum (Page 2010; Piepzna-Samarasinha 2016). As Leah Lakshmi Piepzna-Samarasinha (2016) explains, the movement "centres disabled wisdom that does indeed want access to medicines, adaptive technology, and other things that improve our energy, mobility, or immune systems, but also believes sick and disabled and mad and neurodivergent bodies are a normal part of the continuum of being human, full of wisdom, cripskills, adaptability, and cripscience." Healing focused on "original wounds" of settler colonialism and slavery and ongoing violences of war, racial capitalism, and border imperialism represents a shift away from health as individualized overcoming (Breedlove 2020; Carter et al. 2013). Instead, healing is understood as integrated with freedom struggles "lift[ing] up resiliency and survival practices that center the collective safety and emotional, physical, spiritual, environmental and mental wellbeing of communities" (Raffo 2019, 10). As with other strands of health activism, issues of cooptation and cultural appropriation loom (Carter et al. 2013; Raffo 2019), yet the movement's emphasis on nourishment, strengthening interdependence, and fostering communities of care offers irresistible possibilities for living and healing otherwise (Piepzna-Samarasinha 2018; Breedlove 2020).

33

Heteronormativity

Scott L. Morgensen

Heteronormativity refers to a social method for arranging sexual status unequally. The study of heteronormativity inherits and builds on the legacy of Gayle Rubin (1984) and others who directed sexuality studies to study the cultural production of hierarchical sexualities. Rubin's work extended Michel Foucault's account of the invention of sexuality discourse within European sexual science (Foucault 1978). Rubin and Foucault teach that defining sexuality as a characteristic of types of people is the first act of a form of power that then conditions how sexualities become ranked along hierarchical lines. Sexuality thus refers not only to a way of taxonomizing persistent subjectivity but also to a technology for creating forms of knowledge, including self-knowledge.

Queer theorists proposed the idea of heteronormativity to highlight a form of power that uplifts heterosexuality by marginalizing sexualities outside its mold. This power is normative because it sets and enforces rules: more than just describing heterosexuality as normal, it polices conformity to heterosexual norms. Queer theorists use heteronormativity to study how heterosexuality enters power relationships with any sexual life that appears queer (strange, out of place) in relation to heterosexuality (Warner 1993; Jagose 1996). Heteronormativity also illuminates trans life by addressing how binary sex gets entrenched within sexual norms, although trans theorists have critiqued the failure of queer theory to fully account for the investments of trans studies or for distinctions between cis and trans life (Prosser 1998;

Stryker 2004). Heteronormativity thus is a core, if incomplete, concept that queer theory provides to gender and sexuality studies for the relational analysis of marginal and normalized sexuality.

The concept of heteronormativity meets its limits, however, if we project it across societies or histories. Queer theorists of early modern and medieval Europe (Dinshaw 1999; Freccero 2006) examine desires that are not explained by heterosexuality's modern logics of binary sex or biologically determined drives. Queer scholars further argue for reading European sexual history not self-referentially but in relation to Black, Indigenous, and all peoples worldwide who for centuries confronted Europe's racial, colonial, capitalist, and imperial power (Thomas 2007; Arondekar 2009). On recognizing, with Greg Thomas, that "the culture which constructs sexuality in the 'First World' is itself constructed in and for white racist empire" (Thomas 2007, 8), we must ask if heteronormativity as an analytic can conceptually account for such power relations and for its own emergence within them.

Strategies of racial capital, colonization, slavery, empire, and eugenics rooted societies in Europe and worldwide in intimate but often geographically distanced relations of marginalization and normalization long before the invention of sexuality discourses and in ways that informed the rise of heteronormativity as a mode of governance. Gendered and sexual frames map Europe's shift from Old to New World modes of empire and enslavement (Martinez 2008; H. Bennett 2018), which in turn produced settler colonialism and transatlantic slavery in the Americas (Byrd 2011; T. King 2019) as well as global capitalism, franchise colonization, empire, migrations, and diasporas (Spivak 1999; Stoler 2002; Mohanram 2007; N. Shah 2011). Hortense Spillers explains that chattel slavery, having "ungendered" Black female embodiment, sexualized the eviction of

Blackness from the human at the foundations of race and rule in the Americas ([1987] 2003, 68). Deborah Miranda (Costanoan Ohlone) portrays the sexualized colonization of Indigenous peoples and lands as context for the attempted "gendercide" of Indigenous gender diversity during the establishment of white settler supremacy (2010, 2013). These and related precedents for modern sexuality reside not in Europe or even in "the West"—which Edouard Glissant reminds us "is not in the West. It is a project, not a place" (1989, 2). They rest, rather, in the intimacies (Lowe 2015) of landed relations of violence linking European, African, Asian, Arab, and Indigenous American and Pacific peoples across centuries, all of which condition the present and future of modernity.

Modern sexuality discourses that emerged in European and white settler sexual science thus imported and innovated on colonial and imperial norms that already policed bodies and desires throughout the world. White supremacy had made heteropatriarchy a standard for western civilization: sexual differentiation reflected divine and state power in the white patriarch's possessive rule of colonized lands and peoples, the enslaved, and the nuclear family for profit (Moreton-Robinson 2015; Snorton 2017; Rifkin 2011; Day 2016). Queer theorists show that sexual science extended this project when it assigned a primitive sexual nature to racialized and colonized peoples (McClintock 1995; Sharpe 2010) or associated white sexual deviants with crossing the boundaries of Blackness or Indigeneity (Somerville 2000; Morgensen 2011). Jonathan Katz (1995) notes that sexual science first described "heterosexuality" as a deviation from moral restrictions of sexuality to procreative marriage, but it took more than recasting heterosexuality as sexually normal to turn it into a disciplinary system.

Eugenics specifically adapted heterosexuality to white supremacy by proposing and uplifting a normal sexual body within whiteness, thereby disabling other embodied lives and desires and deploying white normality at the center of national culture, economics, and law (Carter 2007; Herzog 2011; see also McRuer 2006). When sciences of transsexualism normalized heterosexuality by requiring trans people seeking transition to present as straight, they upheld cis-passing white heterosexuality as the acceptable embodiment amid ongoing violence against Black, racialized, and Indigenous trans people and trans practices that rejected norms (Skidmore 2011; Namaste 2015). Formed from these processes, heteronormativity distinguished normal from deviant sexuality not among diverse yet equal human beings but by tying normal sexuality to whiteness and placing sexual deviance along or beyond the boundaries of whiteness. Yet a door remained open to acceptance by appealing to whiteness, as when white sexual and gender minorities organized as good consumers, spouses, parents, or citizens and through this "homonormativity" (Duggan 2004) embraced a white nation, even policing its imagined racial and sexual Others in the spirit of what theorists call "homonationalism" (Puar 2007).

Appreciating these histories reveals that projecting heteronormativity as universal hinges on its links with white supremacy. Even embracing heterosexuality has not guaranteed access to heteronormativity for colonized or racialized peoples, whose appeals to heteronormativity may be read as impositions or reinventions (R. Ferguson 2004, 87; Cohen 1997; Denetdale 2017; L. Simpson 2017)—for the appearance of heteronormativity outside whiteness represents an innovation on heteronormativity's origin within and for whiteness (R. Ferguson 2005). To invoke heteronormativity in gender and sexuality studies, then, we must take an interest in the modern violences that condition it. Narrating it apart from race, colonialism, capital, or empire suggests an interest not in heteronormativity (as we now know it) but in some version of sexuality insulated by whiteness, which also would invite us to evade race in our account of it (Frankenberg 1994). And if that occurred, our account would simply fulfill heteronormativity's proper function: to propagate sexuality discourses that normalize white supremacy within modern life.

34

Heterosexuality
Jane Ward

When most people think about heterosexuality, they think about sexual and romantic partnerships between women and men, and consequently, they imagine that heterosexuality has an eternal history, a presence as long as human existence itself. But as historians of sexuality have pointed out, the actual history of heterosexuality is far more complicated because while heterosexual *behavior* has been an enduring and fundamental feature of human experience, the same cannot be said of heterosexual *identity*, which has a short and remarkably inconstant history (Blank 2012; Katz 1995; Foucault [1978] 1990).

For starters, it may come as a surprise that there were no "heterosexuals" until the late nineteenth century. This is because the terms *heterosexual* and *homosexual* did not exist until European physicians—all white men—coined and published them in medical journals in the 1860s. But even more striking is the fact that influential European sexologists, such as the Viennese doctor Richard von Krafft-Ebing, asserted that normal sexuality was motivated by an instinct to procreate, and therefore any sex acts that did not result in procreation were unhealthy and in need of medical correction—including many kinds of heterosexual sex. Because women and men could engage in sex acts together that did not result in conception (oral sex, anal sex, genital touching, and so on), the term *heterosexuality* was conceived, alongside *homosexuality*, as a perversion and a medical *disorder*—a far cry from its current meaning! Heterosexuality was an "abnormal or perverted appetite toward the opposite sex," and even as late as 1923, Merriam-Webster's dictionary defined heterosexuality as "a morbid (or unhealthy and abnormal) sexual passion for one of the opposite sex" (Katz 1995, 92).

But heterosexuality would undergo a public relations makeover just a few years later, one that would shape how people viewed sexuality throughout the twentieth century and into our own. Krafft-Ebing argued that perhaps when men and women have sex, even if they are engaged in nonreproductive sex acts, they are motivated by an innate, if unconscious, instinct to procreate. Voilà! Even when men and women might appear to be engaging in perverse sex acts with one another, they are actually doing something normal, even noble. Following this line of thinking, Krafft-Ebing redefined heterosexuality from a perversion to a healthy sexual impulse. By the 1930s, with agreement from American and European sexologists, heterosexuality became the gold standard for normal and natural sexuality; in 1934, its definition in Webster's dictionary changed to "a manifestation of sexual passion for one of the opposite sex; normal sexuality" (Katz 1995, 92).

These debates about procreation aside, scholars have also documented that patriarchy and white supremacy gave heterosexual relationships of past eras a different form and meaning than they possess today. In the American colonies, marriage was an economic and cultural imperative in which white women were compelled to submit to sex with husbands to produce male heirs and to do so for the good of the family, the church, and the newly forming nation (Blank 2012; Pateman 1988). White women held no property or custody rights and were frequently raped by their husbands, their desire and consent deemed irrelevant to the marital contract (Ward 2020; Block 2006). This construction of heterosexual sex—as an economic contract and an obligation controlled by white men—significantly constrained white women's opportunities to identify and express agentic heterosexual desire and foreclosed this possibility altogether for enslaved Black women, whose bodies were white men's property, to be subjected to frequent rape and torture (Hartman 2019; Block 2006; Spillers [1987] 2003). By contrast, women of privilege (wealthy white women, women of high status) were sometimes perceived as delicate and virtuous, deserving of men's chivalry and gentle seduction. But even in such cases, it was men who were ostensibly driven by an innate heterosexual desire, while women needed to be coaxed into sexual surrender or compliance. The point here is that what we now call heterosexuality was, not long ago, a compulsory arrangement benefitting white men—not a sexual orientation characterized by consenting and mutual sexual attraction between women and men "in love" or even in lust. In fact, as some nineteenth-century commentators understood it, this latter way of thinking about heterosexuality was dangerous, as it allowed for women's sexual agency and stood to threaten men's patriarchal power: "If a woman can satisfy a man's desire, he may become enamored of her, develop an affection bordering on love, and consequently, become subordinate to her" (Najmabadi 2005, 159).

It is important to note that sexological efforts to classify heterosexuality as an identity and cultural ideal occurred alongside the proliferation of the white supremacist sciences of the nineteenth and twentieth centuries, such as craniometry and eugenics. Both projects drew upon the other to invent hierarchies of health and morality and consequently created new ways to discipline people's bodies and desires in the service of racial, patriarchal, and socioeconomic hierarchies (Carter 2007; Somerville 2000). By declaring that procreative sex secured one's place among the ranks of the sexually normal, sexologists ensured that women's reproductive and sexual labor remained tied to men (G. Rubin

[1975] 1997). By constructing normal sexuality as that which occurred between dominant men and passive women in the private confines of marriage, sexologists also reinforced the dehumanization of African Americans, Native people, and immigrants who did not, or could not, organize their lives around a heteropatriarchal family structure (Spillers [1987] 2003; R. Ferguson 2004). The heterosexual ideal also pushed sexual freedom and experimentation underground, compelling people to be disciplined workers and predictable consumers who restricted their passionate impulses to the domestic sphere (Hartman 2019; R. Ferguson 2004; D'Emilio [1983] 1993). Moreover, the normative force of heterosexuality sent ripple effects around the globe, as it became a sharpened symbolic tool in the arsenals of imperialism, settler colonialism, and Jim Crow. White lawmakers in the United States, for instance, argued that Jim Crow segregation was a means of protecting vulnerable white women from the ostensible excesses of Black sexuality but would later also justify war and military occupation overseas by declaring the United States a proponent of women's sexual freedom.

As twentieth-century sexologists succeeded at establishing romantic and companionate heterosexual marriage as the ideal form of modern love, they also went about describing appropriate behavior for men and women in courtship and marriage. Here, too, the project of defining healthy heterosexual marriage in the United States was a racial project, as the most popular marriage books of the early twentieth century were written by proponents of the white supremacist eugenics movement, such as Havelock Ellis, William Robinson, Marie Stopes, and Harland William Long. These early marriage manuals sought to address any obstacles, including white men's violence against their wives and wives' resistance to sex with their husbands, that might prevent the flourishing of white families. These texts reveal yet another contradiction in the romantic narrative about eternal heterosexual love: they describe a status quo in which men and women commonly made each other miserable. For example, in 1903, the British sexologist and eugenicist Havelock Ellis explained that a husband naturally takes "a certain pleasure in manifesting his power over a woman by inflicting pain upon her [which is a] . . . quite normal constituent of the sexual impulse in man. . . . The pain he inflicts, or desires to inflict, is really part of his love, and . . . is not really resented by the woman on whom it is exercised" ([1903] 1998, 108–9). Marie Stopes, a British eugenicist, wrote at length about her concern that most new brides were repelled by the revelation of their husbands' naked bodies and "driven to suicide and insanity" by "the horror of the first night of marriage" ([1918] 1998, 118). William Robinson (1922, 25–26), another early twentieth-century eugenicist and sexologist, hoped that his marriage advice manuals would address the widespread "disgust," "deep hatred," and "desire for injury and revenge" that heterosexual couples felt for one another. Other sexologists promoted "hygiene" products—soaps, perfumes, makeup, douches, and bleaching—as the key to marital happiness, foreshadowing what would later become a multimillion-dollar beauty industry designed, in large part, to grease the wheels of heterosexual attraction.

With the rise of psychology at midcentury, efforts to normalize the difficulty of heterosexual relationships shifted focus away from men's and women's repellent bodies and toward their "opposite" personalities. The 1980s and 1990s were witness to a powerful backlash against feminist research on the social construction of gender, exemplified by the phenomenal best seller *Men Are from Mars, Women Are from Venus* (J. Gray 1992), which successfully circulated the idea that men and women are so fundamentally different that they might as well be from two different planets. Rejecting feminist efforts to redistribute gendered power and reimagine masculinity, popular wisdom about heterosexuality took for granted that the long-term success of straight relationships depended on women's willingness to tolerate and even eroticize men's limitations. Countering this logic, straight feminists worked to push heterosexuality in more liberatory directions but often ended up concretizing the gender binary in the process. For instance, in 1992, feminist writer Naomi Wolf called for a new mode of straightness she called "radical heterosexuality," which would require men to disavow patriarchal privilege, abolish legal marriage, and ensure women's financial independence. But alongside this vision, Wolf (1992, 30) doubled down on gender essentialism, explaining that women and men are so different, or at least so differently socialized, that they are, for all intents and purposes, in a "cross-cultural relationship."

In recent years, queer critiques of heterosexuality have emphasized the pervasive dysfunction of heterosexuality, characterized by straight women's "hetero pessimism" (Seresin 2019) and "cruel optimism" (Berlant 2011), or their disappointed resignation about their relationships with men and their attachment to a system reliant on their own suffering, respectively. Queer writers have speculated that "queering" straight sex practices—via BDSM, polyamory, "pegging" (women's anal penetration of men)—might be a direct path toward the alleviation of heterosexual misery (Shippers 2016; Glickman and Emirzian 2013). Others have focused less on how straight people's *sex* practices might be queered and more on the queering of straight ways of life by disavowing marriage and child-centeredness and valuing friendships and chosen family as much or more than blood connections (Halberstam 2012). Others have argued that "queering" is not what straight culture needs at all, but rather it must strive to achieve a "deeper" form of heterosexuality, wherein straight men

"like women so much that they actually like women" (Ward 2020, 155). While efforts to transform heterosexuality are varied in theory and approach, what is clear is that heterosexuality—as a sexual orientation characterized by a complex swirl of desire and misogyny, forged through centuries of patriarchy—remains a work in progress.

35

Identity

Joshua Chambers-Letson

The singularity of the word *identity* belies how identity is experienced as an inherent plurality. This statement has concrete political implications for femme, queer, and other minoritarian ways of being in the world. Critical theorist Hortense Spillers writes that "questions of identity [a]re neither automatic nor unfraught, but [a]re, instead, shot through with regimes of difference" (Spillers 2003, 9). Such a conception of identity stands in distinction to the dominant western political and epistemological tradition, in which it is routinely defined as self-similarity—a kind of sameness and even sovereignty of self forged against other axes of (exteriorized) difference. Take the reduction of identity to a discourse of "absolute and essential sameness" or "oneness" in the *Oxford English Dictionary* (*OED*), for instance (*OED Online*, "identity," n.d.). When identity is understood as a mode of (self)sameness that defines "who or what a person or thing is," the identity of the self routinely becomes defined against the difference of the other (who or what a person or thing is *not*).

With a conception of identity as selfsameness, the distinction between self and other, interior and exterior, and even between "friend and enemy" becomes the grounds of political exercise, the framework for establishing political hierarchy and achieving political disenfranchisement. This has led dominant thinkers in queer, psychoanalytic, and political theory to frame difference as a problem and even an antagonism to be attacked, disciplined, or destroyed within the realm of both the psychic (Bersani and Phillips 2008) and the

political (Schmitt [1927] 2007). Within the overlapping orders of white supremacy, cis-heteropatriarchy, and racial capitalism, the identity of a particular subject (man) is established as the golden mean, made abstract and universal, just as it is defined against the (violently regulated) differences of Black, brown, femme, queer, trans, Indigenous, or minoritarian ways of being in the world (Spivak 1999; Wynter 2003; Byrd 2011; Weheliye 2014; Z. Jackson 2020). The result is what Homi Bhabha describes as a "differentiating order of otherness" (2004, 64) that, he argues, organizes the uneven distribution of political power, resources, knowledge, violence, life, and death chances along and through identitarian axes such as race, gender, and sexuality.

For Judith Butler (following Michel Foucault), identity (and in particular, gender identity) is "produced precisely through the regulatory practices that generate coherent identities through the matrix of coherent gender norms" ([1990] 1999, 23; Foucault [1978] 1990). Certain identities ("coherent," but we could also say dominant sexual, gender, racial, and class-based forms of identity) are valued and elevated or protected as others are suppressed, devalued, exploited, and elided. The traditions of feminist and queer theory have long interrogated the political conditions that are productive of and produced by and instrumentalize identitarian axes such as race, gender, and sexuality (A. Y. Davis 1981; Lowe 1996; Spillers [1987] 2003; C. Reddy 2011). Along other lines, particularly in performance studies, scholars have tracked the methods through which the minoritarian practices of (re)making and undoing identity open up differential horizons of possibility for being in the world, if not for altogether new possibilities of what "being" and "world" might mean (Joseph 1999; Shimakawa 2002; McMillan 2016; Ruiz 2019; Muñoz 2020).

When minoritarian, queer, and feminist forms of political intervention are dismissed as "identity politics," it is helpful to remember that Black feminisms, woman of color feminisms, and queer of color critique have long contended that "identity politics" exist in response to the "differentiating orders of otherness" that constitute the various and overlapping regimes of white supremacy, cis-heteropatriarchy, racial capitalism, imperialism, and colonialism. The Combahee River Collective's insistence that "the most profound and potentially the most radical politics come directly out of our own identity, as opposed to working to end somebody else's oppression," was grounded in the Collective's "experience and disillusionment within [feminist] liberation movements, as well as their experiences on the periphery of the white male left, which in turn led to the need to develop a politics that was antiracist, unlike those of white women, and antisexist, unlike those of Black and white men" (Combahee River Collective [1977] 2015, 211). Identity politics, in the Combahee's frame, emerge out of necessity and in response to both the dominant and minoritarian cultures' ordering of the political along lines of identity. It is for this reason that Spillers asserts that the critique of "identity politics" has missed the mark: "The critique of 'identity politics' has positioned the wrong objects in its sights; it needs to ask, more precisely, how *status* is made and pay attention to *that* because *that* is the dialectic that plays here" (Spillers 2003, 21).

Considered thus, identity politics are best described as tools that queers, feminists, trans folk, and people of color have been forced to develop in response to the dominant social order. This is a social order produced by and productive of social hierarchy as well as the uneven distribution of power, resources, and life chances along axes of identity. The task is not to mount a defense of identity politics or even to promote a coherent or transparent conception of identity. It is, rather, to manipulate and deploy the performative force of identity in a strategic effort—echoing Gayatri Spivak's conception of, and later disavowal of the notion of, strategic essentialism (1988, 1999)—that critically elucidates how the master's house is made by and through identity as part of the ongoing effort to dismantle the many houses of the many masters (Lorde [1984] 2007b).

To this end, queer and feminist theorists have long contended that the "persistence and proliferation" (J. Butler [1990] 1999, 24) of differential practices of identity/identities in excess and refusal of desired norms (which is to say, in refusal of sameness and absolute singularity of "coherent identity" and sovereign selfsameness) both critique and reterritorialize the differentiating orders of otherness. Kimberlé Williams Crenshaw's foundational theorization of the intersectional forms that identity takes reformulated the politics of identity to recognize and account for the "difference *within* groups [that] contributes to tension among groups" ([1991] 1995, 357) as well as the forms of identitarian difference that may cut across or through a single being.

For performance theorist José Esteban Muñoz, building directly on the work of woman of color feminists (Norma Alarcón, Gloria Anzaldúa, Cherríe Moraga, Audre Lorde, and Chela Sandoval, in particular), the making of minoritarian identity is always already a practice of making "*identities-in-difference*" (Muñoz 1999, 6–7; Alarcón 1996, 129). The performative constitution of identity, in this sense, becomes a practice of navigating, surviving, thwarting, reterritorializing, and revising the political effects of the differentiating orders of otherness. Queer and trans transfigurations of gender and sexual identity may rearticulate understandings of identity as that which refuses selfsameness and the fixity of solid form to give way toward fluid ways of being and becoming that are constituted through difference and incommensurability.

Identity, here, is a practice that is never reducible to singularity, sameness, and exclusion but instead transitional and transformational, responsive, relational, and fluid (K. Green 2016; Santana 2017). This is not, as C. Riley Snorton (2016, 92) cautions, to assume that a politics of difference is inherently radical and liberating. It is instead to recognize the politics of difference that cohere in all discourses of identity and to account for the power effects that surface as a result. To conceptualize identity as inherently plural, being "shot through with regimes of difference" rather than as an experience of sovereign selfsameness, is thus to understand identity as a practice (one that is rich with internal contradiction, antagonism, and flow) rather than an ontology.

36

Imperialism
Shelley Streeby

Imperialism has long been a keyword for gender and sexuality studies, especially if we take Indigenous, Black, transnational, and woman of color feminisms and queer of color theories as the field's starting point and its foundational moment. In these scholarly conversations, imperialism has two primary meanings. The first refers to the expansion of a nation-state through force and violence into territories, contiguous or noncontiguous, by taking over land or "holding political dominion or control over dependent territories," as the *Oxford English Dictionary* (*OED Online*, "imperialism," n.d.) puts it, or some combination of the two. The second meaning focuses on what the *OED* refers to as "the extension and maintenance of a country's power or influence" through "commercial imperialism, economic imperialism; cultural, dollar, linguistic imperialism." Both land and influence-based forms of imperialism, which often overlap in practice, are inseparable from gender and sexuality in terms of how imperial nation-states and sites of empire are imagined as well as in imperialism's entanglement with formations of race, gender, and sexuality, such as the white patriarchal family, in struggles over land and political, economic, and cultural power.

In the 1970s and 1980s, US women of color theorized the inseparability of race, gender, sexuality, imperialism, and anti-imperialism. In *Sister Outsider*, Audre Lorde ([1984] 2007c) ends by analyzing the 1983 US invasion of Grenada, where her mother was born. Lorde situates this invasion in the context of a "160-year-old course of action called the Monroe Doctrine," in the name of which "america has invaded small Caribbean and Central American countries over and over again since 1823, cloaking these invasions under a variety of names" (181). She reminds readers that thirty-eight such invasions happened before 1917 and that in 1897, US marines landed in Puerto Rico to fight the Spanish-American War and never left. Relatedly, in their multiform *This Bridge Called My Back: Writings by Radical Women of Color*, to which Lorde also contributed, co-editors Cherríe Moraga and Gloria Anzaldúa (1981) amplify the voices of a number of anti-imperialist Black, Latina, Native American, and Asian American women. Toni Cade Bambara wrote the foreword to the first edition of *Bridge*, celebrating the "fashioning of potent networks of all the daughters of the ancient mother cultures" in the face of the "divide and conquer tactics of this moment" (vi), including the temporary offering of relative privileges to minority groups, such as "South Vietnamese and white Cubans," who "the government has made a commitment to in its greedy grab for empire" (vii). *Bridge* also included the Combahee River Collective's ([1977] 2015) "A Black Feminist Statement," which calls for "the destruction of the political-economic systems of capitalism and imperialism as well as patriarchy" (213).

Moraga called *Bridge*'s writers "veteranas of the Chicano, Black Power, Asian American, and American Indian Movement" and the "anti-war/anti-imperialist movement against the US involvement in Vietnam" (1981, xvi), thereby highlighting how the Vietnam War was a critical flash point for contributors from groups whose histories were shaped by US, European, and Asian imperialisms; that served in disproportionate numbers in the war; and that were active in the antiwar movement. These transimperial connections are made throughout *Bridge* by Black feminists, such as Lorde, Bambara, and Clarke, as well as Chicanas, including

Anzaldúa and Moraga, and other Latinas, such as Rosario Morales, who calls herself "puertorican and US american, working-class & middle class, housewife and intellectual, feminist, marxist, and anti-imperialist" (Moraga and Anzaldúa 1981, 97). *Bridge* shows how imagining a "Third World feminist future" (liii) defined in opposition to US military and economic imperialism at home and abroad also hailed Mitsuye Yamada, who calls herself a "Third World" and "Asian Pacific American" (74) woman, and Lakota writer Barbara Cameron, who refers to herself as both "Third World" and "Native American" even as she criticizes some versions of Third Worldism for being too "narrow" (51) and not making enough space for Indigenous people. For her part, Anzaldúa writes that her "vision of radical Third World feminism" is that "women on the bottom throughout the world" can create an "international feminism" based on working with "*El Mundo Zurdo, the left-handed world*: the colored, the queer, the poor, the female, the physically challenged" (218). A classic text of woman of color feminism, *Bridge* theorizes how gender, sexuality, and collectivities beyond nations and empires were shaped by antiwar and anti-imperialist commitments and movements, especially opposition to US imperialism.

Another body of work that made imperialism central to gender and sexuality studies was one by the Birmingham School of Cultural Studies, which in the 1980s questioned the nonrecognition of how British imperialism shaped popular white racisms in first-wave cultural studies scholarship. This critique was made very powerfully in the Centre for Contemporary Cultural Studies' (CCCS; 1982) collective book *The Empire Strikes Back: Race and Racism in 70's Britain*, co-authored by Hazel Carby, a key figure in the history of Black transnational feminist theory who, in England at the beginning of her career, contributed two essays and pushed the CCCS to analyze gender and sexuality in relation to race, nation, and empire. Her essay "Schooling in Babylon" criticizes the "imperialist reasoning" Black students faced in English schools and analyzes the gendered dynamics of representing Black family structures as pathological when British imperialism is simultaneously celebrated and erased (Carby 1982a). The essay "White Women Listen! Black Feminism and the Boundaries of Sisterhood" affiliates with *Bridge* as Carby (1982b) cites the Combahee River Collective and Audre Lorde to raise the subject of white women's roles in imperialism and colonialism and the power they wield because of their race. Also foundational was Carby's 1985 work reconstructing the world of nineteenth-century US Black women writers, including the political thought of 1890s Black feminists such as Anna Julia Cooper, Frances Harper, and Pauline Hopkins, who theorized interrelations between imperialism and domestic racism; Carby suggests that Cooper, for instance, believed "imperialism linked all those oppressed under the domination of the United States" (1982a, 188). In Carby's memoir, coming full circle, the story of the "everyday ties, relations and intricate interdependencies of empire and colonialism" (2019, 1) is told through the history of her family, especially her Jamaican father, who served in the British Royal Air Force, and white Welsh mother, who was raised in rural poverty. Here Carby repeats an insight from Stuart Hall about how the celebration of the British imperial past and the nonacknowledgment of imperial violence shape white perceptions of British national identity and Black people, as she explores "how people are inscribed into ideologies of empire and beliefs of whiteness that enable them to feel superior even when desperately poor" (2).

In England, empire was publicly recognized in Empire Days that Carby vividly remembers her mother celebrating, even as imperialism's effects on the present were repressed. In the United States, however, imperial amnesia was foundational to Cold War ideologies that opposed US democracy to Soviet imperialism and imagined empire building as at most only a brief episode in a long history of the United States benevolently extending to unenlightened others the benefits of progress and modernity. The idea that the United States was not imperialist was shaken, however, by the Vietnam War, US intervention in Central America in the 1980s, and in the early 1990s, the Columbus quincentennial and wars in the Middle East, which made imperialism newly visible, provoking an imperial turn across several fields of scholarship. Connecting "internal categories of gender, race, and ethnicity" to "the global dynamics of empire-building" (Kaplan and Pease 1993, 16), *Cultures of US Imperialism*, an anthology co-edited by literary scholars Amy Kaplan and Donald Pease, centered imperialism in US history and culture despite a long tradition of scholarship defining American uniqueness as antithetical to imperialism. Kaplan's introduction recognized the work of an emergent Chicano studies that was beginning to "redress" the conceptual limits of the "frontier, by replacing it with the borderlands" (16) theorized by Anzaldúa (1987) just a few years earlier in *Borderlands / La Frontera: The New Mestiza*, which posits connections among psychological, sexual, and spiritual borderlands and the physical borderland of the Texas–US Southwest / Mexican border and makes queerness and language central to unsettling frontier frameworks and white mythologies of an anti-imperial United States. Kaplan's (2002) *Anarchy of Empire in the Making of US Culture* also contributed to American studies' imperial turn, especially "Manifest Domesticity," where she explores how nineteenth-century white women writers famous for creating a middle-class culture of sentiment connected domesticity to imperialism.

In the 1990s and 2000s, Black transnational anti-imperialist feminist thought continued to significantly impact gender and sexuality studies as writers such as Sylvia Wynter and M. Jacqui Alexander responded to old and new forms of US imperialism in the Middle East and the Caribbean. The work of Wynter—a Jamaican playwright, philosopher, and literary scholar who came to the United States in 1974 to teach Third World literature at the University of California, San Diego, before moving to Stanford and then back to Jamaica—asks readers to confront multiple histories of imperialism, conquest, genocide, and slavery encoded through gender and sexuality and undergirding violent European ideologies of the human across the Americas (McKittrick 2015). In her generative text *Pedagogies of Crossing: Meditations on Feminism, Sexual Politics, Memory, and the Sacred*, Alexander (2005), who moved from Trinidad and Tobago to work as a professor in the United States and Toronto before returning to her birthplace to start the Tobago Centre for the Study and Practice of Indigenous Spirituality, cites the US 1991 Gulf War and the 2003 US invasion of Iraq as examples of "the seismic imperial shifts that characterize this moment" (2). Both US wars involved military power but focused more on securing control over oil than taking over land. Alexander considers US imperialism in terms of military interventions, militarism expanding throughout societies, economic policies, tourism, and the imperial university. Along with analyzing US rescue narratives in Afghanistan and how imperial military service shapes race and sexuality outside the metropole, Alexander emphasizes "the production and maintenance of sexualized hegemony" (4) through state institutions and everyday life. Thinking about erotic autonomy as a politics of decolonization in relation to feminism, tourism, and the state in the Bahamas, Alexander names "imperial desire" (11) fueled by capitalism as a problem but insists on the role of state power in combination with capitalism. She also anatomizes a "citizenship for empire" in the Caribbean, which connects political and national belonging to militarism and state power and contrasts it with a "citizenship for self-determination" (3), which breaks with imperial structures to imagine new forms of belonging. She tracks "new structures of imperialism such as structural adjustment" (272) and the "ideological trafficking" (12) among capitalism, the state, and knowledge production in the academy while insisting that "to ignore the centrality of imperialism is to continue to live a dangerous privilege that only the analytic habit of mistakenly conflating capitalism and democracy can confer" (252). Alexander credits the "confluence of different geographies of feminism" (4) and "belatedly with a 'queer' theorizing both inside and outside the academy" (9) with inspiring her theories of gender, sexuality, race, and imperialism, writing after Anzaldúa's death that "with Chicanas and Puertorriquenas" and the other *Bridge* writers, she shared a "sensibility of a politicized non-belonging" (263) from the United States that became a source of connection and interdependence.

Woman of color and transnational feminist theory also shaped early twenty-first-century research on intimacies of empire, which analyzes the "intimate" spheres of sexual, reproductive, and household relations as sites of empire. Building on work such as Carby's and Kaplan's, anthropologist and historian Ann Laura Stoler's (2006) edited collection *Haunted by Empire: Geographies of Intimacy in North American History* showcases emergent scholarship on intimacies of North American imperial cultures, with essays focusing on the politics of prostitution, transnational adoption in Latin America, state policies on hygiene, and other examples in which bodies, families, sexualities, households, and imperialisms are entangled.

Nayan Shah, for instance, explores how in the early twentieth-century US West, controversies over marriages of Hindu migrant laborers reveal how imperial states administer intimate ties in legislation, judicial trials, and registration and licensing procedures, as they decide which unions will be sanctioned; this work is an example of queer of color critique, which emerged in the mid-2000s as a field that explicitly built on woman of color and transnational feminism to analyze linkages among sexuality, gender, race, nation, labor, and intersections of identity and struggle. Another contribution to the "intimacies of empire" conversation that explicitly builds on woman of color and transnational feminism is Lisa Lowe's (2015) *Intimacies of Four Continents*, which focuses on the "circuits, connections, associations, and mixings of differentially laboring peoples" (21) that materialized in response to multiple imperialisms in the nineteenth-century Caribbean and how liberal-imperial powers divided up humanity into categories of "geography, nation, caste, religion, gender, sexuality, and other social differences" (7). Lowe theorizes the convergence of older forms of military and economic imperialism with British free trade imperialism and "new forms of imperial sovereignty exercised through 'rule of law,' 'order and progress,' and 'keeping the peace' in the colonial world" (107) as well as an "Anglo-American imperial settler imaginary" that "continues to be elaborated today, casting differentiated peoples across the globe in relation to liberal ideas of civilization and human freedom" (8).

Lowe's theorizing of an Anglo-American "imperial settler imaginary" suggests how imperialism is a force within imperial states and not just outside their boundaries, a point that Native studies scholar Maureen Konkle (2008) makes central to her 2006 analysis of US "liberal-imperialism," a form of imperialism that presents itself as benevolent and civilizing, requiring "paternalistic authority over the colonized" (299), including education and reform programs, while erasing Indigenous ownership and Indigenous political society. Chickasaw theorist Jodi Byrd similarly emphasizes US empire's ties to Enlightenment liberal political and economic thought as she analyzes the "racial, gendered, classed, and sexed normativities of an imperialism that has arisen out of an ongoing settler colonialism" (2011, 20). Arguing that "bringing indigeneity and Indians front and center to discussions of US empire as it has traversed Atlantic and Pacific worlds is a necessary intervention at this historical moment" (xiii), Byrd criticizes poststructuralist theory, postcolonial work on imperial intimacies, and American studies scholarship on intersections of imperialism, race, gender, and sexuality for too often relegating "American Indians to the side of the already-doneness that begins to linger as unwelcome guest to the future" (20). In *Mark My Words: Native Women Mapping Our Nations*, Seneca scholar Mishuana Goeman (2013) broadens the focus to analyze mappings of "an imperial imaginary" (20) in Canada as well as the United States and how Native women (re) mapped spaces of the economic, political, and social, including Mohawk writer E. Pauline Johnson, who provided ways to think about "imperial expansion through intimate relationships" and provoked "a much-needed discussion of race, gender, and nation" (85). Lenape theorist Joanne Barker insists on the importance of holding on to "harsher terms" such as *imperialism* because they facilitate a more precise understanding of current militarized violence and, like Byrd, suggests that "the empire/imperialism of the nation-state" must be at the forefront of a critical analysis in order to understand the "current structure" and "social formation" of the United States as a "global force" in "relation to Indigenous peoples within its various kinds of borders" (2014a). The essays in Barker's (2017) edited collection *Critically Sovereign: Indigenous Gender, Sexuality, and Feminist Studies*, much like those in *Bridge*, bring together

Indigenous and feminist perspectives to address the inherent and ongoing violences of imperialist formations in the United States and Canada and to consider coalitional action and decolonial futures.

In the twenty-first century, new interdisciplinary scholarship illuminates how old and new forms of imperialism intersecting with gender and sexuality colonize the future through speculative instruments of accumulation, such as debt, financial derivatives, and war scenarios, and how insurgent speculative practices create other pathways diverging from imperialism. Melinda Cooper (2008) suggests that since the 1980s, the life sciences have "played a commanding role" in US "economic and imperialist self-invention" (4), particularly through a new "debt imperialism" (12) deeply interconnected with the gender, sex, and race fundamentalisms of white Christian "right to life" politics. In a kind of "speculative reinvention of the future" (11) without foundations, since the 1971 shift to the US treasury bill as the international monetary standard, Cooper argues, "the world's greatest power derives its funds from an influx of perpetually renewed debt" (30) that never has to be paid because of US military power; meanwhile, other nations are forced to undertake austerity measures. In response to the uncertainties about whether this debt will be reterritorialized within the United States and to the precariousness of this lack of a foundation outside of military power for speculative instruments of accumulation, evangelical fundamentalists increasingly supportive of US military interventions in the Middle East struggle to "impose the property form in and over the uncertain future" (171), with the "unborn" representing "the future American nation in its promissory form, the creative power of debt recontained within a sexual politics of family life" (168). Aimee Bahng's (2018) work clarifies how, in such speculative forms of imperialism, "temporality gets narrativized in the service of imperial conquest" in ways that range historically from "the fantastical maps that facilitated the settler colonial conquest of the Americas" to contemporary derivatives markets, with their "calculation and redistribution of projected risk and volatility," which render the future "terra nullius, emptied of its true uncertainty, filled with securitized risk, and sanctified by a positivist accounting of projection" (12). At the same time, Bahng calls attention to how speculative practices from below "participate in the cultural production of futurity" (2) by "excavating forgotten histories of science and empire" and "seeking out queer affinities that belie privatized futures" (7) and the imperial world order's modes of securitization. Ronak Kapadia (2019) similarly analyzes the production of futurity in the "speculative practices" (166) of diasporic Palestinians across a range of "modes of expressive culture aligned with social justice movements" (165) that "underscore and move us beyond the power of imperial and settler security state control," thereby portending "the queer feminist fugitive ends of US empire and its forever wars" (152). As it has in times of war, state violence, militarism, and deepening international economic inequalities and in response to the leadership of anti-imperialist movements, holding on to the "harsher" term *imperialism* has once again taken on special urgency for scholars of gender and sexuality.

37

Indigeneity

Shannon Speed

The definition of the term *Indigeneity* would seem at first glance to be straightforward, meaning "Indigenousness" or "state of being Indigenous." The suffix *-ity* added to the noun *Indigene* forms an abstract noun that refers to a state or condition of being. In practice, however, the term is far more complex, as it begs the question of what it means to be "Indigenous" in the first place and in turn evokes difficult questions of authenticity and belonging, questions powerfully shaped by centuries of settler state dynamics of Native elimination. Due to its coconstitutive relationship with the settler state, "Indigeneity" is also intimately entangled with race, gender, land, and sovereignty in ways that are often ideologically obscured. Adding to the contentious nature of the term is that fact that what it describes troubles other popular and scholarly notions, such as the "postcolonial." Further, while it is often used as such, "Indigeneity" is not precisely equivalent to "Indigenousness." If it were, we would not have need of two terms. Rather, "Indigeneity" evokes a belonging in a larger, indeed global, collectivity of people who share in some form that state of being Indigenous as against the non-Indigenous. Let's unpack this.

As Audra Simpson succinctly states, "To speak of Indigeneity is to speak of colonialism" (2007, 67). Indigenous people were simply *people* prior to colonial invasion. The term itself arose much later in the context of twentieth-century international organizing, particularly at the International Labor Organization (ILO) and the United Nations, and it is significant that in the ILO

Convention—the first international agreement on Indigenous rights—the definition of Indigenous peoples is based on "descent from the populations which inhabited the country, or a geographical region to which the country belongs, at the time of conquest or colonization" (ILO, n.d., article 1b). *Indigeneity* is thus defined in terms of originality to a place and in relation to colonization. The fact that the term *Indigeneity* exists at all speaks to the ongoing nature of that colonial occupation because if Indigenous peoples were not colonized, there would be no need to define them in relation to the colonizer. In his theorization of settler colonialism, Patrick Wolfe famously noted that it is "a structure, not an event" (2006, 387), highlighting the persistent, ongoing nature of colonial projects.

A fundamental aspect of settler colonialism is a "logics of elimination" (Wolfe 2006, 388) that has always sought to "destroy to replace," or dispossess Indigenous peoples of land and replace them as rightful occupiers (Meissner and Powys Whyte 2017). This eliminatory logic has contributed greatly to creating the fraught context in which what it means to be Indigenous and who qualifies to belong in this category are defined. Because settler states deployed racial logics based on notions of blood purity to the quest for elimination, race is inseparable from Indigenous identity in complicated ways. For example, in the United States, the racialization of Indigenous people employed the opposite logic of that applied to Black people. The one-drop rule that asserted one "drop" of Black blood made one Black worked in reverse for Native peoples—one drop of non-Native blood rendered them non-Indigenous (Kauanui 2008; Meissner and Powys Whyte 2017). "Blood quantum" (later conflated with DNA; see TallBear 2013) became an important defining characteristic of Indigeneity, at first imposed and regulated by the federal government and later handed down to tribes. While the US experience is unique, in all settler states, racial mixing has served as a form of erasure, disqualifying or complicating claims to Indigenous identity or rights (see, e.g., Saldaña-Portillo 2016; S. Jackson 2012). Further, as Harris has cogently argued, because the legal racialization of both Natives in the service of seizure and appropriation of land and Blacks in the service of seizure and appropriation of labor and because Native elimination serves land dispossession and facilitates white settler replacement, both Indigeneity and Blackness are bound up in legal constructs justifying white property ownership (C. Harris 1993; see Moreton-Robinson 2015 for Australia).

Just as Indigeneity cannot be defined absent an understanding of race, it also cannot be understood without an analysis of settler colonialism as a gendered process (Arvin, Tuck, and Morrill 2013). Foundationally, gender violence has always been constitutive of settler colonization, both materially through forced miscegenation and symbolically, as the brutal taking of Native women's bodies paralleled the ruthless appropriation of their lands (L. Hall 2009; Barker 2014b; Deer 2014; Million 2013). The settler imposition of heteropatriarchal norms, which TallBear refers to as "settler sexualities," was part of the settler drive to undermine the strength of Indigenous kinship networks and construct "monogamous, couple-centric nuclear famil[ies] co-produced with private property, including the partitioning of tribal land base into individually owned allotments held under men's names" (2013, 6; see also Morgensen 2010, 2012). Heteropatriarchy is thus an operating logic of settler capitalism that constructs Indigenous peoples in highly gendered ways. Settler-imposed patriarchal norms have led to gender inequities in politics of belonging, as some Tribal Nations have adopted membership rules based on patrilineal and not matrilineal descent (see Curry 2001 for an examination of the notable case of *Santa Clara Pueblo v. Martinez*).

In these processes, race, through blood quantum, is bound up with gender dynamics in ways that intersectionally disadvantage Indigenous women who have repeatedly brought this question to the fore in contexts from the community level to the international, particularly in organizing at the UN Indigenous Women's Forum (Kuokkanen 2012; see Corntassel 2007 for critical perspective). Further, the heteronormative nature of this colonial logic conditioned the formation of modern sexuality. As Morgensen has analyzed, "[Settlers] constructed diverse practices of gender and sexuality as signs of a general primitivity among Native peoples . . . [and] produced a colonial necropolitics that framed Native peoples as queer populations marked for death. Colonization produced the biopolitics of modern sexuality that I call 'settler sexuality': a white national heteronormativity that regulates Indigenous sexuality and gender by supplanting them with the sexual modernity of settler subjects" (2010, 106). Settler-imposed norms of gender and sexuality thus shape the modern experience of Indigenous individuals and communities in multiple and ongoing ways.

However, while the settler state constitutes Indigeneity in various ways, it is important to note that Indigeneity also constitutes the settler state. As Povinelli writes, "The sociological figure of the indigenous (the first or prior) person is necessary to produce the modern western form of nation-state sovereignty even as it continually undermines this same form" (2011b, 13). Kauanui also flagged the constitutive (and contestatory) nature of Indigeneity for settler states in what she calls "enduring Indigeneity": "The operative logic of settler colonialism may be to 'eliminate the native' . . . but indigenous peoples exist, resist, and persist; and . . . settler colonialism is a structure that endures indigeneity, as it holds out against it" (2016, para. 1). Thus, the settler state constructs itself and its sovereignty against its Indigenous Other, an Other with a "prior" claim to sovereignty (Povinelli 2011b).

The ongoing nature of settler structures and the enduring nature of Indigeneity engender an inherent tension with the notion of postcoloniality, leading to what Byrd and Rothberg refer to as an "uncompleted dialogue between postcolonial and indigenous perspectives" (Cook-Lynn 1997, 4). As they note, the existence of Indigenous peoples experiencing current colonial occupation presents challenges to both the periodicity and the presumptions contained in the "post": in short, the notion that colonialism is over (Cook-Lynn 1997). Pointing out the multiple ways that this is not the case, Weaver concludes his examination of postcolonial theory by noting, "As long, however, as Western nation-states remain kleptocracies based on the taking of native lands, as long as autochthones are denied sovereignty and are pushed toward assimilation into the dominant culture, the postcolonial moment for indigenous peoples will not have arrived" (2000, 235).

Perhaps due to its emergence in the context of global Indigenous organizing, the term *Indigenous* carries a further implication—that of belonging in a global community of Indigenous as against non-Indigenous peoples. As Merlan writes, "The term *indigenous*, long used to distinguish between those who are 'native' and their 'others' in specific locales, has also become a term for a geocultural category, presupposing a world collectivity of 'indigenous peoples' in contrast to their various 'others'" (2009, 303). This sense is captured in the work of Chadwick Allen (2017) on what he calls "trans-Indigeneity," for example, in which he suggests replacing our dominant conceptions of vertical Indigenous–settler relations with lateral Indigenous connections. For some scholars, this sense of Indigeneity undermines the specificity of Indigenous experience in specific contexts. Further, it can tend to result

in the homogenization of Indigeneity based on external (settler) imaginings, often tied to "cultural alterity, marginality, physicality and morality, which leave an increasing number of people vulnerable to accusations of inauthenticity" (Paradies 2006, 355). There are thus tensions inherent in the work that the word does of highlighting shared experience, at the expense of specificity, that may in some circumstances have unintended consequences.

Interesting questions also manifest when Indigenous people migrate. It should be noted that Indigenous people have always migrated—since long before European colonial invasion—though colonialism has in many ways accelerated these types of movement. The common and somewhat reified notion that Indigeneity is inherently tied to a direct relationship to ancestral lands from time immemorial is often reinforced by national and international laws that base Indigenous land claims on proving such a relationship (Hale 2006). However, while for some Indigenous people the relationship to their ancestral lands has not been ruptured by colonial processes, for many others, it has. Those who have migrated due to forced removal, relocation policies, wars, environmental issues, or other reasons—whether they have moved from rural to urban settings or crossed settler-imposed borders—may thus experience challenges to their authenticity as Indigenous people (Blackwell, Boj López, and Urrieta 2017; Fujikane and Okamura 2008; Ramirez 2007).

Here I have very briefly presented only a few of the complex and coconstitutive intersections of Indigeneity with race, gender, sexuality, globalization, and mobility/migration and pointed to the ways each of these affects the matter of belonging inherent in the term. While none of these can be ignored, perhaps the most important aspect of Indigeneity is this: indigeneity "refers to a person's status or responsibilities, self-perceived or delegated by others, as a member or descendent of one or more Indigenous peoples or communities" (Meissner and Powys Whyte 2017, 1). This type of definition emphasizes one's relationships, responsibilities, and engagements within a community or Tribal Nation rather than externally (all too often settler) defined criteria—a definition that refers to the way one lives in relation to and in the world. Indigenous feminists have been vocal in forefronting relations to community, to land, and to sovereignty as key to lived Indigeneity (Chirix García 2003; L. Hall 2009; Weir 2017; Tzul [2015] 2019; Arvin, Tuck, and Morrill 2013). In so doing, Indigenous feminists have also challenged dominant modes of feminist theorizing by "attending to Indigenous feminist ontology, epistemology, ethics and politics" (Weir 2017, 257). Thus by affirming relationality as a defining aspect of Indigeneity, Indigenous feminists have reclaimed Indigenous perspective and voice from what were, in political practice and in scholarly analyses, all too often western-based conceptions of what it means to be Indigenous.

38

Intersectionality

Jennifer C. Nash

Intersectionality appears in women's studies programs' and departments' mission statements, as a touchstone of queer and feminist activist work, in NGO metrics for assessing the fundability of various efforts, and in the neologisms of diversity and inclusion offices at universities and corporations alike. It is hailed as a transformative theory, an interdisciplinary method, and the cure for feminism's and society's ailments, and it is bemoaned as a toxin that might poison contemporary feminism because of its imagined demand to account for complex power structures and multiple identity positions. Perhaps no term has circulated in feminist theory and politics with the speed and intensity of *intersectionality*, which now stands as a shorthand for the field-defining and programmatic ambitions of women's studies and fields that are in solidarity with academic feminism. More than anything, intersectionality has become the preeminent location of a dense set of feminist desires, longings that reveal the continued centrality of racial anxieties to feminist practice.

Intersectionality has come to be treated by some as a synonym for *Black feminism* and for *Black woman*, even though, as I reveal here, its critical itinerary is far more complex. It is often celebrated as precisely what can disrupt so-called white feminism and even save feminism from its racial exclusivity. This essay reflects on how a term that instantiated a feminist project attentive to the fundamental simultaneity of multiple structures of domination—to how race, gender, class, and sexuality collaborate to shape the most spectacular and most invisible aspects of our lives—has come to be the central keyword of contemporary feminist theory and practice, one recruited to perform so much work and for so many competing intellectual and political projects, investments, and commitments.

While this essay is largely focused on intersectionality's place in the US academy, it is crucial to note that in the wake of Donald Trump's 2016 election, intersectionality has enjoyed its largest and most visible public stage. It was hailed as a necessary intervention in feminist politics, one that could explain how and why US white women voted for Trump and one that could construct a feminist platform attentive to power's workings on marginalized bodies. Flavia Dzodan's (2011) assertion that "my feminism will be intersectional or it will be bullshit" has traveled far from the context in which she was writing to stand as a general plea for the urgency of intersectionality to rescue feminism from a conception of gender that neglects its imbrication with race, class, and sexuality; from a narrow conception of equity; and from a vision of justice that fails to see the intimate connections among myriad forms of violence, from police brutality to environmental racism, from Black maternal mortality to sexual harassment. This vision of a capacious and robust feminism committed to all forms of justice has come to seem even more urgent as white women—often described as a homogenous category—are represented as more invested in upholding white supremacy than in laboring for gender equity and thus as in need of either committing themselves to intersectionality to rescue themselves or surrendering the feminist banner entirely. In this same context of political urgency, intersectionality was described as something that could dismantle feminist unity—if such a thing ever existed—in the wake of the election. If feminists fought over how to construct an "intersectional" women's march, some felt that they were not

directing attention toward the actual source of violence: the Trump administration. *Intersectionality*, perhaps unlike any other term in feminist theory, has a robust life inside and outside of the university, even as its connotations and political aspirations can vary across these sites.

Legal scholar and critical race feminist Kimberlé Williams Crenshaw coined the term *intersectionality* in two foundational articles that mapped the legal invisibility of Black women in multiple doctrinal contexts, including antidiscrimination, domestic violence, and rape laws. In "Demarginalizing the Intersection of Race and Sex" (Crenshaw 1989), she describes the specific ways that Black women's experiences of discrimination—experiences that are often simultaneously raced and gendered—are, because of the legal system's very design, rendered invisible and thus left without redress. As Crenshaw notes, a doctrinal insistence that Black women fit their experiences of harm into frameworks that center either race or gender "guarantees that their needs will seldom be addressed" (1989, 150). Intersectionality is a tool for exposing how law's architecture hinges on the invisibility of Black women's experiences of violence and reveals that the challenge for Black feminist theory and politics is to develop a juridical grammar that can make visible—and even redressable—this harm. Intersectionality is also an analytic that asks how we might reconceptualize discrimination, harm, violence, and power around the experiences of the multiply rather than the singly marginalized. Crenshaw notes, "It is somewhat ironic that those concerned with alleviating the ills of racism and sexism should adopt such a top-down approach to discrimination. If their efforts instead began with addressing the needs and problems of those who are most disadvantaged and with restructuring and remaking the world where necessary, then others who are singularly disadvantaged would also benefit" (167). For

Crenshaw, the Black woman is the quintessentially multiply marginalized figure; her very body is evidence of how power structures collude to subordinate the most vulnerable. If law were to center its efforts to alleviate discrimination on Black women, the most marginalized bodies, it would effectively secure freedom for everyone.

In a second article, "Mapping the Margins: Intersectionality, Identity Politics, and Violence against Women of Color," Crenshaw (1991) offered another articulation of intersectionality that tethered it to the political and the representational. For Crenshaw, political intersectionality describes how "women of color are situated within at least two subordinated groups that frequently pursue conflicting political agendas" (1252). The continued organization of US politics around race or gender often leaves women of color "splitting [their] political energies" or "finding themselves without a singular group, cause, or organization that speaks to their political needs and desires" (1252). Moreover, the continued association of feminism with white women and of antiracist work with Black men shores up the political invisibility of Black women. Crenshaw's concept of representational intersectionality roots itself in an analysis of debates around the obscenity charges levied against the rap group 2 Live Crew in 1990. Crenshaw returns to the debates around the obscenity charges, insisting both on the necessity of a recognition of the violence Black patriarchy inflicts on Black women and on the urgency of recognizing that condemnations of 2 Live Crew's music had little investment in protecting Black women from sexual harm.

While Crenshaw is largely cited—and celebrated—as coining *intersectionality*, many Black feminists have underscored that the Black feminist intellectual tradition has been marked by an investment in thinking about race and gender as coconstitutive and Black women as subjects marked by standing in a densely trafficked intersection. If Crenshaw's analysis foregrounded the legal implications of standing "in the intersection," other Black feminist scholars have brought different disciplinary tools and methods to bear on the project of thinking about power's complex and simultaneous workings. For example, the Combahee River Collective's ([1977] 2015) Marxist Black lesbian investment in thinking race, gender, class, and sexuality together is now often hailed as a critical predecessor to Crenshaw's work, even as Crenshaw's work was particularly oriented toward the juridical. Combahee notes, "We believe that sexual politics under patriarchy is as pervasive in Black women's lives as are the politics of class and race. We also often find it difficult to separate race from class from sex oppression because in our lives they are most often experienced simultaneously" (79). Black feminist work by Frances Beal ([1969] 2008, 176) on "double jeopardy" highlights the extractive violence capitalism inflicts on Black women and calls for "creating new institutions that will eliminate all forms of oppression for all people. We must begin to rewrite our understanding of traditional personal relationships between man and woman." Deborah King (1988) builds on Beal's conception of "jeopardy" to describe the interactive and "multiplicative" relationship among structures of domination. She notes, "The modifier 'multiple' refers not only to several, simultaneous oppressions but to the multiplicative relationships among them as well. In other words, the equivalent formulation is racism multiplied by sexism multiplied by classism" (47). This work, along with crucial contributions by Evelyn Brooks Higginbotham and others, collectively marks crucial nodes of Black feminist theorizing on the simultaneity of power's workings.

If *intersectionality* is a term that generates intense feminist feelings, scholars wrestle not just with the term's current valance but with the term's origins and genealogies and with how credit should be allocated for intersectionality's invention and now near dominance in feminist theory. The preoccupation with crediting intersectionality's innovators particularly circulates in Black feminist theoretical writings as part of a larger Black feminist critique of the university's cannibalization of Black women scholars, uptake of Black women's work, and refusal to cite Black women. Ann duCille, for example, describes her ambivalence about Black feminism's representation as an "anybody-can-play pick-up game performed on a wide-open, untrammeled field" (duCille 1994, 603), one where scholars with little training in Black feminist histories produce work that fails to honor—or even mention—earlier scholarship written by Black women. Underpinning this critique is a concern with the material labor Black women performed in institutionalizing Black feminist studies—labor that, as myriad Black feminists have indicated, quite often kills Black women academics. In Barbara Christian's analysis of Black feminism's location in the academy, she warns that we must "be clear about the dire situation that African American women academics face" (2007, 214), and Grace Hong—drawing on Christian's work—writes, "So many of the black feminists of Christian's generation have died—struck down by cancer and other diseases" (2008, 96). The collective sense that Black feminist work is chic while the Black women who produced the work remain uncited has generated a collective contemporary effort to #CiteBlackWomen, a plea to critically interrogate which work is placed at the center of the field and to honor Black women's scholarly contributions.

The labor of excavating intersectional histories has been taken up with considerable urgency in the last five years by scholars, including Brittney Cooper and Vivian May. This effort has often been marked by a political desire to recover Black women's intellectual histories, a term Cooper invests in to elevate Black women's

theoretical, political, and creative work. This scholarly push to historicize intersectionality has also been underpinned by a refusal to succumb to the presentism of many contemporary feminist conversations about intersectionality by insisting on the long roots of the term and its preoccupations. Cooper and May have collectively reminded us of the crucial contributions of Mary Church Terrell, Anna Julia Cooper, Fannie Lou Hamer, and Sojourner Truth to intersectional theorizing, thus stretching intersectional genealogies at least a century before they are often thought to begin. Yet their efforts have also cemented the idea that intersectional thinking is all that Black feminist theory has generated rather than one of multiple analytics and preoccupations that have marked centuries of critical thought. As much as reading the intersectional canon as a long one is productive, we might also ask how we would understand Black feminist theory anew if we read its varied preoccupations, including around experimental writing, questions of the self and subjectivity, love, intimacy, friendship, and vulnerability.

What the genealogical approach to intersectionality has revealed is that Black feminist theory has a long history of thinking about time and power together. Black feminist theory has developed a conception of power attuned to simultaneity, to how structures of domination collaborate, recruit each other, and work in collusion to secure the positions of the dominant and the marginalized. In the same way that Black feminist theory has developed a powerful palimpsestic conception of history, one attentive to how past and present coexist, intersectionality suggests another way that Black feminists foreground the temporal as a crucial axis for a robust understanding of the social world.

While the excavation of these genealogies has often unfolded under the mantle of revealing that Black feminists have long thought intersectionally, even before

Crenshaw's articles coined the term that has become ubiquitous, I ask what might happen if we consider the generative tensions and disconnects among these varied conceptions of thinking about power's workings. What might a Marxist Black feminist conception of power like Combahee's offer us that is distinct from a conception of power like Higginbotham's that is rooted in Black feminist historiographical work? What might it mean to think about how Black feminists have advanced and refused conceptions of power as multiplicative, additive, or exponential in their attempts to capture the lived experience of multiple marginalization? Rather than reading intersectionality as an end point in a Black feminist progress narrative, how might we hold on to the varied and distinctive theoretical and political possibilities advanced in this different work? If we read this archive as one that marks Black feminist productive debate about how to understand power, identity, and domination and how to conceptualize the self in relation to experiences of marginalization, we see a rich, endlessly complex Black feminist conversation that exceeds a rehearsal of the mutually constitutive nature of structures of domination.

If recent years have been marked by an intense interest in intersectional genealogies, they have also been marked by intense commitment by Black feminists to mark intersectionality's roots and histories in Black feminist thought. This project—which in other work, I have described as an affective manifestation of the movement of intersectionality to the center of women's studies—has also had the effect of obscuring the intersectional thinking of woman of color feminist scholars and activists who might not identify as Black. Rather than thinking about intersectionality as solely the territory and legacy of Black feminists, what might it mean to read the term alongside other analytics and moves that have attempted to think about power, including transnational feminist theory, mestizaje, and subaltern? If we think about Gloria Anzaldúa and Mari Matsuda, for example, as intersectional practitioners who introduce analytics including borders, land, Indigeneity, and accent into their work, we might enhance and complicate intersectional theory and praxis. It might also be generative to probe why these terms have not had the dominance in women's studies that intersectionality has and to consider what has been opened up and foreclosed by this. What might it mean, for example, for Black feminists to think with the idea of the subaltern or alongside the innovations of transnational feminist theory, which has often imagined subjects other than US Black women?

Intersectionality as a keyword in feminist studies—and in Black feminist studies—has also often produced a frictional relationship with queer studies and queer of color studies that regularly imagine themselves as developing theories and methods that jettison identity and its imagined pitfalls in favor of other ways of thinking about collectivities, power, and the felt experiences of marginalization. In this narration of the relationship between feminist theory and queer theory, queer theory is often described—or self-described—as the cutting edge, as the locus of urgent political and theoretical work, and feminist theory is often cast as, at the very least, outdated in its ongoing attachments to categories including identity and "woman." Queer theory's attention to affect, touch, and sensation thinks about bodies' relationships with each other, with space, with objects, and with the forms of togetherness that make survival and living possible in the face of indescribable quotidian and spectacular violence. At the same time, queer theory has largely disavowed identity—to the extent that such a disavowal is actually possible—often reading identitarian projects as wedded to fixity, to stasis, to woundedness. Intersectionality's imagined attachment to the identitarian, and Black woman's imagined role as the quintessentially identitarian identity category, has made some queer scholars imagine it as something that is attached to a vision of politics deemed belated, antiquated, or perhaps even problematic. What the friction between queer theory and feminist theory has revealed about intersectionality is that it is a term loaded with aspiration, that one must declare a position in relationship to it, and that it is thought to be both past and future simultaneously.

What intersectionality offers is one framework of Black feminist thought, as well as a key reminder that feelings are centrally important to academic feminism's institutional lives and that the analytics that are central to our practice are loaded with our desires, longings, wishes, anxieties, and phobias. The fact that intersectionality has come to signify so much, to be saturated with meaning and thus devoid of any particular meaning, and to be a term around which feminists identify or disidentify, declare their allegiance or disavow, suggests that *intersectionality* as a keyword is distinctive in the intensity of feminist feelings it produces. Rather than join those arguing in the declarative tense for its significance to feminist thought, this essay attempts to map the critical attachments we have to intersectionality's history, present practice, and future use for gender and sexuality studies.

39

Intersex

Sean Saifa Wall

I believe that it is the responsibility and duty of artists and activists to be the documentarians of their time. Activists, when leading with integrity and social responsibility, are the linchpins of our society, constantly reminding us to strive for what is just and equitable. In her book *Hunger*, Roxane Gay (2018) shares the story of how her body interacts with society at large and with the medical establishment in particular. After reading her memoir, I was impressed by how she put the desire for and repulsion of fat bodies into a larger theoretical framework and also how she critiqued society's treatment and marginalization of fat people. Although intersex activism and fat positivity are separate issues, I feel that my work as an activist is to make real the experiences of intersex people who have been harmed by the medical establishment.

I am intersex. I was born with one of at least thirty-five intersex traits called androgen insensitivity syndrome (AIS) that physically identified me as different at birth. AIS is a spectrum intersex trait where infants have varying levels of responsiveness to testosterone. As a result, infants can appear with a genital variance that encompasses typical female genitals and atypical male genitals. I was born with a small penis and undescended testes. The doctors at Columbia Presbyterian Hospital in New York City wanted to do surgery on my days-old body, but my mother refused. She was able to shield me from castration until the doctors told her that my testes, which they referred to as gonads, were cancerous and had to be removed. *This lie has been told to many*

AIS patients assigned female at birth who have been subject to castration. For insurance purposes, my surgery was coded as an orchiectomy, which is the removal of the testicles. Despite the fact that I was assigned female at birth and identified as female at the time, the insurance company had no qualms about covering this surgery in 1992, a time when transgender women were denied the same procedure.

Even though I was born with atypical genitals, having atypical genitals is not what defines intersex people. The United Nations and global intersex community have defined intersex as a set of sex characteristics or traits (which include gonadal, chromosomal, hormonal) that are atypical for males and females (Intersex Society of North America, n.d., 2). Although intersex people account for 1.7 percent of the human population, genetic traits cannot be narrowly defined, and to be honest, we really don't know who is intersex. Intersex people who have bodies that are atypical at birth or whose variations manifest in adolescence are subject to medically invasive procedures; however, people can have typical genitals and still have chromosomes or hormones that function differently. For example, a person assigned male at birth with typical male genitals could actually have XX chromosomes, which are associated with female sex characteristics. As a society, we are very uncomfortable with sex and sexuality but simultaneously obsessed with genitals. We refer to people's genitals in order to determine what bathroom they should use or where they should be incarcerated. Intersex and trans experiences force us to reckon with our assumptions of biological sex and gender identity.

Although our understanding of intersex people is increasing, our practices and treatment of intersex people have changed very little since the late 1950s. I use this time period as a marker to show how, from this point, the pathologization of intersex people became intertwined with harmful surgical interventions. At Johns Hopkins University in Baltimore, Maryland, for instance, from 1966 to 1970, Dr. John Money and Dr. Anke Ehrhardt coined the term *gender role* to differentiate biological sex from gender (Program for the Study of LGBT Health, n.d.; Money and Ehrhardt 1972). The concept of gender role allowed for an understanding of trans identities; however, Ehrhardt and Money tested the relationship between gender role, surgery, and socialization in the assigned gender on intersex children. Elizabeth Reis and Suzanne Kessler spoke to this issue in their collaborative essay "Why History Matters: Fetal Dex and Intersex" when they share, "The impulse to 'correct' the genitals of infants and toddlers, as opposed to adults, began in the 1950s. John Money and his colleagues, Joan and John Hampson, advanced a rationale for choosing gender and performing surgery that came to define intersex management for the next 50 years and, despite some resistance, has not been abandoned altogether" (2010, 58–59). Despite numerous accounts by former patients about how early medical interventions are harmful as well as an international call for delaying surgery until a person is old enough to consent, these surgeries persist even today.

As an intersex person who has survived medical violence, I didn't know that Ehrhardt, who provided psychological counseling to me after surgery, created the medical standards that harm intersex children. I didn't understand the extent of Money and Ehrhardt's legacy until I connected with other intersex people. The early survivors of intersex surgeries shared with each other horrific stories of multiple genital surgeries and how these surgeries, combined with secrecy and shame, traumatized them. They were often told by doctors that they were "rare" and would never meet another intersex person, and this often left them feeling alone and isolated. Some, like Georgiann Davis, activist and academic scholar, didn't know what had happened to them as children; Davis didn't discover the truth of her body until she secured her medical records at age nineteen (G. Davis 2015). She eventually sought out support from other intersex people, which is the basis of her book *Contesting Intersex*.

Others, such as Bo Laurent, channeled their anger into activism. Laurent (formerly known as Cheryl Chase) founded the Intersex Society of North America (ISNA) in 1993. ISNA started as a support group but then became an activist group (ISNA, n.d.). Whereas doctors did not listen to former patients, ISNA centered the experiences of adult intersex survivors and challenged doctors on their mistreatment of intersex children. During this time, some of the early leaders of the intersex movement emerged: Lynnell Stefani Long, Hida Viloria, Emi Koyama, Max Beck, Thea Hillman, Jim Ambrose, David Cameron, Peter Trinkl, and Angela Moreno Lippert, to name a few. Their message then was the same as it is today: give intersex children autonomy over their own bodies. ISNA's legacy supported the emergence of other intersex organizations in the United States, such as Bodies Like Ours, cofounded by Betsy Driver; the Intersex Initiative in Oregon, founded by Emi Koyama; and more recently, groups such as interACT, the Houston Intersex Society, and the Intersex Justice Project (IJP).

In 2016, I cofounded IJP alongside Pidgeon Pagonis and Lynnell Stefani Long, because we wanted to prioritize the leadership of people of color (POC) in the intersex movement. Based on our experiences, we recognized that the contributions of women, Black people, POC, and queer people in social justice spaces were often disregarded and co-opted, and we wanted something different for the intersex movement. Starting in 2016, we issued a statement on Intersex Awareness Day, which falls on October 26 of every year (Pagonis

and Wall 2016). In that statement, we asserted our self-determination as intersex POC and lifted up the work of other movements that we were connected to. We use direct action as a tool to pressure surgeons, doctors, and hospitals to stop cosmetic, medically unnecessary surgeries on intersex infants and children. We believe that intersex children and adults should consent to procedures that affect their bodies.

In July 2020, after a three-year campaign by IJP, the Lurie Children's Hospital in Chicago issued an apology to intersex people who were harmed by them: the hospital also agreed to a moratorium on intersex genital surgeries for at least six months. This victory is accurately captured in the words of the late Juan Evans, radical Black trans organizer: "When we fight, we win!" (Hennie 2015). Despite attempts by the medical establishment to erase the beauty of intersex variations, we are still here. Intersex activism is not just about challenging doctors to stop intersex genital surgeries but for doctors and parents to honor consent. We are advocating not only for consent but for our right to be respected as humans. As activists, we will continue to fight until intersex children and adults are safe from harm.

40

Justice

Emily Thuma and Sarah Haley

Justice is undoubtedly a central, if rarely explicitly defined, concept in the institutional and intellectual life of gender and sexuality studies. Most feminist, gender, queer, sexuality, and women's studies programs and departments across the United States name social justice as a foundational pillar of their curriculum and mission. Reflective of the significant number of scholars in the field who research, write, and teach about social justice movements, the National Women's Studies Association themed its 2018 and 2019 annual meetings, respectively, "Just Imagine, Imagining Justice" and "Protest, Justice, and Transnational Organizing." Such invocations of social justice index gender and sexuality studies' roots in liberation movements of the 1960s and 1970s as well as the field's continued commitment to praxis (theory in and through action) and social transformation. Here we highlight only three of the critical imaginaries of justice that animate gender and sexuality studies scholarship and activism today: economic justice, reproductive justice, and prison industrial complex abolition.

During the social movement era of the 1960s and 1970s, Black women radicals were in the vanguard of movements for gendered economic justice. Through their campaigns for domestic workers' rights, welfare rights, and "wages for housework," grassroots activists advanced a robustly intersectional politics of economic transformation. According to one report, members of the National Welfare Rights Organization (NWRO) commonly signed their letters with the closing "Bread, Justice & Dignity" (Rogin 1970). Ruby Duncan, a leader

in the Nevada welfare rights movement, ran for Nevada State Assembly on a "Bread and Justice" ticket. She and other Black women brought "the first library, medical clinic, daycare center, job training office, and senior citizen housing complex" to the predominantly Black side of Las Vegas under the organizing banner "Operation Life," and they were integral in transforming the labor movement through their work with the powerful Culinary Workers Union in the city (Orleck 2005, 2). For the NWRO—an organization that, according to historian Premilla Nadasen (2009), centered Black women in a radically expansive vision of Black power—the concept of gender justice *as* economic justice animated their struggle. The meaning of justice in relation to income, dignity, and bread is embedded in the famous rebuke from NWRO leader Johnnie Lee Tillmon (1972): "Welfare is like a super-sexist marriage. You trade in a man for the man." "Welfare warriors" like Duncan and Tillmon conceptualized economic justice as freedom from forms of domestic control that reside at the nexus of the intimate and the structural. For the NWRO, the policy incarnation of gendered economic justice was a guaranteed adequate income for all (Nadasen 2009).

As the NWRO powerfully exemplifies, feminist refusals of economic subordination put forward the most powerful visions of economic transformation when centering interlocking vectors of power. From enslaved women's rebellion, to domestic worker organizing at the turn of the twentieth century, to the landmark theorizing and activism of, among others, Ella Baker, Marvel Cooke, Beulah Richardson, Eslanda Robeson, and the Sojourners for Truth and Justice in the early Cold War era, Black women's resistance movements have exploded the work/home public/private divide and single-axis understandings of economic, racial, and sexual subordination (A. Y. Davis 1981; Glymph 2008; Hunter 1997; Ransby 2003; Gore 2011; McDuffie 2011). This was, as the Combahee River Collective argued in 1977, informed by a "need to articulate the real class situation of persons who are not merely raceless, sexless workers, but for whom racial and sexual oppression are significant determinants in their working/economic lives" (Combahee River Collective [1977] 2015, 213; Nakano Glenn 1985; Hong 2006; U. Taylor 2017; Bohrer 2019). The gendered, sexual, and racial specificity of the category of the worker that defined Combahee's Black feminist socialism was also critical to foundational 1970s and 1980s Marxist critiques of the sexual division of labor and attendant social movements that demanded justice in relation to the home, such as the international wages for housework movement. Other housing justice movements—such as the struggle over public housing in Baltimore (R. Y. Williams 2004) and the New York City tenants' movement, in which old and new left and Black feminist activists were central to a radical revisioning of the city (Gold 2014)—exemplified the centrality of the home to demands for racial, gender, and economic justice.

If an analysis of reproductive labor has been foundational to economic justice feminism, an analysis of economic subordination has been a key pillar of the movement for reproductive justice. Historians have produced influential analyses of reproductive violence and control as critical modalities of racial capitalism (J. Morgan 2004; Sharpe 2010; Hartman 2016; Ivy 2016; Cooper Owens 2018). Germinated by Black, Indigenous, Latina, and multiracial feminist organizations such as the Third World Women's Alliance, the Committee to End Sterilization Abuse, Women of All Red Nations, and Sister-Song, the framework of reproductive justice is a critical rejoinder to the rhetoric of individual choice that has defined mainstream reproductive rights advocacy. This frame, as Loretta Ross and Rickie Solinger (2017, 9) pithily summarize, "splices reproductive rights with social justice." It offers a human rights conception of reproductive self-determination as not only the right to abortion and contraception but also the right to have children, the right to parent children "in safe and healthy environments," and the right of "sexual autonomy and gender freedom for every human being" (9). Taking a kaleidoscopic view, reproductive justice activists and scholars have illuminated the inextricable ties between reproduction and racial oppression, poverty, colonization, ableism, and heteronormativity and transformed what constitutes a "reproductive rights issue" (D. Roberts 1997; Briggs 2002; INCITE! 2006; Kafer 2013; D.-A. Davis 2019; Theobald 2019). Today's reproductive justice struggles are manifold and increasingly intersecting with forces of criminalization—from fetal protection laws (Goodwin 2020) to compulsory sterilization of fertile persons in immigrant and state prisons (Cohn 2020). Indeed, as Dorothy Roberts (2015) writes in *Dissent* magazine, "true reproductive freedom requires a living wage, universal health care, and the abolition of prisons."

As in the context of reproductive politics, activists and scholars working in the realms of disability and trans politics have adopted "justice" as a suffix to challenge a solely "civil rights–based strategy, where assimilation into, and replication of, dominant institutions are the goals" (Cohen 1997, 437). Movements for reproductive justice, disability justice, and trans justice share several definitional commitments: a refusal of single-issue politics, an emphasis on coalition and alliance building, a methodology of "looking to the bottom" (Matsuda 1987, 324) of social hierarchies and centering those most vulnerable, and an aim of root-level, or radical, societal transformation (Audre Lorde Project 2014; Mingus 2010; Spade 2011; Sins Invalid 2015).

Scholars and activists thus increasingly refuse to cede the term *justice* to the criminal justice system, renaming the latter the criminal punishment system, the criminal legal system, the criminal *in*justice system, or simply the criminal system. These rhetorical strategies signal a desire to reclaim and reimagine justice and to refuse the carceral state's "monopoly on justice" (Tuck and Yang 2016, 9). As the authors of *Queer (In)justice: The Criminalization of LGBT People in the United States* write of their divestment from the phrase *criminal justice system*, "This system has not produced anything remotely approximating justice for the vast majority of people in the United States—particularly for people of color, poor people, immigrants, and queers—since its inception, but rather bears major responsibility for the continuing institutionalization of severe, persistent, and seemingly intractable forms of violence and inequality" (Mogul, Ritchie, and Whitlock 2011, xx).

Histories of feminism, gender, and sexuality have demonstrated that one of the most intractable injustices of the criminal punishment system is its central role in the production and reproduction of ideologies of racialized gender and sexual normativity. Regimes of gendered carceral violence have historically been disproportionately imposed upon Black, Afro-Latinx, Latinx, and Indigenous communities, who in turn have contested norms and practices of racialized gender violation at the hands of carceral agents, such as police and guards, demanding that justice look like new conceptions of gender and sexuality. Whether in jails, federal/immigrant detention prisons, state prisons, or convict labor camps, criminalized Black, brown, and Indigenous women, girls, and queer, trans, and nonbinary people have faced both the inherent violence of imprisonment and targeted forms of institutionalized brutality, including rape, whipping, forced reproduction, reproductive health neglect, and the denial of gender-affirming medical care (L. Ross 1998; Gross 2006; Kunzel 2008; Hicks 2010; LeFlouria 2015; Haley 2016; McDonald 2017; LeBrón 2019; Speed 2019).

Scholars have also interrogated the role of feminist movements in "the buildup of America's prison nation" (Richie 2012, 103). In the context of a metastasizing carceral state and retreating welfare state, many feminist campaigners against sexual and domestic violence across the 1970s, 1980s, and 1990s increasingly embraced law enforcement protection and punitive justice as frontline solutions and found strange bedfellows in get-tough politicians and lawmakers (Gottschalk 2006; Bumiller 2008; Deer 2009; Bernstein 2010; Richie 2012; Gruber 2020; Kim 2020). Advocates, for example, successfully pressed for policies that required police officers to make an arrest if they had probable cause of domestic violence (mandatory arrest laws), required prosecutors to bring criminal charges against abusers regardless of the wants of the victim ("no-drop" laws), and increased the severity of punishments for sex crimes. This "carceral creep," as Mimi Kim (2020) terms it, culminated in the decidedly procriminalization 1994 Violence Against Women Act (VAWA)—part of the mammoth Clinton Crime Bill that sharpened and expanded the tools of racialized mass incarceration. With its funding priorities of encouraging arrest and prosecution, VAWA institutionalized a carceral feminist politics of "social justice as criminal justice" (Bernstein 2010, 58) that remains dominant today.

LGBT activism for expanding laws against hate crimes, or bias-motivated crimes, to include sexual orientation, gender expression, and gender identity has followed this same carceral grain since the 1980s (Hanhardt 2013). Activists saw criminal justice as a means of punishing and deterring anti-LGBT violence, as well as wielding the expressive power of the law to transform social norms of gender and sexuality. Yet queer and trans critics have debunked the purported deterrent effects of hate crime laws and argued that such laws not only fail to "actually increase the life chances of the people they purport-edly protect" but bolster and expand a criminal legal system, which, in turn, "constantly reproduces the same harmful systems (racism, sexism, homophobia, transphobia, ableism, xenophobia) that advocates of these laws want to eliminate" (Spade 2011, 45; see also Snorton and Haritaworn 2013). Moreover, just as VAWA was nested under a big-tent crime bill that fu-eled mass incarceration, LGBT hate crime legislation at the federal level took the form of an amendment to the 2010 National Defense Authorization Act, an annual appropriations act that handed the Depart-ment of Defense a record-shattering $680 billion that year. Exemplars of what Chandan Reddy (2011, 2) calls "freedom with violence," VAWA and the Mat-thew Shepard and James Byrd Jr. Hate Crimes Pre-vention Act fastened feminist and LGBT antiviolence campaigns to the engines of state violence.

Crucially, radical feminists and queers of color and their allies have protested and documented from the 1970s onward that the most socially marginalized of survivors—those especially vulnerable to carceral state violence—bear the myriad costs of feminist and LGBT politics that equate justice with punishment (A. Y. Davis 1976; Richie 1996, 2012, 2017; INCITE! 2006; Spade 2011; Hanhardt 2013; Palacios 2016; Love and Protect and Survived and Punished 2017; Thuma 2019). These strands of anticarceral antiviolence ac-tivism and scholarship offer up an altogether differ-ent conception of social justice rooted in a praxis of prison abolition.

In the catalytic 2001 manifesto "Statement on Gender Violence and the Prison-Industrial Complex," members of the national prison abolitionist organiza-tion Critical Resistance and the national feminist of color antiviolence organization INCITE! offered not only a searing critique of the violence and limits of criminal justice but also a vision of a just future in which "safety and security will not be premised on violence or the threat of violence; it will be based on a collective commitment to guaranteeing the survival and care of all peoples" (Critical Resistance-INCITE! 2008). Since this clarion call, existing and emergent organizations, the majority led by feminists of color, have coalesced into a grassroots movement for transformative justice (Bierria, Rojas, and Kim 2010; Palacios 2016; Kim 2020; Russo 2018). Transformative justice refuses a crime logic that treats people who cause harm as monstrous and aberrant individuals in need of punishment. It instead approaches gender and sexual violence as socially pro-duced phenomena that require not only individual but collective accountability and deep social change. As adrienne maree brown (2020, chap. 25) describes in the recent collection *Beyond Survival: Strategies and Stories from the Transformative Justice Movement*, this movement advances "justice practices that go all the way to the root of the problem and generate solutions and heal-ing there, such that the conditions that create injustice are transformed."

Radical feminist and queer imaginings of justice, then, are the outgrowth of what Cathy J. Cohen has described as transformational political work—the work of "link[ing] our intersectional analysis of power with concrete coalitional work" (1997, 461). As she makes clear, gender and sexual justice must make capacious-ness a core political value and strategy. Prison industrial complex abolition, as a theory of power and the future in terms of and perhaps even beyond justice, is "delib-erately everything-ist; it's about the entirety of human-environmental relations," in the words of Ruth Wilson Gilmore (Kushner 2019). The "everything-ist" character of abolition marks it as deeply feminist, a theory that necessarily and centrally questions the production of normative sexuality and gender as carceral toxins, a cartography if not a blueprint for the realization of feminist demands for new economies, new social and political environments, new modes of reproduction and social reproduction, new practices of living, and new forms of relation.

41

Labor

Jan M. Padios

She sits at the table, reading a book. She sits at the table with a man, embracing him as he looks down at a newspaper. She sits at the table with two friends, somber, then smiling. She stands alone at the table. She looks straight into the camera's lens.

In her renowned *The Kitchen Table Series*, artist Carrie Mae Weems conveys the intimacies, meditations, and struggles of a Black woman's everyday life by placing her at the figurative center of the household: the kitchen table. In these twenty black-and-white images, the woman worries alongside the man, who never looks up from his dinner plate or paper; she does battle with a little girl over what may be homework; she gets her hair done as she takes solace in a cigarette and a glass of wine. The focus on domesticity also begs the question of what the woman encounters in the world outside her household and what it takes to return to this table every day and night. We do not see the woman in a factory, office, or field, but we can understand from these images that her life is constituted by labor, along with pleasure and desire.

Beginning a discussion of *labor* from within a woman of color's household means necessarily considering how labor is a gendered and racialized process of creating not only economic value but life and self. An analysis of labor, gender, and sexuality from various critical feminist perspectives—women of color, Black, transnational, and Indigenous—thus crosses the boundaries between paid and unpaid work, between household and workplace, between the need to make ends meet and the need for a secure place to sleep, healthy food and water, and good schools. Indeed, nine years before Weems debuted her series, Barbara Smith, influenced by Audre Lorde, began Kitchen Table Press as a way to publish the work of feminist and lesbian women of color. Unlike in Marx's ([1867] 1992) *Capital*, volume 1, in which a table is just another commodity treated alongside coats, iron, and corn, the table in critical feminist perspective is a site of labor, family, community, and grassroots struggle (Williams-Forson 2006; Parker et al. 2019).

Most approaches to the study of labor adopt a baseline definition of *labor* as purposeful, effortful activity that effects change in the world. At first blush, this description seems large enough to hold all manner of intentional human action: we do labor when we make the table, set the table, or struggle to pay bills at the table. In the history of the United States, however, much of the scholarly literature, intellectual debate, and political struggle regarding labor has privileged the labor of men, and the labor of white men in particular, who have been said to "directly" produce value in capitalism as an economic system. This focus is not just the result of the racialized and gendered structure of intellectual and political work (i.e., white male intellectuals and organizers focusing on other white men). The definition of labor *as value generating activity* is tied to John Locke's *labor theory of property*, which helped white settlers socially construct the idea of cultural differences between themselves and Native Americans, who were said not to be properly working the land on which they lived. In turn, this approach to land and labor became part of the ideological tool kit of manifest destiny, leading to the genocide and violent relocation of Native Americans on the North American continent in the nineteenth century.

If the definition of labor as only that which directly creates the economic value of a commodity or property is thus part of the framework of white supremacy, then bringing labor, gender, and sexuality together compels us to recognize what is outside that frame and how to push against it. The history of the US welfare rights movement and its articulation with and differences from the movement for labor rights is a powerful model for how this analysis and intervention have come together. As organizers and scholars have shown, women of color have long been coerced by poverty and racism into domestic work with white families or agriculture labor on white-owned fields and were therefore denied state-based benefits to industrial workers, such as social security (G. West 1981; Quadagno 1996; Nadasen 2005; Kornbluh 2007; Sharpless 2013). Women of color were also pushed out of industry after World War II, have been relegated to government jobs, and in the later twentieth century, were confined to deskilled clerical work (C. Jones [1949] 1995; V. Green 2001). Indeed, the history of labor in US communities of color is part and parcel of the struggle for greater recognition and equal treatment of the productive and socially reproductive energies of men and women by society and the state. The term *social reproduction* refers to the processes by which households, relationships, knowledge, and bodies are maintained so society itself can be reproduced (Bhattacharya 2017). Social reproduction is the labor of the kitchen table.

A discussion of labor based in the history of welfare rights, with its intersecting analysis of poverty, racial oppression, punitive state policies, and labor, thus complicates dominant narratives of US feminism. The latter has tended to privilege the stories of white liberal women who in the late 1960s and 1970s began fighting for the opportunity to work outside the home and for the recognition of domestic work, childcare, and marital heterosexual relations as socially reproductive work that indirectly created economic value by giving birth to and maintaining the workforce. Although the political visions of US-based liberal white women have overlapped with Marxist feminists—including radical autonomist Marxist movements based in Italy (Dalla Costa and James [1972] 1975)—their attentions have often differed from many women of color welfare rights activists who fought for structural changes that would afford them the kind of domestic security available to white families, such as the ability to stay at home and care for their own children and families. Without an analysis of the shared and divergent burdens placed on women of color and white women, the former can only ever have been seen as "having it worse" than the latter rather than facing unique circumstances of work and labor because of race.

Accounts of labor focused on women of color have also shown how the US nation-state has historically relied on their oppression and coercion to meet economic and social priorities. For example, between Reconstruction and the dawn of World War II, African American, Mexican, Asian, and Hawaiian women were relegated to low-wage work in agriculture and industry in the South, Southwest, and Hawai'i, respectively (Nakano Glenn 2002). In more recent decades, as neoliberal globalization has unevenly and unjustly restructured workers' lives, making them increasingly more vulnerable and precarious, new accounts of gender, labor, and transnational migration have emerged. While some focus on the autonomy and wage-earning potential of women in global industries (Anwary 2017), others have characterized women in the Global South as well as immigrant women in the Global North as a new proletariat class working in global capitalism's obscured geography of export processing zones, maquiladoras, and sweatshops (Lacsama and Aguilar 2004; P. Ngai 2005; Ong 2006; Wright 2006). Such research demonstrates how the work and labor of young, often migrant, women are crucial to the manufacture and movement of goods along the "global value chain" or "the global assembly line," ostensibly neutral terms that obscure women's experiences of global capitalism and hide the dangerous settings in which they work. Women have died from unsafe conditions in factories in South Asia (F. Ahmed 2004), been raped and murdered in border towns where *maquiladoras* are often situated (Livingston 2004), and been subjected to new or intensified patterns of domestic violence as a result of their shifting socioeconomic status more broadly (Miedem and Fulu 2018). Indeed, the globalization of production—with its overall lack of worker protections, violation of worker rights, and everyday forms of sexual harassment—raises crucial questions about the intersection of labor and gendered violence as well as how women cope, organize, and resist (Islam and Hossain 2015; Lindio-McGovern and Wallimann [2009] 2016; Chang and Poo 2016).

A feminist woman of color focus on globalization and labor also shows us what happens when our metaphorical kitchen table is challenged by the process of migration. By the end of the twentieth century, for example, tens of thousands of women were leaving their home countries each year, going to work in domestic labor for affluent families in major cities like Hong Kong, London, and Los Angeles (Hondagneu-Sotelo [2001] 2007; Parreñas [2001] 2015; Lan 2006). The internalization of an already racialized structural feature of US households (see the discussion of welfare rights and domestic workers above) has presented extreme challenges for women who continue to care for and maintain ties with their own families and communities across borders. The global appropriation of Filipino labor, for example, has led to the emergence of transnational families, where care is delivered across borders through technology and social media—the kitchen table made virtual (Francisco 2018).

Woman of color feminist theory, welfare rights history, and historical accounts of labor focused on women of color have been crucial for defining labor as a collective, historical experience shaped by race, gender, and sexuality. Approaches to labor such as these place stress on the local, regional, national, and global structural conditions that give rise to workers' experiences as well as how migrant and immigrant labor is intrinsic to capitalism. Moreover, woman of color feminist practice, with its attention to the way women of color disidentify with or contest the normative institutions of the state (including those related to work and labor), holds important promise for coalitional politics with racialized immigrant workers (Hong 2006; Mohanty 2003).

If we zoom back in on the kitchen table, we can also sense the labor of the gendered, racialized, and sexualized bodies of those of us who gather there. Indeed, the focus on bodies and labor from feminist and queer perspectives has led to vital conversations about work, law, technology, and reproduction. For example, as feminist movements gained both ground and nuance in the 1970s and 1980s, conflicts over *sex work* emerged too. Gender and sexuality studies literature on sex work makes a number of important distinctions for this conversation—namely, that sex work should not be reduced to prostitution or conflated with sex trafficking (S. Shah 2014); sex work encompasses a wide swath of paid labor related to sexuality, including pornographic entertainment (Miller-Young 2014); and the meaning of sex work changes with economic shifts, whether due to gentrification of cities (Bernstein 2007), or increased military presence, or underdevelopment (Enloe 1990; Tadiar 2004). What is clear from the literature is that productive discussions of sex work should address the specifics of the labor process of the work itself—literally, how sex workers provide the services they do and under what conditions. Also clear from the literature, especially research that looks beyond the United States,

is that for many poor people, the search for sex work is linked to the search for other social necessities, including housing and water (S. Shah 2014).

Another approach combining the study of sexuality, gender, and labor explores jobs or workplaces in which workers' sexual identities and/or gender performance are meaningful in some way. Thanks to a number of ethnographic and historical studies of workplaces around the world, we now have a more profound understanding of how and why Caribbean women, Native American women, or queer Filipino workers can be found doing jobs in outsourced tech-related industry (C. Freeman 2000; Nakamura 2014; David 2015; Padios 2018). The latter kind of approach makes clear what even ostensibly classic Marxists texts like Harry Braverman's *Labor and Monopoly Capital* could not, which is why, as technology breaks down labor into more and more deskilled work, the jobs tend to be taken up by women and people of color. As these discussions progress, we will begin to better understand and confront the myriad ways gender and sexuality matter to the workplace, including how work is a site for not only the production of value but also trauma, as the experiences of "nontraditional" or LGBTQ workers in the trades show (M. Benitez 2021). Such approaches require accounts of both the empirical and nonempirical consequences of trauma, as called for by woman of color feminism (Anzaldúa 1987) and felt theory (Million 2009).

Just as gender studies ought to not be reduced to the study of women and sexuality studies need not be limited to sex, a gender and sexuality studies approach to labor does not have to take women workers or sexual commerce as primary objects of study. Discussions emerging from queer studies, for example, have focused on *affect* and *affective labor*—terms that generate much argumentation. No matter where we pitch our tents in the vast landscape of debates about affect (e.g.,

Is it precognitive? How is it different from emotion?), we can recognize the increasing need in the twenty-first century for a way to talk about the intangible but still profoundly harrowing aspects of labor, including the emotional labor required of workers in the service economy (Takeyama 2016; Padios 2018) or the work of building community within social movements. Indeed, within queer studies, we can find small but strong efforts to think about sexuality in relation to capitalism and Marxist theory and thus, to a limited extent, labor (Hennessy 2000; Floyd 2009; Wesling 2012). Queer studies also shows us ways to understand modes of working and living that take place within late capitalism's interstitial and marginal spaces, such as "messy" queer immigrant households (Manalansan 2014). Furthermore, Black feminist theory and queer theory in particular give us ways to talk about labor that move beyond a concern with capital relations or power and instead understand labor as a process of, for example, Black gay men making sense of themselves within mainstream culture that denies their very being (Bost 2019).

It is crucial to see these discussions of labor, gender, and sexuality not as niche conversations within a larger discussion of labor that one can jettison to "elective" knowledge but as fundamentally challenging and enhancing knowledge about and theories of labor. Scholars of gender and sexuality studies have been instrumental in challenging the idea of free labor within capitalism, of expanding the notion of what counts as value-producing labor, of illuminating large oppressive systems related to labor, of fighting for the redistribution of wealth and the security of households in relation to labor, and of pushing on the term itself.

Feminist science studies has been particularly influential in this regard because beyond asking what else we might fit under the umbrella term of *labor*, or the broader social spectrum on which we should place labor, feminist science and technology studies (STS) scholars attempt to establish a new vocabulary for difficult-to-define processes, including gestational surrogacy (Vora 2015). While the latter keeps faith with earlier efforts to understand reproductive labor in relation to political economy—including the birth of African American children into US slavery (J. Morgan 2004)—the questions raised by the processes of biological reproduction across multiple bodies and borders make clear that the definition of *labor* as the process of giving birth and as *value-producing* activity is becoming more complex. Feminist STS conversations are also emerging around artificial intelligence, automation, and robots—perhaps the most hegemonic association with the term *labor* today—to ask how they are implicated within racial capitalism, dispossession, and patriarchy (Atanasoski and Vora 2019).

As suggested by the movement of this *Keywords* entry from Weems's kitchen table to the world and back again, one of the most important tenets of a critical approach to labor, gender, and sexuality is that *labor* cannot be bracketed as a single category of experience or an analytic framework. Given the actual lived labors of Indigenous, poor, imprisoned, and/or colonized peoples, an understanding of labor is integral to but not set apart from the study of capitalism, patriarchy, the state, social reproduction, welfare, social movements, and community. For imprisoned Black women in the nineteenth and twentieth centuries, for example, "freedom" was contingent on first becoming convict laborers or domestic workers—work that cannot be separated from the larger system that gave rise to Jim Crow modernity (Haley 2016).

Unlike discussions of labor that define it simply *in opposition* to capital or management, feminist approaches to labor—like feminist approaches to the world more generally—look at labor *in relation* to various factors of life. Although we cannot study labor without looking at the political and economic structure of society, we must track where our "vital energy" (Vora 2015) goes and how it is reproduced. Being attuned to labor in gender and sexuality studies means studying and sensing how labor may be organized, appropriated, and oppressed in relation to race, gender, sexuality, and citizenship as modes of human experience and categories of personhood but also how we might better recognize and combine the many labors of our lives to build sustainable social relations and selves.

42

Lesbian

Jeanne Vaccaro and Joan Lubin

"Lesbians are not women," declared lesbian feminist theorist Monique Wittig (1980, 111). Wittig's statement captures a persistent problem that the figure of the lesbian illuminates, bringing to light the frictions between sex, gender, and sexuality as well as nature, culture, and embodiment. If lesbians are not women, what on earth are they?

One might reasonably assume that the term *lesbian* names a type of woman. And yet that has proven to be anything but a straightforward assumption. If the relationship between lesbian and woman is not self-evident, why is that? If those two terms can't be resolved by the logics of synonymy or hierarchy, why not? What vectors of identity, experience, and embodiment organize the difference between lesbian and woman? Wittig's statement implicates the lesbian in an intersectional matrix of difference. Unpacking her provocation requires a recognition that sex and gender have a complicated relation, shaped by race, ability, class, religion, and region, among other aspects of subjectivity and experience. The history of the lesbian as keyword is thus necessarily a history of the uneven terrain of oppression and struggle in which this figure has taken on different meanings in different times and places for different people.

While Wittig proposed a distinction between lesbians and women as a liberatory rallying cry, others have concurred that lesbians are not women with very different motivations. Historically, lesbians have been both pathologized as sexual deviants and desexualized as women—the supposed schizophrenic result of a patriarchal construction of what counts as "normal" female sexuality. Lesbianism could not be reconciled with hegemonic conceptions of womanhood that rely on a fantasy of heteronormative feminine chastity, ignoring the complexity of female desire. For this reason, relations among women that seemed to threaten the normative patriarchal social order have historically been dismissed with desexualized terms like *Boston marriage*, *romantic friendship*, or *spinsters* or familiar vocabularies of obfuscation like *roommates* or *best friends*. Unlike sodomy laws that criminalized sexual activity between men, the presumption of female frigidity meant that in most places, lesbianism was not officially illegal. This both enabled a flourishing of desire and relationships among women and rendered that flourishing mostly unintelligible to observers both then and now.

Even when sex between women has been acknowledged, the scientific vocabularies devised to describe it speak to an enduring confusion about the status of the lesbian vis-à-vis the category woman. Late-nineteenth century sexologists did not use the term *lesbian*, favoring instead a vocabulary of *invert* and *pervert*, which obscured female desire by pathologizing its gendered expression. So-called inverts were presumed pathological masculine subjects who fell out of the category woman, while their feminized lovers, so-called perverts, were paternalistically diagnosed as innocent prey to the invert's twisted fantasies and thus supposedly eligible for rehabilitation into normative femininity. In other words, sexology attempted to make sense of lesbianism by superimposing upon it the gendered sex roles of heteropatriarchy.

This early sexological articulation of a typology of lesbian genders has left a lasting impression. It remains difficult for many to understand lesbianism without reducing it to a parody of heterosexual relations. While the vocabulary of *invert* and *pervert* may sound arcane

now, one can nonetheless hear its echoes in the common inquiry "Which one of you is the man?" In the 1950s, working-class lesbian bar culture made "butch" and "femme" roles central to lesbian life. While butch-femme is one logic of lesbian desire, it is one among infinite possibilities. This was true at the time and is in ample evidence now with a proliferation of lesbian genders of all sexes, including trans and nonbinary identities. The polymorphously perverse scene of lesbianism did not always sit well with feminist political organizing. As the women's movement gained traction in the ensuing decades, the purity politics around "woman" as the subject of feminism brought butch-femme roles in for scorn that was nominally feminist but more nearly a racist and classist bid for respectability politics. The mainstream (white middle-class) feminist critique of butch-femme failed to account for the gendered effects of structural racism and economic inequity, making for a missed opportunity for intersectional gay liberation that centers antiracism and anticapitalism in its understanding of sexual politics.

Many second-wave heterofeminists questioned the status of the lesbian relative to patriarchy, positing an idealized vision of lesbianism as, in the words of Cherríe Moraga and Amber Hollibaugh (1981, 58), a "struggle-free, trouble-free zone" outside of oppressive social structures. Not only is this a romantic fantasy; it also conceals the ways that lesbians are often exceptionally subject to patriarchal oppression because of their non-normative relation to the category woman, which does not so much exempt them from misogyny as provoke it. According to the mainstream women's movement, lesbianism was an elective political identification—and as such, it was constantly under threat of erosion by the unruliness of actual lesbian desire. Betty Friedan (author of *The Feminine Mystique*) infamously referred to lesbians in the women's movement as a "lavender menace"

(Brownmiller 1970, 230). The women's movement tried to tame the lavender menace by instrumentalizing lesbianism as "the practice of feminist theory" (K. King 1994, 125).

As the status of lesbians was being debated by the mainstream women's movement, lesbians themselves were active in a much broader scene of new social movements, civil rights, and gay liberation. The 1970s saw a glut of lesbian cultural production, the print culture of self-actualization. Imagining a lesbian future prompted a search for lesbian pasts. For example, *Sappho Was a Right-On Woman: A Liberated View of Lesbianism* (Abbott and Love 1972) begins with this declaration: "The Lesbian is one of the least known members of our culture" (13).

The dearth of official knowledge about lesbians sent many looking for their own cultural touchstones. The ancient Greek isle of Lesbos, among other utopian sites, has taken on the status of mythic origin in the face of archival silences. Some of the first studies of lesbianism undertaken by lesbians attempted to generate lists of lesbians past as a bulwark against present erasure. Counter-archival projects such as the Lesbian Herstory Archives are testaments to ways lesbian knowledge and history rely on community, oral, anecdotal, and ephemeral or "nonofficial" histories, sometimes called *herstories*.

More recently, the question of whether lesbians are or are not women has a new resonance, as radical feminism has become synonymous with trans-exclusionary politics in the cultural imaginary. However, the notion that lesbians are not women might logically suggest lesbianism as the category most hospitable to trans inclusion and trans affirmative politics, opening up a critical space of possibility between sex, gender, and sexuality. *Trans* and *lesbian* share an unsettled relation to the term *woman*, which makes the fact that trans-exclusionary radical feminists have weaponized lesbianism particularly devastating as a missed opportunity for solidarity.

Lesbians are a paradox, always already passé and yet never quite substantiated in the first instance. In the present, the term *lesbian* has an unstable status where it names both an archaic identity and also an as yet totally unresolved inquiry into the possibilities that inhere in the differences between sex, gender, and sexuality. The possibilities very well may be infinite, if we can resist being reductive about it.

43

Masculinity

Jack Halberstam

It is easy to forget that until very recently, masculinity was understood solely in terms of the behaviors, activities, and political positions associated with the experience of being a man. So sutured to one another were men and masculinity, in ways that are not true for women and femininity, that there were very few ways of speaking or thinking about masculinity that did not affirm manhood on the one hand and define itself against womanhood on the other. Masculinity, furthermore, named a racial project of power and domination in which normative masculinity attached to whiteness while Black, Asian, or Latinx masculinities bore the weight of representing excess or insufficiency. It is not the case that these hegemonic versions of masculinity are now a thing of the past, and yet the twenty-first century has been marked by very clear shifts in the meanings, functions, and understandings of men and masculinity. Social media–based movements like #MeToo have, in the first two decades of the twenty-first century, offered platforms for deep critiques of the "boys will be boys" mentality that has granted powerful men impunity in relation to unwanted sexual advances on women. And as descriptions and accounts of widespread sexual harassment, assault, and abuse entered the viral world of online circulation, discussions that may have happened in small groups in earlier eras now became loud, ubiquitous, insistent. Meanwhile, trans manhood, once a stealth form of embodiment with only scant visibility, became a legible, credible, and influential new articulation of masculinity and manhood and in some cases offered deep critiques of the gender binarism and its seemingly inevitable connection to compulsory heterosexuality.

Historians of gender have offered clear narratives about the emergence of white manhood as a marker of modern power. Gail Bederman (2008) and George Mosse (1998), in particular, have offered accounts of North American and European masculinities, respectively, that explore and explain the suturing of white men to webs and networks of governance in the beginning of the twentieth century. In different ways and with reference to different archives, Mosse and Bederman have offered detailed and complex histories of "manhood" and "masculinity" in relation to a nexus of other discourses about racial dominance and civilization. With reference to slavery in the United States and the Holocaust in Europe, Bederman and Mosse propose that traditional concepts of white manhood formed the foundations for contemporary understandings of national belonging. White men and boys at the beginning of the twentieth century were seen as representatives of the strength of the nation, and they represented the civilizing force of culture that was understood to be one of the central principles of colonial rule. Accordingly, notions of virility, cultivated in the Boy Scouts and on sports teams, linked bodily health and strength to racially inflected principles of fortitude, restraint, moderation, and eventually, purity. And while the fascist German Männerbund of the 1930s was the most obvious and disastrous application of these ideas about political power, masculine strength, and racial purity, some version of racial masculinity propped up even the most apparently anodyne structures of family, fatherhood, and manliness in North America and Europe.

The definitions of manhood and masculinity that were formed in the first part of the twentieth century separated out white men and boys from everyone else. White middle-class men imagined then, and still imagine themselves now, as under threat from feminism, homosexuality, subaltern masculinities, and masculinities of color. Indeed, much of what we experience in contemporary North America as public violence emerges from male paranoia about female sexuality, Black masculinity, and so-called foreigners. However, as one of the many feminist activist groups proposed in the last decade, time's up on the immunity that white men have enjoyed from any sense of having to reckon with what it might mean to organize social life around other forms of power, new understandings of masculinity, and different valuations of wealth, bodily strength, and gender relations.

Just to name a few of the most obvious changes that have impacted our daily experiences of sex and gender, in the late twentieth and early twenty-first centuries, we have seen a massive decline in the prevalence and dominance of monogamous marriage and a huge rise in divorce and diverse households. In the United States, we have also witnessed a new and startling visibility of transgender communities and individuals as well as new levels of acceptance for normative gays and lesbians. And while the acceptance of gay marriage has probably stabilized some conventions of intimacy, the emergence of categories like "nonbinary" and "gender nonconforming" has made the gender binary seem anachronistic. Since gender and sexuality works like a matrix, changes in any part of that system produce deep structural changes elsewhere too. Given all the changes, then, to family, intimacy, relationality, gender norms, and sociality in an age of social networks, digital media, and multiscreened media, it is neither likely nor possible that principles of kinship, desire, and embodiment that went unquestioned in earlier periods will organize people's feelings about family, partnership, and identity today.

I recently read, of my own volition, Karl Ove Knausgaard's (2016) six volumes of *My Struggle*. While women have been writing about the minor, the domestic, the importance of small nothings for centuries, Knausgaard figured out how to turn nothing into something, and by resignifying one of the most notorious literary memoirs of the twentieth century—namely, Hitler's *Mein Kampf*—he deployed the charisma of masculinist fascism to tell a supposedly small and antifascist story. In an era of #MeToo and at a time when all kinds of gendered people would like to bring patriarchy crashing down, it is kind of amazing that Knausgaard is the literary sensation that he is. Volume 4 of *My Struggle*, after all, is all about his experiences as a teacher in a remote Norwegian village. And while he has some great things to say about teaching, both its tedium and its unexpected pleasures, he mostly feels exasperated by being so close to forbidden fruit—namely, the young, adolescent girls he teaches. I am not standing in moralistic judgment at these thoughts; after all, they mostly remain in the realm of thought and fantasy. Rather, I am interested in the anatomy of patriarchy and male desire that the novels give us and how little seems to have been written on that, and never mind on the relation between male desire, patriarchy, and fascism. Fascism, I am willing to claim, lives on in this geometry of masculinity: forbidden fruit, the desire for very young women, the anger directed at even slightly older women, and the simultaneous desire to destroy all of them.

And yet despite all these changes, Knausgaard's struggles are with writing, with women, with sex, and with family. The world, it seems, does not always lay itself at his feet in the way that another writer who summarized his life under the title of *My Struggle* or *Mein Kampf* expected it to. And while Knausgaard's masculinity is not the same as Hitler's and while his investment in manhood is not obviously fascist, still the gender hierarchies that support and are supported by white supremacy have their role to play in ordinary white manhood today. What a difference a decade or two have made to gender norms, and yet white masculinity, against all odds, goes marching on.

44

Matter
Mel Y. Chen

The phrase *Black Lives Matter* (BLM), from the movement originating in 2013, shifts between a critique of Black lives taken *as* matter (understood as inhuman or subhuman) and the sense that Black lives, with queer and trans lives at their center, have consequence. These statements suggest two of the definitions used for materiality itself—one, a Marxist analysis pointing to the potency of a proletariat class under racial capitalism, for instance, and two, the racialization of a seemingly ordinary relationship between life and its material constituents.

I am writing in June 2020 as the movement has invigorated multiple forms of reckoning around anti-Blackness and police violence and given force to prison abolition, economic and environmental justice, racial and health justice, and other linked movements. The BLM phrase would seem to borrow without interference on the immutable structure of a word like *matter* and its fixed senses. However, the ongoing use of language always informs the meaning a word eventually acquires, a point made in discussions of performativity (Austin 1975). Use can also become critique, as with *queer*; words matter and also perform mattering (J. Butler 1996). The racist description of nonwhite human lives regularly participates in the rendering of (and correlates with the capitalist treatment of) many racialized lives as dehumanized matter, authorizing consonant imaginations; consider the devastating and systemic rendering of immigrants as massed animals, as in the naming of "hordes" coming to the United States from Latin and

Central America, or the violent representation of trans women of color with the third-person pronominal "it" as opposed to "she."

This keyword entry reflects on the linguistic and material politics of the word *matter* itself and what they might reveal about uses of "matter" today, in both scholarly and political contexts. I might have begun the entry with a move seemingly appropriate to the genre: an opening philological turn to the *Oxford English Dictionary* (*OED*), which retains an oddly persuasive power by gesturing to the authoritative English-language resource—odd in light of the anti-institutional bent of critical theory or cultural studies' take on keywords. But given the *OED*'s tendency to abstraction, which would seem to be the opposite of matter itself, we might ask if there is any danger in establishing an *OED* basis for the noun *matter*.

Immediately, *matter*'s *OED* synonym *substance* raises caution. When should one accept an interchangeable relationship between, say, a linguistic *substantive*, such as a noun category, and a claim to *importance* or *consequence*, as is found in the verb? As it turns out, the characteristic turn to substance mirrors the structure of desire within the noun *matter*'s own etymology, or linguistic history: we seek substance when we seek origins. In turn, those origins confer significance upon the thing itself. Digging deeper into the *OED*, we find that *matter* etymologically derives from earlier words meaning "wood" or "building material" as well as a philosophical sense of matter as distinguished from or unlike mind or form; this philosophical sense in turn derives from mother (mater) as both tree trunk and source of branches or offshoots. In the first noun-1 etymology, a French borrowing derives from the Latin for wood, "material of which a thing is made"; in the second, a philosophical sense of *potential* is distinguished from (and a necessary companion to) *form*, potential that is itself understood through a maternal reproductive idiom that poses the mother/mater as its generative source.

What isn't represented in this noun-1 form is the sense of *importance*; rather, that sense is best registered in the verbal form, as in "that matters." How did matter (noun) expand to matter (verb)? We can trace the movement from noun to verb as a common process in semanticization, known as *verbalization*: a substantive noun becomes addressable by its associated verb. This leads us to ask, *When* did matter come to matter? Was it due to the recognitions of capitalism, for which according to Marx raw materials came to acquire value? Was it, furthermore, genocidal settlement, under which the possession and refiguration of land and people were artifices that could be assigned significance? Was it through animism, a widespread and often sustained Indigenous approach to the life and agency of things, including ones thought of in western habits as nonliving? Was it the understanding that ancestries (such as mater) *are* potentials so that the energetic sources for things must necessarily have great importance?

While the *OED* orders definition by frequency first, it can also reflect minoritarian uses, albeit ones that usually fall, in its order of priority, to the bottom. The long-standing feminist and queer critiques of a standard language's encoding of sexual, gender, and racial orders would imply that turning in opening gestures to the *OED* is therefore most likely to trace a history of significance that coconspired with heteropatriarchal colonialism. It is also susceptible to lending, as in the structure of matter itself, significance to anything seen as "originary" or "early." It is not a neutral reference.

Hence the many contestations around matter and society. Returning to the more capacious sense of "matter" inherent to the phrase *Black Lives Matter*, I hear in this political call a linguistic echo forward and backward, a sensory—which is to say, material—touch across the Black trans and queer lives and temporalities that, according to its founding theorizers, are at the heart of why the movement *matters*. Thinking even more broadly, if generativity is at the heart of matter, then matter has a diachronic and not synchronic cast: it moves across time, producing new meaning. Whether or not this diachronicity is viewed strictly as a question of reproduction (as originating in the *mater*), questions of sexuality should be seen as germane to the BLM movement and particular modes of life and world making (Leong 2016).

Black Lives Matter is not simply a demand for significance; it is inevitably also a claim about what is a countable life and an opposition to dehumanization. Against racism's ravenous principles of selection and exception by which Blackness is made to acquire specific toxic material character, the Black materialisms of recent scholarship detail an ontological completism by which Blackness is a *fundamental*, rather than excluded, material: the mother/mater (out) of which distinctiveness can ever come to be, bringing with it a critique of white ideologies of self- or Christian-rendered ethereal creation (Z. Jackson 2020).

Matter is thus intrinsically in conversation with the question of humanness. The humanisms of the settler and colonial projects have, by an accumulated sleight of hand, turned "human" into a much more selective group than an image of the species might suggest, rendered hierarchically across disability, gender, race, class, age; the remainder, as feminists, students of race and materiality, Indigenous scholars, and more have shown, were projected as "nature" or "stuff." This isn't entirely true, condition by condition; for some racist dehumanizations, a tension remains with humanness that intensifies the violence. But one can identify, out of these histories, a charmed circle of animacy that effectively pushes many humans and many animals, on the one hand, into a suspended zone of nonhumanness and, on the other hand, into conversation with a generative potential that is electrified by things inhuman.

45

Methods

Matt Brim and Amin Ghaziani

How do scholars create new knowledge in gender and sexuality studies? How do we work with interviewees, key texts, and other data sources while putting not only protocols but political commitments into practice? More broadly, How do we *do* gender and sexuality studies? These questions, each of which asks how we do something, point to the topic of methods.

Methods may seem like a set of standard protocols for collecting and analyzing data. Feminist researchers count, survey, interview, transcribe, and code. They, like others, use qualitative approaches, quantitative techniques, and critical lenses to understand culturally and historically significant phenomena. But does academic inquiry always require an ordered approach? The answer is no. In fact, gender and sexuality scholarship recognizes *disorder* as generative. Interdisciplinary feminist scholars have long mixed different types of research methods, resulting in a blossoming and blurring of fields. Likewise, rather than dismissing outlier data or trying to straighten up its unruly subjects, scholars who work in the emerging field of "queer methods" exploit the possibilities that arise from the "messiness" of LGBTQI social life (Browne and Nash 2010; Ghaziani and Brim 2019; Love 2019). When Latinx ethnographers work in their field sites, lesbian literary scholars offer close readings, Indigenous linguists curate archives, and queer of color geographers map Black life, we can see how many scholars have retooled long-standing methods to respond to the needs of the marginalized researchers and projects that have redefined the field

of gender and sexuality studies. Linda Tuhiwai Smith's *Decolonizing Methodologies* exemplifies this dynamic, both deconstructing "research" as a dangerous colonial project that has caused suffering and, against that history, orienting Indigenous researchers' methodologies within "the wider framework of self-determination, decolonization and social justice" (1999, 4) that does not merely study but saves lives.

Methods of feminist inquiry can also be messy because they are inseparable from the political investments that orient our work toward social justice (Wiegman 2012). Ponder for a moment the confluence of method and politics that animates the question, How do we count the transgender population (Doan 2019)? In parsing this inquiry, "How do we count?" morphs into "Ought we count?" A survey grounded in the principle of self-determination would ask participants to fill in the words they themselves use to imagine their (a)gender identities rather than force them to choose from a list of only partial possibilities that would inevitably undercount the population (Beemyn and Rankin 2011; Kolysh 2019). The title of the recent collection *Other, Please Specify: Queer Methods in Sociology* (Compton, Meadow, and Schilt 2018) captures the sense of otherness that survey participants regularly experience as well as the possibilities that arise from writing ourselves into a study *on our own terms*.

The protocols of gender and sexuality studies reflect not only researchers' decisions about how to collect data but more fundamentally their own understandings about what counts as evidence. Eschewing traditional methods for critically valuing subcultural work, José Esteban Muñoz suggests that scholars with ties to queer of color and outsider art communities can perceive in the fleeting experience of performance a remainder that he calls "ephemera as evidence" (1996). Extending Muñoz's insights about evidence and urban studies,

Ryan Stillwagon and Amin Ghaziani show how Indigenous and queer people of color use temporary "pop-up" events to promote unique place-making efforts. Working in the field of Black queer studies, Phillip Brian Harper (2005) similarly pieces together "the evidence of felt intuition" as he names a phenomenological method of making meaning out of the very real but often unvoiced erotics of Black gay male embodied experience. Likewise, where the historical archive of Black life under slavery fails, Saidiya Hartman invents the method of "critical fabulation" (2008b, 11) to fashion narratives of the past that are both impossible and imperative for navigating the dangers and joys of "the afterlife of slavery" (2008a).

Whereas western epistemologies and scholarship have produced protocols that privilege empirical observations in the guise of the "scientific method," gender and sexuality researchers often draw on Indigenous and nonwestern knowledge systems to understand world making (Haraway 1991; Reid-Pharr 2016; TallBear 2013). Here, "collectivity" names a method of inquiry that is marked by shared thought and negotiated action, particularly for transnational and woman of color feminism in the Global South, the African diaspora, and borderland communities within national frames (Anzaldúa 1987; Combahee River Collective [1977] 2015). In fact, a firsthand example of collective methods of knowledge creation is the volume you are holding.

We look back to the early groundbreaking collection *All the Women Are White, All the Blacks Are Men, but Some of Us Are Brave: Black Women's Studies* to make two final points about feminist and queer methods. While Akasha (Gloria T.) Hull, Patricia Bell Scott, and Barbara Smith ([1982] 2015) build the field of Black women's studies around the experiences of "ordinary" and "unexceptional" Black women in communities, under capitalism, in prison, in the domestic sphere, as mothers, and as lesbians (xxii), they somewhat contentiously argue that "naming and describing our experience are important initial steps, but not alone sufficient to get us where we need to go" (xxi). To buttress experience, they turn to feminist, radical, and analytical *methods* to guide the field. In this productive tension, we see that the methods of *But Some of Us Are Brave* are determined by a larger *methodology* or theory of method: *Black feminist scholarship must be conducted in the name of Black women's total liberation.* Finally, at the end of their introduction, Hull and Smith list seventeen recommendations for the future of Black women's studies. The first seven items demand funding, beginning with "funding of individual research by Black women scholars" (xxxiii). These priorities remind us that the question of method—the *how* of research—is inseparable from the resources we require to do our work. Methods are class-based material practices as well as enactments of protocols and political commitments. In this context, sharing resources between rich and poor institutions—and gender and sexuality studies college programs—is a vital feminist, antiracist, and queer method for challenging elitism in the university (Brim 2020).

46

Migration

Lisa Sun-Hee Park

The study of modern human migration takes place across multiple disciplines and engages a wide variety of methodologies, and yet issues of gender and sexuality have largely been understood as marginal to this pivotal area of research. This essay highlights key contributions regarding migration by gender and sexuality scholars. First, research on women's migration experiences has opened new historical understandings of national inclusion and exclusion. Second, critical, queer, and trans migration studies approaches have scrutinized normativity in ways that have produced new and generative questions regarding state-based rights and policies. Third, and relatedly, this critique has forced us to rethink such fundamental social concepts as citizenship, belonging, and borders.

To begin, we know that migration is not a haphazard event. Rather, patterns of human migration follow established global political, economic, and military linkages. Saskia Sassen's (1990, 1999) work has been pivotal in countering the myth of migration as an indiscriminate flow, or "mass invasion," of the global poor. And while the sources, routes, and numbers of transnational migration may have changed over time in accordance to shifts in capital, technology, and military priorities, its integral role in providing the labor essential for the global economy remains constant. For example, Kitty Calavita (2008) and Ruth Milkman (2006) explain how a surge in demand for migrant women's labor occurred in the 1970s and 1980s as the service sector largely replaced traditional manufacturing industries in the United States. Also, during this time, deindustrialization, capital flight, economic restructuring, and the dismantling of labor unions resulted in declining wage levels, an increase in income inequality, and a growing sense of instability. As the presence of migrant women increased during those unsettling times, they were met with particular anxiety and disdain.

Initially, feminist research on migration sought to address the neglect of women's specific experiences of migration. Rachel Silvey (2004) explains that this effort then shifted to examine the intersections between gender and other axes of difference, which led to the development of innovative theoretical approaches for exploring power relations embedded in changing migration patterns. Silvey (2004, 1) writes, "As a result, it has helped to explain the political dynamics driving the feminization of both internal and international migration flows, as well as the absolute and proportional increase of women of color participating in global migration flows in recent decades" (see also Gabaccia 1994; Fujiwara 2008; Hondagneu-Sotelo 1999; Manalansan 2006; Segura and Zavella 2007).

Migrant women are viewed as necessary but burdensome to the nation-state. Historically, US immigration law has enforced strict dependency on the part of women on men or state institutions as a requirement for admission. Generally, they were allowed to enter as someone's wife, daughter, or mother or recruited as a worker by a particular industry or institution. Women rarely migrated alone for much of US history, and independent, low-income migrant women experienced particular forms of intense scrutiny and suspicion. At the same time, dependency upon public programs was considered irresponsible and a marker of personal deficiency. For example, Martha Gardner (2009, 89) writes that between 1880 and 1924, the federal immigration law of public charge (meaning "public burden") was used as a common category of exclusion for vast numbers of women who were deported as potential paupers for "moral, marital, physical, and economic deficiencies." Vaguely defined, public charge was an administrative law that targeted migrants who were deemed to be or had the possibility of becoming a burden on the state.

Pregnancy was deemed a public charge offense for many low-income or unmarried migrant women. While laws against poverty were usually applied to both men and women immigrants, public charge singled out women as the social mores of the early twentieth century linked immorality and indigence, and subsequently, poverty alleviation policies increasingly focused on women's morality and their "proper" role within the family (Gardner 2009). During this same time, a racial taxonomy in which Europeans were placed at the top was accepted as scientific fact and formed the basis of a vigorous eugenics movement in the United States. Used to rationalize Jim Crow segregation, anti-Asian discrimination, and colonial ventures into Latin America and the Pacific, eugenic logic, as described by Alexandra Stern ([2005] 2016), also undergirded the application of public charge law.

By the end of the Great Depression and the beginning of World War II, public charge designations largely disappeared from the federal immigration agency's exclusionary repertoire. The harrowing realization of the application of eugenic logic in the death camps of the Holocaust contributed to its submersion from public view. Public charge law lay largely dormant until the mid-1990s, when it reappeared with new health care fraud detection programs in California (Park 2011). Once again, reproduction by low-income migrant women was targeted—this time from Latin America and Asia. Migrant women who had used public health insurance, for which they were eligible, for their prenatal care and delivery were accused by federal immigration

authorities of becoming a public charge. At that time, however, immigrant legal advocates were able to push back and pressure the US Citizenship and Immigration Services to clarify the definition of public charge and limit its applicability (Park 2011). Consequently, the fraud detection program was quietly dismantled. Eighteen years later, public charge resurfaced once again with the election of Donald Trump, providing further evidence of its potential as a powerful tool in its strategic ambiguity and relatively quiet location on the outskirts of public notice.

In analyzing such state-based policies, critical, queer, and trans migration frameworks have been productive in decentering normative understandings of migration that reinforce national economic and political rationalities. These approaches are part of a new direction in the study of migration that takes seriously the insights and sensitivities produced by migrant activist movements and struggles. For example, in the US context, undocumented migrant youth, many wearing the identity moniker "undocuqueer," have drawn attention to the ways that previous calls to migrant belonging based on good family values and economic contributions reinforce nation-state norms and a dichotomy between good and bad migrants in which only a select few are worthy (Chávez 2013; Chávez and Masri 2020).

Critical, queer, and trans migration studies counters research that positions migrants as solely a problem to be solved or objects to be studied. Instead, these critical approaches frame migrants and their experiences as key sources of knowledge from which to trace forms of power. For instance, Lisa Lowe (1996, 8) argues that the "immigrant," in their relational and oppositional construction to the "citizen," is a generative site for critique of the nation and its laws. As Karma R. Chávez (2013, 10) notes, "Queers and migrants have been attacked through shared logics of scapegoating, threat, and deviance." Chávez writes that this shared experience positions queers, migrants, and queer migrants "in relation to the US nation-state as strangers who exist largely outside national imaginaries of belonging and as subjects who cannot formally access the state as citizens." In Chavez's writing, we see that retaining a critical stance is key: rather than working toward inclusion into the same social system that has created the condition of their exclusion, such approaches value the migrant subject position as a source of knowledge production from which to challenge the powerful disciplinary requirements of normativity.

In his book *Contagious Divides: Epidemics and Race in San Francisco's Chinatown*, Nayan Shah (2001) operationalizes the term *queer*, rather than simply as a synonym for *homosexual identity*, to question normative family formations as the basis of citizenship and cultural belonging. He writes, "The analytical category of queer upsets the strict gender roles, the firm divisions between public and private, and the implicit presumptions of self-sufficient economics and intimacy in the respectable domestic household" (13). This is in line with Siobhan Somerville's (2005) assessment that queer studies has pushed our understanding of migration by investigating not only queers crossing borders but also how ideologies of the nation actually queer particular migrants, regardless of their sexual orientation. For instance, Somerville presents a "queer" reading of the public oath required as part of the naturalization process. She writes that naturalization (as opposed to birthright citizenship) is a contractual relationship based on mutual consent between the migrant and the state and notes, "Perhaps not coincidentally, in form, language, and effect, the oath of allegiance has similarities to traditional vows of marriage: both are speech acts that transform the speaker's legal status; both use the language of 'fidelity' and 'obligation';

and both establish an exclusive—one might even say 'monogamous'—relationship to the other party" (662). If, as Eithne Luibhéid (2002, x) argues, the immigration control apparatus itself is "a key site for the production and reproduction of sexual categories, identities, and norms within relations of inequality," then we come to understand citizenship and national belonging as an intimate act and migration as a fundamental effort of the state to reproduce itself. Similarly, Jacqueline Stevens (1999) points out that the state, in attempting to reproduce itself, is embedded in the sexual. Trans scholars of migration similarly call attention to the ways gender nonconformity functions as a dense site of state surveillance, whether as a reason to include or exclude one at national borders (Beauchamp 2019; Rand 2005; Shakhsari 2014).

In this way, citizenship and its multiple variations of national belonging have served as productive concepts that complicate rather than celebrate narratives of national membership, particularly within gender and sexuality studies. Leti Volpp (2017, 2) argues that citizenship has evolved in tandem with the western nation-state. As a presumptively masculine and heteronormative condition, women and the sexual and gender nonnormative have long been considered unfit candidates for citizenship. And as citizenship stretches to incorporate new bodies, Volpp argues, it also "excludes fresh targets of unbelonging." She writes, "Which persons have been recognizable as citizens, and what attendant rights they can enjoy, has been highly gendered since the foundation of the very notion of nation-state citizenship. . . . Immigration admission has never been open to undesirable subjects" (4).

Here, the contributions of critical, queer, and trans migration approaches are apparent in providing greater analytical depth of the implicit normative assumptions embedded in "inclusion." As Bonnie Honig (2001) argues, migrant labor has been vital not only for global capital growth but also in its ability to reinforce a national identity of equality and meritocracy, which functions to obscure the reality of a "differential inclusion" based on race, class, gender, and sexuality. Yen Le Espiritu (2003, 47) defines differential inclusion as a process "whereby a group of people is deemed integral to the nation's economy, culture, identity, and power—but integral only or precisely because of their designated subordinate standing." For instance, homophobia has been an effective method in establishing and justifying particular racial groups as inferior. In his analysis of Asian American masculinity, David Eng (2001, 17) notes that "the acquisition of gendered identity in liberal capitalist societies is always a racialized acquisition and that the exploitation of immigrant labor is mobilized not only through the racialization of that labor but through its sexualizing."

Differential inclusion as a concept problematizes the implications of institutional power in the experiences of migrants who must navigate the contradictory expectations of national membership. In reality, immigrants are already included into the nation: as low-wage temporary workers. True assimilation would disrupt the necessary foreignness of low-wage workers—meaning the foreignness and accompanying lack of rights and belonging that help maintain lower wages. And yet the goal of assimilation must be upheld in maintaining the exceptional national image of the United States as a land of equal opportunity and capitalist democracy. It is an aspirational goal with powerful disciplinary potential. In this way, low-wage migrant workers are precariously trapped with paradoxical relations formed by discourses of inclusion, assimilation, and dependency.

47

Movements

Soyica Diggs Colbert

Movement is the politicized version of performance because the term carries two connotations in the twentieth century that are distinct from performance: (1) collective action and (2) perpetual change. Movement remains tethered to social organization and in motion. In terms of gender and sexuality studies, movement draws from the theoretical context in which the idea that the consolidation of repeated actions (performance) over time constitutes identity (J. Butler [1990] 1999; Roach 1996; E. Johnson 2003; D. Brooks 2006). Judith Butler (2007) argues in "Performative Acts and Gender Constitution" that history, power, and repetition produce gender as a performative—the crystallized, hailing, regulatory force of identity categories and social positions. Performance shapes the individual because it renders them answerable to an ideal, which, as Butler explains, becomes sedimented as a performative. Performatives—such as gender roles or other identitarian categories and "reiterations of stylized norms, and inherited gestural conventions from the way we sit, stand, speak, dress, dance, play, eat, hold a pencil and more" (Madison 2014, viii)— exert social force through the perception of their stability, through the idea that they are stable and not in flux. Paradoxically, performatives accrue value through repetition inherent to performance. Butler's formulation thus depends on a logic of accumulation. Over time, the appearance of identity flattens the "internally discontinuous" (J. Butler 2007, 154) aspects of gender in order to produce continuity. Joseph Roach offers a similar rendering of the term *performance*, explaining, "[It] offers a substitute for something else that preexists it. Performance, in other words, stands in for an elusive entity that it is not but that it must vainly aspire both to embody and to replace" (1996, 3). Although the filling of the vacancies, as he explains, never amounts to a perfect replica, the desire attached to performatives conceals inconsistencies.

As I argue in *Black Movements*, "Although it is easy to analogize Butler's rendering of gender performance to race, the preface to the 1999 edition of her book *Gender Trouble* warns against such easy alignments. Her admonition gives us room to consider how the performances that constitute blackness disrupt the accumulative time associated with gender performance" (Colbert 2017, 6). That certain identities challenge the accumulative logic of performance calls attention to how the term helps explain certain manifestations of gender but does not fully account for identity. As a related term, *movement* participates in the formation of collective identity through embodied action but as perpetual change, not repetition. An act could qualify as a performance or a movement depending on its relationship to prior acts and the contexts for its enactment. Thinking in terms of gender and sexuality, the understanding of becoming a woman—and not only a white heteronormative woman, coinciding with postcolonial independence movements and the burgeoning civil rights movement—charges the word with the flow of ideas between activists, artists, and intellectuals. Movement calls attention to the collective and at times asynchronous work of formation.

In the mid-twentieth century, in the midst of the Cold War, independence movements abroad and the civil rights movement in the United States established a foundation for woman of color feminism and the LGBT rights movement. Following the Allied victory in World War II, the US's rhetoric of expansive freedom being tied to capitalist democracy began to show signs of strain as young Black, brown, and white people organized to expand voting rights to all citizens, allow individuals of all races to participate in the markets, and desegregate schools, neighborhoods, and public places. The agitation for Black people's full participation in democratic and capitalist systems produced an urgency that many Americans felt alongside the anxiety and dread of possible nuclear war. This time period, what Lorraine Hansberry (2001) calls "an affirmative period of history," led politicians, artists, and intellectuals to reconsider some of their fundamental presumptions about life, living, and the possibility of human transformation.

Alongside the burgeoning political movements that would define the mid and late twentieth century, in the 1950s, intellectuals—including, Jean-Paul Sartre, Frantz Fanon, Hansberry, and Simone de Beauvoir—began to question the nature of identity and how it figured in forming collectives. This questioning led to de Beauvoir's now well-known assertion "One is not born, but rather becomes, a woman" ([1949] 1989, 267). De Beauvoir's statement reflects her understanding of women as a distinctive group formed through being in the world. This phenomenological understanding of womanhood resonates with Fanon's articulation of the social formation of Blackness. The idea of becoming, through word and deed, set the foundation for late twentieth-century political movements (civil rights, postcolonial rights, women's rights, and LGBT rights) to shift the place or position of identity into a series of actions rather than a static innate quality. The force of these actions also must be understood at the intersection of meanings and as a part of collective histories. Understanding identity as a changing position or posture puts pressure on ontological, or essentialized, renderings of race, gender, and sexuality. The coincident political movements of the 1960s and 1970s ushered along philosophical articulations that later became installed in institutional organizations, including women's studies departments and later gender and sexuality studies departments.

Gender and sexuality studies begins with, as, and in, movement. In the late twentieth century, the movements for political and civil rights helped usher forth the institutionalization of gender and sexuality studies in colleges and universities. *Political movement* can be defined as "a series of actions on the part of a group of people working toward a common goal" (F. Griffin 2013, 16–17). Although not routinely used to discuss gender identity, the physical meaning of the word *movement*—"a change in position," place, or posture—has implications for how we understand the study of gender and sexuality. The multiple meanings of *movement* (political, a change in position, and artistic) come to bear for the term as a keyword of gender and sexuality studies because it is through movement that gender and sexuality come into being historically, institutionally, and politically.

Woman of color feminism coincided with the development of women's and gender studies departments and the intellectual labor of writers that used artistic production to form the basis of political organizing. As a result, the anthology became a useful form of production to gather feminist voices in a shared project. In one of the most important of these collections, *This Bridge Called My Back: Writings by Radical Women of Color*, co-editor Cherríe Moraga describes the production of the collection as a journey. She writes, "It is probably crucial to describe here the way this book is coming together, the journey it is taking me on. The book still not completed and I have traveled East to find it a publisher" ([1981] 1983, xiii). Her travels from the West to the East Coasts also include her navigating Boston and its suburbs. Moving in the segregated city, she notes, "Take Boston alone, I think myself and the feminism my so-called sisters have constructed does nothing to help me make the trip from one end of town to another. Leaving Watertown, I board a bus and ride it quietly in my light flesh to Harvard Square, protected by the gold highlights my hair dares to take on, like an insult, in this miserable light" (xiii). The acknowledgment of her light-skinned privilege and how it affords her liberty to navigate the city calls to mind the ongoing policing of space even post de jure segregation and the way migration functions as another form of movement that defines gender and polices sexuality.

Moraga's political organizing requires that she navigate the coast and the city, bringing the two forms of movement together. But her meditation also calls to mind the fugitive movement of other earlier and contemporary feminists. She explains, "*I transfer and go underground. Julie told me the other day how they stopped her for walking through the suburbs. Can't tell if she's a man or a woman, only know that it's Black moving through that part of town. They wouldn't spot her here, moving underground*" ([1981] 1983, xiii). The undercommons serves as a reservoir for activity and less fettered movement. It also allows for the flourishing and feeding of identities that move less freely above. Moraga concludes emphasizing the importance of the undercommons as a space off the grid to organize: "I hear there are some women in this town plotting a *lesbian* revolution. What does this mean about the boy shot in the head is what I want to know. I am a lesbian. I want a movement that helps me make some sense of the trip from Watertown to Roxbury, from white to Black. I love women the entire way, beyond a doubt" (xiv). Moraga's use of the word *trip* calls attention to how travel functions in both a philosophical and a physical sense.

As Moraga will articulate, part of the movement that she desires requires learning to forge bonds across personal and political differences and physical distances. Describing her relationship with Barbara Smith, she says, "*Sisters* . . . I earned this with Barbara. It is not a given between us—Chicana and Black—to come to see each other as sisters. This is not a given. I keep wanting to repeat over and over and over again, the pain and shock of difference, the joy of commonness, the exhilaration of meeting through incredible odds against it" ([1981] 1983, xiv). Moraga ends the essays by explicating the title of the volume. She suggests the foundation of the movement, even as she remains in motion, is her physical body and its labor. The writing of women of color serves as a bridge for connection. She explains, "It is about physical and psychic struggle. It is about intimacy, a desire for life between all of us, not settling for less than freedom even in the most private aspects of our lives. A total vision. For women in this book, I will lay my body down for that vision. *This Bridge Called My Back*. In the dream, I am always met at the river" (xix). The final sentence of her meditation explains how women of color get over the troubled waters that divide them. Her emphasis on the physical as a mode of surrogation rather than stasis animates conversations about how race comes to matter alongside gender, class, and sexuality. The body stands in for but does not become the destination of the movement. Or as Moraga writes, echoing existentialist thinkers, "I am talking about believing that we have the power to actually transform our experience, change our lives, save our lives. Otherwise, why this book? It is the faith of activists I am talking about" (xviii). The movement emerges between women's active collaboration, their coordinated movement, resulting in not only collectivity but also art. The shift from having an identity to performing an identity does not emerge fully, however, until Butler's (1989) critical philosophical engagement in *Gender Trouble*.

In the interim between the inauguration of women's and gender studies programs through the activism and art of woman of color feminists and the incorporation of these programs into institutions, communities of color lost some of their coherence. The emergence of Black studies, ethnic studies, women's and gender studies, and queer of color critique within universities coincides with neoliberalism and the hyperindividualization of labor. As a result, the systematic integration of Black and brown people and of women into white institutions became understood as a response to individual excellence rather than long-standing and ongoing histories of systemic exclusion. Such framing made requirements on what types of difference could become legible in white institutional spaces. The collective action of woman of color feminists enabled the incorporation of a chosen few in institutions of higher learning and left room for later generations of scholars to consider how race and gender circulate within these new but very familiar economic contexts. Put another way, the women and people of color who gained access to white institutions as a result of collective organizing were told by the institutions that their merit garnered admission and served as justification for their singularity. The exceptional ones became the standard-bearers and expression of the movements.

The toggling back and forth between individual performance—in this case, of excellence—and collective movement shaped discussions in the late twentieth century of identity and its manifestations. In "Feeling Brown, Feeling Down: Latina Affect, the Performativity of Race, and the Depressive Position," José Esteban Muñoz considers how "*racial performativity* is intended to get at an aspect of race that is 'a doing.' More precisely, I mean to describe a political doing, the effects that the recognition of racial belonging, coherence, and divergence present in the world" (2006, 678–79). His focus on race as a doing, which aligns with understandings of movement in a physical and political sense, seeks to produce "a project that imagines a position or narrative of being and becoming that can resist the pull of identitarian models of relationality" (677). This assertion may seem to be at direct odds with the work of women of color feminists as represented by *This Bridge Called My Back*, but instead, Muñoz invites us to remember the intramural organizing that led to the mid and late twentieth-century movements. He contends that "feeling brown . . . is descriptive of the ways in which minoritarian affect is always, no matter what its register, partially illegible in relation to the normative affect performed by normative citizen subjects" (679). As a result, they are meant not to describe a way of knowing but rather to approach a form of being articulated through doing. He says, "Brownness is a mode of attentiveness to the self for others that is cognizant of the way in which it is not and can never be whiteness" (680).

Recalling the form and function of movement as aesthetic practice, Muñoz emphasizes the importance of turning to art to locate the feelings that serve as the basis for relation in the wake of multiculturalism. These aesthetic movements serve as the fodder and foundation for different forms of political organizing that must manifest themselves through purposeful practices of return and the recognition that the work will at least partially take place underground. Muñoz explains, "Aesthetic practices and performances offer a particular theoretical lens to understand the ways in which different circuits of belonging connect, which is to say that recognition flickers between minoritarian subjects" (2006, 679–80). For Muñoz, these circuits produce the possibility "to see the other in alterity as existing in a relational field to the self" (681). This ability to behold the other necessitates the type of work that Moraga maps but must be, as Muñoz suggests, apprehended in contemporary contexts.

The temporal movement of return, in this case, seeks to redirect the movements that have been channeled into the reformation of white institutions back into the Black and brown contexts of their formation and cultivation. To return, in this context, may be to find something that never existed at all but also to redefine possibility. Muñoz argues, quoting Hortense Spillers, "The reparation staged in Spillers' theoretical work is informed by a desire to return to another place that she describes as 'old-fashioned.' *Old-fashioned* is associated with the nonsecular belonging that in turn is associated with the history of the Black church (2003). Spillers explicitly desires a secular space where such relationality is possible, but *old-fashioned* is not only deployed in its conventional usage, it is also written in a psychic sense—the desire for a moment before communities of color lapsed into functional impasse" (2006, 682–83). By the early aughts, the period in which Muñoz writes his essay, the idea of minoritarian coalition as a mode of political organizing and social movement seemed to have run its course, particularly given the purported exhaustion with identity politics and the lack of coherence within racialized groups. Muñoz offers a reconsideration of the direction for movements, recovering spaces off the grid and remembering that movement has always included a doing, an undoing, and becoming at the same time.

48

Performativity

Tavia Nyong'o

Performativity is one of the most consequential and contested ideas to emerge from feminist and queer theory. For better or worse, "queer performativity" was one of the signal queer theory catchphrases of the 1990s, and it continues to reverberate today, even as the heavily linguistic theory from which it emerged has given way to a subsequent turn to affect, new materialism, and ecological approaches. But where did performativity come from? In the midcentury language philosophy of J. L. Austin, the performative speech act was a way of noticing that language did things in the world, which is to say, it was a way of noticing that linguistic statements could not be reduced to transparently true or false descriptions of "the real" (as some of Austin's fellow thinkers held). Austin (1975) originally sought to classify speech acts in terms of whether they were "performative" or "constative"—that is, whether they did things or merely described them. Yet in the end, he concluded that all language contained aspects of performative force in it. This conclusion opened the way for a subsequent philosopher, Jacques Derrida, to give speech act theory a deconstructive emphasis. In order for speech to do something, to act as a force, Derrida argued, it paradoxically must cite some precedent within language that granted that act intelligibility.

Although the performative speech act has been extensively debated within critical theory since its inception, the advent of queer performativity in the 1990s gave the idea a second life. In her well-known book *Gender Trouble*, feminist philosopher Judith Butler ([1990]

1999) helped inaugurate queer theory in part by drawing from this philosophical tradition to argue that "woman" is a performative speech act rather than a biological essence or even a sociocultural known. Prior to Butler, feminist theory had debated the sex/gender distinction, to be sure, with many coming to understand sex as biological and gender as cultural. But Butler's emphasis on performativity implied that the sex/gender distinction itself was in need of deconstruction and that "woman" was itself a citation without a stable original. In order to make the speech act "woman" coherent, a set of conventions and expectations must be imposed and enforced. Paradoxically, gender's status as citation also opens out the potential for the gender nonconforming to disrupt those expectations by refusing to "do" their gender correctly. Most famously, Butler pointed to drag queens as making evident the performativity of gender through satire and theatricality.

In another famous book, *Epistemology of the Closet*, literary critic Eve Kosofsky Sedgwick (1990) made parallel deconstructive moves with regard to the modern discourse of sexuality, focusing her attention primarily on how that discourse was powerfully structured by what it could and could not say about male homosexuality. The closet was Sedgwick's paradigm for describing the context in which certain speech acts became framed within a binarism of the speakable and unspeakable. The closet as a metaphor operates as a source of hidden knowledge that can nonetheless be presumed upon "in a pinch." Taxonomizing the binarisms she repeatedly encountered in modern letters, in which one term is typically privileged and the other stigmatized, Sedgwick showed how reliably queerness was attached to the stigmatized term. Where Butler's influence on theories of queer performativity can be seen most particularly where questions of norms and their transgressions are posed, Sedgwick's influence is more acutely felt where questions of the tacit and unspoken are broached.

Although less frequently cited in the context of queer studies, the groundbreaking essays of Hortense Spillers might also be said to offer a Black feminist account of performativity, one steeped in the psychoanalytic traditions from which Sedgwick and Butler also draw. In "Mama's Baby, Papa's Maybe," Spillers ([1987] 2003) intervened within white feminist theory by outlining how the Middle Passage violently ungendered Black bodies. Spillers's intervention effected a shift toward an analytics of the flesh as an index of the "real" of race held outside language and the symbolic order. Ordinary language philosophy tends to presume a speaking subject who possesses bodily integrity within a mutually intelligible community of speakers. The analytics of the flesh, by contrast, places this presumption under scrutiny. Where gender for Butler is a citation without an original and sexuality for Sedgwick is an epistemology of the tacitly known, race for Spillers is the formative rupture of flesh out of which modern genders and sexualities become thinkable. This framework has consequences for scholars who draw on performativity in order to show how race is an effect of language. Indeed, Spillers employs both feminism and psychoanalysis to step outside the normative western patriarchal understanding of language and the symbolic order and to envision elements of a Black feminist performativity.

Although performativity, as I've suggested, remains associated with the linguistic turn of the 1980s and 1990s, contemporary gender and sexuality studies continues to confront the power of language to do things: its capacity to make and not just describe social worlds. For many skeptics, however, the framework of performativity remains *too* linguistic, neglecting embodied and material experience. While this criticism is valid, it may also reproduce a binarism—between words and things—that is less helpful than it initially seems. Today we routinely face questions of misgendering, deadnaming, and even aspects of so-called callout culture that might all potentially be thought through using performativity. The postmillennial emphasis on epistemic violence—on the power of words to wound—certainly owes a lot to the assumption that language has performative, and not merely descriptive, force. Even the dominance of the digital over how we identify and communicate our race, sex, and gender today is powerfully inscribed by the grammar of the computer languages in which programs are written; our networked utterances are shaped by what is legible and opaque to the platforms they occur on. Algorithmic culture, with its tireless tracking, sorting, and repacking of our individual preferences back to us, may even be digitally enhancing our sense of performative efficacy. Whatever the case may be, it seems there will be a future for the performative just so long as there is a history of past utterances to be drawn on for citational (and revisionary) force.

49

Porn

Lynn Comella

Pornography is defined as any "material (such as writings, photographs, or movies) depicting sexual activity or erotic behavior in a way that is designed to arouse sexual excitement" (Harchuck 2015, 13). Pornography is protected by the First Amendment, making it different from obscenity, which is speech about sex that falls outside First Amendment protections (Heins 1993). The line between pornography and obscenity is a thin one, and the US Supreme Court struggled throughout the twentieth century to define obscenity in legally precise ways (Strub 2010, 2013). The 1973 Supreme Court decision in *Miller v. California* (413 U.S. 15 (1973)) affirmed the place of local community standards for judging whether a text or image is obscene and maintained that such material must lack any "serious literary, artistic, political, or scientific value," establishing the legal standard that continues to be used today.

Pornography has for centuries been a flash point for cultural anxiety, controversy, and regulation. In the 1970s, pornography emerged as an especially contentious battleground for feminists. It was a decade marked by the release of the controversial film *Deep Throat*, the rise of "porno chic" (Bronstein and Strub 2016), and a growing sexual consumer culture that put sexuality "on/scene" in new and more explicit ways (L. Williams 2004). These shifts were facilitated by changing sexual mores and norms borne out by 1960s countercultural movements and the loosening of obscenity laws, which enterprising filmmakers and publishers readily

seized upon (Schaefer 2014). As pornography's reach expanded, more people were inspired to join the fight against it.

Feminist efforts to combat pornography grew out of larger calls for media reform that took aim at sexist and violent imagery in popular culture, such as advertising imagery for the Rolling Stones' 1976 album *Black and Blue*, which featured a bound and bruised woman (Bronstein 2011). Over time, feminists began to focus more narrowly on pornography and its perceived dangers. Throughout the 1970s, they generated petitions, staged protests, and founded influential activist organizations, such Women Against Violence in Pornography and Media and Women Against Pornography, which took direct aim at the pornography industry.

Antipornography feminists were forceful in their denunciations of what they saw as pornography's intrinsically sexist and harmful effects (see Lederer 1980). Andrea Dworkin theorized that pornography "conditions, trains, educates and inspires men to despise women, to use women, to hurt women" (1980, 289). Drawing a link between images and actions, Robin Morgan famously asserted that "pornography is the theory and rape is the practice" (1980, 139). These and similar views dominated national conversations about pornography and informed legislative and legal efforts to restrict sexual speech, awkwardly aligning the feminist antipornography movement, according to its critics, with the political goals of religious conservatives and the power of the state (Duggan and Hunter 1995; Vance 1997).

By the early 1980s, a countermovement led by lesbian sex radicals and anticensorship feminists was emerging. "Pro-sex" feminists—or sex-positive feminists, as they would come to be known—championed people's fundamental right to sexual freedom, pleasure, and autonomy and challenged the idea that sex and sexual imagery were "zones of special danger to women" (Caught Looking 1988, 10). They critiqued what they saw as the oversimplification of the problem of pornography, including antipornography activists' reliance on essentialist theories of gender difference that positioned men as aggressors and women as victims, and rejected reductive ideas about media representation that failed to account for "multiple, contradictory, layered and highly contextual meanings" (Duggan and Hunter 1995, 7).

These dueling positions, which would become known as the feminist sex wars, reached fever pitch at the 1982 Barnard College Scholar and Feminist Conference, "Towards a Politics of Sexuality" (Vance 1984; Comella 2008; Bronstein 2015). Conference organizers saw the event as an opportunity to restore a sense of balance to feminist conversations about sexuality that had been almost entirely eclipsed by the focus on sexual danger and harm. They wanted to highlight erotic diversity, including how gender, race, and class intersect to shape women's sexual lives, and argued that feminism needed robust analyses that could speak "as powerfully in favor of sexual pleasure as it does against sexual danger" (Vance 1984, 3).

Controversy began to brew in the days leading up to the conference. Angered by what they saw as their exclusion from the conference program, antipornography feminists denounced the event and accused organizers of silencing them. They staged a protest on the day of the conference in which they handed out leaflets attacking by name individual organizations and speakers who, according to them, promoted "antifeminist" and "patriarchal sexuality," actions that led to public rebuke and charges of McCarthyism (Nestle 1987). While those involved in the conference planning had expected debate, they had not anticipated the vicious and personal nature of the attacks. The Barnard conference was a defining moment in feminist struggles over pornography.

It signaled "an end to an uncontested anti-pornography politics" (Bronstein 2011, 307) and ignited a period of sustained, and at times deeply personal, conflicts about "good" versus "bad" sexual desires and forms of expression that continue to reverberate today (see G. Rubin [1984] 2011).

By the mid-1980s, technological shifts had also begun to transform the porn industry. Adult video had overtaken film as pornography's dominant format, moving the viewing of adults-only fare from public theaters into the privacy of people's homes (Alilunas 2016). The affordability of video technology and desktop publishing created new opportunities for pornographers to experiment with making different kinds of sex media for new and more diverse audiences and niche categories, including racial fetishism.

The emergence of women- and queer-run porn companies, such as Femme Productions and Fatale Video, and lesbian publications like *On Our Backs* and *Bad Attitude*, all of which were founded in 1984, upended the idea that pornography was the sole purview of men and paved the wave for the eventual rise of queer porn (see Nagle 1997; Henderson 1999; Royalle 2013; Rednour and Strano 2015). Feminist pornographers foregrounded female pleasure and lesbian eroticism, giving rise to alternative pornographic conventions and aesthetics as well as new business models that tapped into a burgeoning sex-positive economy and distribution network (Comella 2013, 2017; Queen 2015). These images not only disrupted the hegemony of the male gaze but challenged the idea that pornography was a monolithic and fixed system of meaning in which women were positioned solely as passive objects rather than active agents and authors of their own desires.

Interest in the academic study of pornography also began to grow during this decade. The publication of Linda Williams's book *Hard Core: Power, Pleasure and the*

"Frenzy of the Visible," which positioned pornography as just another "genre among other genres" ([1989] 1999, 120), helped legitimize pornography as a topic worthy of academic inquiry. *Hard Core* quickly became a foundational text in the porn studies canon and remains an important touchstone for researchers interested in understanding pornography's history, industrial organization, distribution models, and modes of consumption and reception (see Attwood and Smith 2014; L. Williams 2014).

The field of porn studies has evolved from a focus on the hard-core heterosexual films that were the subject of Williams's book to include research on many different porn and porn-adjacent subgenres (H. Butler 2004; Waugh 1996; Ecoffier 2009; Schaefer 1999; Gorfinkel 2017), technological transformations (Alilunas 2016; Heffernan 2015; Attwood 2010; K. Jacobs 2007), labor and production practices (Miller-Young 2014; Berg 2017; Stardust 2019; A. Jones 2020), and questions of audiences and spectatorship (C. Smith 2007; Neville 2018). Researchers have explored pornography's wider contexts of distribution and reception (Delany 1999; Comella 2013) and examined the "specific places it is produced, distributed, and consumed" (Juffer 1998, 14).

Today, porn studies is a growing interdisciplinary field with its own academic journal and professional organizations. Pornography "holds a mirror up to the culture" (Kipnis 1998, 157), and studying it can provide important insights into larger political, economic, and social processes, including how pornography produces and reinscribes class distinctions (Penley 2004; Kipnis 1999), the complexities of race and desire (K. Mercer 1994; Fung 1991; Shimizu 2007; Miller-Young 2014; Nash 2014; Cruz 2016), the politics of queer and trans representation (Hill-Meyer 2013; Trouble 2014; Pezzutto and Comella 2020; Richardson 2020; Strub 2020; R. Goldberg 2020), and the varied experiences of those working both in front of and behind the camera (Jiz Lee 2015; Del Rio and Pezzutto 2020; Threat and Comella 2020).

Over the years, feminist porn has moved from the margins and into the cultural mainstream, deepening our understanding about gendered spectatorship and desire (see Taormino et al. 2013). Feminist and queer pornographers have expanded the kinds of sexual images that are available in pornography. Their films often feature ethnically diverse and queer bodies of all shapes and sizes, exploding the very identity categories that typically define how pornography is made and marketed. In a media culture in which queer and trans representations are still limited, pornography is one of the few places where marginalized people can see images of themselves and their desires reflected back at them. Black lesbian porn producer Shine Louise Houston sees her films as a "site of production for a queer discourse of sexuality" (Houston 2014, 118). Genderqueer porn performer Jiz Lee (2013, 275) notes that queer porn is one of the few venues where queer people can tell their stories on their own terms.

The porn industry has changed in other ways too. The traditional studio system has waned, the result of economic and technological shifts, including rampant piracy and the availability of free internet porn. Pornography is no longer as profitable as it once was. Instead, many performers now work from home across a number of different platforms, using shoots with bigger companies as advertisements for their cam work and custom clip sales (Del Rio and Pezzutto 2020). Adult webcamming and clip sites, such as OnlyFans and ManyVids, allow for personalized content, greater interactivity, and performer control and are increasingly popular and profitable segments of the adult industry (Comella 2016; Pezzutto 2018). According to one researcher, today's porn stars are better thought of as "porntropreneurs," small business owners who are responsible for shooting and marketing their own content and building and maintaining their personal brands across a number of different social media platforms (Pezzutto 2019). For today's porn performers, the demand to always be "on" and provide fans with intimate glimpses into their everyday lives can be extremely labor intensive.

By the late 1990s, federal obscenity cases began to dwindle, in large part because of the challenges of pursuing them in the internet age. A number of US states have declared pornography to be a public health crisis, blaming porn for everything from rising divorce rates to erectile dysfunction (Glazer 2016). Social media companies—such as Tumblr, which banned all adult content from its platform in 2018—are now playing an active role in what some see as a new era of internet censorship (Bronstein 2020). Battles over pornography continue to inform academic research, public discussions, and legislative efforts to regulate sexually explicit media, reminding us that porn remains a "perennial little melodrama in which, though new players have replaced old, the parts remain much as they were first written" (Kendrick 1987, xiii).

50

Property
K-Sue Park

While the English word *property* still retains the meaning of a quality or trait belonging to a thing from its Old French derivation, its now more dominant use to signify a thing "owned" or a "possession" appears to have been rare before the seventeenth century. During that century, when the English colonization project came into full bloom, the Anglo adaptation of this term made this second usage common. At the same time, the parameters of things that could be owned under English law expanded dramatically, and what it meant to "own" or "possess" them underwent a sea change in the colonies. More specifically, as the English entered into and became dominant in the Atlantic slave trade, the "things" that could be property within that legal tradition extended to include human beings, and where owning land had long primarily meant one had the rights to its *use* value, it increasingly meant the right to access monetary value through it, especially by pledging it as security for debts. These evolutions in the Anglo-American understanding of "property" occurred over and against the freedom and dignity of African and Indigenous people and relationships to lands as places and homes (see Goeman 2008). In other words, the production of these qualitatively new forms of "property" depended on dispossession, or extreme violence enacted on the basis of racial hierarchies (see Bhandar 2018; Nichols 2020). By normalizing this violence through the capture and subjugation of African people and the theft of Native Nations' lands, colonists created a thoroughly racialized and sexually disciplined social order, within which property continues to circulate.

The material and conceptual limits of the term *property* are partly defined by law and change with the law. In the Anglo-American tradition, the law has largely, though not exclusively, constructed property rights as a "bundle"—a panoply of different entitlements or private interests in property, whose trade produces the market itself. Given these conditions, critical analyses of property, especially those that focus on private property and the state, should attend to history—and in particular, the ways that the legal construction of property transformed in the English colonies. Private property in the colonies developed in ways radically different from private property in England because of the dramatically different public law interventions and frameworks that shaped its development. This entry focuses on two of the most significant legal frameworks that shaped the character and dynamics of "property" in the colonies and later in the United States and thus the dominant paradigm for property around the globe. These frameworks are (1) the racial mandate of the Doctrine of Discovery, which authorized both conquest and enslavement as means of producing property, and (2) the system of incentives that promised settlers Native Nations' land in return for their occupation, which deputized heteronormative nuclear families to perform the labor of conquest and thereby further the interests of the state.

The Doctrine of Discovery and its interpretation in the English colonies help explain how the development of "property" in the Americas produced a society riven by racial distinctions and driven by the willingness of self-interested heteronormative family units to engage in profitable forms of violence. The Doctrine of Discovery is a public international law doctrine of war that authorized and ordered conquest and enslavement on the basis of distinctions between tiers of humanity that were characterized as religious, cultural, civilizational, and racial. On the basis of different canon law justifications formulated during the Crusades, in 1452, Pope Nicholas V issued the papal bull *Dum Diversas*, which directed King Afonso V of Portugal to "capture, vanquish, and subdue the saracens, pagans, and other enemies of Christ"; to "put them into perpetual slavery"; and "to take all their possessions and property." He followed with the bull *Romanus Pontifex* in 1455, which explicitly extended dominion over nonwestern peoples' lands to the Catholic nations of Europe (Nicholas V 2017). Subsequent bulls developed the Doctrine of Discovery not only to authorize the seizure of people and land in Africa and the Americas but to rank the entitlement of European nations to do so, beginning with Portugal and Spain. Over the following centuries, the Dutch Republic, France, and England, under the auspices of self-issued charters and grants, further adapted the Doctrine of Discovery to enter into this European competition to conquer non-European nations' lands.

The racial violence authorized by the Doctrine of Discovery produced the two forms of property that would encompass the vast majority of assets and wealth in the mainland English colonies by the time of the Revolutionary War: land and enslaved persons. The Virginia Company's first charter from the Crown in 1606—which expressed the hope that the colonists would "in time bring the Infidels and Savages, living in those Parts, to human Civility, and to a settled and quiet Government" (Avalon Project, n.d.)—"granted" the homelands of the Powhatan Confederacy, the Monacan, the Cherokee, the Wampanoag, and others to two groups of English investors. The first enslaved people brought to the colony of Virginia in 1619 were captured in Angola by the Portuguese, acting under the Doctrine of Discovery as well. In 1662, the colony passed a law establishing that enslaved status would follow "the condition of the mother" (Thorpe 1909), contravening the English common law rule that status should follow the condition of the father. This rule of *partus sequitur ventrem* spread across the colonies to tie bondage to birth and race (J. Morgan 2018); antimiscegenation laws aimed at preserving racial purity reinforced this division of status so that Black women's reproductive as well as agricultural labor became key to the production of property under this legal regime (J. Morgan 2004). The racial violence deployed to dispossess Native Nations of land and Africans of their freedom produced a new kind of value in this property that was dependent on race—that is, land did not have monetary value on the colonial market unless white people occupied it at the time of its sale or projected in the future; human beings did not become property except because of being Black. The fact that these forms of property depended on the subordination of nonwhites for their creation and their value meant that their production deeply racialized colonial society and its political economy.

Further, European nations had wide discretion under the broad mandate of the Doctrine of Discovery to experiment with strategies for taking actual possession of Native Nations' lands. In North America, English colonial companies and governments uniquely relied on nuclear families, a kinship formation that colonists imported from England, to settle lands in order to formalize their claims. More specifically, they incentivized settler families to occupy lands with the promise of granting them ownership of those lands. They deputized private individuals to perform racial violence, enforce racial distinctions, and maintain value in the "property" they thereby produced. The perception of abundant available lands, in an era when lands meant wealth and could promise subsistence for a family, lured floods of immigrants to the American frontier, where they engaged in direct combat with the inhabitants of the land, destroyed the environments upon which Native people depended for subsistence, purchased enslaved people in a bid to build their wealth, and reproduced their own forces. Nuclear families moved to the frontier to spread disease, chase away the game, and use force to defend the plots of land on which they built homesteads against the claims of Native Nations.

As a result, marriage was key to "the potential military strength of any American border settlement" and "the capacity of the frontier for war," as frontier historian Frederic Paxson notes, because "in nearly every case the unit working on the frontier was a young married couple" (1924, 37). Again, colonial laws profoundly shaped the ways heteronormative families who were or would be racialized as white helped construct property, not only by promising them title to land in exchange for occupying it for a period of years through headright policies, land grants, and subsidies, but also by encouraging marriages in settlements. During the early years, few women traveled to North America from England, but colonists soon decided that "commercial profits and economic development required stabilized communities rather than rapid exploitation"; trading companies therefore began "to bring women to America to stimulate the formation of families" (Abramovitz 1988, 45). Trading companies aimed to induce farmers to invest in their homesteads rather than returning to Europe and offered incentives in the form of additional land or servants to men who brought wives or married. In 1619, for example, the Virginia House of Burgesses allotted husbands an equal land share for their wives; between 1620 and 1622, in an effort to "make the men there more settled and less moveable," the Virginia Company of London sent 140 women to the colony to increase "the supply of free white women." Pennsylvania and Massachusetts both offered land to women themselves, but Massachusetts prohibited unmarried adults from living outside family units or established households, and Maryland in 1634 threatened to repossess land from women who did not marry within seven years. Laws such as these *made* marriage the "lynchpin" of the colonial social order and the "centerpiece" of its economic system (Abramovitz 1988, 53; Kessler-Harris 1982, 4).

The importance of nuclear families in constituting the labor force of conquest cannot be overstated. Neither English troops nor the "tiny" US Army, before the Civil War, had the funds or personnel to carry out the direct seizure of Native Nations' lands. The greater the numbers of colonists, the more politically and economically valuable land could be settled and held by their collective forces. Colonial governments and companies prioritized the recruitment of immigrants for this reason, making migration policy—governing incentives for white immigration, forced importation of Black people, and Native removal—a fundamental dimension of colonization. After immigrating, white women's reproductive labor also played a key role in building colonists' capacity for force: by 1700, "natural increase" had become "the key factor in white population growth" (Perkins 1980, 1–2); Benjamin Franklin cited early marriage and large families as the chief explanations for American growth and estimated that the typical number of children per family doubled that in England and in the rest of Europe. Colonial laws of marriage, inheritance, and paternity cultivated women's dependence, and nuclear families in colonial communities were governed by a patriarch who controlled the reproductive and domestic labor of women and children. Women performed unpaid household work, such as tending livestock, household production for family consumption, and market sales, and legally had to surrender any income they earned to the male head of household;

children's labor was property that could be sold to others for a price.

The colonial political economy in the United States therefore drew upon a division of labor between the public and the private on both the state and familial levels: the private economy of the family powered the public agenda of conquest; laws that sought to harness the self-interest of white family units deputized them as an informal colonial militia. This role of the nuclear family in *creating* property both furthered state-engineered expansion and created peculiarly personal stakes in the project of empire. The land settler families conquered was a long series of homestead plats—the quintessential "property" of the American Dream—whose defense inevitably meant *domestic* defense to their armed owners. The racial construction of property historically invested whites and those who sought to attain whiteness in acts of racial violence that produced wealth—extracting lands and the reproductive and agricultural labor of enslaved people. It invested them in the project of maintaining the colonial racial social order as a part of the preservation of the property they helped create and, therefore, as Cheryl Harris (1993) has elaborated, in their own whiteness as a specific form of property itself. Thus, settler families acted in tandem with colonial governments and then the United States to produce a highly specific political economy founded on the private construction of "property" through racial violence, while their rapid accumulation of lands and enslaved people accelerated the expansion of those markets and general assault on Native and Black lives and lifeworlds at once.

51

Queer

Chandan Reddy

We tell a story about *queer* that goes like this: Once a slur used to shame and stigmatize same-sex desire, radical LGBT activists, artists, and academics in the 1990s reclaimed it as a term of gender subversion, antirespectability, and antinormativity (J. Butler 1993b). Today, *queer* consolidates these dispositions and is put to use by varied people who take umbrage with binary sexual and gender identities, such as straight or gay, male or female, normal or abnormal, cisgender or transgender. Those who seek more to disturb, shatter, or undermine the heteronormative cultural order than to be included or represented by that culture and order especially claim the term (Halberstam 2011). Against "second-wave" feminist constructs of the personal as political, many use *queer* to stress cultural subjectivities and lives foreclosed by both dominant society's and feminists' imaginaries of the "personal" or the "intimate." The feminist sex wars of the 1980s, out of which some important strands of queer theory developed, pivoted precisely on the exclusion of certain modes of gendered embodiment, sexual desire, and pleasure. And yet, however destabilizing or agonistic assertions of queerness against cultural inclusion and political representation are or appear to be, they are not always in and of themselves political or related to a specifically counter-hegemonic political project or set of meanings. Indeed, the word's usage by some as a social identity and term of belonging is as tied to maintaining a liberal or nationalist order as defying it (Eng, Halberstam, and Muñoz 2005; Puar 2007).

For others, queer—especially when used in conjunctions such as *queer of color*, *queer Latinx*, *Black queer*, and so on—signifies a broad, if at times contradictory, set of political critiques and alternative ideologies *within* LGBT politics and *among* intersectional feminist movements. These orientations may also intersect with movements organized against intimate violence, prisons, immigration restrictions, policing, economic exploitation, casteism, global warming, environmental degradation, extractive industries, and land-based occupation or those for reproductive, HIV, and disability rights; sex work legalization; domestic work unionization; racially equitable social reproduction in housing, childcare, food, health, and transportation; Native sovereignty; decolonization; and community empowerment. Constructed from genealogies of Black radical, women of color, and varied Third World feminisms, queer in these instances is a contingent formation and construct, actively linking gender and sexual insubordinations and deviance to racial capitalist and heteropatriarchal orders (M. J. Alexander 1997; Cohen 1997; R. Ferguson 2004).

Naming varied and even contradictory attitudes and dispositions, *queer* is a word actively in formation, with continuously emergent and nonidentical uses of the word now a crucial feature. Tracking the term's etymology offers a valuable genealogy that can interrogate the story that the "we" of queer studies once told. While some posit that the English-language usage of the term began in the sixteenth and seventeenth centuries, there are uses and etymologies of the word before that, including the German word *quer* or the Middle High German *twer*, meaning "cross," "oblique," "perverse," or "wrong-headed." Other etymologies of the word point to the Middle and Old Irish *quár* or Modern Irish *quaire*, both used to describe "crooked," "bent," "hollow," "curved," or "bowed" human and topographical features as well as objects, such as weapons or implements (*Oxford English Dictionary Online*, "queer," n.d.).

This etymology of the "English" word *queer*'s derivation from "foreign tongue(s)" disturbs notions of bounded, homogenous, or closed linguistic and national communities. These residual histories are reopened by emergent uses of the term today. A number of scholars, cultural workers, and activists, especially in or in relation to the Global South, use the term's linguistic impropriety to index a range of gender-variant, dissident, or nonnormative sexual formations, including sexual identities forged out of local linguistic communities and Indigenous and vernacular languages (Macharia 2020). In doing so, they seek to eschew grounding political claims or cultural and social rights demands through notions of authenticity, heritage, or exclusive tradition. Both diasporic and Global South activists, scholars, and cultural workers are precisely drawn to *queer*'s dubious origins and apparent foreignness always already *within* national society as a moniker for gathering together varied nonbinary sexualities and genders, including most especially culturally Indigenous and nonwestern "same-sex" sexual subjectivities (Whitehead 2018).

The use of queer to name various local "same-sex" formations—signaled in conjunctions such as queer migration or queer Indigeneity—is not necessarily an appropriation or misrepresentation of culturally specific sexualities. Rather, in these instances, queer is used to challenge both the state's capture of national culture, borders, and communities for its own legitimacy and heteropatriarchal genealogies of history and communal membership (Luibhéid and Chávez 2020; Driskill et al. 2011). Indeed, some nonwestern states—such as Singapore—offer nominal rights and recognition to gays and lesbians to promote the state's capacities for flexible governance among globalizing flows of productive and human capital (Lim 2005). Other state formations, like Iran, India, and Pakistan, offer legal recognition and certain welfare entitlement to "transgender," "intersex," "hijra," or "third genders" without or even in antagonism to offering similar state "sanction" to lesbian- and gay-identified persons (Najmabadi 2014; Narrain 2004). In their efforts to unify temporality, space, culture, and embodiment within the order of territoriality and sovereignty, postcolonial states and some Indigenous governments proscribe "queer" formations—that is, groupings of the perverse that disrupt nationalist norms—as inauthentic, imported, or contrary to a venerated past or precolonial essence. In and against these postcolonial statist and heteropatriarchal efforts, queer is actively deployed by diasporic and Global South activists and cultural workers, not as another appropriation of the multiplicity of nonwestern same-sex sexualities, but as a term that designates political and epistemological efforts to demarginalize "nonnormative" local and vernacular sexualities restrictively incorporated by the postcolonial state or within heteropatriarchal histories. In this sense, the term *queer*—such as in the formulation *queer diaspora*—signals a challenge to these statist and postcolonial nationalist efforts to control the lives and meaning of local instances of sexual "nonnormativity" in ways that do not disturb national norms, incorporating some "queer" sexualities while marking other expressions of same-sex, cross-gender, or nonnormative desire as "impossible" (Nabutanyi 2020).

Critical formulations such as "queer diaspora" or "queer Africa" refuse these selective practices of recognition and denial of same-sex formations. They use queerness to name dissident coherencies and connections between recognized and disavowed formations of so-called LGBT subjects across the Global South and its diasporas. Building up intersectional feminist politics, diasporic collaborations, and transnational solidarities, naming these nonwestern formations as "queer" is a call to recompose both avowed and denied modes of the locally perverse within suppressed genealogies of the colonial, global, or regional (Gopinath 2018). By challenging postcolonial nationalist political ideologies and desires that promote fantasies of purity, the restoration of an imagined past, or a moral and kinship order capable of norming global capitalist social relations, these emergent uses of queer in the postcolonial context stress the racializing and necropolitical capacities of postcolonial states, positing queer modes of relatedness as their contradictory expression and critique (Rao 2020, 27–32; Manalansan 2008).

These usages of queer across the Global South and in connection to the "South in the North" (such as racialized poor, Indigenous, and working-class diasporic communities), though still emergent, actively construct alternative routes and genealogies for the term, just as women of color, intersectional, and Third World feminist alliances before them seized and redeployed the category of "woman" to construct antiuniversalist modes of global political engagement (Ochoa 2011; Hobson 2016, 120–54).

This emergent sense of queer is today often obscured by more visible and commercialized understandings of queer as cutting-edge, cosmopolitan, and globally mobile. Here, instead of theoretical meanings of the term as nonnormative or at odds with the dominant, queer is refigured to promote a new class formation within the Global South. Far from being a moniker for multiple forms of perverse embodiment and experiences of disidentification, a distinct class of sexual subjects in the Global South—often elite, urban, and steeped in educational and cultural institutions hybridized by the culturalscapes of global capitalism—claim queer to assert their equality and contemporaneity with LGBTQ people in the Global

North. Despite and, perhaps, because of this more visible use of the term for expressing cosmopolitan identification, persistent emergent uses of queer to describe new political formations and modes of relatedness that disrupt geopolitical, legal, and cultural orderings remain important and instructive.

For example, in contemporary India, queer circulates as both an expression of an urbane English-dominant cultural subjectivity and a moniker for a radical and complex coalition of sexual and gender groups across classes, castes, languages, religions, and regions. When used as a moniker for a coalition of nonnormative same-sex desiring groups, the term *queer* references both those who identify with the sociolinguist construct gay, lesbian, and queer and those who identify with vernacular forms of so-called same-sex desire, such as "hijra," "kothi," and "kinnar." Those who seek to conserve "queer" as the possession of hypermodern, mobile, and cosmopolitan persons living in the major cities of the Global South actively distance the term and themselves from vernacular sexualities, like "kothi" or "hijra," which they figure as "backward," remnants of "customary" or "traditional" parts of society out of step with the modern. In almost diametric contrast, the coalitional use of queer to name both so-called cosmopolitan and vernacular sexualities specifically targets and undermines the cultural and political efforts at such categorical separation, all the while negotiating the hierarchies of power and privilege within such coalitional spaces and efforts. In its coalitional usage, queer names the coeval force of cosmopolitan and vernacular, "modern," and "customary" modes of same-sex desire in constructing the present and the field of political life. By refusing the ideologies that would segregate and fix vernacular sexualities within the past or in "traditional practices and customary orders," these coalitional efforts seek to construct an LGBTQ politics out of suppressed genealogies of the present within which struggle and change can be pursued.

This tendency to overlook emergent diasporic, Indigenous, and Global South habitations of queer is abetted by tendencies within US and European queer and feminist studies that stress "queer" as a western-metropolitan construction disseminated to the postcolonial world, a notion of cultural circulation and exchange that continues to map globality through modernist binaries of core and periphery (El-Tayeb 2011). Yet if we return to the etymology of the term, we can interrogate these constructs of queerness that, however inadvertently, reproduce dominant and hegemonic social and historical perspectives on power and social change. As we have seen, most etymologies posit queer as Celtic in origin and say that it infiltrated English speech in the seventeenth century as a result of the British colonial domination of Ireland. Irish sailors "contracted" to work on British sailing ships, the crucial system of transport that furnished the goods and wealth of European bourgeois society, are cited, in particular, as the probable source for its dissemination into English (Sayers 2010, 18). Borrowed from a so-called lowly, minor, and backward colonized language, perhaps the term has always had a racialized charge, earlier than any sexualized connotations, due to the mode by which it entered the English vernacular.

Indeed, queer scholars of color have reactivated the term's evocation of racial difference, minor identities, and vernacular performance. E. Patrick Johnson, in speaking of Black queer knowledges and modes of flourishing, has argued for "quare studies," a phonetics and vernacular performance of difference that challenges a notion of "proper" usage or genealogy and reverses the belief that minor or racialized formations of "queer" are derivative copies or imitations of a supposedly prior "major culture," white bourgeois sexualities, and their

field of study. Instead, like the term's colonized origin, "quare" studies draws attention to distinct, subjugated, and so-called minor knowledges as sources for contemporary Black relationalities and nonnormativities, evidence both of longer genealogies of queerness yet to be reckoned with and of material Black cultures as irreconcilable with genealogies of queerness that stress institutional histories of nation and globe (E. Johnson 2001).

In continuity with its seventeenth-century origins, in the nineteenth century, Herman Melville, a touchstone author for literary queer theory, used the term liberally in his nautical works about the multiracial laboring cultures of colonized, Indigenous, and white seafarers as a worker's slang for "strange," "peculiar," and "odd." Used as much to describe persons as inanimate things and structures, queer condensed meanings of anachrony (or out of the order of time) with displacement and contiguity (or out of place). A residual use of the term, queer denotes figures, passions, and relationalities that disturb a sense of temporal and spatial continuity used to stabilize a social order, what contemporary queer scholars have refocused as a critique of "reproductive futurism" or "chrononormativity" (L. Edelman 2004; E. Freeman 2010).

By the early twentieth century, along the docks of major imperial and global ports, such as New York City, London, or Marseille, men began using the term to describe their explicitly sexual interest in other men, initiating the term's now dominant meaning as an attitude or disposition with specific regard to sexual desire (McKay 2020). Men looking for sex with straight men, whom they called "trade" or "normal men," used "queer" to describe their same-sex attractions and to distance and distinguish themselves from the "fairies," "inverts," "faggots," and "sissies" with whom they shared the streets and sex markets (Chauncey 1994, 101–27). Many working-class people in urban metropoles used the term to denote same-sex sexual dispositions without necessarily imbuing the term with "pathological"—that is, medicalized—connotations. As men and women arrived to cities like London, calling themselves "queer" was a means to differentiate themselves from the gendered inverts that also roamed the city. In the popular and vernacular presses across the globe, queer became associated with perverse desires, male or female, especially those that their readers associated with "same-sex" desire (Houlbrook 2006). On December 1, 1928, the front-page of the *Chicago Defender*—a leading paper in the Black vernacular press—proclaimed, "*Woman Slain in Queer Love Brawl*," recounting the violent end of a love triangle among three Black women on Chicago's South Side (Woolner 2015, 415; my emphasis).

Tracking queer through the interwar years is instructive about important relays, shifts, and divergences between vernacular and institutional meanings now mostly taken for granted. For instance, the vernacular use of queer began to designate a sexual type defined by same-sex desire and distinguished from the gender inverts with whom queers were sometimes grouped in vernacular spaces. Simultaneous with this vernacular development, the United States, like other European states, developed an extensive "straight" administrative state apparatus that codified binary gender and sexuality, with homosexuality marked as human abnormality or pathology (Foucault 1978; Canaday 2011). Vernacular sexual cultures were imbricated in these disciplinary and institutional developments, often via middle-class and elite white men who had access to both (Mumford 1997). Men who called themselves queer as part of an urban sexual vernacular distinguished their racialized masculinity from the problematic femininity of fairies and sissies. Male sexual desire for another male, while outside the charmed circle of normal desire, could still be within the charmed circle of normal gender and race as defined by modern institutions (N. Shah 2012). As white masculinity accrued moral entitlements and material goods in public and economic life unavailable to all others, queer men demeaned these cross-gendered, feminine-of-center embodiments and bristled against the ideology and "archaic" regime of desire that would "confuse" same-sex desire with the "comical" cross-gender formations of sissies, pansies, male impersonators, butches, and other cross-gendered subjects (Chauncey 1994). Nonetheless, vernacular uses of queer were distinct from institutional discourses of sexuality and state power, used to identify oneself or others within a perverse economy of bodies and pleasures (Halberstam 1997).

Black modernist writer Nella Larsen (2001) played with the multiple and ungovernable connotations of the term during this moment of formation in her literary works *Quicksand* and *Passing*. She paid special attention to its racialized connotation—between vernacular and institutional meanings, racialized "low-culture" pleasures and middle-class pathologizations, perverse attachments and sexual identity. In the later novella, Irene Redfield, a paragon of middle-class respectability, frets over the troubling development of one of her sons, declaring to her husband, "I'm terribly afraid he's picked up some queer ideas about things—some things—from the older boys, you know." "Queer ideas?" her husband asks, as if the term's now multiple and ambiguous meanings required the user's clarification. "D' you mean ideas about sex, Irene?" (Larsen 2001, 220). At the intersection of race and gender, queerness ignites fears of sexual waywardness, a vernacular disruption of middle-class discipline (R. Ferguson 2004). By the Cold War era, with the installation of US militarism globally, queer was firmly installed within an institutional order. In vernacular use, queer pejoratively named perverse bodies and attachments with the force to create shame, stigma, fear, and violence. Such meanings developed from the institutional, legal, and administrative bureaucracies fully in place in society that produced the binary gender and sexuality they regulated. At the same time, affirmative vernacular uses persisted as means to designate the self. Importantly, in light of the institutional development of heteronormative society, this affirmative use gained recalcitrant, even oppositional, force. Unlike metropolitan white men's use of the term in the interwar years to distinguish themselves from fairies, inverts, and the like, the communal, recalcitrant, and oppositional usage of the term was maintained especially by racially mixed gender nonconforming women, butches, and other working-class trans subjects (Kennedy and Davis 1993), the very gendered formations against whom white masculinity appropriated the term for itself.

In other words, by the mid-twentieth century, queer marked the ability of social existence—now thoroughly institutionalized—to produce both bodily and psychological precarity through the construction of sexuality as the essence of self. And it was a metonym in the vernacular for nominating one's "self" as part of dense vernacular sexual economies and spaces—like the lesbian bar—that had other epistemologies of sex, gender, and relatedness (Lorde 1982; Anzaldúa 2000). Soon, by the late twentieth century, radical and global feminisms that developed from contradictions in institutional spaces—like law and policy—strategized for the use of state power for feminist ends. The working-class butches, racialized bulldaggers, and feminist sex radicals who maintained the vernacular circulation of queer were more often figured as self-alienated women by radical feminism, the detritus of the destructive powers of patriarchal society, and the false consciousness of the working classes rather than as groups with subjugated knowledges (Moraga and Hollibaugh 1981; Jaleel 2013).

Today, verb and noun forms—queering and queerness—are broadly used to describe activity that upends or destabilizes a structure, order, or practice from within, defamiliarizing previously stable objects and experiences ranging from gender and sexuality to movies and gaming. Yet here we have emphasized how in relation to racialized sexualities globally, the term expresses changing but always definite and specific connections and divergences between vernacular and institutional histories, modes of discourse, and knowledge. Rarely is the vernacular a unified and fully alternative knowledge; rather, it is shot through with the categories and beliefs of institutions, just as institutions rely on and appropriate vernacular styles and practices, even as they discredit vernacular life. Queerness marks that interface, not to "recover" the vernacular or make it whole in the face of institutions. Nor does queerness pose vernacular formations as necessarily oppositional, let alone political. Rather, queerness expresses those instances where vernacular sociability—progressively obscured by institutional discourses—becomes a resource for undoing and unbuilding the categories and structures that produce dominant modes of relatedness, in order to interrogate received accounts of the past and to reimagine what variety of struggles might be possible in the present (Lowe 2015). As a process and element of practical consciousness actively in formation, queerness is activated by those vernacular practices of relatedness always already existing within defined and globalizing modes of life.

52

Race

Keywords Feminist Editorial Collective

In the United States, race is a colonial project forged in Indigenous dispossession and African enslavement. It has been shaped through multiple historical events, including independence from the British colonial sovereign, rapid western expansion and further dispossession, the internal ethical and capitalist crisis of the Civil War, the false promises of emancipation, the absorption of Mexican states and peoples into the US Southwest, the conscription of indentured Asian laborers subsequently subjected to anti-immigration laws and antisedition surveillance, the brutality of the Jim Crow South, the achievement of desegregation during the civil rights movement of the 1950s and 1960s, and the liberalization of immigration law to end racial quotas in 1965. Many tellings of the history of race in the United States go on to claim that those civil rights efforts resulted in the establishment in the early 1970s of ethnic studies programs and American Indian studies curricula at universities where students could finally learn the histories and cultures of diverse peoples of color with connected but different relationships to the United States.

As programs in ethnic and women's studies began to get institutionalized, though, the state and the academy alike found ways to fold multiculturalism into their liberal self-images, substituting insurgent demands (for the redistribution of power, wealth, and access to education, for example) for investments in equal representation. By reducing the initiatives of oppositional movements to the pursuit of inclusion, universities redirected demands for justice into normative pursuits of "excellence and uplift" (R. Ferguson 2012, 7). Equality supplanted equity as the goal, and color blindness, which asserts that all people, regardless of race, have equal opportunity before the law, became the law of the land. Throughout this history, white supremacy has worked through hierarchical taxonomies of race and gender, presenting such categories as biologically determined, dehumanizing those who did not fall under the ever-changing historical category of normative whiteness. This keyword entry pushes beyond such understandings of race that settle into the complacencies of liberal multiculturalism, color blindness, and biological determinism.

In this essay, we tell the story of racial struggle and racial discourse, especially as these overlap with stories of gender and sexuality, with a focus on the US context. As a collective of Black, Native, Jewish, Arab, Latinx, Asian, and white women, queers, and trans people consciously writing together in the tradition of feminist collectivity, we speak relationally, across our differences of positionality and opinion, to challenge the stability of racial categories and the narratives told about race. One of the most enduring of these "common sense" narratives we refute is biological essentialism: the belief that biologically, humans can be categorized into fixed races based on phenotypical differences, such as skin color, hair texture, and facial features. The idea of race as biological emerged with the Enlightenment-era impulse to classify and order all species and alongside a political desire to prove that social hierarchies reflect "natural" human hierarchies. This served to rationalize the apparent contradiction between Enlightenment ideas of liberty and equality and the violence of enslavement and colonial expansion (Schiebinger 2004, 145). Nineteenth-century biologists such as Louis Agassiz debated whether all humans belonged to the same species;

anatomists measured skulls and dissected bodies, often of non-European, enslaved, or Indigenous people, hypothesizing that cranial shape and size could provide empirical evidence for racial ranking and intelligence (Stepan 1991; TallBear 2013, 34). Well into the twentieth century, eugenicists relied on a biological conception of race to argue for the extinction and social control of people deemed outside of white, able-bodied, heterosexual norms. Many often assume that eugenic science is distinct from scientific projects that deploy racial categories. Black feminists, though, argue that all attempts to ground race in biology are complicit in scientific racism (D. Roberts 2011, 27).

With the mapping of the Human Genome Project through the 1990s, scientists proved that humans, as a species, share 99.9 percent of our DNA with each other—that is, race has no real scientific or genetic basis. But new forms of racial categorizing have emerged, and many still rely on a notion that biological race is something real. Corporations like 23andMe can analyze our genetic ancestry to hypothesize about which continents and regions our distant ancestors came from, producing data that reproduces and relies on preexisting racial categories. Genetic ancestry testing can be used to shed light on lost genealogical information, particularly for people with enslaved or displaced ancestors (A. Nelson 2016), but DNA is also fetishized. For example, Indigenous DNA is assumed to be geographically, and thus genetically, isolated. Geneticists, worried that Indigenous DNA would soon "vanish" through urbanization, migration, and displacement, have called for urgent projects to collect Indigenous "genetic signatures" (TallBear 2013, 2–3; D. Roberts 2011, 66). Assumptions about the distribution of particular genetic mutations across "racial" categories result in medical racial profiling (D. Roberts 2011, 211). These ongoing practices make clear that the idea of race as biology is still treated as factual within science, affecting social policy and political decision-making.

And yet racial categories have always been unstable, manufactured, and re-created to support different state agendas. For instance, while Jewish, Irish, Italian, and other ethnic European populations were assimilating into US categories of whiteness during the Jim Crow era, the color line between whites and nonwhites intensified. Maintaining that line relied on increased surveillance and disciplining of Black and other nonwhite people to maintain strict separation between perceived racial groups—a separation that, despite its passage into law as a doctrine of "separate but equal," nonetheless served to maintain racial hierarchy (*Plessy v. Ferguson*, 163 U.S. 537 (1896)). Racial segregation obscured the fact that innumerable white men had already crossed the color line not only by raping enslaved women during plantation slavery but also through various parallel forms of enslavement, including the "fancy trade," in which fair-skinned women of African and European descent were sold into enslavement specifically for sex work (Baptist 2001; Finley 2020). People who have been deemed racially ambiguous are often at the center of heightened dramas of racial categorization: the argument in *Plessy v. Ferguson* pivots on Homer Plessy's ability to pass as white and exert his private right—not that of the state—to categorize his race (Karcher 2016).

This was not to be, however, for Plessy or anyone else. Even after emancipation, the idea of *partus sequitur ventrem*, the 1662 colonial Virginia law stipulating that the racial status of the child follows that of the mother, persisted. Prior to 1865, under that legal precedent, the children of forced or unequal encounters across the racial line were considered Black and thus both enslaved and available for sale by their biological fathers and white owners of human property. The gendering of such genetic inheritance within this history of coerced and profit-based reproduction reveals that the idea of blood family kinship as a fundamental American value (i.e., "family value") across time is a historical deception specifically geared toward upholding "family" as something that only pertains to white families in which a male is "head of household."

Often assumed to be the gathering of racial "facts" by a "neutral" bureaucratic arm of a rational and disinterested nation-state, the US census offers a case study in how relations of power, property, and gender—not biology—underlie the identification and consolidation of racial categories. The first census was conducted in 1790 within the sixteen states and territories that then composed the United States. Of these sixteen, five states had already adopted gradual emancipation for enslaved African peoples. The first census divided people into categories of free white, parsed by age and gender; free Other; and enslaved. American Indians were not counted, defined instead as members of "foreign nations" governed under the constitution's commerce clause. While not officially defined, the census category "head of family" was assumed to be white and male, and married women who lived with these men were counted as their legal property.

Notably, the first census only categorized gender for free peoples, mainly to identify probable property ownership and potential military labor as the settler state sought to stabilize itself. Enslaved peoples were grouped together under one racialized but ungendered category—a process that Hortense Spillers has marked as one of the fundamental violences against African peoples perpetuated by the Middle Passage (Spillers [1987] 2003). In the 1860 census, American Indian men were counted as the head of the household to determine how already limited land allotments were handed out. This move, in conjunction with the Indian Wars and further expansions of the United States that violently domesticated Indian land and bodies, strategically worked to undermine tribal structures and further dispossess Indigenous women of their traditional ownership of land. The very founding of the United States as a settler colonial state relied on the exclusion of Indigenous peoples from the category of human as racialized non-Christian peoples, a transplanting of the early modern category of heretic into a new taxonomy (Wynter 1995). These invented taxonomies rationalized the use of force to deny Indigenous sovereignty and self-determination and thus to dispossess Indigenous peoples of their land and resources. After the Civil War and with the reservation system implemented, other major shifts in the census categories occurred, including the breakdown of Black into eight different categories (S. Lee 1993), the most derogatory of which would last until the 1930s.

At the same time, American Indians who occupied rich land and resource areas were categorized by US legislation into systems of blood quantum or gendered lineal descent, designed to effect their statistical disappearance through intermarriage and consequent transfer of wealth to white landowners. As land dispossession accelerated, these fertile lands were often given first to immigrants originating from "Anglo-Saxon" countries, then to poor whites in the post–Civil War South, and later to ethnic minorities whose property-owning status facilitated their assimilation into whiteness. Marriage and heteropatriarchy continued to structure the inheritance of property and control of labor: non-Black American Indian women were encouraged to marry white men for oil or land rights to pass into white hands. The myth of the American Indian grandmother, famously used by Elizabeth Warren's claims to Cherokee ancestry, stems from these early attempts to gain oil rights in Oklahoma and the West by claiming American Indian status (Justice 2019).

What counts as race on the census has changed with each iteration. Even as "white" is an option for racial identification on the census, it is rarely considered to be racial. The definition of whiteness has never been coherent. Although "free white" continued as a category after the first census, European Jewish people and Irish and Italian immigrants were racialized as outside of "white" until the early twentieth century. As these groups accrued economic, political, and cultural power, however, they were folded into the category of whiteness, even as Jewish people continued to suffer anti-Semitism (Ignatiev 1995; Frye Jacobson 1999). Whiteness can even be appropriative itself, as in the example of attributing Aryan heritage to Polynesians to allow white settlers to "claim Polynesian peoples, culture, and crucially lands, as their own heritage—because they were descendants of Aryans" (Arvin 2019b, 45). The 1980 census explicitly noted that Hispanic/Latinx identity is not a race, even though people descended from lands to the south of the United States (who could be white, brown, Black, and/or Indigenous) have been targets of racist violence and exclusion since prior to the first census. As of 2021, Middle Eastern and North African (MENA) people are still considered Caucasian, or white, on the census. And yet the racialized gendering of Arab and particularly Arab-Muslim peoples, across the scale from mass entertainment to state policy and particularly the stereotypes of women as victims and men as terrorists, continues. Racist violence toward MENA people has steadily risen since September 11, 2001, alongside a state of ongoing war against the Middle East, or what some scholars refer to as state Islamophobia (Abdulhadi, Alsultany, and Naber 2011). These examples of conflicted ascendency into whiteness underscore both the malleability of racial categories and what Cheryl Harris has argued is the equation of whiteness both with property and as property (C. Harris 1993; Eng 2010). Overall, the lessons of census history are twofold. First, racial categorization has always been about political and material ends. Second, there is no such thing as a racial categorization without gendered ramifications, and vice versa.

In an effort to intervene in both biologizing and individualizing notions of race that inform liberal multicultural state projects like the census, Michael Omi and Howard Winant called on scholars to attend to the "racial formation" of the United States. The idea of racial formation enables examination of how forms of structural racism, such as housing precarity, police brutality, and anti-immigrant legislation, mutually produce inequality through their everyday administrative functioning (Omi and Winant 1986). Race—which is paradigmatically distinct from ethnicity, religion, nationality, and class while overlapping with them—has less to do with origin stories than it does with a set of processes that shape one's access to health care, education, and social services; how one passes through social structures such as traffic policing, border crossing, or academic grading; or the siting of voting booths, polluting facilities, and amenities. Thus, like gender and sex, race may be both social (produced within conditions and structures shared with others) and constructed (based on arbitrary and sometimes contradictory assumptions that cannot provide any evidence for their truth status). Even as race is a social construct, it is also materially quite real and made manifest through everyday acts and social structures. Furthermore, racism, understood to exist structurally across legislative, ideological, and economic sectors, is an ideology that must assume the existence of race in order to implement the uneven distribution of resources. As Ruth Wilson Gilmore argues, racism can be defined as the "state-sanctioned or extralegal production and exploitation of group-differentiated vulnerability to premature death" (2007, 28).

Racial discrimination has always proceeded alongside the disciplining of nonnormative gender and sexuality, often with devastating consequences. As scholars of sexuality working in the field of Indigenous studies have shown, this was a strategy honed and sharpened during the early days of European settler colonialism in the Americas. Hernán Cortés, for instance, set his dogs to tear apart Indigenous peoples who did not conform to the gender binary or to heterosexuality (Miranda 2010). Settler records are full of accounts of the Inquisition punishing people for sexual transgressions such as sodomy, a category that encompassed many different sexual acts that were not reproductive intercourse between a cis male and a cis female (Tortorici 2018). The intensified racialization and policing of sexual minorities coincided with the emergence of the clinical category of the homosexual in the late nineteenth century and into the new postemancipation United States (Somerville 2000). In this regime, Black hypersexualization led to stereotypes of Black male and female promiscuity and sexual appetite in addition to the idea that racialized people had an inherent tendency to be lesbian, bisexual, or homosexual. As the segregation of the Jim Crow era escalated, the idea of Black masculinity was rescripted to depict Black men as virile sexual threats to the sexual sanctity of white women. The mere idea that Black men might desire or even look at white women was enough to lead to lynchings (such as the 1955 murder of Emmett Till) and race riots (such as the Greenwood Massacre in Tulsa, Oklahoma, in 1921). In such hierarchies of racialized gender formation, the designation of correct "manhood" or "womanhood" is inevitably reserved for whites. If ideals of normative cis womanhood cohered around whiteness (Schuller 2018), sexual deviance was also used to demarcate racial hierarchy, and vice versa.

The capaciousness of stereotypes to accommodate contradictions in racialized gender and sexuality is evident across a range of examples. For instance, the Page Law of 1875 blocked the immigration of Chinese women, primarily by prohibiting prostitutes while also making it nearly impossible for Chinese women to prove they were not sex workers. The so-called bachelor societies of the late nineteenth century then naturalized the effeminization of Asian masculinity by pointing to the gendered forms of labor, such as laundry and cooking, that Chinese men had to do. Asian Americans have since been figured as simultaneously a model minority excelling at assimilation and a perpetual foreigner forever suspect of betraying US national allegiances, as both sexually too passive or too aggressive but always exotically available for exploitation. Such contradictory dynamics can also be seen in turning attention to that status of Mexicans in the United States. When the US government launched the "bracero" guest worker program in 1942, Mexican laboring men were championed for their docile demeanor and tireless contributions to the US economy, even as "zoot suiters"—mostly Mexican American but also Black and Filipino youth who wore flamboyant, gender-bending attire—were brutalized by police, local government, and members of the military for their perceived laziness, extravagance, and threat to the nation-state during wartime (Flores 2020). Depending on what kind of enemy or what kind of labor was required or needed to be disavowed, racialized gender and sexuality have constantly shifted to uphold the economic and ideological systems of the nation-state.

From the nineteenth to mid-twentieth century, such racialized sexualities and their perceived deviances became more officially pathologized, often in the name of public health as applied to national immigration control. For example, at both Ellis and Angel Islands, the immigration ports on the East and the West Coasts, respectively, migrants, especially those from places other than northern and western Europe, were closely scrutinized for signs of disease and any perceived gender or sexual nonnormativity, which could lead to exclusion (Rand 2005). Depictions of Asians as both sterile and a "medical menace" due to their presumed sexual immorality (N. Shah 2001) led to mass killings and the forced removal of Asians from their homes—a practice that would, at the executive order of the president during World War II, put Japanese Americans in internment camps, where they were subjected to routine, dehumanizing physical inspections. In 1991, when Haitians fled a coup, the US government detained and processed them on Guantánamo Bay, Cuba, where some three hundred who supposedly tested positive for HIV were left to languish in a detention camp for nearly two years—their sexually transmitted disease, poverty, and Blackness depicted as a triple threat to the US state (Paik 2016). In the mid-twentieth century, the federally funded Moynihan Report leveraged racist social science to pathologize single Black mothers and make the specious claim that restoring patriarchal masculinity to Black men was key to solving racial inequality. The infamous report sought to render heterosexual Black women gender nonnormative and laid the grounds for the stereotype of the welfare mom, who became a central symbol in neoliberal arguments for dismantling the economic protections of the liberal welfare state (Cohen 2004).

In addition to the creation and deployment of controlling images that justify brutal immigration and economic policies, keeping racialized groups in seeming competition with one another for fair wages and better working conditions is another strategy that serves the ends of capitalism. The contradiction between the indisputable evidence of racial categorization across history and the later emergence of white-centered class consciousness moved historians working within the Black radical tradition to develop the term *racial*

capitalism (E. Williams 1994; C. Robinson [1983] 2019). According to this movement, capital has a tendency "not to homogenize but to differentiate—to exaggerate regional, subcultural, and dialectical differences into racial ones" (C. Robinson [1983] 2019, 26). The concept of racial capitalism has been useful for queer and woman of color historical materialists who point out that racial groups excluded from citizenship have been the "surplus labor" of US capitalism: these are populations that can easily be put out of work during recessions or austerity and reintegrated into the workforce during a boom. Differentiating racial groups through sexual and gendered nonnormativity has allowed capital to both enfold difference within capital as surplus labor and exploit and undervalue that labor.

These disparate histories demonstrate why some scholars, in particular those practicing queer of color critique, have moved away from thinking of race as static and toward analyzing racialization as process Queer of color critique involves looking at the combinations of affects, sensations, behaviors, discourses, and gestures to see not only how something or someone came to be designated as racialized and gendered but also what effects those labels have produced. The question is about not what race is but rather how race feels or what race does or, even more specifically, how different peoples or individuals do race (Puar 2007; Musser 2018; Muñoz 1999, 2020; J. Rodríguez 2014). Sometimes affiliated with affect or performance studies, this approach notably features an insistence on the importance of the organic and nonorganic in relation to racialization and sensation: here the question of biology becomes an issue not of racial essence but of the complexity of the physical, neurological, and emotional experience of being a body that is susceptible to an ideological environment shaped by racism, capitalism, and cisgender normativity.

Simultaneously structural in analysis and scalable down to the level of bodies and communities., such an approach to race does not deny the existence of biology or materiality, but it does refute racial-biological essentialism entirely. This methodology also focuses on the pleasures, joys, ecstasies, and experiences of shared ways of being that also constitute being a racialized body. Read in these modes, *race* becomes a keyword for being in community that can be utopian in its practices and imagined beyond the constraints of and damages incurred by rac*ism*. In this mode, the answer to addressing racism becomes not imagining a postracial world or pretending to be color-blind but imagining a world of more race, more community, more being in relation, and even being in common within difference together (Glissant 1990; Lorde [1984] 2007a).

53

Religion
Tazeen M. Ali

Religion has often been categorized as a source of oppression and constraint in public discourse. Take, for example, policy debates in the United States about curtailing women's reproductive rights and LGBTQ rights; in these kinds of debates, particularly in progressive responses to these debates, religion is typically associated with justifying oppression. In reality, however, both religious and secular frameworks can and have been utilized with great success to advance all manners of subjugation and violence, whether through oppressive foreign and domestic policies, discriminatory laws, or military interventions.

Yet certain religious communities—Muslims, Orthodox Jews, Mennonites, Amish, and other conservative Christians, for example—bear sociopolitical stigmas in the US context, not least because their female adherents may adopt styles of dress and demeanor that set them apart from the dominant white Protestant culture in the United States. These differences in clothing or customs can mark such communities as outsiders whose compatibility with western liberal values such as individualism, freedom, and capitalism is called into question. Similar attitudes permeate research on gender and sexuality as well as the policies that result from that research. Consequently, religion is either rendered suspect in the broader struggle for gender justice or otherwise overlooked as a productive category of inquiry by feminist and queer academics and activists alike.

Scholar Elizabeth Castelli, for instance, has called attention to how religion "has rarely been included in the litany of qualifiers ('race, class, culture, ethnicity/ nationality, sexuality') by which 'women' becomes an ever-more marked and differentiated category" (2001, 4–5). This is despite the groundbreaking interventions of feminist scholars who attest to the significance of religion within matrices of identity and power. Within the field/discipline of religious studies, many works that have focused on formal religious institutions, scriptural exegeses, and legal frameworks have, perhaps inadvertently, suggested that religion belongs exclusively in the realm of elite men, who have historically dominated positions of religious authority. By contrast, the study of lived religion, generated by scholars such as Robert Orsi (1997) and R. Marie Griffith (1997) in the 1990s, has opened up frameworks to study "everyday" religious actors and examine the various other spaces where diverse actors "do" religion outside of formal institutions. The lived religion approach, as Nancy Ammerman states, "has resulted in an outpouring of work documenting the religious activities of people—women, migrants, queer people, and others who had previously been ignored" (2020, 10). Consequently, academic focus on lived religious communities in their varied configurations has offered rich possibilities for the study of religion and gender in women's lives in productive ways. These studies do not disregard analysis of scriptures and formal institutions but rather foreground religious communities' relationships to them in practice. Furthermore, the framework of lived religions gives scholars a vantage point to examine new forms of exegeses as they emerge and new institutions as they are built.

Islam in particular has served as a site of contestation over the place of women and equality in modern liberal societies. Some US feminists' turn to global issues in the 1990s signaled a shift whereby the plight of women overseas, in places like Afghanistan, took center stage over domestic issues. Abu-Lughod (2013, 7) argues

that in order to divert from the stagnant aims of feminism in the United States, impaired by charges of racism, as well as conservative backlash to advancements in education and employment, "American feminists began to focus on spectacularly oppressive practices that were easy to mobilize around: female genital cutting, enforced veiling, or the honor crime" to cement their status as moral saviors and facilitate a narrative of US exceptionalism. In the wake of 9/11, the moral savior complex of white US feminist groups in their commitment to "liberating" Muslim women only further intensified and facilitated public support for war on terror policies, including aggressive military campaigns in Muslim-majority nations like Afghanistan and Iraq despite the fact that these interventions further harm women (Hirschkind and Mahmood 2002). The notion of saving Muslim women from Islam's oppressive hold serves as a renewed manifestation of Spivak's phrase "White men saving brown women from brown men" (1993, 93), which was written to describe one of the central justifications of British colonial rule in South Asia. More recently, the increase in state Islamophobia in the United States since 2016 through policies like the Muslim ban has also resulted in rising incidents of anti-Muslim violence. Despite how Islamophobic rhetoric in the United States continues to emphasize their oppression by Islam, Muslim women of color are disproportionately targeted by such violence. Moreover, white liberal feminist narratives that promote the idea of Muslim women in need of liberation attribute their oppression to religion while neglecting to consider material conditions of poverty, war, political corruption, or other aspects of inequality that are the inevitable result of modernity and global capitalism.

Many groundbreaking academic studies on Islam and women have pushed back on white feminism's liberal narratives, effectively dismantling the enduring trope of the oppressed Muslim woman and the concept of Islam as inherently antimodern. For example, historical accounts related to Islam and gender in Egypt and Iran have highlighted how the encounters between Muslim-majority states and colonial powers have often exacerbated women's social and economic conditions. As these societies shifted to adopt patriarchal structures of the nuclear family and companionate marriage, women were coerced into sacrificing their kinship networks in the service of nation-state building (L. Ahmed 1992; Najmabadi 2005). Other studies have demonstrated that Muslim women exercise agency in their religious engagements, use religious norms to their universal betterment, or otherwise subvert patriarchal control in creative ways (Mahmood 2004; Rouse 2004). These works have illuminated how Muslim women in countries such as Egypt and the United States work to promote Islamic sensibilities in the public sphere through their participation in piety movements and mosques, engagements in religious revivalism, and formal membership in Islamist political parties. Significantly, these studies further highlight how Muslim women as full agents critique, reject, and resist the various processes of secularization in their particular contexts, defying academic and activist notions of Islam as inherently opposed to the liberal ideals of rational choice and freedom.

In the context of colonial North America, Native Americans resisted Catholic and Protestant missionizing efforts from European colonists. Their Indigenous religious beliefs and customs often included female deities and matrilineal kinship structures. With respect to the Indigenous populations that did convert, Mónica Díaz (2011) shows how Native American women asserted their agency and authority within the Catholic Church. These women resisted hegemonic power through the colonial structure itself in their activities within missions, convents, schools, and churches. Likewise, the institution of the Black church served as a site of decolonization and resistance to white supremacy, and Evelyn Brooks Higginbotham (1993) shows how Black Baptist women occupied central roles in advocating for desegregation, voting rights, and education in the late nineteenth and early twentieth centuries.

Black Muslims in the United States have also deployed religion as a way to resist white supremacy and counter women's vulnerable status. Through both ethnographies and historical analyses, scholars have shown how African American Muslim women embrace particular Islamic sensibilities that may stand in contrast to secular liberal norms with respect to their choices of conservative dress, embrace of patriarchal gender roles within the family, and participation in polygynous marital arrangements for a variety of reasons. These reasons include these women's relationships to religion as a source of empowerment, spiritual fulfillment, and community support as well as a part of their broader rejection of a racist US state steeped in white supremacy (Rouse 2004; Majeed 2015; U. Taylor 2017; Chan-Malik 2018). Outside of the United States, religion has similarly been deployed as a tool of decolonization. Amina Jamal (2013, 13) suggests that Muslim women's cultivation of religious subjectivities in places like Pakistan should be understood as a "necessary part of the project of decolonization" rather than simply a reactive response to western domination. These practices include promoting religious education as well as forms of governance and legal systems rooted in Islamic teachings.

Other studies have emphasized how the secular state apparatus has been implicated in harms against Muslim women. In Bangladesh, for example, where foreign aid is an integral part of the secular government's infrastructure, microcredit initiatives endorsed by US-funded NGOs are championed as a mode of rural

Muslim women's empowerment against economic dependency on corrupt and misogynistic local religious elites. This is despite the fact that such programs drive borrowers deeper into debt and social stigma while benefiting lenders through prohibitive interest rates (Karim 2014). Such patterns demonstrate the shortcomings of emphasizing linkages between religion and Muslim women's oppressive conditions without due attention to how they themselves often view their religious identities as sources of empowerment. Moreover, these Muslim women also highlight how secular governing bodies and principles can also exacerbate and perpetuate the same material inequalities.

What to say, then, of the inequalities that religious women around the world undoubtedly confront within their communities of faith that are steeped in patriarchal norms? How can we as students and scholars engage in critiques of gender oppression within religious communities without perpetuating the reductive notion that religion necessarily constrains and subjugates women, queer communities, and other vulnerable populations? Aysha Hidayatullah and Judith Plaskow (2011) argue against the problematic trend among religious feminists to critique other religions' treatment of women as a foil to promote how their own traditions uphold women's status. Writing as Jewish and Muslim feminist academics in the United States, Plaskow and Hidayatullah, respectively, highlight how the marginalization of religious women extends beyond status in their own religious communities into their wider exclusion in a Christian-dominated academy and culture. In studies of already marginalized groups, then, what are the best practices to address gender-based discrimination and violence without rendering them even more vulnerable to erasure under white Christian hegemony? With respect to the study of Islam, how can we address issues such as domestic violence, gendered norms of

honor and shame, and marginalization of women, queer, and nonbinary Muslims in worship spaces without adding fuel to the global climate of Islamophobia?

To approach these questions, it is useful to reflect on Kimberlé Crenshaw's (1989, 1991) concept of intersectionality to understand the limitations of single-issue frameworks, which do not account for the multidimensional experiences of women, especially in communities of color. Sa'diyya Shaikh (2013) advocates for the multiple critique method in the study of Islam and gender, which is an intersectional approach that simultaneously accounts for a multiplicity of inequalities and their interactions with one another—that is race, class, colonial status, sexuality. A number of scholarly works on Islam and gender continue to demonstrate the utility and promise of this approach through their investigations of sexual ethics, domestic violence, anti-Black racism in Muslim communities, and Islamophobia and by confronting patriarchal scriptures. Engaging with internal critiques of sexism within the Islamic tradition while simultaneously keeping in mind the global imperial context in which ideas of Islam, women, and identity circulate is critically important in providing a more complete picture of how the categories of religion, gender, and sexuality intersect and relate to each other.

54

Reproduction

Aren Z. Aizura

In feminist politics, reproduction generally connotes two intimately related concepts. First is biological reproduction: relating to human bodies' capacities to menstruate, produce sperm or ova, and gestate. The second meaning is social reproduction: how we care for and maintain the bodies, minds, and capacities of ourselves and others. Colonial and imperial societies have instrumentalized reproduction in both social and biological forms to concretize racial, gender, and sexual orders that divide humans into those elevated and ideal citizens for whom reproduction is valued or encouraged and those for whom reproduction is understood as undesirable or threatening to social order, such as immigrants or people in the Global South. One useful way to think about reproduction is as *stratified*, a term sociologist Shellee Colen coined to show how the mundane and intimate acts of both social and biological reproduction differ "according to inequalities that are based on hierarchies of class, race, ethnicity, gender, place in a global economy, and migration status" ([1995] 2006, 380).

While some people might claim that both social and biological reproduction pertain mainly to cis women, or people with uteruses, the political value making of reproduction affects everyone, regardless of gender. Thus, in this essay, I do not speak of women as the primary subjects of social or biological reproduction. While cis women's bodies have been a battleground for political struggles around reproduction, we are all affected by reproductive struggles. Feminist, queer, trans, and disability movements have contributed to understanding reproductive capacities not as natural or biological instincts but as socially and technologically constructed, commodified, and always contested (Murphy 2012; Bridges 2011).

The right to reproduce, or not, is one such constellation. Almost all nation-states had criminalized abortion, widely believed to be a sin, by the end of the nineteenth century. European colonial powers also imposed criminalization of abortion in colonial states (Berer 2017). While modern medical techniques made abortion procedures much safer, criminalization made it more difficult to access and increased the number of complication-related deaths. Thus, during the twentieth century, feminists around the world demanded safe and legal access to abortion and contraception and comprehensive access to knowledge about sexual health and reproduction.

Using a rights framework to think about reproduction has many limitations. The focus on *rights* is shaped by a demand for individual autonomy and "choice"; this reflects a preoccupation with liberalism in which individual rights are understood as paramount (Ginsburg and Rapp 1991, 317). Black, Indigenous, and people of color have historically been excluded from the category of rights-bearing subjects, which means that often only whiteness can make a successful claim for reproductive rights. When we understand abortion and contraception as the primary reproductive rights, we exceptionalize those procedures—they appear to stand alone, outside of a context or history. Feminist science and technology studies has instead understood abortion and contraception along a spectrum of technologies that can control, enhance, or regulate conception and birth, including fertility treatments, IVF, sperm and ova donation, and sex selection of embryos (Mamo 2007; Thompson 2005).

The history of reproductive rights has also been about regulating the reproductive capacities of particular people, including those who are Black, people of color, poor, Indigenous, and disabled. Enslavement, central to the formation of the United States as a nation-state, situated Black women's reproduction as central to reproducing an enslaved labor force; meanwhile, enslaved women were refused right or recognition of motherhood and often torn away from their children (J. Morgan 2004; S. Turner 2017). Conversely, ideas about maintaining racial and class order were saturated with preventing childbearing in populations deemed unfit. In the late nineteenth century, English demographer Thomas Malthus argued that poverty was caused by high birth rates, which led to efforts to control reproduction via abstinence and late marriage campaigns, preventing poor or disabled people from marrying, and removing social safety nets to force poor or unemployed people into work (Linda Gordon 2002). Margaret Sanger, who in the early twentieth century advocated for access to contraception, drew on eugenicist arguments that birth control would prevent the "multiplication of the unfit" and hasten "racial betterment" (D. Roberts 1997, 74). Sanger believed that "mental and physical defect, delinquency, and beggary" (73) could be prevented through birth control as a public health measure. Sanger strategically built coalitions with eugenicists in order to further birth control campaigns; their goal was to extinguish Black, immigrant, Indigenous, and disabled people through birth control (Schuller 2018, 173; Saxton 2006, 106).

These eugenicist ideas carried into the twentieth century as reproductive technologies such as contraception, abortion, and sterilization became more widely available. In the 1960s, decolonization and independence movements in the Global South flourished; meanwhile, Global North development policies and continuing colonial extraction contributed to high rates of poverty and disease in colonized states, which were fast becoming known as the "Third World." US government agencies framed the combination of poverty and high birth rates in these regions as a national security threat and named it "overpopulation." Rather than looking to the structural conditions of racial capitalism, the history of colonization, enslavement, and white supremacy, which have contributed to keeping Black, Indigenous, and people of color communities in poverty, governments saw these communities as burdens on the state who had to be disciplined through reproductive interventions. Widespread sterilization campaigns were tested in Puerto Rico (Briggs 2002); on the US mainland, sterilization campaigns targeted Puerto Rican, Latinx, Black, and Indigenous communities. Sterilization became the fastest-growing method of birth control in the United States: between 1970 and 1980, the number of sterilizations increased from two hundred thousand to more than seven hundred thousand, many of these on women of color. Doctors who performed sterilizations sometimes neglected basic consent procedures or failed to inform women that hysterectomy or tubal ligation was not reversible. However, in an ethnography of New York–based Puerto Rican women who obtained *la operación*, Iris Lopez reminds us that women accessed sterilization for diverse reasons; they were neither free agents exercising liberal choice nor powerless victims. Poor women, she argues, exercise reproductive agency within multiple dimensions of oppressive social, cultural, and individual circumstances (2008, xii). White supremacist governments also attacked Black women's reproduction outside of medical forms of birth control (D. Roberts 1997, xi). Racist myths scapegoating Black mothers as "welfare queens," irresponsible and unfit to parent, helped Democrats pass a 1996 law restricting social safety nets along with an increase in laws criminalizing drug use during pregnancy, abortion, or stillbirth by poor women and women of color.

Evidencing the history of resistance, the 1960s and 1970s feminists in the Puerto Rican nationalist Young Lords Party and Black Panther Party campaigned to end sterilization abuse of women of color and fought for community control of hospitals and clinics (A. Nelson 2011, 130). The reproductive justice movement is a more recent response to these forms of violence. The word *justice* replaces the language of rights to point to how individual access to reproductive choice takes place within social and economic contexts. As an analytic, reproductive justice weaves reproductive access with social justice, focusing on the right to parent and access sexual and gender autonomy free of white supremacy, anti-Blackness, or carcerality in safe and healthy environments with a social safety net (Ross and Solinger 2017, 9). Reproductive justice is a key part of multiple intersectional movements: from enacting Indigenous self-determination over land, bodies, and language through teaching about Indigenous forms of reproductive care; to HIV prevention in queer and trans communities of color; to the fight to free Black women incarcerated because they defended themselves against intimate partner violence (Ross and Solinger 2017).

The beauty of reproductive justice analytics is that they take the racialization of social reproduction as the basis for an intersectional feminist politics. Social reproduction is something we all do, and in a Marxist sense, it refers to the abstract forms through which workers' lives are replenished. Thus we arrive at the term *reproductive labor*, encompassing a range of terms—care work, domestic work, affective labor, service work, housework—and including the labor of buying and preparing food; doing laundry, dishes, and cleaning; birthing, feeding, and socializing children; providing emotional support and care to partners, family members, and friends; and sex. Reproductive labor may be paid or unpaid, but it is almost always devalued as something women are naturally good at.

When Marxists talk about the gendered division of labor, they mean the truism that men are expected to work for wages ("productive" labor) while women are expected to keep house and raise children ("reproductive" labor; Dalla Costa and James [1972] 1975). Traditional Marxism saw the class division between workers and bosses, or capital, as the main social fault line within capitalism and the wage as the instrument that kept workers oppressed. But Marxist feminists argued that the wage men brought home controlled not only paid labor ("productive" work) but also unpaid women's work, or reproductive labor. Reproductive labor keeps both families and capital going—and, they argued, it is completely undervalued.

But these divisions of labor into "productive" and "reproductive" are historically specific, racialized, and classed. The twentieth-century postwar idea of the "family wage"—the idea that men were the principal workers in a household while women stayed home to raise children—applied mainly to middle-class white workers. Anyone outside that circle not only needed every adult to bring in wages but often did not arrange their family relationships in a nuclear family model at all. This has not been lost on Black, Indigenous, and woman of color feminists. In 1981, Angela Davis (1981, 132) pointed out that Black women did not experience the same relationship to the figure of the housewife as white women. Reproductive labor is also divided racially, as Evelyn Nakano Glenn (1992, 3) points out, and thus understanding the labor exploitation of women of color and how racial divisions set white and women of color feminists against each other requires an interlocking theory of labor, race, gender, and sexuality.

In a US historical context, reproductive labor is central to understanding the afterlife of slavery and the history of racial capitalism in the United States (Hartman 2016, 167). During enslavement, Black women were forced to do manual labor alongside men; according to Hortense Spillers, gender differentiation itself was withheld as a property of the human, from which Black women were excluded (1987, 67). Spillers writes that "'kinship' loses meaning, *since it can be invaded at any given and arbitrary moment by the property relations*" (74). Thus the lines between the private household and the public market that define the domestic as the primary site of reproductive labor in white households have never applied to Blackness. In the South postemancipation, freed Black women often moved into unpaid or underpaid domestic work in white households; working as housekeepers, maids, nannies, and wet nurses, Black women's labor reproduced white security, wealth, and freedom (Hartman 2016, 170). The sexual violence and exploitation meted out by white householders (both men and women) functioned to maintain Black women's captivity (Hunter 1997, 106). Meanwhile, in the Southwest, Chicana women were overrepresented as domestic workers. In California and Hawaiʻi, Chinese and later Japanese immigrant men worked in domestic service (Nakano Glenn 1992, 9). Indian boarding schools taught white homemaking skills to Indigenous young people to coerce them into entering the workforce in low-paid domestic and laboring jobs (O'Neill 2019; M. Jacobs 2007). This is consistent with assimilatory tactics used in other settler colonies—for example, Australia, where Indigenous girls removed from their families by missions were trained as maids for white setter households (Haskins and Scrimgeour 2015; Besley 2016).

All these historical conditions contribute to the current global market for care labor and domestic work, which still requires femme-subjectified workers to perform work that is considered unskilled and thus low paid and low valued. This can be described as feminized labor, which Rosemary Hennessy describes thus: "When the marks of femininity accompany the exchange of labor power for a wage, they offer a tacit promise to the buyer that the supervision of the physical life and living personality of the bearer of this labor power is out of her hands" (2006, 390). Global North feminist gains in employment equality have meant that domestic work, childcare, and eldercare are often outsourced to low-paid immigrant and Black women, creating a "care chain" where immigrant women domestic workers often rely on other family members or even lower paid workers to raise their own children (Hochschild 2000; Nadasen 2017). Immigrant women overwhelmingly perform the majority of domestic work in the Global North; visa conditions and temporary work permits can be used to racialize and further exploit immigrants by tying their survival to compliance with brutal working conditions and low pay. The scripts of both the housewife's blissful feminine domesticity and the liberal feminist narratives of women's increasing independence have relied on Black and Indigenous women and women of color to literally do the dirty work for both housewives and middle-class professional women. In this sense, the Marxist feminist rejoinder to liberal feminists who invested in workplace equality—that housework should be paid and that women were not always interested in work outside the home or refusing care—cannot work unless feminists start at the bottom, fighting for justice in all workplaces and for all domestic workers, paid and unpaid.

As they are usually taught, these feminist analyses of domestic work assume that the heterosexual nuclear family and gendered division of labor are universal. But too often, political debates about reproduction renaturalize gender even as it comes under question. Cis women are assumed to be the logical subjects of reproductive labor struggles, while the heterosexual couple is imagined as the basic unit of divisions of labor and of reproducing the nation-state materially by gestating children. To queer or trans (as a verb) reproductive labor means unshackling reproductive capacities from heteronormativity and gender normativity. Martin Manalansan (2008) intervenes in this heteronormativity when he points out that the "chain of care" paradigm always assumes that "domestic = family = heterosexual woman = care and love." He asks what happens when we include "such queer creatures as gay men, single and married women with no 'maternal instinct,' and transgendered persons into the mix." We might also look to how trans and queer understandings of family look different, whether through the nonbiological bonds of "queer family" or through queer and trans parenting, pregnancy, and child-rearing (cárdenas 2016; Lampe, Carter, and Sumerau 2019; Mamo 2007).

However, there's an important caveat, which is that we must refuse to exceptionalize the queerness and transness of reproduction. It is not sufficient to claim that queer and trans reproduction—whether social or biological—is radical. Queer and trans of color critique, woman of color feminism, reproductive justice frameworks, and disability studies can inform an analysis that also looks at how queer reproduction can replicate white supremacy. And while nowadays families can include two moms, two dads, or multiple gender-diverse parental figures, the family as an instrument of social control continues to have significant power. Previously, the nationalist family form positioned normative gender as a key part of familial integrity, designed to reproduce racial divisions of property (C. Harris 1993). Melinda Cooper (2017, 9) argues that neoliberal economic policies have used the family as a symbol of economic security, focusing on inheritance, property, and investments that are regulated through biological or kinship ties rather than individual accumulation of wages. Thus, the family functions to shift economic responsibility for people's care and livelihood from the state to the private and domestic sphere. Dismantling welfare also placed a new emphasis on the family and the private sphere as sites of social reproduction. While families that reproduce heteronormative and gendered divisions of labor are rewarded, racial capital also rewards any families that reproduce these property relations and unjust distribution of wealth, whether queer, trans, or heterosexual.

Thus, it is crucial to look to conceptual frameworks that do not exceptionalize and that can make space for trans and queer social and biological reproduction at the same time as they resist reinstating the biological family. Queering reproduction may mean abolishing the family form altogether (T. Lewis 2018). There is a rich history within feminist politics of cultivating shared and communal parenting, from polymaternal practices (T. Lewis 2018) to revolutionary mothering practiced in a context where Black mothering is criminalized (Gumbs, Martens, and Williams 2017, 121). As Alexis Pauline Gumbs, China Martens, and Mai'a Williams point out, "Black mothering is already a queer thing" (119).

Trans people have also established long-standing mutual aid networks that enact much-needed care and social reproduction denied by oppressive racial and gender orders, particularly biological family but also trans-exclusive social services (Gleeson 2017; Raha 2017; Malatino 2019b). These mutual aid networks emerge because "the normative and presumed centers of a life have fallen out, or never were accessible to or desired by us in the first place" (Malatino 2019b, 2); they might include activities from communal housing for precarious or unhoused trans women to collective fundraising for medical, social, and legal needs to solidarity support for incarcerated trans people. Following novelist Torrey Peters, Malatino proffers the frame of t4t, trans for trans, as a quasi-separatist form of mutual aid between trans people that is "antiutopian, guiding a praxis of solidarity in the interregnum" (Malatino 2019a, 656). "Small acts guided by a commitment to trans love" (656) sit in tension with each other, always emergent within a racial capitalist social order that understands Black and Indigenous queer and trans life as disposable and deviant. Treva Ellison describes such Black queer and trans social reproduction as "werqing it": "to exercise power through the position of being rendered excessive to the project of the human and its dis/organizing social categories: race, gender, sexuality, and class" (2017, 1).

Utopian or anticapitalist forms of mutual aid as reproductive labor can also be found in disability justice. Disability justice movements have emphasized the importance of care webs that are "for us and by us" and that do not rely on the state (Piepzna-Samarasinha 2018, 33). Park McArthur and Tina Zavitsanos (2013) point to forms of "conviviality" and care that do not form through exchange or transactional modes; they argue for cripping understandings of labor, debt, and interdependency. This work reveals interdependence and interconnectedness as necessary, beautiful, and part of honoring reproductive labor as something produced not only within the family but with and for strangers. Sandy Grande points to the decolonial potentials of care and social reproduction in foregrounding "relations of responsibility, collectivity, mutuality, and reciprocity," central to Indigenous protocols and practices (2018, 173). To think of any form of reproduction adequately, we need a vision for thinking about labor, care, and reproductive capacities in ways that not only enable self-determination as well as sexual and bodily autonomy for everyone but also refuse anti-Blackness, settler colonialism, nationalism, and the insidious forms through which these forces have sought to regulate reproduction across the centuries.

55

Securitization

Neel Ahuja

In some of its earliest usages in the English common law tradition, the term *security* referred to the incorporation of a collateral object—property, currency, or even persons—into a social pledge, court requirement, or financial obligation; in the phrasing of the *Oxford English Dictionary* (*OED*), a *security* may refer to "property pledged (or, occasionally, a person held) to guarantee someone's good conduct, appearance at court at a specified time, or fulfillment of some other obligation" (*OED Online*, "security," n.d.). The fact that the noun *security* has for some five hundred years signaled the reservation of property, including in some cases enslaved or incarcerated human beings, as a type of backing for a contract or requirement of a legal authority suggests that security has a relationship to both the rise of the state and the types of economic contact, appropriation, circulation, and mobility embedded in capitalist systems of property and exchange. The process of securitization refers to transformations in a subject, system, or state that are conceived as reducing the risk of harm or danger emerging from some specific social or environmental context. Securitization may take place on many scales and for many types of entities, ranging from an individual human to a financial contract to an institution, social system, or state apparatus. Across them all, securitization implies protecting the object of security by deploying a future-oriented temporality that balances investments in preventative measures in the short term in order to manage possible harm in the long term (Lakoff 2008).

Because humans may appear as both the agents who initiate securitization and the objects whose repression guarantee it, securitization is rife with structured inequalities across the fields of racial, gender, sexual, class, and species differences; to put it plainly, some people or groups are the beneficiaries of security's efforts at containment and others are targeted by them. This is not only so for those humans who are criminalized and thus subjected to the threat of carceral containment at the behest of the law, glimpsed in the *OED*'s above reference to bail. It is also apparent in the history of settler colonialism in North America, which involved the establishment of property relations that transformed Indigenous relationships to the land and, in the process, involved technologies like fences, armed policing, and allotments that destroyed native ecologies and accelerated genocide in order to securitize white colonists' property in land (Dunbar-Ortiz 2014). In such processes, security not only involves the claiming of space and the rendering of it as "domestic" in the process of colonization; it also allows white colonists the ability to accumulate wealth based on expropriated land.

Securitization emerges widely as a keyword within gender and sexuality studies, often as a process that requires critique because it configures relations of power that may be naturalized as a protective social order. For socialist feminists of the 1970s who focused on the problem of women's alienated reproductive labor, the institution of contract marriage in the Euro-American nuclear family cynically deployed the fiction that women traded household and sexual labor for either love or economic security in order to actually prop up a system that reproduced gender domination and that exploited feminized labor (Federici 1975). More recently, feminist and queer theorists engaging with the post-9/11 US security state have argued that racist and US American exceptionalist notions of western gender and sexual freedom have been used to justify new forms of imperial militarism that masquerade as security, particularly through US interventions in Muslim-majority countries and enhanced surveillance of Muslims in the United States. In the process, they construct the idea of Islam as a threat to liberal freedom through its gender and sexual repression (Puar 2007). A related process appears in critiques of queer urban spatialities, where gentrification and racist policing are possible outcomes of the development of what appear as neighborhoods devoted to sexual freedom and inclusion (Hanhardt 2013). Such critiques have touched the gender and sexuality studies classroom itself, as universities increasingly become sites where students assert the need for autonomy from sexual violence and argue for new forms of design that attend to the effects of trauma and disability caused by gender discrimination (Hanhardt et al. 2020).

Keeping the violence inherent to the form of security in mind, it is possible to consider how securitization as a process of capital accumulation and state expansion implies a relationship between myths of freedom and myths of self-defense. The thing that requires security is one whose ability to sustain the integrity of a way of living is able to manage unpredictable risks arising from an environment. As such, modern securitization becomes an imperative for governance of the self and the population, suggesting a biopolitics, a relationship between embodied needs of subjects and the politically managed capabilities of the population or species. According to Michel Foucault, "Freedom is nothing but the correlative of the deployment of the apparatuses of security," experienced as "the possibility of movement, change of place, and processes of circulation of both people and things" (2007, 48–49). Given that this ideological association between freedom and security allows the agents of capitalism and militarism the power to define violence as the basis of human flourishing, it should

be no surprise that with the launch of the post-9/11 wars and the expansion of the security state, US officials suggested both that the war on terror was the best way to secure freedom and that freedom itself could be realized by the maintenance of the US patterns of consumerism (Bush 2001; Dudziak 2003, 44–45). To the extent that securitization appears today as increasingly technological and integrated into all facets of everyday life, it nonetheless continues to serve a long-standing function of ensuring that certain forms of racialized property and value are able to reproduce.

56

Settler Colonialism

Manu Karuka

Settler colonialism is colonization by replacement. This replacement occurs at different levels, including politics, the law, culture, economics, technology, demographics, and ecology. Since Europe initiated its invasion of the Americas, settler colonialism has spread across the earth, becoming a primary vehicle of imperialism (Byrd 2011). In North America, a long Indigenous feminist tradition has analyzed the particular kinds of relationships that settler colonialism produces, which result in isolation, scarcity, and mass death. Indigenous feminists have emphasized the kinds of relationships that have been necessary to survive settler colonialism (Byrd 2019b; LaDuke 2015; A. Simpson 2018; TallBear 2019). Joanne Barker has theorized the "polity of the Indigenous," which she defines as "the unique governance, territory, and culture of Indigenous peoples in unique and related systems of (non)-human relationships and responsibilities to one another" (2017, 7). Indigenous feminist critiques of settler colonialism prioritize relationships and relatedness, drawing attention to ongoing processes of transformation (processes, in turn, that manifest through relationship and relatedness).

Settler colonialism operates at different scales, ranging across geographies. In northern, eastern, and southern Africa, decolonization struggles won resounding victories against settler colonialism during the second half of the twentieth century. With an eye toward defeating settler colonialism, we would do well to study those victories and to learn from the worlds they built (Kelley 2017). In this essay, I will briefly consider the history of women's participation in the Algerian Revolution in relation to Indigenous feminist scholarship from North America. Algerian women's role in the anticolonial struggle has tended to be downplayed in historical and cultural memory (Sawers 2014, 95–96). Outrage against French torture of captured Algerian women militants, in fact, galvanized international opinion against the brutality of the colonial state (Perego 2015, 354–56). Through their anticolonial militancy, Algerian women began to dismantle their gendered oppression (Gauch 2002, 122). And yet one of the larger questions raised in engaging this history is precisely about the reinforcement of Algerian women's oppression following the victory against colonialism (Faulkner 1996).

While settler colonialism centers on the control and capture of territory, scholars have analyzed the effects of these dynamics on culture and consciousness (Barker 2018b; Goeman 2008; Pasternak 2017; Silko 1998). Sarah Hunt writes, "Indigeneity is . . . lived, practiced, and relational. Yet Indigenous knowledge is rarely seen as legitimate on its own terms, but must be negotiated in relation to pre-established modes of inquiry" (2014, 29). Because settler colonialism requires more than the occupation of territory, struggles against settler colonialism occur within the bodies and consciousness of anticolonial militants. Anticolonial consciousness develops through a refusal to collaborate with settler colonialism. To refuse collaboration is to seek anticolonial forms of organization, posing questions that presume the impermanence of colonialism, thereby developing anticolonial consciousness (Arvin 2019a; Leroy 2016; A. Simpson 2014).

As Audra Simpson argues, "This practice of refusal . . . revenges the conceit of easy politics, of the very notion that Indigenous peoples had all things been equal would have consented to have things taken, things stolen from them" (2017, 29). Practical work toward decolonization (including theoretical work and collective study) repudiates core justifications for colonialism itself. Settler colonialism destroys existing worlds. It offers paternalistic concepts like progress, responsibility, and protection as justification for genocide. Settler colonialism informs a theory of society rooted in hoary theological fantasies of male birth. In fact, classical liberal theories of society derived foundational concepts from readings of reports about settler colonialism in the Americas (Muthu 2003, 31–36; Nichols 2020, 32, 156–57).

Settler colonialism is not a point of origin. It is, instead, a point of departure, marked by reaction to the collective relationships in and with land that preceded invasion and that persists in changed form after invasion (Byrd 2019a; Stark 2016; Vimalassery, Pegues, and Goldstein 2016). Against settler colonial reaction, anticolonial struggle takes root in what Amilcar Cabral referred to as the distinct "historical processes" of colonized peoples (1969, 96). This is not some kind of timeless essence. It is instead a dialectical relationship between groups of people and the lands where they live, between past ways of life and present struggles. Settler colonialism is a relationship of reaction to Indigenous peoples' historical processes (Adams 1995; Barker 2011, 19–22; Denetdale 2009; Kauanui 2018, 2–3; Teves 2018, 3). For this reason, engaging Indigenous intellectual traditions is a core necessity for the critical study of settler colonialism. Noenoe Silva describes this work as a "sustained reading of the works of our intellectual predecessors, those before us in the unending genealogy of indigenous thought" (2017, 211). The fuller understanding that can be cultivated from such sustained reading is a crucial aspect of reanimating the historical process, which, as Cabral insisted, is the essence of decolonization.

Frantz Fanon described colonialism in Algeria as "rationally pursued mutilation," a mutilation that registered in Algerians' bodies and psyches, a mutilation of the historical process that shaped Algerian collective life (1965, 65). Recent projects of "redress" and "reconciliation" by settler states like Canada leave the fact of colonial occupation, of this "rationally pursued mutilation," undisturbed (Coulthard 2014; A. Simpson 2016, 2020). By nurturing collective relationships and commitments, anticolonial struggle undoes that mutilation (L. Simpson 2017). Dian Million has found that in settler colonial contexts, healing processes raise questions about the nature and status of nations and, especially, of the centrality of Indigenous women in defining nations and nationhood (2013, 123–24). In the Algerian Revolution, young Algerian women militants participated in new forms of collectivity. Colonialism fostered relationships of isolation and vulnerability, relationships that had long appeared to be timeless features of everyday life. At grave risk, these young militants affirmed new kinds of relationships that prioritized decolonized futures.

Over the past decade, Indigenous mass movements across North America have also asserted new relationships, prioritizing decolonized futures. Women have been at the heart of the Idle No More, #MMIW (missing and murdered Indigenous women), and #NoDAPL (Dakota Access Pipeline) movements, engaging gendered solidarity and retaking Indigenous public space. Idle No More protested the Canadian government's removal of environmental protections, overwhelmingly on First Nations lands or unceded territory, for the benefit of Canadian mining and pipeline corporations. The movement involved flash mob round dances, reshaping spaces of consumerism like shopping malls, and negotiating acts of control from mall security and police forces in order to create spaces of Indigenous collectivity (Fitzgerald 2015, 111–16; Simpson, Walcott, and Coulthard 2018; Webber 2016, 4–5; Weir 2017, 31–33).

Dina Gilio-Whitaker has argued that Idle No More's environmentalist politics proceeded from assertions of Indigenous self-determination and the political primacy of Indigenous treaty rights (2015, 867–68).

Activists bearing witness to missing and murdered Indigenous women have emphasized bodily sovereignty to contest the role of the settler state and corporations in fostering violence against Indigenous women and the persistent absence of justice (Harjo, Navarro, and Robertson 2018). For example, the website of the Canadian MMIW coalition affirms that their collective efforts are necessary because "police and governments have failed to acknowledge, listen, or act despite Indigenous women, Two-Spirit and Trans people that have continued to disappear or be murdered" (Mack and Na'puti 2019, 355–58).

At Standing Rock, women played a central role in the rapid creation of community institutions that propelled the water protectors movement, reenlivening long histories of women's leadership in community governance and anticolonial resistance (Estes and Dhillon 2019, 28–29). While alert to the ideological and logistical challenges of camp life at Standing Rock, Sarah Sunshine Manning writes, "In virtually just weeks, an entire city of thousands was born out of the hopes, cooperation, and imaginations of healthy and motivated individuals yearning for something more in this world, while aiming, ultimately, to stop the Dakota Access Pipeline" (2019, 297–98).

Anticolonial struggle disrupts colonialist desires for tradition-bound, coherent colonial subjects. Jodi Byrd (2018, 134) has drawn out how symbolic attention to "appropriative and fetishized Indigeneity" enables a "disavowed acknowledgement" of settler colonialism and racism. She argues that "desire for indigeneity" underlies the everyday reproduction of colonial possession. Decolonization necessitates a disruption of such "erotic terrains" (Byrd 2017, 225–26). Byrd concludes, "The queer in Indigenous studies . . . challenges the queer of queer studies by offering not an identity or a figure necessarily, but rather an analytic that helps us relocate subjectivity and its refusals back into the vectors of ongoing settler colonialism" (225–26).

Algerian women's participation in the Algerian Revolution remade the self through participation in collective struggle. New relations of anticolonial struggle brought new gendered realities into being (L. R. Gordon 2015, 101). In this process, the veil itself became a useful tool to manipulate colonial gendered assumptions in the service of decolonization. Algerian militants, regardless of their own gender identities, consciously subverted the occupiers' presumptions about how Algerian women dressed in public and what kind of threat they posed to colonial power in order to advance the decolonization struggle. The gender identity of the person under the veil was less relevant to the decolonization struggle than the gendered assumptions of French military and police power. Maneuvering those assumptions enabled Algerian militants to carry weapons and explosives or to act as lookouts for larger groups of militants walking behind them, knowing that if they were caught, they would be imprisoned and likely tortured (Haddour 2010, 71–72).

Decolonization, as Mishuana Goeman has noted, is a spatial process (2013, 158–59). Rather than extending from Indigenous communities, with their distinct forms of relationship in and with place, settler colonialism imposes its own structures over Indigenous places. For example, Aileen Moreton-Robinson has examined how Australian beach culture has remade the beach from Indigenous land to a space of white masculinity (2015, 37–44). Settler colonialism reorganizes places by surrounding Indigenous collective life, in a kind of siege warfare against the land itself, and the people who live in relationship to it (Estes 2019). Decolonization involves breaking the settlers' siege. For young Algerian militants, this necessitated overcoming inner fears in order to move through the colonizers' city, confronting the hostile world of colonial occupation, personified in its violent police and vigilante forces. Fanon understood these physical and mental movements as "breaches" of colonialism, overcoming fear and despair, "distilled day after day by a colonialism that has incrusted itself with the *prospect of enduring forever*" (1965, 52–53; my emphasis).

Collective struggle against settler colonialism involves a theory of the future against an endless colonial present. As Anne Spice writes, "Indigenous blockades, checkpoints, and encampments slow and disrupt flows of extractive capital and the ideological project of settler sovereignty while also strengthening alternative relations that tend to the matter beyond what is usually considered the 'built environment'" (2018, 48). Anticolonial struggle involves realizing the possibilities of liberated futures into actually existing, concrete features of the world today. Relationships in and with land are at the heart of this process (Barker 2018a; Cornell 2001, 32; de Leeuw and Hunt 2018).

Anticolonial struggle entails a "new dialectic of the body and of the world" (Fanon 1965, 59). New unities are forged in the crucible of this dialectic. Elisabeth Armstrong writes, "Political unity, as the organizational transformation of solidarity, is a prerequisite, and not merely the necessary evil, of revolutionary struggle" (2002, 7). The concept of settler colonialism raises the question of how to build the political unity that will be necessary to achieve its defeat. In its "Principles of Unity," the Red Nation has affirmed the centrality of cultivating unity for its vision of struggle, declaring that "we seek to not just challenge power, but to build power. We are not simply a negation of the nightmarish colonial present—colonialism, capitalism, heteropatriarchy, imperialism, and white supremacy—we are the embodiment and affirmation of a coming Indigenous future, a future in which many worlds fit" (Red Nation, n.d.).

57

Sex

Amber Jamilla Musser

Sex is everywhere and also elusive. This essay focuses on sex as it relates to physical practices, intimacies, and regulations, even as the parameters of these are always shifting. On the one hand, people's ability to access sex has been considered a hallmark of personal freedom and societal liberation. On the other hand, sex is also a site of intense regulation, and the questions of what is permissible sex, who is allowed to have it, and what counts as sex have generated a lot of debate. As a keyword in gender and sexuality studies, talking about *sex* means talking about gender, subjectivity, sexuality, pleasure, privacy, race, colonialism, and the erotic. When one is talking about sex, one is always implicitly talking about power.

In his analysis of power and subjectivity, the French philosopher Michel Foucault ([1978] 1990) argued that sexual practices have, since the late nineteenth century, been imagined to reveal the most essential part of each person. This means that sexuality, how one describes one's sexual preferences, was intimately connected with one's identity, and sex was believed to be an important way to express selfhood. This tight linkage has had many effects—chief among them the belief that sexual revolution leads to greater freedoms. In Anne Koedt's ([1968] 1970) essay "The Myth of the Vaginal Orgasm," for example, we see an argument that one of the primary components of gendered oppression is the prioritization of penetrative sex and male pleasure. "Gender parity" meant emphasizing the importance of the clitoris and teaching women to access their own sexual

pleasure. Queer activists have also sought to broaden the category of socially acceptable sex by working to destigmatize nonmonogamy and casual sex in addition to nonheterosexual sex acts. Using the framework that access to sex constitutes a human right, disability activists have argued for the importance of sex surrogates and other forms of sex therapy as integral to sexual citizenship.

Activating these connections between sex, liberation, subjectivity, and citizenship, however, also illuminates the fact that the question of access is predicated on thinking about sex through a framework of consent, as something that one can say yes or no to. It does not take into account the numerous ways that sex has been used as a tool of coercion, both interpersonally and by the state. Here, we can think about the use of rape as a war tactic as well as forced practices of reproduction. In these analyses, sex is not about pleasure but about intimidation, domination, or even annihilation of others (Spillers [1987] 2003). To be embedded in these sexual scenes is to be disempowered. In response to the legacy of enslavement, for example, some strands of Black feminism have enacted a politics of silence around sex in order to reject these racialized projections of hypersexuality, preferring to dwell in the possibilities of respectability rather than get mired down in the dangers of sex (Hammonds 2004).

These two perspectives on sex are part of the tension between public and private that thinking sex occasions. Accordingly, sex is seemingly both something that occurs between people (private) and something that has greater significance in the sphere of the social (public). Importantly, when sex is imagined to be public, it is subject to greater regulation, but what this means varies tremendously. Arguments to destigmatize sex practices posit these practices as private. In the United States, arguments to decriminalize sodomy, for example, were based on broadening the right to privacy. In *Lawrence v. Texas* (539 U.S. 558 (2003)), Justice Kennedy argued that gay couples had the same expectation of privacy as heterosexual couples, and so sodomy, the way that the US legal system defined nonheterosexual sex, was implicitly protected by these same rights. However, this prioritization of sex in a domestic setting and between a presumptively monogamous couple highlights what kind of sex and whose sex is rendered public. Gayle Rubin ([1984] 2011) gives us a framework to see how sex outside the confines of domesticity, transactional sex, children's sex, and intergenerational sex is stigmatized. Alongside this, we can see how access to a private domestic space is dependent on other factors, including capital, age, citizenship, and race. Those who have a more tenuous grasp on the private—those who lack property or those who are reliant on the state for housing or food—are similarly subject to more surveillance and regulation of their sex lives through programs that have included the forced implantation of contraceptive devices and even forced sterilization.

This relationship between the regulation of sex, privacy, and property is itself an extension of the logics of settler colonialism and colonialism. Mark Rifkin (2011) argues that the naturalization of heterosexuality and binary gender is an extension of the domination of settler colonialism. One result of this is the assumption that sex is always penetrative and between men and women. Other frameworks for thinking about sex and gender have consequently been devalued and even criminalized. In India, for example, Jyoti Puri (2016) traces the criminalization of sodomy to British colonialism, and Kim TallBear (n.d.) asks us to see monogamy and the state's privileging of it as part of these residues of domination.

Introducing alternate frameworks for thinking about what constitutes sex (and gender) allows us to think about what has been legible as sex, particularly since most conversations about it have assumed the presence of a penis and penetration. Sex with other objects or body parts has not always been classified as sex. We see this omission in debates about how lesbians have sex and if they actually do and in questions about whether oral sex is "really sex." Discounting these acts as sex renders certain sexualities not only devalued but also less protected by the state. However, people have also used these foreclosures to think about other ways that sex might signify so some forms of sex are not always linked to disempowerment but can be used to find other modalities of pleasure and being. This is the case in some forms of BDSM and racialized sex play. Additionally, there are also those who are working with decolonized theorizations of sex. One of these models moves away from a focus on sex as genital toward thinking about the erotic. This puts sex into conversation with spirituality and/or other systems of knowledge that escape the logic of property, objectification, and privacy (Lorde [1984] 2007e).

58

Sexuality

Durba Mitra

Nothing seems more natural than the idea of "sexuality." *Sexuality* is a term used to describe the state of being sexual and sexual activity and as an expression of sexual interest, especially when it is seen as excessive. In common parlance, the word *sexuality* can denote an individual expression of sexual desire or can mean one's sexual preference or orientation. Yet critical scholarship has demonstrated that sexuality is far more complicated. Indeed, the idea that sexuality is a natural or purely biological trait is much more a product of history than one might imagine.

Sexuality studies, an interdisciplinary field of knowledge that emerged in the 1960s and 1970s, argues that sexuality has always been a project of knowledge and power. It explores how states, institutions, and societies make knowledge about sexual forms, practices, and identities. Perhaps the most cited study on sexuality is French theorist Michel Foucault's 1976 volume (English translation in 1978) *The History of Sexuality: An Introduction*, volume 1. Foucault's famous study has a deceptively simple title. His project, purportedly a history of the concept, gives no simple or easy definition of sexuality. Foucault subverts any commonsense understanding of Christianity and modern bourgeois societies as repressive of sexual pleasures and behaviors. Instead, he treats sexuality as a recent phenomenon linked to the rise of the individual and social identity, a term critical to understanding the complex history of state power and the radical transformation of the modern subject in western civilization. As Foucault shows in his lifelong project on the technologies of modern disciplinary knowledge and power, modern sexuality created an inextricable link between sexual desires and identities and facilitated them into a large-sale project of creating and naturalizing classifications for people as part of new forms of power that governed everyday life and death.

The critical study of sexuality has since proliferated across many fields—history, literature, sociology, anthropology, and the interdisciplinary fields of American studies; ethnic studies; Black studies; women's, gender, and sexuality studies; queer studies; transgender studies; and more. Scholars have investigated the emergence of heterosexual norms, the condemnation and regulation of homosexuality, asexuality as a radical critique of the scientific naturalization of sexuality, and the critical place of gender performance in the making of sexuality (G. Rubin [1984] 2011; J. Butler [1990] 1999). Gender and queer studies scholars have studied homosexuality and queer sexualities in relation to histories of urbanization, migration, capitalism, and identity.

In the history of the interdisciplinary fields of study that address sexuality, it is worth highlighting major theoretical interventions by women of color scholars who deepened the study of sexuality to focus on intersecting questions of race, class, gender, enslavement, and colonialism. Angela Davis's foundational 1971 study of American slave societies demonstrates how sexuality and the undoing of kin networks are essential to understanding reproductive labor and exploitation at the heart of slavery in the United States (A. Y. Davis 1971, 1981). Gayatri Chakravorty Spivak—who in 1985 provocatively asked, "Can the subaltern speak?"—raises questions about the limits of recuperating marginalized histories of sexuality that are fragmented or occluded in dominant archives produced in the aftermath of colonialism (Spivak 1988; Arondekar 2009). Hortense Spillers, in her 1987 essay "Mama's Baby, Papa's Maybe," places the origins of sexuality at the moment of enslavement, critically reframing the sexing and sexualization of enslaved peoples through the concept of "flesh" (Spillers 1987). Gloria Anzaldúa, in her 1987 *Borderlands / La Frontera: The New Mestiza*, innovatively reconceptualizes queer Chicanx sexuality as a mutable idea across spatial, racial, and sexual formations. In her work in the 1990s and 2000s, Sylvia Wynter (1995, 2003) links sexual difference and sexuality to the Christian imperial project, settler genocide of Indigenous peoples, and the long-term effects of bondage on African diasporic peoples in their forced migration across the Atlantic. These feminist scholars have transformed fields by arguing that sexuality cannot be understood without critical engagement with territorial expansion and slavery, the gendering of bodies, racism, and power.

Contemporary gender and sexuality studies demonstrates that when sexuality is denaturalized as an ahistorical fact, what emerges instead are complex histories based in domination and the social construction of sexual and racial difference. These histories link sexuality to colonial state power and exclusionary projects of racial domination based in systems of normative heterosexuality, Christian morality, territorial possession, and forced labor systems of slavery and indenture. Scholars of settler colonialism, slavery, and modern imperialism have argued that sexuality was critically fundamental for modern colonial projects of imperial sovereignty, settler colonialism, and the forced subjugation and bondage of people (Stoler 1995; Wynter 2003; Arondekar 2009; Rifkin 2011). It is thus imperative to think globally, to critically engage the racial history of sexual difference and the multiplicity of gender formations, and to foreground race and colonial empires in the study of heteronormative as well as queer sexualities and their political formations (Arondekar and Patel 2016; Snorton 2017; Amin 2017).

These studies show how sexuality must be explicitly situated in histories of slavery and colonial knowledge projects about enslaved and colonized bodies. Yet in many studies, the colonial origins of the concept of sexuality itself have been overlooked. The colonial origins of sexuality can be found in the late eighteenth century in the British Empire, when the English term *sexuality* itself began to be regularly used and circulated, etymologically emerging as a distinct word in the 1770s and 1780s in the natural sciences. This period saw the height of the African slave trade across the Atlantic, initiated by the Portuguese and Spanish more than two centuries before and expanded by the British across the globe. To understand the colonial origins of the keyword *sexuality*, one might begin this history in the city of Calcutta, the capital of the British Empire, when William Jones (1746–94), a jurist and philologist, was learning the ancient Indian language of Sanskrit. Jones argued that learning Sanskrit was essential to rule the newly conquered peoples who lived in the Indian subcontinent. He insisted that ancient Sanskrit texts must be used by the British to create a new system of law to govern the timeless "Hindoo" people of the subcontinent (Mitra 2020).

In the 1770s, Jones decided to practice his Sanskrit translation skills by writing a poem 287 couplets long based on his interpretation of Mahabharata that he titled *The Hindu Wife; or, The Enchanted Fruit*. In it, Jones analogized a major character from Mahabharata—Draupadi—with Eve in the Garden of Eden. In the following excerpt, Jones animates the sexuality of Draupadi in mocking verses that caricatured Indian society for an English audience. He contrasted the polygamous Muslims of his time to the polyandrous story lines of Hindus in Mahabharata:

Preposterous! That one biped vain
Should drag ten housewives in his train,

And stuff them in a gaudy cage,
Slaves to weak lust, or potent rage!
Not such the Dwapar Yug! Oh then
ONE BUXOM DAME MIGHT WED FIVE MEN.

    True History, in solemn terms,
This Philosophic lore confirms;
For *India* once, as now cold *Tibet*,
A groupe unusual might exhibit,
Of several husbands, free from strife,
Link'd fairly to a single wife!
Thus Botanists, with eyes acute
To see prolific dust minute,
Taught by their learned northern Brahmen
[Linneas]
To class by *pistil* and by *stamen*,
Produce from nature's rich dominion
Flow'rs *Polyandrian Monogynian*,
Where embryon blossoms, fruits, and leaves
Twenty prepare, and ONE receives. (W. Jones 1876, 3)

The polyandry of the "Hindu" woman Draupadi was to be differentiated from "caged" Muslim women who were "slaves" of the polygamous Muslim men. Jones built on common tropes of oppressive sexuality used to critique colonized Muslims across Central Asia, South Asia, and North Africa and stereotyped Muslim women as oppressed by a perverse religion (Said 1978).

Jones utilizes the language of natural science to explain Draupadi's "unusual" sexual whims. She is the pistil of the flower, the part of the plant that he genders female. The many men who sought to fertilize the Indian woman are the "stamen" essential for women to bear "fruit" (Subramaniam 2014, 2019; LaFleur 2018). Jones takes the ideas of a scientific sexual difference based in two distinct sexes from famed botanist and zoologist Carl Linnaeus's (1707–88) taxonomy, who he cites in the poem's footnotes. He explicitly

combines Linnean Latin taxonomical terms used solely for plants—"Polyandrian" and "Monogynian," many men for one woman (*poly-*, "many," and *andro-*, "men," paired with *mono-*, "one," and *gyno-*, "woman")—to categorize Indians by their polyandrous sexual excess where one woman held sway over and had sex with many men (W. Jones 1876). In contemporary scholarship, Jones is remembered primarily for "discovering" the link between Indo-European languages. He is not cited as a key thinker in the history of sexuality. Yet even this brief look at his knowledge project reveals critical insights into how the idea of sexuality was essential for the colonial enterprise of creating knowledge based in the rule of colonial difference (P. Chatterjee 1993).

The colonial translation project, based in moral claims about women's subordination and the weakness of their will in the face of backward patriarchal "customs," framed colonized peoples as ruled by unconscious sexual whims, overabundant sexual desires, and oppressive sexuality based in understandings of timeless "custom" (Mitra 2020). Jones's 1782 critique of Indian society as naturally and perversely polygamous set forth an agenda of dramatic social and legal reforms against polygamy among both colonial officials and Indian reformers for the following two hundred years. Sexuality in this moment emerges as a concept that intimately linked European territorial expansion to the racial subjugation of peoples through pseudoscientific ideas of civilizational difference.

In the one hundred years that followed Jones's knowledge project, much of the world experienced the intimate violence of European imperial domination, building on centuries of settler colonial domination and resource extraction across continents (Lowe 2015). The forced bondage of peoples and the settler colonial expansion and genocide of Indigenous peoples across the Americas had by the late eighteenth century expanded rapidly and spanned the modern world to many parts of Asia, North Africa, sub-Saharan Africa, and Australia (Du Bois 1945; Wynter 1995). Claims to sexual sovereignty became a primary domain for colonial critiques of colonized peoples as well as claims to autonomy and anticolonial claims to sovereignty by people of color around the world.

In the nineteenth century, multiple forms of knowledge flourished that built on the work of these colonial philologists. The natural and social sciences focused on sexuality based in ideas of racial difference, systematizing the comparative study of languages, texts, and civilizations. Perhaps the most significant among these fields is the nineteenth-century discipline of ethnology, often called "race science," which centered sexuality as the primary marker of civilizational development. Ethnologists compared different societies and peoples by evaluating and placing them on a linear grid of evolution, from "primitive" sexuality (found in so-called tribal societies) to modern-day monogamy (found in Europe and its diaspora; Rusert 2017; Mitra 2020). Another field of knowledge associated with the historical study of sexuality is the field of sexology, or the idea of the science of sexuality, a discipline that emerged in the nineteenth century in Europe and across the colonial world. Sexology built on philology, ethnology, and the natural sciences to systematically study human sexuality (Doan and Bland 1998; Fuechtner, Haynes, and Jones 2017; Mitra 2019). A related discipline is psychoanalysis, a field invented by Austrian neurologist Sigmund Freud. Built on key ethnological ideas of sexual evolution, totemism, bride capture, and the incest taboo, Freud theorized sexuality as an individual's "state of being." With the emergence of the psychoanalytic study of the mind in 1896, sexuality emerged in new domains of study that saw it as key to an individual's mental or personality traits rather than as a reflection of social structures.

These racist and patriarchal forms of knowledge were not only perpetuated in the domain of scholarly books. Ethnology was also disseminated and consumed by Europeans and Americans through the display of peoples as representative of stages of civilization. The nineteenth century was a foundational moment in modern race science, where the public display of people became a popular way to explain the excessive sexualities of "other" people. Early examples of human display can be found in the display of multiple Black African women, perhaps most famously in the example of a Khoekhoe woman who is recorded in archives through the Dutch name Saartjie Baartman (Qureshi 2004; Crais and Scully 2010; R. Mitchell 2019). The name Saartjie (anglicized as Sara) is a diminutive word, and Baartman, literally "bearded man," also could denote a "servant" or "savage." This woman was inscribed into history through a name with racist connotations, the "diminutive savage." She was born sometime in the 1780s, just as Jones was characterizing Indian sexuality as nonhuman through botanical terminology. A woman from southern Africa who traveled to England and France, she was put on display to perform as the "Hottentot Venus," an exaggerated, fake persona of hypersexual physicality invented for a European audience. She died in her midthirties in France, far from her place of birth. During her life, she was exploited as an object of public scrutiny and fascination, and after her death, she was dehumanized and scientifically objectified, studied as anatomical specimen by the famed French natural scientist Georges Cuvier, who, like Jones's favorite naturalist Linnaeus a hundred years before Cuvier, utilized the natural sciences to create sexualized taxonomies of nonwhite people.

The exaggerated and profoundly racist understandings of sexuality that Saartjie Baartman came to represent for Europe in name and image shaped a system of knowledge that spurred ideologies in the natural and human sciences for years to come—including race theory, anthropology, history, and sociology, as well as biology, anatomy, and botany. In her life, she may have resisted or taken advantage of her systematic objectification. Yet the archives of her life give us little understanding of her choices and experience, as she is recorded into history only by those people who described and viewed her. Almost two centuries after her passing, South Africans after the end of apartheid repatriated the labeled remains of Baartman back to South Africa and conducted a burial ceremony that reflected a complex politics of decolonization (Crais and Scully 2010).

From Jones and the woman named Baartman, we learn not only of the racist ideologies that formed early scientific studies of sexuality but also of the challenge of writing histories of colonized peoples who fought to survive and endure a world of painfully racist and sexist exploitation and forced migration, whose perspectives are often erased from archives. The political afterlives of these colonial histories of sexuality are alive today in ongoing struggles for decolonization in societies permanently shaped by slavery and colonization. Told in this interlinking history of colonialism, this woman and the history of display and the repatriation of her remains appear as another critical origin for understanding the emergence of the keyword *sexuality*.

Sexuality was a project of knowledge for colonial travelers, administrators, sociologists, scientists, and slaveholders who argued that the social behaviors, forms of reproduction, and desire and will of Black and brown people—most of the people of the world—were outside of modern civilization. In European and American depictions in writings, art, and exhibitions, the bodily practices of colonized people consistently appeared as deviant and backward, from the "perverse" homosexuality in Orientalist depictions of the Arab world to racist understandings of women as promiscuous and submissive from India, China, Japan, to the Philippines; to distorted depictions of racial effeminacy and homosociality of men in East and Southeast Asia; to the dehumanization and hypersexualization of Indigenous, Latinx, African, and African diasporic peoples. These sexual ideologies were used to justify systematic structures of gendered and sexual violence.

Today, the word *sexuality* also denotes the idea of sexual identity, linked to ideas of sexual orientation and preference. The emergence of the concept of sexual identity is intimately linked to the rise of the concept of the individual from the eighteenth century, which emerges out of liberal political philosophy deeply invested in imperial expansion. By the second half of the twentieth century, sexual identity was seen as a natural—indeed, essential—way to understand one's self. Ideas of sexual identity become particularly politically powerful in 1960s social movements, and by the 1980s, there were new categories and acronyms of sexual identity that were mobilized for social and political rights. For example, communities, activists, and eventually policy makers utilize the acronym "LBGTQI+" (lesbian, bisexual, gay, transgender, queer, intersex, nonbinary, and more) to designate historically marginalized and nonnormative, nonheterosexual sexualities. These politicized ideas of sexual identities have defined a powerful terrain of protest and social movements for rights through the twenty-first century, including ongoing work to decriminalize homosexuality in colonial-era laws, the persistence of the global HIV/AIDS crisis, advocacy for gay marriage, and urgent global movements for transgender rights.

Sexuality appeared as a word exactly in the moment when Europeans sought to secure their dominance through projects of territorial expansion and ideological control. From this brief sojourn into specific histories of the keyword *sexuality*, the term appears not as some natural trait or a matter of one's sexual preference. From sexuality studies, we learn that sexuality is not natural at all. Rather, sexuality is a deeply politicized idea that is essential to systematic projects of difference and social exclusion in the modern world. At its most groundbreaking, scholarship today critiques knowledge projects that create norms of sexuality that naturalize whiteness, cis bodies based in constructed ideas of sexual difference, and heterosexual, patriarchal monogamy while simultaneously objectifying, condemning, and dehumanizing the sexuality of "other" people—be they Black, Native, homosexual, transgender, people in bondage, or people who continue to live under colonial conditions. Understanding the keyword *sexuality* through its colonial history helps one understand how modern societies define ideas of the individual and norms of sexual choice, pleasure, and identity in exclusionary terms while condemning most people as deviant, dangerous, backward, and incapable of appropriate forms of sexuality. Today, *sexuality* as a term remains a contested site of racism and decolonization. The continued investigation of its colonial origins in disciplinary thought offers new directions for scholars to think about how to decolonize sexuality. These histories also help us think anew about the critical place of sexuality in ongoing projects of social and political liberation.

59

Sex Work
Heather Berg

What do we mean when we call sex "work"? For sex worker activist Carol Leigh, who is credited with coining the term in the late 1970s, and for the activists and scholars who soon took it up, *sex work* was a destigmatizing term to describe the range of ways people exchange sexual services for money—full-service sex work / prostitution, professional BDSM, porn performance, erotic dance/stripping, and phone sex. New forms of sex work have emerged since, and today, "sex work" includes digital sexual labors such as webcam performance and paid app-based sexting. Leigh wanted a term that would bridge internal hierarchies and bring these workers together in the struggle against criminalization, violence, and social stigma. From the porn set to the street corner, workers could find common cause. Leigh wanted to avoid both euphemistic terms (such as *escort* and *call girl*) and the shaming ones weaponized by cops, scolds, criminologists, and doctors who treated sex workers as pathological curiosities. "Sex work," Leigh says, "acknowledges the work we do rather than defines us by our status" (1997, 203). Leigh is not the first person to frame sex work as *work*. Sex workers, using many names for themselves and called many things by outsiders, have long talked about what they do as a job. At the turn of the twentieth century, Black sex workers framed their labor in clear economic terms: "I've got to make my livin'" (Blair 2018, 236). "Sex work" tries to bring diverse sexual labors together without pretending that they are the same.

Sex workers experience social stigma, policing, and interactions with consumers differently depending on their industry, historical moment, and social location. Race, class, citizenship, gender, and age structure working conditions and risk within sex industries. Racist and discriminatory hiring practices and consumers' sense that people of color's sexual labor is worth less create extreme inequalities in income and working conditions in erotic dance (S. Brooks 2010), porn performance (Miller-Young 2014), and webcam work (A. Jones 2020). Full-service sex workers working on the street or in massage parlors, who are more likely to be poor and working-class or women (both cis- and transgender) and queer people of color, face greatest risks of police abuse and violence from perpetrators who target vulnerable communities (Dewey 2011, 120). Undocumented migrants are criminalized regardless of the legal status of their industry, and abusive bosses, clients, and police know that migrants may avoid reporting violence, theft, or extortion for fear of deportation (Agustín 2007, 31). "Sex work" hopes to acknowledge these differences and unite workers across them in order to combat stigma, improve working conditions, and fight surveillance from the state.

But sex work—the term and the thing itself—is not only about risk. Sex workers are often creative hustlers, keen navigators of interpersonal dynamics, and skilled community organizers. They have had to be, with no help from the institutions (such as labor law, police, and established labor unions) that protect workers with more relative privilege and little support from progressives (such as mainstream feminists, immigration and civil rights activists, and advocates for the working poor) who often ally with other marginalized people. Rather than ally with workers to improve working conditions, concerned outsiders, especially feminists, often attempt to "rescue" sex workers through arrest, deportation, and forced rehabilitation (Agustín 2007). Critiquing this tendency, sex workers demand labor rights rather than rescue.

In the absence of external supports, sex workers often develop creative strategies for improving their own conditions. Across industries, they regularly develop ways of sharing information, such as "bad date" lists that warn other in-person sex workers to avoid abusive clients, internet chat rooms that share strategies for making money in webcam work, and informal networks among porn performers that teach newcomers how to reduce health risks on set. Sex workers also organize in more formal ways, building labor unions (Gall 2012; Hardy and Rivers-Moore 2018; Kotiswaran 2011), lobbying for better policy (Chateauvert 2013; Mgbako 2016), and administering peer-to-peer medical care (P. Newman 2003; Majic 2014). "Sex workers are fierce fighters because their jobs demand perspicacity [and] persistence," writes Melinda Chateauvert, and "these skills have also made them canny political activists" (2013, 4). The term *sex work* signals not just shared points of vulnerability but also this shared craftiness and grit.

Sex work thinkers continue to debate what counts as sex work. Should it include those who do "survival sex" by exchanging sex for housing, drugs, or other material goods? What, really, is the difference between exchanging sex for cash one uses to pay the rent and exchanging it in lieu of rent? Don't most people work in order to survive? And as Marxist feminists have long argued, is traditional marriage not grounded in exchanging sex for security (Fortunati 1981)? Should "sex work" include undocumented migrants (Kempadoo, Sanghera, and Pattanaik 2005) or underage people who do commercial sex (Showden and Majic 2018), or are these actors "victims of sex trafficking" because work is something that only adults with work authorization can do? Some thinkers want to reserve "sex work" for adults who freely choose their work, while others argue that for most workers (in sex work as in other jobs), choice feels more like being "forced to choose" among limited options (Doezema 1998).

Whether or not you are already familiar with sex work, where you land in these debates says a lot about what you think about work. Some feminists reject the term *sex work* altogether because they believe it normalizes something that is actually violent exploitation (Barry 1996, 67). If you think that work is a good thing, and your race, class, gender identity, and citizenship status allow you to experience work as generally nonviolent, this makes sense. Many sex work thinkers do not think "work" is good, however. Under racial capitalism, they say, all work is exploitative, but workers also struggle against this exploitation. To frame sexual labor as work places it squarely in the context of political economic shifts. Here, scholars focus on the work in sex work in order to explore its connections to global economic flows (D. Brennan 2004; Hoang 2015; G. Mitchell 2015) and the shift from industrial to postindustrial economies (Bernstein 2007; Dewey 2011).

Calling sex "work" can suggest that it is work like any other. For some thinkers, this is a good thing, and they highlight the commonalities among sex work and other forms of intimate and emotional labor, such as massage, domestic labor, and therapy (Boris and Parreñas 2010; Wolkowitz 2013). "The world's oldest profession is also the world's oldest form of affective labor," writes Melissa Ditmore (2007, 167). Feminists who believe that commercialized sexuality is uniquely exploitative object to this suggestion, arguing that unlike domestic labor, for example, sex work represents sexual violence and the "outsourcing of women's subordination" (Jeffreys 2009, 291). This "hostile worlds view" (Zelizer 2005, 22) posits sexuality as a particularly poor fit with commerce and assumes that sex can and should be completely detached from economy.

Sex work may be different from other forms of intimate labor for another reason—workers might experience it as *less* exploitative. LaShawn Harris, for example, describes Black sex workers in the Progressive Era who did sex work to avoid "break[ing] my back scrubbing floors" (2016, 139), while Prabha Kotiswaran describes contemporary Indian sex workers' critiques of "the abject nature of other work options" (2011, 216). The 1970s group Black Women for Wages for Housework argued that the state targets sex workers because they refuse "to settle for the sweatshop just because the Man tells us it's a 'respectable' job" (1977, 7). At the same time, we learn that the boundaries between sex work and nonsex work are porous—workers move in and out of and combine sex work and other forms of labor (S. Shah 2014).

There are more divisions still around what "worker" means. "Work" can suggest domination, classed struggle, or legitimacy, and thus sex workers might emerge as victims, agents in creative struggle, or responsible wage earners under an ostensibly just system. Sex workers of color who sometimes perform racist tropes can be framed as the quiet victims of racial capitalism, or they can be seen as creatively reappropriating its terms by putting hypersexuality to work (Miller-Young 2010). "Worker" could mean someone with a strong work ethic whose industry should be celebrated (Weeks 2011, 67), or it could mean a hustler who finds crafty ways to take more from the job than it takes from them. Porn performers might film for directors just to advertise their more lucrative side hustles, subverting managers' attempts to make money from their labor (Berg 2021). Work, then, might be a site of both exploitation and resistance, not one or the other.

Ideas about whether sex work is work and what work means shape regulatory approaches to it. Supporters of partial criminalization or the "Nordic model," aimed at ending demand for sexual services, argue that it rightly treats workers as abuse victims and targets perpetrators. But workers and researchers say that, like full criminalization, the Nordic model endangers workers by forcing them to work underground (Smith and Mac 2018). Criminalization through antitrafficking efforts also has unintended consequences. First, it can distract from the reality that labor trafficking is much more common in industries such as agriculture and domestic work (D. Brennan 2014, 12). Second, stricter national borders make migrants more dependent on smugglers and more likely to be caught in debt bondage to them (Kempadoo, Sanghera, and Pattanaik 2005; Parreñas 2011). And third, antitrafficking initiatives depend on arrest for "diversion," exposing workers to state surveillance and carceral violence. Some critique feminist support for criminalization, as what Elizabeth Bernstein (2010, 21) calls "carceral feminism," wherein feminists rally behind the punitive state.

Two legal alternatives attempt to remedy the harms of full and partial criminalization. The first, legalization, establishes special permitting and regulations for sex work. In Chiapas's state-run brothels, for example, workers submit to a state-run test for sexually transmitted infections, work in a designated zone of the city, and forfeit a portion of their earnings to the state (Kelly 2008). This approach helps workers protect themselves from client and police abuse. However, it presents sex workers, but not their clients, as a threat to public health and exposes them to regulations other people who have sex do not confront (Katsulis 2009, 83). And it creates a two-tier system, since undocumented migrants cannot access the limited benefits of working in a legal regime. And a third issue is that it directs profits away from workers and to business owners and the state (McClintock 1993, 5).

Another approach is decriminalization, in which sex work is subject to the same laws governing other forms of labor. In New Zealand's decriminalized context, for example, workers can report violence or theft, access health care without concern that the state will have access to their medical records, and unionize to agitate for better conditions. Sex workers overwhelmingly prefer this approach (Smith and Mac 2018), and human rights organizations such as Amnesty International recommend it (Amnesty International 2016). They do not, however, suggest that decriminalization solves all the problems sex workers confront. "Standard workplace law will almost certainly fail sex workers" (A. D. Davis 2015) for the same reason that low wages, racism, and health risk remain present in mainstream jobs.

This is why anticapitalist sex work thinkers argue that a critique of the commodification of sex needs to be a critique "of the commodification of everything" (Hardy 2013, 56). Some suggest that there is already a hint of this future in sex work, which for some workers feels like a departure from the daily tedium of most jobs. Here, LaMonda Horton-Stallings (2015, 20) warns that the "sex work is work" line risks obscuring the radical ways it breaks rules about work. "Can we move beyond 'sex work is work,'" the sex worker theorist suprihmbé asks, "to 'sex work is (anti)work'?" (2018). Sex workers wrestle with these tensions as they work to pay the bills in ways that sometimes feel just like other jobs, sometimes feel much harder, and sometimes feel like moments of escape. In the process, they reveal the cracks in nonsex work, unpaid sex, and a system in which we all work because there is rent to pay.

60

Sovereignty

Joanne Barker

This iteration of my work on sovereignty is cognizant of its framing as a keyword in a series published by New York University Press. The press is located within Lenapehoking, the historic territory of the Lenape people. As a Lenape scholar, I hold this representation accountable to the people from whose territory it is published.

Sovereignty is a word that registers varying contested ways of conceptualizing, evaluating, and negotiating the terms of our social relations and conditions with one another, other than humans, the land, and water. By thinking through two discrete and opposed claims on what sovereignty means and how sovereignty matters—by white supremacy and by Indigenous feminism—it is possible to understand in part the difficult terrain of racialized, gendered, and sexualized social contestations that inform its continued significance. I begin with a definition.

The United Nations defines sovereignty as a set of inherent, fundamental human rights to governance that belong to the state (a polity under a system of governance) and to the individual (a person). State sovereignty is associated with collectively held rights to self-governance, territorial integrity, natural resource control, economic self-sufficiency, and cultural autonomy. These rights are anchored to the principle of noninterference from foreign governments and militaries, defining an inherent right to independence and autonomy from invasion and occupation. Nonstate polities,

including thousands of Indigenous groups around the world, are understood to possess the collective rights akin to those reserved for sovereign states. The individual is similarly understood to possess basic human rights "regardless of race, sex, nationality, ethnicity, language, religion, or any other status" (United Nations, n.d.). These rights include "the right to life and liberty, freedom from slavery and torture, freedom of opinion and expression, the right to work and education, and many more" (United Nations, n.d.). States and nonstate polities are obligated to protect individual sovereignty; individuals are seen as righted to define and constitute the state sovereignty of which they are members. These mutual obligations and rights are codified in state constitutions defining the structure and process of governance and participation.

White supremacists appropriate sovereignty to advance racist and misogynist ideologies of identity, belonging, freedom, and liberty. These ideologies inform and unite seemingly unrelated sociopolitical movements, including antiabortion and anti-immigration. Both are grounded in eugenics, a belief that genetics (inheritance) determines intelligence and prosperity. They argue that undesirable genetic qualities can be strategically bred out or deported from a society in the name of its progress. Progress is almost always cast and measured in the capitalist terms of property, wealth, status, and entitlement.

Antiabortion movements often seek to regulate reproduction rates among population groups they believe represent inferior genetics. These groups include the mentally ill, criminals, the poor, and nonwhites. Regulatory measures involve sterilization, financial compensation for women on welfare who use contraceptives, withholding or curtailing welfare aid to women who become pregnant, the distribution of unsafe contraceptives, and foreign investments in "Third World" countries that employ sterilization.

At the same time, antiabortion advocates seek to advance reproduction among whites by the restriction of abortion rights and access to health care, including the imposition of bans on heartbeat and late-term abortions, the criminalization of doctors who perform abortions, and the criminalization of women who have miscarriages or abortions. During a debate in Sterling, Virginia, in October 2019, Republican delegate candidate Bill Drennan, running in Virginia's eighty-seventh delegate district against Democrat Suhas Subramanyam, responded to a question about gun violence by saying that the real problem in the country was abortion, proposing to put ankle bracelet monitors on pregnant (ostensibly white) women to ensure they would not get abortions. There are now over sixty-five state bills being vetted or that have passed that restrict reproductive choice and health care access, with nine states seeking to ban all forms of abortion.

These efforts align with those of adoption and foster care movements that take children from Indigenous, Black, Central American migrant, and other racialized groups and place them with white families. The movements are frequently populated by conservative Christians who envision a sovereign state and individual citizen governed by and for white heteronormative free market capitalists in the name of God. Wealth and prosperity are perceived as signs of not only good genetics but God's blessings for living a good life. They claim themselves as descendants of the country's Christian founders, the only righted citizens of the sovereign state, holding strongly to Confederate monuments and public spaces as marking their inherited blessings from above (Barker 2015).

On August 12, 2017, white nationalists from over thirty-five states across the United States held a well-coordinated Unite the Right rally in Charlottesville, Virginia. The occasion was the removal of a monument to Confederate General Robert E. Lee. Counterprotests, including those organized by Black Lives Matter, antiracist activists, and students, challenged the rally's mandate. Violence including stabbings, beatings, and shootings resulted in the death of one woman and the hospitalization of over twenty. The police did not intervene.

The heavily armed protesters chanted "White lives matter," "You will not replace us," and "Blood and soil" as they attacked counterprotestors during their marches through Charlottesville. "Blood and soil" is a phrase "popularized by the prominent Nazi theorist Richard Walther Darré in 1930, three years before he became Hitler's minister of food and agriculture. Darré maintained that the preservation of the Nordic race was inextricably tied to Germany's agrarian population. The idea painted farmers as national heroes who protected the purity of Germany" (Epstein 2017; Hatewatch Staff 2017). The purity linked an idealized agrarian past to a future world hegemony ruled by Nazi Germany. "Blood and soil" was codified in a 1933 law that required farmers to possess a certificate proving they were a member of the Aryan race in order to keep their farms and qualify for various programs.

White nationalists fear demographic shifts in the country and mobilize against immigration rights. Every count and projection indicates the United States will become "minority white" by 2045. "Hispanics" are already the largest minority group in the electorate; they now surpass Black eligible voters for the first time in US history. This is coupled with the fact that the number of immigrants in the United States is at a record high of 13.6 percent (though twenty-five other countries have higher shares of immigrants than the United States, including Australia, New Zealand, and Canada). While immigration from Mexico is on the decline, immigration from Central and South America and elsewhere is on the rise in direct consequence of US foreign policy. According to the Southern Poverty Law Center (SPLC), as of summer 2020, there were about fifty bills seeking to restrict, regulate, and fund anti-immigration laws before the US Congress. Most of these bills are written and/or sponsored by anti-immigrant hate groups like the California Coalition for Immigration Reform (CCIR). The CCIR, founded by Barbara Coe, was a cosponsor of California's 1994 Proposition 187, which denied public services to "illegal" immigrants and their children before it was found unconstitutional in 1999. Coe has claimed to have exposed a "secret plan" by Mexican immigrants to take over the Southwest and advocates for the military to seal the US-Mexican border.

The racism that fuels anti-immigration movements is inseparable from the misogyny that fuels antiabortion, and vice versa. Both are rooted in a fear of "white genocide" in the face of international immigration and migration realities, shifting national populations and economies, and people's empowered choices to be single and/or childless. The Federation for American Immigration Reform (FAIR), founded by John Tanton, subsidizes dubious studies about the alleged links between race and intelligence. They claim that "Dan Stein, the group's executive director, has warned that certain immigrant groups are engaged in 'competitive breeding' aimed at diminishing white power" (SPLC, n.d.). Garrett Hardin, a FAIR board member, has argued that "aiding starving Africans is counterproductive and will only 'encourage population growth'" (SPLC, n.d.). These racisms and sexisms are affected across antiabortion and anti-immigration efforts to protect the entitlements, privileges, and status of white heteronormativity and its core place in the constitution and exercise of an imperialist and neoliberal state sovereignty.

Indigenous feminist claims on sovereignty pose a unique challenge to this state sovereignty and the racist and sexist ideologies on which it is built (A. Simpson 2014; Goeman 2013; Denetdale 2006; Denetdale 2009). On the one hand, the claims define a territorial-based governance and relationality that involves a deep "caretaking" and nonhierarchical responsibility to land, water, and other-than-human beings (Kimmerer 2013; TallBear 2016, 2019; TallBear and Willey 2019). Decentering humans and individual rights discourses in notions of relationship and responsibility, it offers anticapitalist valuations of the land, bodies, and kinships that respect the radical necessity of difference and the revolutionary necessity of possibilities for kin- and love-making in other-than-compulsory monogamy, heteronormative, and homonormative ways.

On the other hand, Indigenous feminist claims on sovereignty invariably pit Indigenous territories, governments, and people against an imperialist and neoliberal state sovereignty that asserts indiscriminate rights over all lands and bodies in the name of fulfilling a divine mandate it inflects through hyperbolic registers of accumulative freedom and happiness (Pasternak 2017). This state requires the distorted presence or erasure of Indigenous people from the land and from the state's history to not only keep imperialism and neoliberalism in place but maintain the lie of its structural and moral rationale. Indigenous feminist claims on sovereignty mark the core place of sexual violence in the state's deployment of the military and police to suppress political opposition and engage in or cover-up murder, rape, child theft, and incarceration (A. Simpson 2016; Beardall 2019). It helps us understand futures and spaces not contained by graveyards or fated by nostalgia.

In her series "Thunder up Above," Navajo artist Wendy Red Star places Indigenous people in metallic-clad dress overlooking the terrains of other worlds (Star, n.d.). In "Indigenous Futurisms Mixtape," Revolutions Per Minute opens with a NASA countdown that fades into the words of Seneca author John Mohawk addressing regional and global conflicts over climate catastrophe and then moves through future-thinking electronic tracks by A Tribe Called Red, Kelela, Silver Jackson, Erykah Badu, and others (Revolutions Per Minute 2014). In *Deer Woman: An Anthology*, co-editors Elizabeth LaPensée, Weshoyot Alvitre, Patty Stonefish, Allie Vasquez, and Rebecca Naragon gather short fiction and comics reinterpreting Deer Woman stories in opposition to current structures of colonial gender violence (LaPensée et al. 2017).

The reclamation of the relevance of Indigenous cultural teachings and practices in the claims of Red Star, Revolutions Per Minute, and *Deer Woman* on the future and otherworlds simultaneously refutes the "last of" narratives that situate Indigenous peoples in a romantic but insignificant past and offers a lived alternative to the imperialist violences and neoliberal ideologies of state sovereignties in the present. This future-oriented valuation of Indigenous life is especially significant not only because it refutes the distortions and erasures of Indigenous peoples within the narratives of a state sovereignty obligated to fantastical tales of its progress requiring Indigenous injury and death but because it registers the continued relevance of Indigenous territories, governance, and cultures to Indigenous peoples in the present.

As represented by the confluence of Indigenous antipipeline/antiextraction capitalism, antipolice violence, and antisexual violence efforts throughout the United States and Canada, this present embodies the way Indigenous feminist claims on sovereignty refute the analytic, organizational, or social partitioning of sovereignty from gender and sexuality. Indigenous feminist analytics have *always already* been attuned to the extraconstitutional rights of Indigenous peoples to sovereignty and self-determination, emerging from organizing efforts for treaty and territorial rights, for environmental and food justice, for cultural autonomy, and against gender- and sexual-based discrimination violence, including child theft (Barker 2006).

These understandings of collective sovereignty inform Indigenous feminism's conceptualization of individual sovereignty not as a set of rights but as a defining of relationship in responsibility. In *Braiding Sweetgrass*, Robin Wall Kimmerer examines Indigenous relationality in the context of human and plant interactions (Kimmerer 2013). Through biology and story, Kimmerer shows how the lifework of plants, including sweetgrass, pecans, and strawberries, are represented in Indigenous teachings not only as animated symbols but as teachers of reciprocity, collaboration, synchronicity, and unity. For instance, pecan trees have a unique mast fruiting cycle and shared production of enzymes in defense against insect attacks that embodies their unity (in the production of nuts) and cooperation (in shared defense). Indigenous teachings draw lessons from the ways pecan trees work together to understand the importance of reciprocity and strategies for survival. So not only do pecan trees provide a source of protein during long winter months; they teach humans how to live in the world. In reciprocity, humans are obligated to protect plants and the land. Kimmerer writes, "We reciprocate the gift" of life and teaching "by taking care of the grove, protecting it from harm, planting seeds so that new groves" continue to thrive, shade, and feed the world (2013, 21). In "Why Interspecies Thinking Needs Indigenous Standpoints," Kim TallBear argues that Indigenous relationality includes humans, animals, thunder, water, stones, plants, fungi, microbes, and others as sentient, thinking beings (TallBear 2011; see Hogan 1996, 2018). In "American Indian Metaphysics," Vine Deloria Jr. writes

SOVEREIGNTY   JOANNE BARKER

that Indigenous teachings offer "the realization that the world, and all its possible experiences, constitute[s] a social reality, a fabric of life in which everything had the possibility of intimate knowing relationships because, ultimately everything was related" (Deloria 2001, 2). The orientation of Indigenous feminism is not to a long-lost past that is miraculously made relevant today but to the ongoing reconstitution and practice of cultural teachings in the now.

This now is a huge concept that wonders what sovereignty does and not merely what its definition has been. Musing over Indigenous queer ethics, Billy-Ray Belcourt wonders,

> Sovereignty is a charismatic concept, which means that it galvanizes inquiry en masse. It swallows up a host of meta-concepts that do not stand the test of intellectual time like it does. So, it is not just that we experience multi-faceted forms of oppression that "race" itself cannot fully account for; it is also that we participate in relational practices that agitate the body or the nation as inviolable containers for political life. Anything can become a site of severance, even the concepts to which we are most devoted. There are, of course, two valences of severance at play here: the ways in which we are made vulnerable to a host of political violences as a symptom of state power, and the ways in which we are beholden to others for our survivability—think Butler's generative claim that the ontological condition of being in the world is that we are in it with others, that we are made and unmade by those around us. (Belcourt and Nixon 2018)

This making and unmaking reverberates in Indigenous feminist claims on a sovereignty unanchored to western political theology and rearticulated through ethical concerns about the terms and conditions of our relations to one another. Therein, sovereignty is starved of its obligations to racial capitalism and registers instead the potential for mapping the multiple ways we are beholden to one another for our very lives.

61

Space

Michelle Daigle and Margaret Marietta Ramírez

Summer 2020 was a moment of mass reckoning. The pandemic amplified inequalities already existing across the globe, and the killing of George Floyd by Minneapolis police officers reignited a movement for Black lives that has reverberated across North America and well beyond. As we weave a conception of "space," we sit with the significance of monuments aggrandizing the "founding fathers" of genocide, slavery, and conquest being torn from their pedestals and dragged through the streets. To topple these figures along the same waterways where colonial ships once departed and arrived, on the same streets where Black and Indigenous lives have and continue to be massacred, calls attention to the importance of space, both in how power functions and in how relations between peoples emerge.

Our theorizing of space arises from these instances of unrest and upheaval, for space is laden with histories of conquest and resistance that demand our attention. Drawing from Tiffany Lethabo King's theorizing in *Black Shoals*, we use the term *conquest* here as a "grammar and a frame . . . to register the always already intersectional violence of anti-Blackness, slavery and its afterlife, and genocide at the same time" (2019, 68). While imperfect, we utilize the term *BIPOC* in this essay and specifically reference Black and Indigenous peoples when appropriate, as this differentiation is necessary to address particular embodied geographies and spatialized experiences of conquest. As Dionne Brand powerfully articulates in a piece published in the *Toronto Star*

in July 2020, the viral pandemic has laid bare the structural pandemic of anti-Black racism. She writes, "I know, as many do, that I've been living a pandemic all my life; it is structural rather than viral; it is the global state of emergency of antiblackness. What the COVID-19 pandemic has done is expose even further the endoskeleton of the world" (2020). Anti-Blackness, along with colonial genocide, discursively and materially shapes spatial ideologies and practices, naturalizing a white heteronormative cisgendered property-owning male subject, while BIPOC, queer, trans, and poor peoples have been made to be out of place through the ways they have been racialized, gendered, and sexualized. As Katherine McKittrick (2006) theorizes, practices of subjugation and conquest are spatial acts as racial, class, and sexual hierarchies become naturalized into our everyday landscapes, yet Black, Indigenous, and anticolonial relations continually navigate, refuse, and respatialize their surroundings through acts of place making and movement. That is, spaces of conquest are not merely experienced but constantly remade and reenvisioned within the global conditions of anti-Blackness and genocide.

A crucial task in conceptualizing space is recognizing how the violent conditions of conquest have shaped the spatial formation of places. Geographic sites such as nation-states, borders, private property, reservations, neighborhoods, prisons, schools, and so on fix, contain, and surveil people through racialized, gendered, and classed logics and practices. Space, as it is conveyed in geographic thought, is much more than a container—it is the material substance through which power is transmitted and through which relations are made. Space is never neutral and reflects the structures of power that human societies are founded upon, saturating geographic locations and relations with meaning. Without collapsing distinct racialized and gendered experiences, it is necessary to understand how colonial and capitalist grammars function as genocidal, anti-Black, gendered, and classed totalities that are imbued across space.

Therefore, space cannot be understood apart from power and conquest. We situate our conceptualizations of space from the rich genealogies of Black, Indigenous, and Latinx feminist and queer theories, for these literatures have always already been geographic, whether or not the discipline of geography has recognized their contributions to spatial theory. Theorists such as Mishuana Goeman (2013), Katherine McKittrick (2006), and Mary Pat Brady (2002) provide exceptionally rich insights into how Chicana, Indigenous, and Black women's discourses and practices contest spatial formations of conquest and produce alternative political, economic, and social relations that embody decolonial futures in the present. To echo Brady, Black, Indigenous, and women of color do not merely respatialize place but understand it to be imbued with collective possibilities by "seeing and feeling space as performative and participatory" (2002, 6). Similarly, Goeman's careful reading of Indigenous women writers in *Mark My Words* foregrounds the imaginative and transformative landscapes that are molded through their lived stories. We follow these brilliant thinkers not only to build a conceptualization of space that attends to the ongoing subjugation of BIPOC, queer, trans, and poor peoples' lives under conquest but also to insist that these "alternative" spatial genealogies offer integral frames to understand space itself. Situating our thinking alongside these theorists, we begin to understand the fluidity of space and how conquest and liberation traverse bounded geographic notions of scale. Colonial patriarchal categorizations of rural and urban, public and private, home and work, state and body, are unnecessarily rigid when we situate our thinking from Black and Indigenous genealogies, for their relations with land, water, labor, and each other extend beyond these binaries,

forming multiscalar conceptions of and relations to place. As McKittrick asserts, "One way to contend with unjust and uneven human/inhuman categorizations is to think about, and perhaps employ, the alternative geographic formulations that subaltern communities advance" (2006, xix). Following these theorists, an attention to space thus enables one to analyze the world through the complex social relations that emerge from sites of conquest and empire as well as to make sense of the alternate renderings of the world that emerge from subaltern relations.

Across scale, human lives, particularly Black, Indigenous, and migrant lives, are seen as sites of extraction, where racial capitalism renders a profit. In the words of Ruth Wilson Gilmore, "What's extracted from the extracted is *the* resource of life—time. If we think about this dynamic through the politics of scale, understanding bodies as places, then criminalization transforms individuals into tiny territories primed for extractive activity to unfold—extracting again time from the territories of selves. This process opens a hole in a life, furthering, perhaps to our surprise, the annihilation of space by time" (2017, 227). These carceral modes of extraction disproportionately criminalize Black, Indigenous, migrant, and poor peoples across the "terrain of racial capitalism" (227), forming vast carceral geographies that are upheld by white supremacist and colonial ideologies and continually devalue and dehumanize Black and Indigenous life. As King stresses, Black and Indigenous feminist and queer theories illuminate the multiple and intersecting modes of oppression that shape their humanity, down to the fleshy embodiments of what she calls a "conquistador humanism, which requires Black and Indigenous dehumanization" and renders Black and Indigenous bodies "as spaces of death" (2019, 16). BIPOC women, queer, and trans peoples have been subjugated to sexual and gender-based violence, as colonialism and racial capitalism require the conquest of racialized and gendered bodies and justify their ongoing criminalization, incarceration, and genocide (Spillers 1987; Fregoso and Bejarano 2010; Hunt 2015; A. Simpson 2016; Ellison 2016; Maynard 2017; L. Simpson 2017).

Confronting conquistador violence across space starts and ends with the everyday, organized, and intimate ways that BIPOC mediate, disrupt, and refuse conquest and carcerality. Thinking of the body as a "tiny territory" not only suggests that the body is a site of conquest or extraction but also recognizes how each body or life offers its own intimate geography that holds the capacity to ripple outward. Drawing from McKittrick (2019), these tiny territories also tell us of the "livingness" that is embodied on the streets, in the bush, at the kitchen table, in our artistic and creative labors, and through the ways we relate to one another. As Sarah Hunt and Cindi Holmes write, intimate relations illuminate how large-scale sites of resistance such as "rallies, protests and blockades" exist because of "the daily actions undertaken by individual Indigenous people, families, and communities (who) often go unacknowledged but are no less vital to decolonial processes" (2015, 157–58). Intimate spatial relations begin to crumble the impasses between Black, Indigenous, and POC life, allowing us to see and feel the ways that we come together to weave the fabric of radical transformative change.

If the political mobilizations of summer 2020 have reexposed the interconnected spaces of oppression across the globe, they also reveal shared desires for freedom. The movement for Black lives has offered up a renewed grammar for abolition, and as Gilmore writes, "Abolition geography starts from the homely premise that freedom is a place" (2017, 227), and it is by building together in and across place that we cultivate relationships to sustain our mutual liberation.

Putting liberation into practice is necessarily slow work, for power dynamics can be reproduced in organizing spaces if rushed. Bringing Nishnaabeg theorist Leanne Betasamosake Simpson's (2017) writing into relation with our years of thinking, organizing, and caring alongside/for each other, we find that to weave constellations of coresistance across space and difference requires that we also create a collective language, sharing stories and intimacies so as to trust one another in our work toward liberation (Daigle and Ramírez 2019). This weaving of liberatory intimacies builds solid foundations for abolitionist and decolonial work, through which tiny territories of mutual aid can grow into constellations that hold vast political power across space. As Leanne Simpson writes, constellations form within particular communities, such as within and across the plurality of Indigenous places, but true liberation can only happen as star systems meet each other to form constellations. It is then that "the fabric of the night sky changes: movements are built, particularly if constellations of coresistance create mechanisms for communication, strategic movement, accountability to each other, and shared decision-making practices" (2017, 218). Through this metaphor, we can see how space embodies "'the product of interrelations . . .' 'spheres of possibility,' and is 'always under construction' or a 'simultaneity of stories-so-far'" (Goeman 2013, 6, citing Massey 2005). Space is quite literally made up of constellations of interrelation, always in formation.

As Goeman notes, a consideration of space is "of utmost importance in decolonization projects" (2013, 6), and abolition and decolonization require the dismantling of oppressive power structures that affect our lives in the everyday. This transformative work starts at an embodied scale, as mass movements cannot be built without the mutual recognition, trust, and accountability that arise from ethical intimacies. Building interrelationships is coconstitutive to more visible forms of on-the-ground political organizing. Abolitionist and decolonial futures cannot happen without the intimate, at times messy, work that is not always reckoned with or acknowledged in liberatory theory and activism. This work is often feminized, displaced, and depoliticized and can be seen as accessorial despite being a crucial component of organizing. These intimate labors, too, are political and gendered spaces.

Black and Indigenous feminist and queer thinkers offer some of the most radical theorizations of freedom through an attention to intimate life. Drawing from Audre Lorde, King writes how erotic chaos is crucial to decolonization, where "the erotic is a 'measure between the beginnings of the sense of self and the chaos of our strongest feelings'" (2019, 144). Bringing Lorde's thinking into dialogue with Cree poet and theorist Billy-Ray Belcourt's (2017) discussion of sex, King continues, "The erotic is a powerful space in which, Lorde suggests, we engage the threat and our fear of difference to come to a place that allows us to be with and for one another. . . . Lingering with and in the erotic is a generative way to enter into conversations about sovereignty, coalition, and ethics on different terms" (147–48). Here, the intimate and the erotic offer a grounded space where constellations come into formation. Erotic chaos unmoors us and moves us closer to new forms of knowledge and ways of being together, and perhaps this chaotic and erotic space is also queer. As José Esteban Muñoz so sharply theorized, queerness is invested in futurities, for "queerness is essentially about the rejection of a here and now and an insistence on potentiality on concrete possibility for another world" (2009, 1). As intimate, erotic, and queer constellations form, monuments of conquest come tumbling down, and streets are animated by rallies, blockades, teach-ins, and artistic labors by and for Black, Indigenous, and POC life. Through these intimacies, spaces of conquest become unraveled and remade—intimate, erotic, and embodied dialogue cradles the embers of mutual recognition so that structures of conquest can be dismantled at a larger scale. We need to build trust to build movements, as erotic chaos unmoors and allows for liberatory intimacies to emerge. Our interrelations traverse time and space and give meaning to space itself, rippling out to mold a multitude of interconnected places. Space sculpts our everyday lives and foments power structures across scale, but space is always also being disentangled and rewoven, constellations forming, matter realigning, to bring new worlds into being.

62

Sports

Jennifer Doyle

In 2004, Celaya FC, a second-division men's soccer team in Mexico, attempted to sign striker Maribel Domínguez to a contract. Fédération Internationale de Football Association (FIFA), the sport's international governing organization, stepped in with an official prohibition and the assertion, "There must be a clear separation between men's and women's football" (Tuckman 2005). The memo prohibited Domínguez, who captained the women's national team, from playing in even exhibition games with the men's squad. Domínguez is hardly alone. Although Calgary Foothill team management felt she had earned her place on the squad, in 2017, the Canadian goalkeeper Stephanie Labbé was barred from playing with the men's team for the same reason (Turk 2018).

In recent years, the fight for equity in sports has been in the spotlight: tennis players have fought for equal prize money, soccer players for equal playing conditions, and basketball players for media coverage. Stories of women fighting to compete with and against men pop into our headlines as anomalies. In 2017, in advance of a downhill World Cup event, for example, ski racer Lindsey Vonn fought to be allowed to compete in the men's event (Pennington 2017). In this sport, men and women rarely race the same course, and women's courses are shorter. There is no clear reason for this, other than making it materially difficult to compare the capacities of men and women ski racers. Vonn's petition was denied; authorities invoked the same principle used by FIFA: the separation between men's and women's sports

must be clear. Similarly, in 2011, the International Association of Athletics Federations (IAAF) declared that marathon records set by women running alongside men would no longer count as women's records. A woman paced by a man, it seems, cannot call her speed her own (Longman and Macur 2011).

The more one thinks about these rules, the stranger they seem: For what is the problem, really, if Lindsey Vonn wants to race the men's course? Why do men and women ski different courses? Why should it matter if, in a marathon, a woman is paced by a man when everyone who does not lead the entire field over the duration of the race is paced by *someone*. In the New York Marathon, for example, it is not as if all men finish in front of all women. Is a personal record set by a nonelite male runner not his alone if he is running behind a woman? Or is this only an issue for the fastest woman in the world? If so, then why?

The sports world as we know it depends on fictions of absolute difference between men and women and naturalizes the violence of the processes through which these distinctions are drawn (Travers 2008). It takes an enormous amount of effort to produce these fictions. Behind statements like "There must be a clear separation between men's and women's football" is an array of cultural practices that articulate and reinforce a gender binary and that, furthermore, present the condition of being a woman athlete as a form of debility. We see this, for example, in resistance to supporting endurance events for women runners and swimmers. Women ran the 800 m race in the 1928 Olympics, and then not again until 1960, as the men governing the sport felt it was dangerous to allow women to run longer distances. The Olympics only began to feature races 1500 m or longer in 1980. Women compete in a heptathlon rather than a decathlon. The 1500 m freestyle swim, an event in which men have competed since 1904, was only introduced to the Summer Olympics schedule in 2020 (A. Gordon 2017). There is no Tour de France for women (Cross 2018). At most tennis tournaments, men and women play three sets. In Grand Slam events, however, men play five (Gibbs 2016). This used to be explained as an accommodation for women's weakness (even given that women competed in a five-set final for the Women's Tennis Association tournament from 1984 until 1998), but today—a real sign of how much things are changing—critics have begun to argue that men will be spared injury and enjoy longer careers if they play the same number of sets as women (L. Wagner 2018). In other words, the determination to materialize a difference between the capacities of men and women tennis players may actually just be bad for the game.

The fight for gender equity at the highest levels of sports is of paramount importance. But in the day-to-day practice of sports, we find even deeper forms of gender trouble. Gender policing is a defining feature of dominant sports cultures and impacts nearly every person who has ever played a sport—the harassment of male athletes within team hazing rituals and the normalization of homophobia and misogyny are defining characteristics of the homosocial spaces of many men's sports (Luther 2016; Messner and Sabo 1994). Trans athletes are treated as an existential threat, especially to women's sports (Anderson and Travers 2017). Gay men often stay in the closet: coming out risks shutting down that player's access to training, high-level competition, and commercial endorsement. Women's sports has had its own forms of closeting (P. Griffin 2011); in the United States, much has changed as high-profile athletes like Megan Rapinoe (soccer) and Brittney Griner (basketball) have insisted on their queerness as a defining feature of their public profiles. Nevertheless, gender policing in women's sports is often startling in its violence. Girls are told not to play certain sports because it will make their legs and arms too thick, their shoulders too broad. Boyish girls may be mocked and bullied by teammates who coerce them into feminizing their appearance to ward off the accusations that they are gay. This policing often concentrates on Black women athletes. In sports, the centrality of anti-Black racism to gender policing is all too clear. This is a painful, enduring feature of public discourse about the tennis players Venus and Serena Williams (Rankine 2015) and shapes discourse about athletes in diverse sports, from track and field (Nyong'o 2010) to basketball and figure skating (Rand 2013).

The organizations that govern a wide range of sports allow the gender identity of women athletes to be challenged by anyone—a competitor, teammate, sports official. Those athletes may then be subjected to invasive, humiliating examinations in which their sexual characteristics are studied, measured, and squared against charts developed by scientists who see their work as protecting women's sports from masculine intrusion. That process is not only misogynist: it is deeply racist and has long had horrifying consequences for especially Black and brown women from the Global South (Karkazis and Jordan-Young 2018; Padawer 2016; Ross and Forsyth 2020). The year 2019 marked the ten-year anniversary of the hounding of the South African runner Caster Semenya by the IAAF, which governs track and field. Semenya, a gender nonconforming track star, is one of the greatest athletes of her generation. The organization crafted a rule prohibiting women with naturally occurring testosterone levels above a certain marker from competing in the 800 m and 1500 m events—the two events in which Semenya competes. This rule and its accompanying enforcement policies are based on arguments rejected by the medical community and denounced by human rights organizations—these arguments reinforce an association of testosterone with men, obscure female and genderqueer masculinities, and gerrymander the category "woman athlete" in order to exclude specific Black genderqueer women. Unfortunately, these rules have migrated out of the sports world and now provide the template for antitrans legislation making its way through various state legislatures in the United States (Kliegman 2020).

I have thus far focused on negative effects of gender segregation in sports. However, the importance and necessity of women's sports, as a space apart within a patriarchal culture, is widely felt by diverse athletes. Activists organize access to sports for girls as a means for supporting their health and sense of autonomy and power. Antirape activists and scholars advocate for training in combat sports as a means for empowering girls and women to fight. These community-based initiatives link embodiment, agency, and liberty as counterpressures to a world organized around the dismantling of feminine motility (Gorely, Holroyd, and Kirk 2003; I. Young 1980). Intentional, feminist, and LGBT sports practices can be as inclusive (and as contentious) as gender studies itself (Caudwell 2006b). A history of women's participation in a particular sport within a particular region offers the reader not only a grim survey of the degree to which women's sports has been suppressed but an inspiring account for the endurance of women's sports in the face of that opposition (J. Williams 2003; Ring 2010; Elsey and Nadel 2019).

Sports history offers powerful counterexamples to the patriarchal and segregationist structures of mainstream commercial sports. The grassroots, amateur space of feminist and LGBTQ sports leagues can foster an inclusive, open environment for people exiled from mainstream sports cultures (Caudwell 2006a). Ethnic leagues provide essential spaces of belonging for communities ignored by mainstream sports, spaces within which men of color collectively navigate a range of oppressive and policing forces (Thangaraj 2010; Trouille

2013). In the decade that Jackie Robinson led the desegregation of baseball by playing for the Dodgers, Black women (excluded from professional women's baseball, which was whites-only) played for men's teams in the Negro league and, in fact, were important to the league's marketing (A. R. Davis 2016). Increasingly, sports studies scholars are turning their attention to these minor, amateur spaces—within those stories are important, often intensely gendered, histories of community formation and rebellion.

Sports is less a keyword in gender studies than *gender* is *the* keyword for *sports*. Looking beyond the two-gender model imposed by the organizations governing sports, we discover that the very category "sport" emerges from a wide set of activities that might fall under categories like exercise, fitness, play, leisure, and labor (J. Williams 2014). When we begin to think about the culture of specific sports, we see that there is not one athletic form of masculinity but many—the masculinity of the paradigmatic boxer is quite different from that of the baseball player. The masculinity of the paradigmatic gymnast is different from that of the wrestler. The femininity of the figure skater is quite different from the gymnast or track athlete. Individual athletes are different. Men and women and cis, trans, and genderqueer people share relationships to gender in and through sports—this has always been true, but it becomes true in new and transformative ways as sports allow for more gender diversity and as people coach, train, and compete with and against each other as differently gendered athletes.

63

State

A. Naomi Paik

On November 24, 2019, the International Day for the Elimination of Violence Against Women, thousands of women sang "Un violador en tu camino" (A rapist in your path) in front of the national stadium of Santiago, Chile, a site notorious for the torture and disappearances executed by the Pinochet dictatorship. The protestors performed a dance that evoked the sexual violence inflicted during interrogations, historically linking the Pinochet era and the present. They dressed in clothing, complete with blindfolds, highlighting the ways police subject protestors to blinding violence with pellets aimed at eyes. They performed the song, which ironically twists the Chilean police anthem "A friend in your path," as part of the nationwide protests ignited by a fare hike in public transit but fed by decades of neoliberal governance that has made Chile one of the most privatized economies with some of the worst income inequality in the world. As one protest motto proclaims, "This is not about thirty pesos, but about thirty years" (Rioja 2019). As ordinary Chileans rose up, the state cracked down, with police violence leading to thousands of arrests and injuries, at least twenty deaths, and hundreds of human rights violations, including rape and forced stripping.

These protest performances highlight the state's role in enabling capitalist extraction; deploying cultural forms, like the police anthem, to foster consent for its rule; and inflicting violence when that consent breaks down. The protests also demonstrate how feminist activism—which has spread through Latin America, North America, Europe, Africa, and Asia—can build solidarity across borders. This example of feminist activism offers one entry point to reflect on the complex political formation and set of institutions, agents, and relationships of power that we have come to know as the state.

Thinking about the state is difficult. Even the semantics work against clarifying its meaning. To talk about "the state" suggests that "it" is a singular object of study. (This semantic challenge recurs throughout this essay too.) But the state is internally divided, made up of many moving parts, many of which do not work together seamlessly, some of which actually oppose each other, even as, together, they marshal intense power. "Unsystematic," "without a center," and "generally unconscious," "state domination works through its ubiquitous power rather than through tight, coherent strategies," as Wendy Brown (1995, 179) highlights. Yet even if incoherent, the state performs functions that no other social formation does, organizing and condensing multiple practices into a system of rule. While we cannot approach it as a coherent object of analysis, we also cannot neglect the state. Since it is not a single entity, it makes sense to approach it less by what it is and more by what it does and how it operates.

Among the many lines of power the state draws together, the most obvious may be its coercive force. Indeed, coercion is central to Max Weber's oft-cited definition: "A state is that human community which (successfully) always claims to the monopoly of legitimate physical violence within a certain territory" ([1994] 2003, 311). According to Weber (and earlier theorists like Machiavelli and Hobbes), what is specific to the state, as opposed to other political formations that reign over human communities existing within a specific territory, is its "'right' to use violence" (Weber [1994] 2003, 311) that is *perceived* to be legitimate. Nonstate actors, like vigilantes, can deploy violence only insofar as the state allows it; otherwise, the state would use its own coercive powers to discipline those illegitimate uses of force. But violence, too, is an amorphous concept that can take many forms—a bullet, tear gas canister, or prison cell but also the structural violence inflicted not by particular agents of aggression but by social arrangements that harm people by depriving them of essential needs and ultimately abridge not only the quality of life but also its duration.

While the state is defined by this "right," violence is hardly the only mechanism through which the state exerts its authority. A state must garner the consent of its subjects and thus also functions by educating and fostering conditions in which most people adopt the values and "common sense" of a ruling class. Such ruling-class ideologies (i.e., that work in and of themselves as value) achieve hegemony if people so thoroughly adopt them as to think they are unquestionable.

Legal systems, for example, establish and enforce rules for engaging with each other. But they also shape and express societal norms and thus perform an ideological function. As critical race theorists argue, the law plays a "constitutive social role" because "social interests do not exist outside the law, but depend on it for content and form" (Crenshaw et al. 1996, xxiv). Legal discourses tell narratives about the state, its subjects, and our relations to each other. For example, as Kimberlé Crenshaw argues, efforts to pass the Violence Against Women Act (VAWA) relied on narratives that highlighted white women's subjection to domestic violence. VAWA could pass legislative muster only by suppressing Black women's experiences of domestic violence, thus continuing their devaluation as "less believable or less important" (Crenshaw 1991, 1271). VAWA highlights how the United States values differently gendered and racialized people as worthy or unworthy. Furthermore, VAWA has failed to prevent gender-based violence, even as it

has hardened state coercion by increasing punishments for sex crimes. Unlike other narratives, legal discourses are backed up by the state's "right" to violently enforce them.

The law also tells narratives about itself—that it is an objective arbiter of justice. Different minoritized groups have thus worked through the law to compel state-level change, as seen in movements that achieved civil rights legislation and Supreme Court decisions. But seeking legal redress through the state, particularly for wrongs committed *by* the state, is contradictory. Such efforts not only risk occluding how the law functions to control people but can also affirm the idea that the state provides guardianship. Even that guardianship can exert power over those subjected to it.

The state is "double-sided" and thus constitutes a site of struggle. It wields its self-legitimized violence and denies the right to self-defense against it. Yet it also "enlarges social and cultural possibilities; it enables people to enter new terrains" (S. Hall 2016, 164). While the state organizes its functions to facilitate the smooth operations of capitalism, it is no mere servant to hegemonic interests. Such (reductive Marxist) approaches that dismiss the welfare state as a "ruse of the capitalist class" also dismiss the organized struggle of millions of people who fought "to win from the State what was owed them" (164). *And yet* even the welfare state operates to regulate its subjects. Public schools provide free education and also train a future workforce in compliant behaviors while enforcing codes of dress and conduct, "zero-tolerance" policies (i.e., against drug possession), and so on. Other social workers determine eligibility for public benefits (disability, food aid, health care, etc.) by examining people's private lives and finances. "The state that gives out benefits also snoops on its recipients," Stuart Hall ([1984] 2017, 230) notes. This snooping extends the ideologies of race, class, gender, sexuality, and other social formations that inform the decisions of welfare state agents as they determine who deserves access to resources. In the United States, discourses like the infamous Moynihan Report (Moynihan 1965) have blamed demands for welfare services not on eviscerated economies or systemic inequalities but on the deviant structure of women-led, father-absent Black households that defied heteropatriarchal norms. Though designed as part of a liberal program to eradicate poverty, the report is mired in racist, patriarchal assumptions that ultimately cast Black women as objects of state surveillance. Even the welfare state, which provides resources, inflicts an intrusive structural violence on its recipients.

Indeed, the experience of the welfare state as a snooping meddler into private life and the identification of welfare with poor people of color fostered consent for the neoliberal evisceration of the welfare state in the mid to late twentieth century. Political leaders and economists like Margaret Thatcher and Milton Friedman could sell gutting social safety nets in ways that spoke to people, even those who relied on welfare services, in terms of their everyday lives—liberating them from government intrusions and the too-high taxes that ultimately support "welfare queens" living for free off the backs of working people.

The dismantling of the welfare state did not just happen. It was catalyzed under specific historical conditions: the multiple social and political economic crises in the late 1960s and early 1970s—notably, the global revolts against capitalism in anticolonial and revolutionary movements (Third World, feminist, queer, Indigenous, etc.) and the 1973 global economic recession. The welfare state got blamed for the crash. To resolve this crisis, neoliberal advocates argued, the state needed to drop this economic "interference" and instead facilitate the workings of the market, which best determines not only how the economy functions but also how the

government should operate and how individuals should organize their lives. Neoliberal ideology shifted thinking about the proper role of the state. As Brown argues, "With neoliberalism, the political rationality of the state becomes economic in a triple sense: the economy is at once model, object, and project. That is, economic principles become the model for state conduct, the economy becomes the primary object of state concern and policy, and the marketization of domains and conduct is what the state seeks to disseminate everywhere" (2015, 62). The purported goal of this shift was to make the state as small as possible, via deregulation, privatization, and devolving state capacities to local governments and sectors of civil society, like the homes and nonprofit organizations called upon "to fill in the caring gaps that the obliterated welfare state has left vacant," as Elizabeth Bernstein (2012, 250) states.

These neoliberal transformations congealed the "anti-state state," which, as Ruth Wilson Gilmore argues, "dismisses any agency or capacity that government might use to guarantee social well-being" (2007, 245). The antistate state is not diminishing but reallocating its capacities from ensuring the social good to disciplining those who threaten the social order—"surplus" populations left behind by gutted economies as well as those who resist capitalist exploitation and state oppression. This is why the antistate state is "built on prison foundations," with the rate of incarceration in the United States quadrupling since the 1970s to more than 2.2 million people imprisoned in the early 2000s (Gilmore 2007, 245). This reorganization of state power is ideologically driven not only by the "folk devil" of the welfare cheat but also by the boogeyman of the criminal—the gang member, terrorist, thug, "illegal" immigrant, or border crosser—which harnesses consent for the proliferation of state tactics of social control. Against this boogeyman, the state needs "to stand firm, not to give in, to restore authority to the government," Hall argues. "This theme of national unity and authority provided the all-important positive face to the more negative themes of law and order" ([1978] 2017, 166). The neoliberal devolution of state power does not mean the state is no longer significant; it remains a major player in global economic and political affairs and a powerful symbol of political collective identity and security.

State power has never operated solely through formal state agencies. Instead, an expanded notion of the state encompasses political and civil society. The neoliberal state's devolution of capacity to local governments, households, nonprofits, and so on also helps multiply "the potential sites of social conflict and constituencies for change" (S. Hall [1990] 2017, 127). These opportunities for conflict and change are politically neutral; they can be mobilized in progressive or revanchist ways depending on how they are engaged. Even mobilizations framed as feminist can move in either direction. Carceral feminist strategies, for example, illustrate how levers of state power—both within and beyond formal state bureaucracies—can work to shore up state power while undermining social justice for people of all genders, including women.

Carceral feminism, following Bernstein (2010, 58), entails "a vision of social justice as criminal justice, and of punitive systems of control as the best motivational deterrents" for gender-based and sexual violence. Its proponents look to collaborate with the state agencies of social control that are strengthening under neoliberalism. As neoliberal states rely ever more on these collaborations with agencies beyond the state, they operate in terms of interest convergence—limiting their support to those social issues that align with already existing political agendas, like border security, prison and policing regimes, or warfare. While framed as protecting women, carceral feminism advances neoliberal ideologies that view punishment as social justice and deploys the levers of power made available by the antistate state. It seeks to control *individual* perpetrators in order to solve the *social* problem of sexual and gender-based violence. It thereby strengthens the idea that the state protects victims of this violence. Carceral feminists have thus argued for antitrafficking laws that harden border enforcement in ways that do not protect but subject migrants, including trafficked sex workers, to greater surveillance, detention, and deportation. Similarly, laws like VAWA and mechanisms like sex offender registries do little to make potential survivors safe from sexual harm but justify and bolster the state's capacities for criminalization and social control.

As the abolitionist organization Critical Resistance and the feminist of color collective INCITE! argue, this dependence on the carceral state, in fact, has disempowered "women's ability to organize collectively to stop violence and invested this power within the state" (Critical Resistance-INCITE! 2008). These organizers acknowledge the appeal of turning to the carceral state given the absence of alternative means of seeking justice and emphasize the dire need to create real strategies for addressing the multifaceted patriarchal violence that permeates so many people's lives. The track record of carceral feminism shows that trying to deploy the tools of the carceral state does nothing to empower people or create conditions of bodily autonomy and dignity. Indeed, it is paradoxical, since, as Mariame Kaba, Dean Spade, and other feminist organizers have argued, the (carceral) state is a rapist.

The thousands of women who have performed "Un violador" know this point well. Their performances identify sexual and gender-based violence as the expected outcome of patriarchal social orders and the state agents that propagate them—by inflicting such violence, blaming survivors, and offering impunity to perpetrators. Created by the feminist collective Las Tesis and based on the scholarship of Argentinian feminist Rita Segato, "Un violador," as mentioned, twists the Chilean police slogan "A friend in your path." It also ironically quotes the police anthem, highlighting how the cop watching over the "innocent girl" stalks her while using her innocence to discipline the bandit and to legitimize the existence of the police. But it is, in fact, "your loving cop" that is the rapist: "The oppressive state is a rapist" (Merelli 2019). "Un violador" exposes how the state sustains the patriarchal powers at the root of sexual violence. While first igniting in Chile, the performance has spread like wildfire over a vast expanse. The song's global reach makes sense. Since patriarchal violence, supported and inflicted by the state, is global, so too is its opposition. The reach of "Un violador" signals a broad, deep criticism of neoliberal statecraft while forging emergent, potential collectivities, imaginaries, and solidarities rooted in feminist politics. Contrary to carceral feminist approaches, these protestors identify the state not as their protector but as an assailant of antifeminist, gender-based oppression.

These demonstrations also show the state as a bundle of contradictory forces and agents that work to organize the social, political, and economic—largely in service of capital but having to garner hegemony through cultural and ideological work and ultimately backed up by the violence it will always claim is legitimate. Indeed, the protests in Chile and elsewhere struggle not only to dismantle the oppressive state that shoots people in the eyes and sexually assaults those it criminalizes but also to expand the collective investments in the social good, like public transportation, education, and health care. At the same time, seizing the state, on its own, will not lead to liberation. "You don't change the world by taking over the state," Silvia Federici argues. Instead, "let's give up the idea of electing the right person and let's work on building forms of resistance and alternative forms of production from below. That is the road to creating a new world and not wasting time delegating to the state, even to the progressive state" (2016, 211). Federici emphasizes that real change comes less from seizing the state, even as the state is an important site of struggle, and more from deep, democratic organizing among ordinary people. Indeed, one of the most pernicious effects of neoliberal statecraft and ideology has been the dedemocratization of social life ("there is no such thing" as society) and fostering of an "abject, unemancipatory, and anti-egalitarian subjective orientation" among vast numbers of people (W. Brown 2006, 703). Contesting this trend requires building real democratic power, which, as Hall argues so well, "is the real passage of power to the powerless, the empowerment of the excluded" ([1984] 2017, 237). This work must take place across a wide range of social sites, including those located within the state. But it is the people, and not the state, who can realize the democratization of public life that the future requires.

64

Subaltern

Susan Koshy

The term *subaltern* has traveled widely, mutating as it has animated political projects and academic interventions across several continents. Originally a late-medieval term for peasants and vassals and later for low-ranked military troops of peasant background, it was adapted by Marxist philosopher and politician Antonio Gramsci (1978) to refer to subordinated groups and classes in his analysis of the "Southern Question" in Italy. His overarching concern was to produce "a methodology of subaltern historiography, a history of the subaltern classes, and a political strategy of transformation based upon the historical development and existence of the subaltern" (M. Green 2002, 3). Gramsci's analysis of subalternity in relation to domination and uneven development had a major impact on thinkers grappling with colonialism and its legacies in the Global South.

More than fifty years later, Gramsci's concept of the subaltern was reworked by the Subaltern Studies Collective, a group of historians of South Asia that was founded in 1982 and led by Ranajit Guha. The collective sought to counter the elitist bias in South Asian historiography by centering the perspective of nonelite groups, using the term to refer to a shifting mass of groups subordinated along lines of caste, class, gender, religion, and culture. Although their early writings asserted the autonomy and determinate social identities of subaltern groups, their later work explored "how subalternity was constituted by dominant discourses" (Prakash 1994, 1480). Their historiographic methods evolved to grapple with how the disciplinary conventions of western

history—such as the need for written or verifiable records, or the authority accorded official colonial records and translations, or the reliance on native informants as transparent sources of cultural information—impeded the retrieval of subaltern histories. In another crucial innovation, the collective channeled the Gramscian scrutiny of the relationship between intellectuals and subaltern groups toward cultivating a reflexivity about the Eurocentrism of their discipline. In particular, they sought to name their fraught position as postcolonial subjects who inhabited the structures of western domination they sought to undermine and their social difference from the groups whose histories they recorded. This awareness informed their archival methods as they drew on unconventional sources such as oral narratives, rumors, or popular memory; critically reevaluated administrative documents and reports; and read both colonial and nationalist sources against the grain. Their historical accounts treated the discontinuity of subaltern presence in the records as evidence of "both the necessary failure of subalterns to come into their own and the pressure they exerted on discursive systems that, in turn, provoked their suppression and fragmentation" (Prakash 1994, 148).

Largely missing from their work, especially in the first four volumes of the *Subaltern Studies* journal, was attention to women as historical agents or to questions of gender and sexuality. A notable exception was Ranajit Guha's (1987) essay "Chandra's Death," which reads a colonial legal case involving the death of a low-caste Bagdi widow as a recessive instance of subaltern gender solidarity. By far the most influential and ambitious feminist intervention into the Subaltern Studies project was Gayatri Chakravorty Spivak's landmark essay "Can the Subaltern Speak?" The essay appeared in three different versions: it was first published in *Wedge* (Spivak 1985), then reprinted as a chapter in the edited volume

Marxism and the Interpretation of Culture (Spivak 1988), and later revised to address criticisms and misappropriations in Spivak's (1999) book *A Critique of Postcolonial Reason*. Spivak's passionate declaration in the essay that the subaltern cannot speak, which she later qualified as "inadvisable" in her revised version, expresses her dismay at the barriers to hearing subaltern women from the periphery "because of their muting by heterogeneous circumstances" (308). The three case studies in her essay illustrate this historical and ideological muting in sites as various as colonial records and family memory. In one example, Spivak points to how colonial debates between British officials and Hindu men about the practice of Hindu widow sacrifice represent women as either an imperial object of protection to be freed from religious traditions or the good Hindu wife willing to die for her husband. Applying a feminist deconstructive approach, Spivak seeks not to recover the authentic voices of the widows but to examine the conditions that prevent them from being heard. Consequently, she argues that the silencing of the subaltern is not merely a matter of their absence from the record, which can be readily solved by "information retrieval"; it is a problem of reading, for which the methods of literary analysis can be deployed.

Throughout her work, Spivak insists that the subaltern is not a synonym for oppression but a figure of radical exclusion from cultural and political power. As Rosalind Morris explains, subalternity is not so much an identity as a predicament in Spivak's work; it names "a structured place from which the capacity to access power is radically obstructed" (2010, 8). A further complexity in her work on the gendered subaltern is her stipulation that the subordination of women is overdetermined, meaning that it has multiple crosscutting sources and cannot be reduced to a single indicator such as class position. Thus, her examples of subalternity include middle-class or elite women, whose gendering cuts off their access to representation under certain conditions. The fluidity of Spivak's usage signals the cultural complexities and historical contingency of gender and sexual subordination.

The revised version of her essay updates the discussion to situate subalternity in contemporary globalization, noting that the "new subaltern" emerges at numerous sites across the international division of labor, including among the rural and urban subproletariat, unorganized or permanently casual women workers, or women targeted by microfinance lenders. Spivak's shift from the national to the transnational gendered subaltern has inspired a rich vein of transnational feminist scholarship (Koshy 2005; A. Roy 2010; Cheah 2010). Nevertheless, scholars of contemporary globalization have questioned the usefulness of subalternity for understanding contemporary modes of biopolitical power that operate not through exclusion but through affective capture and incorporation (Cheah 2010). They have also tried to retool the concept to track the subaltern's passage into hegemonic circuits and to examine the multiple sites of interaction between dominant and subordinate groups in a global economy (Franco 2010).

Spivak's writings and the work of other prominent members of the collective, such as Dipesh Chakrabarty, Partha Chatterjee, and Gyan Prakash, brought this work to the attention of scholars in the US academy in the late 1980s, where it influenced the development of South Asian history, postcolonial literary studies, development studies, ethnic studies, and feminist, queer, and more recently, trans studies. In this work, the subaltern is variously read as the figure that exceeds Eurocentric frames; that defies western paradigms of civilization, modernization, and development; that cannot be conscripted as the "self-consolidating other" of the western subject; and that eludes dominant gender and sexual norms. Spivak's critique has encouraged vigilance about relying on undifferentiated categories such as the Third World woman or the postcolonial subject. Equally, her work has warned about the propensity for metropolitan white feminists, postcolonial diasporics, or the Indigenous elite to serve as proxies for subaltern groups in the Global South (Spivak 1999, 276–77). Her insistence that the study of subalternity entails the responsibility of unlearning privilege has inspired work in feminist, queer, and trans theory that recognizes the implication of investigators in their objects of knowledge. Feminist, queer, and trans scholarship is especially attuned to the processes by which dominant institutions but also progressive movements hail some subjects while muting others. Thus, recent work in trans studies examines how the contemporary production of the transgender subject of rights casts prisoners, sex workers, and people of color as subaltern trans subjects (Namaste 2000; Spade 2011; Aizura 2012).

A few years after subaltern studies scholarship entered the US academy, it inspired allied projects in other regions of the "Third World," most notably Latin America, the Caribbean, and Africa. The term's South-South passage bore with it "the seeds for a method of post-orientalist comparison" (Mallon 1994, 1494) that has yielded a rich body of work. The Latin American Subaltern Studies Group's (1993, 118) founding statement embraces the term's travels, describing the subaltern as a "mutating, migrating subject" with changing, situational meanings. They attest that this flexibility enables the category "to access the vast (and mobile) array of the masses," especially in periods of change (121). Revealingly, the concept's uptake across the South followed the collapse of revolutionary utopian projects of anticolonial nationalism or socialism in these regions. During this transitional moment, "the historical failure of the nation to come to its own," a

key thematic of subalternist work on India, resonated strongly in the peripheries (Guha 1988, 43). Subalternity offered a timely analytic for grappling with "the complex nature of social disorganization" in developing countries battered by structural adjustment programs, ecological depredations, racial division, and sectarianism and in populations not yet represented by states (I. Rodríguez 2000, 47). Furthermore, feminist and queer scholarship on the gendered and sexed subaltern highlighted the internal fissures within subaltern groups and the interlocking systems of domination that cast such subjects deeply in shadow, occupying a status between subject and object.

Although the South Asian collective's work gained traction across the Global South, scholars in Indigenous studies questioned the adequacy of models based on the history of territorial colonialism in India for addressing ongoing colonialism in settler colonial states like Australia, the United States, and Canada (Byrd 2011; Byrd and Rothberg 2011). Indigenous critics highlighted the neglect of problems of Indigeneity in the discussions of subalternity in the South. Despite these reservations, scholars in American Indian and Indigenous studies recouped subalternity, especially its Spivakian strain, to theorize both Indigenous refusal and negotiation with mechanisms of multicultural recognition and legal incorporation into settler colonial states (A. Simpson 2008; Coulthard 2014; D. Turner 2006; Povinelli 2002). In particular, subalternity as a figure for radical alterity, for what is incommensurable with or untranslatable into dominant languages and social forms, has been used to reassert Native sovereignty and reinvigorate Indigenous lifeways, cosmogonies, kinship systems, and relationships to the land and to the nonhuman world (A. Simpson 2008; Coulthard 2014; Tuck and Yang 2012).

65

Subjectivity

Greta LaFleur

What does it mean to be a subject—to be a subject *of* or to be subject *to*? What does it mean, what does it feel like, to be hailed—*interpellated*, as some theorists have termed it—as a subject? And what is the relationship between being a *subject* and having a *subjectivity*?

To understand how *subjectivity* has been queried, considered, and deployed in thinking and writing in gender and sexuality studies, then, it might be best to simply start with the meaning of the term itself. The etymological root of *subjectivity* is the recognizable term *subject*, which is both a noun and a verb; the verb, in English, is one of those that changes meaning slightly depending on the preposition with which it is paired, usually "of" or "to." To be subject *of*, then, is to exert a certain organizing force on the world around you. To be subject *to*, on the other hand, describes the experience of being organized by the energies of something else: a person, an organization, a knowledge structure, and so on. In short, being the *subject of* or being *subject to* describes different relationships to power.

So if a *subject*, as an idea, might indicate some sort of relationship to the wielding of power, then what is subjectivity? Perhaps unexpectedly, *subjectivity* is not merely the sum of the various inflections of *subject* (to, of, etc.). *Subjectivity* can name a range of ideas. While *subject of* and *subject to* can describe any sort of entity, including but not limited to a person—a contract subject to approval, the subject of study, etiquette and manners are subject to regional cultural values—*subjectivity* almost always refers to the subjective experience of a person or a group of people. So what is the relationship between the experience of being a *subject of* and *subject to* and that of our own subjective experience? Gender and sexuality studies has, historically, had much to say about this very question.

One of the most important things to understand is that *subjectivity*, as a term, has been used to both name and theorize a range of highly individuated and ineluctably collective or social forms of experience, from those as seemingly universal as perception, knowledge, and emotion to those as highly culturally and regionally specific as social oppression or experiences of interior life. Because gender and sexuality studies, as a field, evolved largely out of women's studies, the question of what types of subjective experiences—either individual or collective—might be unique to *women* has long constituted an important site of inquiry for scholars. In the work of feminist philosophers Gayatri Chakravorty Spivak and Judith Butler, for example, each has posed the question, What, if anything, can *women* be said to share (Spivak 1988; J. Butler [1990] 1999)?

A range of scholarly voices during the 1970s, 1980s, and 1990s were wrestling with the same question. As interdisciplinary fields such as women's studies and ethnic studies began to find permanent homes in universities, woman of color feminists such as Barbara Smith and Demita Frazier pushed back against hegemonic understandings of "woman" as a singular formation or collection of subjective experiences. The world- and self-making structures of racialization, class stratification, and national belonging or unbelonging, these thinkers argued, rendered the subjective experience of gender multifaceted, striated by a wide range of structural powers. Race, ethnicity, gender (including cis, nonbinary, or trans), class, nationality, disability or ability, age, religion, and many more vectors of experience are usually *also* vectors of social power, naming what we might be *subjects of* and/or *subject to*. We might then also consider Black feminist accounts of intersectionality as theories of subjectivity as well.

Alongside and building on the first voices in woman of color feminism were other critiques of universalizing theories of "womanhood" or gender writ large. Attention to the multimodal effects of power on subjective experience also revealed how structures such as heterosexuality informed the lived understanding of gender. Thinkers such as Adrienne Rich or the French philosopher Monique Wittig paid particular attention to the political economy of heterosexuality in their writings, imagining how heterosexuality, as a powerful structure that organized lived experience and made meaning out of interactions between men and women, influenced one's own experience of womanhood. Echoing the logic of some woman of color feminist thought, Wittig's landmark 1980 essay "The Straight Mind" concludes with the assertion that the term "'woman' has meaning only in heterosexual systems of thought and heterosexual economic systems. Lesbians," she thus argues, "are not women" (1980, 32). Instead of imagining subjectivity as forged primarily in relation to structures of social power, however, other French feminists such as Luce Irigaray and Hélène Cixous relied on theories of subject formation derived from psychoanalysis and linguistics, considering the entwined roles of body, psyche, language, and culture in the forging of individual and collective subjectivities.

But how is *subjectivity* used to make sense of the experiences of gender and of sexuality? The most important thing to remember about the approach to subjectivity in *queer theory*—a field that by many accounts grew out of woman of color feminist theory, especially thinkers such as Cherríe Moraga, Audre Lorde, June Jordan, Toni Cade Bambara, Barbara Christian, and Gloria Anzaldúa, as well as early scholarship in the history of sexuality—is

that subjectivity, especially sexual subjectivity, is not stable, fully knowable, or predictable. Early queer theory was especially interested in the dynamism of the subject and of subjectivity more broadly, its ability to change and its inability to be known in advance. Judith Butler, for example, famously theorized gender, sexuality, and even the psyche as performative, features of experience that must be compulsively and unrelentingly performed, over and over again, in order to achieve any sense of coherence and stability.

Butler's sense that even subjectivity or psyche may be performative, rather than a kind of material truth about a person that emanates from and is housed in the body itself, draws from one of the many theories of subjectivity that gained traction in gender and sexuality studies in the 1980s but that received special attention in the US American scholarly community: Michel Foucault's ([1978] 1990) understanding of the relationship between sexuality and subjectivity that appears in *The History of Sexuality*, volume 1. Foucault's understanding of the emerging bind between sexuality and subjectivity is complicated, but one of the main things that any student of gender and sexuality studies should understand about Foucault is that he was incredibly suspicious of *sexuality* as a form of identity-based experience. For Foucault, *sexuality* is the result of a system of what he terms *discipline*—an effect of what he termed *savoir-pouvoir*, "power/knowledge"—that combined the power/knowledge of the law, medicine, religion, and other socially disciplinary forces over time to give us a vocabulary for naming the "truth" of our bodies, souls, and desires. The result is that naming our sexual desires or orientations has become a major idiom of telling the truth about ourselves. Consider the idea of "coming out": if a person is "out" as queer or trans, some believe that this means that the person is being not only more honest with the people around them but even more honest with themselves. Foucault argues that this sense of truth telling that inheres in the way we narrate our experiences of sexuality is a descendant of the Catholic confessional, a practice that keeps us surveilling ourselves. For Foucault, *sexuality* is a tactic of subjectification, a way of making us obedient subjects that watch ourselves so the state does not have to (or doesn't have to as closely). Many scholars have advanced important and apt critiques of Foucault that address the shortcomings in his later work, especially his failure to think about racial hierarchies, colonialism, and slavery. Foucault's work has nonetheless been so influential in the first twenty years of the development of queer theory in the United States, however, that it is probably still helpful to have some familiarity with his thinking.

In short, social theories of power deriving from US American woman of color feminism, international womanist feminism, and French social theory influenced the emergence of early queer theory in the United States by advancing a critical sense of the *contingency* of not only sexual practice, sexual identity, and sexual subjectivity but subjectivity as a whole. As a result, queer theory and the social theory from which it draws tend to understand queerness (and the sexuality it may or may not imply) as contextual, subject to the recognition or misrecognition, regard or disregard, of peoples, institutions, and structures in the environment.

No scholarship demonstrated this more clearly than landmark essays by Cathy J. Cohen and Gayle Rubin. Cohen's (1997) still widely taught "Punks, Bulldaggers, and Welfare Queens: The Radical Potential of Queer Politics?" importantly argued that lesbian and gay people may not actually be the proper subjects of queer theory; in fact, Cohen argues, lesbians and gays are not always queer at all. Cohen suggests instead that queerness is a *position*, not a stable state of being or identity, relative to dominant orders of power, whether they be the economy, the state, the family, or structures of knowledge like recognizable binary gender. Punks, bulldaggers, and welfare queens—gay or not—actually pose more of a threat to state, gendered, and economic structures of power, Cohen argues, than, for example, monied white gay people. For Cohen and the many scholars who followed in her footsteps, queerness is portable, never securely or consistently attached to any particular subjectivity.

Finally, for some scholars, subjectivity *itself* is a political problem of which we should all be very suspicious. These thinkers are, in a sense, both building upon and announcing a significant departure from the scholarship described above. If woman of color feminists, for example, sought to refuse universalist or implicitly white supremacist understandings of womanhood by insisting on the experiential and highly racialized particularities of all gender, we might read this as something of a strategic use of the idea of subjectivity toward the ends of developing an antiracist feminism. But thinkers such as Lee Edelman and Leo Bersani have insisted on a much more critical stance in relation to subjectivity, citing subjectivity itself as a means of disciplining our very *being* into making us recognizable, social, and thus exploitable by power. In queer theory, what is termed the *antisocial turn* explored the possibility of developing an antagonistic relationship to subjectivity in the 1980s through the first decade of the 2000s, touting the refusal of the organization of one's psychic energies into the clean contours of *subjectivity* as a queer stance relative to both psychoanalytic and poststructuralist theories of power.

Certain Black feminist theorists such as Sylvia Wynter have advanced something akin to this critique as well, arguing that what many US American theorists term *the subject* is just as problematically universalizing of a formulation as the idea of "woman" was for feminists in the 1970s and 1980s. Arguing that the intellectual history of the subject as an idea emerged from a European world that centered white, enfranchised, propertied men, Wynter suggests that the philosophical ideal of what she calls Man (and with it the architecture of his subjective experience) has become overrepresentative of *all* subjective experience. In this sense, Wynter's work and scholarship that builds on it suggest that there are margins or an outside to the experience or structure that theorists call *subjectivity*, one that cannot entirely be accounted for, even by work in gender and sexuality studies, indebted as much of it is to the canonical (western) philosophical tradition that has overrepresented itself as universal and global.

Gender and sexuality studies scholarship, then, has theorized subjectivity, like power, in profoundly ambivalent terms. No power, as Michel Foucault teaches, is entirely oppressive or entirely productive; it is always both, and so too is subjectivity. Understanding how gendered and sexual experience can both structure subjective experience *and* be structured by it reveals what gender and sexuality studies has contributed to much larger questions about power, being, and experience—some of the key questions for humanistic inquiry today.

66

Temporality

Elizabeth Freeman

In July 2017, Representative Maxine Waters (D-CA) repeated the phrase "reclaiming my time" in the face of attempts to run down the clock on her questions as chair of the House Financial Services Committee. A procedural move, this statement nevertheless captured the nation's attention, for it succinctly invoked the time stolen from people of color and women of all races, foregrounding time as a vector of control. Though we are conditioned to see time as a neutral substance through which we simply move in a forward direction, in academic discourse, the term *temporality* registers the collective patterning of stasis and change according to various regimes of power: the politics of our *experience* of time. Disciplinary tools as various as the whip in slavery, total quality management in capitalism, and domestic violence in the household have ensured that vulnerable bodies wait or move according to the dictates of others. Even within seemingly benign settings like homes and schools, bodies are trained to sleep, to wake up, to eat, to work, to have sex (or not), and to follow myriad activities keyed to maximum productivity in a process I have called "chrononormativity" (E. Freeman 2010). Moreover, the state organizes lives according to a deeply cisgendered and heteronormative time line: it registers the dates of birth, marriage, and death; pays many benefits according to a generational logic; and so on (Halberstam 2005). And national culture organizes the rhythms and life narratives of human populations through gender and sexuality in a process Dana Luciano (2007) calls "chronobiopolitics." Finally, entire academic fields, most notably anthropology and history, have been predicated on the idea that some cultures exist outside of modern time (Fabian 1983), and imperial and colonial ventures have depended on this social-evolutionary model of uneven development (Fanon [1952] 2008). In response to these dominant temporal paradigms, overlapping feminist, queer, and transgender theories—explicitly and implicitly anticolonial—have insisted on reimagining possible relations between past, present, and future.

Julia Kristeva's (1981) "Women's Time" was an early feminist theorization of how time is cast in gendered ways. For Kristeva, the "masculine" time of nationhood is forward-moving, linear, and prospective, while (white) women are relegated to cyclical activities or eternal, monumental time. But this dichotomy cannot fully explain the position of women of color, who have been historically barred from the cyclical scene of the domestic and the sacred time of the eternal. Woman of color feminisms, then, have from the beginning sought to theorize time as heterogeneous. Audre Lorde (1982), for example, coins the term *biomythography* to combine her personal story, collective history, and eternalizing myth into a narrative form for her Black lesbian life, while Cherríe Moraga (1993) critiques and remobilizes earlier Chicano-nationalist uses of the precolonial time of Aztlán to theorize contemporary antipatriarchal forms of love and belonging. Another version of monumental time inflects the work of Afropessimist Black theorists who have insisted that European modernity itself took shape against mass Black death and ontological nonbeing (see, e.g., Wilderson 2010). But feminist scholars in Black studies have also speculated on the futures that might emerge from this condition of timeless nonrelationality. Hortense Spillers (1987), for example, demonstrates that the destruction of captive Africans' kinship, gender identities, and sexual meanings and

practices left the enslaved person with no recognized ancestry and no claims on the future in the idiom of parenthood—but she also asks if the negating generational legacy in which slavery followed the condition of the mother might be the basis for an insurgent Black female future. Saidiya Hartman (1997, 2008a, 2019) traces how the afterlife of slavery continues to render Black people, especially women, into property. But more broadly connecting Black futures to seemingly negated pasts, she also engages in speculative, imaginative reconstructions of histories that are unavailable in the archives.

At first glance, queer theory seems divided between an antisocial stance that renounces the possibility of collectively built futures and a prosocial utopianism. Lee Edelman (2004) dispenses with futurity altogether, arguing that it is girded by a reproductive sexuality and child-centeredness threatened by queers, who have served as avatars of death. Edelman thus enjoins us to commit to that ahistorical, structural position by renouncing political claims on tomorrow. But other theorists use negated or foreclosed pasts as the material for alternative presents and/or a future "imagined otherwise" (Chuh 2003, 151). Judith Butler (1997), for example, reclaims melancholia as the condition of heterosexual subjectivity itself: Butler argues that the child, foreclosed from desiring the same-sex parent, internalizes that parent as its own disciplining gender. Heather Love (2009) looks to a shared history, interpreting early twentieth-century European Americans' attachments to discarded and obsolete gender/sexual categories as bids against a homogenizing modernity and an emerging fixed divide between hetero- and homosexuality. In a similar vein, in explicit disagreement with Edelman, José Esteban Muñoz (2009) argues that ephemeral moments of sociability in the past (and occasionally the present) augur a political future that cannot be solidified in the here and now, especially for queers of color. Kara Keeling (2019) focuses on queer temporalities and/as Black futures, the latter term preserving both the plurality of tomorrows and the suggestion of financial risk. Keeling argues that experimental social relations among queers of color produce possibilities that cannot be accounted for by chrononormativities and the power interests they serve (32). Aimee Bahng (2018) also plays on the dual financial and temporal sense of "futures," arguing that speculative fictions by migrants and other queers of color redress the foreshortening of their lives by late-stage capitalism.

In transgender studies, the earliest questions about temporality circulated around narrative: transgender subjects could only access gender-affirming care by claiming to have always felt like the "opposite" gender and to desire a linear transition from one gender to another, and Jay Prosser (1998) describes transgender autobiography as a counterpoint to this medicalized narrative. Theories of feminist and queer "crip temporality" have likewise described living aslant to medical temporalities of prognosis and cure (Kafer 2013), while trans theorists have continued to clarify how time is lived and felt by gender nonconforming people. Jacob Lau (2016), for example, has coined the term *trans temporality* to describe the many ways that transgender lives do not accord with medical and other cisnormative time lines. Other transgender theorists continue to ask such temporally inflected questions as how to account for transgender children and people of color who do not appear in the historical record (Gill-Peterson 2018) or how generationality is disrupted when people transition in their later years (Lavery 2019). Most expansively, Susan Stryker and Aren Z. Aizura (2013, 217) gesture toward a "trans-historicity" that can both indicate lines of affiliation between gender nonconformities of the past and present and disrupt linear-historical, causal

accounts. A brilliant example of this historiographical method is C. Riley Snorton's (2017) *Black on Both Sides*, which draws from Spillers to locate transgender history in the Middle Passage: even as Black people were torn from their own natal genders and sexual lifeways and reduced to pure flesh, he argues, the resulting mutability of their genders contained the seeds of trans embodiment. Snorton's work sees, in the very history of anti-Blackness, possibilities for present-tense and future Black genders and in doing so reclaims what seems like an irrecoverably stolen time.

67

Trans
Jacob Lau

A critical genealogy of the keyword *trans* must start with the question of what appears as trans and why. Where we start defining how trans emerges shapes what is allowed to fall under the so-called umbrella of trans. For instance, if we understand trans to be an identity involving a person's relationship to legal and medical definitions of gender and/or sex stemming from Europe and the United States during the nineteenth and twentieth centuries but do not consider how legal and medical institutions are already informed by a much longer history of disciplinary colonial, imperial, racist, ableist, and classist state technologies, then our definition of trans will not be intersectional or critically engaged. This brings to the fore questions of methodology, interdisciplinarity, and field emergence of trans as a site of knowledge as well as gender and sex identities and subjectivities.

Since the 1990s, *trans* as a term has become a contested site of knowledge formation in the field of gender and sexuality studies. In similar ways to *queer*, the emergence of *trans* draws from a long tradition of politicized identities, intersectional power formations, and social processes that challenge both the potential and the limitations of political, social, disciplinary, and economic sex, gender, and sexual epistemologies (how we know what we know), ontologies (states of being), and historicities (which historical figures we chose to highlight and how we choose to write history). While more popular understandings of trans focus on transgender representation in the media—particularly who is producing content about people with trans identities and what is produced knowledgewise about transness (which tends to ask questions about trans identity and subjectivity)—what is more important is who we draw from to define both the field of knowledge constituting trans and what the term includes.

In that spirit, this essay will look at three conversations/contestations as genealogical modes of studying "trans" that bring us to central conversations informing trans as a site of knowledge today. The conversations/modes of contention discussed in this entry are as follows: social/cultural/economic organization of sex/gender systems, narratives of medicalization, and trans of color critique. It should be noted that these are not the only ways to approach "trans," but historically, as the field of trans studies has emerged, they are primary ways of tracing both its roots and its future potentialities.

We can start with the oft-quoted *Oxford English Dictionary* definition of the Latin prefix *trans-* to look at the capacities of trans as an intersectional site for gender and sexual knowledge. Meaning "across," "beyond," and "through," *trans-* is usually juxtaposed as the opposite of the prefix *cis-*, which means "on the same side as." While the prefix *trans-* refers to movement across a bounded position, *cis-* implies a stasis or lack of movement. *Trans* as a prefix for *sex* (transsex) and *sexuality* (transsexuality) referred mainly to a binaristic and medicalized view of gender and sex transition (as will be explained later). *Trans* became attached to *gender* in the 1990s, producing the term *transgender*, popularized by transgender and communist activist Leslie Feinberg (2013) in hir pamphlet *Transgender Liberation: A Movement Whose Time Has Come.* "Transgender" in Feinberg's vision was a political identity and a critique of a social order that only recognized two genders that "naturally" arise from two sexes. Feinberg's understanding of transgender covered a spectrum of genders, was rooted in collective political movements, and connected transgender oppression (genderphobia) to other systemic oppressions such as colonialism and capitalism. However, as Native studies scholar Mark Rifkin has argued, Feinberg also positioned a generically characterized Indigenous cultural acceptance of gender and sexual nonnormativity as a predecessor to current iterations of transgender, which "resists state-sanctioned violence without actually contesting the terms of settler governance," a move that has continued to be problematically replicated in various disciplinary engagements within trans studies (Rifkin 2011, 239; for a further critique of the romance of the universal transgender Native, see Towle and Morgan 2002). Around the same time Feinberg published hir pamphlet, feminist and queer critiques of the assumption of a direct correspondence of gender with the pronounced sex of the body (i.e., that someone is a girl if they have been assigned a female sex at birth) were being theorized in ways that opened the door for queer and trans theorists to further challenge the supposed inherent connections between a sex and gender with past interpretations of embodiment (J. Butler [1990] 1999; Salamon 2010).

Recent work in trans studies has demonstrated the insufficiency of mapping binaristic gender and/or sex within the transition-as-movement model or thinking trans and cis as oppositional, identity, and body-bound (Enke 2012). The developmental narrative of progress locates transness in the process of a subject's social identity and embodied change from one gender to another. We would do well to suspend belief in assigning what counts as trans to that narrative, which replicates norms of binaristic embodied sex and fetishizes a hierarchy of transness. This belief unthinkingly replicates colonial, imperialist, and ableist ideologies of normative human development (from infantile to adult, from diseased to cured, from primitive to civilized, from alien to citizen). Rather than begin from an understanding of trans as that which shows movement from one gender or sex to "the other," which reinscribes sex and gender essentialist paradigms and understands social, cultural, and embodied transitioning as the key to transness, it is helpful to instead critique those baseline assumptions underlining the political economy of trans by looking at critical genealogies of what cultural anthropologist Gayle Rubin called "the sex/gender system." That is, dominant and colonial economic, cultural, and social systems of sex and gender (macro-level analysis of oppression) have created normative interpretations of the body. The implication of this is that our understandings of transness have been formed through the intersectional lens of race, class, ableism, and nation.

Building largely from Friedrich Engels's ([1884] 1978) work on the origin of gendered divisions of labor in Anglo Euro-American kinship systems based on the ability to hold private property, Gayle Rubin described the social, political, and economic organization of modern kinship systems into what she calls "a political economy of sex" ([1975] 1997, 27). This colonial sex/gender system functioned as a way to distinguish women as a second class of gendered and sexual person who was exchanged by men to shore up their economic, political, and social capital.

Rubin's idea of the political economy of sexuality and gender through patriarchal kinship is further complicated by the history of human enslavement as discussed by women of color, specifically Black feminists (Spillers [1987] 2003; Truth [1851] 1995; Combahee River Collective [1977] 2015; A. Y. Davis 1971). To understand how the sex/gender system arose within the intersectional context of racial and gender capital, it is also important to consider the role of colonialism and specifically settler colonialism. The colonial sex/gender system functioned as a weapon to discipline and control colonized and enslaved people; that is, people who departed from or did not conform to it were dispossessed of land and/or the ownership of their own bodies. For instance, Deborah Miranda rereads the archive to discuss how the killing of Indigenous *joyas* by Spanish colonialist Vasco Núñez de Balboa on September 23, 1513, was an act of gendercide rather than just homophobia, arguing, "To call it gendercide would certainly require rethinking the assimilation of Euro-American cultural values and the meaning of indigenous community" (2010, 260). Even the word *joya* was a pejorative created by Spanish colonizers for Indigenous people who did not adhere to binary European notions of gender. However, what this demonstrates is that in some of the earliest depictions of the violence of first contact, the colonial sex/gender system's distinguishing normative from nonnormative ideologies of gender functioned as a disciplining setter technology, which has been largely unacknowledged or ignored by the larger field of trans studies, as Indigenous trans scholars have pointed out (Pyle 2018).

Without an understanding of how racism, colonialism, and imperialism have shaped and continue to shape sex/gender systems within capitalism and other economic systems, we cannot grasp a larger understanding of transness. More recent discussions birthing a critical trans politics and analytics emerge from this understanding that gender, sex, and sexuality are constituted not solely from within an economic system but also through the material realities of how personhood was extended only to certain groups of people based on race, ethnicity, class, nationality, citizenship, ability, and Indigeneity (Spade 2011).

Another crucial historical conversation of understanding *trans*'s relationship with gender and sexuality studies is through the emergence of trans within sexology and psychology, producing medical models of transsexuality and transvestism (an outdated term for people who dress differently than their assumed gender from their sex assigned at birth). Coined by David O. Cauldwell in 1949, *transsexual* became a psychologically and socially deviant type of person whose gender identity differed from the sex (and naturally assumed gender) they were assigned at birth. While the actual first text advocating for the ethical treatment of transsexuals came before Cauldwell (Michael Dillon's [1946] *Self: A Study in Ethics and Endocrinology*), "Psychopathia Transexualis" had the Foucaultian effect of putting a name on a deeply felt desire and later organizing groups of people with that common feeling under a marginalized identity (Meyerowitz 2002; Stryker 2017). While Cauldwell's text problematically framed transsexuality through the discourse of pathology, endocrinologist Harry Benjamin's (1966) *The Transsexual Phenomenon* became a more widely read medical text advocating for the treatment of trans people's bodies to fit their minds. Benjamin's text also served to create a medical diagnosis for "true" transsexuality, which replicated heteronormative and cisnormative ideologies of gender and sexuality. The cultural impact of sexology's understandings of transsexuality cannot be understated. To this day, much of what is popularly understood as "trans" largely comes from this medicalized diagnostic discourse. What is widely considered the field-forming essay for trans studies in academia, Sandy Stone's (1992) "The *Empire* Strikes Back: A Posttranssexual Manifesto" unpacks the legacies of disappearing a trans subject's gender history to give a "consistent" uniform gender past. However, it is important to contextualize this as only one conversation about the term *trans*, and it does not take into account the replication of larger colonial frameworks and racialized histories of gender and sex nonnormativity, for which Stone's essay has been critiqued (Bhanji 2012).

Work in trans of color critique, a discrete knowledge formation stemming from the intersectional analysis of woman of color feminisms (referenced earlier) and critical race theory, challenges the assumptions forming the academic field of trans studies. The field-forming works making up queer of color analysis and critique (Cohen 1997; R. Ferguson 2004; Muñoz 1999) made the argument that like women of color, queer of color as an organizing analysis and identity formation came from reading histories of sexuality against the grain of modes of whiteness through which they were articulated. That is, cultural production and the archives of history often leave out or pass over marginalized sexual, gendered, and racialized subjects, and bringing an intersectional critical race lens asks questions about why most early histories of trans (medical or not) have centered white historical figures (such as Christine Jorgensen, Jan Morris, and Lili Elbe). Trans of color critique not only recovers history and cultural work by trans of color figures and asks that they be included in canonical histories of trans (Snorton 2017; Gill-Peterson 2018; Ellison et al. 2017) but also posits that those canonical histories have been built from a radically different understanding of gender and sex subjectivity. By positioning trans of color and in particular trans femmes of color figures at the center of analyses of power, trans of color critique asks not only how bodies are assumed and aligned with normative ideologies of sex and gender but which bodies and how that assumption and alignment adhere to intersectional structural oppressions and long-operating histories of whiteness, classism, racism, settler colonialism, and imperialism.

As the understanding of trans has detached from purely medicalized and social movement–based understandings of sex (transsexuality) and gender (transvestite/transgender), trans has become less attached to an embodied identity-based definition and, like queer, more a political positionality in opposition to normative regulations of embodiment. For example, trans asks many similar questions about state and medical interventions on defining normative bodily capacity (what a body can do and how environments are more or less accessible and accommodating to diverse embodiments) aligning with questions asked by disability studies and in particular crip studies. Eli Clare has discussed the importance of thinking about the ways socially stigmatizing diagnoses in the *Diagnostic and Statistical Manual* should be thought of through a lens of self-determination by trans scholars and activists and less as something pathological (Clare 2013). Conversations about gender "potty parity" in bathrooms when framed through conversations about accessibility open trans to wider historical questions about how bathrooms have been a site of not only gender policing and discrimination but racial policing as well (H. Davis 2017).

Two more recent developments in the field involve asking if *trans* can behave as a verb like *queer*. That is, scholars have asked if like "queering" literature, film, history, or visual culture, one can "trans" them too. This has been asked not just in studies of cultural production but in feminist science studies at the biochemical level (Preciado 2013) and in animal studies (M. Chen 2012; Hayward and Weinstein 2015) and has demonstrated its limitations when applied to analogies with race (Bow 2009). Trans of color critique has offered the ideology of "tranifesting" (transformative manifesting; Ellison and Green 2014) as a different collective trans approach to "transing," which has drawn its share of skeptics (Chu and Drager 2019). However, these trenchant critiques suggest that it may be more helpful to think about trans as an adjective rather than a verb, as a modifying descriptor of a figure, object, or field of knowledge rather than an action, state, or occurrence. This can be seen through the question of the asterisk (trans*), the prefix (trans-), and how acknowledging trans has modified the names of other fields of study (such as Latinx studies rather than Latina/o studies). As gender and sexuality studies continues giving greater heed to positionalities that have held up the field but been marginalized, trans will continue articulating its citational limits through how the term is written. As the work of trans continues to modify its subjectivities, modes of relation, and surrounding academic landscape, the citational history of the term will continue to echo with the force of its complex, contestatory, and multigenealogical lineage.

68

Transnational

Evren Savci

The term *transnational* entered feminist studies terminology in the 1990s, emerging out of a desire for studies of gender and sexuality to address asymmetries in globalization processes. Transnational feminism purposefully set itself apart from "international" and "global" feminisms—rejecting the reified cartographies and national borders of the former and the dismissal of nation-states and the universalizing gesture of the latter (Swarr and Nagar 2010). By contrast, transnational approaches emphasize the political function of borders while they expose their constructedness and porousness. Under historical circumstances where global capitalism is imagined to undermine national borders, scholars have noted that states, and therefore borders, have been unevenly impacted by processes of global neoliberalization: while some states have waned in power, others have grown stronger (Grewal 2005). While globalization may have increased the flows of capital and technologies across borders and thereby created the conditions for an uncritical celebration of increased mobility, it did not result in equal mobility for all bodies (C. Kaplan 2002). Scholars have also problematized the suggestion that the "global" constitutes a moment of decentralization of power, underlining that such deterritorialization, or delinking of power from territorial bounds, has been followed by various reterritorializations, or remapping of power, especially through asymmetrical travels of culture and media (Grewal 2005). In other words, the fact that US "culture" is now widely mediated and detached from the physical space of the United States or that many jobs are now outsourced and capital is offshored does certainly not culminate into the US empire's inability to consolidate and exercise economic, cultural, and military power worldwide (Grewal 2005).

A transnational approach to gender and sexuality thus can be understood as a demand to take the transnational connections that produce global asymmetries into account as we grapple to make sense of one of the core questions of the field—that of identity and difference. Transnational feminism shares many concerns and interests with Black feminism, US woman of color feminism, and Third World feminism (Mendoza 2016; Nash 2019a; Patil 2013; Soto 2005). Nash in particular traces the coeval emergence of transnational feminism and Black feminism as critical to US women's studies in the 1990s and questions whether transnational feminism and intersectionality, a central category emerging from Black feminist intellectual and activist genealogies, should be treated as separate analytics (Nash 2019a). Similarly, Asian American and Latinx feminist genealogies have always engaged either the border or immigrant flows as central to their political engagements. By contrast, Indigenous feminisms, particularly those rooted in the study of space, note that simply to travel within the borders of any nation-state in the Americas is to travel transnationally between unceded Indigenous Nation spaces (Anzaldúa 1987; Goeman 2013; Lowe 1996).

If feminist and queer studies have analyzed the production of sameness/identity and difference and how they are rendered intelligible, transnational approaches urge us to ask, How do we understand difference as an important and complex social reality that is not to be reified or erased? How do we keep the centrality of power in our analyses without relying on or reifying North/South or West/East binaries? Grewal and Kaplan (1994)

have invited us to think about hegemony—that is, social, cultural, economic, or ideological dominance—as multiple and *scattered* under conditions of transnational connectivity. Some people live under abysmal conditions in locations deemed "the center," facing severely decreased life chances, and economic upper classes and elites reside in all the "peripheries." Transnational feminism proposes that we seek to understand the connections and collusions of interest between different patriarchies, fundamentalisms, authoritarianisms, and racisms worldwide without a recourse to modernist tropes of progress and modernity versus backwardness and tradition.

Approaching gender and sexuality transnationally, scholars analyze how fantasies about masculinity and femininity intertwined with race and ethnicity play a key role in the unfolding of the global political economy, including tourism and transnational marriage economies (M. J. Alexander 2005; Hoang 2015; Lowe 1996; G. Mitchell 2011; Salzinger 2004; Schaeffer-Grabiel 2005); in structuring various forms of transnational reproductive labor, such as transnational surrogacy and care work (Hondagneu-Sotelo [2001] 2007; Vora 2015); and in systems of global securitization and militarization (Hochberg 2015; C. Kaplan 2018; Puar 2007; Terry 2017). For instance, instead of understanding the prison industrial complex as a domestic matter, scholars have asked about the transnational linkages between the architectures and organizations of prisons, trainings of prison guards, and development of torture techniques (Briggs 2014; A. Y. Davis 2016; Lazreg 2008). Transnational approaches to gender and sexuality also help illuminate that understandings of what are considered investmentworthy, respectable, or desirable are always already transnational. For instance, such approaches show how allegedly feminist calls for investment in the education of "Third World Girls" through philanthrocapitalism are shot through with logics of population control as well as predicated upon the presumed low value of Third World Girls, rendering them a worthy site of investment (Murphy 2012–13).

While transnational feminist and queer studies analyze the gendered and sexual implications of various flows of bodies, goods, technologies, labor, and capital across the globe, this is adamantly not an approach to studying an exotic "elsewhere" that lies beyond Northern America, which is imagined as the default location and "home" of the knowledge producer (Grewal 2005). Transnational feminisms are as invested in showing the constructed nature of "elsewhere" and "home" as they are in rejecting the colonial knowledge paradigm, in which "elsewhere" has served a site of knowledge extraction. Yet this is not accomplished in a way that overlooks the current transnational power asymmetries at play with regard to knowledge production, such as the global dominance of the US academy, especially in gender and sexuality studies, or the fact that most "top-ranked" journals publish only in the English language. Neither is it to forget the deeply troubling histories of studying "elsewhere" in Northern America / western Europe–based scholarship that has taken such forms as colonial anthropology and Cold War area studies. In fact, the fields of transnational feminist and queer studies continuously grapple with concerns about who gets to be a subject versus an object of knowledge production by interrogating problems of voice, representation, and citationality (who reads and who is read) and by looking critically at the entanglements of legitimizing institutions of knowledge, such as the university, with its neoliberal capitalist logics of multicultural incorporation. Yet despite these concerns, transnational connectivity and its power asymmetries have been and continue to be a current reality under which gender, sexual, class, and race politics unfold. Transnational gender and sexuality studies, then, is concerned with not whether but *how* politics of location will be handled and how our scholarship can be grounded in locality without reifying that locality. In other words, how can our questions be location-specific and not location-bound (Alexander and Mohanty 2010)?

Not reifying the local, a commitment of transnational feminist and queer work, is accomplished through insisting on historicizing and complicating the local by showing that all localities feature multiple and contradictory values and asymmetries of power and a rejection of radical alterity by illustrating the deep transnational connections everywhere (Alexander and Mohanty 2010). Since emphasizing the particularity of "local" often serves to reproduce the universality of the center, which is often the Euro-American "West" (Hua 2011), showing the messy, multiple, and transnational nature of the "local" becomes crucial to transnational analysis. Further, as Caren Kaplan (1994) has pointed out, nontransnational analyses that rely on these binaries often conflate western with white. Amanda Swarr and Richa Nagar have also warned against the use of a villain/victim dichotomy where, for instance, the villain global is imagined to swallow the victimized "local," and the local heroically resists the global. This framework risks rendering power differentials invisible *within* the geographies deemed as local (Swarr and Nagar 2010). To make this point differently, Mohanty (1988) argues we cannot imagine globalization or modernization to effect an Egyptian upper-class housewife and her house cleaner similarly—which is precisely what an uncritical and nontransnational understanding of locality or of "Egyptian women" as a category would have us do. The failure of universal "woman of color" or "queer of color" categories combined with the transnationalization and complication of "the local" exposes the inadequacy of center/periphery models and West/non-West binaries.

Transnational feminist and queer studies is also steeped in a strong rejection of cultural relativism that would reduce nations, especially the "non-West," to "cultures." This reification often results in positioning of the "non-West" (its "cultures," "traditions," and "religions") as radical alterity to be then met with "Western tolerance" and in tropes such as the "objectification of so-called Third World Women as privileged signifiers of difference" (Grewal and Kaplan 1994, 21; Abu-Lughod 2002). The problem with categories such as "Third World woman" is not only that this figure has historically been imagined as "ignorant, poor, uneducated, tradition-bound, religious, domesticated, family-oriented, victimized etc." but also that as a reified category, it has been used to produce "Third World difference" as an ahistorical, essential, and homogenous empirical reality (Mohanty 1988, 65). Transnational analyses insist that access to any tradition has been made impossible by the historical colonial cultural contact and contemporary "claims to a pure indigenous tradition are spurious" (Abu-Lughod 1998, 255). Therefore, those who claim to act on behalf of tradition or religion, whether they are located in geographies territorialized as the North or the South, are subjects and products of modernity themselves (Moallem 2005).

To conclude, two important issues facing scholars engaging in transnational approaches to the study of gender and sexuality are worth highlighting. The first one is that queer studies is admittedly a newer field than feminist studies, and it has a shorter history of producing transnational scholarship (Aizura 2018; Liu 2015; Mitra 2020; Shakhsari 2020) that extends beyond the work that focuses on queer diasporas (Eng 2001; Gopinath 2005; Manalansan 2003). While there is a longer history of anthropology of sexualities that has analyzed locations outside of the US and western Europe, much of that work has remained loyal to modernist center/periphery models, modern/traditional binaries, and East/West distinctions. Perhaps as a result, the field has not yet seen a similar critique of "queer of color" to the one produced by transnational feminists about the global deployment of "woman of color." As Grewal and Kaplan note, all identification requires "an elision of material difference in favor of a fantasized similarity" (Grewal and Kaplan 1996, 12), and as queer studies further transnationalizes, it will likely produce analyses of the limits of "queer of color" applied globally. Moreover, Petrus Liu has drawn our attention to the role "cultural difference" has played in queer theory's unconscious, especially given the heavy reliance on gender and sexual variation "across cultures" in order to establish the socially and culturally constructed nature of gender and sexuality (Liu 2015). Discussions of whether queer is appropriate to apply to "nonwestern" contexts overlook the fact that cultural difference has informed queer studies' epistemic unconscious from the very start, even in scholarship that was seemingly not speaking of racial, ethnic, or "cultural" difference. If sexual difference has necessitated cultural comparability, then we must pause and ask, What work have "cultural Others" been asked to do to liberate the West from the "heterosexism of the Symbolic"? (Liu 2015, 23). This inquiry invites transnational queer studies to investigate how "elsewhere" has always formed the constitutive outside of the field.

The second related issue is the fact that "global English" remains the dominant language of discussions of transnational genders and sexualities. This is not only or necessarily because most feminist and queer studies scholarship is produced in Northern America but (also) because global English has become *the* language of global academia and publishing. Here it is equally important to problematize (a) the English-centeredness of the academy and ask what that implies for fields such as queer studies that have followed the poststructuralist proposal that language is constitutive of the real and (b) the homolingual address (Sakai 1997) that informs much academic work today, including studies of gender and sexuality. Translation studies scholars argue that it is precisely the homolingual address that produces the effect of languages as natural, ahistorical, easily identifiable as autonomous and comparable objects with particular attributes and erases polyglot histories as well as violent erasures of Indigenous languages and reduction of many forms to "dialect" (Gal 2006; Gramling 2016; Makoni and Pennycook 2007; Mezzadra and Sakai 2014). Homolingual address, which often features an ahistorical understanding of language, also makes it possible to equate languages with national cultures, which further enable theories of the coloniality of the circulation of terms such as *gay*, *lesbian*, *feminist*, or *queer*. Finally, translation studies scholars also criticize the heavily discursive treatment of language, which ignores the hermeneutical dimension of language, the fact that communication is always full of disjunctures and "messages" often do not arrive in ways that they are supposed to (Sakai 1997). All these points invite us to ask, What are the limitations of transnational scholarship of gender and sexuality given the English-centered homolingual address of scholarship?

When we reject center-periphery models, understand hegemonies as scattered, and embrace a heterolingual view of language, we are better equipped to think about circulation of concepts, terms, and ideologies of gender and sexuality outside of the binary of epistemic colonization versus local Indigenous resistance. None of these are to suggest that transnational approaches to gender and sexuality are flawless—transnational feminist scholars have cautioned against producing a feminist teleology where all feminist criticism culminates in "transnational feminism" as the superior form (Swarr and Nagar 2010). They have also warned that

transnational is not immune to becoming a normativizing gesture (Alexander and Mohanty 2010). Therefore, transnationality is better thought of as not a master solution to the existing shortcomings of studies of gender and sexuality but a currently productive approach that can help us ask important questions about global historical asymmetries of power. Since transnational feminist scholars are acutely aware of the dangers of any one approach becoming paradigmatic, it is also a keyword that we will hopefully know how to move away from when it no longer serves the feminist and queer critical ends it currently does.

69

Two Spirit

Elton Naswood

Two Spirit is a contemporary term that American Indian / Alaska Native and Indigenous individuals may use to self-identify. The use of this term to name oneself may be in addition to using such mainstream identifications as lesbian, gay, bisexual, transgender, and queer (LGBTQ) with a traditional and cultural understanding of gender roles and identity. *Two Spirit* was first adopted in 1990 by attendees, activists, and elders in attendance at the third International Native Gay/Lesbian Gathering held in Winnipeg, Canada. The embracing of this term at the gathering arose out of discussions for the need to have a specific and empowering cultural term defined by Native LGBTQ people themselves. By adopting the term *Two Spirit*, the community sought to disavow the colonized and anthropological term *Berdache*—a derogatory French word meaning "a boy kept for homosexual practices" or "male prostitute."

The cultural context of Two Spirit is from the Anishinaabe, and the term encompasses the fluidity of having both female and male spirits within one person. As such, a Two Spirit person would have culturally prescribed spiritual and social roles in the community. Prior to colonial contact, a majority of Indigenous communities in the Americas had alternative non-binary gender roles and community responsibilities based on the individuals' gender and not their sexuality, with each person playing their part to benefit the community as a whole rather than their individual selves. As a community health care advocate, I often state that "what you do outside your tipi is more important that what you do inside your tipi," thus explaining how community responsibility in Indigenous contexts compares to the potential individuality of expressing one's sexuality/sexual orientation within a solely American perspective.

Oral traditions reveal that Two Spirit people existed as deities and/or sacred beings in Indigenous communities. For example, among the Navajo people, who are my community, our creation stories include the cultural figure of the Nádleeh. As I related in the documentary *As They Are: Two Spirit People in the Modern World* (Garrido and Tohme 2009),

> I had heard a story from my mother's eldest sister, who played the role of grandmother, if you will. And she had told me a story that I remember, that I recall, that long ago when the Navajo world [began], within the Navajo people, there was a separation of the sexes, and that there was an argument between man and woman. And then, at that time, the men went to one side of the river and the women went to the other side of a river. And, it was the nádleeh, it was the more effeminate less masculine men, that brought the sexes together, and that because of the nádleeh, our people survived. If it wasn't for the nádhleehs, we wouldn't be the people we are today. (Estrada 2011, 173)

My role in my family and community is still seen as that of a negotiator, an advisor. I have participated in ceremonial settings to assist with male-oriented roles (i.e., chopping wood, hauling water, etc.) as well as in female-oriented roles (cooking, organizing, caregiving), which is accepted by the community. I accept these responsibilities as a Navajo gay male and *Nádleeh*, as they are instilled in me through our Navajo creation stories, through family and community acceptance, and by Navajo culture generally.

After European contact with Indigenous peoples, our gender identities dramatically changed. Primarily through organized religions like Christianity, acculturation, homophobia, and transphobia were introduced into and adopted by Indigenous communities. Yet there still exist resilient Two Spirit identities, some of which have even seen a resurgence. Language, words, and meanings are significant for the cultural survival of Indigenous peoples. There still exist, in Tribal Nations, words that are utilized to describe Two Spirit / Native male and female gender identities—such as *Nádleeh* (Navajo), *Winkte* (Lakota), *Boté* (Crow), and *Lhamana* (Zuni), to name a few (Jacobs, Thomas, and Lang 1997). Among the Tongva Nation in Southern California, there is a specific term for transgender individuals, which is *Kuuyat* (Naswood and Jim 2012). Additionally, among the Lakota people, the Winkte are viewed as sacred people whose androgynous nature is an inborn character trait or the result of a vision. The Winkte are given the ceremonial responsibility of naming a newborn within the tribe, a practice still prevalent today.

The *Two Spirit* term has also significantly allowed for structural and social change among our communities and agencies. The term has recently been adopted by and utilized in our health care facilities and the Indian Health Service. For example, the term is now used on intake forms for patients and also while providing professional trainings on Indigenous LGBTQ–Two Spirit identities and cultural awareness for clinical staff and physicians. This is a cultural shift that instills knowledge among care providers and builds trust, which, in turn, empowers our Native LGBTQ–Two Spirit community to access health services.

For far too long, western colonial concepts of gender and sexuality have superseded the worldview of Indigenous gender identities. Accordingly, even the term *Two Spirit* has been appropriated by non-Indigenous individuals. This is inappropriate, as it is an identification that is only for our way of knowing and being, specific to our worldview and cultural contexts. To be Native is a foremost identity for us and is then typically followed by gender and other identities. These composite identities are held as a revered responsibility and make us accountable to our communities in our roles as Two Spirit persons. As a Navajo and a Two Spirit, gay male, Nádleeh individual, I hold that the historical, cultural, and contemporary aspects of Indigenous gender identity are important not only to Native people but also to non-Native settler people. Resident upon our lands, non-Natives must understand that the cultural identities of Native people are the essence of who we are as Indigenous people, as Native LGBTQ–Two Spirit people. These gender and cultural identities, which we sustain and hold sacred, are the *hózhó*, the "balance," of our cultural worldviews in how we see our place on this earth and our responsibilities for continued survival.

70

Woman

Kyla Schuller

In 1995, home in Northern California during my first year of college, I sat on my parents' sofa flipping through one of the house's most treasured possessions: a set of red-and-gold 1984 *World Book* encyclopedias. I was in the middle of the *W* volume when an entry labeled *"Woman"* gave me pause. "A woman can have many roles in society," the entry opened, "including doctor, secretary, or homemaker." Several pages followed, illustrated with black-and-white stock photographs of women performing various occupations. Sensing something was amiss, I returned to the shelf and pulled the *M* volume. Under the header *"Man,"* only three short words appeared: "See *'Human Being.'*"

It was an early moment of feminist awakening. Here, faced with allegedly impartial knowledge, I finally confronted a dynamic I had been studiously repressing below the surface of my own consciousness. Euro-American culture positioned "woman" as an object to be studied and defined while positioning "man" as the universal human subject. Woman was a role in society; man was society itself. Woman as a concept in the West carries the weight of centuries of Othering. "Woman" figures as the muse, the natural, the object, the body, the question, while man is the writer, the social, the subject, the mind, the given. Woman is always the art, rarely the artist. Or according to my grandfather's favorite joke, "Women are meaner than people."

Keyword and encyclopedia entries don't typically present the reader with a fleshy author with a history of her own—they emanate from an all-knowing, locationless position that is at once everywhere and nowhere at all. Donna Haraway calls this fantasy of contextless, seemingly omniscient knowledge "a god trick" (1988, 582). Yet knowledge itself changes when "woman" moves from an object of inquiry to a producer of knowledge. The delusion of disembodied authority drops away. Individual, context-specific, subjective modes of knowing come into view as feminist modes of inquiry. As the opening anecdote of this keyword entry hopes to suggest, feminist inquiry challenges and displaces traditional forms of knowledge that venerate the mythical possibility of context-free objectivity. Feminist theorists have developed influential approaches, including "situated knowledges," "feminist standpoint theory," and "strong objectivity," that reject the myth of neutral knowledge and propose multiply located, subaltern, or self-reflexive methods that build on the researcher's specific subject position and implicit biases rather than fantasize them away (Haraway 1988; Hartsock [1983] 2004; Harding 2005).

But is the central task of gender and sexuality studies as a knowledge project therefore to transform woman from an object into a subject, from the nonperson into one of the people? And should fighting for the rights of women be the preeminent goal of feminism? These questions rock the field of gender and sexuality studies and feminist social movements. The term *woman* and the various official discourses that have produced it, from scientific and medical studies to legal documents and political platforms, spurred my personal feminist awareness. *Woman* was also the term that mainstream feminism initially consolidated around, whether in 1848 at the first woman's rights convention led by Elizabeth Cady Stanton in Seneca Falls, New York, or a century later in philosopher Simone de Beauvoir's provocation that "one is not born, but rather becomes, a woman" ([1949] 1989, 267). For liberal feminists, feminism is the fight for political and social equality between women and men (Stanton [1854] 2007; Adichie 2014). Yet as de Beauvoir implies, "woman" is not a stable anatomical category, nor is it a neutral descriptor of an identity. Woman is a product of culture. Despite its seeming naturalness, *woman* is a keyword: a term that carries the baggage of history that it is the task of scholarship to unpack. Woman as a concept emerged from a matrix of empire, racial thinking, and capitalism, dynamics that continue to churn below the surface of the term, as I explore below. Many white feminists since at least the time of de Beauvoir often emphasize that woman is the cultural role assigned to the female sex. Woman, in this view, is a *gender*, a social script produced over time that stems entirely from cultural norms. Female, by contrast, is a *sex*, a physiological and anatomical category rooted in biological difference. Since the origins of this sex/gender distinction in 1970s theory, the idea that "woman" is a set of cultural expectations, while "female" is a putatively natural biological fact, has inspired the theory of social constructionism. Woman, understood to be a cultural role, opens up the vantage that the social expectations assigned to women, such as the domestic tasks of raising children and maintaining the domestic sphere, are elaborate scripts staged upon female bodies—rather than the unassailable result of deep biological difference. The social construction of gender includes the production of woman as a category, Judith Butler ([1990] 1999) famously argues. Legal rights and protections are not merely applied to women, she suggests, but invent the category of woman in the first place through delineating a group of people defined by their distinct legal status.

Feminist theory insists that our basic categories of knowledge are constructed by culture—which includes the discipline of biology as well. Imagining sex/gender as thoroughly distinct phenomena positions gender, and woman, as a purely cultural process that is scripted on to a static, biologically inert body (Chodorow [1980] 1990; Oakley 1972). But is the cultural really a binary opposite of the biological, in which no interaction of any kind takes place between the two realms? Much feminist theory—including poststructuralist feminism, feminist science studies, intersectional feminism, and trans studies—questions this sex/gender binary (Plumwood 1989; J. Butler 1993a; Moraga 1994; Preciado 2013). These theorists argue that social processes in fact have biological impact, such as in the form of trauma that accumulates as memories persisting over generations or as brain plasticity that explains the formation of neuronal connections based on repeated experiences (Hirsch 2012; Fausto-Sterling 2012). These perspectives ask us to consider the possibility that "woman" is a social role that, over time, manifests in the way our bodies think, move, and feel. Cultural ideas about what makes a woman take physical shape, for example, as medical protocols that approach intersex babies as untenable bodies that must undergo immediate surgical "correction." Biological and cultural processes are always intertwined, including sex and gender, according to these theorists (Frost 2016).

If woman is made, not born, then who made woman? How do its origins impact its usage in gender and sexuality studies today? In other words, what machinations of power do we tacitly accept when we embrace "woman" and "man" as natural categories of identity that are later subject to unequal treatment—rather than concepts that themselves result from hierarchy and power? From the perspective of critical gender and sexuality studies, woman is the invention of politics and history rather than a transparent identity tied to basic biological fact. According to this view, "woman" is the result of the ruthless binary logic that all bodies are divided into one of two categories, woman or man. Woman as a category does not preexist sexism; rather, woman as a category is one of sexism's major accomplishments.

A historical approach to "woman" reveals how the intertwined forces of racism and sexism produced the concept in the first place. Before the nineteenth century, bodies were generally seen as more alike than different (Russett 1989). Male, female, and intersex bodies were ascribed with the same general features, albeit with distinct variations. Historian Thomas Lacquer writes that in the eighteenth century, the vagina was deemed an internal penis, a structure fundamentally similar to the genitalia of men (Lacquer 1990). In the nineteenth century, a wide variety of genital appearances and secondary sex characteristics were classified as hermaphrodite, or what we now call intersex, a designation that was more or less deemed a natural variation of human development (Fausto-Sterling 2000).

Amid a backdrop of European empires carving up Africa and Asia and US settler colonialism taking over Native lands, a new logic of sex differentiation emerged hand in hand with new ideas of race in the mid-nineteenth century. In this new paradigm, both race and sex were matters of deep biological difference and inequality, hierarchies that suited the political project of empire in which whites were assuming political control over populations of color. Scientists and others argued that the sex binary of male/female and the cultural roles of man/woman were advanced evolutionary specializations that only the so-called civilized white race had attained. Scientists came to see the male and female sexes as distinct evolutionary specializations in four key ways: anatomical structure, physiological function, mental capacity, and emotional development (Russett 1989). As the feminist evolutionary theorist Antoinette Brown Blackwell put it in 1875, "Sex means differentiation in every process of body and mind," down to "every hair of the head," but allegedly only the civilized had

achieved this level of binary difference (1875, 221). To put it even more bluntly: woman, as a physical and cultural state of being, was defined as an elite achievement of whiteness (Schuller 2018).

By the early twentieth century, the intersex category was drastically narrowed so that only a tiny fraction of the population fit its criteria—in effect, it pathologized intersex bodies and designated them for immediate surgical treatment. By contrast, these new medical protocols further normalized the sex binary as seemingly the only legitimate form of bodily sex (Fausto-Sterling 2000).

Whose interests were served by this new logic of absolute binary difference between white women and white men? In the United States, as white settlers pushed West and the government broke treaty after treaty to transform communal Indigenous ecologies into white private property, the racial politics of "woman" played a key role in settler colonialism. Anthropologists and others argued that Native society was too primitive to have evolved distinct social roles for women; Native women were thus squaws and drudges. White women reformers such as Alice Fletcher took it as their special task to "save" Native females, elevating them into the status of women by relieving them of the burden of labor (Pascoe 1990; L. Newman 1999). Meanwhile, enslavement created a similar dynamic in whites' views of Black communities, where womanhood was a status they reserved for white enslavers and refused to grant to enslaved workers (Carby 1987). Hortense Spillers's (1987) famous essay "Mama's Baby, Papa's Maybe" makes precisely this point. Transatlantic slavery, she argues, consigned Blackness to the position of raw, physical resource and was stripped of the social roles of woman or man, leaving enslaved peoples in a bare state of unsexed existence.

Meanwhile, influential scientists, writers, and others, both men and women, assigned white women to the private sphere and protected them from labor while assigning white men to the public sphere of politics and capitalism. The ideal that white women should be restricted to the hearth and home, softening the effects of the brutal demands of the marketplace and extending their domestic influence by civilizing alleged primitives, was underwritten by the new biological logic that their bodies were thoroughly distinct from that of white men and of all people of color. The logic of "woman" was a key element of white supremacy.

This leaves feminists today with a thorny dilemma. Since woman as a category was articulated as a specialization of whiteness, not as a universal aspect of female existence, should feminists today be rallying around "woman"? Can we liberate woman from its history as a function of whiteness? For some feminists of color, such as Brittney Cooper (2017), organizing as Black women is important because of the common experiences Black women presently face as well as their historic exclusion from the category of woman. On the other hand, some white feminists uphold the equality between women and men as the entire project of feminism, a hierarchy of purpose that ends up sidelining other aspects of power such as race and capitalism and thereby reinforcing the idea that woman is equal to white (Sandberg and Scovell 2013). Others suggest that different histories require different activist tactics: while it may be strategic for Black women and other women of color to organize as women, white women have a responsibility to understand how other dynamics of power are equally central to their experiences as women and to organize beyond the category of gender. Still others increasingly want to be free of the binary logic of male/female, in part because of its colonial and racial history. "Femme," "masc," and "nonbinary" are among the new categories that attempt to break out of the historically sedimented terms *woman* and *man* and offer new modes of identity and

collectivity. Woman thus exists in complicated relationship to other key terms, such as *female* and *nonbinary*.

As with any identity-based political project, "woman" as the rallying point of feminism opens up difficult questions of who counts and who doesn't count in the group. Feminist scholarship and activism have often policed the category of woman, arguing that only those assigned female at birth can lay claim to the identity of woman (Raymond 1979). This position denies the right of trans women to be included in the category of women. Others, who imagine themselves as trans allies, nonetheless use phrases like "women and trans women" that reveal an implicit bias in which only the cisgender, meaning those whose gender identity corresponds with the sex identity they were assigned at birth, can lay claim to "woman," unmodified. A third position embraces the right of any person, trans identified or not, to identity as a woman. These debates, in which some wish to restrict the category of women and others to expand it, echo the nineteenth-century debates that restricted the category of woman to whiteness.

Given the trouble with woman as a political category, how else can feminism organize its political project around the rights of women? Gender and sexuality studies, the successor to what was initially called women's studies, takes that problem head-on by shifting its central object of analysis from "woman" to power. Rather than examining the role of women in society and issues of identity and representation in politics and culture, it looks at how gender, capitalism, colonialism, racism, sexuality, ability, and other forces of power organize our social structures and cultural practices and how these seep into our very flesh in ways both limiting and enabling. Rather than looking strictly at the products of power as they show up in categories such as woman, we also take a step back and examine how gender consolidates within a dense network of economics, science, politics, and other phenomena in the first place. Woman from this perspective is not merely a role in society, documentable with black-and-white photographs of secretaries and doctors: it is an invitation to investigate how power has materialized over centuries and to what ends.

References

Abbott, Sidney, and Barbara Love. 1972. *Sappho Was a Right-On Woman: A Liberated View of Lesbianism*. New York: Stein & Day.

Abdulhadi, Rabab, Evelyn Alsultany, and Nadine Naber, eds. 2011. *Arab and Arab American Feminisms: Gender, Violence, and Belonging*. Syracuse, NY: Syracuse University Press.

Abel, Elizabeth. 2009. "Bathroom Doors and Drinking Fountains: Jim Crow's Racial Symbolic." *Critical Inquiry* 25 (3): 435–81.

Abramovitz, Mimi. 1988. *Regulating the Lives of Women: Social Welfare Policy from Colonial Times to the Present*. Boston: South End.

Abu-Lughod, Lila. 1990. "The Romance of Resistance: Tracing Transformations of Power through Bedouin Women." *American Ethnologist* 17, no. 1 (February): 41–55.

———. 1998. "The Marriage of Feminism and Islamism in Egypt: Selective Repudiation as a Dynamic of Postcolonial Cultural Politics." In *Remaking Women: Feminism and Modernity in the Middle East*, edited by Lila Abu-Lughod, 243–69. Princeton, NJ: Princeton University Press.

———. 2002. "Do Muslim Women Really Need Saving? Anthropological Reflections on Cultural Relativism and Its Others." *American Anthropologist* 104 (3): 783–90.

———. 2009. "Dialects of Empowerment: The International Circuitry of the Arab Development Report 2005." *International Journal of Middle Eastern Studies* 41:83–103.

———. 2013. *Do Muslim Women Need Saving?* Cambridge, MA: Harvard University Press.

Adams, Howard. 1995. *A Tortured People: The Politics of Colonization*. Penticton, Canada: Theytus.

Adichie, Chimamada Ngozi. 2014. *We Should All Be Feminists*. New York: Fourth Estate.

Agard-Jones, Vanessa. 2012. "What the Sands Remember." *GLQ: A Journal of Lesbian and Gay Studies* 18 (2–3): 325–46.

Agustín, Laura María. 2007. *Sex at the Margins: Migration, Labour Markets and the Rescue Industry*. London: Zed.

Ahmed, Leila. 1992. *Women and Gender in Islam: Historical Roots of a Modern Debate*. New Haven, CT: Yale University Press.

Ahmed, Fauzia Erfan. 2004. "The Rise of the Bangladesh Garment Industry: Globalization, Women, Workers, and the Voice." *NWSA Journal* 16 (2): 34–45.

Ahmed, Sara. 2004. *The Cultural Politics of Emotion*. Edinburgh: Edinburgh University Press.

———. 2006. *Queer Phenomenology: Orientations, Objects, Others*. Durham, NC: Duke University Press.

———. 2014. *Willful Subjects*. Durham, NC: Duke University Press.

———. 2017. *Living a Feminist Life*. Durham, NC: Duke University Press.

Aizura, Aren Z. 2012. "The Persistence of Transsexual Travel Narratives." In *Transgender Migrations: The Bodies, Borders, and Politics of Transition*, edited by Trystan T. Cotten, 139–56. New York: Routledge.

———. 2018. *Mobile Subjects: Transnational Imaginaries of Gender Reassignment*. Durham, NC: Duke University Press.

Aizura, Aren Z., Trystan Cotton, Carsten Balzer / Carla LaGata, Marcia Ochoa, and Salvador Vidal-Ortiz. 2014. "Introduction: Decolonizing the Transgender Imaginary." *TSQ: Transgender Studies Quarterly* 1 (3): 308–19.

Alaimo, Stacy. 2016. *Exposed: Environmental Politics and Pleasures in Posthuman Times*. Minneapolis: University of Minnesota Press.

Alarcón, Norma. 1981. "Chicana's Feminist Literature: A Re-vision through Malintzin / or Malintzin Putting Flesh Back on the Object." In *This Bridge Called My Back: Writings by Radical Women of Color*, edited by Cherríe Moraga and Gloria Anzaldúa, 202–11. Watertown, MA: Persephone.

———. 1990. "The Theoretical Subject(s) of *This Bridge Called My Back* and Anglo-American Feminism." In *Making Face, Making Soul: Haciendo Caras; Creative and Critical Perspectives by Feminists of Color*, edited by Gloria Anzaldúa, 356–59. San Francisco: Aunt Lute.

———. 1994. "Conjugating Subjects: The Heteroglossia of Essence and Resistance." In *Another Tongue: Nation and Ethnicity in the Linguistic Borderlands*, edited by Alfred Arteaga, 125–38. Durham, NC: Duke University Press.

———. 1996. "Conjugating Subjects in the Age of Multiculturalism." In *Mapping Multiculturalism*, edited by Avery F. Gordon and Christopher Newfield, 127–48. Minneapolis: University of Minnesota Press.

Alexander, M. Jacqui. 1997. "Erotic Autonomy as a Politics of Decolonization: An Anatomy of Feminist and State Practice in the Bahamas Tourist Economy." In *Feminist Genealogies, Colonial Legacies, Democratic Futures*, edited by M. Jacqui Alexander and Chandra Talpade Mohanty, 63–100. New York: Routledge.

———. 2005. *Pedagogies of Crossing: Meditations on Feminism, Sexual Politics, Memory, and the Sacred*. Durham, NC: Duke University Press.

Alexander, M. Jacqui, and Chandra Talpade Mohanty. 1997. *Feminist Genealogies, Colonial Legacies, Democratic Futures*. New York: Routledge.

———. 2010. "Cartographies of Knowledge and Power: Transnational Feminism as Radical Praxis." In *Critical Transnational Feminist Praxis*, edited by Amanda Lock Swarr and Richa Nagar, 23–45. Albany: State University of New York Press.

Alexander, Michelle. 2012. *The New Jim Crow: Mass Incarceration in the Age of Colorblindness*. New York: New Press.

Alilunas, Peter. 2016. *Smutty Little Movies: The Creation and Regulation of Adult Video*. Berkeley: University of California Press.

Allen, Chadwick. 2017. *Trans-Indigenous: Methodologies for Global Native Literary Studies*. Minneapolis: University of Minnesota Press.

Allen, Jafari S. 2011. *¡Venceremos? The Erotics of Black Self-Making in Cuba*. Durham, NC: Duke University Press.

———. 2012. *Black Queer Diaspora: A GLQ Special Issue*. Durham, NC: Duke University Press.

Allen, Paula Gunn. 1986. *The Sacred Hoop: Recovering the Feminine in American Indian Traditions*. Boston: Beacon.

Amaya, Hector. 2013. *Citizenship Excess: Latino/as, Media, and the Nation*. New York: New York University Press.

Amel, VJ Um. 2014. "Voice of a Cyborg." vjumamel.com. July 18, 2014.

Amin, Kadji. 2017. *Disturbing Attachments: Genet, Modern Pederasty, and Queer History*. Durham, NC: Duke University Press.

Ammerman, Nancy T. 2020. "Rethinking Religion: Toward a Practice Approach." *American Journal of Sociology* 126 (1): 6–51.

Amnesty International. 2016. *Amnesty International Policy on State Obligations to Respect, Protect and Fulfil the Human Rights of Sex Workers*. POL 30/4062. London: Amnesty International.

Anderson, Eric, and Ann Travers, eds. 2017. *Transgender Athletes in Competitive Sports*. New York: Routledge.

Anguksuar / Richard LaFortune. 1997. "A Postcolonial Perspective." In *Two-Spirit People: Native American Gender Identity, Sexuality and Spirituality*, edited by Sue-Ellen Jacobs, Wesley Thomas, and Sabine Lang, 217–22. Urbana-Champaign: University of Illinois Press.

Anwary, Afroza. 2017. "Globalization, Women Factory Workers of Bangladesh and Their Autonomy." *Géneros* 6 (3): 1389–1413.

Anzaldúa, Gloria. 1987. *Borderlands / La Frontera: The New Mestiza*. San Francisco: Aunt Lute.

———, ed. 1990. *Making Face, Making Soul: Haciendo Caras; Creative and Critical Perspectives by Feminists of Color*. San Francisco: Aunt Lute.

———. 2000. *Interviews/Entrevistas*. Edited by Ana Louis Keating. New York: Routledge.

Appel, Hana. 2017. "Toward an Ethnography of the National Economy." *Cultural Anthropology* 32:294–322.

Armstrong, Elisabeth. 2002. *The Retreat from Organization: US Feminism Reconceptualized*. Albany: State University of New York Press.

Armstrong, Jeanette. 1998. "Land Speaking." In *Speaking for the Generations: Native Writers on Writing*, edited by Simon Ortiz, 175–94. Tucson: University of Arizona Press.

———. 2007. "Native Perspectives on Sustainability: Jeannette Armstrong (Syilx)." By David E. Hall. Native Perspectives on Sustainability. October 21, 2007. www.nativeperspectives.net.

Arondekar, Anjali. 2009. *For the Record: On Sexuality and the Colonial Archive in India*. Durham, NC: Duke University Press.

Arondekar, Anjali, and Geeta Patel. 2016. "Area Impossible: Notes toward an Introduction." *GLQ: A Journal of Lesbian and Gay Studies* 22 (2): 151–71.

Arquette, Mary. 2000. "The Animals." In *Words That Come before All Else*, edited by Haudenosaunee Environmental Task Force, 82–101. Akwesasne, NY: Haudenosaunee Environmental Task Force.

Arvin, Maile. 2019a. "Indigenous Feminist Notes on Embodying Alliance against Settler Colonialism." *Meridians: Feminism, Race, Transnationalism* 18 (2): 335–57.

———. 2019b. *Possessing Polynesians: The Science of Settler Colonial Whiteness in Hawai'i and Oceania*. Durham, NC: Duke University Press.

Arvin, Maile, Eve Tuck, and Angie Morrill. 2013. "Decolonizing Feminism: Challenging Connections between Settler Colonialism and Heteropatriarchy." *Feminist Formations* 25 (1): 8–34.

Atanasoski, Neda, and Kalindi Vora. 2019. *Surrogate Humanity: Race, Robots, and the Politics of Technological Futures*. Durham, NC: Duke University Press.

Atleo, E. Richard. 2002. "Discourses in and about the Clayoquot Sound: A First Nations Perspective." In *A Political Space: Reading the Global through Clayoquot Sound*, edited by Warren Magnusson and Karena Shaw, 199–208. Minneapolis: University of Minnesota Press.

Attwood, Feona, ed. 2010. *Porn.com: Making Sense of Online Pornography*. New York: Peter Lang.

Attwood, Feona, and Clarissa Smith. 2014. "Porn Studies: An Introduction." *Porn Studies* 1:1–6.

Audre Lorde Project. 2014. "A Decade of Resistance." June 17, 2014. https://alp.org.

Austin, J. L. 1975. *How to Do Things with Words*. Oxford: Clarendon.

Avalon Project. n.d. "The First Charter of Virginia; April 10, 1606." Accessed July 2, 2021. https://avalon.law.yale.edu.

Bacchetta, Paola, Sunaira Maira, and Howard Winant, eds. 2019. *Global Raciality: Empire, Postcoloniality, Decoloniality*. New York: Routledge.

Bahng, Aimee. 2018. *Migrant Futures: Decolonizing Speculation in Financial Times*. Durham, NC: Duke University Press.

Bailey, Marlon. 2013. *Butch Queens Up in Pumps: Gender, Performance, and Ballroom Culture in Detroit*. Ann Arbor: University of Michigan Press.

Bailey, Moya, and Whitney Peoples. 2017. "Articulating Black Feminist Health Science Studies." *Catalyst: Feminism, Theory, Technoscience* 3 (2). https://doi.org/10.28968/cftt.v3i2.28844.

Balderrama, Francisco E., and Raymond Rodríguez. 1995. *Decade of Betrayal: Mexican Repatriation in the 1930s*. Albuquerque: University of New Mexico Press.

Ball, Matthew. 2016. *Criminology and Queer Theory: Dangerous Bedfellows?* London: Palgrave Macmillan.

Bang, Megan, Lawrence Curley, Adam Kessel, Ananda Marin, Eli S. Suzukovich III, and George Strack. 2014. "Muskrat Theories, Tobacco in the Streets, and Living Chicago as Indigenous Land." *Environmental Education Research* 20 (1): 37–55.

Baptist, Edward E. 2001. "'Cuffy,' 'Fancy Maids,' and 'One-Eyed Men': Rape, Commodification, and the Domestic Slave Trade in the United States." *American Historical Review* 106 (5): 1619–50. https://doi.org/10.2307/2692741.

Barad, Karen. 2007. *Meeting the Universe Halfway: Quantum Physics and the Entanglement of Matter and Meaning*. Durham, NC: Duke University Press.

Baril, Alexandre. 2015. "Transness as Debility: Rethinking Intersections between Trans and Disabled Embodiments." *Feminist Review* 111 (1): 59–74.

Barker, Joanne. 2006. "Gender, Sovereignty, and the Discourse of Rights in Native Women's Activism." *Meridians: Feminism, Race, Transnationalism* 7 (1): 127–61.

———. 2011. *Native Acts: Law, Recognition, and Cultural Authenticity*. Durham, NC: Duke University Press.

———. 2014a. "Decolonize This: Joanne Barker's Critical Notes on 'Settler Colonialism.'" *mexmigration* (blog). January 14, 2014. http://mexmigration.blogspot.com.

———. 2014b. "Gender." In *The Indigenous World of North America*, edited by Robert Warrior, 506–24. New York: Routledge.

———. 2015. "Self-Determination." *Critical Ethnic Studies* 1 (1): 11–26.

———, ed. 2017. *Critically Sovereign: Indigenous Gender, Sexuality, and Feminist Studies*. Durham, NC: Duke University Press.

———. 2018a. "Decolonizing the Mind." *Rethinking Marxism* 30 (2): 208–31.

———. 2018b. "Territory as Analytic: The Dispossession of Lenapehoking and the Subprime Crisis." *Social Text* 36 (2): 19–39.

Barry, Kathleen. 1996. *The Prostitution of Sexuality*. New York: New York University Press.

Bataille, Georges. 1985. *Visions of Excess: Selected Writings, 1927–1939*. Edited by Allan Stoekl. Minneapolis: University of Minnesota Press.

———. 1999. "Abjection and Miserable Forms." In *More and Less*, edited by Sylvère Lotringer and Chris Kraus, 8–13. Los Angeles: Semiotext(e).

Battiste, Marie. 2000. *Reclaiming Indigenous Voice and Vision*. Vancouver: University of British Columbia Press.

Baynton, Douglas. 2001. "Disability and the Justification of Inequality in American History." In *The New Disability History: American Perspectives*, edited by Paul Longmore and Lauri Umansky, 33–57. New York: New York University Press.

Beal, Frances M. (1969) 2008. "Double Jeopardy: To Be Black and Female." *Meridians: Feminism, Race, Transnationalism* 8 (2): 166–76.

Beardall, Theresa Ysabel Rocha. 2019. "Transactional Policing: Reframing Local Police-Community Relations through the Lens of Police Employment." PhD diss., Cornell University.

Beauchamp, Toby. 2019. *Going Stealth: Transgender Politics and US Surveillance Practices*. Durham, NC: Duke University Press.

Beauvoir, Simone de. (1949) 1989. *The Second Sex*. Edited and translated by H. M. Parshley. New York: Vintage.

Beckert, Sven, and Seth Rockman. 2018. *Slavery's Capitalism: A New History of American Economic Development*. Philadelphia: University of Pennsylvania Press.

Bederman, Gail. 2008. *Manliness and Civilization: A Cultural History of Gender and Race in the United States, 1880–1917*. Chicago: University of Chicago Press.

Beemyn, Genny, and Susan Rankin. 2011. *The Lives of Transgender People*. New York: Columbia University Press.

Belcourt, Billy-Ray. 2017. "Indigenous Studies beside Itself." *Somatechnics* 7 (2): 182–85.

Belcourt, Billy-Ray, and Lindsay Nixon. 2018. "What Do We Mean by Queer Indigenous Ethics?" *Canadian Art*, May 23, 2018. https://canadianart.ca.

Belsey, Catherine. 1980. *Critical Practice*. New York: Routledge.

Benitez, M. 2021. "Becoming Our Labor: Non-traditional Workers in the Blue-Collar Workforce." PhD diss., University of Maryland, College Park.

Benjamin, Harry. 1966. *The Transsexual Phenomenon*. New York: Julian.

Benjamin, Ruha. 2013. *People's Science: Bodies and Rights on the Stem Cell Frontier*. Stanford, CA: Stanford University Press.

Ben-Moshe, Liat. 2020. *Decarcerating Disability: Deinstitutionalization and Prison Abolition*. Minneapolis: University of Minnesota Press.

Ben-Moshe, Liat, and Allison C. Carey. 2014. *Disability Incarcerated: Imprisonment and Disability in the United States and Canada*. New York: Palgrave Macmillan.

Bennett, Brian. 2020. "Why President Trump Wants to Frame COVID-19 as a 'Foreign Virus.'" *Time*, March 11, 2020. https://time.com.

Bennett, Herman L. 2018. *African Kings and Black Slaves: Sovereignty and Dispossession in the Early Modern Atlantic*. Philadelphia: University of Pennsylvania Press.

Bennett, Jane. 2010. *Vibrant Matter: A Political Ecology of Things*. Durham, NC: Duke University Press.

Benton-Banai, Edward. 2008. *Anishinaabe Almanac: Living through the Seasons*. M'Chigeeng, Canada: Kenjgewin Teg Educational Institute.

Berer, Marge. 2017. "Abortion Law and Policy around the World: In Search of Decriminalization." *Health and Human Rights* 19 (1): 13–27.

Berg, Heather. 2017. "Porn Work, Feminist Critique, and the Market for Authenticity." *Signs: Journal of Women in Culture and Society* 42 (3): 669–92.

———. 2021. *Porn Work*. Chapel Hill: University of North Carolina Press.

Berger, Dan, Mariame Kaba, and David Stein. 2017. "What Abolitionists Do." *Jacobin*, August 17, 2017. www.jacobinmag.com.

Bergeron, Suzanne. 2003. "The Post Washington Consensus and Economic Representations of Women in Development in the World Bank." *International Feminist Journal of Politics* 5 (3): 397–419.

Berlant, Lauren. 1997. *The Queen of America Goes to Washington City: Essays on Sex and Citizenship*. Durham, NC: Duke University Press.

———. 2011. *Cruel Optimism*. Durham, NC: Duke University Press.

Berlant, Lauren, and Michael Warner. 1998. "Sex in Public." *Critical Inquiry* 24 (2): 547–66.

Bernstein, Elizabeth. 2007. *Temporarily Yours: Intimacy, Authenticity, and the Commerce of Sex*. Chicago: University of Chicago Press.

———. 2010. "Militarized Humanitarianism Meets Carceral Feminism: The Politics of Sex, Rights, and Freedom in Contemporary Antitrafficking Campaigns." *Signs: Journal of Women in Culture and Society* 36 (1): 45–71.

———. 2012. "Carceral Politics as Gender Justice? The 'Traffic in Women' and Neoliberal Circuits of Crime, Sex, and Rights." *Theory and Society* 41 (3): 233–59.

Bersani, Leo. 1987. "Is the Rectum a Grave?" *October* 43:197–222.

Bersani, Leo, and Adam Phillips. 2008. *Intimacies*. Chicago: University of Chicago Press.

Besley, Joanna. 2016. "'Speaking to, with and About': Cherbourg Women's Memory of Domestic Work as Activist Counter-Memory." *Continuum* 30 (3): 316–25.

Bettie, Julie. 2014. *Women without Class: Girls, Race, and Identity*. Berkeley: University of California Press.

Bey, Marquis. 2017. "The Trans*-ness of Blackness, the Blackness of Trans*-ness." *TSQ: Transgender Studies Quarterly* 4 (2): 275–95.

———. 2019. "Black Fugitivity Un/gendered." *Black Scholar* 49 (1): 55–62.

Bhabha, Homi K. 2004. *The Location of Culture*. London: Routledge.

Bhandar, Brenna. 2018. *Colonial Lives of Property*. Durham, NC: Duke University Press.

Bhanji, Nael. 2012. "Trans/scriptions: Homing Desires, (Trans) sexual Citizenship and Racialized Bodies." In *Transgender Migrations: The Bodies, Borders, and Politics of Transition*, edited by Trystan T. Cotten, 157–75. New York: Routledge.

Bhattacharya, Tithi. 2017. *Social Reproduction Theory: Remapping Class, Recentering Oppression*. London: Pluto.

Bierria, Alisa, Clarissa Rojas, and Mimi Kim, eds. 2010. "Community Accountability: Emerging Movements to Transform Violence." Special issue, *Social Justice* 37 (4).

Blackwell, Antoinette Brown. 1875. *The Sexes throughout Nature*. New York: G. P. Putnam's Sons.

Blackwell, Maylei, Floridalma Boj López, and Luis Urrieta. 2017. "Critical Latinx Indigeneities." *Latino Studies* 12 (2): 126–37.

Black Women for Wages for Housework. 1977. "Money for Prostitutes Is Money for Black Women." Edited by Laura Renata Martin. *Lies* 1:6–8. www.liesjournal.net.

Blair, Cynthia M. 2018. *I've Got to Make My Livin': Black Women's Sex Work in Turn-of-the-Century Chicago*. Chicago: University of Chicago Press.

Blank, Hanne. 2012. *Straight: The Surprisingly Short History of Heterosexuality*. New York: Beacon.

Blassingame, John. 1979. *The Slave Community: Plantation Life in the Antebellum South*. Oxford: Oxford University Press.

Block, Sharon. 2006. *Rape and Sexual Power in Early America*. Chapel Hill: University of North Carolina Press.

Bocking, Stephen. 1997. *Ecologists and Environmental Politics: A History of Contemporary Ecology*. New Haven, CT: Yale University Press.

Bohaker, Heidi. 2006. "'Nindoodemag': The Significance of Algonquian Kinship Networks in the Eastern Great Lakes Region, 1600–1701." *William and Mary Quarterly* 63 (1): 23–52.

Bohrer, Ashley J. 2019. *Marxism and Intersectionality: Race, Gender, Class and Sexuality under Contemporary Capitalism*. Bielefeld, Germany: transcript Verlag.

Bois, Yves-Alain, and Rosalind Krauss. 1997. *Formless: A User's Guide*. Cambridge, MA: MIT Press.

Borden, Lizzie, dir. 1983. *Born in Flames*. New York: First Run Features. DVD.

Boris, Eileen, and Rhacel Salazar Parreñas, eds. 2010. *Intimate Labors: Cultures, Technologies, and the Politics of Care*. Stanford, CA: Stanford University Press.

Bost, Darius. 2019. *Evidence of Being: The Black Gay Cultural Renaissance and the Politics of Violence*. Chicago: University of Chicago Press.

Bow, Leslie. 2009. "Transracial/Transgender: Analogies of Difference in *Mai's America*." *Signs: Journal of Women in Culture and Society* 35 (1): 75–103.

Brady, Mary Pat. 2002. *Extinct Lands, Temporal Geographies: Chicana Literature and the Urgency of Space*. Durham, NC: Duke University Press.

Brah, A. 1996. *Cartographies of Diaspora: Contesting Identities*. London: Routledge.

Brand, Dionne. 2020. "On Narrative, Reckoning and the Calculus of Living and Dying." *Toronto Star*, July 4, 2020.

Breedlove, Caitlin. 2020. "Future: Spiritual and Political Mandates for Our Future. Discussion with Susan Raffo, Cara Page, Anjali Taneja, Erica Woodland, and Shira Hassan." *Fortification*, May 1, 2020. Podcast audio. https://fortification.libsyn.com.

Brennan, Denise. 2004. *What's Love Got to Do with It? Transnational Desires and Sex Tourism in the Dominican Republic*. Durham, NC: Duke University Press.

———. 2014. *Life Interrupted: Trafficking into Forced Labor in the United States*. Durham, NC: Duke University Press.

Brennan, Teresa. 2004. *The Transmission of Affect*. Ithaca, NY: Cornell University Press.

Brewer, Holly. 2005. *By Birth or Consent: Children, Law, and the Anglo-American Revolution in Authority*. Chapel Hill: University of North Carolina Press.

Bridges, Khiara. 2011. *Reproducing Race: An Ethnography of Pregnancy as a Site of Racialization*. Berkeley: University of California Press.

Briggs, Laura. 2002. *Reproducing Empire: Race, Sex, Science, and U.S. Imperialism in Puerto Rico*. Berkeley: University of California Press.

———. 2014. "Making Race, Making Sex: Perspectives on Torture." *International Feminist Journal of Politics* 16 (4): 1–20.

———. 2017. *How All Politics Became Reproductive Politics: From Welfare Reform to Foreclosure to Trump*. Berkeley: University of California Press.

Brim, Matt. 2020. *Poor Queer Studies: Confronting Elitism in the University*. Durham, NC: Duke University Press.

Bronstein, Carolyn. 2011. *Battling Pornography: The American Feminist Anti-pornography Movement, 1976–1986*. Cambridge: Cambridge University Press.

———. 2015. "Clashing at Barnard's Gates: Understanding the Origins of the Pornography Problem in the Modern American Women's Movement." In *New Views on Pornography: Sexuality, Politics, and the Law*, edited by Lynn Comella and Shira Tarrant, 57–76. Santa Barbara, CA: Praeger.

———. 2020. "Pornography, Trans Visibility, and the Demise of Tumblr." *TSQ: Transgender Studies Quarterly* 7 (2): 240–54.

Bronstein, Carolyn, and Whitney Strub, eds. 2016. *Porno Chic and the Sex Wars: American Sexual Representation in the 1970s*. Amherst: University of Massachusetts Press.

Brooks, Daphne. 2006. *Bodies in Dissent: Spectacular Performances of Race and Freedom, 1850–1910*. Durham, NC: Duke University Press.

Brooks, Joanna. 2010. "Our Phillis, Ourselves." *American Literature* 82 (1): 1–28.

Brooks, Siobhan. 2010. *Unequal Desires: Race and Erotic Capital in the Stripping Industry*. Albany: State University of New York Press.

brown, adrienne maree. 2020. "How We Learned (Are Learning) Transformative Justice." In *Beyond Survival: Strategies and Stories from the Transformative Justice Movement*, edited by Ejeris Dixon and Leah Lakshmi Piepzna-Samarasinha, 321–24. Oakland, CA: AK.

Brown, Jacqueline. 2005. *Dropping Anchor, Setting Sail: Geographies of Race in Black Liverpool*. Durham, NC: Duke University Press.

Brown, Rita Mae. 1995. "Reflections of a Lavender Menace. (Lesbians Left Out of Women's Movement)." *Ms.* 6 (1): 40.

Brown, Wendy. 1995. *States of Injury: Power and Freedom in Late Modernity*. Princeton, NJ: Princeton University Press.

———. 2006. "American Nightmare: Neoliberalism, Neoconservatism, and De-democratization." *Political Theory* 34 (6): 690–714.

———. 2015. *Undoing the Demos: Neoliberalism's Stealth Revolution*. Brooklyn: Zone.

Browne, Kath, and Catherine J. Nash, eds. 2010. *Queer Methods and Methodologies*. Farnham, UK: Ashgate.

Brownmiller, Susan. 1970. "Sisterhood Is Powerful." *New York Times*, March 15, 1970.

Bruyneel, Kevin. 2007. *Third Space of Sovereignty: The Postcolonial Politics of US-Indigenous Relations*. Minneapolis: University of Minnesota Press.

Buffalohead, Priscilla K. 1983. "Farmers Warriors Traders: A Fresh Look at Ojibway Women." *Minnesota History* 48 (6): 236–44.

Bullard, Robert D. 1990. *Dumping in Dixie: Race, Class, and Environmental Quality*. Boulder, CO: Westview.

Bumiller, Kristin. 2008. *In an Abusive State: How Neoliberalism Appropriated the Feminist Movement against Sexual Violence*. Durham, NC: Duke University Press.

Bush, George W. 2001. "Text: President Bush Addresses the Nation." *Washington Post*, September 20, 2001. www.washingtonpost.com.

Butler, Heather. 2004. "What Do You Call a Lesbian with Long Fingers?" In *Porn Studies*, edited by Linda Williams, 167–97. Durham, NC: Duke University Press.

Butler, Judith. 1986. "Sex and Gender in Simone de Beauvoir's *Second Sex*." *Yale French Studies*, no. 72, 35–49. https://doi.org/10.2307/2930225.

———. (1990) 1999. *Gender Trouble: Feminism and the Subversion of Identity*. New York: Routledge.

———. 1990. "Imitation and Gender Insubordination." In *The Lesbian and Gay Reader*, edited by Henry Abelove, Michele Aina Barale, and David M. Halperin, 307–20. New York: Routledge.

———. 1993a. *Bodies That Matter: On the Discursive Limits of "Sex."* New York: Routledge.

———. 1993b. "Critically Queer." *GLQ: A Journal of Lesbian and Gay Studies* 1 (1): 17–32.

———. 1994. "Against Proper Objects." *differences: A Journal of Feminist Cultural Studies* 6, nos. 2–3 (Summer/Fall): 1–26.

———. 1996. *Excitable Speech: A Politics of the Performative*. New York: Routledge.

———. 1997. *The Psychic Life of Power: Theories in Subjection*. Stanford, CA: Stanford University Press.

———. 2007. "Performative Acts and Gender Constitution: An Essay in Phenomenology and Feminist Theory." In *The Performance Studies Reader*, edited by Henry Bial, 154–66. New York: Routledge.

Byrd, Jodi A. 2011. *The Transit of Empire: Indigenous Critiques of Colonialism*. Minneapolis: University of Minnesota Press.

———. 2017. "Loving Unbecoming: The Queer Politics of the Transitive Native." In *Critically Sovereign: Indigenous Gender, Sexuality, and Feminist Studies*, edited by Joanne Barker, 207–28. Durham, NC: Duke University Press.

———. 2018. "'Variations under Domestication': Indigeneity and the Subject of Dispossession." *Social Text* 36 (2 (135)): 123–41.

———. 2019a. "To Hear the Call and Respond: Grounded Relationalities and the Spaces of Emergence." *American Quarterly* 71, no. 2 (June): 337–42.

———. 2019b. "Weather with You: Settler Colonialism, Antiblackness, and the Grounded Relationalities of Resistance." *Critical Ethnic Studies* 5 (1–2): 207–14.

Byrd, Jodi A., and Michael Rothberg, eds. 2011. "Between Subalternity and Indigeneity." *Interventions: International Journal of Postcolonial Studies* 13 (1): 1–12.

Cabral, Amilcar. 1969. *Revolution in Guinea: Selected Texts*. New York: Monthly Review.

Cacho, Lisa Marie. 2012. *Social Death: Racialized Rightlessness and the Criminalization of the Unprotected*. New York: New York University Press.

Calavita, Kitty. 2008. "Deflecting the Immigration Debate: Globalization, Immigrant Agency, 'Strange Bedfellows,' and Beyond." *Contemporary Sociology* 37 (4): 302–5.

Califa, Pat, and Robin Sweeney, eds. 1996. *The Second Coming: A Leatherdyke Reader*. Los Angeles: Alyson.

California Scholars for Academic Freedom. 2020. "Trump's Executive Order on Antisemitism Is Only Meant to Suppress Palestine Solidarity on Campus." January 7, 2020. https://mondoweiss.net.

Canaday, Margot. 2011. *The Straight State: Sexuality and Citizenship in Twentieth-Century America*. Princeton, NJ: Princeton University Press.

Cannon, Loren. 2019. "Trans Directed Injustice." In *Ethics, Left and Right: The Moral Issues That Divide Us*, edited by Bob Fischer, 428–36. Oxford: Oxford University Press.

Carby, Hazel. 1982a. "Schooling in Babylon." In *Empire Strikes Back: Race and Racism in 70's Britain*, edited by Centre for Contemporary Cultural Studies, 181–210. London: Routledge.

———. 1982b. "White Women Listen! Black Feminism and the Boundaries of Sisterhood." In *Empire Strikes Back: Race and Racism in 70's Britain*, edited by Centre for Contemporary Cultural Studies, 211–34. London: Routledge.

———. 1985. "'On the Threshold of Woman's Era': Lynching, Empire, and Sexuality in Black Feminist Theory." *Critical Inquiry* 12 (1): 262–77.

———. 1987. *Reconstructing Womanhood: The Emergence of the Afro-American Novelist*. New York: Oxford University Press.

———. 2019. *Imperial Intimacies: A Tale of Two Islands*. London: Verso.

cárdenas, micha. 2016. "Pregnancy: Reproductive Futures in Trans of Color Feminism." *TSQ: Transgender Studies Quarterly* 3 (1–2): 48–57.

———. 2017. "Dark Shimmers." In *Trap Door: Trans Cultural Production and the Politics of Visibility*, edited by Reina Gossett, Eric A. Stanley, and Johanna Burton, 161–81. Cambridge, MA: MIT Press.

Carey, Allison C. 2009. *On the Margins of Citizenship: Intellectual Disability and Civil Rights in Twentieth-Century America*. Philadelphia: Temple University Press.

Carrillo, Jo. 1981. "And When You Leave, Take Your Pictures with You." In *This Bridge Called My Back: Writings by Radical Women of Color*, edited by Cherríe Moraga and Gloria Anzaldúa, 66–67. Watertown, MA: Persephone.

Carrington, Kerry. 2015. *Feminism and Global Justice*. New York: Routledge.

Carroll, Clint. 2014. "Native Enclosures: Tribal National Parks and the Progressive Politics of Environmental Stewardship in Indian Country." *Geoforum* 53:31–40.

Carter, Julian. 2007. *The Heart of Whiteness: Normal Sexuality and Race in America*. Durham, NC: Duke University Press.

Carter, Tieraney, Rico Kleinstein Chenyek, M'kali-Hashiki, Marcelo Felipe Garzo Montalvo, Leah Lakshmi Piepzna-Samarasinha, and Jonah Aline Daniel. 2013. "'A Babe-ilicious Healing Justice Statement' from the BadAss Visionary Healers (BAVH)." *Nineteen Sixty Nine* 2 (1). https://escholarship.org.

Caserio, Robert L., Lee Edelman, Judith Halberstam, José Esteban Muñoz, and Tim Dean. 2006. "The Antisocial Thesis in Queer Theory." *PMLA* 121 (3): 819–28.

Castelli, Elizabeth. 2001. "Women, Gender and Religion: Troubling Categories and Transforming Knowledge." In *Women, Religion and Gender: A Reader*, edited by Elizabeth Castelli, 3–28. New York: Palgrave.

Caudwell, Jayne. 2006a. *Sports, Sexualities, and Queer Theory*. London: Taylor & Francis.

———. 2006b. "Women Playing Football at Clubs in England with Socio-political Associations." *Soccer & Society* 7 (4): 423–38.

Caught Looking. 1988. *Caught Looking: Feminism, Pornography and Censorship*. Seattle: Caught Looking.

Cavanagh, Sheila. 2010. *Queering Bathrooms: Gender, Sexuality, and the Hygienic Imagination*. Toronto: University of Toronto Press.

Center for HIV Law and Policy. 2020. *Map: HIV Criminalization in the United States*. Brooklyn: Center for HIV Law and Policy. www.hivlawandpolicy.org.

Centre for Contemporary Cultural Studies (CCCS), ed. 1982. *Empire Strikes Back: Race and Racism in 70's Britain*. London: Routledge.

Chang, Grace, and Ai-Jen Poo. 2016. *Disposable Domestics: Immigrant Women Workers in the Global Economy*. Chicago: Haymarket.

Chan-Malik, Sylvia. 2018. *Being Muslim: A Cultural History of Women of Color in American Islam*. New York: New York University Press.

Chateauvert, Melinda. 2013. *Sex Workers Unite: A History of the Movement from Stonewall to Slutwalk*. Boston: Beacon.

Chatterjee, Indrani, ed. 2004. *Unfamiliar Relations: Family and History in South Asia*. New Delhi: Permanent Black.

Chatterjee, Partha. 1993. *The Nation and Its Fragments*. Princeton, NJ: Princeton University Press.

Chauncey, George. 1994. *Gay New York: Gender, Urban Culture, and the Making of the Gay Male World, 1890–1940*. New York: Basic Books.

Chávez, Karma R. 2013. *Queer Migration Politics: Activist Rhetoric and Coalitional Possibilities*. Urbana: University of Illinois Press.

Chávez, Karma R., and Hana Masri. 2020. "The Rhetoric of Family in the US Immigration Movement: A Queer Migration Analysis of the Central American Child Migrant 'Crisis.'" In *Queer and Trans Migrations: Dynamics of Illegalization, Detention, and Deportation*, edited by Eithne Luibhéid and Karma R. Chávez, 209–25. Urbana: University of Illinois Press.

Cheah, Pheng. 2010. "Biopower and the New International Division of Reproductive Labor." In *Can the Subaltern Speak? Reflections on the History of an Idea*, edited by Rosalind C. Morris, 179–212. New York: Columbia University Press.

Chen, Jian Nao. 2019. *Trans Exploits: Trans of Color Technologies and Technologies of Movement*. Durham, NC: Duke University Press.

Chen, Mel Y. 2012. *Animacies: Biopolitics, Racial Mattering, and Queer Affect*. Durham, NC: Duke University Press.

Cheng, Anne Anlin. 2000. *The Melancholy of Race: Psychoanalysis, Assimilation, and Hidden Grief*. Oxford: Oxford University Press.

Chess, Simone, Alison Kafer, Jessi Quizar, and Mattie Udora. 2004. "Calling All Restroom Revolutionaries!" In *That's Revolting! Queer Strategies for Resisting Assimilation*, edited by Mattilda Bernstein Sycamore, 216–35. Brooklyn: Soft Skull.

Chettiar, Inimai, and Pyiya Raghavan. 2019. "Ending Mass Incarceration: Ideas from Today's Leaders." Brennan Center for Justice, May 16, 2019. www.brennancenter.org.

Chiang, Howard, and Alvin K. Wong. 2016. "Queering the Transnational Turn: Regionalism and Queer Asias." *Gender, Place & Culture* 23 (11): 1643–56. https://doi.org/10.1080/0966369X.2015.1136811.

Child, Brenda J. 2012. *Holding Our World Together: Ojibwe Women and the Survival of Community*. New York: Penguin.

Chirix García, Emma Delfina. 2003. *Alas y raíces, afectividad de las mujeres mayas. Rik'in ruxik' y ruxe'il, ronojel kajowab'al* [Roots and wings, Mayan women's affectivity]. Guatemala City: Grupo de Mujeres Kaqla, Nawal Wuj.

Chodorow, Nancy Julia. (1980) 1990. "Gender, Relation, and Difference in Psychoanalytic Perspective." In *Essential Papers on the Psychology of Women*, edited by Claudia Zanardi, 420–36. New York: New York University Press.

Christian, Barbara. 1987. "The Race for Theory." *Cultural Critique* 6:51–63.

———. 2007. "Diminishing Returns: Can Black Feminism Survive the Academy?" In *New Black Feminist Criticism, 1985–2000*, edited by Gloria Bowles, M. Guilia Fabi, and Arlene Keizer, 204–15. Urbana: University of Illinois Press.

Chrystos. 1988. *Not Vanishing*. Vancouver: Press Gang.

Chu, Andrea Long, and Emmett Harsin Drager. 2019. "After Trans Studies." *TSQ: Transgender Studies Quarterly* 6 (1): 103–16.

Chuh, Kandice. 2003. *Imagine Otherwise: On Asian Americanist Critique*. Durham, NC: Duke University Press.

Clare, Eli. 2009. *Exile and Pride: Disability, Queerness and Liberation*. Cambridge, MA: South End.

———. 2013. "Body Shame, Body Pride: Lessons from the Disability Rights Movement." In *The Transgender Studies Reader 2*, edited by Susan Stryker and Aren Z. Aizura, 261–65. New York: Routledge.

———. 2017. *Brilliant Imperfection*. Durham, NC: Duke University Press.

Clarke, Adele E., Janet K. Shim, Laura Mamo, Jennifer Ruth Fosket, and Jennifer R. Fishman. 2003. "Biomedicalization: Technoscientific Transformations of Health, Illness, and US Biomedicine." *American Sociological Review* 68 (2): 161–94.

Cochran, Patricia Longley, and Alyson L. Geller. 2002. "The Melting Ice Cellar: What Native Traditional Knowledge Is Teaching Us about Global Warming and Environmental Change." *American Journal of Public Health* 92 (9): 1404–9.

Cohen, Cathy J. 1997. "Punks, Bulldaggers, and Welfare Queens: The Radical Potential of Queer Politics?" *GLQ: A Journal of Lesbian and Gay Studies* 3 (4): 437–65.

———. 1999. *The Boundaries of Blackness: AIDS and the Breakdown of Black Politics*. Chicago: University of Chicago Press.

———. 2004. "Deviance as Resistance: A New Research Agenda for the Study of Black Politics." *Du Bois Review: Social Science Research on Race* 1, no. 1 (March): 27–45.

Cohn, Erika, dir. 2020. *Belly of the Beast*. San Francisco: ITVS.

Colbert, Soyica Diggs. 2017. *Black Movements: Performance and Cultural Politics*. New Brunswick, NJ: Rutgers University Press.

Colen, Shellee. (1995) 2006. "'Like a Mother to Them': Stratified Reproduction and West Indian Childcare Workers and Employers in New York." In *Feminist Anthropology: A Reader*, edited by Ellen Lewin, 380–96. Malden, MA: Blackwell.

Collins Dictionary. n.d. s.v. "de-." Accessed June 12, 2021. www.collinsdictionary.com.

Combahee River Collective. (1977) 2015. "A Black Feminist Statement." In *This Bridge Called My Back: Writings by Radical Women of Color*, edited by Cherríe Moraga and Gloria Anzaldúa, 210–18. Albany: State University of New York Press.

Combs, Barbara Harris. 2016. "Black (and Brown) Bodies Out of Place: Towards a Theoretical Understanding of Systemic Voter Suppression in the United States." *Critical Sociology* 42 (4–5): 535–49.

Comella, Lynn. 2008. "Looking Backward: Barnard and Its Legacies." *Communication Review* 11 (3): 202–11.

———. 2013. "From Text to Context: Feminist Porn and the Making of a Market." In *The Feminist Porn Book: The Politics of Producing Pleasure*, edited by Tristan Taormino, Celine

Parreñas Shimizu, Constance Penley, and Mireille Miller-Young, 79–93. New York: Feminist Press.

———. 2016. "Selling Intimacy Online: Inside the World of a Las Vegas Webcam Studio." *Vegas Seven*, January 21–27, 2016, 17–18.

———. 2017. *Vibrator Nation: How Feminist Sex-Toy Stores Changed the Business of Pleasure*. Durham, NC: Duke University Press.

Compton, D'Lane, Tey Meadow, and Kristen Schilt, eds. 2018. *Other, Please Specify: Queer Methods in Sociology*. Berkeley: University of California Press.

Contreras, Irina. 2012. "Descado en Los Angeles: Cycles of Invisible Resistance." In *Beyond Walls and Cages: Prisons, Borders, and Global Crisis*, edited by Jenna M. Loyd, Matt Mitchelson, and Andrew Burridge, 325–36. Athens: University of Georgia Press.

Cook-Lynn, Elizabeth. 1997. "Who Stole Native American Studies?" *Wicazo Sa Review* 12 (1): 9–28.

Cooper, Brittney. 2017. *Beyond Respectability: The Intellectual Thought of Race Women*. Urbana: University of Illinois Press.

Cooper, Frederick, and Jane Burbank, eds. 2011. *Empires in World History: Power and the Politics of Difference*. Princeton, NJ: Princeton University Press.

Cooper, Frederick, and Ann Laura Stoler, eds. 1997. *Tensions of Empire: Colonial Cultures in a Bourgeois World*. Berkeley: University of California Press.

Cooper, Melinda. 2008. *Life as Surplus: Biotechnology and Capitalism in the Neoliberal Era*. Seattle: University of Washington Press.

———. 2017. *Family Values: Between Neoliberalism and the New Social Conservatism*. New York: Zone.

Cooper Owens, Deirdre. 2018. *Medical Bondage: Race, Gender, and the Origins of American Gynecology*. Athens: University of Georgia Press.

Cornell, Drucilla. 2001. "The Secret behind the Veil: A Reinterpretation of 'Algeria Unveiled.'" *Philosophia Africana* 4 (2): 27–35.

Corntassel, Jeff. 2007. "Partnership in Action? Indigenous Political Mobilization and Co-optation during the First UN Indigenous Decade (1995–2004)." *Human Rights Quarterly* 29 (1): 137–66.

Cornwall, Andrea, Elizabeth Harrison, and Ann Whitehead. 2007. "Gender Myths and Feminist Fables: The Struggle for Interpretive Power in Gender and Development." *Development and Change* 38 (1): 1–20.

Cott, Nancy. 2003. *Public Vows: A History of Marriage and the Nation*. Cambridge, MA: Harvard University Press.

Coulthard, Glen. 2014. *Red Skin, White Masks: Rejecting the Colonial Politics of Recognition*. Minneapolis: University of Minnesota Press.

Cox, Aimee Meredith. 2015. *Black Girls and the Choreography of Citizenship*. Durham, NC: Duke University Press.

Cox, Alexandra B. 2017. "On the Durability of Carceral Logics: A Review of Three New Works." *Critical Criminology* 25:479–81.

Crais, Clifton, and Pamela Scully. 2010. *Sara Baartman and the Hottentot Venus: A Ghost Story and a Biography*. Princeton, NJ: Princeton University Press.

Crawford, Lucas. 2015. *Transgender Architectonics: The Shape of Change in Modernist Space*. Burlington, VT: Ashgate.

Crawford, Robert. 1980. "Healthism and the Medicalization of Everyday Life." *International Journal of Health Services* 10 (3): 365–88.

Crenshaw, Kimberlé. 1989. "Demarginalizing the Intersection of Race and Sex: A Black Feminist Critique of Antidiscrimination Doctrine, Feminist Theory and Antiracist Politics." *University of Chicago Legal Forum* 1:139–67.

———. (1991) 1995. "Mapping the Margins: Intersectionality, Identity Politics, and Violence against Women of Color." In *Critical Race Theory: The Key Writings That Formed the Movement*, edited by Kimberlé Crenshaw, Neil Gotanda, Gary Peller, and Kendall Thomas, 357–83. New York: New Press.

———. 1991. "Mapping the Margins: Intersectionality, Identity Politics, and Violence against Women of Color." *Stanford Law Review* 43 (6): 1241–99.

Crenshaw, Kimberlé, Neil Gotanda, Gary Peller, and Kendall Thomas. 1996. *Critical Race Theory: The Key Writings That Formed the Movement*. New York: New Press.

Cross, Kim. 2018. "The Real Reason There Is No Tour de France for Women." *Outside*, July 23, 2018.

Cruz, Ariane. 2016. *The Color of Kink: Black Women, BDSM, and Pornography*. New York: New York University Press.

Currans, Elizabeth. 2017. *Marching Dykes, Liberated Sluts, and Concerned Mothers: Women Transforming Public Space*. Urbana: University of Illinois Press.

Curry, Lucy A. 2001. "A Closer Look at *Santa Clara Pueblo v. Martinez*: Membership by Sex, by Race, and by Tribal Tradition." *Wisconsin Women's Law Journal* 16:161–214.

Cvetkovich, Ann. 2003. *An Archive of Feelings*. Durham, NC: Duke University Press.

———. 2012. *Depression: A Public Feeling*. Durham, NC: Duke University Press.

Cwynar-Horta, Jessica. 2016. "The Commodification of the Body Positive Movement on Instagram." *Stream: Interdisciplinary Journal of Communication* 8 (2): 36–56.

Daigle, Michelle, and Margaret Marietta Ramírez. 2019. "Decolonial Geographies." In *Keywords in Radical Geography: Antipode at 50*, 78–84. Toronto: Wiley.

Dalla Costa, Mariarosa, and Selma James. (1972) 1975. *The Power of Women and the Subversion of the Community*. Bristol, UK: Falling Wall.

David, Emmanuel. 2015. "Purple-Collar Labor: Transgender Workers and Queer Value at Global Call Centers in the Philippines." *Gender & Society* 29, no. 2 (April): 169–94.

Davis, Adrienne D. 1999. "The Private Law of Race and Sex: An Antebellum Perspective." *Stanford Law Review* 51 (9): 221–28.

———. 2015. "Regulating Sex Work: Erotic Assimilationism, Erotic Exceptionalism, and the Challenge of Intimate Labor." *California Law Review* 5:1195–1276.

Davis, Amira Rose. 2016. "No League of Their Own: Baseball, Black Women, and the Politics of Representation." *Radical History Review* 125:74–96.

Davis, Angela Y. 1971. "Reflections on the Black Woman's Role in the Community of Slaves." *Black Scholar*, December 7, 1971, 2–15.

———. 1976. "Racism and Contemporary Literature on Rape." *Freedomways* 16, no. 1 (Winter): 25–33.

———. 1981. *Women, Race and Class*. New York: Random House.

———. 1989. *Women, Culture, and Politics*. New York: Random House.

———. 2016. *Freedom Is a Constant Struggle: Ferguson, Palestine, and the Foundations of a Movement*. Chicago: Haymarket.

Davis, Dána-Ain. 2019. *Reproductive Injustice: Racism, Pregnancy, and Premature Birth*. New York: New York University Press.

Davis, Georgiann. 2015. *Contesting Intersex: The Dubious Diagnosis*. New York: New York University Press.

Davis, Heath Fogg. 2017. *Beyond Trans: Does Gender Matter?* New York: New York University Press.

Day, Iyko. 2016. *Alien Capital: Asian Racialization and the Logic of Settler Colonial Capitalism*. Durham, NC: Duke University Press.

Dean, Jodi. 2009. *Democracy and Other Neoliberal Fantasies: Communicative Capitalism and Left Politics*. Durham, NC: Duke University Press.

Dean, Tim. 2009. *Unlimited Intimacy: Reflections on the Subculture of Barebacking*. Chicago: University of Chicago Press.

de Brey, Cristobal. 2017. Report on the Condition of Education 2017 (*or* NCES 2021-144). Washington, DC: National Center for Education Statistics at IES.

Decena, Carlos Ulises. 2011. *Tacit Subjects: Belonging and Same-Sex Desire among Dominican Immigrant Men*. Durham, NC: Duke University Press.

DeClue, Jennifer. 2016. "Let's Play: Exploring Cinematic Black Lesbian Fantasy, Pleasure, and Pain." In *No Tea, No Shade: New Writings in Black Queer Studies*, edited by E. Patrick Johnson, 216–38. Durham, NC: Duke University Press.

Deer, Sarah. 2009. "Decolonizing Rape Law: A Native Feminist Synthesis of Safety and Sovereignty." *Wicazo Sa Review* 24 (2): 149–67.

———. 2014. *The Beginning and End of Rape: Confronting Sexual Violence in Native America*. Minneapolis: University of Minnesota Press.

Delany, Samuel. 1999. *Times Square Red, Times Square Blue*. New York: New York University Press.

de Lauretis, Teresa, ed. 1991. "Queer Theory: Gay and Lesbian Sexualities." Special issue, *differences: A Journal of Feminist Cultural Studies* 3 (2).

de Leeuw, Sarah, and Sarah Hunt. 2018. "Unsettling Decolonizing Geographies." *Geography Compass* 12:e12376.

Deloria, Vine, Jr. 2001. "American Indian Metaphysics." In *Power and Place: Indian Education in America*, edited by Vine Deloria Jr. and Daniel R. Wildcat, 1–6. Golden, CO: Fulcrum.

Deloria, Vine, and James Treat, eds. 1999. *For This Land: Writings on Religion in America*. New York: Routledge.

DeLoughrey, Elizabeth. 2010. *Routes and Roots: Navigating Caribbean and Pacific Island Literatures*. Honolulu: University of Hawai'i Press.

———. 2013. "The Myth of Isolates: Ecosystem Ecologies in the Nuclear Pacific." *Cultural Geographies* 20 (2): 167–84.

Del Rio, Korra, and Sophie Pezzutto. 2020. "Professionalism, Pay, and the Production of Pleasure in Trans Porn." *TSQ: Transgender Studies Quarterly* 7 (2): 262–67.

D'Emilio, John. (1983) 1993. "Capitalism and Gay Identity." In *The Lesbian and Gay Studies Reader*, edited by Henry Abelove, Michele Aina Barale, and David Halperin, 467–76. New York: Routledge.

Denetdale, Jennifer Nez. 2006. "Chairmen, Presidents, and Princesses: The Navajo Nation, Gender, and the Politics of Tradition." *Wicazo Sa Review* 24 (2): 9–28.

———. 2009. "Securing Navajo National Boundaries: War, Patriotism, Tradition, and the Diné Marriage Act of 2005." *Wicazo Sa Review* 24 (2): 131–48.

———. 2017. "Return to 'The Uprising at Beautiful Mountain in 1913': Marriage and Sexuality in the Making of the Modern Navajo Nation." In *Critically Sovereign: Indigenous Gender, Sexuality, and Feminist Studies*, edited by Joanne Barker, 69–98. Durham, NC: Duke University Press.

Dennis, Jeffery P. 2018. *The Myth of the Queer Criminal*. New York: Routledge.

Desai, Karishma. 2020. "Life Skills as Affective Labour: Skilling Girls with Gendered Enterprise." *South Asia: Journal of South Asian Studies* 43 (4): 705–22.

Dewey, Susan. 2011. *Neon Wasteland: On Love, Motherhood, and Sex Work in a Rust Belt Town*. Berkeley: University of California Press.

Díaz, Mónica. 2011. "Native American Women and Religion in the American Colonies: Textual and Visual Traces of an Imagined Community." *Legacy* 28 (2): 205–31.

Diaz, Robert, Marissa Largo, and Fritz Pino, eds. 2017. *Diasporic Intimacies: Queer Filipinos and Canadian Imaginaries*. Chicago: Northwestern University Press.

Diedrich, Lisa. 2016. *Indirect Action: Schizophrenia, Epilepsy, AIDS, and the Course of Health Activism*. Minneapolis: University of Minnesota Press.

Dillon, Michael. 1946. *Self: A Study in Ethics and Endocrinology*. London: William Heinemann Medical Books.

Dinshaw, Carolyn. 1999. *Getting Medieval: Sexualities and Communities, Pre- and Postmodern*. Durham, NC: Duke University Press.

Ditmore, Melissa. 2007. "In Calcutta, Sex Workers Organize." In *The Affective Turn: Theorizing the Social*, edited by Patricia Clough and Jean Halley, 170–86. Durham, NC: Duke University Press.

Dixon, Deborah P. 2014. "The Way of the Flesh: Life, Geopolitics and the Weight of the Future." *Gender, Place & Culture* 21 (2): 136–51.

Doan, Laura, and Lucy Bland, eds. 1998. *Sexology in Culture: Labelling Bodies and Desires*. Chicago: University of Chicago Press.

Doan, Petra. 2019. "To Count or Not to Count: Queering Measurement and the Transgender Community." In *Imagining Queer Methods*, edited by Amin Ghaziani and Matt Brim, 121–42. New York: New York University Press.

Doezema, Jo. 1998. "Forced to Choose: Beyond the Voluntary v. Forced Prostitution Dichotomy." In *Global Sex Workers: Rights, Resistance, and Redefinition*, edited by Kamala Kempadoo and Jo Doezema, 34–50. New York: Routledge.

Douglas, Mary. 1966. *Purity and Danger: An Analysis of Concepts of Pollution and Taboo*. London: Routledge & Keagan Paul.

Doyle, Jennifer. 2013. *Hold It against Me: Difficulty and Emotion in Contemporary Art*. Durham, NC: Duke University Press.

———. 2015. *Campus Sex, Campus Security*. Cambridge, MA: MIT Press.

Driscoll, Catherine. 2002. *Girls: Feminine Adolescence in Popular Culture and Cultural Theory*. New York: Columbia University Press.

Driskill, Qwo-Li. 2005. *Walking with Ghosts: Poems*. Cambridge, MA: Salt.

———. 2016. *Asegi Stories: Cherokee Queer and Two Spirit Memory*. Tucson: University of Arizona Press.

Driskill, Qwo-Li, Chris Finley, Brian Joseph Gilley, and Scott Lauria Morgensen. 2011. *Queer Indigenous Studies: Critical Interventions in Theory, Politics, and Literature*. Tucson: University of Arizona Press.

Driskill, Qwo-Li, Daniel Heath Justice, Deborah A. Miranda, and Lisa Tatonetti, eds. 2011. Introduction to *Sovereign Erotics: A Collection of Two Spirit Literature*, edited by Qwo-Li Driskill, Daniel Heath Justice, Deborah A. Miranda, and Lisa Tatonetti, 1–30. Tucson: University of Arizona Press.

Dru Stanley, Amy. 1998. *From Bondage to Contract: Wage Labor, Marriage, and the Market in the Age of Slave Emancipation*. Cambridge: Cambridge University Press.

Du Bois, W. E. B. 1935. *Black Reconstruction in America, 1860–1880*. New York: Harcourt, Brace.

———. 1945. *Color and Democracy: Colonies and Peace*. New York: Harcourt, Brace.

duCille, Ann. 1994. "The Occult of True Black Womanhood: Critical Demeanor and Black Feminist Studies." *Signs: Journal of Women in Culture and Society* 19 (3): 591–629.

Dudziak, Mary. 2003. *September 11 in History: A Watershed Moment?* Durham, NC: Duke University Press.

Duggan, Lisa. 2004. *The Twilight of Equality: Neoliberalism, Cultural Politics, and the Attack on Democracy*. Boston: Beacon.

Duggan, Lisa, and Nan Hunter. 1995. *Sex Wars: Sexual Dissent and Political Culture*. London: Routledge.

Dunbar-Ortiz, Roxanne. 2014. *An Indigenous People's History of the United States*. New York: Beacon.

Durazo, Ana Clarissa Rojas. 2006. "The Medicalization of Domestic Violence." In *Color of Violence: The INCITE! Anthology*, edited by INCITE! Women of Color Against Violence, 179–90. Cambridge, MA: South End.

Dworkin, Andrea. 1980. "Pornography and Grief." In *Take Back the Night: Women on Pornography*, edited by Laura Lederer, 286–91. New York: Morrow.

Dzodan, Flavia. 2011. "My Feminism Will Be Intersectional or It Will Be Bullshit." Tiger Beatdown, October 11, 2011. www.tigerbeatdown.com.

Ecoffier, Jeffrey. 2009. *Bigger Than Life: The History of Gay Porn Cinema from Beefcake to Hardcore*. Philadelphia: Running Press.

Edelman, Lee. 1994. *Homographesis: Essays in Gay Literary and Cultural Theory*. New York: Routledge.

——. 2004. *No Future: Queer Theory and the Death Drive*. Durham, NC: Duke University Press.

Edelman, Peter. 2019. *Not a Crime to Be Poor: The Criminalization of Poverty in America*. New York: New Press.

Edwards, Erica. 2015. "Sex after the Black Normal." *differences: A Journal of Feminist Cultural Studies* 26 (1): 141–67.

Edwards, Laura. 2009. *The People and Their Peace: Legal Culture and the Transformation of Inequality in the Post-Revolutionary South*. Chapel Hill: University of North Carolina Press.

Ehlers, Nadine, and Leslie R. Hinkson, eds. 2017. *Subprime Health: Debt and Race in US Medicine*. Minneapolis: University of Minnesota Press.

Ehlers, Nadine, and Shiloh Krupar. 2019. *Deadly Biocultures: The Ethics of Life-Making*. Minneapolis: University of Minnesota Press.

Ellis, Havelock. (1903) 1998. "Studies in the Psychology of Sex, Vol. III: Analysis of the Sexual Impulse." In *Sexology Uncensored: The Documents of Sexual Science*, edited by Lucy Bland and Laura Doan, 108–9. Chicago: University of Chicago Press.

Ellison, Treva. 2016. "The Strangeness of Progress and the Uncertainty of Blackness." In *No Tea, No Shade: New Writings in Black Queer Studies*, edited by E. Patrick Johnson, 323–45. Durham, NC: Duke University Press.

——. 2017. "The Labor of Werqing It: The Performance and Protest Strategies of Sir Lady Java." In *Trap Door: Trans Cultural Production and the Politics of Visibility*, edited by Tourmaline, Eric. A. Stanley, and Johanna Burton, 1–22. Cambridge, MA: MIT Press.

——. 2019. "Black Femme Praxis and the Promise of Black Gender." *Black Scholar* 49 (1): 6–16. https://doi.org/10.1080/00064246.2019.1548055.

Ellison, Treva, and Kai M. Green. 2014. "Tranifest." *TSQ: Transgender Studies Quarterly* 1 (1): 222–25.

Ellison, Treva, Kai M. Green, Matt Richardson, and C. Riley Snorton. 2017. "We Got Issues: Toward a Black Trans*/Studies." *TSQ: Transgender Studies Quarterly* 4 (2): 162–69.

Elsey, Breda, and Joshua Nadel. 2019. *Fútbolera: A History of Women and Sports in Latin America*. Austin: University of Texas Press.

El-Tayeb, Fatima. 2011. *European Others: Queering Ethnicity in Postnational Europe*. Minneapolis: University of Minnesota Press.

Emirbayer, Mustafa, and Ann Mische. 1998. "What Is Agency?" *American Journal of Sociology* 103 (4): 962–1023.

Eng, David L. 2001. *Racial Castration: Managing Masculinity in Asian America*. Durham, NC: Duke University Press.

——. 2003. "Transnational Adoption and Queer Diasporas." *Social Text* 21 (3): 1–37.

——. 2010. *The Feeling of Kinship: Queer Liberalism and the Racialization of Intimacy*. Durham, NC: Duke University Press.

Eng, David L., Jack Halberstam, and José Muñoz. 2005. "What's Queer about Queer Studies Now?" *Social Text* 23 (3–4 (84–85)):1–17.

Eng, David L., and Shinhee Han. 2018. *Racial Melancholia, Racial Dissociation: On the Social and Psychic Lives of Asian Americans*. Durham, NC: Duke University Press.

Engels, Friedrich. (1884) 1978. "The Origin of the Family, Private Property, and the State." In *The Marx-Engels Reader*, 2nd ed., edited by Robert C. Tucker, 734–59. New York: W. W. Norton.

Enke, A. Finn. 2012. "The Education of Little Cis: Cisgender and the Discipline of Opposing Bodies." In *Transfeminist Perspectives in and beyond Transgender and Gender Studies*, edited by A. Finn Enke, 60–77. Philadelphia: Temple University Press.

Enloe, Cynthia. 1990. *Bananas, Beaches, and Bases: Making Feminist Sense of International Politics*. Berkeley: University of California Press.

Epstein, Adam. 2017. "Blood and Soil: The Meaning of the Nazi Slogan Chanted by White Nationalists in Charlottesville." *Quartz*, August 13, 2017. https://qz.com.

Erevelles, Nirmala. 2006. "Disability in the New World Order." In *Color of Violence: The INCITE! Anthology*, edited by INCITE! Women of Color Against Violence, 25–31. Cambridge, MA: South End.

——. 2014. "Crippin' Jim Crow: Disability, Dis-location, and the School-to-Prison Pipeline." In *Disability Incarcerated: Imprisonment and Disability in the United States and Canada*, edited by Liat Ben-Moshe, Chris Chapman, and Allison C. Carey, 81–100. New York: Palgrave Macmillan.

Escobar, Arturo. 1995. *Encountering Development: The Making and Unmaking of the Third World*. Princeton, NJ: Princeton University Press.

——. 2018. *Design for the Pluriverse: Radical Interdependence, Autonomy and the Making of Worlds*. Durham, NC: Duke University Press.

Escobar, Martha D. 2016. *Captivity beyond Prisons: Criminalization Experiences of Latina (Im)migrants*. Austin: University of Texas Press.

Espiritu, Yen Le. 2003. *Homebound: Filipino American Lives across Cultures, Communities, and Countries*. Berkeley: University of California Press.

Essig, Laurie. 2014. "Trigger Warnings Trigger Me." *Chronicle of Higher Education*, March 10, 2014. http://chronicle.com.

Estes, Nick. 2019. *Our History Is the Future: Standing Rock versus the Dakota Access Pipeline, and the Long Tradition of Indigenous Resistance*. Brooklyn: Verso.

Estes, Nick, and Jaskiran Dhillon. 2019. "Traditional Leadership and the Oceti Sakowin: An Interview with Lewis Grassrope." In *Standing with Standing Rock: Voices from the #NoDAPL Movement*, edited by Nick Estes and Jaskiran Dhillon, 24–36. Minneapolis: University of Minnesota Press.

Estrada, Gabriel S. 2011. "Two Spirits, Nádleeh, and LGBTQ2 Navajo Gaze." *American Indian Culture and Research Journal* 35 (4): 167–90.

Evans, Monica. 1993. "Stealing Away: Black Women, Outlaw Culture and the Rhetoric of Rights." *Harvard Civil Rights–Civil Liberties Law Review* 28 (2): 263.

Fabian, Johannes. 1983. *Time and the Other: How Anthropology Makes Its Object*. New York: Columbia University Press.

Fajardo, Kale. 2011. *Filipino Crosscurrents: Oceanographies of Seafaring, Masculinities, and Globalization*. Minneapolis: University of Minnesota Press.

Fanon, Frantz. (1952) 2008. *Black Skin, White Masks*. Translated by Richard Philcox. New York: Grove.

———. 1965. *A Dying Colonialism*. New York: Grove.

Farrow, Kenyon. 2016. "Beyond Tuskegee: A Case for a Racial Justice Agenda in Treatment and Research." Treatment Action Group. Accessed June 21, 2021. www.treatmentactiongroup.org.

Faulkner, Rita A. 1996. "Assia Djebar, Frantz Fanon, Women, Veils, and Land." *World Literature Today* 70 (4): 847–55.

Fausto-Sterling, Anne. 2000. *Sexing the Body: Gender Politics and the Construction of Sexuality*. New York: Basic Books.

———. 2012. *Sex/Gender: Biology in a Social World*. New York: Routledge.

Federici, Silvia. 1975. *Wages against Housework*. Bristol, UK: Power of Women Collective and the Falling Wall.

———. 2004. *Caliban and the Witch*. Brooklyn: Autonomedia.

———. 2016. "'Our Struggle Will Not Succeed Unless We Rebuild Society': Interview with Silvia Federici." By Alana Moraes and Maria A. C. Brant. *SUR: International Journal on Human Rights* 13 (24): 203–13.

Feimster, Crystal. 2009. *Southern Horrors: Women and the Politics of Rape and Lynching*. Cambridge, MA: Harvard University Press.

Feinberg, Leslie. 2013. "Transgender Liberation: A Movement Whose Time Has Come." In *The Transgender Studies Reader 2*, edited by Susan Stryker and Aren Z. Aizura, 221–36. New York: Routledge.

Ferguson, James. 1990. *The Anti-politics Machine: "Development," Depoliticization and Bureaucratic Power in Lesotho*. Cambridge: Cambridge University Press.

Ferguson, Roderick A. 2004. *Aberrations in Black: Toward a Queer of Color Critique*. Minneapolis: University of Minnesota Press.

———. 2005. "Of Our Normative Strivings: African American Studies and the History of Sexuality." *Social Text* 23 (3–4): 85–100.

———. 2012. *The Reorder of Things: The University and Its Pedagogies of Minority Difference*. Minneapolis: University of Minnesota Press.

———. 2019. *One Dimensional Queer*. Cambridge: Polity.

Fiereck, Kirk, Neville Hoad, and Danai S. Mupotsa, eds. 2020. "Time Out of Joint: The Queer and the Customary in Africa." Special issue, *GLQ: A Journal of Lesbian and Gay Studies* 26 (3).

Finley, Alexandra J. 2020. *An Intimate Economy: Enslaved Women, Work, and America's Domestic Slave Trade*. Chapel Hill: University of North Carolina Press.

Finney, Carolyn. 2014. *Black Faces, White Spaces: Reimagining the Relationship of African Americans to the Great Outdoors*. Chapel Hill: University of North Carolina Press.

Firmat, Mariana Ruiz. 2018. "Reproductive Health and Our Environment." In *Feminisms in Motion: Voices for Justice, Liberation, and Transformation*, edited by Jessica Hoffman and Daria Yudacufski, 207–16. Oakland, CA: AK.

Fischel, Joseph. 2016. "Transcendent Homosexuals and Dangerous Sex Offenders: Sexual Harm and Freedom in the Judicial Imaginary." *Duke Journal of Gender Law and Policy* 17:277–311.

———. 2019. *Screw Consent: Toward a Better Politics of Sexual Justice*. Oakland: University of California Press.

Fisher, Berenice, and Joan Tronto. 1990. "Toward a Feminist Theory of Caring." In *Circles of Care: Work and Identity in Women's Lives*, edited by Emily K. Abel and Margaret Nelson, 35–62. Albany: State University of New York Press.

Fisher, Simon. 2016. "Pauli Murray's Peter Panic: Perspectives from the Margins of Gender and Race in Jim Crow America." *TSQ: Transgender Studies Quarterly* 3 (1–2): 95–103.

———. 2019. "Challenging Dissemblance in Pauli Murray Historiography, Sketching a History of the Trans New Negro." *Journal of African American History* 104 (2): 176–200.

Fitzgerald, Stephanie J. 2015. *Native Women and Land: Narratives of Dispossession and Resurgence*. Albuquerque: University of New Mexico Press.

Flatley, Jonathan. 2008. *Affective Mapping: Melancholia and the Politics of Modernism*. Cambridge, MA: Harvard University Press.

Flores, Lisa A. 2020. *Deportable and Disposable: Public Rhetoric and the Making of the "Illegal" Immigrant*. State College: Penn State University Press.

Flores, William V., and Rina Benmayor, eds. 1997. *Latino Cultural Citizenship: Claiming Identity, Space, and Rights*. Boston: Beacon.

Floyd, Kevin. 2009. *The Reification of Desire: Toward a Queer Marxism*. Minneapolis: University of Minnesota Press.

Ford, Jesse, and Dennis Martinez. 2000. "Traditional Ecological Knowledge, Ecosystem Science, and Environmental Management." *Ecological Applications* 10 (5): 1249–50.

Fortunati, Leopoldina. 1981. *The Arcane of Reproduction: Housework, Prostitution, Labor and Capital*. Translated by Hilary Creek. Brooklyn: Autonomedia.

Foster, Hal, ed. 1998. *The Anti-aesthetic: Essays on Postmodern Culture*. New York: New Press.

Foster, Laura A. 2018. *Reinventing Hoodia: Peoples, Plants, and Patents in South Africa*. Seattle: University of Washington Press.

Foucault, Michel. (1978) 1990. *The History of Sexuality*. Vol. 1, *An Introduction*. New York: Vintage.

———. 2007. *Security, Territory, Population: Lectures at the College de France, 1977–1978*. Translated by Graham Burchell. Houndmills, UK: Palgrave.

Fraiman, Susan. 2003. *Cool Men and the Second Sex*. New York: Columbia University Press.

Francisco, Valerie. 2018. *The Labor of Care: Filipina Migrants and Transnational Families in the Digital Age*. Urbana: University of Illinois Press.

Franco, Jean. 2010. "Moving on from Subalternity: Indigenous Women in Guatemala and Mexico." In *Can the Subaltern Speak? Reflections on the History of an Idea*, edited by Rosalind C. Morris, 213–24. New York: Columbia University Press.

Frankenberg, Ruth. 1994. *White Women, Race Matters: The Social Construction of Whiteness*. Minneapolis: University of Minnesota Press.

Freccero, Carla. 2006. *Queer/Early/Modern*. Durham, NC: Duke University Press.

Freedman, Estelle. 2013. *Redefining Rape: Sexual Violence in the Era of Suffrage and Segregation*. Cambridge, MA: Harvard University Press.

Freeman, Carla. 2000. *High Tech and High Heels in the Global Economy: Women, Work, and Pink-Collar Identities in the Caribbean*. Durham, NC: Duke University Press.

Freeman, Elizabeth. 2010. *Time Binds: Queer Temporalities, Queer Histories*. Durham, NC: Duke University Press.

Fregoso, Rosa Linda, and Cynthia L. Bejarano, eds. 2010. *Terrorizing Women: Feminicide in the Américas*. Durham, NC: Duke University Press.

Freud, Sigmund. 1905. *Three Essays on Sexuality*. London: Hogarth.

Friedkin, William, dir. 1973. *The Exorcist*. Burbank, CA: Warner Bros. Pictures. DVD.

Frost, Samantha. 2016. *Biocultural Creatures: Toward a New Theory of the Human*. Durham, NC: Duke University Press.

Frye Jacobson, Matthew. 1999. *Whiteness of a Different Color: European Immigrants and the Alchemy of Race*. Cambridge, MA: Harvard University Press.

Fuechtner, Veronika, Douglas E. Haynes, and Ryan M. Jones, eds. 2017. *A Global History of Sexual Science, 1880–1960*. Berkeley: University of California Press.

Fujikane, Candace, and Jonathan Y. Okamura. 2008. *Asian Settler Colonialism: From Local Governance to the Habits of Everyday Life in Hawai'i*. Honolulu: University of Hawai'i Press.

Fujiwara, Lynn. 2008. *Mothers without Citizenship: Asian Immigrant Families and the Consequences of Welfare Reform*. Minneapolis: University of Minnesota Press.

Fung, Richard. 1991. "Looking for My Penis: The Eroticized Asian in Gay Porn." In *How Do I Look? Queer Film and Video*, edited by Bad Object-Choices, 145–68. Seattle: Bay Press.

Gaard, Greta. 1997. "Toward a Queer Ecofeminism." *Hypatia: A Journal of Feminist Philosophy* 12 (1): 114–37.

Gabaccia, Donna. 1994. *From the Other Side: Women, Gender, and Immigrant Life in the US, 1820–1990*. Bloomington: Indiana University Press.

Gagnon, John H., and William Simon. 1967. *Sexual Deviance*. New York: Harper & Row.

———. (1973) 2017. *Sexual Conduct: The Social Sources of Human Sexuality*. Reprint. New York: Routledge.

Gal, Susan. 2006. "Migration, Minorities, and Multilingualism: Language Ideologies in Europe." In *Language Ideologies, Policies and Practices: Language and the Future of Europe*, edited by Clare Mar-Molinero and Patrick Stevenson, 13–27. Basingstoke, UK: Palgrave.

Gall, Gregor. 2012. *An Agency of Their Own: Sex Worker Union Organizing*. Winchester, UK: Zero Books.

Galtung, Johan. 1969. "Violence, Peace, and Peace Research." *Journal of Peace Research* 6 (3): 167–91.

Gardner, Martha. 2009. *The Qualities of a Citizen: Women, Immigration, and Citizenship, 1870–1965*. Princeton, NJ: Princeton University Press.

Garland-Thomson, Rosemarie. 2002. "Integrating Disability, Transforming Feminist Theory." *NWSA Journal* 14 (3): 1–32.

———. 2005. "Feminist Disability Studies." *Signs: Journal of Women in Culture and Society* 30 (2): 1557–87.

Garrido, Mike, and Tarek Tohme. 2009. "As They Are: Two Spirit People in the Modern World." Indigenous Wellness Research Institute, April 6, 2012. YouTube video, 18:18. www.youtube.com/watch?v=AYGxZL870ZE.

Gauch, Suzanne. 2002. "Fanon on the Surface." *Parallax* 8 (2): 116–28.

Gay, Roxane. 2018. *Hunger: A Memoir of (My) Body*. New York: Harper Perennial.

Genovese, Eugene. 2011. *Roll, Jordan, Roll: The World the Slaves Made*. New York: Vintage.

George, Rosemary Marangoly. 1998. "Recycling: Long Routes to and from Domestic Fixes." In *Burning Down the House: Recycling Domesticity*, 1–20. Boulder, CO: Westview.

Georgelou, Konstantina. 2014. "Abjection and *Informe*: Operations of Debasing." *Performance Research: A Journal of the Performing Arts* 19 (1): 25–32.

Germon, Jennifer. 2009. *Gender: A Genealogy of an Idea*. New York: Palgrave.

Gershenson, Olga. 2010. "The Restroom Revolution: Unisex Toilets and Campus Politics." In *Toilet: Public Restrooms and the Politics of Sharing*, edited by Harvey Molotch and Laura Noren, 191–207. New York: New York University Press.

Ghaziani, Amin, and Matt Brim. 2019. "Queer Methods: Four Provocations for an Emerging Field." In *Imagining Queer Methods*, edited by Amin Ghaziani and Matt Brim, 3–27. New York: New York University Press.

Gibbs, Lindsay. 2016. "Why Women Don't Play Best of Five Matches at Grand Slams." Think Progress, May 27, 2016. https://archive.thinkprogress.org.

Gilio-Whitaker, Dina. 2015. "Idle No More and Fourth World Social Movements in the New Millennium." *South Atlantic Quarterly* 114 (14): 866–77.

Gill, Lyndon. 2018. *Erotic Islands: Art and Activism in the Queer Caribbean*. Durham, NC: Duke University Press.

Gilliard, Dominique DuBois. 2018. *Rethinking Incarceration: Advocating for Justice That Restores*. Downers Grove, IL: InterVarsity.

Gilligan, Carol. 1982. *In a Different Voice: Psychological Theory and Women's Development*. Cambridge, MA: Harvard University Press.

Gill-Peterson, Julian. 2018. *Histories of the Transgender Child*. Minneapolis: University of Minnesota Press.

Gilmore, Ruth Wilson. 2007. *Golden Gulag: Prisons, Surplus, Crisis, and Opposition in Globalizing California*. Oakland: University of California Press.

———. 2017. "Abolition Geography and the Problem of Innocence." In *Futures of Black Radicalism*, edited by Gaye Theresa Johnson and Alex Lubin, 225–40. Brooklyn: Verso.

———. 2021. *Change Everything: Racial Capitalism and the Case for Abolition*. Chicago: Haymarket.

Gilroy, Paul. 1993. *The Black Atlantic: Modernity and Double Consciousness*. Cambridge, MA: Harvard University Press.

Ginsburg, Faye, and Rayna Rapp. 1991. "The Politics of Reproduction." *Annual Review of Anthropology* 20 (1): 311–43.

Glazer, Sarah. 2016. "Pornography: Does It Pose a Public Health Crisis?" *CQ Researcher* 26 (37): 865–88.

Gleeson, Jules Joanne. 2017. "Transition and Abolition: Notes on Marxism and Trans Politics." *Viewpoint*, July 19, 2017. www.viewpointmag.com.

Glickman, Charlie, and Aislinn Emirzian. 2013. *The Ultimate Guide to Prostate Pleasure*. Minneapolis: Cleis.

Glissant, Edouard. 1989. *Caribbean Discourse: Selected Essays*. Charlottesville: University of Virginia Press.

———. 1990. *Poetics of Relation*. Ann Arbor: University of Michigan Press.

Glymph, Thavolia. 2008. *Out of the House of Bondage: The Transformation of the Plantation Household*. New York: Cambridge University Press.

Goeman, Mishuana. 2008. "From Place to Territories and Back Again: Centering Storied Land in the Discussion of Indigenous Nation-Building." *International Journal of Critical Indigenous Studies* 1 (1): 23–38.

———. 2009. "Notes toward a Native Feminism's Spatial Practice." *Wicazo Sa Review* 24 (2): 169–87.

———. 2013. *Mark My Words: Native Women Mapping Our Nations*. Minneapolis: University of Minnesota Press.

Goffman, Erving. 1963. *Stigma: Notes on the Management of Spoiled Identity*. New York: Simon & Schuster.

Gold, Roberta. 2014. *When Tenants Claimed the City: The Struggle for Citizenship in New York City Housing*. Urbana: University of Illinois Press.

Goldberg, Jonathan. 2010. *Sodometries: Renaissance Texts, Modern Sexualities*. New York: Fordham University Press.

Goldberg, RL. 2020. "Staging Pedagogy in Trans Masculine Porn." *TSQ: Transgender Studies Quarterly* 7 (2): 208–21.

Gonick, Marnina. 2006. "Between 'Girl Power' and 'Reviving Ophelia': Constituting the Neoliberal Girl Subject." *NWSA Journal* 18 (2): 1–23.

Goode, Erich. (1978) 2016. *Deviant Behavior*. New York: Routledge.

Goodley, Dan. 2014. *Dis/ability Studies: Theorising Disablism and Ableism*. New York: Routledge.

Goodwin, Michele. 2020. *Policing the Womb: Invisible Women and the Criminalization of Motherhood*. Cambridge: Cambridge University Press.

Gopinath, Gayatri. 2005. *Impossible Desires: Queer Diasporas and South Asian Public Cultures*. Durham, NC: Duke University Press.

———. 2018. *Unruly Visions: The Aesthetic Practices of Queer Diaspora*. Durham, NC: Duke University Press.

Gordon, Aaron. 2017. "Finally, the Olympics Will Let Women Swim 1,500 Meters." Vice, June 9, 2017. www.vice.com.

Gordon, Lewis R. 2015. *What Fanon Said: A Philosophical Introduction to His Life and Thought*. New York: Fordham University Press.

Gordon, Linda. 2002. *The Moral Property of Women: A History of Birth Control Politics in America*. Champaign: University of Illinois Press.

Gore, Dayo F. 2011. *Radicalism at the Crossroads: African American Women Activists in the Cold War*. New York: New York University Press.

Gorely, Trish, Rachel Holroyd, and David Kirk. 2003. "Muscularity, the Habitus and the Social Construction of Gender: Towards a Gender-Relevant Physical Education." *British Journal of Sociology of Education* 24 (4): 429–48.

Gorfinkel, Elena. 2017. *Lewd Looks: American Sexploitation Cinema in the 1960s*. Minneapolis: University of Minnesota Press.

Gossett, Che. 2012. "We Will Not Rest in Peace: AIDS Activism, Black Radicalism, Queer and/or Trans Resistance." In *Queer Necropolitics*, edited by Jin Haritaworn, Adi Kuntsman, and Silvia Posocco, 31–50. New York: Routledge.

Gottschalk, Marie. 2006. *The Prison and the Gallows: The Politics of Mass Incarceration in America*. New York: Cambridge University Press.

Gould, Jon B., and Richard A. Leo. 2010. "One Hundred Years Later: Wrongful Convictions after a Century of Research." *Journal of Criminal Law and Criminology* 100 (3): 825–68.

Gramling, David. 2016. *The Invention of Monolingualism*. New York: Bloomsbury.

Gramsci, Antonio. 1978. "Some Aspects of the Southern Question." In *Selections from Political Writings (1921–1926)*, translated by Quintin Hoare, 421–62. New York: International.

Grande, Sandy. 2018. "Aging, Precarity, and the Struggle for Indigenous Elsewheres." *International Journal of Qualitative Studies in Education* 31 (3): 168–76.

Grandin, Greg. 2019. *The End of the Myth: From the Frontier to the Border Wall in the Mind of America*. New York: Metropolitan.

Gray, John. 1992. *Men Are from Mars, Women Are from Venus*. New York: HarperCollins.

Gray White, Deborah. 1999. *Ar'n't I a Woman? Female Slaves in the Plantation South*. New York: W. W. Norton.

Green, Kai M. 2016. "Troubling the Waters: Mobilizing a Trans* Analytic." In *No Tea, No Shade: New Writings in Black Queer Studies*, edited by E. Patrick Johnson, 65–82. Durham, NC: Duke University Press.

Green, Marcus. 2002. "Gramsci Cannot Speak: Presentations and Interpretations of Gramsci's Concept of the Subaltern." *Rethinking Marxism* 14 (3): 1–24.

Green, Venus. 2001. *Race on the Line: Gender, Labor, and Technology in the Bell System, 1880–1980*. Durham, NC: Duke University Press.

Grewal, Inderpal. 1997. *Home and Harem: Nation, Gender, Empire, and the Culture of Travel*. Durham, NC: Duke University Press.

———. 2005. *Transnational America: Feminisms, Diasporas, Neoliberalisms*. Durham, NC: Duke University Press.

———. 2013. "Outsourcing Patriarchy: Feminist Encounters, Transnational Mediations, and the Crime of 'Honor Killings.'" *International Feminist Journal of Politics* 15 (1): 1–19.

Grewal, Inderpal, and Caren Kaplan. 1994. *Scattered Hegemonies: Postmodernity and Transnational Feminist Practices*. Minneapolis: University of Minnesota Press.

———. 1996. "Warrior Marks: Global Womanism's Neocolonial Discourse in a Multicultural Context." *Camera Obscura: Feminism, Culture, and Media Studies* 13 (3 (39)): 4–33.

Griffin, Farah Jasmine. 2013. *Harlem Nocturne: Women Artists and Progressive Politics during World War II*. New York: Basic Books. Kindle.

Griffin, Pat. 2011. *Strong Women, Deep Closets: Lesbians and Homophobia in Sports*. Champaign, IL: Human Kinetics.

Griffith, Marie. 1997. *God's Daughters: Evangelical Women and the Power of Submission*. Berkeley: University of California Press.

Grignon, Jeff, and Robin Wall Kimmerer. 2017. "Listening to the Forest." In *Wildness: Relations of People and Place*, edited by Gavin Van Horn and John Hausdoerffer, 67–74. Chicago: University of Chicago Press.

Gross, Kali. 2006. *Colored Amazons: Crime, Violence, and Black Women in the City of Brotherly Love, 1880–1910*. Durham, NC: Duke University Press.

Grosz, Elizabeth. 1994. *Volatile Bodies: Toward a Corporeal Feminism*. Bloomington: Indiana University Press.

Gruber, Aya. 2020. *The Feminist War on Crime: The Unexpected Role of Women's Liberation in Mass Incarceration*. Berkeley: University of California Press.

Guenther, Lisa. 2019. "Critical Phenomenology." In *50 Concepts for a Critical Phenomenology*, edited by Gail Weiss, Ann V. Murphy, and Gayle Salamon, 11–16. Evanston, IL: Northwestern University Press.

Guha, Ranajit. 1987. "Chandra's Death." In *Subaltern Studies V*, edited by Ranajit Guha, 135–65. New Delhi: Oxford University Press.

———. 1988. "On Some Aspects of the Historiography of Colonial India." In *Selected Subaltern Studies*, edited by Ranajit

Guha and Gayatri Chakravorty Spivak, 37–44. Oxford: Oxford University Press.

Gumbs, Alexis Pauline. 2010. "We Can Learn to Mother Ourselves: The Queer Survival of Black Feminism 1968–1996." PhD diss., Duke University.

Gumbs, Alexis Pauline, China Martens, and Mai'a Williams. 2017. *Revolutionary Mothering: Love on the Front Lines*. Oakland, CA: PM Press. www.pmpress.org.

Gupta, Akhil. 1998. *Postcolonial Developments: Agriculture in the Making of Modern India*. Durham, NC: Duke University Press.

Gutiérrez, Elena. 2008. *Fertile Matters: The Politics of Mexican-Origin Women's Reproduction*. Austin: University of Texas Press.

Haag, Pamela. 1999. *Consent: Sexual Rights and the Transformation of American Liberalism*. Ithaca, NY: Cornell University Press.

Haddour, Azzedine. 2010. "Torture Unveiled: Rereading Fanon and Bourdieu in the Context of May 1958." *Theory, Culture & Society* 27 (7–8): 66–90.

Haga, Kazu. 2020. *Healing Resistance: A Radically Different Response to Harm*. Berkeley, CA: Parallax.

Halberstam, Jack. 1997. "Who's Afraid of Queer Theory?" In *Class Issues: Pedagogy, Cultural Studies, and the Public Sphere*, edited by Amitava Kumar, 256–74. New York: New York University Press.

———. 2005. *In a Queer Time and Place: Transgender Bodies, Subcultural Lives*. New York: New York University Press.

———. 2011. *The Queer Art of Failure*. Durham, NC: Duke University Press.

———. 2012. *Gaga Feminism: Sex, Gender, and the End of Normal*. Boston: Beacon.

Hale, Charles. 2006. "Activist Research v. Cultural Critique: Indigenous Land Rights and the Contradictions of Politically Engaged Anthropology." *Cultural Anthropology* 21 (1): 96–120.

Haley, Sarah. 2016. *No Mercy Here: Gender, Punishment, and the Making of Jim Crow Modernity*. Chapel Hill: University of North Carolina Press.

Hall, Kim Q. 2011. *Feminist Disability Studies*. Bloomington: Indiana University Press.

Hall, Lisa Kahaleole. 2009. "Navigating Our Own 'Sea of Islands': Remapping a Theoretical Space for Hawaiian Women and Indigenous Feminism." *Wicazo Sa Review* 24 (2): 15–38.

Hall, Stuart. (1978) 2017. "1970: The Birth of Law and Order Society." In *Selected Political Writings: The Great Moving Right Show and Other Essays*, edited by Sally Davidson, David Featherstone, Michael Rustin, and Bill Schwarz, 158–72. Durham, NC: Duke University Press.

———. (1984) 2017. "The State: Socialism's Old Caretaker." In *Selected Political Writings: The Great Moving Right Show and Other Essays*, edited by Sally Davidson, David Featherstone, Michael Rustin, and Bill Schwarz, 223–37. Durham, NC: Duke University Press.

———. 1990. "Cultural Identity and Diaspora." In *Identity: Community, Culture, Difference*, edited by Jonathan Rutherford, 222–37. London: Lawrence & Wishart.

———. (1990) 2017. "The First New Left: Life and Times." In *Selected Political Writings: The Great Moving Right Show and Other Essays*, edited by Sally Davidson, David Featherstone, Michael Rustin, and Bill Schwarz, 117–41. Durham, NC: Duke University Press.

———. 2016. *Cultural Studies 1983: A Theoretical History*. Durham, NC: Duke University Press.

Halley, Janet. 2016. "The Move to Affirmative Consent." *Signs: Journal of Women in Culture and Society* 42 (1): 257–79.

Halperin, David M. 1989. "Is There a History of Sexuality?" *History and Theory* 28 (3): 257–74.

———. 2007. *What Do Gay Men Want? An Essay on Sex, Risk, and Subjectivity*. Ann Arbor: University of Michigan Press.

Hammami, Rema. 2019. "Follow the Numbers: Global Governmentality and the Violence against Women Agenda in Palestine." In *Governance Feminism: Notes from the Field*, edited by Janet Halley, Prabha Kotiswaran, and Rachel Rebouché, and Hila Shamir, 479–503. Minneapolis: University of Minnesota Press.

Hammonds, Evelynn. 2004. "Black (W)holes and the Geometry of Black Female Sexuality." In *The Black Studies Reader*, edited by Jacqueline Bobo, Cynthia Hudley, and Claudine Michel, 313–26. New York: Routledge.

Hanhardt, Christina B. 2013. *Safe Space: Gay Neighborhood History and the Politics of Violence*. Durham, NC: Duke University Press.

Hanhardt, Christina B., Jasbir Puar, Neel Ahuja, Paul Amar, Aniruddha Dutta, Fatima El-Tayeb, Kwame Holmes, and Sherene Seikaly. 2020. "Beyond Trigger Warnings: Safety, Securitization, and Queer Left Critique." *Social Text* 38 (4): 49–76.

Hansberry, Lorraine. 2001. "Your Play Is Performed." In *Lorraine Hansberry Audio Collection: A Raisin in the Sun, to Be Young Gifted and Black, and Lorraine Hansberry Speaks Out*. Read by Ruby Dee and James Earl Jones. New York: Caedmon Records.

Haraway, Donna. (1985) 1991. "A Cyborg Manifesto: Science, Technology, and Socialist-Feminism in the Late Twentieth

Century." In *Simians, Cyborgs and Women: The Reinvention of Nature*, 149–81. New York: Routledge.

———. 1988. "Situated Knowledges: The Science Question in Feminism and the Privilege of Partial Perspectives." *Feminist Studies* 14:575–99.

———. 1991. *Simians, Cyborgs, and Women: The Reinvention of Nature*. New York: Routledge.

———. 2003. *The Companion Species Manifesto: Dogs, People, and Significant Otherness*. Chicago: Prickly Paradigm.

———. 2016. *Staying with the Trouble: Making Kin in the Chthulucene*. Durham, NC: Duke University Press.

Harchuck, Kimberly A. 2015. "Pornography and the First Amendment Right to Free Speech." In *New Views on Pornography: Sexuality, Politics, and the Law*, edited by Lynn Comella and Shira Tarrant, 9–36. Santa Barbara, CA: Praeger.

Harding, Sandra G. 2005. "Rethinking Standpoint Epistemology: What Is 'Strong Objectivity'?" In *Feminist Theory: A Philosophical Anthology*, edited Ann E. Cudd and Robin O. Andreased, 218–36. Oxford: Blackwell.

———. 2008. *Sciences from Below: Feminisms, Postcolonialisms, and Modernities*. Durham, NC: Duke University Press.

Hardy, Kate. 2013. "Equal to Any Other, but Not the Same as Any Other: The Politics of Sexual Labour, the Body, and Intercorporeality." In *Body/Sex/Work: Intimate, Embodied and Sexualized Labour*, edited by Carol Wolkowitz, Rachel Laura Cohen, Teela Sanders, and Kate Hardy, 43–58. Hampshire, UK: Palgrave Macmillan.

Hardy, Kate, and Meghan Rivers-Moore. 2018. "Compañeras de La Calle: Sex Worker Organising in Latin America." *Moving the Social: Journal of Social History and the History of Social Movements* 59:97–113.

Haritaworn, Jin, Adi Kuntsman, and Silvia Posocco. 2013. "Murderous Inclusions." *International Feminist Journal of Politics* 15 (4): 445–52.

Harjo, Joy. 1983. "Remember." In *She Had Some Horses*, 40. New York: W. W. Norton.

Harjo, Laura, Jenell Navarro, and Kimberly Robertson. 2018. "Leading with Our Hearts: Anti-violence Action and Beadwork Circles as Colonial Resistance." In *Keetsahnak / Our Missing and Murdered Indigenous Sisters*, edited by Kim Anderson, Maria Campbell, and Christi Belcourt, 279–303. Edmonton, Canada: University of Alberta Press.

Harper, Phillip Brian. 2005. "The Evidence of Felt Intuition: Minority Experience, Everyday Life, and Critical Speculative Knowledge." In *Black Queer Studies: A Critical Anthology*, edited by E. Patrick Johnson and Mae G. Henderson, 106–23. Durham, NC: Duke University Press.

Harris, Anita. 2004. *Future Girl: Young Women in the Twenty-First Century*. New York: Routledge.

Harris, Cheryl. 1993. "Whiteness as Property." *Harvard Law Review* 106 (8): 1707–91.

Harris, LaShawn. 2016. *Sex Workers, Psychics, and Numbers Runners: Black Women in New York City's Underground Economy*. Urbana: University of Illinois Press.

Hartman, Saidiya. 1997. *Scenes of Subjection: Terror, Slavery, and Self-Making in Nineteenth-Century America*. New York: Oxford University Press.

———. 2008a. *Lose Your Mother: A Journey along the Atlantic Slave Route*. New York: Macmillan.

———. 2008b. "Venus in Two Acts." *Small Axe* 12 (2): 1–14.

———. 2016. "The Belly of the World: A Note on Black Women's Labors." *Souls: A Critical Journal of Black Politics, Culture and Society* 18 (1): 166–73.

———. 2019. *Wayward Lives, Beautiful Experiments*. New York: W. W. Norton.

Hartman, Saidiya, and Frank B. Wilderson III. 2003. "The Position of the Unthought." *Qui Parle* 13 (2): 183–201.

Hartsock, Nancy. (1983) 2004. "The Feminist Standpoint: Developing the Ground for a Specifically Feminist Historical Materialism." In *The Feminist Standpoint Theory Reader: Intellectual and Political Controversies*, edited by Sandra Harding and Merrill B. Hintikka, 35–54. New York: Routledge.

Haskins, Victoria, and Anne Scrimgeour. 2015. "'Strike Strike, We Strike': Making Aboriginal Domestic Labor Visible in the Pilbara Pastoral Workers' Strike, Western Australia, 1946–1952." *International Labor and Working-Class History* 88:87–108. https://doi.org/10.1017/S0147547915000228.

Hatewatch Staff. 2017. "Flags and Other Symbols Used by Far-Right Groups at Charlottesville." Southern Poverty Law Center, August 12, 2017. www.splcenter.org.

Haworth, Abigail. 2016. "Forced to Be Fat." *Marie Claire*, April 19, 2016. www.marieclaire.com.

Hawthorne, Camilla. 2019. "Black Matters Are Spatial Matters: Black Geographies for the Twenty-First Century." *Geography Compass* 13 (11): 1–13.

Hayward, Eva, and Jami Weinstein. 2015. "Introduction: Tranimalities in the Age of Trans* Life." *TSQ: Transgender Studies Quarterly* 2 (2): 195–208.

Heffernan, Kevin. 2015. "Seen as a Business: Adult Film's Historical Framework and Foundations." In *New Views on Pornography: Sexuality, Politics, and the Law*, edited by Lynn Comella and Shira Tarrant, 37–56. Santa Barbara, CA: Praeger.

Heins, Marjorie. 1993. *Sex, Sin and Blasphemy: A Guide to America's Censorship Wars*. New York: New Press.

Helmreich, Stefan. 1992. "Kinship, Nation, and Paul Gilroy's Concept of Diaspora." *Diaspora: A Journal of Transnational Studies* 2 (2): 243–49.

Henderson, Lisa. 1999. "Lesbian Pornography: Cultural Transgression and Sexual Demystification." In *The Columbia Reader on Lesbians and Gay Men in Media, Society and Politics*, edited by Larry Gross and James D. Wood, 506–17. New York: Columbia University Press.

Hennefeld, Maggie, and Nocholas Sammond, eds. 2020. *Abjection Incorporated: Mediating the Politics of Pleasure and Violence*. Durham, NC: Duke University Press.

Hennessy, Rosemary. 2000. *Profit and Pleasure: Sexual Identities in Late Capitalism*. New York: Routledge.

———. 2006. "Returning to Reproduction Queerly: Sex, Labor, Need." *Rethinking Marxism* 18 (3): 387–95.

Hennie, Matt. 2015. "Friends Mourn Death of Trans Atlanta Activist." Project Q, July 17, 2015. www.projectq.us.

Henningsen, Kadin. 2019. "Cis, or Cisgender." In *Global Encyclopedia of Lesbian, Gay, Bisexual, Transgender, and Queer (LGBTQ) History*, edited by Howard Chiang, 357–63. Farmington Hills, MI: Charles Scribner's Sons.

Hernández, Kelly Lytle, Khalil Gibran Muhammad, and Heather Ann Thompson. 2015. "Introduction: Constructing the Carceral State." In "Historians and the Carceral State." Special issue, *Journal of American History* 102, no. 1 (June): 18–24.

Herring, Scott. 2010. *Another Country: Queer Anti-urbanism*. New York: New York University Press.

Herzig, Rebecca. 2015. *Plucked: A History of Hair Removal*. New York: New York University Press.

Herzog, Dagmar. 2011. *Sexuality in Europe: A Twentieth Century History*. Cambridge: Cambridge University Press.

Hicks, Cheryl D. 2010. *Talk with You like a Woman: African American Women, Justice, and Reform in New York, 1890–1935*. Chapel Hill: University of North Carolina Press.

Hidayatullah, Aysha A., and Judith Plaskow. 2011. "Beyond Sarah and Hagar: Jewish and Muslim Reflections on Feminist Theology." In *Muslims and Jews in America: Commonalities, Contentions, and Complexities*, edited by Reza Aslan and Aaron Hahn Tapper, 159–72. New York: Palgrave McMillan.

Higginbotham, Evelynn Brooks. 1993. *Righteous Discontent: The Women's Movement in the Black Baptist Church, 1880–1920*. Cambridge, MA: Harvard University Press.

———, ed. 2001. *The Harvard Guide to African American History*. Edited by Evelynn Brooks Higginbotham. Cambridge, MA: Harvard University Press.

Hill, Susan. 2017. *The Clay We Are Made Of: Haudenosaunee Land Tenure on the Grand River*. Winnipeg: University of Manitoba Press.

Hill-Meyer, Tobi. 2013. "Where the Trans Women Aren't: The Slow Inclusion of Trans Women in Feminist and Queer Porn." In *The Feminist Porn Book: The Politics of Producing Pleasure*, edited by Tristan Taormino, Celine Parreñas Shimizu, Constance Penley, and Mireille Miller-Young, 155–63. New York: Feminist Press.

Hinton, Elizabeth. 2016. *From the War on Poverty to the War on Crime: The Making of Mass Incarceration in America*. Cambridge, MA: Harvard University Press.

Hirsch, Marianne. 2012. *The Generation of Postmemory: Writing and Visual Culture after the Holocaust*. New York: Columbia University Press.

Hirschberg, Claire E. 2015. "'A Village Can't Be Built in a Jail' Carceral Humanism and Ethics of Care in Gender Responsive Incarceration." Senior thesis, Scripps College. *Scripps Senior Theses* (655). https://scholarship.claremont.edu.

Hirschkind, Charles, and Saba Mahmood. 2002. "Feminism, the Taliban, and the Politics of Counter-insurgency." *Anthropological Quarterly* 75 (2): 339–54.

Hoang, Kimberly. 2015. *Dealing in Desire: Asian Ascendancy, Western Decline, and the Hidden Currencies of Global Sex Work*. Berkeley: University of California Press.

Hobson, Emily. 2016. *Lavender and Red: Liberation and Solidarity in the Gay and Lesbian Left*. Berkeley: University of California Press.

Hochberg, Gil Z. 2015. *Visual Occupations: Violence and Visibility in a Conflict Zone*. Durham, NC: Duke University Press.

Hochschild, Arlie Russell. 2000. "Global Care Chains and Emotional Surplus Value." In *On the Edge: Living with Global Capitalism*, edited by Will Hutton and Anthony Giddens, 130–46. London: Jonathan Cape.

Hocquenghem, Guy. (1972) 1993. *Homosexual Desire*. Durham, NC: Duke University Press.

Hogan, Linda. 1996. *Dwellings: A Spiritual History of the Living World*. New York: Simon & Schuster.

———. 2018. "The Radiant Life with Animals." In *Traditional Ecological Knowledge: Learning from Indigenous Practices for Environmental Sustainability*, edited by Melissa K. Nelson and Daniel Shilling, 188–212. Cambridge: Cambridge University Press.

Holland, Sharon. 2000. *Raising the Dead: Reading of Death and (Black) Subjectivity*. Durham, NC: Duke University Press.

Hollibaugh, Amber. 1984. "Desire for the Future: Radical Hope in Passion and Pleasure." In *Pleasure and Danger: Exploring Female Sexuality*, edited by Carole S. Vance, 401–11. Boston: Routledge & Kegan Paul.

Hondagneu-Sotelo, Pierrette. 1999. "Introduction: Gender and Contemporary US Immigration." *American Behavioral Scientist* 42 (4): 565–76.

———. (2001) 2007. *Doméstica: Immigrant Workers Cleaning and Caring in the Shadows of Affluence*. Berkeley: University of California Press.

Hong, Grace Kyungwon. 2006. *The Ruptures of American Capital: Women of Color Feminism and the Culture of Immigrant Labor*. Minneapolis: University of Minnesota Press.

———. 2008. "'The Future of Our Worlds': Black Feminism and the Politics of Knowledge in the University under Globalization." *Meridians: Feminism, Race, Transnationalism* 8 (2): 95–115.

Honig, Bonnie. 2001. *Democracy and the Foreigner*. Princeton, NJ: Princeton University Press.

hooks, bell. 1989. *Talking Back: Thinking Feminist, Thinking Black*. Boston: South End.

Horton-Stallings, LaMonda. 2015. *Funk the Erotic: Transaesthetics and Black Sexual Cultures*. Urbana: University of Illinois Press.

Hoskin, Rhea Ashley. 2019. "Can Femme Be Theory? Exploring the Epistemological and Methodological Possibilities of Femme." *Journal of Lesbian Studies* 25 (1): 1–17.

Houlbrook, Matt. 2006. *Queer London: Perils and Pleasures in the Sexual Metropolis, 1918–1957*. Chicago: University of Chicago Press.

Houston, Shine Louise. 2014. "Mighty Real." *In Porn after Porn: Contemporary Alternative Pornographies*, edited by Enrico Biasin, Giovanna Maina, and Federico Zecca, 117–20. Milan: Mimesis International.

Hua, Julietta. 2011. *Trafficking Women's Human Rights*. Minneapolis: University of Minnesota Press.

Hull, Gloria T. Akasha, Patricia Bell Scott, and Barbara Smith, eds. (1982) 2015. *All the Women Are White, All the Blacks Are Men, but Some of Us Are Brave: Black Women's Studies*. Old Westbury, NY: Feminist Press.

Hunt, Sarah. 2014. "Ontologies of Indigeneity: The Politics of Embodying a Concept." *Cultural Geographies* 21:27–32.

———. 2015. "Violence, Law, and the Everyday Politics of Recognition." Paper presented to the Native American and Indigenous Studies Association (NAISA), Washington, DC.

Hunt, Sarah, and Cindy Holmes. 2015. "Everyday Decolonization: Living a Decolonizing Queer Politics." *Journal of Lesbian Studies* 19 (2): 154–72.

Hunter, Tera. 1997. *To 'Joy My Freedom: Southern Black Women's Lives and Labors after the Civil War*. Cambridge, MA: Harvard University Press.

———. 2017. *Bound in Wedlock: Slave and Free Black Marriage in the Nineteenth Century*. Cambridge, MA: Harvard University Press.

Hurston, Zora Neale. 1935. *Mules and Men*. Philadelphia: J. B. Lippincott.

Hurtado, Aida. 2003. "Theory in the Flesh: Toward an Endarkened Epistemology." *International Journal of Qualitative Studies in Education* 16 (2): 215–25.

Ibarra, Xandra. n.d. "About." Accessed June 15, 2021. www.xandraibarra.com.

Ignatiev, Noel. 1995. *How the Irish Became White*. New York: Routledge.

Igoe, Jim. 2004. *Conservation and Globalization: A Study of the National Parks and Indigenous Communities from East Africa to South Dakota*. Boston: Cengage Learning.

INCITE!, ed. 2006. *Color of Violence: The INCITE! Anthology*. Cambridge, MA: South End.

INCITE! Women of Color Against Violence. 2008. "Statement on Gender Violence and the Prison-Industrial Complex." INCITE! Accessed July 25, 2021. https://incite-national.org/incite-critical-resistance-statement/.

Innes, Robert Alexander. 2013. *Elder Brother and the Law of the People: Contemporary Kinship and Cowessess First Nation*. Winnipeg: University of Manitoba Press.

International Labor Organization (ILO). n.d. "C169—Indigenous and Tribal Peoples Convention, 1989 (No. 169)." Accessed June 25, 2021. https://ilo.org.

Intersex Society of North America (ISNA). n.d. "What's the History behind the Intersex Rights Movement?" Accessed April 1, 2020. https://isna.org.

Irigaray, Luce. (1977) 1985. *The Sex Which Is Not One*. Ithaca, NY: Cornell University Press.

———. 1993. *An Ethics of Sexual Difference*. Translated by Gillian C. Gill. Ithaca, NY: Cornell University Press.

Islam, Md Saidul, and Md Ismail Hossain. 2015. *Social Justice in the Globalization of Production*. London: Palgrave Macmillan.

Ivy, Nicole. 2016. "Bodies of Work: A Meditation on Medical Imaginaries and Enslaved Women." *Souls: A Critical Journal of Black Politics, Culture and Society* 18 (1): 11–31.

Jackson, Sarah J., Moya Bailey, and Brooke Foucault Welles. 2020. *#HashtagActivism*. Cambridge, MA: MIT Press.

Jackson, Shona. 2012. *Creole Indigeneity: Between Myth and Nation in the Caribbean*. Minneapolis: University of Minnesota Press.

Jackson, Zakiyyah Iman. 2020. *Becoming Human: Matter and Meaning in an Antiblack World*. New York: New York University Press.

Jacobs, Harriet Ann. (1861) 2009. *Incidents in the Life of a Slave Girl: Written by Herself*. Cambridge, MA: Harvard University Press.

Jacobs, Katrien. 2007. *Netporn: DIY Web Culture and Sexual Politics*. Lanham, MD: Rowman & Littlefield.

Jacobs, Margaret. 1999. *Engendered Encounters: Feminism and Pueblo Cultures, 1879–1934*. Lincoln: University of Nebraska Press.

———. 2007. "Working on the Domestic Frontier: American Indian Domestic Servants in White Women's Households in the San Francisco Bay Area, 1920–1940." *Frontiers: A Journal of Women Studies* 28 (1–2): 165–99.

———. 2009. *White Mother to a Dark Race: Settler Colonialism, Maternalism, and the Removal of Indigenous Children in the American West and Australia, 1880–1940*. Lincoln: University of Nebraska Press.

Jacobs, Sue-Ellen, Wesley Thomas, and Sabine Lang. 1997. *Two-Spirit People: Native American Gender Identity, Sexuality, and Spirituality*. Urbana: University of Illinois Press.

Jagose, Annamarie. 1996. *Queer Theory: An Introduction*. New York: New York University Press.

Jaimes Guerrero, Marie Anna. 1997. "Civil Rights versus Sovereignty: Native American Women in Life and Land Struggles." In *Feminist Genealogies, Colonial Legacies, Democratic Futures*, edited by M. Jacqui Alexander and Chandra Talpade Mohanty, 101–21. New York: Routledge.

Jain, Sarah Lochlann. 2007. "Living in Prognosis: Toward an Elegiac Politics." *Representations* 98 (1): 77–92.

Jakobsen, Janet R. 1998. "Queer Is? Queer Does? Normativity and the Problem of Resistance." *GLQ: A Journal of Lesbian and Gay Studies* 4 (4): 511–36.

Jaleel, Rana. 2013. "Weapons of Sex, Weapons of War: Feminisms, Ethnic Conflict and the Rise of Rape and Sexual Violence in Public International Law during the 1990s." *Cultural Studies* 27 (1): 115–35.

Jamal, Amina. 2013. *Jamaat-e-Islami Women in Pakistan: Vanguard of a New Modernity?* Syracuse, NY: Syracuse University Press.

Jeffreys, Sheila. 2009. *The Industrial Vagina: The Political Economy of the Global Sex Trade*. London: Routledge.

Johnson, E. Patrick. 2001. "'Quare' Studies, or (Almost) Everything I Know about Queer Studies I Learned from My Grandmother." *Text and Performance Quarterly* 21 (1): 1–25.

———. 2003. *Appropriating Blackness: Performance and the Politics of Authenticity*. Durham, NC: Duke University Press.

———. 2018. *Black. Queer. Southern. Women: An Oral History*. Chapel Hill: University of North Carolina Press.

Johnson, Walter. 1999. *Soul by Soul: Life inside the Antebellum Slave Market*. Cambridge, MA: Harvard University Press.

———. 2003. "On Agency." *Journal of Social History* 37 (1): 113–24.

———. 2013. *River of Dark Dreams: Slavery and Empire in the Cotton Kingdom*. Cambridge, MA: Belknap Press of Harvard University Press.

———. 2020. *The Broken Heart of America: St. Louis and the Violent History of the United States*. New York: Basic Books.

Jones, Angela. 2020. *Camming: Money, Power, and Pleasure in the Sex Work Industry*. New York: New York University Press.

Jones, Claudia. (1949) 1995. "An End to the Neglect of the Problems of the Negro Woman!" In *Words of Fire: An Anthology of African American Feminist Thought*, edited by Beverly Guy-Sheftall, 107–24. New York: New Press.

Jones, William. 1876. *The Hindu Wife; or, The Enchanted Fruit*. London: Trübner.

Joseph, May. 1999. *Nomadic Identities: The Performance of Citizenship*. Minneapolis: University of Minnesota Press.

Juffer, Jane. 1998. *At Home with Pornography: Women, Sex, and Everyday Life*. New York: New York University Press.

Justice, Daniel Heath. 2019. "Elizabeth Warren and the Enduring Myth of Cherokee Identity with Daniel Heath Justice." February 24, 2019, in *Medicine for the Resistance*, podcast.

Kaba, Mariame, and Shira Hassan. 2019. *Fumbling towards Repair: A Workbook for Community Accountability Facilitators*. Chicago: Project Nia.

Kabeer, Naila. 1994. *Reversed Realities: Gender Hierarchies in Development Thought*. London: Verso.

Kafer, Alison. 2013. *Feminist, Queer, Crip*. Bloomington: Indiana University Press.

Kapadia, Ronak. 2019. *Insurgent Aesthetics: Security and the Queer Life of the Forever War*. Durham, NC: Duke University Press.

Kaplan, Amy. 2002. *The Anarchy of Empire in the Making of US Culture*. Cambridge, MA: Harvard University Press.

Kaplan, Amy, and Donald Pease, eds. 1993. *Cultures of US Imperialism*. Durham, NC: Duke University Press.

Kaplan, Caren. 1994. "The Politics of Location as Transnational Feminist Practice." In *Scattered Hegemonies: Postmodernity and Transnational Feminist Practices*, edited by Inderpal Grewal and Caren Kaplan, 137–52. Minneapolis: University of Minnesota Press.

———. 2002. "Transporting the Subject: Technologies of Mobility and Location in an Era of Globalization." *PMLA* 117 (1): 32–42.

———. 2018. *Aerial Aftermaths: Wartime from Above*. Durham, NC: Duke University Press.

Karcher, Carolyn L. 2016. *A Refugee from His Race: Albion W. Tourgée and His Fight against White Supremacy*. Chapel Hill: University of North Carolina Press.

Karim, Lamia. 2011. *Microfinance and Its Discontents: Women in Debt in Bangladesh*. Minneapolis: University of Minnesota Press.

———. 2014. "Demystifying Microcredit: The Grameen Bank, NGOs, and Neoliberalism in Bangladesh." In *Theorizing NGOs: States, Feminisms, and Neoliberalism*, edited by Victoria Bernal and Inderpal Grewal, 193–217. Durham, NC: Duke University Press.

Karkazis, Katrina, and Rebecca M. Jordan-Young. 2018. "The Powers of Testosterone: Obscuring Race and Regional Bias in the Regulation of Women Athletes." *Feminist Formations* 30 (1): 1–39.

Katsulis, Yasmina. 2009. *Sex Work and the City: The Social Geography of Health and Safety in Tijuana, Mexico*. Austin: University of Texas Press.

Katz, Jonathan Ned. 1995. *The Invention of Heterosexuality*. New York: Plume.

Kauanui, J. Kēhaulani. 2008. *Hawaiian Blood: Colonialism and the Politics of Sovereignty and Indigeneity*. Durham, NC: Duke University Press.

———. 2016. "'A Structure, Not an Event': Settler Colonialism and Enduring Indigeneity." *Lateral* 5 (1). https://doi.org/10.25158/L5.1.7.

———. 2018. *Paradoxes of Hawaiian Sovereignty: Land, Sex, and the Colonial Politics of State Nationalism*. Durham, NC: Duke University Press.

Kawagley, Angayuqaq Oscar. 2006. *A Yupiaq Worldview: A Pathway to Ecology and Spirit*. Longrove, IL: Waveland Press.

Kearney, Mary Celeste. 2009. "Coalescing: The Development of Girls' Studies." *NWSA Journal* 21 (1): 1–28.

Keeling, Kara. 2007. *The Witch's Flight: The Cinematic, the Black Femme, and the Image of Common Sense*. Durham, NC: Duke University Press.

———. 2019. *Queer Times, Black Futures*. New York: New York University Press.

Kelley, Robin D. G. 2017. "The Rest of Us: Rethinking Settler and Native." *American Quarterly* 69 (2): 267–76.

Kelly, Patty. 2008. *Lydia's Open Door inside Mexico's Most Modern Brothel*. Berkeley: University of California Press.

Kempadoo, Kamala, Jyoti Sanghera, and Bandana Pattanaik, eds. 2005. *Trafficking and Prostitution Reconsidered: New Perspectives on Migration, Sex Work, and Human Rights*. Boulder, CO: Paradigm.

Kendrick, Walter. 1987. *The Secret Museum: Pornography in Modern Culture*. New York: Penguin.

Kennedy, Elizabeth Lapovsky, and Madeline D. Davis. 1993. *Boots of Leather, Slippers of Gold: The History of a Lesbian Community*. New York: Routledge.

———. 2014. *Boots of Leather, Slippers of Gold: The History of a Lesbian Community*. 2nd ed. New York: Routledge.

Kessler-Harris, Alice. 1982. *Out to Work: A History of Wage-Earning Women in the United States*. Oxford: Oxford University Press.

Khanna, Ranjana. 2003. *Dark Continents: Psychoanalysis and Colonialism*. Durham, NC: Duke University Press.

Khoja-Moolji, Shenila. 2018. *Forging the Ideal Educated Girl: The Production of Desirable Subjects in Muslim South Asia*. Berkeley: University of California Press.

Kim, Mimi E. 2020. "The Carceral Creep: Gender-Based Violence, Race, and the Expansion of the Punitive State, 1973–1983." *Social Problems* 67 (2): 251–69.

Kimmel, Michael, and Gloria Steinem. 2014. "'Yes' Is Better Than 'No.'" *New York Times*, September 4, 2014.

Kimmerer, Robin. 2013. *Braiding Sweetgrass: Indigenous Wisdom, Scientific Knowledge and the Teachings of Plants*. Minneapolis: Milkweed Editions.

King, Deborah K. 1988. "Multiple Jeopardy, Multiple Consciousness: The Context of a Black Feminist Ideology." *Signs: Journal of Women in Culture and Society* 14 (1): 42–72.

King, Katie. 1994. *Theory in Its Feminist Travels*. Bloomington: Indiana University Press.

King, Tiffany Lethabo. 2019. *The Black Shoals: Offshore Formations of Black and Native Studies*. Durham, NC: Duke University Press.

Kipnis, Laura. 1998. "Pornography." In *The Oxford Guide to Film Studies*, edited by John Hill and Pamela Church Gibson, 153–57. Oxford: Oxford University Press.

———. 1999. *Bound and Gagged: Pornography and the Politics of Fantasy in America*. Durham, NC: Duke University Press.

Kliegman, Julie. 2020. "Idaho Banned Trans Athletes from Women's Sports. She's Fighting Back." *Sports Illustrated*, June 30, 2020.

Knausgaard, Karl Ove. 2016. *My Struggle*. New York: Farrar, Straus & Giroux.

Know Your IX. n.d. "Know Your IX." Accessed September 2016. www.knowyourix.org.

Koedt, Anne. (1968) 1970. "The Myth of the Vaginal Orgasm." In *Radical Feminism: A Documentary Reader*, edited by Barbara A. Crow, 371–77. New York: New York University Press.

Kogan, Terry. 2007. "Sex Separation in Public Restrooms: Law, Architecture, and Gender." *Michigan Journal of Gender and Law* 14 (1): 1–57.

Kolysh, Simone A. 2019. "Everyday Violence: Catcalling and LGBTQ-Directed Aggression in the Public Sphere." PhD diss., Graduate Center of the City University of New York.

Konkle, Maureen. 2008. "Indigenous Ownership and the Emergence of US Liberal Imperialism." *American Indian Quarterly* 32 (3): 297–323.

Koopman, Colin. 2012. *Genealogy as Critique: Foucault and the Problems of Modernity*. Bloomington: Indiana University Press.

Kornbluh, Felicia. 2007. *The Battle for Welfare Rights: Politics and Poverty in Modern America*. Philadelphia: University of Pennsylvania Press.

Koshy, Susan. 2005. "The Postmodern Subaltern: Globalization Theory and the Subject of Ethnic, Area, and Postcolonial Studies." In *Minor Transnationalism*, edited by Françoise Lionnet and Shu-mei Shih, 109–31. Durham, NC: Duke University Press.

Kothari, Ashish, Ariel Salleh, Arturo Escobar, Federico Demaria, and Alberto Acosta, eds. 2019. *Pluriverse: A Postdevelopment Dictionary*. New Delhi: Tulika.

Kotiswaran, Prabha. 2011. *Dangerous Sex, Invisible Labor: Sex Work and the Law in India*. Princeton, NJ: Princeton University Press.

Koyama, Emi. 2002. "Cissexual/Cisgender." Eminism.org, June 7, 2002. www.eminism.org.

Kristeva, Julia. 1981. "Women's Time." Translated by Alice Jardine and Harry Blake. *Signs: Journal of Women in Culture and Society* 7 (1): 13–35.

———. 1982. *Powers of Horror: An Essay on Abjection*. New York: Columbia University Press.

Kunzel, Regina G. 2008. *Criminal Intimacy: Prison and the Uneven History of Modern American Sexuality*. Chicago: University of Chicago Press.

Kuokkanen, Rauna. 2012. "Self-Determination and Indigenous Women's Rights at the Intersection of International Human Rights." *Human Rights Quarterly* 34 (1): 225–50.

Kushner, Rachel. 2019. "Is Prison Necessary? Ruth Wilson Gilmore Might Change Your Mind." *New York Times Magazine*, April 17, 2019.

Kwa, Chung Lin. 1989. "Mimicking Nature: The Development of Systems Ecology in the United States, 1950–1975." PhD diss., University of Amsterdam.

Lacquer, Thomas. 1990. *Making Sex: Body and Gender from the Greeks to Freud*. Cambridge, MA: Harvard University Press.

Lacsamana, Anne E., and Delia D. Aguilar. 2004. *Women and Globalization*. London: Humanities.

LaDuke, Winona. 2015. *All Our Relations: Native Struggles for Land and Life*. Chicago: Haymarket.

LaFleur, Greta. 2018. *The Natural History of Sexuality in Early America*. Baltimore: Johns Hopkins University Press.

La Fountain-Stokes, Lawrence. 2009. *Queer Ricans*. Minneapolis: University of Minnesota Press.

Lakoff, Andrew. 2008. "The Generic Biothreat, or, How We Became Unprepared." *Cultural Anthropology* 23 (3): 399–428.

Lampe, Nik M., Shannon K. Carter, and J. E. Sumerau. 2019. "Continuity and Change in Gender Frames: The Case of Transgender Reproduction." *Gender & Society* 33 (6): 865–87.

Lan, Pei-Chia. 2006. *Global Cinderellas: Migrant Domestics and Newly Rich Employers in Taiwan*. Durham, NC: Duke University Press.

LaPensée, Elizabeth, Weshoyot Alvitre, Patty Stonefish, Allie Vasquez, and Rebecca Naragon, eds. 2017. *Deer Woman: An Anthology*. Albuquerque: Native Realities.

LaPier, Rosalyn R. 2017. *Invisible Reality: Storytellers, Storytakers, and the Supernatural World of the Blackfeet*. Lincoln: University of Nebraska Press.

Larsen, Nella. 2001. *The Complete Fiction of Nella Larsen*. New York: Random House.

Latin American Subaltern Studies Group. 1993. "Founding Statement." *boundary 2* 20 (3): 110–21.

Lau, Jacob. 2016. "Between the Times: Trans-Temporality, and Historical Representation." Unpublished PhD diss., University of California, Los Angeles.

Lavery, Grace. 2019. "The Old-School Transsexual and the Working-Class Drag Queen." Stage Mirror, November 4, 2019. https://grace.substack.com.

Law, Victoria. 2014. "Against Carceral Feminism." *Jacobin*, October 17, 2014. www.jacobinmag.com.

Lawrence, Bonita, and Enakshi Dua. 2005. "Decolonizing Antiracism." *Social Justice* 32 (4): 120–43.

Lazreg, Marnia. 2008. *Torture and the Twilight of Empire: From Algiers to Baghdad*. Princeton, NJ: Princeton University Press.

LeBrón, Marisol. 2019. *Policing Life and Death: Race, Violence, and Resistance in Puerto Rico*. Oakland: University of California Press.

Lederer, Laura, ed. 1980. *Take Back the Night: Women on Pornography*. New York: William Morrow.

Lee, Jiz. 2013. "Uncategorized: Genderqueer Identity and Performance in Independent and Mainstream Porn." In *The Feminist Porn Book: The Politics of Producing Pleasure*, edited by Tristan Taormino, Celine Parreñas Shimizu, Constance Penley, and Mireille Miller-Young, 273–78. New York: Feminist Press.

———, ed. 2015. *Coming Out like a Porn Star: Essays on Pornography, Protection, and Privacy*. Berkeley, CA: ThreeL Media.

Lee, Joon Oluchi. 2005. "The Joy of the Castrated Boy." *Social Text* 23 (3–4 (84–85)): 35–56.

Lee, Sharon M. 1993. "Racial Classifications in the US Census: 1890–1990." *Ethnic and Racial Studies* 16 (1): 75–94.

LeFlouria, Talitha L. 2015. *Chained in Silence: Black Women and Convict Labor in the New South*. Chapel Hill: University of North Carolina Press.

Leigh, Carol. 1997. "Inventing Sex Work." In *Whores and Other Feminists*, edited by Jill Nagle, 223–31. New York: Routledge.

Leo, Brooklyn. 2020. "The Colonial/Modern [Cis] Gender System and Trans World Traveling." *Hypatia: A Journal of Feminist Philosophy* 35 (3): 454–74.

Leong, Diana. 2016. "The Mattering of Black Lives: Octavia Butler's Hyperempathy and the Promise of the New Materialisms." *Catalyst: Feminism, Theory, Technoscience* 2 (2). https://doi.org/10.28968/cftt.v2i2.28799.

Lerman, Amy E., and Vesla M. Weaver. 2014. *Arresting Citizenship: The Democratic Consequences of American Crime Control*. Chicago: University of Chicago Press.

Leroy, Justin. 2016. "Black History in Occupied Territory: On the Entanglements of Slavery and Settler Colonialism." *Theory & Event* 19 (4): 1.

Lesko, Nancy. 2012. *Act Your Age! A Cultural Construction of Adolescence*. New York: Routledge.

Levine, Phillipa. 2003. *Prostitution, Race, Politics: Policing Venereal Disease in the British Empire*. London: Routledge.

Lewis, Sydney Fonteyn. 2012. "'Everything I Know about Being Femme I Learned from *Sula*,' or Toward a Black Femme-inist Criticism." *Trans-Scripts* 2. https://sites.uci.edu.

Lewis, Talila. 2018. "Disability Justice in the Age of Mass Incarceration: Perspectives on Race, Disability, Law and Accountability." Lecture, Syracuse College of Law, Syracuse, NY, March 29, 2018.

Li, Stephanie. 2011. *Something Akin to Freedom: The Choice of Bondage in Narratives by African American Women*. Albany: State University of New York Press.

Li, Tania Murray. 2017. "After Development: Surplus Population and the Politics of Entitlement." *Development and Change* 48 (6): 1247–61.

Lickers, Henry. 1997. "Can't See the Forest for the Trees: A Native American's Perspective." In *Biodiversity: Toward Operational Definitions: The 1995 Plum Creek Lectures*, edited by Nick Baker, 39–53. Missoula: University of Montana School of Forestry. www.cfc.umt.edu.

Light, Caroline. 2017. *Stand Your Ground: A History of America's Love Affair with Lethal Self-Defense*. Boston: Beacon.

Lim, Eng Beng. 2005. "Glocalqueering in New Asia: The Politics of Performing Gay in Singapore." *Theatre Journal* 57 (3): 383–405.

Lindio-McGovern, Ligaya, and Isidor Wallimann. (2009) 2016. *Globalization and Third World Women: Exploitation, Coping, and Resistance*. London: Routledge.

Linton, Eliza Lynn. 1868. "The Girl of the Period." *Saturday Review*, March 1868.

Liu, Petrus. 2015. *Queer Marxism in Two Chinas*. Durham, NC: Duke University Press.

Livingston, Jessica. 2004. "Murder in Juárez: Gender, Sexual Violence, and the Global Assembly Line." *Frontiers: A Journal of Women Studies* 25 (1): 59–76.

Locke, John. 1689. *Two Treatises of Government*. London: Andrew Millar.

———. 2014. *Second Treatise of Government: An Essay concerning the True Original, Extent and End of Civil Government*. Hoboken, NJ: John Wiley & Sons.

Loftsdottir, Kristin. 2016. "International Development and the Globally Concerned European Subject." *Interventions* 18 (2): 234–50.

Lomawaima, K. Tsianina. 1994. *They Called It Prairie Light: The Story of Chilocco Indian School*. Lincoln: University of Nebraska Press.

Longman, Jeré, and Juliet Macur. 2011. "For Women's Road Records, No Men Allowed." *New York Times*, September 21, 2011. www.nytimes.com.

Loomba, Ania. (1995) 2015. *Colonialism/Postcolonialism*. New York: Routledge.

Lopez, Iris. 2008. *Matters of Choice: Puerto Rican Women's Struggle for Reproductive Freedom*. New Brunswick, NJ: Rutgers University Press.

Lorde, Audre. 1982. *Zami: A New Spelling of My Name*. Freedom, CA: Crossing.

———. (1984) 2007a. "Age, Race, Class and Sex: Women Redefining Difference." In *Sister Outsider: Essays and Speeches*, 114–23. Berkeley, CA: Crossing.

———. (1984) 2007b. "The Master's Tools Will Never Dismantle the Master's House." In *Sister Outsider: Essays and Speeches*, 110–13. Berkeley, CA: Crossing.

———. (1984) 2007c. *Sister Outsider: Essays and Speeches*. 2nd ed. Berkeley, CA: Crossing.

———. (1984) 2007d. "The Transformation of Silence into Action." In *Sister Outsider: Essays and Speeches*, 36–40. Berkeley, CA: Crossing.

———. (1984) 2007e. "Uses of the Erotic: The Erotic as Power." In *Sister Outsider: Essays and Speeches*, 53–59. Berkeley, CA: Crossing.

———. 2011. *Zami: A New Spelling of My Name; A Biomythography*. Berkeley, CA: Crossing.

Losh, Elizabeth. 2019. *Hashtag (Object Lessons)*. New York: Bloomsbury Academic.

Love, Heather. 2009. *Feeling Backward: Loss and the Politics of Queer History*. Cambridge, MA: Harvard University Press.

———. 2015. "Doing Being Deviant: Deviance Studies, Description and the Queer Ordinary." *differences: A Journal of Feminist Cultural Studies* 26 (1): 74–95.

———. 2019. "'How the Other Half Thinks': An Introduction to the Volume." In *Imagining Queer Methods*, edited by Amin Ghaziani and Matt Brim, 28–42. New York: New York University Press.

Love and Protect and Survived and Punished. 2017. *#Survivedandpunished: Survivor Defense as Abolitionist Praxis*. N.p.: Love and Protect and Survived and Punished. https://survivedandpunished.org.

Lowe, Lisa. 1996. *Immigrant Acts: On Asian American Cultural Politics*. Durham, NC: Duke University Press.

———. 2015. *The Intimacies of Four Continents*. Durham, NC: Duke University Press.

Loyd, Jenna M. 2014. *Health Rights Are Civil Rights: Peace and Justice Activism in Los Angeles, 1963–1978*. Minneapolis: University of Minnesota Press.

Luciano, Dana. 2007. *Arranging Grief: Sacred Time and the Body in Nineteenth-Century America*. New York: New York University Press.

Lugones, María. 2003. "Purity, Impurity, and Separation." In *Pilgrimages/Peregrinajes: Theorizing Coalition against Multiple Oppressions*, 120–48. Lanham, MD: Rowman & Littlefield.

———. 2007. "Heterosexualism and the Colonial/Modern Gender System." *Hypatia: A Journal of Feminist Philosophy* 22 (1): 186–209.

———. 2010. "Toward a Decolonial Feminism." *Hypatia: A Journal of Feminist Philosophy* 25 (4): 742–59.

Luibhéid, Eithne. 2002. *Entry Denied: Controlling Sexuality at the Border*. Minneapolis: University of Minnesota Press.

Luibhéid, Eithne, and Lionel Cantú, eds. 2005. *Queer Migrations: Sexuality, US Citizenship, and Border Crossings*. Minneapolis: University of Minnesota Press.

Luibhéid, Eithne, and Karma R. Chávez, eds. 2020. *Queer and Trans Migrations: Dynamics of Illegalization, Detention, and Deportation*. Urbana: University of Illinois Press.

Luther, Jessica. 2016. *Unsportsmanlike Conduct: College Football and the Politics of Rape*. Brooklyn: Akashic Books.

Macharia, Keguro. 2020. "Belated: Interruption." *GLQ: A Journal of Lesbian and Gay Studies* 26 (3): 561–73.

Mack, Ashley Noel, and Tiara R. Na'puti. 2019. "'Our Bodies Are Not Terra Nullius': Building a Decolonial Feminist Resistance to Gendered Violence." *Women's Studies in Communication* 42 (3): 347–70.

MacKinnon, Catharine, and Reva B. Siegel, eds. 2008. *Directions in Sexual Harassment Law*. New Haven, CT: Yale University Press.

Maclear, Kyo. 2018. "Something So Broken: Black Care in the Wake of Beasts of the Southern Wild." *ISLE: Interdisciplinary Studies in Literature and Environment* 25 (3): 603–29.

Madison, D. Soyini. 2014. Foreword to *Black Performance Theory*, edited by Thomas F. DeFrantz and Anita Gonzalez, vii–ix. Durham, NC: Duke University Press.

Mahmood, Saba. 2004. *Politics of Piety: The Islamic Revival and the Feminist Subject*. Princeton, NJ: Princeton University Press.

Maira, S. 2002. *Desis in the House: Indian American Youth Culture in New York City*. Philadelphia: Temple University Press.

Majeed, Debra. 2015. *Polygyny: What It Means When African American Muslim Women Share Their Husbands*. Gainesville: University Press of Florida.

Majic, Samantha. 2014. *Sex Work Politics: From Protest to Service Provision*. Philadelphia: University of Pennsylvania Press.

Makoni, Sinfree, and Alastair Pennycook. 2007. *Disinventing and Reconstituting Languages*. Clevedon, UK: Multilingual Matters.

Malatino, Hil. 2019a. "Future Fatigue." *TSQ: Transgender Studies Quarterly* 6 (4): 635–58.

———. 2019b. *Trans Care*. Minneapolis: University of Minnesota Press.

Mallon, Florencia E. 1994. "The Promise and Dilemma of Subaltern Studies: Perspectives from Latin American History." *American Historical Review* 99 (5): 1491–1515.

Mamo, Laura. 2007. *Queering Reproduction*. Durham, NC: Duke University Press.

Manalansan, Martin F., IV. 2003. *Global Divas: Filipino Gay Men in the Diaspora*. Durham, NC: Duke University Press.

———. 2006. "Queer Intersections: Sexuality and Gender in Migration Studies." *International Migration Review* 40 (1): 224–49.

———. 2008. "Queering the Chain of Care Paradigm." *Scholar and Feminist Online* 6 (3). http://sfonline.barnard.edu.

———. 2014. "The 'Stuff' of Archives: Mess, Migration, and Queer Lives." *Radical History Review* 120:94–107.

Manalansan, Martin F., IV, and A. Cruz-Malave, eds. 2002. *Queer Globalizations: Citizenship and the Afterlife of Colonialism*. New York: New York University Press.

Mani, Bakirathi. 2012. *Aspiring to Home: South Asians in America*. Palo Alto, CA: Stanford University Press.

Mani, Lata. 1998. *Contentious Traditions: The Debate on Sati in Colonial India*. Berkeley: University of California Press.

Mann, Barbara Alice. 2006. *Iroquoian Women: The Gantowisas*. New York: Peter Lang.

Manning, Sarah Sunshine. 2019. "Standing Rock: The Actualization of a Community and a Movement." In *Standing with Standing Rock: Voices from the #NoDAPL Movement*, edited by Nick Estes and Jaskiran Dhillon, 290–300. Minneapolis: University of Minnesota Press.

Maracle, Lee. 2015. *Memory Serves*. Edmonton, Canada: NeWest.

Marine, Susan, and Z. Nicolazzo. 2020. "Campus Sexual Violence Prevention Educators' Use of Gender in Their Work: A Critical Exploration." *Journal of Interpersonal Violence* 35 (21–22): 5005–27.

Martensen, Kayla Marie. 2020. "Review of Carceral State Studies and Application." *Sociology Compass* 14 (7): e12801.

Martinez, Maria Elena. 2008. *Genealogical Fictions: Limpieza de Sangre, Religion, and Gender in Colonial Mexico*. Stanford, CA: Stanford University Press.

Marx, Karl. (1867) 1992. *Capital*. Vol. 1. New York: Penguin.

Marx, Karl, and Friedrich Engels. (1848) 1998. *The Communist Manifesto: A Modern Edition*. London: Verso.

Massad, Joseph. 2008. *Desiring Arabs*. Chicago: University of Chicago Press.

Massey, Doreen B. 2005. *For Space*. London: Sage.

Masulo, Karen. 2015. "Personal Violence, Public Matter: Evolving Standards in Gender-Based Asylum Law." *Harvard International Review* 36 (2): 45–48.

Mathiesen, Sara. 2016. "Equality vs Reproductive Risk: Women and AIDS Activism and False Choice in the Clinical Trials Debate." *Signs: Journal of Women in Culture and Society* 41:579–601.

Matsuda, Mari. 1987. "Looking to the Bottom: Critical Legal Studies and Reparations." *Harvard Civil Rights–Civil Liberties Law Review* 22:323–99. http://hdl.handle.net.

Maynard, Robyn. 2017. *Policing Black Lives: State Violence in Canada from Slavery to the Present*. Winnipeg: Fernwood.

Mbembe, Achille. 2019. *Necropolitics*. Durham, NC: Duke University Press.

McArthur, Park, and Constantina Zavitsanos. 2013. "Other Forms of Conviviality: The Best and Least of Which Is Our Daily Care and the Host of Which Is Our Collaborative Work." *Women & Performance: A Journal of Feminist Theory* 23 (1): 126–32.

McClintock, Anne. 1993. "Sex Workers and Sex Work: Introduction." *Social Text* 37:1–10.

———. 1995. *Imperial Leather: Race, Gender and Sexuality in the Colonial Contest*. New York: Routledge.

McCurry, Stephanie. 1995. *Masters of Small Worlds: Yeoman Households, Gender Relations, and the Political Culture of the Antebellum South Carolina Low Country*. New York: Oxford University Press.

McDonald, CeCe. 2017. "'Go beyond Our Natural Selves': The Prison Letters of CeCe McDonald." *TSQ: Transgender Studies Quarterly* 4 (2): 243–65.

McDuffie, Eric. 2011. *Sojourning for Freedom: Black Women, American Communism, and the Making of Black Left Feminism*. Chapel Hill: University of North Carolina Press.

McGregor, Deborah. 2005. "Traditional Ecological Knowledge: An Anishnabe Woman's Perspective." *Atlantis: Critical Studies in Gender, Culture & Social Justice* 29 (2): 103–9.

McKay, Claude. 2020. *Romance in Marseille*. New York: Penguin.

McKittrick, Katherine. 2006. *Demonic Grounds: Black Women and the Cartographies of Struggle*. Minneapolis: University of Minnesota Press.

———, ed. 2015. *Sylvia Wynter: On Being Human as Praxis*. Durham, NC: Duke University Press.

———. 2019. "Living Just Enough for the City, Volume VI, Black Methodology." Keynote presented to the GenUrb: Feminist Explorations of Urban Futures, Toronto.

McMillan, Uri. 2016. *Embodied Avatars: Genealogies of Black Feminist Art and Performance*. New York: New York University Press.

McRobbie, Angela, and Jenny Garber. 1976. "Girls and Subcultures: An Exploration." In *Resistance through Rituals: Youth Subcultures in Post-war Britain*, edited by Stuart Hall and Tony Jefferson, 209–22. London: Hutchinson.

McRuer, Robert. 2006. *Crip Theory: Cultural Signs of Queerness and Disability*. New York: New York University Press.

McTighe, Laura. 2012. "The War on Drugs Is a War on Relationships: Crossing the Borders of Fear, Silence, and HIV Vulnerability in the Prison-Created Diaspora." In *Beyond Walls and Cages: Prisons, Borders, and Global Crisis*, edited by Jenna Loyd, Matt Mitchelson, and Andrew Burridge, 301–14. Athens: University of Georgia Press.

McTighe, Laura, and Deon Haywood. 2017. "'There Is No Justice in Louisiana': Crimes against Nature and the Spirit of Black Feminist Resistance." *Souls: A Critical Journal of Black Politics, Culture and Society* 19 (3): 261–85.

Meissner, Shelbi Nahwilet, and Kyle Powys Whyte. 2017. "Theorizing Indigeneity, Gender, and Settler Colonialism." In *Routledge Companion to the Philosophy of Race*, edited by Paul C. Taylor, Linda Martín Alcoff, and Luvell Anderson, 1–21. New York: Routledge.

Mendoza, Breny. 2016. "Coloniality of Gender and Power: From Postcoloniality to Decoloniality." In *The Oxford Handbook of Feminist Theory*, edited by Lisa Disch and Mary Hawkesworth, 100–121. New York: Oxford University Press.

Meneley, Anne, and Don Kulick. 2005. *Fat: The Anthropology of an Obsession*. New York: Tarcher.

Mercer, John. 2012. "Power Bottom: Performativity in Commercial Gay Pornographic Video." In *Hard to Swallow: Hard-Core Pornography on Screen*, edited by Feona Attwood, 215–28. New York: Columbia University Press.

Mercer, Kobena. 1994. "Skin Head Sex Thing: Racial Difference and the Homoerotic Imaginary." In *Welcome to the Jungle: New Positions in Black Cultural Studies*, 171–219. New York: Routledge.

Merck, Mandy. 2000. *In Your Face: 9 Sexual Studies*. New York: New York University Press.

Merelli, Annalisa. 2019. "Learn the Lyrics and Dance Steps for the Chilean Feminist Anthem Spreading around the World." *Quartz*, December 2, 2019. https://qz.com.

Merlan, Francesca. 2009. "Indigeneity: Global and Local." *Current Anthropology* 50 (3): 303–33.

Messner, Michael, and Donald F. Sabo. 1994. *Sex, Violence and Power in Sports: Rethinking Masculinity*. Freedom, CA: Crossing.

Meyerowitz, Joanne. 2002. *How Sex Changed: A History of Transsexuality in the United States*. Cambridge, MA: Harvard University Press.

Mezzadra, Sandro, and Naoki Sakai. 2014. "Introduction." *Translation: A Transdisciplinary Journal* 4:9–27.

Mgbako, Chi. 2016. *To Live Freely in This World: Sex Worker Activism in Africa*. New York: New York University Press.

Miedem, Stephanie Spaid, and Emma Fulu. 2018. "Globalization and Theorizing Intimate Partner Violence from the Global South." In *The Palgrave Handbook of Criminology and the Global South*, edited by Kerry Carrington, Russell Hogg, John Scott, and Máximo Sozzo, 867–82. London: Palgrave Macmillan.

Mignolo, Walter D. 2007. "Introduction: Coloniality of Power and De-colonial Thinking." *Cultural Studies* 21 (2–3): 155–67.

Mikulic, Matej. 2019. "US Health Expenditure as Percent of GDP 1960–2019." Statista, 2019. www.statista.com.

Miles, Tiya, and Sharon P. Holland, eds. 2006. *Crossing Waters, Crossing Worlds: The African Diaspora in Indian Country*. Durham, NC: Duke University Press.

Milkman, Ruth. 2006. *L.A. Story: Immigrant Workers and the Future of the U.S. Labor Movement*. New York: Russell Sage Foundation.

Miller-Young, Mireille. 2010. "Putting Hypersexuality to Work: Black Women and Illicit Eroticism in Pornography." *Sexualities* 13 (2): 219–35.

———. 2014. *A Taste for Brown Sugar: Black Women in Pornography*. Durham, NC: Duke University Press.

Millett, Kate. 1970. *Sexual Politics*. London: Rupert Hart-Davis.

Million, Dian. 2009. "Felt Theory: An Indigenous Feminist Approach to Affect and History." *Wicazo Sa Review* 24 (2): 53–76.

———. 2013. *Therapeutic Nations: Healing in an Age of Indigenous Human Rights*. Tucson: University of Arizona Press.

Mingus, Mia. 2010. "Changing the Framework: Disability Justice." *Resist Newsletter* 19 (6): 1–2.

Minich, Julie Avril. 2014. *Accessible Citizenships: Disability, Nation, and the Cultural Politics of Greater Mexico*. Philadelphia: Temple University Press.

———. 2016. "Enabling Whom? Critical Disability Studies Now." *Lateral: Journal of the Cultural Studies Association* 5, no. 1 (Spring). https://doi.org/10.25158/L5.1.9.

Miranda, Deborah. 2010. "The Extermination of the Joyas: Gendercide in Spanish California." *GLQ: A Journal of Lesbian and Gay Studies* 16 (1–2): 253–84.

———. 2013. *Bad Indians: A Tribal Memoir*. Berkeley, CA: Heyday.

Mitchell, Gregory. 2011. "TurboConsumers™ in Paradise: Tourism, Civil Rights, and Brazil's Gay Sex Industry." *American Ethnologist* 38 (4): 666–82.

———. 2015. *Tourist Attractions: Performing Race and Masculinity in Brazil's Sexual Economy*. Chicago: University of Chicago Press.

Mitchell, Robin. 2019. *Venus Noire: Black Women and Colonial Fantasies in Nineteenth-Century France*. Athens: University of Georgia Press.

Mitchum, Preston, and Aisha C. Moodie-Mills. 2014. *Beyond Bullying: How Hostile School Climate Perpetuates the School-to-Prison Pipeline for LGBT Youth*. Washington, DC: Center for American Progress. www.ncjrs.gov.

Mitra, Durba. 2019. "Review Essay: Sexual Science as Global History." *Gender & History* 31, no. 2 (June): 500–510.

———. 2020. *Indian Sex Life: Sexuality and the Colonial Origins of Modern Social Thought*. Princeton, NJ: Princeton University Press.

Moallem, Minoo. 2005. *Between Warrior Brother and Veiled Sister: Islamic Fundamentalism and the Politics of Patriarchy in Iran*. Berkeley: University of California Press.

Modleski, Tania. 1991. *Feminism without Women: Culture and Criticism in a Postfeminist Age*. London: Routledge.

Moeller, Kathryn. 2018. *The Gender Effect: Capitalism, Feminism, and the Corporate Politics of Development*. Oakland: University of California Press.

Mogul, Joey, Andrea Ritchie, and Kay Whitlock. 2011. *Queer (In)justice: The Criminalization of LGBT People in the United States*. Boston: Beacon.

Mohanram, Radhika. 2007. *Imperial White: Race, Diaspora, and the British Empire*. Minneapolis: University of Minnesota Press.

Mohanty, Chandra Talpade. 1988. "Under Western Eyes: Feminist Scholarship and Colonial Discourses." *Feminist Review* 30 (10): 61–88.

———. 2003. *Feminism without Borders: Decolonizing Theory, Practicing Solidarity*. Durham, NC: Duke University Press.

Molina, Natalia. 2014. *How Race Is Made in America: Immigration, Citizenship, and the Historical Power of Racial Scripts*. Berkeley: University of California Press.

Mollow, Anna. 2015. "Disability Studies Gets Fat." *Hypatia: A Journal of Feminist Philosophy* 30 (1): 199–216.

———. 2017. "Unvictimizable: Toward a Fat Black Disability Studies." *African American Review* 50 (2): 105–21.

Molloy, Sylvia, and Robert McKee Irwin, eds. 1998. *Hispanisms and Homosexualities*. Durham, NC: Duke University Press.

Money, John, and Anke A. Ehrhardt. 1972. *Man and Woman, Boy and Girl: The Differentiation and Dimorphism of Gender Identity from Conception to Maturity*. Baltimore: Johns Hopkins University Press.

Money, John, Joan Hampson, and John Hampson. 1955a. "Hermaphroditism: Recommendations concerning Assignment of Sex, Change of Sex, and Psychologic Management." *Johns Hopkins Medical Journal* 97 (4): 284–300.

———. 1955b. "Hermaphroditism, Gender, and Precocity, in Hyper-Andrenocorticism: Psychologic Findings." *Bulletin of the Johns Hopkins Hospital* 96:253–54.

Moore, Alison. 2009. "Colonial Visions of 'Third World' Toilets: A Nineteenth-Century Discourse That Haunts Contemporary Tourism." In *Ladies and Gents: Public Toilets and Gender*, edited by Olga Gershenson and Barbara Penne, 105–25. Philadelphia: Temple University Press.

Moraga, Cherríe. 1981. Preface to *This Bridge Called My Back: Writings by Radical Women of Color*, edited by Cherríe Moraga and Gloria Anzaldúa, xiii–xx. Watertown, MA: Persephone.

———. (1981) 1983. Preface to *This Bridge Called My Back: Writings by Radical Women of Color*, 2nd ed., edited by Cherríe Moraga and Gloria Anzaldúa, xiii–xix. New York: Kitchen Table: Women of Color Press.

———. 1993. "Queer Aztlán: The Re-formation of Chicano Tribe." In *The Last Generation: Prose and Poetry*, 145–74. Boston: South End.

———. 1994. *Heroes and Saints and Other Plays*. Albuquerque: West End.

———. 2011. *A Xicana Codex of Changing*. Durham, NC: Duke University Press.

Moraga, Cherríe, and Gloria Anzaldúa, eds. 1981. *This Bridge Called My Back: Writings by Radical Women of Color*. Watertown, MA: Persephone.

Moraga, Cherríe, and Amber Hollibaugh. 1981. "What We're Rollin around in Bed With." *Heresies* 12:58–62.

Moreton-Robinson, Aileen. 2015. *The White Possessive: Property, Power, and Indigenous Sovereignty*. Minneapolis: University of Minnesota Press.

Morgan, Jennifer L. 2004. *Laboring Women: Reproduction and Gender in New World Slavery*. Philadelphia: University of Pennsylvania Press.

———. 2018. "Partus Sequitur Ventrem." *Small Axe* 22 (1): 1–17.

Morgan, Robin. 1980. "Theory and Practice: Pornography and Rape." In *Take Back the Night: Women on Pornography*, edited by Laura Lederer, 134–40. New York: Morrow.

Morgensen, Scott Lauria. 2010. "Settler Homonationalism: Theorizing Settler Colonialism within Queer Modernities." *GLQ: A Journal of Lesbian and Gay Studies* 16 (1–2): 105–31.

———. 2011. *Spaces between Us: Queer Settler Colonialism and Indigenous Decolonization*. Minneapolis: University of Minnesota Press.

———. 2012. "Theorising Gender, Sexuality and Settler Colonialism: An Introduction." *Settler Colonial Studies* 2 (2): 2–22.

Morris, Monique W. 2019. "Countering the Adultification of Black Girls." *Educational Leadership* 76 (7): 44–48.

Morris, Rosalind C. 2010. Introduction to *Can the Subaltern Speak? Reflections on the History of an Idea*, edited by Rosalind C. Morris, 1–18. New York: Columbia University Press.

Morrison, Toni. (1987) 1988. *Beloved: A Novel*. New York: Plume.

Mosse, George L. 1998. *The Image of Man: The Creation of Modern Masculinity*. Oxford: Oxford University Press.

Moynihan, Daniel Patrick. 1965. *The Negro Family: The Case for National Action*. Washington, DC: Office of Policy Planning and Research.

Mulla, Sameena. 2014. *The Violence of Care: Rape Victims, Forensic Nurses, and Sexual Assault Intervention*. New York: New York University Press.

Mumford, Kevin. 1997. *Interzones: Black/White Sex Districts in Chicago and New York in the Early Twentieth Century*. New York: Columbia University Press.

———. 2019. *Not Straight, Not White: Black Gay Men from the March on Washington to the AIDS Crisis*. Chapel Hill: University of North Carolina Press.

Muñoz, José Esteban. 1996. "Ephemera as Evidence: Introductory Notes to Queer Acts." *Women & Performance: A Journal of Feminist Theory* 8 (2): 5–16.

———. 1999. *Disidentifications: Queers of Color and the Performance of Politics*. Minneapolis: University of Minnesota Press.

———. 2006. "Feeling Brown, Feeling Down: Latina Affect, the Performativity of Race, and the Depressive Position." *Signs: Journal of Women in Culture and Society* 31 (3): 675–88.

———. 2009. *Cruising Utopia: The Then and There of Queer Futurity*. New York: New York University Press.

———. 2020. *The Sense of Brown*. Edited by Joshua Chambers-Letson and Tavia Nyong'o. Durham, NC: Duke University Press.

Muñoz Martínez, Monica. 2018. *The Injustice Never Leaves You: Anti-Mexican Violence in Texas*. Cambridge, MA: Harvard University Press.

Murphy, Michelle. 2012. *Seizing the Means of Reproduction: Entanglements of Feminism, Health, and Technoscience*. Durham, NC: Duke University Press.

———. 2012–13. "The Girl: Mergers of Feminism and Finance in Neoliberal Times." *Scholar and Feminist Online* 11 (1–2). http://sfonline.barnard.edu.

———. 2017. *The Economization of Life*. Durham, NC: Duke University Press.

Murray, Stephen O. 2002. *Homosexualities*. Chicago: University of Chicago Press.

Musser, Amber Jamilla. 2014. *Sensational Flesh: Race, Power, and Masochism*. New York: New York University Press.

———. 2018. *Sensual Excess: Queer Femininity and Brown Jouissance*. New York: New York University Press.

Muthu, Sankar. 2003. *Enlightenment against Empire*. Princeton, NJ: Princeton University Press.

Nabutanyi, Edgar Fred. 2020. "(Un)Complicating Mwanga's Sexuality in Nakisanze Segawa's *The Triangle*." *GLQ: A Journal of Lesbian and Gay Studies* 26 (3): 439–54. https://doi.org/10.1215/10642684-8311786.

Nadasen, Premilla. 2005. *Welfare Warriors: The Welfare Rights Movement in the United States*. New York: Routledge.

———. 2009. "'We Do Whatever Becomes Necessary': Johnnie Tillmon, Welfare Rights, and Black Power." In *Want to Start a Revolution? Radical Women in the Black Freedom Struggle*, edited by Dayo F. Gore, Jeanne Theoharis, and Komozi Woodard, 317–38. New York: New York University Press.

———. 2017. "Rethinking Care: Arlie Hochschild and the Global Care Chain." *WSQ: Women's Studies Quarterly* 45:124–28. https://doi.org/10.1353/wsq.2017.0049.

Nagel, Mechthild. 2018. "Policing Families: The Many-Headed Hydra of Surveillance." *APA Newsletter for Feminism and Philosophy* 17 (2): 2–11.

Nagle, Jill. 1997. "First Ladies of Feminist Porn: A Conversation with Candida Royalle and Debi Sundahl." In *Whores and Other Feminists*, edited by Jill Nagle, 156–66. New York: Routledge.

Nair, Janaki. 1996. *Women and Law in Colonial India: A Social History*. Delhi: Kali for Women.

Nair, Yasmin. 2015. "How to Make Prisons Disappear: Queer Immigrants, the Shackles of Love, and the Invisibility of the Prison Industrial Complex." In *Captive Genders*, edited by Eric A. Stanley and Nat Smith, 123–40. Oakland, CA: AK.

Najmabadi, Afsaneh. 2005. *Women with Mustaches and Men without Beards: Gender and Sexual Anxieties of Iranian Modernity*. Berkeley: University of California Press.

———. 2014. *Professing Selves: Transsexuality and Same-Sex Desire in Contemporary Iran*. Durham, NC: Duke University Press.

Nakamura, Lisa. 2014. "Indigenous Circuits: Navajo Women and the Racialization of Early Electronic Manufacture." *American Quarterly* 66, no. 4 (December): 919–41.

Nakano Glenn, Evelyn. 1985. "Racial Ethnic Women's Labor: The Intersection of Race, Gender, and Class Oppression." *Review of Radical Political Economics* 17 (3): 86–108.

———. 1992. "From Servitude to Service Work: Historical Continuities in the Racial Division of Paid Reproductive Labor." *Signs: Journal of Women in Culture and Society* 18 (1): 1–43.

———. 2002. *Unequal Freedom: How Race and Gender Shaped American Citizenship and Labor*. Cambridge, MA: Harvard University Press.

———. 2010. *Forced to Care: Coercion and Caregiving in America*. Cambridge, MA: Harvard University Press.

Namaste, Viviane. 2000. *Invisible Lives: The Erasure of Transsexual and Transgendered People*. Chicago: University of Chicago Press.

———. 2015. *Oversight: Critical Reflections on Feminist Research and Politics*. Toronto: Canadian Scholars.

Narrain, Arvind. 2004. "The Articulation of Rights around Sexuality and Health: Subaltern Queer Cultures in India in the Era of Hindutva." *Health and Human Rights* 7 (2): 142–64.

Nash, Jennifer. 2014. *The Black Body in Ecstasy: Reading Race, Reading Pornography*. Durham, NC: Duke University Press.

———. 2019a. *Black Feminism Reimagined: After Intersectionality*. Durham, NC: Duke University Press.

———. 2019b. "Pedagogies of Desire." In "Sexual Politics, Sexual Panics." Special issue, *differences: A Journal of Feminist Cultural Studies* 30, no. 1 (May): 197–227.

Naswood, Elton, and Mattee Jim. 2012. "Mending the Rainbow: Working with the Native LGBT / Two Spirit Community." PowerPoint presented at the Thirteenth National Indian Nations Conference, Agua Caliente reservation, CA, December 2012. http://tribal-institute.org.

National Center for Transgender Equality. 2016. *The Report of the 2015 US Transgender Survey*. Washington, DC: National Center for Transgender Equality. https://transequality.org.

Nelson, Alondra. 2011. *Body and Soul: The Black Panther Party and the Fight against Medical Discrimination*. Minneapolis: University of Minnesota Press.

———. 2016. *The Social Life of DNA: Race, Reparations, and Reconciliation after the Genome*. Boston: Beacon.

Nelson, Jennifer. 2003. *Women of Color and the Reproductive Rights Movement*. New York: New York University Press.

Nestle, Joan. 1987. *A Restricted Country*. Ithaca, NY: Firebrand.

———. 1992. "The Femme Question." In *The Persistent Desire: A Butch-Femme Reader*, edited by Joan Nestle, 138–46. Boston: Alyson.

———. 1997. "Butch-Femme Relationships: Sexual Courage in the 1950s." In *Que(e)rying Religion: A Critical Anthology*, edited by Gary Comstock and Susan E. Henking, 323–29. New York: Continuum.

Neville, Lucy. 2018. *Girls Who Like Boys Who Like Boys: Women and Gay Male Pornography and Erotica*. London: Palgrave.

Newman, Louise Michele. 1999. *White Women's Rights: The Racial Origins of Feminism in the United States*. New York: Oxford University Press.

Newman, Peter. 2003. "Reflections on Sonagachi: An Empowerment-Based HIV-Preventive Intervention for Female Sex Workers in West Bengal, India." *Women's Studies Quarterly* 31 (1/2): 168–79.

Ngai, Mae M. 2004. *Impossible Subjects: Illegal Aliens and the Making of Modern America*. Princeton, NJ: Princeton University Press.

Ngai, Pun. 2005. "The Social Body, the Art of Discipline and Resistance." In *Made in China: Women Factory Workers in a Global Workplace*, 77–108. Durham, NC: Duke University Press.

Ngai, Sianne. 2005. *Ugly Feelings*. Cambridge, MA: Harvard University Press.

Nguyen, Hoang Tan. 2014. *A View from the Bottom: Asian American Masculinity and Sexual Representation*. Durham, NC: Duke University Press.

Nicholas V., Pope. 2017. "Romanus Pontifex: (Granting the Portuguese a Perpetual Monopoly in Trade with Africa); January 8, 1455." Papal Encyclicals Online, 2017. www.papalencyclicals.net.

Nichols, Robert. 2020. *Theft Is Property! Dispossession and Critical Theory*. Durham, NC: Duke University Press.

Niranjana, Tejaswini. 2006. *Mobilizing India: Women, Music, and Migration between India and Trinidad*. Durham, NC: Duke University Press.

Nirta, Caterina. 2014. "Trans Subjectivity and the Spatial Monolingualism of Public Toilets." *Law Critique* 25:271–88.

Noddings, Nel. 1984. *Caring: A Feminine Approach to Ethics and Moral Education*. Berkeley: University of California Press.

Norris, Zach. 2020. *We Keep Us Safe: Building Secure, Just, and Inclusive Communities*. Boston: Beacon.

Nunn, Ryan, Jana Parsons, and Jay Shambaugh. 2020. "A Dozen Facts about the Economics of the US Health-Care System." Brookings Institute, March 10, 2020. www.brookings.edu.

Nyong'o, Tavia. 2010. "The Unforgivable Transgression of Being Caster Semenya." *Women & Performance: A Journal of Feminist Theory* 20 (1): 95–100.

Oakley, Ann. 1972. *Sex, Gender and Society*. London: Temple Smith.

Oboler, Suzanne, ed. 2006. *Latinos and Citizenship: The Dilemma of Belonging*. New York: Palgrave.

Ochoa, Marcia. 2011. "Pasarelas y 'Perolones': Mediaciones Transformistas en la Avenida Libertador de Caracas." *Íconos. Revista de Ciencias Sociales*, no. 39, 123–42.

Oldenburg, Veena. 2002. *Dowry Murder: The Imperial Origins of a Cultural Crime*. New Delhi: Oxford University Press.

Omi, Michael, and Howard Winant. 1986. *Racial Formation in the United States*. 1st ed. New York: Routledge & Kegan Paul.

O'Neill, Colleen. 2019. "Testing the Limits of Colonial Parenting: Navajo Domestic Workers, the Intermountain Indian School, and the Urban Relocation Program, 1950–1962." *Ethnohistory* 66 (3): 565–92. https://doi.org/10.1215/00141801-7517958.

Ong, Aihwa. 2006. *Neoliberalism as Exception: Mutations in Citizenship and Sovereignty*. Durham, NC: Duke University Press.

Orleck, Annelise. 2005. *Storming Caesar's Palace: How Black Mothers Fought Their Own War on Poverty*. Boston: Beacon.

Orsi, Robert. 1997. "Everyday Miracles: The Study of Lived Religion." In *Lived Religion in America: Toward a History of Practice*, edited by David Hall, 3–21. Princeton, NJ: Princeton University Press.

Owens, Camille. 2020. "Blackness and the Human Child: Race, Prodigy, and the Logic of American Childhood." PhD diss., Yale University.

Owens, Emily. 2015. "Fantasies of Consent: Black Women's Sexual Labor in 19th C. New Orleans." PhD diss., Harvard University.

———. 2019. "Keyword 7: Consent." In "Sexual Politics, Sexual Panics." Special issue, *differences: A Journal of Feminist Cultural Studies* 30 (1): 148–56.

Oxford English Dictionary Online (*OED Online*). n.d. s.v. "colonialism (*n.*)." Accessed July 2, 2021. www.oed.com.

———. n.d. s.v. "identity (*n.*)." Accessed June 9, 2021. www.oed.com.

———. n.d. s.v. "imperialism (*n.*)." Accessed July 2, 2021. www.oed.com.

———. n.d. s.v. "queer (*adj.* 1), (*adj.* 2), (*n.* 1), (*v.* 1), and (*v.* 2)." Accessed June 14, 2021. www.oed.com.

———. n.d. s.v. "security." Accessed June 21, 2021. www.oed.com.

Padawer, Ruth. 2016. "The Humiliating Practice of Sex-Testing Female Athletes." *New York Times Magazine*, June 28, 2016. www.nytimes.com.

Padios, Jan M. 2018. *A Nation on the Line: Call Centers as Postcolonial Predicaments in the Philippines*. Durham, NC: Duke University Press.

Page, Cara. 2010. "Reflections from Detroit: Transforming Wellness and Wholeness." INCITE!, August 5, 2010. https://incite-national.org.

Pagonis, Pidgeon, and Sean Saifa M. Wall. 2016. "A Statement from Intersex People of Color on the 20th Anniversary of Intersex Awareness Day." *Pidgeon Pagonis*, October 26, 2016. www.pidgeonismy.name.

Paik, A. Naomi. 2016. *Rightlessness: Testimony and Redress in US Prison Camps since World War II*. Chapel Hill: University of North Carolina Press.

Painter, Nell. 2009. *The History of White People*. New York: W. W. Norton.

Palacios, Lena. 2016. "'Something Else to Be': A Chicana Survivor's Journey from Vigilante Justice to Transformative Justice." *Philosophia* 6 (1): 93–108.

Paradies, Yin C. 2006. "Beyond Black and White: Essentialism, Hybridity and Indigeneity." *Journal of Sociology* 42 (4): 355–67.

Park, Lisa Sun-Hee. 2011. *Entitled to Nothing: The Struggle for Immigrant Health Care in the Age of Welfare Reform*. New York: New York University Press.

Parker, Barbara, Jennifer Brady, Elaine Power, and Susan Belya, eds. 2019. *Feminist Food Studies: Intersectional Perspectives*. Toronto: Women's Press.

Parreñas, Rhacel Salazar. (2001) 2015. *Servants of Globalization: Migration and Domestic Work*. Stanford, CA: Stanford University Press.

———. 2011. *Illicit Flirtations: Labor, Migration, and Sex Trafficking in Tokyo*. Stanford, CA: Stanford University Press.

Pascoe, Peggy. 1990. *Relations of Rescue: The Search for Female Moral Authority in the American West, 1874–1939*. New York: Oxford University Press.

Pasternak, Shiri. 2017. *Grounded Authority: The Algonquins of Barriere Lake against the State*. Minneapolis: University of Minnesota Press.

Patel, Alphesh Kantilal. n.d. "La Chica Boom's Failed, Decolonial Spictacles." Hemispheric Institute. Accessed June 8, 2021. https://hemisphericinstitute.org.

Patel, Geeta. 2017. *Risky Bodies and Techno-intimacy*. Seattle: University of Washington Press.

Pateman, Carol. 1988. *The Sexual Contract*. Palo Alto, CA: Stanford University Press.

Patil, Vrushali. 2013. "From Patriarchy to Intersectionality: A Transnational Feminist Assessment of How Far We've Really Come." *Signs: Journal of Women in Culture and Society* 38 (4): 847–67.

Patton, Cindy. 1990. *Inventing AIDS*. New York: Routledge.

Patton, Cindy, and Benigno Sánchez-Eppler, eds. 2000. *Queer Diasporas*. Durham, NC: Duke University Press.

Paxson, Frederic L. 1924. *The History of the American Frontier, 1763–1893*. Boston: Houghton Mifflin.

Penley, Constance. 2004. "Crackers and Whackers: The White Trashing of Porn." In *Porn Studies*, edited by Linda Williams, 309–31. Durham, NC: Duke University Press.

Penner, Barbara. 2013. *Bathroom*. London: Reaktion.

Pennington, Bill. 2017. "Lindsey Vonn May Get Her Chance to Race against Men in 2018." *New York Times*, September 27, 2017. www.nytimes.com.

Perego, Elizabeth. 2015. "The Veil or a Brother's Life: French Manipulations of Muslim Women's Images during the Algerian War, 1954–62." *Journal of North African Studies* 20 (3): 349–73.

Perkins, Edwin J. 1980. *The Economy of Colonial America*. New York: Columbia University Press.

Peterson, Emily E., Nicole L. Davis, David Goodman, Shanna Cox, Carla Syverson, Kristi Seed, Carrie Shapiro-Mendoza, William M. Callaghan, and Wanda Barfield. 2019. "Racial/Ethnic Disparities in Pregnancy-Related Deaths—United

States, 2007–2016." *Morbidity and Mortality Weekly Report* 68 (35): 762.

Petti, Alessandro, Sandi Hilal, and Eyal Weizman. 2014. *Architecture after Revolution*. Berlin: Sternberg.

Pezzutto, Sophie. 2018. "Why Adult Video Stars Rely on Camming." *Conversation*, November 21, 2018. https://theconversation.com.

———. 2019. "From Porn Performer to Porntropreneur: Online Entrepreneurship, Social Media Branding, and Selfhood in Contemporary Trans Pornography." *AG about Gender: International Journal of Gender Studies* 8 (16): 30–60.

Pezzutto, Sophie, and Lynn Comella. 2020. "Trans Pornography: Mapping an Emerging Field." *TSQ: Transgender Studies Quarterly* 7 (2): 152–71.

Piepzna-Samarasinha, Leah Lakshmi. 2016. "A Not-So-Brief Personal History of the Healing Justice Movement, 2010–2016." *MICE*, no. 2. http://micemagazine.ca.

———. 2017. "Femme Futures." *Hematopoiesis Press*, no. 2. https://poets.org.

———. 2018. *Care Work: Dreaming Disability Justice*. Vancouver, Canada: Arsenal Pulp.

Pinto, Samantha. 2020. *Infamous Bodies: Early Black Women's Celebrity and the Afterlives of Rights*. Durham, NC: Duke University Press.

Pitts-Taylor, Victoria. 2016. *The Brain's Body: Neuroscience and Corporeal Politics*. Durham, NC: Duke University Press.

Plumwood, Val. 1989. "Do We Need a Sex/Gender Distinction?" *Radical Philosophy* 51 (2): 2–11.

Potter, Claire. 2014. "Inside the Red Zone: The College Rape Season." *Chronicle of Higher Education*, July 13, 2014.

Potter, Hillary. 2015. *Intersectionality and Criminology: Disrupting and Revolutionizing Studies of Crime*. London: Routledge.

Povinelli, Elizabeth A. 2002. *The Cunning of Recognition: Indigenous Alterities and the Making of Australian Multiculturalism*. Durham, NC: Duke University Press.

———. 2011a. *Economies of Abandonment: Social Belonging and Endurance in Late Liberalism*. Durham, NC: Duke University Press.

———. 2011b. "The Governance of the Prior." *Interventions* 13 (1): 13–30.

Prakash, Gyan. 1994. "Subaltern Studies as Postcolonial Criticism." *American Historical Review* 99:1475–90.

Pratt, Richard. 1973. "The Advantages of Mingling Indians with Whites." In *Americanizing the American Indians: Writings by the "Friends of the Indian," 1880–1900*, edited by Francis Paul Prucha, 260–71. Cambridge, MA: Harvard University Press.

Preciado, Paul B. 2013. *Testo Junkie: Sex, Drugs, and Biopolitics in the Pharmacopornographic Era*. Translated by Bruce Benderson. New York: Feminist Press.

Price, Margaret. 2015. "The Bodymind Problem and the Possibilities of Pain." *Hypatia: A Journal of Feminist Philosophy* 30 (1): 268–84.

Program for the Study of LGBT Health. n.d. "Ehrhardt—Program for the Study of LGBT Health." Accessed May 25, 2020. www.lgbthealthprogram.org.

Prohaska, Ariane, and Jeffrey R. Jones. 2017. "Fat Sexuality as Deviance." In *Routledge Handbook on Deviance*, edited by Stephen E. Brown and Ophir Sefiha, 272–81. New York: Routledge.

Prosser, Jay. 1998. *Second Skins: The Body Narratives of Transsexuality*. New York: Columbia University Press.

Pryor, Jaclyn. 2017. *Time Slips: Queer Temporalities, Contemporary Performance, and the Hole of History*. Evanston, IL: Northwestern University Press.

Puar, Jasbir K. 2007. *Terrorist Assemblages: Homonationalism in Queer Times*. Durham, NC: Duke University Press.

———. 2017. *The Right to Maim: Debility, Capacity, Disability*. Durham, NC: Duke University Press.

Pulley, Anna. 2013. "Femmepire Records: Jewelle Gomez on Adornment and the Point of Feminism." *SF Weekly*. Accessed July 1, 2021. https://archives.sfweekly.com.

Puri, Jyoti. 2016. *Sexual States: Governance and the Struggle over the Antisodomy Law in India*. Durham, NC: Duke University Press.

Pyle, Kai. 2018. "Naming and Claiming: Recovering Ojibwe and Plains Cree Two-Spirit Language." *TSQ: Transgender Studies Quarterly* 5 (4): 574–88.

Quadagno, Jill. 1996. *The Color of Welfare: How Racism Undermined the War on Poverty*. Rev. ed. New York: Oxford University Press.

Queen, Carol. 2015. "Good Vibrations, Women, and Porn: A History." In *New Views on Pornography: Sexuality, Politics, and the Law*, edited by Lynn Comella and Shira Tarrant, 179–90. Santa Barbara, CA: Praeger.

Quiroga, José. 2000. *Tropics of Desire: Interventions from Queer Latino America*. New York: New York University Press.

Qureshi, Sadiah. 2004. "Displaying Sara Baartman, the 'Hottentot Venus.'" *History of Science* 42, no. 2 (June): 233–57.

Raffo, Susan. 2019. *Healing Justice: Building Power, Transforming Movements*. New York: Astraea Lesbian Foundation for Justice. www.astraeafoundation.org.

Raghuram, Parvati. 2019. "Race and Feminist Care Ethics: Intersectionality as Method." *Gender, Place & Culture* 26 (5): 613–37.

Raha, Nat. 2017. "Transfeminine Brokenness, Radical Trans-feminism." *South Atlantic Quarterly* 116 (3): 632–46.

Rajunov, Micah, and Scott Duane, eds. 2019. *Nonbinary: Memoirs of Gender and Identity*. New York: Columbia University Press.

Ramirez, Renya. 2007. *Native Hubs: Culture, Community, and Belonging in Silicon Valley and Beyond*. Durham, NC: Duke University Press.

Rand, Erica. 2005. *The Ellis Island Snowglobe*. Durham, NC: Duke University Press.

———. 2013. "Court and Sparkle: Kye Allums, Johnny Wier, and Raced Problems in Gender Authenticity." *GLQ: A Journal of Lesbian and Gay Studies* 19 (4): 435–63.

Rankine, Claudia. 2015. "The Meaning of Serena Williams." *New York Times*, August 25, 2015.

Ransby, Barbara. 2003. *Ella Baker and the Black Freedom Movement: A Radical Democratic Vision*. Chapel Hill: University of North Carolina Press.

Rao, Rahul. 2020. *Out of Time: The Queer Politics of Postcoloniality*. New York: Oxford University Press.

Raymond, Janice. 1979. *The Transsexual Empire: The Making of the She-Male*. Boston: Beacon.

Razack, Sherene. 2008. *Casting Out: The Eviction of Muslims from Western Law and Politics*. Toronto: University of Toronto Press.

Reagon, Bernice Johnson. 1983. "Coalition Politics: Turning the Century." In *Home Girls: A Black Feminist Anthology*, edited by Barbara Smith, 356–68. New York: Kitchen Table: Women of Color Press.

Reardon, Jenny. 2002. *Race to the Finish: Identity and Governance in an Age of Genomics*. Princeton, NJ: Princeton University Press.

Reddy, Chandan. 2011. *Freedom with Violence: Race, Sexuality, and the US State*. Durham, NC: Duke University Press.

Reddy, Vanita. 2016. *Fashioning Diaspora: Beauty, Femininity, and South Asian American Culture*. Philadelphia: Temple University Press.

Red Nation. n.d. "Preamble: Principles of Unity." Accessed December 21, 2020. https://therednation.org.

Rednour, Shar, and Jackie Strano. 2015. "Steamy, Hot, and Political: Creating Radical Dyke Porn." In *New Views on Pornography: Sexuality, Politics, and the Law*, edited by Lynn Comella and Shira Tarrant, 165–77. Santa Barbara, CA: Praeger.

Rege, Sharmila. 2003. *Writing Caste, Writing Gender*. New Delhi: Zubaan.

Reid-Pharr, Robert. 2016. *Archives of Flesh: African America, Spain, and Post-humanist Critique*. New York: New York University Press.

Reis, Elizabeth, and Suzanne Kessler. 2010. "Why History Matters: Fetal Dex and Intersex." *American Journal of Bioethics* 10 (9): 58–59.

Repo, Jemima. 2015. *The Biopolitics of Gender*. Oxford: Oxford University Press.

Revolutions Per Minute. 2014. "Indigenous Futurisms Mixtape." November 22, 2014. http://rpm.fm.

Richardson, Matt. 2020. "Ajita Wilson: Blaxploitation, Sexploitation, and the Making of Black Womanhood." *TSQ: Transgender Studies Quarterly* 7 (2): 192–207.

Richie, Beth E. 1996. *Compelled to Crime: The Gender Entrapment of Battered Black Women*. New York: Routledge.

———. 2012. *Arrested Justice: Black Women, Violence, and America's Prison Nation*. New York: New York University Press.

———. 2017. *Invisible No More: Police Violence against Black Women and Women of Color*. Boston: Beacon.

Rifkin, Mark. 2011. *When Did Indians Become Straight? Kinship, the History of Sexuality, and Native Sovereignty*. New York: Oxford University Press.

Ring, Jennifer. 2010. *Stolen Bases: Why American Women Don't Play Baseball*. Urbana: University of Illinois Press.

Rioja, Romina A. Green. 2019. "'Until Living Becomes Worth It: Notes from the Chilean Uprising." Abusable Past, November 1, 2019. www.radicalhistoryreview.org.

Rios, Victor. 2011. *Punished: Policing the Lives of Black and Latino Boys*. New York: New York University Press.

Rist, Gilbert. 2008. *The History of Development: From Western Origins to Global Faith*. London: Zed.

Roach, Joseph. 1996. *Cities of the Dead: Circum-Atlantic Performance*. New York: Columbia University Press.

Roberts, Dorothy. 1997. *Killing the Black Body: Race, Reproduction, and the Meaning of Liberty*. New York: Vintage.

———. 2006. "Feminism, Race, and Adoption Policy." In *Color of Violence: The INCITE! Anthology*, edited by INCITE! Women of Color Against Violence, 42–52. Cambridge, MA: South End.

———. 2011. *Fatal Invention: How Science, Politics, and Big Business Re-create Race in the Twenty-First Century*. New York: New Press.

———. 2015. "Reproductive Justice, Not Just Rights." *Dissent*, October 6, 2015. www.dissentmagazine.org.

Roberts, Monica. 2009. "Cisgender Isn't an Insult." *TransGriot* (blog), July 10, 2009. http://transgriot.blogspot.com.

Robinson, Cedric. (1983) 2019. *Black Marxism: The Making of a Black Radical Tradition*. Chapel Hill: University of North Carolina Press.

Robinson, William. 1922. *Married Life and Happiness, or Love and Comfort in Marriage*. New York: Eugenics.

Rodney, Walter. 1972. *How Europe Underdeveloped Africa*. London: Bogle L'Ouverture.

Rodríguez, Ileana. 2000. "Cross-Genealogies in Latin American and South Asian Subaltern Studies." *Nepantla: Views from South* 1 (1): 45–58.

Rodríguez, Juana María. 2003. *Queer Latinidad: Identity Practices, Discursive Spaces*. New York: New York University Press.

———. 2011. "Queer Sociality and Other Sexual Fantasies." *GLQ: A Journal of Lesbian and Gay Studies* 17 (2–3): 331–48.

———. 2014. *Sexual Futures, Queer Gestures, and Other Latina Longings*. New York: New York University Press.

Rodríguez, Richard T. 2009. *Next of Kin: The Family in Chicano/a Cultural Politics*. Minneapolis: University of Minnesota Press.

Rogin, Richard. 1970. "Now It's Welfare Lib." *New York Times*, September 27, 1970.

Rosaldo, Renato. 1997. "Cultural Citizenship, Inequality, and Multiculturalism." In *Latino Cultural Citizenship: Claiming Identity, Space, and Rights*, edited by William V. Flores and Rina Benmayor, 27–38. Boston: Beacon.

Rose, Chloë Brushwood. 2002. "Introduction: A Brazen Posture." In *Brazen Femme: Queer Femininity*, edited by Chloë Brushwood Rose and Anna Camilleri, 11–15. Vancouver: Arsenal Pulp.

Rosen, Hannah. 2009. *Terror in the Heart of Freedom: Citizenship, Sexual Violence, and the Meaning of Race in the Postemancipation South*. Chapel Hill: University of North Carolina Press.

Ross, Loretta, and Rickie Solinger. 2017. *Reproductive Justice: An Introduction*. Berkeley: University of California Press.

Ross, Luana. 1998. *Inventing the Savage: The Social Construction of Native American Criminality*. Austin: University of Texas Press.

Ross, MacIntosh, and Janice Forsyth. 2020. "A Good Fight: How Indigenous Women Approach Boxing as a Mechanism for Social Change." *Journal of Sport and Social Issues* 45 (4): 303–28.

Rouse, Carolyn. 2004. *Engaged Surrender: African American Women and Islam*. Berkeley: University of California Press.

Roy, Ananya. 2010. *Poverty Capital: Microfinance and the Making of Development*. New York: Routledge.

Roy, Deboleena. 2018. *Molecular Feminisms: Biology, Becomings, and Life in the Lab*. Seattle: University of Washington Press.

Royalle, Candida. 2013. "'What's a Nice Girl like You. . . .'" In *The Feminist Porn Book: The Politics of Producing Pleasure*, edited by Tristan Taormino, Celine Parreñas Shimizu, Constance Penley, and Mireille Miller-Young, 58–69. New York: Feminist Press.

Rubin, David. 2017. *Intersex Matters: Biomedical Embodiment, Gender Regulation, and Transnational Activism*. Albany: State University of New York Press.

Rubin, Gayle. (1975) 1997. "The Traffic in Women: Notes on the Political Economy of Sex." In *The Second Wave: A Reader in Feminist Theory*, edited by Linda Nicholson, 27–62. New York: Routledge.

———. (1984) 2011. "Thinking Sex." In *Deviations a Gayle Rubin Reader*, edited by Gayle Rubin, 137–81. Durham, NC: Duke University Press.

———. 2002. "Studying Sexual Subcultures: Excavating the Ethnography of Gay Communities in Urban North America." In *Out in Theory: The Emergence of Lesbian and Gay Anthropology*, edited by Ellen Lewin and William L. Leap, 17–68. Urbana: University of Illinois Press.

Ruiz, Sandra. 2019. *Ricanness: Enduring Time in Anticolonial Performance*. New York: New York University Press.

Rusert, Britt. 2017. *Fugitive Science: Empiricism and Freedom in Early African American Culture*. New York: New York University Press.

Russett, Cynthia Eagle. 1989. *Sexual Science: The Victorian Construction of Womanhood*. Cambridge, MA: Harvard University Press.

Russo, Ann. 2018. *Feminist Accountability: Disrupting Violence and Transforming Power*. New York: New York University Press.

Said, Edward. 1978. *Orientalism*. New York: Pantheon.

Sakai, Naoki. 1997. *Translation and Subjectivity: On "Japan" and Cultural Nationalism*. Minneapolis: University of Minnesota Press.

Sakr, Shereen L. 2015. "A Virtual Body Politic on #Gaza: The Mobilization of Information Patterns." *Networking Knowledge: Journal of the MeCCSA Postgraduate Network* 8 (2). https://doi.org/10.31165/nk.2015.82.373.

Salamon, Gayle. 2010. *Assuming a Body: Transgender and Rhetorics of Materiality*. New York: Columbia University Press.

Saldaña-Portillo, María Josefina. 2016. *Indian Given: Racial Geographies across Mexico and the United States*. Durham, NC: Duke University Press.

Salzinger, Leslie. 2004. "From Gender as Object to Gender as Verb: Rethinking How Global Restructuring Happens." *Critical Sociology* 30 (1): 43–62.

Samois. 1981. *Coming to Power: Writing and Graphics on Lesbian S/M*. Boston: Alyson.

Samuels, Ellen. 2014. *Fantasies of Identification: Disability, Gender, Race*. New York: New York University Press.

Sandberg, Sheryl, and Nell Scovell. 2013. *Lean In: Women, Work, and the Will to Lead*. New York: Knopf.

Sandoval, Chela. 2000. *Methodology of the Oppressed*. Minneapolis: University of Minnesota Press.

Sandoval-Sánchez, Alberto. 2005. "Politicizing Abjection: In the Manner of a Prologue for the Articulation of AIDS Latino Queer Identities." *American Literary History* 17 (3): 542–49.

Sangari, Kumkum, and Sudesh Vaid, eds. 1990. *Recasting Women: Essays in Indian Colonial History*. New Brunswick, NJ: Rutgers University Press.

Santana, Dora Silva. 2017. "Transitionings and Returnings: Experiments with the Poetics of Transatlantic Water." *TSQ: Transgender Studies Quarterly* 4 (2): 181–90.

Sarkar, Tanika. 2002. *Hindu Wife, Hindu Nation*. Bloomington: Indiana University Press.

Sartre, Jean-Paul. 1948. *The Emotions: Outline of a Theory*. Translated by Bernard Frechtman. New York: Philosophical Library.

Sassen, Saskia. 1990. *Mobility of Labor and Capital*. Cambridge: Cambridge University Press.

———. 1999. *Guests and Aliens*. New York: New Press.

Sawers, Catherine. 2014. "The Women of Bataille D'alger: Hearts and Minds and Bombs." *Journal of Middle East Women's Studies* 10 (2): 80–106.

Saxton, Marsha. 2006. "Disability Rights and Selective Abortion." In *The Disability Studies Reader*, 2nd ed., edited by Lennard J. Davis, 105–16. New York: Routledge.

Sayers, William. 2010. "The Etymology of Queer." *ANQ: A Quarterly Journal of Short Articles, Notes and Reviews* 18 (2): 17–19.

Schaefer, Eric. 1999. *Bold, Daring, Shocking, True! A History of Exploitation Films, 1919–1959*. Durham, NC: Duke University Press.

———, ed. 2014. *Sex Scene: Media and the Sexual Revolution*. Durham, NC: Duke University Press.

Schaeffer-Grabiel, Felicity. 2005. "Planetlove.com: Cyberbrides in the Americas and the Transnational Routes of US Masculinity." *Signs: Journal of Women in Culture and Society* 31:331–56.

Schalk, Sami. 2013. "Coming to Claim Crip: Disidentification with/in Disability Studies." *Disability Studies Quarterly* 33 (2). https://dsq-sds.org.

———. 2017. "Disability and Women's Writing." In *The Cambridge Companion to Literature and Disability*, edited by Clare Barker and Stuart Murray, 170–84. Cambridge: Cambridge University Press.

———. 2018. *Bodyminds Reimagined: (Dis)ability, Race and Gender in Black Women's Speculative Fiction*. Durham, NC: Duke University Press.

Schenwar, Maya, and Victoria Law. 2020. *Prison by Any Other Name: The Harmful Consequences of Popular Reforms*. New York: New Press.

Schiebinger, Londa. 2004. *Nature's Body: Gender in the Making of Modern Science*. New Brunswick, NJ: Rutgers University Press.

Schmitt, Carl. (1927) 2007. *The Concept of the Political*. Translated by George Schwab. Chicago: University of Chicago Press.

Schoen, Johanna. 2005. *Choice and Coercion: Birth Control, Sterilization, and Abortion in Public Health and Welfare*. Chapel Hill: University of North Carolina Press.

Schrader, Astrid, Elizabeth R. Johnson, Henry Buller, Deborah Robinson, Simon Rundle, Dorion Sagan, Susanne Schmitt, and John Spicer. 2017. "Considering Killability: Experiments in Unsettling Life and Death." *Catalyst: Feminism, Theory, Technoscience* 3 (2). https://doi.org/10.28968/cftt.v3i2.28849.

Schuller, Kyla. 2018. *The Biopolitics of Feeling: Race, Sex, and Science in the Nineteenth Century*. Durham, NC: Duke University Press.

Schulman, Sarah. 2013. *The Gentrification of the Mind: Witness to a Lost Imagination*. Oakland: University of California Press.

Schur, Edwin M. 1984. *Labeling Women Deviant: Gender, Stigma, and Social Control*. New York: Random House.

Scott, Darieck. 2010. *Extravagant Abjection: Blackness, Power, and Sexuality in the African American Literary Imagination*. New York: New York University Press.

Scott, Joan Wallach. 1986. "Gender: A Useful Category of Historical Analysis." *American Historical Review* 91 (5): 1053–75.

———. 1992. "Experience." In *Feminists Theorize the Political*, edited by Judith Butler and Joan Scott, 22–40. New York: Routledge.

Sedgwick, Eve Kosofsky. 1980. *The Coherence of Gothic Conventions*. New York: Arno.

———. 1990. *Epistemology of the Closet*. Berkeley: University of California Press.

Sedgwick, Eve Kosofsky, and Adam Frank, eds. 1995. *Shame and Its Sisters: A Silvan Tompkins Reader*. Durham, NC: Duke University Press.

Segrest, Mab. 2020. *Administrations of Lunacy: Racism and the Haunting of American Psychiatry at the Milledgeville Asylum*. New York: New Press.

Segura, Denise A., and Patricia Zavella. 2007. *Women and Migration in the US-Mexico Borderlands*. Durham, NC: Duke University Press.

Self, Robert. 2012. *All in the Family: The Realignment of American Democracy in the 1960s*. New York: Hill & Wang.

Sen, Gita, and Caren Grown. 1987. *Development, Crises and Alternative Visions: Third World Women's Perspectives*. London: Monthly Review.

Serano, Julia. 2014. "Julia Serano's Compendium on Cisgender, Cissexual, Cissexism, Cisgenderism, Cis Privilege, and the Cis/Trans Distinction." *Whipping Girl* (blog), December 16, 2014. http://juliaserano.blogspot.com.

Sered, Danielle. 2019. *Until We Reconcile: Violence, Mass Incarceration and Road to Repair*. New York: New Press.

Sered, Susan Starr, and Maureen Norton-Hawk. 2014. *Can't Catch a Break: Gender, Jail, Drugs, and the Limits of Personal Responsibility*. Oakland: University of California Press.

Seresin, Indiana. 2019. "On Heteropessimism: Heterosexuality Is Nobody's Personal Problem." *New Inquiry*, October 9, 2019. https://thenewinquiry.com.

Shah, Nayan. 2001. *Contagious Divides: Epidemics and Race in San Francisco's Chinatown*. Berkeley: University of California Press.

———. 2012. *Stranger Intimacy: Contesting Race, Sexuality, and the Law in the North American West*. Durham, NC: Duke University Press.

Shah, Svati. 2014. *Street Corner Secrets: Sex, Work, and Migration in the City of Mumbai*. Durham, NC: Duke University Press.

Shahani, Nishant. 2016. "How to Survive the Whitewashing of AIDS: Global Pasts, Transnational Futures." *QED: A Journal in GLBTQ Worldmaking* 3 (1): 1–33.

Shaikh, Sa'diyya. 2013. "Feminism, Epistemology and Experience: Critically (En)gendering the Study of Islam." *Journal for Islamic Studies* 33:14–47.

Shakhsari, Sima. 2014. "The Queer Time of Death: Temporality, Geopolitics, and Refugee Rights." *Sexualities* 17 (8): 998–1015.

———. 2020. *Politics of Rightful Killing: Civil Society, Gender, and Sexuality in Weblogistan*. Durham, NC: Duke University Press.

Shange, Savannah. 2019. "Play Aunties and Dyke Bitches: Gender, Generation, and the Ethics of Black Queer Kinship." *Black Scholar* 49 (1): 40–54. https://doi.org/10.1080/00064246.2019.1548058.

Sharma, Aradhana. 2008. *Logics of Empowerment: Gender, Development, and Governance in Neoliberal India*. Minneapolis: University of Minnesota Press.

Sharman, Zena, ed. 2016. *The Remedy: Queer and Trans Voices on Health and Health Care*. Vancouver: Arsenal Pulp.

Sharpe, Christina. 2010. *Monstrous Intimacies: Making Post-slavery Subjects*. Durham, NC: Duke University Press.

———. 2016. *In the Wake: On Blackness and Being*. Durham, NC: Duke University Press.

Sharpless, Rebecca. 2013. *Cooking in Other Women's Kitchens: Domestic Workers in the South, 1865–1960*. Chapel Hill: University of North Carolina Press.

Shelton, Perrē L. 2018. "Reconsidering Femme Identity: On Centering Trans* Counterculture and Conceptualizing Trans*Femme Theory." *Journal of Black Sexuality and Relationships* 5 (1): 21–41.

Shilling, Dan, and Melissa Nelson, eds. 2018. *Traditional Ecological Knowledge: Learning from Indigenous Practices for Environmental Sustainability*. Cambridge: Cambridge University Press.

Shimakawa, Karen. 2002. *National Abjection: The Asian American Body Onstage*. Durham, NC: Duke University Press.

Shimizu, Celine Parreñas. 2007. *The Hypersexuality of Race: Performing Asian/American Women on Screen and Scene*. Durham, NC: Duke University Press.

Shippers, Mimi. 2016. *Beyond Monogamy: Polyamory and the Future of Polyqueer Sexualities*. New York: New York University Press.

Showden, Carisa, and Samantha Majic. 2018. *Youth Who Trade Sex in the US: Intersectionality, Agency, and Vulnerability*. Philadelphia: Temple University Press.

Siddiqi, Dina M. 2009. "Do Bangladesh Sweatshop Workers Need Saving? Sisterhood in the Post-sweatshop Era." *Feminist Review* 91 (1): 154–74.

Silko, Leslie Marmon. 1998. "Interior and Exterior Landscapes." In *Speaking for the Generations: Native Writers on Writing*, edited by Simon Ortiz, 2–24. Tucson: University of Arizona Press.

Silliman, Jael, and Anannya Bhattacharjee, eds. 2002. *Policing the National Body: Race, Gender, and Criminalization*. Cambridge, MA: South End.

Silva, Noenoe K. 2017. *The Power of the Steel-Tipped Pen: Reconstructing Native Hawaiian Intellectual History*. Durham, NC: Duke University Press.

Silvey, Rachel. 2004. "Power, Difference and Mobility: Feminist Advances in Migration Studies." *Progress in Human Geography* 28, no. 4 (August): 1–17.

Simmons, LaKisha Michelle. 2015. *Crescent City Girls: The Lives of Young Black Women in Segregated New Orleans*. Chapel Hill: University of North Carolina Press.

Simpson, Audra. 2007. "On Ethnographic Refusal: Indigeneity, 'Voice' and Colonial Citizenship." *Junctures* 9:67–80.

———. 2008. "Subjects of Sovereignty: Indigeneity, the Revenue Rule, and Juridics of Failed Consent." *Law and Contemporary Problems* 71 (3): 191–216.

———. 2014. *Mohawk Interruptus: Political Life across the Borders of Settler States*. Durham, NC: Duke University Press.

———. 2016. "The State Is a Man: Theresa Spence, Loretta Saunders and the Gender of Settler Sovereignty." *Theory & Event* 19 (4). https://muse.jhu.edu.

———. 2017. "The Ruse of 'Consent' and the Anatomy of Refusal: Cases from Indigenous North America and Australia." *Postcolonial Studies* 20 (1): 18–33.

———. 2018. "Sovereignty, Sympathy, and Indigeneity." In *Ethnographies of US Empire*, edited by Carole McGranahan and John F. Collins, 72–90. Durham, NC: Duke University Press.

———. 2020. "Empire of Feeling." *General Anthropology* 27:1–8.

Simpson, Leanne Betasamosake. 2011. *Dancing on Our Turtle's Back: Stories of Nishnaabeg Re-creation, Resurgence and a New Emergence*. Winnipeg: Arbeiter Ring.

———. 2017. *As We Have Always Done: Indigenous Freedom through Radical Resistance*. Minneapolis: University of Minnesota Press.

Simpson, Leanne Betasamosake, Rinaldo Walcott, and Glen Coulthard. 2018. "Idle No More and Black Lives Matter: An Exchange." *Studies in Social Justice* 12 (1): 75–89.

Sinclair, Niigaan. 2016. "Returning to Ourselves: Two-Spirit Futures and the Now." In *Love beyond the Body, Space and Time: An Indigenous LGBT Sci-Fi Anthology*, edited by Hope Nicholson, 12–19. Winnipeg: Bedside.

Sinha, Mrinalini. 1995. *Colonial Masculinity: The "Manly Englishman" and the "Effeminate Bengali" in the Late Nineteenth Century*. Manchester: University of Manchester Press.

Sins Invalid. 2015. "10 Principles of Disability Justice." September 17, 2015. www.sinsinvalid.org.

Sithole, Tendayi. 2020. *The Black Register*. Cambridge: Polity.

Skidmore, Emily. 2011. "Constructing the 'Good' Transsexual." *Feminist Studies* 37 (2): 270–300.

Smith, Andrea. 2005. *Conquest: Sexual Violence and American Indian Genocide*. Boston: South End.

———. 2010. "Queer Theory and Native Studies: The Heteronormativity of Settler Colonialism." *GLQ: A Journal of Lesbian and Gay Studies* 16 (1–2): 42–68.

Smith, Bonnie G., and Beth Hutchinson, eds. 2004. *Gendering Disability*. New Brunswick, NJ: Rutgers University Press.

Smith, Clarissa. 2007. *One for the Girls: The Pleasures and Practices of Pornography for Women*. Bristol, UK: Intellect.

Smith, Linda Tuhiwai. 1999. *Decolonizing Methodologies: Research and Indigenous Peoples*. London: Zed.

Smith, Molly, and Juno Mac. 2018. *Revolting Prostitutes: The Fight for Sex Workers' Rights*. London: Verso.

Smyth, Cherry, and Judith Roof. 1998. "Butch/Femme: Inside Lesbian Gender." In *Butch/Femme: Inside Lesbian Gender*, edited by Sally Munt, 27–36. London: Cassell.

Snorton, C. Riley. 2016. "Gender Trouble in Triton." In *No Tea, No Shade: New Writings in Black Queer Studies*, edited by E. Patrick Johnson, 83–94. Durham, NC: Duke University Press.

———. 2017. *Black on Both Sides: A Racial History of Trans Identity*. Minneapolis: University of Minnesota Press.

Snorton, C. Riley, and Jin Haritaworn. 2013. "Trans Necropolitics: A Transnational Reflection on Violence, Death and the Trans of Color Afterlife." In *The Transgender Studies Reader 2*, edited by Susan Stryker and Aren Z. Aizura, 66–76. New York: Routledge.

Sojoyner, Damien. 2016. *First Strike: Educational Enclosure in Los Angeles*. Minneapolis: University of Minnesota Press.

Somerville, Siobhan. 2000. *Queering the Color Line: Race and the Invention of Homosexuality in American Culture*. Durham, NC: Duke University Press.

———. 2005. "Notes toward a Queer History of Naturalization." *American Quarterly* 57, no. 3 (September): 659–75.

Soto, Sandra K. 2005. "Where in the Transnational World Are US Women of Color?" In *Women's Studies for the Future*, edited by Elizabeth Lapovsky Kennedy and Agatha Beins, 111–24. New Brunswick, NJ: Rutgers University Press.

Southern Poverty Law Center (SPLC). n.d. "Anti-immigration Groups." Accessed June 19, 2021. www.splcenter.org.

Spade, Dean. 2011. *Normal Life: Administrative Violence, Critical Trans Politics, and the Limits of Law*. Boston: South End.

Speed, Shannon. 2019. *Incarcerated Stories: Indigenous Women Migrants and Violence in the Settler-Capitalist State*. Chapel Hill: University of North Carolina Press.

Spelman, Elizabeth. 1988. *Inessential Woman: Problems of Exclusion in Feminist Thought*. Boston: Beacon.

Spice, Anne. 2018. "Fighting Invasive Infrastructures: Indigenous Relations against Pipelines." *Environment and Society: Advances in Research* 9:40–56.

Spillers, Hortense. 1987. "Mama's Baby, Papa's Maybe: An American Grammar Book." *Diacritics* 17 (2): 64–81.

———. (1987) 2003. "Mama's Baby, Papa's Maybe: An American Grammar Book." In *Black, White, and in Color: Essays on American Literature and Culture*, 203–29. Chicago: University of Chicago Press.

———. 2003. "Introduction: Peter's Pans: Eating in the Diaspora." In *Black, White, and in Color: Essays on American Literature and Culture*, 1–64. Chicago: University of Chicago Press.

Spillers, Hortense, Saidiya Hartman, Farah Jasmine Griffin, Shelly Eversley, and Jennifer L. Morgan. 2007. "'Whatcha Gonna Do?' Revisiting 'Mama's Baby, Papa's Maybe: An American Grammar Book'; A Conversation with Hortense Spillers, Saidiya Hartman, Farah Jasmine Griffin, Shelly Eversley, and Jennifer L. Morgan." *Women's Studies Quarterly* 35 (1/2): 299–309.

Spivak, Gayatri Chakravorty. 1985. "Can the Subaltern Speak? Speculations on Widow Sacrifice." *Wedge*, nos. 7–8 (Winter/Spring): 120–30.

———. 1988. "Can the Subaltern Speak?" In *Marxism and the Interpretation of Culture*, edited by Cary Nelson and Lawrence Grossberg, 271–313. Urbana: University of Illinois Press.

———. 1993. "Can the Subaltern Speak?" In *Colonial Discourse and Post-colonial Theory: A Reader*, edited by Patrick Williams and Laura Chrisman, 66–111. New York: Harvester Wheatsheaf.

———. 1999. *A Critique of Postcolonial Reason: Toward a History of the Vanishing Present*. Cambridge, MA: Harvard University Press.

Stanley, Eric A., and Nat Smith, eds. (2011) 2015. *Captive Genders: Trans Embodiment and the Prison Industrial Complex*. Oakland, CA: AK.

Stanton, Elizabeth Cady. (1854) 2007. "Address to the Legislature of New York, Albany, February 14, 1854." In *Elizabeth Cady Stanton: Feminist as Thinker*, edited by Ellen Carol DuBois and Richard Cándida Smith, 155–69. New York: New York University Press.

Star, Wendy Red. n.d. "Thunder Up Above." Accessed June 19, 2021. www.wendyredstar.com.

Stardust, Zahra. 2019. "From Amateur Aesthetics to Intelligible Orgasms: Pornographic Authenticity and Precarious Labour in the Gig Economy." *AG about Gender: International Journal of Gender Studies* 8 (16): 1–29.

Stark, Heidi Kiiwetinepinesiik. 2012. "Marked by Fire: Anishinaabe Articulations of Nationhood in Treaty Making with the United States and Canada." *American Indian Quarterly* 36 (2): 119–49.

———. 2016. "Criminal Empire: The Making of the Savage in a Lawless Land." *Theory & Event* 19 (4). https://muse.jhu.edu.

Stepan, Nancy Leys. 1991. *"The Hour of Eugenics": Race, Gender and Nation in Latin America.* Ithaca, NY: Cornell University Press.

Stern, Alexandra Minna. (2005) 2016. *Eugenic Nation: Faults and Frontiers of Better Breeding in Modern America*. 2nd ed. Berkeley: University of California Press.

Stevens, Jacqueline. 1999. *Reproducing the State*. Princeton, NJ: Princeton University Press.

Stevenson, Lisa. 2014. *Life beside Itself: Imagining Care in the Canadian Arctic*. Berkeley: University of California Press.

Stewart, Kathleen. 2010. "Afterword: Worlding Refrains." In *The Affect Studies Reader*, edited by Gregory J. Seigworth, Melissa Gregg, and Sara Ahmed, 339–54. Durham, NC: Duke University Press.

Stockton, Kathryn Bond. 2006. *Beautiful Bottom, Beautiful Shame: Where "Black" Meets "Queer."* Durham, NC: Duke University Press.

Stoler, Ann Laura. 1995. *Race and the Education of Desire: Foucault's History of Sexuality and the Colonial Order of Things*. Durham, NC: Duke University Press.

———. 2002. *Carnal Knowledge and Imperial Power: Race and the Intimate in Colonial Rule*. Berkeley: University of California Press.

———. 2004. "Tense and Tender Ties: The Politics of Comparison in North American History and (Post) Colonial Studies." *Journal of American History* 88 (3): 829–65.

———, ed. 2006. *Haunted by Empire: Geographies of Intimacy in North American History*. Durham, NC: Duke University Press.

———. 2010. *Along the Archival Grain: Epistemic Anxieties and Colonial Common Sense*. Princeton, NJ: Princeton University Press.

Stoller, Robert. (1968) 1994. *Sex and Gender: The Development of Masculinity and Femininity*. Vol. 1. New York: Routledge.

Stone, Sandy. 1992. "The *Empire* Strikes Back: A Posttranssexual Manifesto." *Camera Obscura* 10 (2): 150–76.

Stopes, Marie. (1918) 1998. Excerpt from *Married Love*. In *Sexology Uncensored: The Documents of Sexual Science*, edited by Lucy Bland and Laura Doan, 118. Cambridge: Polity.

Story, Kaila Adia. 2016. "Fear of a Black Femme: The Existential Conundrum of Embodying a Black Femme Identity While Being a Professor of Black, Queer, and Feminist Studies." *Journal of Lesbian Studies* 21 (4): 407–19.

Strings, Sabrina. 2019. *Fearing the Black Body: The Racial Origins of Fat Phobia*. New York: New York University Press.

Strub, Whitney. 2010. *Perversion for Profit: The Politics of Pornography and the Rise of the New Right*. New York: Columbia University Press.

———. 2013. *Obscenity Rules: Roth v. United States and the Long Struggle over Sexual Expression*. Lawrence: University Press of Kansas.

———. 2020. "Trans Porn Genealogy beyond the Queer Canon: Kim Christy, Joey Silvera, and the Hetero-industrial Production of Transsexuality." *TSQ: Transgender Studies Quarterly* 7 (2): 174–91.

Stryker, Susan. 2004. "Transgender Studies: Queer Theory's Evil Twin." *GLQ: A Journal of Lesbian and Gay Studies* 10 (2): 212–15.

———. 2008. *Transgender History: The Roots of Today's Revolution.* Berkeley, CA: Seal.

———. 2017. *Transgender History: The Roots of Today's Revolution.* 2nd ed. New York: Seal.

Stryker, Susan, and Aren Z. Aizura, eds. 2013. *The Transgender Studies Reader 2.* New York: Routledge.

Subramaniam, Banu. 2014. *Stories for Darwin: The Science of Variation and the Politics of Diversity.* Urbana: University of Illinois Press.

———. 2019. "Like a Tumbleweed in Eden: The Diasporic Life of Concepts." *Contributions to the History of Concepts* 14, no. 1 (Summer): 1–16.

suprihmbé. 2018. "Can You Be Pro-sex Worker and Anti-sex Work?" Medium, February 2, 2018. https://medium.com.

Swarr, Amanda Lock. 2012. *Sex in Transition: Remaking Gender and Race in South Africa.* Albany: State University of New York Press.

Swarr, Amanda Lock, and Richa Nagar. 2010. *Critical Transnational Feminist Praxis.* Albany: State University of New York Press.

Switzer, Heather. 2010. "Disruptive Discourse." *Girlhood Studies* 3 (1): 137–55.

Sy, Waaseyaa'sin Christine. 2018. "Relationship with Land in Anishinaabeg Womxn's Historical Research." In *Reshaping Women's History: Voices of Nontraditional Women Historians*, edited by Julie A. Gallagher and Barbara Winslow, 227–28. Urbana: University of Illinois Press.

Sycamore, Mattilda Bernstein, ed. 2004. *That's Revolting! Queer Strategies for Resisting Assimilation.* Brooklyn: Soft Skull.

Tadiar, Neferti. 2004. *Fantasy-Production: Sexual Economies and Other Philippine Consequences for the New World Order.* Manila, Philippines: Ateneo de Manila University Press.

Takeyama, Akiko. 2016. *Staged Seduction: Selling Dreams in a Tokyo Host Club.* Stanford, CA: Stanford University Press.

TallBear, Kim. 2011. "Why Interspecies Thinking Needs Indigenous Standpoints." *Cultural Anthropology*, April 24, 2011. https://culanth.org.

———. 2013. *Native American DNA: Tribal Belonging and the False Promise of Genetic Science.* Minneapolis: University of Minnesota Press.

———. 2016. "Making Love and Relations beyond Settler Sexualities." Social Justice Institute UBC, February 24, 2016. YouTube video, 55:39. www.youtube.com/watch?v=zfdo2ujRUv8.

———. 2019. "Caretaking Relations, Not American Dreaming." *Kalfou* 6 (1): 24–41.

———. n.d. Critical Polyamorist (website). Accessed June 19, 2021. www.criticalpolyamorist.com.

TallBear, Kim, and Angela Willey. 2019. "Critical Relationality: Queer, Indigenous, and Multispecies Belonging beyond Settler Sex and Nature." *Imaginations: Journal of Cross-Cultural Image Studies* 10 (1): 5–15.

Tallie, T. J. 2019. *Queering Colonial Natal: Indigeneity and the Violence of Belonging in Southern Africa.* Minneapolis: University of Minnesota Press.

Tambe, Ashwini. 2019. *Defining Girlhood in India: A Transnational History of Sexual Maturity Laws.* Urbana: University of Illinois Press.

Taneja, Anjali, Cara Page, and Susan Raffo. 2019. "Healing Histories: Disrupting the Medical Industrial Complex." Susan Raffo. September 13, 2019. www.susanraffo.com.

Taniwaki, Margie. 2000. "Yellow Peril to Yellow Power." In *Legacy to Liberation: Politics and Culture of Revolutionary Asian Pacific America*, edited by Fred Ho, with Carolyn Antonio, Diane Fujino, and Steve Yip Edinburgh, chap. 8. San Francisco: AK.

Taormino, Tristan, Celine Parreñas Shimizu, Constance Penley, and Mireille Miller-Young, eds. 2013. *The Feminist Porn Book: The Politics of Producing Pleasure.* New York: Feminist Press.

Taylor, Keeanga-Yamahtta, ed. 2017. *How We Get Free: Black Feminism and the Combahee River Collective.* Chicago: Haymarket.

Taylor, Ula Yvette. 2017. *The Promise of Patriarchy: Women and the Nation of Islam.* Chapel Hill: University of North Carolina Press.

Terry, Jennifer. 2017. *Attachments to War: Biomedical Logics and Violence in Twenty-First Century America.* Durham, NC: Duke University Press.

Teves, Stephanie N. 2018. *Defiant Indigeneity: The Politics of Hawaiian Performance.* Chapel Hill: University of North Carolina Press.

Thangaraj, Stanley. 2010. "Ballin' Indo-Pak Style: Pleasures, Desires, and Expressive Practices of 'South Asian American' Masculinity." *International Review for the Sociology of Sport* 45 (3): 372–89.

Theobald, Brianna. 2019. *Reproduction on the Reservation: Pregnancy, Childbirth, and Colonialism in the Long Twen-*

tieth Century. Chapel Hill: University of North Carolina Press.

Thomas, Greg. 2007. *The Sexual Demon of Colonial Power: Pan-African Embodiment and Erotic Schemes of Empire*. Bloomington: Indiana University Press.

Thompson, Charis. 2005. *Making Parents: The Ontological Choreography of Reproductive Technologies*. Cambridge, MA: MIT Press.

Thorpe, Francis Newton, ed. 1909. *The Federal and State Constitutions Colonial Charters, and Other Organic Laws of the States, Territories, and Colonies Now or Heretofore Forming the United States of America*. Washington, DC: Government Printing Office.

Threat, Rae, and Lynn Comella. 2020. "The Politics of Representation: A Photographer's View of the Adult Industry." *TSQ: Transgender Studies Quarterly* 7 (2): 255–61.

Thuma, Emily L. 2019. *All Our Trials: Prisons, Policing, and the Feminist Fight to End Violence*. Urbana: University of Illinois Press.

Tillmon, Johnnie. 1972. "Welfare Is a Women's Issue." *Ms.*, Spring 1972. https://msmagazine.com.

Tinsley, Omise'eke. 2008. "Black Atlantic, Queer Atlantic: Queer Imaginings of the Middle Passage." *GLQ: A Journal of Lesbian and Gay Studies* 14 (2–3): 191–215.

———. 2018. *Ezili's Mirrors: Imagining Black Queer Genders*. Durham, NC: Duke University Press.

Todd, Zoe. 2017. "Fish, Kin and Hope: Tending to Water Violations in Amiskwaciwâskahikan and Treaty Six Territory." *Afterall: A Journal of Art, Context and Enquiry* 43 (1): 102–7.

Tompkins, Kyla Wazana. 2017. "Crude Matter, Queer Form." *ASAP/Journal* 2 (2): 264–68.

Tongson, Karen. 2011. *Relocations: Queer Suburban Imaginaries*. New York: New York University Press.

Toor, Saadia. 2012. "Imperialist Feminism Redux." *Dialectical Anthropology* 36:147–60.

Tortorici, Zeb. 2018. *Sins against Nature: Sex and Archives in Colonial New Spain*. Durham, NC: Duke University Press.

Tourmaline, Eric A. Stanley, and Johanna Burton, eds. 2017. *Trap Door: Trans Cultural Production and the Politics of Visibility*. Cambridge, MA: MIT Press.

Towle, Evan B., and Lynn M. Morgan. 2002. "Romancing the Transgender Native: Rethinking the Use of the 'Third Gender' Concept." *GLQ: A Journal of Lesbian and Gay Studies* 8 (4): 469–97.

Travers, Ann. 2008. "The Sports Nexus and Gender Injustice." *Studies in Social Justice* 2 (1): 79–101.

Trinh, T. Minh-ha. 1986. "Difference: 'A Special Third World Women Issue.'" *Discourse* 8 (Fall): 11–38.

Trosper, Ronald L. 1995. "Traditional American Indian Economic Policy." *American Indian Culture and Research Journal* 19 (1): 65–95.

———. 2002. "Northwest Coast Indigenous Institutions That Supported Resilience and Sustainability." *Ecological Economics* 41:329–44.

Trouble, Courtney. 2014. "Finding Gender through Porn Performance." *Porn Studies* 1 (1–2): 197–200.

Trouille, David. 2013. "Neighborhood Outsiders, Field Insiders: Latino Immigrant Men and the Control of Public Space." *Qualitative Sociology* 36 (1): 1–22.

Truth, Sojourner. (1851) 1995. "Woman's Rights." *Words of Fire: An Anthology of African-American Feminist Thought*, edited by Beverly Guy-Sheftall, 36. New York: New Press.

Tuck, Eve. 2016. "Episode 4: Red and Black DNA, Blood, Kinship and Organizing with Kim TallBear." *Henceforward*, July 25, 2016. Podcast audio. www.thehenceforward.com.

Tuck, Eve, and Rubén A. Gaztambide-Fernández. 2013. "Curriculum, Replacement, and Settler Futurity." *JCT Online* 29 (1): 72.

Tuck, Eve, and K. Wayne Yang. 2012. "Decolonization Is Not a Metaphor." *Decolonization: Indigeneity, Education & Society* 1 (1): 1–40.

———. 2016. "What Justice Wants." *Critical Ethnic Studies* 2 (2): 1–15.

Tuckman, Jo. 2005. "It's a Man's Game." *Guardian*, January 5, 2005. www.theguardian.com.

Turk, Victoria. 2018. "Why Are Elite Female Footballers Barred from Playing with Men?" Wired, November 8, 2018. www.wired.co.uk.

Turner, Dale. 2006. *This Is Not a Peace Pipe*. Toronto: University of Toronto Press.

Turner, Sasha. 2017. *Contested Bodies: Pregnancy, Childrearing, and Slavery in Jamaica*. Philadelphia: University of Pennsylvania Press.

Tyler, Imogen. 2013. *Revolting Subjects: Social Abjection and Resistance in Neoliberal Britain*. London: Zed.

Tzul, Gladys. (2015) 2019. "Sistemas de Gobierno Comunal Indígena: La Organización de la Reproducción de la Vida." In *Antología del Pensamiento Crítico Guatemalteco Contemporáneo*, edited by Ana Silvia Monzón, 71–82. Buenos Aires: CLACSO.

United Nations. n.d. "Human Rights." Accessed June 21, 2020. www.un.org.

US Department of Education. 2011. "Dear Colleague Letter." April 4, 2011. www.ed.gov.

US Department of Justice. 2018. "Matter of A-B-, Respondent." 27 I&N Dec. 316 (A. G. 2018). Interim decision no. 3929. Accessed June 21, 2021. www.justice.gov.

Valentine, David. 2007. *Imagining Transgender: Ethnography of a Category*. Durham, NC: Duke University Press.

Valenzuela, Angela. 1999. *Subtractive Schooling: US-Mexican Youth and the Politics of Caring*. Albany: State University of New York Press.

Vance, Carole S., ed. 1984. *Pleasure and Danger: Exploring Female Sexuality*. Boston: Routledge & Kegan Paul.

———. 1997. "Negotiating Sex and Gender in the Attorney General's Commission on Pornography." In *The Gender/Sexuality Reader: Culture, History, Political Economy*, edited by Roger N. Lancaster and Micaela Di Leonardo, 440–52. London: Routledge.

Vargas, Deborah R. 2014. "Ruminations on Lo Sucio as a Latino Queer Analytic." *American Quarterly* 66 (3): 715–26.

Viego, Antonio. 2007. *Dead Subjects: Toward a Politics of Loss in Latino Studies*. Durham, NC: Duke University Press.

Vimalassery, Manu, Juliana Hu Pegues, and Alyosha Goldstein. 2016. "Introduction: On Colonial Unknowing." *Theory & Event* 19 (4). https://muse.jhu.edu.

Vitale, Alex. 2018. *The End of Policing*. New York: Verso.

Volpp, Leti. 2017. "Feminist, Sexual, and Queer Citizenship." In *The Oxford Handbook of Citizenship*, edited by Ayelet Shachar, Rainer Baubock, Irene Bloemraad, and Maarten Vink, 153–77. Oxford: Oxford University Press.

Vora, Kalindi. 2015. *Life Support: Biocapital and the New History of Outsourced Labor*. Minneapolis: University of Minnesota Press.

Wagner, Laura. 2018. "Men Should Play Three Sets." *Deadspin* (blog), September 5, 2018. https://deadspin.com.

Wagner, Sally Roesch. 2001. *Sisters in Spirit: Haudenosaunee (Iroquois) Influence on Early American Feminists*. Summertown, TN: Native Voices.

Walcott, Rinaldo. 2016. *Queer Returns: Essays on Multiculturalism, Diaspora, and Black Studies*. Toronto: Insomniac.

Wang, Jackie. 2018. *Carceral Capitalism*. South Pasadena, CA: Semiotext(e).

Wang, Sean H. 2017. "Fetal Citizens? Birthright Citizenship, Reproductive Futurism, and the 'Panic' over Chinese Birth Tourism in Southern California." *Environment and Planning D: Society and Space* 35 (2): 263–80.

Ward, Jane. 2020. *The Tragedy of Heterosexuality*. New York: New York University Press.

Warner, Michael. 1993. Introduction to *Fear of a Queer Planet: Queer Politics and Social Theory*, edited by Michael Warner, vii–xxxi. Minneapolis: University of Minnesota Press.

Watkins, Rychetta. 2012. *Black Power, Yellow Power, and the Making of Revolutionary Identities*. Jackson: University Press of Mississippi.

Waugh, Thomas. 1996. *Hard to Imagine: Gay Male Eroticism in Photography and Film from Their Beginnings to Stonewall*. New York: Columbia University Press.

Weaver, Harlan. 2020. *Bad Dog: Pit Bull Politics and Multispecies Justice*. Seattle: University of Washington Press.

Weaver, Jace. 2000. "Indigenousness and Indigeneity." In *A Companion to Postcolonial Studies*, edited by Henry Schwarz and Sangeeta Ray, 221–35. Malden, MA: Blackwell.

Webber, Jeffery R. 2016. "Idle No More." *Historical Materialism* 24 (3): 3–29.

Weber, Max. (1994) 2003. "The Profession and Vocation of Politics." In *Selected Political Writings*, edited by Peter Lassman and Ronald Speirs, 309–68. New York: Cambridge University Press.

Weeks, Kathi. 2011. *The Problem with Work: Feminism, Marxism, Antiwork Politics, and Postwork Imaginaries*. Durham, NC: Duke University Press.

Weheliye, Alexander G. 2014. *Habeas Viscus: Racializing Assemblages, Biopolitics, and Black Feminist Theories of the Human*. Durham, NC: Duke University Press.

Weinbaum, Alys Eve, Lynn M. Thomas, Priti Ramamurthy, Uta G. Poiger, Madeleine Yue Dong, and Tani E. Barlow, eds. 2008. *The Modern Girl around the World: Consumption, Modernity, and Globalization*. Durham, NC: Duke University Press.

Weir, Allison. 2017. *Decolonizing Feminism: Transnational Feminism and Globalization*. Edited by Margaret A. McLaren. New York: Rowman & Littlefield.

Wekker, Gloria. 2006. *The Politics of Passion: Women's Sexual Culture in the Afro-Surinamese Diaspora*. New York: Columbia University Press.

Wendell, Susan. 1996. *The Rejected Body: Feminist Philosophical Reflections on Disability*. New York: Routledge.

Wesling, Meg. 2012. "Queer Value." *GLQ: Journal of Lesbian and Gay Studies* 18 (1): 107–25.

West, Guida. 1981. *The National Welfare Rights Movement: The Social Protest of Poor Women*. New York: Praeger.

West, Isaac. 2010. "PISSAR's Critically Queer and Disabled Politics." *Communication and Critical/Cultural Studies* 7 (2): 156–75.

Western, Bruce, and Becky Pettit. 2010. "Incarceration and Social Inequality." *Daedalus* 139 (3): 8–19.

Weston, Kath. 1993. "Lesbian/Gay Studies in the House of Anthropology." *Annual Review of Anthropology* 22:339–67.

White, Monica. 2011. "Sisters of the Soil: Urban Gardening as Resistance in Detroit." *Race/Ethnicity: Multidisciplinary Global Contexts* 5 (1): 13–28.

Whitehead, Joshua. 2018. "Why I Am Withdrawing from My Lambda Literary Award Nomination." TIA House, University of Calgary, March 14, 2018. www.tiahouse.ca.

Wiegman, Robyn. 2012. *Object Lessons*. Durham, NC: Duke University Press.

———. 2019. "Now, Not Now." In "Sexual Politics, Sexual Panics." Special issue, *differences: A Journal of Feminist Cultural Studies* 30 (1): 1–14.

Wiegman, Robyn, and Elizabeth A. Wilson, eds. 2015. "Queer Theory without Antinormativity." Special issue, *differences: A Journal of Feminist Cultural Studies* 26 (1).

Wilderson, Frank B., III. 2010. *Red, White and Black: Cinema and the Structure of US Antagonisms*. Durham, NC: Duke University Press.

———. 2020. *Afropessimism*. New York: Liveright.

Willey, Angela. 2016. *Undoing Monogamy: The Politics of Science and the Possibilities of Biology*. Durham, NC: Duke University Press.

Williams, Eric. 1994. *Capitalism and Slavery*. Chapel Hill: University of North Carolina Press.

Williams, Jean. 2003. *A Game for Rough Girls? A History of Women's Football in Britain*. London: Routledge.

———. 2014. *A Contemporary History of Women's Sport, Part One: Sporting Women 1850–1960*. London: Routledge.

Williams, Linda. (1989) 1999. *Hard Core: Power, Pleasure and the "Frenzy of the Visible."* Berkeley, CA: University of California Press.

———, ed. 2004. *Porn Studies*. Durham, NC: Duke University Press.

———. 2014. "Pornography, Porno, Porn: Thoughts on a Weedy Field." *Porn Studies* 1 (1–2): 24–40.

Williams, Raymond. (1976) 2014. *Keywords: A Vocabulary of Culture and Society*. Oxford: Oxford University Press.

Williams, Rhonda Y. 2004. *The Politics of Public Housing: Black Women's Struggles against Urban Inequality*. Oxford: Oxford University Press.

Williams, Robert A., Jr. 1990. *The American Indian in Western Legal Thought: The Discourses of Conquest*. New York: Oxford University Press.

Williams-Forson, Psyche. 2006. *Building Houses Out of Chicken Legs: Black Women, Food, and Power*. Chapel Hill: University of North Carolina Press.

Wilson, Ara. 2006. "Queering Asia." *Intersections: Gender, History, and Culture in the Asian Context* 14:1–10.

Wilson, Elizabeth A. 2015. *Gut Feminism*. Durham, NC: Duke University Press.

Wittig, Monique. 1980. "The Straight Mind." *Feminist Issues* 1:103–11.

Woelfle-Erskine, Cleo. 2015. "Thinking with Salmon about Rain Tanks: Commons as Intra-actions." *Local Environment* 20 (5): 581–99.

Wolf, Naomi. 1992. "Radical Heterosexuality." *Ms.* 3 (1): 28–32.

Wolfe, Patrick. 2006. "Settler Colonialism and the Elimination of the Native." *Journal of Genocide Research* 8 (4): 387–409.

Wolkowitz, Carol, ed. 2013. *Body/Sex/Work: Intimate, Embodied and Sexualized Labour*. Houndmills, UK: Palgrave Macmillan.

Wong, Alice. 2020. "Freedom for Some Is Not Freedom for All: COVID-19, Institutions, and Disability Rights." Disability Visibility Project, June 7, 2020. https://disabilityvisibilityproject.com.

Woodson, Carter G. 1933. *The Miseducation of the Negro*. Washington, DC: Associated.

Woolner, Cookie. 2015. "'Woman Slain in Queer Love Brawl': African American Women, Same-Sex Desire, and Violence in the Urban North, 1920–29." *Journal of African American History* 100 (3): 406–27.

Worthen, Meredith G. F. 2016. *Sexual Deviance and Society: A Sociological Examination*. New York: Routledge.

Wright, Melissa. 2006. "Manufactured Bodies." In *Disposable Women and Other Myths of Global Capitalism*, 45–70. New York: Routledge.

Wynter, Sylvia. 1995. "1492: A New World View." In *Race, Discourse, and the Origin of the Americas: A New World View*, edited by Vera Lawrence Hyatt and Rex Nettleford, 5–57. Washington, DC: Smithsonian Institution Press.

———. 1996. "Is 'Development' a Purely Empirical Concept or Also Teleological? A Perspective from 'We the Underdeveloped.'" In *Prospects for Recovery and Sustainable Development in Africa*, edited by Agibou Yansane, 299–316. Westport, CT: Praeger.

———. 2003. "Unsettling the Coloniality of Being/Power/Truth/Freedom: Toward the Human, after Man, Its Overrepresentation—an Argument." *CR: The New Centennial Review* 3 (3): 257–337.

Yazzie, Melanie. 2018. "Decolonizing Development in Diné Bikeyah: Resource Extraction, Anticapitalism, and Relational Futures." *Environment and Society: Advances in Research* 9:25–39.

Young, Hershini Bhana. 2017. *Illegible Will: Coercive Spectacles of Labor in South Africa and the Diaspora*. Durham, NC: Duke University Press.

Young, Iris Marion. 1980. "Throwing like a Girl: A Phenomenology of Feminine Body Comportment Motility and Spatiality." *Human Studies* 3:137–56.

Zelizer, Viviana. 2005. *The Purchase of Intimacy*. Princeton, NJ: Princeton University Press.

Zurn, Perry. 2019. "Waste Culture and Isolation: Prisons, Toilets, and Gender Segregation." *Hypatia: A Journal of Feminist Philosophy* 34 (4): 669–89.

About the Contributors

Kemi Adeyemi (she/her) is Assistant Professor of Gender, Women, and Sexuality Studies and Director of the Black Embodiments Studio at the University of Washington. She is the co-editor of *Queer Nightlife* and author of the forthcoming *Feels Right: Black Queer Women's Choreographies of Belonging in Chicago*.

Anisha Ahuja (she/her) is a PhD Student in Cultural Studies and Women's and Gender Studies at Claremont Graduate University.

Neel Ahuja (he/him) is Associate Professor of Feminist Studies and Critical Race and Ethnic Studies at the University of California, Santa Cruz. He is the author of *Bioinsecurities: Disease Interventions, Empire, and the Government of Species* and the forthcoming *Planetary Specters: Race, Migration, and Climate Change in the Twenty-First Century*.

Hōkūlani K. Aikau (she/her) is Associate Professor in Ethnic Studies and Gender Studies at the University of Utah. She is the author of *A Chosen People, a Promised Land: Mormonism and Race in Hawai'i* and co-editor of *Detours: A Decolonial Guide to Hawai'i*.

Aren Z. Aizura (he/him) is Associate Professor in the Department of Gender, Women, and Sexuality Studies at the University of Minnesota. He is the author of *Mobile Subjects: Transnational Imaginaries of Gender Reassignment* and co-editor of *The Transgender Studies Reader 2*.

Tazeen M. Ali (she/her) is Assistant Professor of Religion and Politics at Washington University in St. Louis. She is the author of "Qur'anic Literacy as Women's Empowerment: Cultivating Interpretive Authority at the Women's Mosque of America," forthcoming in *Journal of the American Academy of Religion*.

Leticia Alvarado (she/her) is Associate Professor of American Studies at Brown University. She is the author of *Abject Performances: Aesthetic Strategies in Latino Cultural Production* and the forthcoming *Cut/Hoard/Suture: Aesthetics in Relation*.

Aimee Bahng (she/her) is Associate Professor of Gender and Women's Studies at Pomona College. She is the author of *Migrant Futures: Decolonizing Speculation in Financial Times* and co-editor of the "Transpacific Futurities" special issue of *Journal of Asian American Studies* (2017).

Joanne Barker (she/her) is Lenape (a citizen of the Delaware Tribe of Indians) and Professor of American Indian Studies at San Francisco State University. She is the editor of the volume *Critically Sovereign*.

Heather Berg (she/her) is Assistant Professor of Women, Gender, and Sexuality Studies at Washington University in St. Louis. She is the author of *Porn Work: Sex, Labor, and Late Capitalism* and "Left of #MeToo" in *Feminist Studies*.

Matt Brim (he/him) is Professor of Queer Studies at the CUNY College of Staten Island. He is the author of *Poor Queer Studies: Confronting Elitism in the University* and *Imagining Queer Methods*.

micha cárdenas (she/her) is Assistant Professor in Art and Design: Games and Playable Media and Critical Race and Ethnic Studies at the University of California, Santa Cruz, where she directs the Critical Realities Studio. She is the co-editor of "Trans Futures," a special issue of *Transgender Studies Quarterly* and author of *Poetic Operations: Trans of Color Art in Digital Media*.

Joshua Chambers-Letson (he/him or no preference) is Professor of Performance Studies at Northwestern University. He is the author of *After the Party: A Manifesto on Queer of Color Life* and *A Race So Different: Law and Performance in Asian America*.

Karma R. Chávez (she/her) works at the University of Texas at Austin and is the author of *Queer Migration Politics*, *Palestine on the Air*, and *The Borders of AIDS*.

Mel Y. Chen (they/them) is Associate Professor of Gender and Women's Studies and Director of the Center for the Study of Sexual Culture at the University of California, Berkeley. They are the author of *Animacies: Biopolitics, Racial Mattering, and Queer Affect* and "Agitation" in *South Atlantic Quarterly*.

Soyica Diggs Colbert (she/her) is Interim Dean of Georgetown University's College of Arts and Sciences and Idol Family Professor of African American and Performing Arts. Colbert is the author of *Radical Vision: A Biography of Lorraine Hansberry*, *Black Movements: Performance and Cultural Politics*, and co-editor of *Race and Performance after Repetition and the Psychic Hold of Slavery*.

Lynn Comella (she/her) is Associate Professor of Gender and Sexuality Studies at the University of Nevada, Las Vegas. She is the author of *Vibrator Nation: How Feminist Sex-Toy Stores Changed the Business of Pleasure* and co-editor of *New Views on Pornography: Sexuality, Politics, and the Law*.

Michelle Daigle (she/her) is Mushkegowuk (Cree), a member of Constance Lake First Nation in Treaty 9, and of French ancestry. She is Assistant Professor in the Centre for Indigenous Studies and the Department of Geography and Planning at the University of Toronto. She is the author of "The Spectacle of Reconciliation: On (the) Unsettling Responsibilities to Indigenous Peoples in the Academy" in *Environment and Planning D: Society and Space* and "Resurging through Kishiichiwan: The Spatial Politics of Indigenous Water Relations" in *Decolonization: Indigeneity, Education & Society*.

Jennifer DeClue (she/her) is Assistant Professor in the Program for the Study of Women and Gender at Smith College. She is the author of *Visitation: Toward a Black Feminist Avant-Garde Cinema* and "Deferral and the Dream: Visualizing the Life and Loves of Lorraine Hansberry" in *GLQ: A Journal of Lesbian and Gay Studies*.

Karishma Desai (she/her) is Assistant Professor of Education at Rutgers University–New Brunswick. She is the author of "Life Skills as Affective Labour: Skilling Girls with Gendered Enterprise" in *South Asia: Journal of South Asian Studies* and "Teaching the 'Third World Girl': Girl Rising as a Precarious Curriculum of Empathy" in *Curriculum Inquiry*.

Jennifer Doyle (she/her) is Professor of English at the University of California, Riverside. She is the author of *Campus Sex, Campus Security* and *Hold It against Me:*

Difficulty and Emotion in Contemporary Art. She has published writing on the gender politics of sports in *Deadspin*, the *New York Times*, the *Guardian*, and Vice.

Finn Enke (they/them) is Professor at the University of Wisconsin–Madison. They are the author of *Finding the Movement: Sexuality, Contested Space, and Feminist Activism* and *Transfeminist Perspectives in and beyond Transgender and Gender Studies*.

Elizabeth Freeman (she/her) is Professor of English at the University of California, Davis. She is the author of *Time Binds* and *Beside You in Time*.

Amin Ghaziani (he/him) is Professor of Sociology and Canada Research Chair in Urban Sexualities at the University of British Columbia. He is the author of *Imagining Queer Methods* and *There Goes the Gayborhood?*

Jules Gill-Peterson (she/her) is Associate Professor of English, with a secondary appointment in Gender, Sexuality, and Women's Studies, at the University of Pittsburgh. She is the author of *Histories of the Transgender Child*.

Mishuana Goeman (she/her), Tonawanda Band of Seneca, is a Professor of Gender Studies, Chair of American Indian Studies, and affiliated faculty of Critical Race Studies in the Law School at the University of California, Los Angeles. She is also the author of *Mark My Words: Native Women Mapping Our Nations* and a Co-PI on two community-based digital projects, *Mapping Indigenous L.A.* and *Carrying Our Ancestors Home*.

Gayatri Gopinath (she/her) is Professor of Social and Cultural Analysis and the Director of the Center for the Study of Gender and Sexuality at New York University.

She is the author of *Impossible Desires: Queer Diasporas and South Asian Public Cultures* and *Unruly Visions: The Aesthetic Practices of Queer Diaspora*.

Sandy Grande (she/her) is Professor of Political Science and Native American and Indigenous Studies with affiliations in American Studies and Philosophy at the University of Connecticut. She is the author of *Red Pedagogy: Native American Social and Political Thought* and "The Standing Rock Syllabus, Refusing the University." She is also a founding member of New York Stands for Standing Rock.

Joshua Javier Guzmán (he/him) is Assistant Professor of Gender Studies at the University of California, Los Angeles. He is a contributor to *Keywords for Latina/o Studies*.

Jack Halberstam (he/him) is Professor of English and Gender Studies at Columbia University. He is the author of *The Queer Art of Failure* and *Wild Things: The Disorder of Desire*.

Sarah Haley (she/her) is Associate Professor of Gender Studies and Director of the Center for the Study of Women, Black Feminism Initiative at the University of California, Los Angeles. She is the author of *No Mercy Here: Gender, Punishment, and the Making of Jim Crow Modernity* and *The Carceral Interior: A Black Feminist Study of American Punishment*. She has worked as a labor organizer with UNITE HERE and is a member of Scholars for Social Justice.

Lisa Kahaleole Hall (she/her) is a multiracial Kānaka Maoli Associate Professor and Director of Indigenous Studies at the University of Victoria. She is the author of "More Than 'Two Worlds:' Black Feminist Theories of Difference in Relation" in *Critical Ethnic Studies* and "Indigenous Women in Print," forthcoming in *The Routledge Handbook of Critical Indigenous Studies*.

Sharon Patricia Holland (she/her) is the Townsend Ludington Distinguished Professor in American Studies and Chair of the Department of American Studies at the University of North Carolina at Chapel Hill. She is the author of *The Erotic Life of Racism* and the forthcoming project "hum:animal:blackness."

Nguyen Tan Hoang (he/him, they/them) is Associate Professor of Literature and Cultural Studies at the University of California, San Diego, and director of the films *Forever Bottom!*, *PIRATED!*, *K.I.P.*, and *I Remember Dancing*. He is the author of *A View from the Bottom: Asian American Masculinity and Sexual Representation*.

Grace Kyungwon Hong (she/her) is Professor of Gender Studies and Asian American Studies as well as the Director of the Center for the Study of Women at the University of California, Los Angeles. She is the author of *Death beyond Disavowal: The Impossible Politics of Difference* and co-editor of *Strange Affinities: The Gender and Sexual Politics of Comparative Racialization*.

Dredge Byung'chu Kang (he/we/they) is Assistant Professor at the University of California, San Diego. He is the author of "Eastern Orientations: Thai Middle-Class Gay Desire for 'White Asians'" in *Theory and Critique* and "Idols of Development: Transnational Transgender Performance in Thai K-Pop Cover Dance" in *Transgender Studies Quarterly*.

Manu Karuka (he/him) is Assistant Professor in American Studies at Barnard College. He is the author of *Empire's Tracks: Indigenous Nations, Chinese Workers, and the Transcontinental Railroad*.

Tiffany Lethabo King (she/her) is Associate Professor in African American Studies and Women's, Gender, and Sexuality Studies at Georgia State University. She is the author of *The Black Shoals: Offshore Formations of Black and Native Studies* and co-editor of *Otherwise Worlds: Against Settler Colonialism and Anti-Blackness*.

Susan Koshy (she/her) is Director of the Unit for Criticism and Interpretive Theory and Associate Professor of English and Asian American Studies at the University of Illinois, Urbana-Champaign. She is the author of *Sexual Naturalization: Asian Americans and Miscegenation* and co-editor of the forthcoming *Colonial Racial Capitalism*.

Greta LaFleur (she/they) is Associate Professor of American Studies at Yale University. She is the author of *The Natural History of Sexuality in Early America* and editor of *Trans Historical: Gender Plurality before the Modern*.

Jacob Lau (he/him) is Assistant Professor of Women's and Gender Studies and the Director of Sexuality Studies at the University of North Carolina at Chapel Hill. He is the editor of *Out of the Ordinary: A Life of Gender and Spiritual Transitions* and author of "His Body of Work, the Work of His Body: The Chronicles of Christopher Lee and Respect after Death" in *Amerasia Journal*.

Jenna M. Loyd (she/her) is Associate Professor in the Department of Geography at the University of Wisconsin-Madison. She is the author of *Boats, Borders, and Bases: Race, the Cold War, and the Rise of Migration Detention in the United States* and *Health Rights Are Civil Rights: Peace and Justice Activism in Los Angeles, 1963–1978*.

Joan Lubin (she/her) is Visiting Scholar in the Society for Humanities at Cornell University. She is the author of the forthcoming *Pulp Sexology: Paperback Revolution, Gay Liberation* and is the co-author of "Learning in Public" in *Women & Performance*.

Julie Avril Minich (she/her) is Associate Professor of English and Mexican American and Latino/a Studies at the University of Texas at Austin. She is the author of *Accessible Citizenships: Disability, Nation, and the Cultural Politics of Greater Mexico* and the forthcoming *Radical Health: Justice, Care and Latinx Expressive Culture*.

Durba Mitra (she/her) is Assistant Professor of Studies of Women, Gender, and Sexuality and the Carol K. Pforzheimer Assistant Professor at the Radcliffe Institute at Harvard University. She is the author of *Indian Sex Life: Sexuality and the Colonial Origins of Modern Social Thought*.

Scott L. Morgensen (he/him) is Associate Professor in Gender Studies and teaches in the Gender Studies Department at Queen's University. He is the author of *Spaces between Us: Queer Settler Colonialism and Indigenous Decolonization* and "Encountering Indeterminacy: Colonial Contexts and Queer Imagining" in *Cultural Anthropology*.

Amber Jamilla Musser (she/her) is Professor at the Graduate Center at the City University of New York. She is the author of *Sensational Flesh: Race, Power, and Masochism* and *Sensual Excess: Queer Femininity and Brown Jouissance*.

Jennifer C. Nash (she/her) is Jean Fox O'Barr Professor of Gender, Sexuality, and Feminist Studies at Duke University. She is the author of *Black Feminism Reimagined: After Intersectionality* and *The Black Body in Ecstasy*.

Elton Naswood (he/him) is the co-coordinator for the National Native HIV Network and was a Senior Program Analyst at the Office of Minority Health Resource Center. He is Navajo, Diné, originally from Whitehorse Lake, New Mexico, on the Navajo Reservation. He is the co-author of "Unique Challenges Facing Native American People Living with HIV" and a contributor to "Dispatches on the Futures of AIDS," in *AIDS and the Distribution of Crises*. He is a member of the Southwest Indigenous Women's Coalition Two Spirit / LGBTQ Advisory Council and the US Leader for the International Indigenous Working Group on HIV/AIDS.

Mimi Thi Nguyen (she/her) is Associate Professor in Gender and Women's Studies at the University of Illinois, Urbana-Champaign. She is the author of *The Gift of Freedom: War, Debt, and Other Refugee Passages* and "The Hoodie as Sign, Screen, Expectation, and Force" in *Signs: Journal of Women in Culture and Society*.

Tavia Nyong'o (he/him) is William Lampson Professor of American Studies at Yale University and member of the Yale Prison Education Initiative. He is the author of *The Amalgamation Waltz* and *Afro-Fabulations*.

Emily Owens (she/her) is David and Michelle Ebersman Assistant Professor of History and in the Center for Study of Slavery and Justice at Brown University. She is the author of "Reproducing Racial Fictions" in *Signs: Journal of Women in Culture and Society* and the forthcoming *The Fantasy of Consent: Violence of Survival in Antebellum New Orleans*.

Jan M. Padios (she/her) is Associate Professor of American Studies at Williams College. She is the author of *A Nation on the Line*.

A. Naomi Paik (she/her) is Associate Professor of Criminology, Law, and Justice and Global Asian Studies at the University of Illinois, Urbana-Champaign. She is the author of *Bans, Walls, Raids, Sanctuary: Understanding US Immigration for the 21st Century* and *Rightlessness: Testimony and Redress in US Prison Camps since World War II*.

K-Sue Park (she/her) is Associate Professor of Law at the Georgetown University Law Center. She is the author of *Money, Mortgages and the Conquest of America* and "Self-Deportation Nation" in *Harvard Law Review*.

Lisa Sun-Hee Park (she/her) is Professor and Chair of Asian American Studies at the University of California, Santa Barbara. She is the author of *Entitled to Nothing: The Struggle for Immigrant Health Care in the Age of Welfare Reform* and co-author of *The Slums of Aspen: Immigrants vs. the Environment in America's Eden*.

Geeta Patel is Professor of Middle Eastern and South Asian Languages and Cultures and Women, Gender, and Sexuality at the University of Virginia and the author of *Lyrical Movements, Historical Hauntings* and *Risky Bodies and Techno-Intimacy*.

Margaret Marietta Ramírez (she/her) is Associate Professor in Geography at Simon Fraser University. She is the author of "City as Borderland: Gentrification and the Policing of Black and Latinx Geographies in Oakland" in *Environment and Planning D* and "Take the Houses Back / Take the Land Back: Black and Indigenous Urban Futures in Oakland" in *Urban Geography*.

Chandan Reddy (he/him) is Associate Professor of Gender, Women, and Sexuality Studies and Comparative History of Ideas at the University of

Washington. He is the author of *Freedom with Violence: Race, Sexuality, and the US State*.

Beth E. Richie (she/her) is Professor of Criminology, Law and Justice, Black Studies, and Gender and Women's Studies at the University of Illinois at Chicago. She is the author of *Arrested Justice* and co-author of the forthcoming *Abolition Feminism Now*.

Evren Savci (she/her) is Assistant Professor at Yale University. She is the author of *Queer in Translation: Sexual Politics under Neoliberal Islam*.

Sami Schalk (she/her) is Associate Professor at the University of Wisconsin-Madison. She is the author of *Bodyminds Reimagined: (Dis)ability, Race and Gender in Black Women's Speculative Fiction*.

Kyla Schuller (she/her) is Associate Professor of Women's, Gender, and Sexuality Studies at Rutgers University, New Brunswick. She is the author of *The Biopolitics of Feeling: Race, Sex, and Science in the Nineteenth Century* and *The Trouble with White Women: A Counterhistory of Feminism*.

Savannah Shange (she/her) is Assistant Professor of Anthropology and Principal Faculty in Critical Race and Ethnic Studies at the University of California, Santa Cruz. She is the author of "Play Aunties and Dyke Bitches: Gender, Generation and the Ethics of Black Queer Kinship" in *The Black Scholar: Journal of Black Studies and Research* and *Progressive Dystopia: Abolition, Antiblackness and Schooling in San Francisco*.

Dina M. Siddiqi (she/her) is Clinical Associate Professor in Liberal Studies at New York University. She is the author of "Logics of Sedition: Re-signifying Insurgent

Labor in Bangladesh's Garment Factories" in the *Journal of South Asian Development* and "Exceptional Sexuality in a Time of Terror: 'Muslim' Subjects and Dissenting/Unmournable Bodies" in *South Asia Multidisciplinary Academic Journal*.

Shannon Speed (she/her) is a citizen of the Chickasaw Nation, Director of the American Indian Studies Center, and Professor of Gender Studies and Anthropology at the University of California, Los Angeles. She is the author of *Incarcerated Stories: Indigenous Women Migrants and Violence in the Settler-Capitalist State* and editor of *Indigenous Women and Violence: Feminist Activist Research in Heightened States of Injustice*.

Shelley Streeby (she/her) is Professor of Ethnic Studies and Literature at the University of California, San Diego. She is the author of *Imagining the Future of Climate Change: World-Making through Science Fiction and Activism* and *Radical Sensations: World-Movements, Violence, and Visual Culture*.

Banu Subramaniam is Professor of Women, Gender, and Sexuality Studies at the University of Massachusetts Amherst. Subramaniam is the author of *Holy Science: The Biopolitics of Hindu Nationalism* and *Ghost Stories for Darwin: The Science of Variation and the Politics of Diversity*.

Ashley Coleman Taylor (she/her) is Assistant Professor at the University of Texas at Austin. She is the author of the forthcoming *Majestad Negra: Race, Class, Gender, and Religious Experience in the Puerto Rican Imaginary*.

Emily Thuma (she/her) is Assistant Professor of Politics and Law at the University of Washington Tacoma. She is the author of *All Our Trials: Prisons, Policing, and the Feminist Fight to End Violence*.

Kyla Wazana Tompkins (she/her) is Associate Professor at Pomona College. She is the author of *Racial Indigestion: Eating Bodies in the Nineteenth Century* and the forthcoming *Deviant Matter: Ferment, Intoxicants, Jelly, Rot*. She is also the author of the article "We Aren't Here to Learn What We Already Know" in the *Los Angeles Review of Books*.

Virgie Tovar (she/her) is host of the podcast *Rebel Eaters Club*. Her podcast examines food and culture with an intersectional feminist lens. She is the author of *You Have the Right to Remain Fat* and *The Self Love Revolution: Radical Body Positivity for Girls of Color*. In 2018, she was named one of the fifty most influential feminists by *Bitch* magazine. She has been featured by the *New York Times*, Tech Insider, BBC, MTV, Al Jazeera, and NPR. She holds a master's degree in sexuality studies with a focus on the intersections of body size, race, and gender.

Jeanne Vaccaro (she/her) is Postdoctoral Fellow in the Department of Gender and Sexuality Studies and in the ONE Archives at the University of Southern California. She is the author of "Canonical Undoings: Notes on Trans Art and Archives" in *Trap Door: Trans Visibility and the Politics of Representation*.

Sean Saifa Wall (he/him) is an intersex activist and public health researcher. He is cofounder and strategist of the Intersex Justice Project, a grassroots organization that is committed to ending intersex genital surgery in the United States. He is also a Marie Skłowdoska-Curie Early Stage researcher based at the University of Huddersfield in England, where he will be pursuing his PhD in sociology with an emphasis on intersex rights and social policy. He is the author of "Black US Sexual and Gender Minority Mental Health" in *The Oxford Handbook of Sexual and Gender Minority Mental Health*.

Jane Ward (she/her, they/them) is Professor of Gender and Sexuality Studies at the University of California, Riverside. She is the author of *The Tragedy of Heterosexuality* and *Not Gay: Sex between Straight White Men*.

Kyle Powys Whyte (he/him) is George Willis Pack Professor of Environment and Sustainability at the University of Michigan. He is the author of "Sciences of Consent: Indigenous Knowledge, Governance Value, and Responsibility" in the *Routledge Handbook of Feminist Philosophy of Science* and "Indigenous Environmental Justice: Anti Colonial Action through Kinship" in *Environmental Justice: Key Issues*. He is an enrolled member of the Citizen Potawatomi Nation.

Angie Willey (she/her) is Associate Professor in Women, Gender, and Sexuality Studies at the University of Massachusetts Amherst. She is the author of *Undoing Monogamy: The Politics of Science and the Possibilities of Biology* and co-editor of *Queer Feminist Science Studies: A Reader*.

Hershini Bhana Young (she/her) is a Professor at the University of Texas at Austin. She is the author of *Illegible Will: Coercive Spectacles of Labor in South Africa and the Diaspora* and the forthcoming *Spasming, Stuttering and Other Ways to Get Off: Differential Embodiment and Alternate Moving Practices in African Diasporic Performance*.

Perry Zurn (he/him) is Assistant Professor of Philosophy at American University. He is the author of *Curiosity and Power: The Politics of Inquiry*.